The Lord of Ārūr
THE TYĀGARĀJA CULT
IN TAMILNĀḌU

THE LORD OF ĀRŪR
THE TYĀGARĀJA CULT
IN TAMILNĀḌU
A Study in Conflict and Accommodation

RAJESHWARI GHOSE

MOTILAL BANARSIDASS PUBLISHERS
PRIVATE LIMITED • DELHI

First Edition: Delhi, 1996

ISBN: 81-208-1391-x

Also available at:

MOTILAL BANARSIDASS

41 U.A. Bungalow Road, Jawahar Nagar, Delhi 110 007
120 Royapettah High Road, Mylapore, Madras 600 004
16 St. Mark's Road, Bangalore 560 001
8 Camac Street, Calcutta 700 017
Ashok Rajpath, Patna 800 004
Chowk, Varanasi 221 001

PRINTED IN INDIA

BY JAINENDRA PRAKASH JAIN AT SHRI JAINENDRA PRESS,
A-45 NARAINA, PHASE I, NEW DELHI 110 028
AND PUBLISHED BY NARENDRA PRAKASH JAIN FOR
MOTILAL BANARSIDASS PUBLISHERS PRIVATE LIMITED,
BUNGALOW ROAD, DELHI 110 007

Preface and Acknowledgements

This book is based on research carried out in India and in England over the years 1980-84. It would not have been possible but for the generous help from many people, only some of whom have been acknowledged here.

I am grateful to the Thañjāvūr Tamil University for their research fellowship for three months in 1982. Dr.V.I. Subramonian, the then Vice-Chancellor, took special interest and made this visiting grant a possibility. This enabled me to meet renowned Tamil̲ scholars. My special thanks to Profs. Veḷḷaivāraṇar, Taṇṭapāṇi Tēcikar, Veṅkaṭarāmiah and Nambi Ārooran for their helpful comments on a paper on the Tyāgarāja cult that I submitted at a seminar held in the University in December 1982.

I am deeply indebted to the Late Dr. Gourināth Śāstrī, then Vice Chancellor, Sampūrṇānand Sanskrit University, Vārāṇasī, who initiated me into the study of Sanskrit in my undergraduate days at Government Sanskrit College, Calcutta, and who kindly invited me to stay with him in Vārāṇāsī in July-August 1983 and introduced me to several Sanskrit Pandits such as Professor V. Dvivedi, Pandit Vaṭuknāth Sāstrī and Paṭṭābhirāma Śāstrī.

Pandit Vaṭuknāth Śāstrī Khiṣṭe not only lent me the unpublished manuscript *Śrīnātha navaratnamālā mañjūṣā* from his private collection but also helped me to understand the difficult passages therein.

The Late Dr. A.V. Jeyachundran, who was the Director of Tirupati Tirumala Museum in 1981, when I met him, and was later associated with the Tiruvāvaṭuturai Ātīn̲am, not only generously opened his vast private library to me but was a constant source of inspiration.

Mu. Ko. Rāman̲, manuscriptologist at the International Institute of Ṯamil̲ Culture, Madras, kindly lent me the four volumes of the *Tiyākarājalīlaikaḷ*. Mr. K.S. Balasubramanian of the Kuppuswami Sastri Research Institute, Madras kindly read the proof of the manuscript and rechecked the references for me.

This work would not have been possible but for the support from the Tiruvārūr Tyāgarājasvāmi Devasthānaṃ and the officiants of the temple. The two *Kurukkals*, the *Ōtuvār* Tilakammā, the scion of the Tēvaraṭiyār family at Tiruvārūr, the *nātasvaram* players, Mr. Dakṣiṇāmūrti of the *Viḻupperumār* family, Mr. Kaṅkātaraṉ, the present-day holder of the honour of *yāṉaiyērumperumpaṟaiyaṉ* and several others helped me to understand the Tiruvārūr temple and its hoary traditions as a part of a living faith. The present trustee Mr. Somasundaram and his father, the Late Mr. Tyagaraja Mudaliar provided me not only their warm hospitality but shared with me their love and understanding of the subject. The Late Mr. Kuñcitapātam of Iñcikkollai patiently explained to me the situation regarding the Madhyāhna Brāhmaṇas at a time when he was critically ill and in bed and inspired me not only with his courage but his tenacity in pursuit of academic precision.

I would like to express special gratitude to Dr. J.R. Marr for generously sharing with me his love and knowledge of Tamiḻ culture. The photographs of the Tārācuram frieze reproduced in this work were also kindly lent to me by Dr. Marr.

The late Mr. Mu. Aruṇācalam, Dr. R. Nagasamy, Director of Tamiḻnadu Archaelogical Department, Prof. K.V. Raman and many others in Madras helped me in various ways in finding source materials. Many scholars such as Herman Kulke from Heidelberg, Prof.Zvelebil from Utrecht and Saskia Kersenbohm Story kindly lent me reprints of their articles and sent me material which was not easily accessible to me in India.

The staff of Thañjāvūr Saraswathi Mahal library were not only cooperative but positively enthusiastic in their support of this project. Special thanks go to Mr. N. Visvanathan, who, if he had his way, would have made me write this book on his 'hero' Shāhāji!

I would like to thank the Centre of Asian Studies, University of Hong Kong for extending their facilities to me as one of their Research Associates.

My parents, late Mr. and Mrs. Naṭarāja Iyer, who were Śrī-Vidyā Upāsakas, instilled in me a certain interest in mysticism and religion and nurtured in me a love of myths and stories, and I do hope that this work conveys a little of their enthusiasm. My brother-in-law the late Mr. Swaminathan, patiently accompanied me to many of the sites and helped me in data collection.

My friends Geetanjali Singh and Nayan Chanda kept prodding me and but for their constant encouragement this book may never have been completed.

Finally, yet foremost, I thank my husband Tushar Ghose for sustaining me emotionally and financially for three years, without whose unfailing help, encouragement and enthusiasm this work would have been impossible.

RAJESHWARI GHOSE

Contents

Preface and Acknowledgements v
A Note on Transliteration xiii
Abbreviations xv
List of Maps, Plates and Illustrations xvii

I. INTRODUCTION **1-10**
What is a Cult? 3
Regional Cults and Hindu Tradition 4
A Note on Methodology 7
Notes 10

II. THE SOMĀSKANDA-VĪTIVIṬAṄKA TYĀGARĀJA: EVOLUTION OF THE ICON, ITS NOMENCLATURE AND SYMBOLIC FUNCTIONS **11-54**
Evolution of the Icon 11
Tyāgarāja Typology 25
Nomenclature of the Deity 29
Viṭaṅka 29
Viṭaṅka in Epigraphy 32
The Name Tyāgarāja 38
The Symbolic Functions 40
Tyāgarāja, The Dancer 40
Tyāgarāja, The Paradigmatic Sovereign 41
The Functional Status of the Processional Image 42
Tyāgarāja's Love of Tamiḻ 42
Tyāgarāja in Paintings 44
Notes 48

III. REGIONAL TOPOGRAPHY AND CULTIC GEOGRAPHY **55-73**
The Sapta Viṭaṅka 57
Tiruvārūr 58
Tirunākaikkāroṇam 60
Tirukkāṟāyil 61
Tirumaṟaikkāṭu 61
Tirunaḷḷāṟu 62

Tiruvāymūr 62
Tirukkōḷili 63
Other Sites 64
Notes 69

IV. THE TYĀGARĀJA ORIGIN MYTH 75-96
The Origin 77
Elaborations and Variants of the Myth 81
Standardised Form of the Myth 82
Notes 91

V. THE TYĀGARĀJA ICONOLOGY: A STUDY OF THE ICON AS A SYMBOL 97-134
Prāṇa 102
The Equation Prāṇa=Ātman 103
The Grammarian's Equation of Prāṇa with Sound Patterns 106
Haṁsa or the Interiorised Identity 107
Auditory Meditations, Sound and Ajapā-Haṁsa 109
The Soteriology of Dance and '*Acapai*' in the Tirumantiram 110
Ajapā and the Evolution of the Speech World 116
Spandana 120
Ajapā, Haṁsa and Śrī-Vidyā 120
Tyāgarāja and Muttusvāmi Dīkṣitar 123
Other Literary References 125
Conclusion 126
Notes 128

VI. RELIGIOUS SYNTHESIS: THE PATTERN, THE PROCESS AND THE AGENTS 135-198
Vedic 135
The Āgamas 138
The Bhakti Movement 143
The Tāntric School 148
The Kāpālikas, Kālamukhas, Pāśupatas and Sacred Networks 149
Pāśupata 156
Somasiddhānta 159
Mattamayūra and the Goḷaki Maṭha 162
Śaiva Siddhānta 167

Māheśvara and Śiva Yogis 168
The Kaula Mārga and Cōmācimāṟaṉār Episode 169
The Two Compendiums of Tyāgarāja's Līlaikaḷ or Divine Sport 181
Conclusion 187
Notes 189

VII. THE TYĀGARĀJA CULT, ITS INSTITUTIONAL FRAMEWORK AND SOCIAL RAMIFICATIONS 199-252
The Temple as a Regulator of Tamil Society: Recent Studies 203
The Nāyaṉmār and Social Challenges 206
The *Tiyākarājalīlaikaḷ* and Other Myths 212
The Age of Experiments and Synthesis 221
The Ritual Officiants: Caste and *Mariyātai* 223
Uvacaṉ 223
The Uvacaṉ's Role in the Tiruvārūr Temple 223
The *Yāṉaiyērumperumpaṟaiyaṉ* 226
The Tēvaraṭiyārs 230
The Viḻuppaṟaiyaṉs 235
The Otuvār, Brahmarāyar and Nāyiṉār 239
Kaikkōḷar 241
Notes 243

VIII. KAṬṬAḶAI MAṬHAS, TEMPLES AND CULTS AS REGULATORS OF SOCIAL STATUS 253-285
Veḷḷāḷa Maṭhas and Temple Trusteeships 253
The Tāṉattār, Maṭhādhipatis and Present Trustees 254
The Tiruvārūr Temple and Arbitration Courts 264
Communal Tensions and their Resolutions 269
Temple Donors and Their Caste Affiliations 277
Notes 282

IX. TYĀGARĀJA AS CULT TYPOLOGY AND LEGITIMIZATION OF POWER 287-364
Vertical Legitimation 288
Horizontal Legitimation 290
Legitimation 290
The Pallava Model of Sovereignty in its Religio-Political Context 291

Incorporative Kingship 295
Sacred Clusters 297
Tyāgarāja Cultic Centres and the Pallavas 299
Tyāgarāja and the Cōḷas 301
Rājarāja I and Dakṣiṇamēruviṭaṅkar 301
Rājarāja and the Cōḻa State Cult 306
Rājēndra I and the State Cult 309
Vīracōḻaṉukkār 311
Rājēndra I and Tyāgarāja 311
The Later Cōḻas and the Revival of Tyāgarāja Myths 316
A Brief Outline of Later Cola History 319
Rājarāja II and Kulōttuṅga III 322
The Succession Issue 322
Maṉunīti Myth and Vikramacōḻa 326
The Antecedents of the Maṉunīti Myth 326
Myths, Epigraphs and Cōḻa Kings 330
The Cōḻa Monarchy and the Tiyākarājalīlaikaḷ 338
Pāṇḍyan Rule 339
The Vijayanagara and Nāyaka Period 341
The Marāṭhās and Tyāgarāja 346
The British Period 349
The Recent Past 350
Notes 354

X. POSTSCRIPT **365-371**

Bibliography **373-400**
Index **401-413**

A Note on Transliteration

Modern names such as Thañjāvūr or Chidambaram have been generally spelt the way they are on modern maps and Railway Station boards. The name of the deity Tyāgarāja has been spelt in the manner in which Sanskrit words are transliterated. When Tamiḻ works dealing with Tyāgarāja are mentioned the *maṇipravāḷa* form of Tiyākarāja has been adopted using the grantha j as most manuscripts use this form. Thus, Tiyākarājalīlaikaḷ has used the j sound. Names like Kulōttuṅga have been spelt with the 'g' as in modern history books but when the name occurs in a Tamiḻ work it has been spelt as Kulōttuṅkaṉ as in *Kulōttuṅkaṉulā*. Certain historic place names like Gaṅgaīkoṇḍacholapuram (as spelt in English on sign boards) appear both as Kaṅkaikoṇṭacōḻapuram and in the modern form depending upon whether they are used as a part of a Tamiḻ work or as they occur in epigraphs. Specific Tamiḻ names and concepts have been transliterated according to the MUTL (Madras University Tamil Lexicon, Madras, 1936) system. Thus Cuntarar or Ñāṉacampantar for Sundara or Jñānasambandha. However certain words like Brāhmaṇa or utsava have been left in their Sanskritic form and not transliterated as 'pirāmaṇar', MUTL fashion. Names like Mucukuntaṉ, when they occur in Tamiḻ have been spelt MUTL fashion but when they occur in Sanskrit, they have been changed to Mucukunda as in *Mucukundasahasranāmam*.

Names in the masculine gender ending in -n in Tamil take on -r as an honorofic. Thus Oṭṭakkūttaṉ becomes Oṭṭakkūttar in an honorofic form. This rule also applies for plural numbers. Thus *pāṇaṉ* becomes *pāṇar* in the plural as well as in the honorofic form as in *yāḻppāṇar*.

Abbreviations

ABORI	*Annals of the Bhandarkar Oriental Research Institute*
ALB	*Adyar Library Bulletin*
ARE	*Annual Report on (South) Indian Epigraphy, 1887*
BISN	A List of the Sanskrit Manuscripts in the Bharatiya Itihasa Samsodhana Mandal, Poona (card index)
BSOAS	*Bulletin of the School of Oriental and African Studies*
CII	*Corpus Inscriptionum Indicarum*
DMK	Drāviḍa Munnetṟa Kaḻakam
EI	*Epigraphia Indica*
IA	*Indian Antiquary*
IESHR	*Indian Economic and Social History Review*
IHQ	*Indian Historical Quarterly*
IOL	India Office Library, London.
JAOS	*Journal of American Oriental Society*
JBORS	*Journal of the Bihar and Orissa Research Society*
JMU	*Journal of Madras University*
JRAS	*Journal of Royal Asiatic Society of Great Britain and Ireland*
JSR	*Journal of Social Research*
MOL	Madras Oriental Library, Manuscript Library and Publications Series, Madras.
QJMS	*Quarterly Journal of Mythic Society*
RASB	*Royal Asiatic Society of Bengal*
SII	*South Indian Inscriptions*
TSML	Tanjore Saraswati Mahal Library, Manuscripts and Publications Series.

List of Maps, Plans and Illustrations

Map of South India
Frontispiece
Ground Plan of Tiruvārūr temple, with major spots marked
Ground plan of Tiruvoṟṟiyūr temple, with major spots marked.
Ground Plan of Tirukkuvaḷai temple, with major spots marked.

Pl.I. Pallava Somāskanda from Mahābalipuram.
Pl.II. Pallava painting of Somāskanda, from Kailāsanatha Temple at Kāñcī, kindly lent by Dr. J.R.Marr.
Pl.III. Marāṭha painting of Somāskanda.
Pl.IV. Somāskanda in the dado of the Rājanārāyaṇa maṇṭapa.
Pl.V. Reclining Viṣṇu with Somāskanda in his bosom, on silver doorway, entrance to Tyāgarāja shrine.
Pl.VI. Reclining Viṣṇu on a niche in the wall.
Pl.VII. Entrance to Tyāgarāja shrine.
Pl.VIII. Hāṭakēśvara, a cavern or nāgabila.
Pl.IX. Paintings of seven replicas of Tyāgarāja in the Tēvāciriyamaṇṭapam.
Pl.X. Ajapā Yantra.
Pl.XI. Pañcamukhavādyam and uvacaṉ playing it.
Pl.XII. Periya maṭam, the paṇṭāracaṉṉiti in white, receiving temple honours during Tyāgarāja processional rite: painting on the wall of Tēvāciriyamaṇṭapam.
Pl.XIII. Yoni pūjā, on pillar.
Pl.XIV. Yāṉaiy ērum perum paṟaiyaṉ, with regalia, the present holder of the honour Mr. Kaṅkātaraṉ and family.
Pl.XV. Icon of Cuntaramūrtināyaṉār.
Pl.XVI. Cuntaramūrtināyaṉār in Marāṭha attire, Nīlōtpalāmpāḷ Shrine.
Pl.XVII. Cōmacimāṟaṉār episode, painted on the lintel of the yāgaśālā.
Pl.XVIII. Cōmācimāṟaṉār episode on the walls of the Nīlōtpalāmpāḷ shrine.
Pl.XIX. Cōḻarāja.
Pl.XX. Maṉunīti's shrine.

Pl.XXI. A festival painted on Tēvāciriya maṇṭapam. XXII
Pl.XXII. The kurukkaḷ Cantiracēkaranāyiṉār (Candraśekhara) at the Tiruvārūr temple. XXIII
Pl.XXIII. Tārācuram frieze. XXIV
Pl.XXIV. Tārācuram frieze. XXV

Chapter One

INTRODUCTION

Was it the day You stood as the Primeval One
Or was it the day that you emerged as the Trinity
Or perchance the day that you overwhelmed the God of Death
Or burnt the God of Love with the eye of fire
Could it be the day the Earth and Heaven appeared
Or the day that you arrested the deer betwixt your fingers
And shared your form with The Woman of divine beauty
Was it before or was it after that
You enshrined yourself at Tiruvārūr?[1]

(Appar, *Tēvāram* VI 247.1)

This was a hymn sung by the poet Appar somewhere in the 7th century A.D. on the entempled form of Śiva as the Lord of Tiruvārūr. The mood expressed in this verse is one of reverence prompted by the antiquity and sacerdotal character of the site. This ancient town, often described as the land fragrant with the perfume of the blue lotus, was regarded by these saint poets as one of the favourite haunts of the 'Tamiḻian' Śiva. It was the birthplace of the Tamiḻ *bhakti* movement. It was here that the saint Cuntarar, with great humility, offered his salutations to a long list of sixty two saints before him in a moving hymn called the *Tiruttoṇṭattokai* or the List of Holy men of Devoted Service. By hailing the Śaiva collective of worshippers as One Body, he canonized them. From then on, the number sixty three, including the hymnist Cuntarar, becomes the fixed number of Tamiḻ Śaiva *bhakti* saints in the canonical literature. It is believed that this hymn was composed by Cuntarar in the Tēvāciriya maṇṭapam at Tiruvārūr.

Tiruvārūr was the *locus sanctus* of the Śaiva *magnum opus*, the *Periya Purāṇam*, a 12th century A.D. work describing the lives of the sixty three saints collectively called the *nāyaṉmār*. The anthology of the works of three of these saints is called the *Tēvāram*. These are often referred to with reverence as the Tamiḻ Vēdam. To the north Indian devotee of the god Śiva, however, the place meant nothing then and it means nothing now.

The centre of pilgrimage in Tiruvārūr is the Tyāgarāja temple named after the processional icon. Tyāgarāja is a trinitarian concept. It includes Śiva, his wife Pārvatī and one of their sons Skanda and is a composite image known in iconographic texts as the Somāskanda. Though bearing a chaste Sanskrit name, the icon is a uniquely Tami<u>l</u> concept and Somāskandas are not found in the north Indian Śiva temples. However this icon is a ritual imperative in all Tamil Śiva temples.

Just an outline of the facts stated above reveals the importance of Tiruvārūr in forging a religio-cultural identity of the ancient Tamil speaking peoples. To the theistic Tamil nationalists of the 19th and 20th centuries, the sacred scriptures of the Śaiva canon, on which they based their Siddhānta faith, also provided the ideology of cultural nationalism. They regarded Śaiva Siddhānta as specially suited to and a product of the Tamil genius. Typical of this group would be J.M. Nallaswami Pillai. There was another stronger movement of Tamil cultural nationalism led by a group calling itself the *Tirāviṭa Kaḻakam*, (D.K. for short in English after the spelling Drāviḍa Kaḻakam adopted by them) which was formed in 1944. They expressed views diametrically opposite to those of Nallaswami Pillai. Their leader E.V. Ramasvami Naicker symbolically threw the *Periya Purāṇam* and other works venerated as the Tamil Vēdam into a huge bonfire along with the *Rāmāyaṇa*. He alleged that these works were racist and casteist. The 'north', 'south' polarity had assumed in their minds both a linguistic and a racial connotation.

It was as a young girl from up north in Rājasthān, on a school vacation while visiting my grandparents in Tiruvārūr, that I first witnessed both the pride in the town as a centre of Tamil culture and the iconoclastic bonfire. Many symbols, I was told, were being consumed by the fire. Tamil culture was being cleansed of all alien import. The term 'alien' included specific concepts of "Āryan", "Sanskritic" and "Brāhmaṇa". The last mentioned category of people were regarded as the repositories of the two earlier categories.[2]

It was a desire to understand a few of the many symbols associated with Tamil consciousness, specially those which reach deep into Tamil history and religion, that prompted this study of a regional cult of Tamilnāḍu, which is uniquely Tamil and yet highly syncretistic.

The subject lent itself to study from three distinct angles:

as an experiment in religious synthesis; as a bridge over zones of social tension and as a legitimiser of political power during different stages of its historical development with varying degrees of success.

The Tyāgarāja mythology, rich and variegated in its texture, focuses attention on several socio-religious confrontations. It records, albeit in the indirect language of myths, the subtle means by which such situations were handled. The cult also acts as a powerful tool for legitimisation of power at different times.

It was extremely interesting to trace the development of the Tyāgarāja cult from this perspective: first under the Pallavas, (mid 6th-late 9th Cen. A.D.), then under the early Cōḻas , (mid 9th-mid 12th) to be followed by the later Cōḻas , (in the latter half of the 12th to early 13th Cen. A.D.), when the empire was in dire distress and desperate for legitimacy. The dates given above are rough political periods and in the case of the Tyāgarāja cult, it does not make a definite impact till the 7th-8th Centuries A.D. It was reinvigorated as a royal cult in the 17th Century A.D. under the Marāṭhā rulers of Thañjāvūr. One thing to bear in mind is that while these angles of the cult are distinctly visible to a modern scholar studying this cult from the outside, to the insider, to the believer, the lines must have been extremely hazy, if at all they did exist. The 'insider' would have in all probability perceived it in a holistic manner.

Thus, even though this is basically a micro study of Tamiḻ Śaiva beliefs and norms as expressed through the unfolding of a cult over a period of thirteen centuries of recorded history, it nevertheless encapsulates to a great extent the intricacies, paradoxes and conundrums of the Tamiḻ cultural ethos.

What is a Cult?

The word 'cult' has acquired considerable notoriety in recent years in the wake of several macabre sub-cultural group activities claiming to be directed by cult leaders. Several studies emphasise the anti-social, anti-familial, anti-intellectual aspects of their belief and the secret society mode of their operation.

This work uses the term cult not quite in the modern sociological sense but in the more archaic sense of the word as derived from the latin 'cultus.' Hence, it defines it broadly as a special aspect of religion organised through common myths, symbols and functionaries, rites, festivals and dance. These commonalities are then woven together to produce a body of ideas and practices resulting in the formation of a group espousing a specific form of the divine. It acquires other specificities depending on the cultural milieu within which it operates.

When one is studying the historical evolution of a cult one is aware that it is not a static body of belief systems, as the above definition would seem to imply. When faced with new challenges there took place a maieutic development from within the cult leading to changes in the relationships between the components of the cult. A classic example is the many vicissitudes through which the medieval Rāma cult of Ayodhyā has gone through within the Hindu context posing, as it does today, a threat to the secular Indian constitution. It has involved enormous adjustments of rites, rituals, personnel, music and dance and worked on several new strategies of recruitment, while invoking some of the more ancient symbols which have deep resonances in the Hindu mind.

In the ancient context the introduction of a new rite, such as the chariot festival, brought enormous pooling of manpower and resources and greater cross caste support for the cult. It also posed the challenge of accommodating disaggregated groups of people coming from various ethnic stocks and disparate levels of cultural expectations. In the context of Hindu theories of caste and pollution the situation called for ideological shifts. The resultant dichotomies between what Turner labels "communitas" and "structure"[3] or the desire to belong to an undivided human society versus the neat, orderly, structural divisions of a functioning society were very pronounced in Hindu cults. A study of the modalities of adjustment leads to a better understanding of the teleological matrix.

Regional Cults and Hindu Tradition

Regional cults are a characteristic feature of Hinduism and over the centuries several cults have evolved all over India. The inherent belief underlying these specific centres of worship is that "holy acts when performed in certain spots acquire special sanctity". The deity manifests itself to the devotees in a particular form, at a particular spot for a specific purpose. It is then pinned to the spot in the minds of the believers and that becomes its permanent abode.[4] The deity may choose to have other abodes and other forms as well, but inhered in that particular form it is deeply rooted to the soil where it was originally believed to have been 'seen', where the hierophany took place. This geocentricity in no way detracted for the believer the transcendental nature of godhead for the *nirguṇa* Brahman (the attributeless godhead) belonged to a totally different plane of religious experience.

The worship of Mīnākṣī - Cuntarēcuvara of Madurai, Jagannātha of Puri, Viṭṭhaldev of Paṇḍharpur, Veṅkaṭeśvara Bālājī of Tirupati and Tyāgarāja of Tiruvārūr are a few of the many examples of regional cults in India. A cult in the Hindu tradition primarily evolves around three factors, viz. *talam* (Skt. *sthala*) meaning sacred space, *tīrtham* or sacred waters and *mūrti* or icon.

The icon, once enshrined, belongs to that temple and to that territory even if the physical structure of the shrine is destroyed. Even if the icon is forced to take refuge elsewhere in times of danger, it still retains its territorial affiliation. Two classic examples that spring to mind are those of the Viṭṭhaldev of Paṇḍharpur and Someśvara of Somnāthpur. The former was secretly moved from place to place to protect it from Muslim iconoclasts and was once even held to ransom by petty thieves. Nonetheless, Viṭṭhaldev remains the Lord of Paṇḍharpur. The Somnāthpur temple was repeatedly razed to the ground by invaders but it in no way detracted its claim to the lordship of Somnāthpur. Another instance is that of Baṅgāru Kāmākṣī, now at Thañjāvūr but originally the lady of Kāñcī and the tutelary deity of the famous music composer Syāma Śāstrī.

It is to such a genre of regional cults that the Tyāgarāja or *sapta viṭaṅka* as it is often called, belongs. It is what Werbner would call a "middle range" cult. He defines it as "more far-reaching than any parochial cult of the little community, yet less inclusive in its belief and membership from a world religion in its most universal form". Their focal centres, he exemplifies, are shrines in towns and villages where people come from various communities to pray, sacrifice or simply as an act of pilgrimage. They are cults which have a religious topography of their own "conceptually defined by the peoples themselves and marked apart from other features of cultural landscape".[5] Cultic sites form the focal points for pilgrimages.

Hindu pilgrim sites are normally classified into *tīrthas* and *pīṭhas*. A *tīrtha* literally means a crossing place or a ford and hence, the waters thereof. The ritual of ablution or the holy dip as it is popularly called, plays an important part. The *tīrtha* of Tiruvārūr is the venerated pond called Kamalālaya. The term *pīṭha* has special connotations in Tāntric terminology. The word means a seat; and to the Tāntrics it means the seat of the goddess, the female aspect forming an important focal point of their worship. The *pīṭha* is associated with several mythological motifs and is regarded as a mystical spot representing several abstruse philosophical doctrines. Thus, on one hand, it has close connection with the mythology of the dismemberment of Satī's body. On the other, it is connected to the metaphysics of the Sanskrit sound system and syllabary, whereby a metaphysical truth is posited in a seed syllable. *Pīṭhas* are associated with calligrams and homologisation processes by which the Tāntric envisages the site as a mystical organ in the macrocosmic body of Devī and/or of her microcosmic adept, the initiated devotee. Most pilgrim sites have imbibed, to a greater or lesser degree, features from the Tāntric tradition. Suffice it to say at this point that there are two pilgrimage traditions, a northern and a southern. Some of these regional pilgrim centres have acquired at different times a decidedly pan-Indian status, attracting pilgrims from all over the country.

Turner traces several tensions in regional cults. He treats them under categories arising from what he calls "exclusiveness vs. inclusiveness", "egalitarianism vs. non-egalitarianism", "generic vs. particularistic relationships" and "peripherality vs. centrality".[6] While Turner's paradigm of analysis has been used in the present study it has had to be modified to make it relevant in the Hindu, Tamiḻ context. Thus for example, caste as a factor in the social structural dimension becomes important given the intimate connection between Hinduism and the caste system. Temples as custodians of Vedic-Āgamic traditions are upholders of the neatly organised and hierarchic system of caste and at the same time as vehicles of the charismatic *bhakti* movement are also means of channelling the spirit of "communitas". Temple cults are thus called upon to uphold the modality of structure with its emphasis on order and often hierarchy and are expected to accommodate the spontaneity and egalitarianism of the saintly brotherhood of devotees, a fraternity which wishes to transcend all limitations imposed by the structure. Such dichotomies are marked in the Tamil̲ cultic tradition in the manner in which the lives and personalities of the saints themselves are portrayed.

Other peculiarly Tamil̲ cultic dichotomies that emerge result from the rather ambiguous relationship between the 'higher' 'Sanskritic' and 'Āryan' tradition and '*autochthonous*,' 'noble' and 'sacred' Tamil̲ experiences. Tyāgarāja is the 'God of the Tamil̲s'. He loves Tamil̲ songs set to music. The doors of a temple that could only be opened by the recitation of Sanskrit hymns could be reopened only by the singing of Tamil̲ hymns. The *Tēvāram* hymnists pride themselves as the propagators of Tamil̲ culture. Appar's attack on the Jains is based amongst other things on what he describes as the "dreadful sound of their language" and both Campantar and Cuntarar heap on them much cultural disdain.[7]

Tyāgarāja is the Lord of Tiruvārūr and of Cōl̲amaṇṭalam and has a special love for the Kāvēri river and the Cōl̲a monarchy. Tiruvārūr was also one of the towns where the early Cōl̲a monarchs were crowned. The Tyāgarāja cult emanated from the centre of Tiruvārūr and by a process of networking linked several, what would then have been, peripheral sites within the central orbit. Thus a Hinduised and Tamil̲ised version of Turner's classificatory scheme was found to be a useful tool of enquiry throughout this study

A Note on Methodology

While groping with several methodological tools with varying degrees of success, it was encouraging to find such gropings legitimised as academic "pursuits of truth" by a school of historians of early south east Asia. They were trying to fit in pieces of evidence into the larger jigsaw puzzle. John Higham distinguishes two approaches—that "which is process oriented and enjoys the pursuit of truth more than the possession of it" and the product oriented one which cares more for the completeness or coherence of the work. The latter methodology, says Higham, is therefore unappreciative of negative findings and unwilling to risk time and effort in methodological experimentation.[8]

Much time and effort have been spent in this work on experimentation and if all loose ends could not be neatly tied, it is because such a task is left for a product oriented scholar to complete!

The Tyāgarāja cult has been studied from iconographical, canonical, anthropological and historical perspectives. The doctrinal and ideological assumptions have been investigated with a special emphasis on the process of synthesis. The social and operational levels of the cult have been placed within the same methodological framework. As layers upon layers of thought patterns were piled upon the cultic symbol, its philosophical paradigms were drawn from many sources such as Vedāntic metaphysics, Brāhmaṇic orthopraxy, Āgamic ritualism and *bhakti* devotionalism, to mention just a few. With the entrance of every new force social adjustments were imperative. In view of the complex nature of the tradition studied and to avoid the dangers of tautology this work has been divided into three broad categories viz. the development of religious ideas, the social shifts and the study of the religious cult as a tool for legitimisation of political power. In spite of considerable care, overlapping and repetition could not be totally avoided.

The variegated nature of the sources consulted necessitated a "toolbox approach". Myths and legends formed part of the source materials. These, as O'Flaherty beautifully describes them "are like a palimsest on which generation after generation has engraved its own messages"[9]. They, therefore need to be deciphered by a different code book each time.

In the case of the Tyāgarāja cult, a complex philosophical system has grown out of metaphorical imageries. These, in turn, are closely linked with myths woven round the deity. In the absence of a regulating ecclesiastic authority, the cultic symbols grew and new ideas were added on without discarding the old, thereby creating a forest of symbols. Wading through this forest has necessitated the use of different methodological guidelines.

An attempt has been made throughout this work to keep the historical perspective and maintain as tight a chronological framework as the nature of materials consulted will permit. As a great deal of the written sources had a long oral antecedent, dating was often arbitrary. The starting point has been the Śaiva canonical literature comprising of the *Tēvāram*, the *Tirumantiram* and other devotional works collectively called the *Tirumuṟai* and the Śaiva hagiography, the *Periya Purāṇam*.

Oṭṭakkūttar, the Cōḻa court poet under three successive monarchs Vikrama Cōḻa (1118-35), Kulōttuṅga II (1136-46) and Rājarāja II (1146-73) composed semi-historical panegyrics on his royal patrons and has also recorded some of the Tyāgarāja myths, which provided a close connection between Cōḻa monarchy and Tyāgarāja, and in so doing, has provided one of the chronological landmarks. Inscriptions of the monarchs of this dynasty also provide interesting examples of legitimising political power in the uncertain times of the 12th century A.D.

However, there is a large body of works such as those which belong to the genre of *padas, stotras, tālāṭṭu, temmāṅku, kuṟavañci* etc., which are extremely difficult to date. Even some works of more classical genre of *ulā* and *kōvai* share this difficulty.

The sources consulted have varied from philosophical texts to compendiums of myths; and from liturgical texts such as the *Mucukundasahasranāmam* to a study of iconography and hence different methods have been adopted to draw an overall picture.

The Tyāgarāja Cult in the context of Temple Cults Today

While some cults belonging to the south Indian tradition such as the Bālāji cult of Tirupati have achieved a pan-Indian status and other more egalitarian cults like the Ayyappaṉ have acquired a more elevated regional status, the Tyāgarāja of Tiruvārūr has sunk into comparative oblivion. A number of factors have contributed to this decline including lack of patronage, bickering between trustees, structural defects of the *kaṭṭaḷai* or trusteeship scheme etc., but above all it has lost its charisma. Failure to survive is as important a social indicator as the success of a cult.

A combination of factors leads to the rise of either a brand new cult such as the Santośīmā cult in recent years or to the revival of an ancient temple cult. In the modern context, where the challenges are of a very different order and mobilisation methods are vastly divergent, what is interesting is to see the persistence of certain motifs in mobilising support. The hierophony, the geocentricity, the use of mobile icons on chariot processions, the myths, the creating of new rituals, the pooling of resources, the resultant tensions, the appeal of religious forces as legitimating agents of political power—all these reappear in new permutations and combinations each time. One cannot escape a sense of *deja vu*. However, a cult like the Rāma cult, reinvigorated at the time of writing, has to take into account the shifting relationship between state values, intelligentsia sensibilities and popular tastes.

Finally, I do hope that I have not succumbed to that occupational disease of the historians which leads to an immoderate conviction of the importance and virtues of the subject studied! It must be remembered that the Tyāgarāja cult is one of the many regional cults of India, not even the most important one in terms of following. Nevertheless, it is its antiquity and historicity that has lent it significance.

NOTES

1. This hymn of Appar is full of mythological allusions. Śiva kicking the god of Death in order to protect his young devotee Mārkaṇḍeya from his fated end, the iconic form of the Ardhanārīśvara, the half man-half woman form of Śiva-Pārvati, and the myth of Śiva burning the god of Love are pan-Indian myths and iconography incorporated from Sanskrit into Tamiḻ. The reference to the "deer" on the other hand is a purely Tamiḻ iconic attribute of Śiva, unknown in north India.
2. In 1927-8 started the campaign of burning the *Manusmṛti*, which was extended in 1942 to include the *Rāmāyaṇa*, followed by the *Periya Purāṇam*. E.V.R, as the founder was fondly called, thundered "Tamil poets of old like Kambar only glorified the Āryans at the cost of the Dravidians and hence no self respecting Tamilian would have any respect for Kambar or other Tamiḻ poets like him. The first act of any future Tamilian government will be to ban the reading of *Kamba Rāmāyaṇam* and set fire to the revolting book which has destroyed the honour of the Tamils" *Mail*, 26th May 1942. The pre-Āryan society was conceived of as a classless, casteless society. They claimed that the "Brāhmaṇas are also foreign to India like the British" (*Nyāya Dīpikā*, January 25th 1923, cited by Barnett, N.R. *The Politics of Cultural Nationalism in India* . The theist Tamiḻ nationalists, on the other hand, gave the upper class non-Brāhmaṇas cultural confidence by claiming the Śaiva Siddhānta, which drew its devotees mostly from the Veḷḷāḷa community, to be superior to Āryan Vedic beliefs.
3. Turner, Victor *Dramas, Fields and Metaphors*, pp. 202 and 282-83. Also *The Ritual Process* pp. 106-7.
4. Bolle, Kees W. "Speaking of a Place" in Kitagawa and Long, Ed. *Myths and Symbols: Studies in Honour of Mircea Elliade*, p. 129
5. Werbner, R. P. Ed. *Regional Cults*, p.ix
6. Turner, Victor, See note 3 above
7. Appar mocks their mantras as "Jñamana, Jñajñana Jñana Jñonam" as gibberish nasal sounds. Campantar's hymns are full of acrimony against the Jainas. A classic example is provided in Tēvāram III.297, where he refers to the filthy Jains who massacre the beautiful Sanskrit of the Āgama texts and chides them as the monkeys who are ignorant of both pure Tamiḻ and chaste Sanskrit.
8. Cited by Kammen, Michael "On Predicting the Past: Potter and Plumb", *Journal of Interdisciplinary History* 7 (Summer 1974) pp. 115-116.
9. O'Flaherty Wendy, *Women, Androgynes and Beasts*, Introduction.

Chapter Two

THE SOMĀSKANDA-VĪTIVIṬAṄKA TYĀGARĀJA: EVOLUTION OF THENICON, ITS NOMENCLATURE AND SYMBOLIC FUNCTIONS

EVOLUTION OF THE ICON

The Tyāgarāja icon, now enshrined at Tiruvārūr in a temple bearing the deity's name,[1] can be regarded as the archetype of all Tyāgarāja images, and there are over a dozen such cultic icons in Tamilnāḍu. No doubt there are minor divergences of style and ornamentation[2] between one Tyāgarāja and the other but the typology is clearly defined by cultic conventions and iconographic injunctions.

The Tyāgarāja is a Somāskanda, but marked apart from others of the same genre solely by its particularistic relationship to and requirements of the cult. Thus, while all Tyāgarāja images *per se* are Somāskandas, the reverse does not necessarily hold true. Shorn of its mythic origin and its unique schemata of grace, emptied of its mystico-esoteric content, bereft of its historic juro-political role and deprived of its 'root'[3] metaphors, which evolve around the twin metaphysical concepts of *'ajapā'* and *haṁsa*, the icon would lose its cultic personality. Not all Somāskandas share in this complex heritage. It is the prerogative of the Tyāgarāja. Thus, though iconographically similar, the Tyāgarāja and Somāskanda are iconologically divergent. Architecturally speaking, when separate shrines are dedicated to the *utsavabera* form of Somāskanda, they are called Tyāgarāja shrines after the celebrated shrine at Tiruvārūr. These became popular in the Thañjāvūr area during the second phase of Cōḻa rule, though Dhaky places it in the last phase.[4]

A detailed discussion of the twin 'root metaphors' referred to above and the conceptual archetype that was evolved will be reserved for the section dealing with iconological symbolism. As the object of this section is to determine the parameters of the cult from an iconographical viewpoint, the main focus is on the visual form of the icon both in its generic Somāskanda and in its particular Tyāgarāja aspects.

Tyāgarāja is a composite icon representing Śiva, his consort Umā and their son Skanda seated on the same throne. The Hindu iconographical texts designate such figures as *Somāskandas,* a Sanskrit compound meaning *sa* (with) Umā and Skanda, the subject Śiva being understood.

In the history of Hindu art, the Somāskanda made its debut as a carved stone panel in the rear walls of the *sanctum sanctorum* of Śaiva temples in Tamilnāḍu during the Pallava period in the 7th century A.D., and became almost the *leitmotif* of their sacred art in the following century.[5] Of all the Pallava images that have survived to the present the Somāskanda panels are by far the most numerous. There are more than forty of them, excluding the remnants of painted Somāskanda panels in the Kailāśanātha temple at Kāñcīpuram[6]. (Pl. II) Most of these belong to the Rājasiṁha period (700-728 A.D.). Very few earlier examples have come to light, and those that have are attributed by K.V. Soundararajan to Mahendra (580-630 A.D.), Mahāmalla (630-668 A.D.) and Parameśvaravarman phase (670-700 A.D.).[7] Lockwood, Siromoney and Dayanand trace the evolution of the Somāskanda sculpture from its earliest representation at the Dharmarāja Ratha at Mahābalipuram through to what is stylistically called the 'Rājasiṁha style', though they believe that "it was his father Parameśvaravarman I who actually initiated the 'Rājasiṁha style' and who was also the author of some of these monuments".[8] (Pl. I)

The Caṅkam literature does not mention the Somāskanda concept although Murukan̲, Kor̲r̲avai, who later merged into the concept of Pārvatī and Śiva, the three members of the Somāskanda trinity were individually known to these writers.[9] The sentiments conveyed by the icon, seems to have been familiar to the author of the *Aiṅkur̲unūr̲u*[10] when he describes the scene of the son dancing between his parents like a fawn. The poet goes into raptures over the picture of domestic felicity. The earliest direct reference to the Somāskanda in the form of the *viṭaṅka* (q.v.) occurs only in the *Tēvāram* literature. The iconic form of the trinity is hinted at in some of the hymns.[11]

Thus, to attempt a brief summary, the earlier cave temples of the Pallava ruler Mahendra (580-630 A.D.) are bare with no sculptures in the niches. It seems highly probable that the trio were either painted or chiselled on the hind wall of the rear sanctum of the Orukāl Maṇṭapam at Tirukkaḻukkunṟam, which belongs to the time of Mahāmalla. On the rear wall of a maṇṭapam adjoining the main chamber are depicted the figures of Brahmā and Viṣṇu flanking what is now an empty space.[12] The empty space was in all probability occupied by a Somāskanda. This presumption rests on the fact that such a composition of deities was popular in Pallava art of the succeeding period. From Parameśvaravarman's time one can be certain of the appearance of the Somāskanda formation.[13] Literary evidence supports the iconographical findings. The repetition of the Somāskanda panels in the time of Rājasiṁha in such regular frequency is an important indicator of the reverence in which the Somāskanda icon was held by this Pallava King, for, in contradistinction to the pre-Rājasiṁha Somāskandas which are found only in the Dharmarāja Ratha and the Rāmānuja Maṇṭapam (now almost a destroyed panel) and in the Orukāl Maṇṭapam referred to above, the Rājasiṁha Somāskanda panels are a regular feature in all Pallava temples.

The Cōḻas continued the iconic tradition of portraying the Somāskanda trinity but the Cōḻa images were more popularly modelled in bronze and served as processional deities. With the Pallavas vanished the tradition of carving them on the back wall of the *sanctum sanctorum*. Thus, to quote Lockwood "As a rule of thumb we can say that if a Śaivite temple has a sculptured Somāskanda panel in its *sanctum* it is almost certainly a temple of the Pallava period". Thus, the tradition of carving a Somāskanda image on the rear wall of the *sanctum* was in vogue from about 700-800 A.D. The ninth century A.D. temple dedicated by Aparājita Pallava to the Lord at Tiruttaṇi and called the Vīraṭṭānēśvara temple followed the same convention and it is presumably the last of the series to do so.[14] Balasubramanian refers to two Cōḻa temples belonging to the Middle period, i.e. 11th century A.D. with such an arrangement. They are mentioned later in the chapter.[15]

One of the most frequently used epithets of the Tyāgarāja icon is *muṉṉilum piṉṉaḻakar*,[16] i.e one whose rear view is more beautiful than his frontal appearance. This description is particularly interesting since the majority of ancient Indian sculptures are done in high relief and, even where the rear is carved, seldom is much attention given to the back. This is true of all stone sculptures, and of several bronzes. The Pallava tradition of carving stone

Somāskandas as high reliefs precludes the possibility that an icon which is specifically described as one whose rear beauty far surpasses the frontal look could be a stone Somāskanda panel. Could it be then that the Tyāgarāja was one of the early processional bronzes of the Pallava period, which has set itself free from its backing for the first time, for all Somāskanda panels referred to above were carved on the rear walls of the *sanctum sanctorum* or in subsidiary shrines, but always placed in a niche so that their back was not visible. Very few Pallava bronzes have survived, and the earliest examples of Somāskanda bronzes now extant can definitely be ascribed only to the Pallava-Cōḻa transition period. This, however, does not preclude the possibility that Pallava Somāskanda bronzes are lost to us. From the *Tēvāram* hymnists we know that the tradition of processional deities or *utsavaberas* was known from Pallava times, as we shall presently see in the context of the use of the term *Viṭaṅka.* An iconographic study of that special class of Somāskandas, called the Ṭyāgarāja, particularly the icon at Tiruvārūr would possibly have shed light on the date of this particular iconic type. Unfortunately, however, a stylistic analysis of the Tiruvārūr icon is not possible because of the esoteric traditions associated with this icon, which believes in keeping the torso of the figure covered.

In the absence of any iconographic clue to the dating of the early Tyāgarāja typology it is found necessary to study the Pallava Somāskanda model, which again can be classified into two groups, pre-Rājasiṁha and Rājasiṁha styles and compare them with the Cōḻa models and the description of this class of icons in the texts.

The pre-Rājasiṁha icons, as seen in the Dharmarājaratha at Mahābalipuram portray Umā in profile, clasping the child Skanda with her left arm. Interestingly enough there is a bronze image of Nīlōtpalāmpāḷ, the consort of Tyāgarāja in Tiruvārūr which portrays her holding the little finger of Skanda who is carried by another woman (Pl.III). This is iconographically very unusual and seems to belong on stylistic grounds to the Late Cōḻa period. The Rājasiṁha panels depict her in a frontal posture resting her body weight on her left hand which is firmly placed on the pedestal. She is not shown clasping Skanda as in the earlier example. The trinity is flanked by Brahmā and Viṣṇu. A detailed cataloguing of the characteristics of pre-Rājasiṁha and Rājasiṁha sculptures has been done by Lockwood.[17]

Lockwood points to the positioning of Śiva's legs as one of the differentiating characteristics between the 'pre-Rājasiṁha' and 'Rājasiṁha' iconic models. In the earlier examples it is his right leg that is down while in the 'Rājasiṁha' specimens it is the left leg that is shown in the posture of ease, resting on the footstool. The positioning of Śiva's hands in the two classes of images are also different. In the earlier examples his lower left hand is portrayed with the fingers closed and resting near his left knee. His lower right forearm is held perpendicularly near his chest in what looks like a *Cin mudrā,* though all the fingers are bent and hence it looks as if the hand is in a loose fist. In the "Rājasiṁha' type Śiva's lower left hand always rests in *Dhyāna mudrā* just above his right ankle which is tucked on the pedestal, while his lower right is held away from his body, almost parallel to the seat. The earlier examples depict hovering *gaṇas,* the latter do not. Skanda in the 'Rājasiṁha' type is depicted with the same hairdo as Umā—a conical coiffure with a pronounced hairline—looking almost like the hairband that separates Khmer sculptures of the early period from the crown. The upper left hand of Śiva in the 'Rājasiṁha' type is held bent touching his left shoulder while the upper right hand holds presumably a *cāmara.* The umbrella, an insignia of royalty, is clearly portrayed in the top left hand corner. Neither of these two classes of Pallava sculptures depict the attributes which are characteristic of the Cōḻa bronzes, viz, axe and the deer. It is only in the panel from the Kailāśanātha temple at Kāñcīpuram in the main *sanctum* of the Rājasiṁheśvara that the two motifs of the axe and the deer appear for the first time. This particular Somāskanda is unique for it differs from the other twentynine examples in this temple itself and from all other Rājasiṁha icons of the trio. The axe and deer attributes appear also in the Mukteśvara at Kāñcīpuram. These however, seem to be definitely attributable to the post-Rājasiṁha period. Yet the Tēvāram composers constantly alluded to the deer in Śiva's hand.

Manuals on sculpture like the *Sakalādhikāram,*[18] *Sārasvatīyam Citrakarmaśāstram,*[19] *Kāśyapam*[20] and *Śilparatnam*[21] describe the Somāskanda icon. So do the *talapurāṇams* dealing with Tyāgarāja shrines. The earliest *talapurāṇams* dealing with the Tyāgarāja cult appear in their written form only from the 16th century A.D. onwards, though undoubtedly they preserve an earlier oral tradition. The *Śilparatnam* is also dated to about the same period.

The *Sakalādhikāram* which is attributed to Agastya presumably, can be dated to the 13th century A.D. The fourteenth chapter of the *Sārasvatīyam* describes the Somāskanda *mūrti* in the following manner: "The Somāskanda should be seated in the *ardhaparyaṅka* pose and should be depicted erect and majestic, full of the quality of dynamism (*rajōguṇa*). His left leg should be shown resting on the pedestal and his right hanging down". This description accords with the 'pre-Rājasiṁha style', i.e. the earlier variety of Somāskandas as far as the placement of the leg is concerned. The *Sārasvatīyam* is a work of iconometry as well and gives detailed description of the proportions to be adopted. The emblems to be held by Śiva are described as the axe and the deer in the upper back hands while three variant *mudrās*, viz *kaṭaka, varada* and *kartarī mudrās* are suggested for the lower two hands. The emphasis here too is on the majesty (*rajōguṇa*), beauty and the expression of *śṛṅgāra* or love. Either an ornate crown or the *jaṭāmukuṭa*, the traditional matted locks of Śiva, is suggested as an appropriate hair arrangement. A crescent moon is prescribed on one side of the diadem and details of ornaments are enumerated. The god according to this text is to be depicted three-eyed. The *Sakalādhikāra* states clearly that Lord Śiva's image should be made according to the scale of *Uttamadaśatāla*, that of Umā according to *Madhyamadaśatāla* and Skanda according to *Uttama pañçatāla*. *Tāla* is a unit and the number of *aṅgulas* (which is a basic unit approximating an inch, though different texts give different calculations) in each *tāla* division is calculable on the basis of "good", "better" and "best" multiples. Thus in the "best" unit called *uttamadaśatāla* there are 124 *aṅgulas*. The others vary according to their being "better" or just "good" in the number of *aṅgulas*. Thus Skanda as a child is to be measured by five *tālas*. Skanda's crown is a *Karaṇḍa Mukuṭa*. Umā could wear one of four types of crown, viz. *Makuṭa, Karaṇḍikā, Keśabandha* and *Kirīṭa*. Umā should be portrayed with a flower in her right hand. It is in the *Kāśyapa Śilpaśāstra* that it is definitely described as a blue lily. Śiva, says the text, should portray the two qualities of *rajas* and *śṛṅgāra*.

Devī, according to the same text (i.e.*Sārasvatīyam)* should be seated on the left of Śiva and one of her long arms should extend to the seat, while the other, the right, should be depicted holding a blue water-lily, hence the name Nīlōtpalāmpāḷ attributed to all the consorts of Tyāgarāja. She should be portrayed as demure and beautiful. Murukaṉ according to the text could be portrayed as either seated between his parents or shown dancing in between his parents. The height of the child is prescribed as one-eighth or one quarter of the height of Śiva.

The *Śilparatna* describes the icon in a similar fashion, except that additionally it prescribes the colour red for the icon. The stress is on the dynamic quality or *rajoguṇa*, and beauty. The colour red and the erotic moods are common characteristics of Murukaṉ, as an independent icon or *pradhānamūrti* and of the Somāskanda trinity. The *Śilparatnam* (Tamiḻ translation) describes Murukaṉ as the 'dwelling place of divine sport' (*Teyvīkamāna viḷaiyāṭṭiṟku ellām iruppiṭam*). The *Kāraṇāgama*[22] interestingly enough prescribed that the gods Brahmā and Viṣṇu, together with their consorts should be seen flanking the main figure, like in the Pre-Rājasiṁha Pallava sculptures. There is a difference in the iconometric proportions suggested in the different texts.

What is interesting is that several attributes are common to Murukaṉ and Śiva even in the *Caṅkam* literature as pointed out by Marr.[23] Even in *Paripāṭal* it is apparent that the Śiva mythology was prominent in the mind of the Skanda hymnologists. The same text refers to an independent temple for Murukaṉ in which Śiva and Śakti were enshrined as subsidiary deities.[24]

The 16th century work the *Kamalālayacciṟappu*[25] describes the image of Somāskanda as commissioned by Viṣṇu and executed by the divine craftsman Viśvakarmā. Śiva is described, as in other works on iconography and sculpture, as three-eyed with a buck on the left hand and an axe on the right with the lower left and right hands in *vara* (boon-giving) and *abhaya* (protection) *mudrās*. Of Śiva's ornaments the crescent moon, the snake and the anklets are particularly emphasised (9.353.5). The fact that they are all three seated on the same platform is made clear, presumably to emphasise the ritual equality of the three members of the trinity. As functionally this was a processional image, it had to be one composite icon, which could also explain their sharing the same throne.

Somāskanda is one of the *līlāmūrti* (forms which the lord is believed to have assumed in order to perform acts of divine sport) and Gopinath Rao enumerates twenty-five such forms.[26] The *Śivarahasyakhaṇḍa*[27] lists thirty-two forms and strangely enough attributes the most mundane *raison d'etre* for the Somāskanda manifestation. It states bluntly that the only reason for worshipping the Somāskanda is for acquiring a progeny.[28] Elsewhere the emphasis is on the beauty, regality and eroticism of the composite deity. Though a trinity, the Śiva element seems to have been the dominant one as the hierarchy of the size of the figures would indicate. This is substantiated by literary references in which Śiva is definitely assigned a higher status. Gradually, however, the Śakti element seems to have taken over with the spread of the Śrī-Vidyā doctrine. Thus, the Somāskanda seems to have started with predominantly Murukaṉ traits, to later acquire a Śiva predominance and finally became a Tāntric emblem of Śiva-Śakti worship.

Somāskanda is today a ritual imperative in all Śiva temples of Tamiḻnāḍu. This composite form is considered as the representative of the chief presiding deity (*mūlavar*), who, by Śaiva tradition, is always an aniconic form of Śiva, the *liṅga*, and is considered fixed and immovable (*acalabera*). The Somāskanda, in contradistinction, is the mobile icon (*calabera*) taken out in processions. Thus the Tyāgarāja of Tiruvārūr is the *utsavabera* of the *acalabera* Valmīkanātha, which is in the aniconic form of the liṅga. It acquired its name Valmīka, as it is believed to have originally been an anthill.

The Somāskanda is a uniquely Tamiḻian concept as no Somāskandamūrtis are found in northern India. "These bronzes", says J.N. Banerjea, portray "in a characteristic manner the great loving adoration for the child Subrahmaṇya (known in Tamiḻ as Murukaṉ) and his parents which the southerners cherished and still cherish".[29] Jouveau-Dubreuil comments in a similar vein "Pārvatī, holding a little child is full of graciousness and motherly love. The moral and social ideas of the Pallava people may be imagined as the Supreme God is represented as a father by the side of his wife and child. The Śiva of the Pallavas is not a terrible and cruel god; he does not inspire fear and terror but shows an example of family life."[30] In this context it is interesting to note that the endearing *Piḷḷaittamiḻ* (babytalk) used in praise of several deities whilst recounting the acts performed during divine childhood, is not in vogue for the god Śiva. The Tamiḻ love of spontaneity and gaiety, according to Dubreuil, led to the creation of the Somāskanda by the Pallavas. While it is true to say that the *bhakti* religion of the *Nāyaṉmār* with its emphasis on divine love and grace did create a tender caring Śiva, they were also aware of the god of the cemeteries, dark and foreboding, an aspect particularly emphasised by Kāraikkāl Ammaiyār.

What is of great significance is that the *Rauravāgama* (Ch. 34) states clearly that the best place, the most auspicious place for a Someśa sculpture is behind the *liṅga* in the *sanctum sanctorum* of the Śiva temple. It describes it under the caption *Someśvarasthāpanā vidhiḥ*. It states *"liṅgasya parabhāge tu garbhagehe viśeṣataḥ"*. This does not occur in any other Āgama. Either this Āgama was one of the early Āgamas or it was simply recording an iconic tradition originated and propagated by the Pallavas. What is important to note is that the image described is that of Someśa not Somāskanda. Ch. 35 states that Somāskanda is a variation of Someśa. Somāskanda can be distinguished from the Someśa of the *Rauravāgama* because of the following major differences: (1) The absence of a Skanda image, (2) Śiva and Umā are seated in separate pedestals, (3) The lower left hand of Śiva is in Siṁhakarṇa not *abhaya* as in Somāskanda images. Could this be the *Umaipaṅkaṉ* of the *Tēvāram* hymnists? Since the Somāskanda is described as a variant, one would have to believe that they were interchangeable icons.

The Somāskanda was given an increased ritual importance by the Cōḻas in his aspect of the *Viṭaṅka*, as testified by the Cōḻa epigraphs, as we shall presently see.

The Somāskanda was evolved during a time when the process of synthesis between the Sanskrit north and the Tamiḻ south was accelerated under royal patronage. It was also an age of religious synthesis. The Pallavas described themselves as *Paramabhāgavatas*, *Parama Śaivas* and *Paramabrāhmaṇyas*. The tradition of including such laudatory portions (*meykīrtis*)[31] in epigraphs of Tamiḻnāḍu was started by the Pallavas. A united Hindu front against the heterodox Jains and Buddhists was much encouraged. Murukaṉ was one of the earliest gods worshipped by the Tamiḻs. He was the god of hunters and of the mountain people; he was regarded as a lover and a warrior. His colour was red and he, as the lord of the forests, was the possessor of the elephant and the peacock as his symbols. Divination and shamanistic dances were associated with him. He was believed to provide rain and keep the earth fertile (*Puṟanāṉūṟu* 143). He was regarded as the god of justice (*Puṟanāṉūṟu* 35: 14). Murukaṉ in the later Caṅkam literature becomes identified with kings and chieftains (*Malaipaṭukaṭām* 651). He becomes the model of a king (*Puṟanāṇṉuṟu*, 16.2). As pointed out by Thangavelu, all the insignias of royalty were attributed to Murukaṉ.[32] The Tamiḻ word *muruku* is associated with beauty and youth in the early lexicons like *Tivākaram* (c.a. 8th century A.D.). Murukaṉ started as the son of Koṟṟavai, the goddess of war and later was assigned a father in Śiva. Murukaṉ is closely associated with the Tamiḻ land and the Tamiḻ language. The mythology of Murukaṉ is largely associated with the Tamiḻ country. Later poets emphasise this close link between Murukaṉ and Tamiḻ culture. These writers were most probably drawing on earlier oral traditions. This tradition of equating Murukaṉ with Tamiḻ has persisted to this day and even the self-proclaimed atheist Annaturai could openly state that Murukaṉ was the god of the *Tirāviṭa Muṉṉētṟa Kaḻakam* (DMK) without raising an eyebrow.[33]

This long digression on the nature and evolution of Murukaṉ is necessary to trace the dominant characteristics in the personality of the syncretistic deity Somāskanda. Many of these characteristics were transferred to Tyāgarāja; he was the god of the Tamiḻs, god of the Cōḻas, and god of fertility; he was the lover and the great god. His colour was red and he had all the insignia of royalty. Mucukuntaṉ,[34] the Cōḻa king who is credited with the bringing of Tyāgarāja to earth was a great devotee of Murukaṉ. This transference of Murukaṉ traits to Śiva was a phenomenon that was familiar in northern India too where, in the post-Gupta period the characteristics of Skanda were transferred to Śiva.[35]

It was in the post-Gupta period that Sanskrit and northern culture began to play an increasingly important role in Tamiḻnāḍu. Gupta influence can be detected in a good deal of Pallava sculptures too, e.g. the *gaṇas* in the Lalitāṅkara Cave Temple at Tiruccirāppaḷḷi.[36] The Pallavas assumed Sanskrit *abhiṣeka* names and claimed descent from *Mahābhārata* heroes such as Aśvatthāmā and the Cōḻas from a whole host of people - Hariścandra, Dilīpa, Raghu, Māndhātā and Śibi. Concessions to local sensitivity were made by linking themselves to the 'Tamiḻ' heroes Mucukuntaṉ, and Maṉunītıcōḻaṉ. The Pāṇḍavas of the *Mahābhārata* were regarded as the ancestors of the Pāṇḍyas. It was also the period when the rulers assumed Sanskrit names and coronation titles. The Pallavas called themselves by names such as Nṛpatuṅga and Aparājita, Mahendravarman and Narasiṁhavarman, etc., and assumed the title *cakravartī* in addition to the Tamil̲ *kōn̲ērimaikoṇṭāṇ*. A similar process was observable in the South East Asian kingdoms, e.g. in Cambodia where kings assumed Sanskritic names. It is interesting to see the process work in the reverse order in contemporary Tamil̲nāḍu, where Sanskrit names are deliberately translated into Tamil̲ and old Tamil̲ names are being revived with a view to emphasising the Tamil̲ identity of the person.

Kor̲r̲avai, the mother of Murukan̲ became the Pārvatī of the Somāskanda pantheon and thus the Pallavas seem to have evolved an excellent visual symbol for the Skanda-Murukan̲, Kor̲r̲avai-Umā and Śiva synthesis. It is, however, interesting to note the subtle difference in the mythic origins of the north Indian Skanda, who to begin with has a father but no mother and the Tamil̲ Murukan̲, who to begin with has a mother but no father. That it was a cult favoured by royalty, presumably to emphasise a close link between divinity and royalty, seems highly probable. The Somāskanda is not only repeated as an iconic symbol but several allusions are made in the Pallava epigraphs by which a Pallava king is identified with Śiva and, thus by inference, the royal family with the sacred trinity. The predominant characteristic of the Somāskanda icon in all texts on iconography is its regal aspect, as we have seen earlier. This theme of the relationship between royalty and divinity will be explored in greater depth in Chapter IX dealing with the rise of the Tyāgarāja cult to the status of a state cult. The *Avantisundarīkathā* of Daṇḍin[37] and the Kailāśanātha Temple Inscription[38] make the metaphor amply clear, wherein Rājasiṁha is compared to Guha (Skanda).

There has been some controversy regarding the function of the Somāskanda bas-reliefs at Mahābalipuram. K.V. Soundararajan believes that the Somāskanda icons were the focus of worship with the *liṅga* evolving at subsequent date. Other scholars question this assumption. This is discussed later in the chapter.

The Cōl̲a, or now presumably lost Pallava Somāskanda, cast in bronze or some perishable material such as clay but made as a mobile icon with the front and rear carefully chiselled, seems to have provided the iconographic model for the Tyāgarāja. An early Cōl̲a bronze of Somāskanda from Tiruvālaṅkāṭu of the 10th century A.D., now in the Madras Museum, [39] largely conforms to the descriptions given in the *śilpaśāstras*. Devī is seen to the left of the Lord with her right leg resting on the seat and the left hanging down. There is a difference in the *mudrā* adopted by Devī; the *Kaṭakahasta* is seen in the icon, while the texts recommend *Varamudrā*.[40] In most of the extant Cōḻa Somāskandas the Skanda is completely missing. In the Tiruvālaṅkāṭu specimen Śiva is shown with his left leg resting on the seat and his right hanging from the seat, with his foot on a stool. This is according to the prescriptions of the *Śilparatna* and accords with the earliest Somāskandas depicted in the Dharmarājaratha at Mahābalipuram, as far as the positioning of the leg of Śiva is concerned. The Cōḻa Śiva portrays a deer on the upper left and an axe on the upper right (though in this particular specimen it looks more ornate than usual). These characteristics were not yet evolved in the Pallava examples though they are fully in accordance with the *Śilparatna* injunctions. The ornaments, the crescent moon on the coiffure, are all strictly in accordance with prescriptions. The Tiruvālaṅkāṭu Somāskanda, unlike the common forms of Somāskanda, is shown carrying a *kapāla* (skull) in his lower right hand and a trident in the lower left. These attributes are also portrayed in an image of Śiva from Tiruvoṟṟiyūr commonly called the *Gauḷīśvara* but which is generally regarded as an image of Lakulīśa.[41] Śiva here is shown holding a *kapāla* in the upper left hand and a *triśūla* (the upper end of which is broken) in his upper right.

That it was the fully evolved variety of Somāskanda that constituted the Tyāgarāja model becomes evident from the description of Tyāgeśa given in the *Kamalālayacciṟappu*. This work is dated 1547 A.D. The iconographical details are repeated in the *Tiruvārūrpurāṇam*. Thus iconographically the Somāskanda evolved in three distinct stages—early Pallava, late Pallava and Cōḻa.

The stylistic and iconographic experimentation with regard to the Somāskanda figures continued well into the middle Cōḻa period with regard to the positioning of the figures, the attributes, etc. Even within the broad typologies of pre-Rājasiṁha and Rājasiṁha, one finds several sub-types as early as at Mahābalipuram. Thus, in the Mahiṣāsuramardinī cave panel both Śiva and Umā are shown resting their feet on the back of Nandī, a feature not present in other representations. At Irāvataneśvara a group of *gaṇas* in supplication is portrayed at the feet of the principal deities and the treatment of the footstool is unique in the Mātaṅgeśvara panel at Kāñcipuram. In all these, Śiva holds a serpent in the upper left hand while the upper right is shown sporting the *Siṁhakarṇa mudrā*. In the Tiruvālaṅkāṭu example a royal parasol is held just over Umā's head.

Some rather unusual Somāskandas come from Periyaveṇmaṇi in South Arcot district and Tirurpaṅkili (Tirurpaiññili of *Tēvāram*).[42] The upper right hand in the Periyaveṇmaṇi example seems to be holding a *triśūla* and the lower right rests on the thigh. The upper left holds what looks like an axe and the lower left is in *Kaṭakahasta*; the figures look very crowded with the knees of Śiva and Pārvatī almost touching each other. It is the left leg of Śiva that almost touches the left leg of Devī, as they both share the same footstool. Devī is in three-quarter profile and is shown holding Skanda with her right hand.

The Tirurppaṅkili specimen, possibly of about the ninth century A.D., is even more unusual in composition.[43] Śiva is shown holding a rosary in his upper left hand while his lower left rests on his lap in *dhyāna mudrā*. His upper right hand holds an antelope and the lower right is held in *Siṁhakarṇa mudrā*. It is his right leg that rests on the footstool. Pārvatī (Umā) is positioned to the right of Śiva which is extremely unusual. She is shown in three-quarter profile. She also holds a rosary in her right hand. The child Skanda is shown standing, depicted as a plump child. At Ecalam, Subrahmaṇya is portrayed in a niche and just above, in a separate niche, are portrayed Śiva and Pārvatī.[44]

Various styles are introduced during this experimental phase. Thus, at Takkōlam, Śiva sits in the 'Pre-Rājasiṁha' stylistic posture whereas Umā is portrayed like in "Rājasiṁha' images. Skanda, unlike the early Pallava specimens, is shown standing. Śiva's attributes are also different, for he holds a rosary and an axe in his back left and right hands respectively.[45]

The Takkōlam model resembles an image in the Tyāgarājasvāmi temple at Tiruvārūr, which is carved on the dado of a later *maṇṭapa*, created out of the long peristylar passage right round the twin shrines of Valmīkanātha and Tyāgarāja (Pl. IV). The cloistered peristyle in the North Eastern corner has some very modern paintings but also has a few stone sculptures telling the story of the advent of Tyāgarāja to earth but these are so heavily stuccoed that it is difficult to determine their date. The pillared verandah itself is presumably of the 11th -12th centuries A.D. and hence the sculptures can also be dated to that period. Śiva is shown here with a rosary and an axe.

Not only do the stone sculptures of Somāskanda betray several iconic types, for even in bronzes, there are several known types. The Tiruvālaṅkāṭu bronze icon, discussed earlier, for example, shows marked differences, with Śiva holding a *kapāla* and *triśūla*.

The Somāskanda of Tiruvāymūr, stylistically betraying both Pallava and Cōḻa treatment of the human anatomy, is the first of the images clearly to define the 'Cōḻa typology' with Śiva seated in full face holding an axe in his upper right and a deer in the upper left, while the lower right is held in *abhaya* and the lower left in *Cinmudrā*. Śiva's right leg is down and to acquire symmetry Umā's left leg is down. The Tiruvāymūr icon betrays the slim elongated and tightly controlled lines of a Pallava sculpture. The faces are heart-shaped with the cheek bones highly emphasised. Skanda is shown standing between his parents. Umā is portrayed wearing drapery with floral designs, a style which travelled to Indonesia and was popular in Central Javanese art.[46] This printed drapery also appears in several Pāla icons. Though this seems like a Pallava-Cōḻa transition piece, yet it looks later than the Somāskanda from Cōṟakuṭi, now in the Madras Museum.[47] Somāskandas from Talaiyālaṅkāṭu, Paṅkal, etc., conform to the Cōḻa inconographic idiom.

Thus, the Somāskanda iconic model for Tyāgarāja seems to have been evolved around the 10th century A.D. This coincides with the period of Rājarāja I. It was Rājendra I who built the Tyāgarāja shrine in stone both at Tiruvārūr and Tiruvoṟṟiyūr as is known from inscriptions.

The literary descriptions in the *Tēvāram* seem to have inspired the sculptors. Thus Śiva holding the axe and deer was known to Campantar (c.a. 7th century A.D.) for he refers to them in *Patikams* 160, 364, 106, etc. The icon holding these attributes is known to us from the 9th-10th centuries A.D., dateable only on stylistic grounds. Earlier specimens may have existed of perishable substance. It is about this same time that Naṭarāja images as high reliefs begin to appear in the Tamiḻ country. Rājarāja I made an image of Naṭarāja, called Āṭavallān of which a precise technical description is given in his Thañjāvūr inscription. From the later

Cōḻa period Naṭarāja shrines became a ritual imperative, much like the Somāskanda icon.

Based on the data we have, it seems reasonable to assume that the Somāskanda icon had a long period of evolution from the late 7th to the early 10th century A.D., first as an idea, then as an experimental form, before it acquired a definite standardised iconography. After this period Somāskandas betray only very minor variations. Their differences lie in the different aesthetic sensibilities of the sculptors rather than differences in iconographic content.

The Tyāgarāja iconic typology, with all its esoteric implications in all probability, evolved around the 12th century A.D. when the Temple religion of Tamiḻnāḍu became to a great extent tinged with Tāntrism (not to be mistaken as *Kaula mārga*, which also existed in some places). It is presumably to this period that we must attribute the mystico-esoteric tradition of embossing a *śrī-cakra* on the icon and the covering of the body and the following of other cult-dictated conventions.

Several paintings of the Tyāgarāja are known from the 18th century A.D. The Marāṭhās of Thañjāvūr (1676-1855) revived the cult and several Marāṭhā paintings on wood, paper and mica have come to light from the different museums and private collections within India and abroad. Before taking up a discussion of Tyāgarāja paintings it would be essential to define the Tyāgarāja typology.

Tyāgarāja Typology

The Tyāgarāja icon at Tiruvārūr, as noted earlier, can be regarded as the prototype of all Tyāgarāja images and the following description is of the icon at Tiruvārūr. All Tyāgarāja icons are wrapped in a mystic, esoteric tradition and as such only the faces of Śiva and Pārvatī are revealed to public view. Presumably because of following the prescribed inconometric proportions by which the recommended height of the Skanda image is one-eighth, one-tenth or one-quarter of the Śiva image,[48] he is completely hidden from view in all the flamboyance of the floral and ornamental decorations in which the icon is decked. In several fully exposed Somāskanda icons too, the Skanda is often missing. There can only be two plausible explanations for this. The Skanda icon, a standing or a dancing image in the Cōḻa Somāskandas was delicately balanced on the pedestal to give it the ethereal quality of a standing or dancing child. It could, therefore, have easily come off its fixture and thus, be either lost or have acquired the status of an independent icon or *pradhānamūrti*, and installed elsewhere. The priests of the Tiruvārūr temple vouch for the existence of a dancing Skanda between his parents.

All that is visible of the Tyāgarāja icon at Tiruvārūr are the following features:[49]

a) An elaborately ornate halo arranged in a highly symmetrical pattern of four horseshoes forming an elegant backdrop to the image, the outer ring of which exhibits alternating motifs of discus and flame, which are interestingly enough the attributes of Viṣṇu and Śiva respectively, the flame in particular being symbolic of the Naṭarāja aspect of Śiva. Thus, the Śiva-Viṣṇu syncretistic aspect is subtly hinted at with this iconic clue.
b) An exquisitely designed bulbous chignon which tops an ornamental crown, with the headgear iteself resembling that of the deity Aiyaṉār, minus his lop-sided tassel. When in full cult attire, he sports an elaborate crown over which are placed little wreaths of flowers topped by a thick band of waterlilies.
c) Two crescent moons, which adorn the two sides of the chignon.
d) Two perfectly circular floral studs, which adorn Śiva's ear lobes.
e) The carefully chiselled face of Śiva with a gentle, benevolent smile.
f) The torso of the deity, which is held so erect that it gives an impression of great height and majesty as it was wont to do and looks like a standing icon rather than a seated one.
g) Strings of horseshoe-shaped garlands, which adorn both the Śiva and Devī images and are not allowed to be knotted on the ends by cultic conventions and are thus called *patis*, (snakes).
h) Gold ornaments inset with precious stones, which adorn the plum-line of the Śiva and Devī icons, for Skanda, as mentioned earlier, is completely hidden from view and so are all attributes of Śiva and Devī.
i) Devī's face and the conical arrangement of her coiffure, which

bears marked resemblance to that of her consort.

j) A curious object to the right of Śiva, which is shaped like a mound and is covered with a cloth on which is painted a *liṅga* on a pedestal. The cloth is called by special name, *Tiyākappaṭṭu*, and is part of the cultic paraphernalia. Two circular stones rest on top of the cloth-covered mound.

k) Two swords are placed diagonally, almost framing the entire group of deities.

l) The ornate throne is decorated with inverted lotus emblems. The centre of this pedestal is occupied by two bulls facing each other. The centre piece, towards which the two bulls gravitate, looks like a lighted flame. On the two corners of the base of the throne are portrayed the sages Patañjali and Vyāghrapāda. This, again, is interesting as these two sages are closely connected with the theme of Śiva's dance at Chidambaram.

The general descriptions of the icon given above are of the Tyāgarāja in full cult attire. When bereft of this flamboyance, as he usually appears in the Bṛhadīśvara temple, Thañjāvūr, the icon is covered with a white cloth, revealing only the faces of Śiva and Umā. Behind the white cloth can be discerned a hard screen giving the general visual impression of an armour plate covered with a white sheet! The general belief expressed in several Tyāgarāja shrines is that a *Śrī-Cakra* adorns the image and this three dimensional *yantra* is covered by the *Tiyākappaṭṭu* or the piece of cloth with the *liṅga* painted on it, referred to earlier in the context of the Tiruvārūr image. The *Śrī-Cakra* emblem is regarded as a power emblem which attracts power to itself, like a magnet attracting pieces of iron, and is hence potentially dangerous in the hands of the unscrupulous or even simply the unwise. Thus, Tyāgarāja, originally a full blooded anthropomorphic representation of Śiva, Umā and Skanda, became more and more abstracted and was reduced in essence to a *Yantra*.[50]

When precisely such an esoteric tradition [51]came into vogue is difficult to determine. An explicit reference to the taboo of beholding the image with a graphic description of all the evil that could befall the curious trespasser is given in the *Tirukkāṟāyiṟpuṟāṇam*.[52] The same work also explains the reasons for this secrecy i.e. that it is an emblem of Śrī-Vidyā, as expressed through the medium of a *Śrī-Cakra.* The Pallava and early Cōḻa Somāskanda with their dominant Śiva traits had gradually been drawn into a Śakti orbit.[53] Tirukkāṟāyil is a *pāṭalpeṟṟa talam* or one visited by the *Tēvāram* hymnists.[54] Ñāṉacampantar has written a hymn on the deity of this place.[55]

An interesting feature in the architectural layout of the Tiruvārūr temple is that the *garbhagṛha,* or what should have been the *garbhagṛha,* is empty. Just behind the Tyāgarāja icon, which is installed in what is called the *devasabhā,* there is a blocked chamber, which is rectangular in shape. The *Vimāna* actually rises over this blocked area. Hence, architecturally this should have been the *garbhagṛha.* There is a waterchute or *praṇāla* emerging from this blocked area, suggesting that the ritual of water ablution or *abhiṣeka* was performed here or was intended to be performed here at the time of the construction of the temple.

The present Tyāgarāja shrine was built of stone by Rājendra I. B.G.L. Swamy in his monograph on Chidambaram suggests that there is a walled-in room at Chidambaram as well, where he believes Yogins sat in meditation. In fact he believes that the *Pratyabhijñā* form of Kashmir Śaivism with its stress on "inward vision" and "light" was prevalent in Chidambaram also. The rectangular shrine in Tiruvārūr could very well have housed a reclining Viṣṇu image. The silver door of the Tyāgarāja temple has a relief of a reclining Viṣṇu (Pl. V). A painting on a niche in the south wall of the shrine portrays a reclining Viṣṇu on whose bosom is enthroned the image of Tyāgarāja (Pl.VI). A real stone Viṣṇu icon could possibly have been housed here exactly as in Chidambaram. It is known that Kulōttuṅga II cast the image of Viṣṇu at Chidambaram into the sea. He was closely connected with the Tiruvārūr temple and instituted over fifty-one special rituals in the temple, as is known from his inscriptions at the temple. He could well have been responsible for uprooting the Viṣṇu image here too and walling in the shrine. This conjecture seems all the more plausible when we remember that Tyāgarāja cult has strong Vaiṣṇava traditions in its myths and rites.

An enigmatic epigraph from Tiruvārūr (S.I.I. Vol. XVII, No.614) refers to certain arrears of money as being due to Śri Ārūrar (i.e. Tyāgarāja). This payment, it is stated, was exempted in lieu of 40 kācu received from servants of Viṣṇu who were pleased to be in the standing posture at Maṉṟakam. This presumably reflects a state of affairs similar to Chidambaram where there are two major cults—the Naṭarāja and the Govindarāja, each with its own ritual personnel enjoying financial autonomy.

NOMENCLATURE OF THE DEITY

Viṭaṅka

In the two previous sections we have seen that Somāskanda was a Pallava innovation and was popular in the Toṇṭaimaṇṭalam region in particular, though examples are also found in Pāṇṭināṭu. The Cōḻas were feudatories of the Pallavas, and they had a special connection with the Somāskanda. So, whether it was a Pallava innovation or whether they appropriated it from the pre-Imperial Cōḻas and incorporated it into their sacred kingship is difficult to determine. In Chapter VII, I have also suggested the possibility that it was a Cōḻa territorial emblem, and was executed by them under Pallava patronage.

The traditional rulers of this area were the Cōḻas, Cēras and Pāṇḍyas, the *mūvēnta vēḷārs.* The Pallavas were outsiders and the Tyāgarāja could well have been one of the sacred motifs of the Early Cōḻas which the Pallavas as their overlords incorporated. There are examples of Somāskanda images in temples of present day Andhra Pradesh and Kerala, but they are all without exception, either built or endowed by the Cōḻas. A very well-known image of Somāskanda comes from Śucīndram. It is now called the Śucīndraperumāḷ and was, according to an inscription in the temple, installed in 1126 A.D. The epigraph describes the icon as "*Umāskandasahita tirumēṉi*" (the divine form along with Umā and Skanda). Śiva in the Śucīndraperumāḷ trinity is portrayed with the usual characteristics, viz. the axe and the antelope in his two upper hands and *abhaya* and *vara mudrās* in his two lower hands.[56]

The enigmatic term *Viṭaṅka* was associated with Tyāgarāja icons and does not seem to have been originally associated with the general Somāskanda *genre* of icons. At present, however, there are a number of temples which bear inscriptional references to *Viṭaṅka* icons. They do not exhibit all the characteristics of the Tyāgarāja typology, inasmuch as they do not conform to the esoteric veiling of the image nor are they aware of the Tyāgarāja myth so crucial to the cultic personality.[57] Whether the original

Tyāgarāja association had been forgotten and a new image of Somāskanda, minus the cult associations, was established at a later date to replace an earlier 'Tyāgarāja' image, it is difficult to determine.[58] A group of seven sacred temples, all in Cōḻamaṇṭalam and all belonging to the Tyāgarāja cult, are commonly referred to as the *sapta Viṭaṅka talaṅkaḷ*, 'the sacred seven *Viṭaṅka* sites'[59]. Again when precisely this group was formed is difficult to determine, but it must have been evolved by the middle Cōḻa period.

Present-day tradition attributes the term *Viṭaṅka* to a *liṅga*, 'made'[60] of precious stone and carefully preserved in a silver casket and ritually placed on the right hand side of the Somāskanda to which daily midday ablutions *(uccikāla abhiṣēkam)* and evening ablutions called *iraṇṭāṅkālam* in Tiruvārūr are performed. It is only after the rituals are complete for the Somāskanda-Tyāgarāja that the presiding deity is anointed, thereby giving a special status to this *utsavabera*. Incidentally, it is interesting to note that daily *abhiṣēkams* are not performed for the Valmīkanātha for he is a *puṟṟu*, or 'anthill', and hence it is believed would disintegrate. A *puṉuku* or special paste of sandalwood, incense powder etc., is applied on the aniconic symbol, i.e. the *liṅga*. This tradition is followed in Tiruvoṟṟiyūr as well and in other places where the *liṅga* is believed to be made of clay, etc. The unguent that is applied on the Tyāgarāja icon is known as *Tyāgavinōdaṉ* and the *Mucukundasahasranāmam* refers to the deity as being pleased with the application of the paste (Invocation 15). This *Viṭaṅka*, which is made of emerald in Tiruvārūr and of other similar precious stones elsewhere[61], is regarded as the subtle form of the Tyāgarāja, the emblem of the transcendental, in contradistinction to the Somāskanda Tyāgarāja icon itself, which belongs to the domain of the immanent.

The term *Viṭaṅka* is now unquestioningly accepted as of Sanskritic origin and etymologically split into *vi+ṭaṅka* 'one made without the use of the chisel' and consequently a *svayaṁbhū* or self-manifested *liṅga* and it is this self manifestation which makes it specially sacred. It seems unlikely that this is what the word meant in earlier times in Tamiḻ literature and epigraphy. It is however difficult to be certain what precisely the *Tēvāram* poets meant when they used this term. The *Madras University Tamiḻ Lexicon* gives several meanings for the word, apart from that of *svayaṁbhū*. It denotes, according to the above work 'a form of beauty', 'a narrow way' (*viṭu* = crack + *taṅkal* = place and therefore *Viṭaṅkal* 'a narrow way') and *Viṭaṅkal* becomes *Viṭaṅkaṉ* in the masculine form, for 'ṉ' is the male suffix. Interesting etymological possibilities were suggested by the linguist, Dr.Veerasamy.[62] The *Piṅkaḷanikaṇṭu* a lexicon popularly attributed to the 9th century A.D., also gives the meaning 'a form of beauty'. It does not refer to the meaning *svayaṁbhū*, as later lexicons do. Professor T. Nadarajan from Jaffna, Sri Lanka, drew my attention to a Tamil book entitled *Kamalālaya Kṣētratattuvam* (neither the name of the author nor the date of publication is available) where the author splits it into *vi* meaning birds and *ṭaṅkayati* meaning abode. So the term *Viṭaṅka* is interpreted as the abode of the birds. The birds are *haṁsa* - a play on words, for the word *haṁsa* denotes not only swans but also in yogic and tāntric parlance, inhalation and exhalation and these in turn have metaphysical significance for the Tyāgarāja cult. This has been taken up for detailed discussion in the chapter on iconology.

The term *Viṭaṅka* or its honorofic form *Viṭaṅkar*, when used in the Śaiva canonical works often has the connotation of something beautiful. Thus in *Tiruvicaipā*[63] occurs the description "*Ārūr ātiyāy vītiviṭaṅkarāy naṭaṅkulāviṉār*". A literal translation would be "As the Primal (Lord) of Ārūr as the beautifier of the streets (He) moved intimately (with the populace)". Appar[64] refers to "*Āruran eṉṉum vīti Viṭaṅkanāy*", "(the Lord) known as Āruran, the beautifier of the streets". In all this it is the deity's *utsavabera* form (as suggested by his sojourning in the streets of Ārūr) that is described. Appar, in the same hymn, describes how the women fell in love with the Lord as he came out in procession. This mood is well in keeping with the descriptions of Ārūrar in Cēramān Peumāḷ's *Tiruvārūr Mummaṇikkōvai*. The *Madras University Tamil Lexicon* gives the additional meaning of the term *Viṭaṅka* as 'one with dissolute habits'.

Cuntarar[65] addresses the deity of Tiruppaiññili as '*āraṇīya Viṭaṅkar*'(the *Viṭaṅkar* of the forest). In the same hymn,[66] while describing the Lord of the place, he uses the expression '*Viṭaṅkāka niṉṟu*', 'standing in an aesthetically pleasing manner'. The same poet, again in his hymn on Tirunākaikkārōṇam refers to the beauty of the Lord with his matted locks let down and moving through the streets (*Viṭaṅkāka vīti viṭai peṟuvīr*)[67]. In the *Periya Purāṇam* of Cēkkiḻār the word *Vīti Viṭaṅkār* is simply used as the name of the deity of Tiruvārūr, who is clearly distinguished from the *mūlattānar* or the presiding deity[68]. In v.276 the word is used again in the compound *caiva viṭaṅku* and it stands according to the commentator C.K. Cupparamaṇimutaliyār for all the visible marks of a Śaiva devotee, which he regards as his embellishments, such as the sacred ash, the rosary, etc.

In Parañcōti muṉivar's *Tiruviḷaiyātaṟ Purāṇam* occurs the phrase *'vēlyeṉa vanta nāyakar cuntara Viṭaṅkarāṉār'* [69]. Here again, it seems the word is used in the sense of a form of beauty. In the litany of the *Mucukundasahasranāmam*, the word is used in a more metaphysical sense,[70] as *virata Viṣṇu samutpanna Viṭaṅkātmasvarūpavate*, with a link to the myth as well, for it describes the *Viṭaṅka* as conceived by Viṣṇu and manifested in the form of the essence *(ātmā)*, *(Viṭaṅkātmasvarūpavate)*; here presumably, the reference is to the essence of godhead and the reference is most probably to the *svayambhū* form. Appar (Tēv.1.9: *Kōyiṟ Tiruniruttam*) invokes the Lord of Tillai as *Paḻitēruṇṭuḻalum Viṭaṅkarvēṭa ciṉṉattiṉāṉ malitillaiyuṭ ciṟṟampalattu naṭṭam*. Here the dancer of Chidambaram is addressed as one who begs and who in the garb of the *Viṭaṅka*, which acts as his distinguishing mark (*ciṉṉam* = sign), etc. Here "Viṭaṅka" possibly refers to his beauteous form, which is his hallmark, his garb.

Viṭaṅka in Epigraphy

The term *Viṭaṅka* occurs several times in epigraphy as well, from the time of the Cōḻas. Rājarāja I set up several *pañcaloha* images and prominent among them were Āṭavallār, Dakṣiṇamēruviṭaṅkar, Tañjai Viṭaṅkar and Mahāmēruviṭaṅkar. Rājarāja I had set up the images to which his sister Kuntavi added by setting up icons of the consorts of Dakṣiṇamēruviṭaṅkar and the Tanjaiviṭaṅkār.[71] Kuntavi, again, is the generous donor of gold vessels and ornaments to the image of Dakṣinamēruviṭaṅkār on various dates between 23rd and 29th regnal years of Rājarāja I[72]. The gifts were most generous, consisting of pearls, corals and lapis lazuli. That the images were processional images becomes clear when a grant is made to decorate the sacred hall (*tiruvaraṅku*), which the consorts of the above mentioned gods occupied when on procession during the sacred festival (*tiruviḻā*). Expenses for food, garlands, etc., we are told, were to be covered by a grant of money deposited with the villagers, which was also expected to cover the expenses of the procession of the two consorts. Umā Paramesvarī seems to be the name of the consort of both Āṭavallār Dakṣiṇamēruviṭaṅkar and Tañjaiviṭaṅkar[73] Another epigraph refers to the grant of Kuntavi to the above-mentioned consorts dated in the regnal years of her nephew Rājendra I.[74] A simliar grant is also made to the Lords Mahāmēruviṭaṅkar and Dakṣiṇamēruviṭaṅkar during Rājendra's rule.[75] One of Rājarāja's wives bears the name Danti Śakti Viṭaṅki.[76]

Another very interesting piece of information is provided by a set of inscriptions[77], wherein it is stated that a group of people designated *niyāyaṉ ciṟuntāṉattu valaṅkai vēlaikkārappaṭaikaḷilār* (the regiment of the right-handed servants attached to the endowment) were attached by royal order to the image of the Dakṣiṇamēruviṭaṅkar and from the interests on an endowment of 125 *kācus* deposited with *brahmadēyas* and *caturvēd-imaṅgalams,* they were to meet the expenses of the deity. It is significant to note in this context that the Devadāsīs of the Tiruvoṟṟiyūr temple were divided into two groups—*valaṅkai* and *iṭaṅkai* and while the *valaṅkai dāsis* danced before the Tyāgarāja, the *iṭaṅkai* danced before Vaṭivuṭaiyammaṉ. This information was provided by the trustee and also independently by the *Kurukkaḷ* of the temple. The different epigraphs referred to above record basically the same information though different grants were made which were deposited in the hands of different *brahmadēyas* and *caturvēdimaṅgalams* but the ritual personnel and the deity to whom the offerings were made remained unaltered.

It is thus from the time of Rājarāja and Rājendra that the term *Viṭaṅka* comes to be regularly used in epigraphs and it is evident from the wording of the epigraphs that the Āṭavallāṇ of Chidambaram and the *Viṭaṅkar* of Thañjāvūr (a concept borrowed from Tiruvārūr) were raised to the status of state cults under the two illustrious Cōla rulers. *Vītiviṭaṅkaṉ* and *Āṭavallāṉ* became the names of standard measures of weight and in a record of the 26th year of Rājarāja I from Tiruvāmattūr it is clearly stated that a surplus was left as a result of measuring paddy by *vītiviṭaṅkaṉ* instead of the standard *Rājakēsari.*[78] The icons at Tiruviṭaṅkaṉ are called Naṭarāja Perumāḷ Māṇikkakkūttar and Āṭalviṭaṅkar.[79] While some writers have equated all the three deities, it seems clear that while the first epithet refers to the Naṭarāja, the term Āṭalviṭaṅkar refers to the Somāskanda. *ARE*

278 of 1907 and 254 of 1907 from Tiruviṭaimarutūr refer to Pañcavan̲ Mahādēvi's endowing (No. 278) and setting up (No. 254) of images of "Umā-Sahita" (possibly the Āṭalviṭaṅkar). This queen was either Rājarāja's wife or Rājendra's of the same name. Uttamacōḻa's wife, Cempiyan̲ Mahādēvi also built a shrine with the image of Tan̲mavitaṅkar at Ar̲aner̲i in Tiruvārūr.[80] Thus the two images foremost in the minds of these 'middle Cōḻa kings' were Vītiviṭaṅkan̲ and Āṭavallār and hence the "*Umā-sahitatirumēn̲i*" must have been a variation of the Somāskanda. Even at Tirupuvan̲am the Somāskanda is prominently enthroned in the *mukha maṇṭapa*. The Tiruviṭaṅkan̲ temple has been assigned to Uttamacōḻa's reign by Douglas Barrett,[81] and so "was built of stone in or around 973 A.D."[82] At this period the predominant deities were Naṭarāja and Tyāgarāja (Vītiviṭaṅkar) and the Āṭal (dance) here therefore refers to the dance of Viṭaṅkar. At Tiruvāymūr, as we shall presently note, is an *āṭalviṭaṅkar* and the site is one of the *saptaviṭaṅka* sites.

An inscription from Tirukkāravācal[83] dated in the 28th regnal year of Rājarāja I, i.e. 1013 A.D. refers to gifts of land by the residents of Mūvūr and in demarcating the boundary it refers to a field south of the Ātiviṭaṅkan̲ canal. The name is of particular interest as the deity of the place is called Ātiviṭaṅkan̲. Stated in a chronological order the next reference is to Tan̲maviṭaṅkar of the 8th regnal year of Rājendra I (1020 A.D.) and comes from the north wall of the Acaleśvara shrine, which belongs to the Tyāgarājasvāmi temple complex in Tiruvārūr. The name Kāraṇai Viṭaṅkār occurs in an epigraph of Rājādhirājadeva I (1018-54 A.D.), from Tiruvor̲r̲iyūr in the suburbs of Madras, yet another of the cult centres. The temple of Āṭipurīśvara (the name of the presiding deity) at Tiruvor̲r̲iyūr, i.e. the actual stone structure, was built by Rājendra I, though the site itself was well known from Pallava times and several Pallava inscriptions of the 9th century A.D. have come to light from here.

Interestingly enough, it was during the time of Rājendra I that the stone temple of *Viṭaṅkar* in Tiruvārūr was also constructed. The name Vītiviṭaṅkar, that of the deity of Tiruvārūr, occurs in several inscriptions from the place.[84] One is dated in the reign of Kulōttuṅga III in the 13th year, i.e. 1190-91[85] and another which does not bear the regnal name of a king has been paleographically dated in the 12th century A.D. Yet another inscription is dated in the 49th year of Kulōttuṅga I, i.e. 1118-1119 A.D. (606 of SII VOL.XVII). Another interesting reference is provided in an inscription dated in the 48th regnal year of Kulōttuṅga I[86] in which reference is made to a Ālaviṭaṅkatēvar, who is described as a deity taken out in procession *(tiruvutsavaṅkaḷ eḻuntaruḷum)*. The name of a dancer of the Tiruvārūr temple complex transferred to Thañjāvūr by Rājarāja I is given as Vītiviṭaṅki and she belonged to the street called Periyataḷiccēri, which was presumably named after the twin temples Valmīka and Tyāgarāja. The latter temple must have existed of brick or mud before being reconstructed of stone under Rājendra I. 680 of 1919 refers to the Vītiviṭaṅka temple being built and endowed in 1012-44 A.D. by Paravai during the reign of Rājendra I.

Several other *Viṭaṅkas* are known from inscriptions such as Puvaṉiviṭaṅkar from Vedāraṇyam[87] in the 15th regnal year of Rājarāja I. From Chidambaram comes the reference to Mēruviṭaṅkar and Tillaiviṭaṅkar.[88] While an epigraph of Kulōttuṅga III's time from Tiruvāymūr refers to Āṭalviṭaṅkar[89]. The Vītiviṭaṅkar of Tiruvārūr is treated as a real personage who speaks and issues an edict, sits and watches a performance in the Tēvācirīyamaṇṭapam and refers to Piḷḷaiyār as 'our son' and to the ruler as 'our friend'. Examples of such first-person usage with reference to deities was prevalent in the 12th-13th century epigraphs and though not a very popular tradition was certainly not unknown. 150 of 1956-57 refers to Aḻakaviṭaṅkaperumāḷ and 164 of 1956-57 to Nākai Aḻakar. The last 2 came from Nāgapaṭṭanam and thus seem to refer to the *Viṭaṅka* of the place. This site is one of the *sapta Viṭaṅka* sites.

From the foregoing discussion several things emerge clearly: (a) The term *Viṭaṅkar* was used by several writers to denote a processional image. (b) From the references to his sitting in the *Tēvācirīya* maṇṭapam, issuing orders, etc., it seems likely that the reference is to an anthropomorphic figure and not an aniconic one. (c) Though no iconographical descriptions of the *Viṭaṅkar* are given either by the *Tēvāram* writers or by the epigraphs, the fact that nowadays processional images are Somāskandas makes it probable that the *Viṭaṅkas* were Somāskandas in the Pallava and Cōḻa times as well. (d) In all present-day temples though the Somāskanda is itself a trinity consisting of Śiva, Devī and Skanda, the epigraphs still refer to the consort of the two *Viṭaṅkar*, and the consorts like the consorts of Tyāgarāja bear the same name at all times. Nīlotpalāmpāḷ is the consort of all Tyāgarājas and Umā Parameśvarī the consort of both the *Viṭaṅkas* referred to in the Thañjāvūr inscriptions. (e) The present-day association of the term *Viṭaṅka* with the *liṅga* of precious stone has a close parallel in the Naṭarāja of Chidambaram, where a *liṅga* made of crystal called the Candramaulīśvara occupies a similar ritual status. Appar describes it as "marked by the *Viṭaṅka.*" Popular tradition, despite denials by the Dīkṣitars of the Naṭarāja temple, ascribes the installation of the *Sphaṭika liṅga* to Śaṅkara and associates it with the Śrī-Vidyā Cult. The close link between the *liṅga* and the Somāskanda in Pallava times has been, as mentioned earlier, the subject of much discussion. To reiterate the earlier argument, the prismatic *liṅgas* placed before the Somāskanda panels in the Pallava temples in all probability represented the transcendental form of the Somāskanda, as pointed out by L'Hernault.[90]

K.V. Soundararajan and K.R. Srinivasan both believe that these were installed later than the time of chiselling of the Somāskanda panel.[91] The reasons given by Soundararajan are:

1) In the Rock-cut caves at Mahābalipuram one would expect a Rock-cut *liṅga* but what is found instead is a separate prismatic *liṅga* individually carved and installed.
2) There is a conspicuous absence of *praṇāla* or water chute to drain the *abhiṣeka* water. Where there are *praṇālas* their alignment is such that they do not match the position of the *liṅga* and were later additions inasmuch as they are crudely cut and the *vārimārga* seems improvised whenever it appears and often, as seen above, does not appear at all.
3) The Atiraṇacanda cave inscription of Rājasiṁha refers to the Somāskanda as installed in the temple.

K.V. Soundararajan emphasises the conspicuous positioning of the Somāskanda at the rear of the chamber and the rather off-centre position of the *liṅga*. A parallel is noticeable at Katirkāmam in Śrī Laṅkā where the focal point of worship is the painted image of Kārttikeya. In place of the liṅga there is a *yantra* of Murukaṉ (i.e. Katirkāma). It is this *yantra* that is taken in procession.[92] The shrine of Śiva at Katikāmam is also similarly treated. The main object of worship being a painted image of Śiva with no *liṅga*.

Thus, the Somāskanda could well have been the main object of worship.[93]

Lockwood, on the other hand, believes that the Somāskanda and the *liṅga* were both objects of worship, at least from the time of Rājasiṁha. As for the absence of *praṇālas* or water chutes, Lockwood believes that the *abhiṣeka* water was presumably collected in a pitcher by the priests. He further suggests that *abhiṣeka* may not have been such an elaborate rite in the early Pallava days. L'Hernault seems to have captured the spirit of the whole composition for she regards the *liṅga* as the representative of the Somāskanda. The two seem to be philosophically inseparable. They stand for *nirguṇa* and *saguṇa, sthūla* and *sūkṣma* forms. Lockwood too generally holds the same view[94] with the added emphasis on God-king identification, which will be discussed in Chapter IX.

The *Rauravāgama* states, as seen earlier, that the Sōmeśa, with its variation, the Somāskanda was carved behind the *liṅga* but unfortunately there is great uncertainty about the age of the *Rauravāgama*. S.R. Balasubrahmanian refers to three temples with such an arrangement in the middle Cōḻa period. They are the Kāyārōhaṇasvāmī temple at Nāgapaṭṭanam and the Vijayālaya Cōḻīśvaram temples at Vikkaṇampūṇṭi and Tiruvīḻimiḻalai. The Kāyārōhaṇasvāmī is one of the *Sapta Viṭaṅkatalaṅkaḷ*. Behind the Kāyārōhana the Somāskanda is carved on the rear wall. L'Hernault[95] refers to several Somāskandas carved "on the ground" behind the *liṅga* in Cōḻa temples. The term "ground" used in the English translation must be taken to mean the lowest level of the rear wall.

The Vītiviṭaṅka mentioned in the *Tēvāram* and *Mucukunda-sahasranāmam* seems to have been a term for both an aniconic and anthropomorphic figure, with transferable identities.

Today the term *Viṭaṅka* refers to a portable *liṅga* made of precious stone. It is described as the *kuṇḍaḻinī* and Tiruvārūr itself is described as the *Mūlādhāra kṣetra*. In the Tāntric system *Kuṇḍalinī* lies coiled like a serpent wound around itself three and a half times and covering the mouth of the *svayaṁbhū liṅga*. It is believed to lie in the *mūlādhāra*. The *Ṣaṭcakranirūpaṇa* (v.50), a Tāntric work, describes the arousal of Kuṇḍalinī as "piercing the centre of the *svayaṁbhū liṅga* the mouth of which is closed and therefore invisible". This *liṅga* (as we know from several Yogic Upaniṣads) when its mouth is opened by the *Kuṇḍalinī* raising and hence uncoiling herself, is finally seen as the resplendent crystal column symbolising the union of Śiva and Śakti in the *brahmarandhra* and is the state of salvation for the yogin. The *liṅga* with its opening blocked by the *Kuṇḍalinī* was well-known to the author of the above work. Thus this crystal or emerald or garnet *liṅga* seems to be a Śrī-Vidyā symbol and the *Mucukundasahasranāmam* is full of references to the Śrī-Vidyā character of the Tyāgarāja cult, a feature emphasised in all Tyāgarāja shrines.

Śrī-Vidyā is one of those schools of Tāntrism which was subscribed to by the Smārta Brāhmaṇas as well as the Śaiva Non-Brāhmaṇa followers of the cult. When precisely Śrī-Vidyā became an established creed in South India is difficult to determine, but the 12th century A.D. has been generally regarded as the age of systematisation of Tāntric beliefs in Tamiḻnāḍu.[96] This was also about the same time when *Kāmakkōṭṭams* or devī shrines were introduced as an integral part of the Tamiḻ Śaiva complex. [97] It was also the period when folk rituals centering around Devī were incorporated into the official canonical faith of Temple worship.[98] The *Saundaryalaharī*, the bible of the Śrī-Vidyā was also presumably composed in the 10th century A.D.[99] and must have become very popular by this period, i.e. the 12th century A.D. This was also the time when the *Mucukundasahasranāmam* with its Śrī-Vidyā-orientation was composed.[100]

Thus the final question one is left to ponder over is what was the *Viṭaṅka* of the *Tēvāram* writers? It seems most likely that it was an object of beauty and was used in that sense of the term and when mingled with Tāntric ideas, the *svayaṁbhū liṅga* of Śaivite philosophical import, became the emblem of *haṁsa*, the resplendent *Kuṇḍalinī* at the end of its soteriological function. The mystery of the *Tēvāram* writers and the epigraphs not describing a Somāskanda image, or for that matter the term *Viṭaṅka*, may have to be explained by some esoteric tradition which forbade the description of those Somāskandas linked with Viṭaṅkas, i.e Tyāgarājas.[101]

The Name Tyāgarāja

In epigraphs the name Tyāgarāja, as the name of the deity, occurs for the first time in a Marāṭhā inscription of Ekoji and is dated 1605 Śaka Era, i.e. 1683 A.D. and comes from Accāḷpuram in

Śīrkāḻi Taluq.[102] The two *Sthalapurāṇa*s (Tam. *talapurāṇa* or pilgrim literature) of Tiruvārūr and that of Tiruvoṟṟiyūr of the 16th century A.D. refer to the name Tyāgarāja. The deity of Tiruvārūr is referred to in all early works as Vītiviṭaṅkaṉ and alternately as Ārūraṉ. That these two names were used as synonyms to refer to the same deity is evident from a number of references in the post 16th century literature. The opening verse of *Tiruvārūrkkōvai* is an invocation of *Vīrattiyākapperumāḷ Vītiviṭaṅkapperumāḷ* (the valorous lord Tyāga, the lord Vītiviṭaṅka).[103] Kumarakurupara describes the deity as *"tērūrnta celva tiyākane Ārūr vītiviṭaṅka"* (the precious Tyāga who gently moves seated on the chariot, the Vitiviṭaṅka of Ārūr).[104] In the 16th-17th century works the nomenclature Tyāgarāja is popularly used to denote the deity of Tiruvārūr. *Tiyākavalli, Tiyākapatākā* were expressions known from Cōḻa epigraphs to describe either the names of people or names of measures.[105] A regiment called the *Tiyākavalli vēlaikkārar* is mentioned in 562 of 1904, 607 of *S.I.I. XVII* dated 1120-21 A.D. The same inscription also mentions a *Tiyāka Vinōtaṉ cālai maṭam.* (a monastery in the street called Tyāgavinoda)

The only work, presumably of an earlier date than the 16th century A.D., to refer to the deity as Tyāgarāja is the *Īṭṭiyeḻupatu*[106] of Oṭṭakkūttar, the 12th century A.D. court poet of three successive Cōḻa monarchs.[107] It is presumably to this period that the *Mucukundasahasranāmam* is dateable and in this liturgical invocation the Tyāgarāja concept is stated in highly Śākta terms.[108]

The epithet *tyāga* is used several times in the *Mucukundasahasranāmam* for describing the deity's 'qualities'. The word *tyāga* is used in the two distinct senses of 'renouncing' or 'abandoning' and 'giving'. While both the above meanings are known to Sanskrit and Tamiḻ, the usage of the word to denote 'charity', 'liberalty', etc., are more commonly used in Tamiḻ than in Sanskrit. Thus, as pointed out by Winslow in his Tamiḻ to English Dictionary,[109] it is used in sentences such as *"avar oruvariṭattilum tiyākam vāṅkuvatillai"* (he does not accept charity from anyone) or in expressions such as *tiyākam kūṟa, tiyākam iṟaikka,* etc., meaning 'to proclaim one's charities' or 'spread one's munificence', etc.[110] Thus, in invocations 132 and 133 of the *Mucukundasahasranāmam* he is described as 'the renouncer of the darkness of ignorance' (*ajñānatimiratyāga*), the abandoner of the *Kāraṇa* or primal cause, i.e.of *karma.* In 134, he is said to have relinquished all characteristics (*upādhi*), thus, referring to his *nirguṇa* state. Invocations 141 and 150 could be interpreted in both ways as giver and renouncer of 'the six aids to meditation' (*adhvāṣaṭka parityāga*) and 'the five *mantras* and the six aids to meditation' (*pañcamantra ṣaḍaṅgādi parityāga*) respectively for he gives these to his followers and by transcending all these limitations has become Tyāgarāja. This is how it has to be explained; otherwise the expression *vidvajjanadhanatyāgine* in 136 does not make sense, for then he becomes the abandoner of the wise (*vidvajjana*). This idea of his having sacrified his pleasures for the welfare of mankind is already suggested by Appar, when he says, "*amarar nāṭāḷātē ārūrāṇṭa airāvaṇamē*" in VI.238.1., where he invokes Tyāgarāja, as one who having given up the rule of the heavens has descended to the earth to rule Ārūr.

Venkaṭamakhin, the 17th century codifier of the seventy-two *melakartā rāgas* in Carnatic music and the court musician of Vijayarāghava explains the meaning of the terms as follows:

> "*caturṇām puruṣārthānām tyāgam yasmāt karotyataḥ*
> *Tyāgarājam iti khyātam Somāskandam upāsmahe*"

I offer my obeisance to Somāskanda, called Tyāgarāja, so called because of his sacrifice for the welfare of the four *puruṣārthas*.[111] Kumarakuruparar in v. 24 of *Tiruvārūr Nāṉmaṇimālai* explains the name as one who has given the universe to Viṣṇu, given all the 'nine' treasures to Kubera, happiness and domestic bliss to his followers and half his body to the virgin and thus earned the epithet Tiyākar (*Kamalai Tiyākareṉpatu iyar ivarukkē takum*). K.V. Raman has pointed out how Kāñcī was known as *Tyāga Maṇṭapa* in the 13th and 14th centuries A.D. He refers to the *Guruparamparā* which describes Kāñcī as Tyāgamaṇṭapa and Śrī Raṅgam as *Bhōga Maṇṭapa*. The *Guruparamparā* has been dated by him in the 13th century A.D. The *Ācāryahṛdayam* of Aḷakiya Maṇavāḷa Nāyaṉār (14th century) also mentions this.[112]

THE SYMBOLIC FUNCTIONS

Tyāgarāja, the Dancer

Though the *Caṅkam* classics make no mention of the dance of Śiva, the *Cilappatikāram* refers to *Koṭukoṭṭi* (and other dances of Śiva)[113] and Kāraikkāl Ammaiyār makes several references. Some of the most frequent epithets used for the deity are : *Acaintāṭiya Perumāḷ* (the gently swaying dancer), *antiyum cantiyum āṭuvār* (the one who dances at morn and the evening), *āṭātuāṭavallār* (the expert dancer who dances without actually dancing)[114] *Iruntāṭalakar* (the beautiful one, who dances while seated), an expression which gets translated into Sanskrit as *āsīnatāṇḍava.*

Other epithets such as *kiṇkiṇikālalakar* (the one with beautifully ankleted feet) and several other epithets suggesting his association with dance are constantly used to describe the deity. That this dance was a part of the eschatology, ontology and soteriology of the cult is clearly discernible in terms like *aiñkaraṇai tāṇṭavaṉ,* (the dancer of the five deeds), *pañcākṣarasūkṣmanaṭanam,* (subtle dance of five syllables)[115]. He is invoked as *haṁsatāṇḍavasuprītāya,* 'one who loves the *haṁsa* dance' etc. This element of the dancer is referred to several times by the *Tēvāram* writers and is not solely applied to Tyāgarāja. Appar addresses the Lord of Araneri at Tiruvārūr as "*āṭavallār*", an epithet popularly attributed to Naṭarāja of Chidambaram by the Cōḻa epigraphs. Appar refers to the Tyāgarāja of Tirukkōḷili as "*Kūttaṉār uṟaiyum Tirukkōḷili*", (the place where the dancer resides). In IV.120.1. Appar again describes the deity as "*Kokkaṟai Kuḻal viṉai Koṭukoṭṭitō āṭum ampoṟ kaḻal aṭikaḷ ārūrar*". Appar sings of Śiva's dance in almost every *patikam.* By Appar's time Tillai had assumed great importance.

Tyāgarāja, the Paradigmatic Sovereign

Irattinacciṅkātipati, 'the Lord of the jewelled throne', *cemporciṅkātipati,* 'the Lord of the golden throne', *siṁhāsaneśvara, Rājarāja, mahārāja,* etc. are some of the oft-repeated descriptions symbolising the grandeur of the monarch. Interesting epithets occur in the *Mucukundasahasranāmam* where Tyāgarāja is described as *rājaveṣadhāra,* 'one who has donned the garb of the king',[116] *pureśa,*'the lord of the city', and what is even more significant as *Anapāya Mahīpāla* and *Anapāya pureśa*[117].

The title *Anapāya* is often used to describe Kulōttuṅga II who was a keen devotee of Tyāgarāja of Tiruvārūr. Tyāgarāja is also alluded to as *Karuṇākara Toṇṭaimāṉ,* who was a real historical personage, a feudatory of Kulōttuṅga I, who conquered Kaliṅga.[118] This is probably the result of a mix-up between the legendary Toṇṭaimāṉ and the historical personage. The legendary Toṇṭaimāṉ is associated with Tirumullaivāyil and the episode of his striking the sacred spot with the hoofs of his horse and finding a bleeding *liṅga* are alluded to by Cuntarar in *Patikam* 69, on the deity of Mullaivāyil. The present *mariyātai* done to the Toṇṭaimāṉs at Tiruvārūr temple is from an endowment which was created by the Toṇṭaimāṉs of Pudukkōṭṭai and named after their overlords the Cētupatis of Ramnad. Beneficiaries of temples and sovereigns regarded as great devotees were often invoked in ritual incantations along with the names of the deity. This is most clearly indicated in the Āgamic rites performed at Rāmēśvaram. In the rites called *Āvāhanam* and *Visarjanam* which are performed before the emblem of the Lord is taken to Devī's bedchamber, the names of the diety are invoked. Along with it are invoked the names of the Cētupatis.

The Functional Status of the Processional Image

Epithets such as *Vītisañcārasundara*, 'the beautiful form of the sojourner of the streets', *āḻittēraḻakar;* the beautiful lord of the *āḻittēr* or the chariot called *āḻi, tērūrntacelvattiyākar*, 'the prosperous lord of the moving chariot', etc., are frequently used to represent his functional aspect. The *Mucukundasahasranāmam* has a number of descriptions of the role of the deity as riding a chariot and it treats the chariot as a huge metaphor to denote several philosophical categories.[119] That Āruran and Vītiviṭaṅkaṉ were synonymous is made amply clear by Appar when he says *"ārūraṉ eṉṉum pavaṉi vīiviṭaṅkaṉai"*,'the Vītiviṭaṅka sojourner known as Āruraṉ' -(Appar IV. 17.6.)

Tyāgarāja's Love of Tamiḻ

Some of the most frequently used epithets for Tyāgarāja are *Tēvāraṅkaṇṭaperumāṉ* 'the Lord, who discovered the *Tēvāram*', *niṟaintacentamiḻccērārūrpati*, 'the Lord of prosperous Ārūr, which is rich in pure Tamiḻ' (*Tyāgeśakuṟavañci* 51). Other epithets include *mūvartamiḻukkukantavaṉ*, 'one who is the object of the Tamiḻ of the trio, meaning the *Tēvāram* trio', (*Tyāgeśakuṟavañci* v.52) and in the *Mucukundasahasranāmam*, interestingly enough his love of the southern culture is described in Sanskrit as *Drāviḍastotratoṣita*, 'lover of the Tamiḻ stotras', *bhakta sundara saṅgīta*, a devotee of Sundara's (Cuntara) music, etc. This transference of Murukaṉ traits to Śiva, as the *teṉṉavaṉ*, the 'southerner' is a characteristic feature of the *Tēvāram* literature and several references are made to the close link between Śiva and Tamil̲. Cuntarar asserts that Śiva is considered a Tamil̲ian *'tamil̲an̲ en̲r̲u pāvikka valla* VII.31.6 or *paṇṇārin̲ tamil̲āy paramāya parañcuṭarē* (VII.24.5.). These are, however, not exclusively applied to Tyāgarāja but to Śiva in general. In the *Sundaramūrti Aṣṭottaraśatanāmāvali* (60-65) Tyāgarāja is addressed as the propagater of Drāviḍa Vidyā, Vyākaraṇa and Sampradāya, i.e. learning, grammar and tradition of the Draviḍian people. He is further described as one worshipped by the Drāviḍas. The nāyan̲mār, particularly Ñān̲acampantar is extremely conscious of the importance of his Tamil̲ identity.

Apart from these epithets there are several ritual objects associated with the Tyāgarāja and several concepts associated with him, which define his role as a sovereign of the Tamil̲ country. He has all the emblems of royalty, an elephant, swords, a throne, a chariot, wealth, a flag, special musical instruments, dancers, retinue and capital city. Tiruvārūr̲ is his capital, Col̲amaṇṭalam his realm, Kāvēri his river etc. This association of Śiva with the sacred geography of Cōl̲amaṇṭalam and the Kāvēri river interestingly enough, finds mention in the Tiruccirāppaḷḷi epigraph of Mahendravarma Pallava [120] (*S.I.I.Vol.I*), where Hara (i.e. Śiva) is reported to have politely asked the king "How could I, while remaining in a temple on earth, see the great land of the Cōl̲as or the river Kāvēri?" and to solve the problem as it were, Mahendra is said to have built him a temple on the lofty mountain. Pārvatī is said to be afraid of Śiva's love for the Kāvēri and so came down to Tiruccirāppaḷḷi to be with her Lord and she gently reminds Śiva that the Pallava is the Lord (husband) of Kāvērī. Here we can see how the Kāvērī is treated as equivalent to the Ganges, for it is the Ganges who is regarded as the second wife of Śiva. Thus the incorporative sacred geography of the Hindus gets extended further south.

While most Tyāgarāja shrines are aware of these epithets and the myths of the cult, there are several temples, where the cultic associations have been completely forgotten. In Tiruvārūr it is still kept alive and so also in the seven *Viṭaṅka* shrines. In Thañjāvūr the *kurukkaḷ*, 'the officiating priest', was very surprised when asked to perform a special *arccan̲ai* (offering) for Tyāgarāja. It was the first time he had been asked to do so in his term of office. Thus, while several shrines now have an icon called Tyāgarāja, these do not really follow all the cultic prescriptions.

Tyāgarāja in Paintings

As mentioned earlier, several late medieval Tyāgarāja paintings have come to light. These are done on mica, wood or paper and are housed in the different museums all over Tamilnāḍu and abroad. The two very well preserved paintings on wood belonging to the Marāṭhā period reproduced in the end of this work come from the Sarasvatī Mahal Library, Thañjāvūr. It is interesting to see the King Serfoji in a place traditionally assigned to Cuntarar standing in supplication before the Tyāgarāja. He stands just behind Viṣṇu and Lakṣmī. This composition occurs in the Nīlōtpalāmpāḷ shrine as well where Serfoji is again depicted in his full Marāṭhā attire of royalty in *anjali mudrā* before the Tyāgarāja icon. (Pl. III)

Several other Tyāgarāja paintings are housed in museums in England and France.[121] The Victoria and Albert Museum has a 19th century painting of God "Tiyāgarāja" on mica (No. 4662-4662 18/20) and another of the same deity on paper from Tiruccirāppaḷḷi dateable to circa 1820 (I.M. 357-1923). The British Museum has a painting of "Tiyākaraja with Goddess" on paper with Telugu inscription (1962-12-31-089). The Bibliotheque Nationale, Paris, has an album of paintings depicting the different pilgrimage sites in Tamilnāḍu and it depicts the car festival at Tirunaḷḷaṟu near Kāraikkāl with the chief deity (Tyāgarāja) being taken in procession.

Apart from these isolated examples of paintings, the ceiling and the inner walls of the Tēvācirīya Maṇṭapam in the Tiruvārūr temples are covered with mural paintings depicting the myth of Tyāgarāja's arrival on earth and narrating the various important events in the life of this cult deity including the description, both pictorial and in writing (for the paintings bear captions), of the important festivals connected with the worship of Tyāgarāja. They are done very much in the Nāyaka style.

The best-preserved sections of this vast mural deal with the Mucukunda legend and are painted on the ceiling. Unfortunately the other set of paintings of Maṉunīticōḻaṉ are in a very bad state of preservation due mainly to rain water seeping through the walls. Whilst the order in which the narrative appears on the walls is mentioned below, the actual evolution of the myth portrayed is discussed in chapter 4.

The Mucukunda narrative is broken into two parts. One part

is painted on the southern end of the ceiling and another set of paintings depicting the same myth is painted on the north west corner of the ceiling. The paintings are divided into sections by means of the inscribed legends below them which describe the event or tell the story portrayed. But for this artificial panelling, the paintings stretch right across the ceiling in a continuous narrative scheme. The script and the colloquial nature of the language used in the labels suggest a fairly late date for the paintings. The earliest date that can be assigned to them on palaeographical and stylistic grounds is the 16th century A.D. It could well belong to the 17th century or even early 18th under Śāhāji II. However comparing it with other Marāṭhā and Nāyaka paintings I am inclined towards the earlier date of the late 16th century A.D.

The contents of the paintings can be briefly described under the following captions:[122]

1. Viṣṇu performing a sacrifice in order to have a son.
2. The birth of a son due to Śiva's blessing.
3. The anger of Devī at being ignored.
4. The release from the curse.
5. The acquisition of the icon by Viṣṇu.
6. His worshipping it in the 'Ocean of Existence'.
7. Indra's war against Valāsura.
8. The meeting of Viṣṇu and Indra.
9. Viṣṇu's helping Indra to overcome the Asura.[123]
10. Indra requesting Viṣṇu to give him the Viṭaṅka.
11. His acquisition of the Viṭaṅka.
12. His taking it back to the heaven and the damsels of heaven performing a dance of invocation to the deity and its installation in Indra's heaven.

The story ends here in the southern section of the ceiling. Here it is important to note that Viṭaṅka of the labels refers to Tyāgarāja.

1. The paintings in the north western section of the ceiling begin by depicting the king "Mucukuntaṉ" (Mucukunda) a monkey-faced king ruling along with his nine warrior confidants in Ayodhyā.
2. His rule is portrayed as being just and joyous. Mucukuntaṉ is shown witnessing a dance performance.
3. An envoy from Indra invites Mucukuntaṉ to accompany him

to heaven.
4. Mucukuntaṉ accompanies him with his army.
5. Scenes of battle between Indra and the Asura and between Mucukuntaṉ and the Asura.
6. The killing of Valāsura by Mucukuntaṉ.
7. Indra and Mucukuntaṉ in heaven.
8. Scenes of heaven.
9. Indra's worship of Tyāgarāja.
10. Mucukuntaṉ asking for the Tyāgarāja image.
11. Indra conspires with Viśvakarmā.
12. The dream of Mucukuntaṉ.
13. Indra's presenting seven identical Viṭaṅkas to Mucukuntaṉ: all seven are Tyāgarājas.
14. His choosing the right one.
15. Mucukuntaṉ's bringing all seven Viṭaṅkas to Tiruvārūr.
16. The festivities in Tiruvārūr—the joy and revelry—the fireworks, dances, etc. These festivals are celebrated at Tiruvārūr. The festivals bear captions such as *'pairavar tiruviḻā'* or even details of events such as *'cuvāmi pavaṉi'*; *'kaikaṭṭumuṟai-kkāri naṭaṉam ceyvatu'*; it gives the time such as *'pūraṭṭāti naṣatu nakṣatril'* (not clear as to the implication of 'naṣatu') or simply the name of the festival such as *'mutaliya mūvar tiruviḻā'* (the festival of the three *Tēvāram* hymnists), *'Kātci koṭutta tiruviḻā'* (the festival of the deity's *darśanam* or sight to the 64 saints).

The captions give the names of *maṭhas* (monastic establishments), like *Periyamaṭam* and details such as *Turvācamaṭam* or *periyamaṭam,* thereby equating the two and portray the *paṇṭāram* (the monk in charge; the word paṇṭāram is used for non-Brāhmaṇa heads of establishments) of this *maṭha* receiving 'honours'. The *periyamaṭam paṇṭāram* is shown wearing white with all the other attributes of a devout Śaiva—the *Vibhūti* (ash) marks on his forehead, forearm, arm and wrist and the white clothes indicate that he belonged in all likelihood to the *Vēḻānkuṟicci maṭam* whose *Paṇṭāram* is called *ajapā paṇṭāram* and is one of the most important trustees of a *Kaṭṭaḷai* or endowment in the Tyāgarāja temple. This *maṭha* with its headquarters at Tiruppukaḻūr is an establishment consisting of married *paṇṭārams,* who in order to show their *gṛhastha* status wear white and not the ochre robes of a Sannyāsin. The plates at the end of this work illustrate several of these scenes.

Interesting labels describe the names of the different fireworks such as *nilā cakra vāṇam*, etc. Temple functionaries such as *muṭṭukkārar, mēḷakkārar*, etc. are mentioned.

The murals betray two distinct styles—one depicting the main icon, which is markedly hieratic, and the other, much more natural, describing the human beings participating in the worship of the icon. The icon itself has acquired a standardised form and looks the same whether it is in an early or a later painting. So the clue to the dating of this painting would have to be sought in the manner of representing the human actors.

I am inclined to date these paintings at a much earlier period than the Marāṭhā paintings delineating the Devī Māhātmyam in the Thañjāvūr temple which decorate the ceilings of the Devī temple. The Thañjāvūr paintings seem to belong to the early 18th century. R. Nagasamy dates them in the reign of Serfoji II in his Tamiḻ work *Kallum collum.*

There is a great difference between the paintings in the Nīlōtpalāmpāḷ shrine at Tiruvārūr and those of the Tēvācirīya maṇṭapam. The latter could well have been painted in the later part of the 16th century A.D. One is tempted to equate it with the rise of the Tarumapuram Ātīṉam and the *Rājaṉ kaṭṭaḷai* (an important endowment in this temple managed by the Ātīṉam), and trace it to the time of the great sectarian leader in Tiruvārūr, Kamalai, ñāṉappirakācar who was a devotee of the Tyāgarāja. However, a firm conclusion on the dating of the Tyāgarāja murals is impossible at this time with the paucity of materials at hand.

C. Sivaramamurti traces painting of the Maṉunīti legend in Lēpākṣi and Peṉukoṇṭa. Maṉunīti was also a figure closely connected with the Tyāgarāja myth. The same author also identifies a monkey faced king at Lēpākṣi with Mucukuntaṉ.[124]

The only Pallava painting of Somāskanda comes from the Kailāsanātha temple at Kāñcīpuram (Pl. II). This depicts the 'Rājasiṁha' type of Somāskandas except that *gaṇas* are depicted on one side at the feet of Śiva and a charming attendant is painted on Pārvatī's side.

NOTES

1. The presiding deity of the temple at Tiruvārūr is Valmīkanātha, while Tyāgarāja is simply the *utsava mūrti* (processional image). Despite this, the temple and the *Devasthānam* (management Board) are both known by the name of Tyāgarāja. In the *Tēvāram*, the main shrine is called *tirumūlattānam* and the Tyāgarāja temple is referred to as the *pūṅkōyil*. Another example of the processional image occupying an important role is in Chidambaram where the temple and *Devasthānam* go by the name of Naṭarāja.
2. Since cult convention forbids the icon to be fully revealed, the visible differences between the various Tyāgarāja images are mainly in matter of ornamentation.
3. For a fuller discussion on the concept of root metaphors and the Tyāgarāja *Vide Infra* Ch. V., Pepper, Stephen C., *World Hypotheses*, Berkeley, University of California, 1942, cited by Turner, Victor *Dramas, Fields and Metaphors*, p. 26, used this expression 'root metaphor' to mean the central essence of a concept. He treats the root metaphor as a set of categories, and people proceed to study all other 'areas of fact' in terms of these categories. Some root metaphors, to quote the author, "have greater power of expansion and adjustment" than others.
4. Dhaky, M.A., and Meister, M.W., *Encyclopaedia of Indian Temple Architecture South India, Lower Drāviḍadēśa*, p. 372.
5. The Pallava Somāskandas and their locations within the Pallava temples at Mahābalipuram, Kāñcīpuram, Tirupparaṅkunṟam, etc., have been discussed by several writers, such as K.V. Soundararajan, "Cult in Pallava Times" and "Rājasiṁha's Temples in Pallava Times", both in *Trans. of Arch.Soc. of South India, 1962-65*, K.R. Srinivasan, *Cave Temples of the Pallavas*, p. 2 ff. and *Some Aspects of Religion as Revealed by Early Monuments and Literature of the South*, Madras, 1960 and Lockwood, M., "Pallava Somāskanda" in Lockwood et al, *Mahābalipuram Studies*. The following list of temples housing Pallava Somāskandas is by no means exhaustive but is an indicator of the prominence given to this image by this dynasty:

   (a) *Rock Cut Shrines* from *Mahābalipuram* and its environs:
   Dharmarājaratha, Rāmānujamaṇṭapam, Mahiṣāsuramardinī Cave (main sculpture), Atiraṇacaṇḍeśvara maṇṭapam at Cāluvaṉkuppam (main + 2 other Somāskandas).

   (b) *Structural Temples* that house Somāskanda Pallava images at *Mahābalipuram*:
   Shore Temples (Kṣatriya Siṁheśvara and Rājasiṁheśvara), at Mahābalipuram, both of which have Somāskandas in niches. The Rājasiṁhēśvara temple has Brahmā and Viṣṇu on the Somāskanda panel itself while the Kṣatriyasimheśvara has Brahmā and Viṣṇu panels on the side walls. Mukuntanāyaṉār Temple of the Rājasiṁha period.

   (c) *At Kāñcīpuram*:
   Mahendravarmeśvara-Kailāsanātha temple has 29 (1 + 28) panels of Somāskandas.
   Airāvatanēśvara has the usual Brahmā-Viṣṇu flanking the Somāskanda.
   Amareśvara has the Somāskanda panel over double pediment.
   Airāvateśvara Somāskanda panel is in the *mukhamaṇṭapa*. Mukteśvara

Somāskanda occupies the whole wall. It is here that Śiva is shown holding an axe (right) and a deer (left) in his upper hands. This is highly stuccoed and could well be a later addition.

Mātaṅgeśvara in the middle of the wall on a low pediment.

pirāvataneśvara.

(d) *Tirukkaḻukkunṟam* in the Pallava country has two Somāskanda panels in the Vedagirīśvara temple. See Srinivasan, K.R., *Cave Temples*, p.105.

(e) At Paṉamalai in South Arcot district, the Tālagirīśvara temple houses a Somāskanda.

This practice was not continued by the successors of the Pallavas and so can well be described as the *leitmotif* of Pallava sacred art.

6. For the painted Somāskanda see Pl. II.
7. Soundararajan, *op.cit.*, p.144 (i.e. Cult)
8. Lockwood, *op.cit.*, pp. 33 and 107 where basically he arrives at three main typologies of Somāskandas, viz. pre-Rājasiṁha, Rājasiṁha and post-Rājasiṁha.
9. Raman, K.V., 'Iconographic Concepts and Forms from Early Tamiḻ Sources' in *Reports of Seminars, Bulletin of the Institute of Traditional Cultures*, Madras, 1957, where he gives a list of forms of Śiva not mentioned in *Caṅkam* works.
10. *Aiṅkuṟunūṟu*, 401. For text see Rajam, E.S. (ed.)., *Aiṅkuṟunūṟu*. This was brought to my attention by Mr. Ratnasabhapati, curator of Thañjāvūr Art Gallery.
11. The *Tēvāram* hymns indirectly refer to the concept such as V.8.38, which referring to Śiva describes him as the great father of beautiful *Murukaṉ* and while describing *Murukaṉ* in the same hymn, verse 5 says "He is with mother overflowing with beauty and sympathy", M. Rajamanikkam, tr. in *The Development of Śaivism in South India* p. 38. Nowhere is the Somāskanda iconography specifically described. In VII. 18 Śiva's daughter-in-law is referred to as a *kuṟava* girl. It is the *Viṭaṅka* that finds frequent mention.
12. Srinivasan, K.R., *op.cit.*, p. 2 ff. and also by the same author, *Indian Temple Styles*.
13. Lockwood, *op.cit.*, pp. 54-55.
14. Srinivasan, K.R., Temple Architecture in South India, in *Temple India*, Madras 1981, p. 59.
15. Balasubramanian, S.R., *Middle Cōḻa Temples*, p. 7.
16. See U. Ve. Cāmināta Aiyar, introduction to *Tiruvārūr Ulā*; in *Tyageśa Kuṟavañci* (v. 20), the expression *'muṉṉilum mummaṭaṅku piṉṉaḻakar'* (one whose rear-view is three times more beautiful) is used. These are, however, late works of the 17th and 18th centuries A.D. respectively.
17. Lockwood, *op.cit.*, p.21.
18. *Sakalādhikāram* attributed to Agastya, pp. 60-72 (2nd Ed. 1973). There are two editions of this work. The earlier one is in Grantha characters and was published by Tanjore Saraswati Mahal Library, Tanjore, 1961 (Tanjore Saraswati Mahal Series No. 92). The more recent edition is in Nāgarī characters and is published as Tanjore Saraswati Mahal Series No. 141, Tanjore, 1973.
19. Subrahmania Sastri, K.S., Ed., *Sārasvatīya Citra Karma Sastra*, Tanjore Saraswati Mahal Series, No. 87, Tanjore, 1960, pp. 138-69.
20. *Kāśyapam*, Tanjore Saraswati Mahal Series, Tanjore, 1960, pp. 258-67. This is in Grantha script and has a Tamiḻ translation.
21. *Śilparatnam*, Vol.II, pp. 3-4. Tanjore Saraswati Mahal Publications, No. 90, Tanjore 1961. In Grantha script and Tamiḻ translation by Devanāthacharya.

22. Cited by Rao, Gopinath, *Elements of Hindu Iconography*, Vol. II, pt. 409.
23. Marr, J.A.R., *Eight Tamil Anthologies*, p. 409.
24. Verse 8.
25. *Kamalālaya cirappu* of Citamparam Kaṅkaṭṭi Śrī Maṟaiñaṉacampantar, 9, 352.
26. Gopinath Rao, T.A.G., *op.cit.*, Vol. II, pt. II, p. 369.
27. *Śivarahasyakhaṇḍa, Upadeśa Khaṇḍa*,Ch. 90. This numbering refers to the printed edition. See Bibliography.
28. *Śivarahasyakhaṇḍa*, Ch.90. Tirumūlar in the middle of a highly mystical exposition suddenly and quite out of context states that Somāskanda is worshipped for acquiring progeny.
29. Banerjea, J.N., *Development of Hindu Iconography*, p. 470
30. Dubreuil, Jouveau, *Iconography of South India*, p. 123.
31. See Subramanian, P., *Meykīrttikal*, p.9. The Sanskrit word *Kīrti* itself, according to the author, was incorporated into Tamil during the Pallava times. *Mey* (Tamil true) *Kīrti* (panegyric in Sanskrit) showed the trend of combining Sanskrit and Tamil. The Pallava *meykīrtis* were in Prākrit and then in Sanskrit and later became bilingual.
32. Thangavelu, M.K., *Concept of the God Muruga in Sangam Literature*, unpublished M.Litt. thesis, University of Madras, 1963, p. 174.
33. See Clothey, *The Many Faces of Murukaṉ*, p. 116.
34. Mucukuntan (Skt. Mucukunda) though known to the Sanskritists through the *Bhāgavata purāṇa* (10.5, 23-24), *Harivaṁśa*, 2. 58. 43-67 and the *Mbh. Udyōga Parva*, Ch. 137, S1,197, was adopted by the Cōḻas as their 'patron king' and was Tamilised and localised and thenceforth associated with Karūr and Tiruvārūr.
35. Banerjea, J.N., op. cit., p. 364.
36. This was kindly brought to my attention by Dr. J.R. Marr.
37. vv. 37-38.
38. *S.I.I.*, Vol.I, pp. 12-14, No.24 (line 5). In this a parallel is drawn between Rājasiṁha and his father and Skanda and his father (i.e. Śiva). See also Paṇamalai Ins., *E.I.*, Vol. XIX., pp. 113-15, vv.3-4. The Raṅgapatākā ins. in *S.I.I.*, Vol. I, pp.23-24, compares the queen to Pārvatī.
39. An excellent photograph of this is included in Sivaramamurti, C., *Art of India*. See also a photograph of this image in Pl. 313 of Balasubramanyam, *Middle Cōḻa Temples*, or Gopinath Rao, *op.cit.*
40. *Sārasvatīyacitrakarmaśāstra* 164. See also *Kāraṇāgama*, cited by Rao, *op.cit.*, vol.II, pt. I,P. 132.
41. See Pl. facing p.285 of Rao *op.cit*
42. L'Hernault, Francoise, *L'Iconographie de subrahmaṇya au Tamilnad* pl.21.
43. *Ibid.*, pl. 22.
44. *Ibid.*, pl. 25.
45. *Ibid.*, pl. 24.
46. See Kempers, Bernet, *Ancient Indonesian Act*, pl. 110.
47. See Sivaramamurti, C., *South Indian Bronzes*, pl. 36b.
48. *Uttara Kāmikāgama* cited by Rao, *op.cit.*, p. 164. See also *Sakalādhikāram*, Ch. VI, V. 26-27. This text ascribed to Agastya is regarded as the sculptural manual of the *Aṁśubhedāgama*.
49. See Frontispiece for a lithograph. Photography of the icon is forbidden.
50. This is interesting since the Viṭaṅka-Tyāgarāja was specially imported to Thañjāvūr from Tiruvārūr by Rājarāja I and made into a state cult. The deity

is almost forgotten now.

51. See Kuppuswamy, Gouri and Hariharan, M., *Glimpses of Indian Music*, Sandeep Prakashan 1982, in which they cite the *patam* by Pāpavināśa Mutaliyār called 'Mukattai Kāṭṭi', which describes this esoteric element of the Tyāgarāja cult. This is in *Bhairavi rāga*. Another composition by the same composer on Tyāgarāja is entitled *Perum Nalla Tiyākar* and is in *Pūrvī Kalyāṇī*.
The *Śrī-cakra* and its relationship to the Tyāgarāja cult has been discussed in Chapter V. This *Yantra* aspect of the image has been suggested as the reason for the esotericism.
52. Vēlucāmi Kavirāyar, *Tirukkāṟāyiṟ Purāṇam* in the Chapter entitled 'Tiyākarācarahasyacarukkam'. (The chapters in this prose rendering are not numbered.)
53. *Ibid.*, Ch. entitled '*Viṭaṅka kapāla vana rahasya*'.
54. The *Tēvāram* singers regard the *Viṭaṅka* as male for he is described as filling the hearts of maidens with love as he proceeds through the streets. In the 16th century *talapurāṇams* the cause of the creation of the Somāskanda Viṭaṅka icon is to appease the wrath of Devī. See Ch. IV. Gradually it accrues more Śāktaic traits.
55. Campantar, *Patikam* II, line 151. The name of the site occurs as a refrain in the end of every stanza.
56. See Pillay, K.K., *The Śucīndram Temple*, p. 119. The person who installed the image was according to K.K. Pillay a Malayāḷi Brāhmaṇa and he believes that he was the predecessor of the latter day Yōgakkāras who wielded great power in the temple. They formed an independent religious corporation (*Saṅkētam*). Śucīndram was built under the Cōḻa influence and thus Somāskanda installers could well have been the cultural mediators or power brokers, a kind of religio-political lobbyists for the Cōḻa cause.
57. There are several such Tyāgarāja sites such as Tiruvoṟṟiyūr, Tiruvāṉmiyūr, Tirukkaccūr, Tiruviḻimiḻalai, etc.
58. Meister, Michael W. and Dhaky, M.A., *Encyclopaedia of Indian Temple Architecture, South India, Lower Drāvidadēśa*, p. 317, defines a Tyāgarāja shrine as one with a separate shrine to the Somāskanda.
59. At present only those sites which formed the original nucleus of seven sites in Cōḻamaṇṭalam conform fully to the *Viṭaṅka* tradition. The geographical locations of these sites and other particulars are discussed in the text in the section on religious topography.
60. The word 'made' has to be understood in the context for the belief is that these *liṅgas* were self-manifested and the word *Viṭaṅka* itself is treated as a synonym of *svayaṁbhū* or self-created.
61. The most popular stones are emeralds and garnets (*marakatam* and *gometakam*), though the Chidambaram *candramaulīśvara* is made of crystal and it seems most likely that it is this, which is referred to as *Tillai Viṭaṅkar* in epigraphs. There is a modern village six miles from Chidambaram called TillaiViṭaṅkaṉ and a 19th century Tamiḻ writer bore the name Tillai Viṭaṅkar.
62. Personal discussion at the International Institute of Tamiḻ Culture, July 1983.
63. Tirmuṟai IX. *Tiruvicaippā, Patikam* 18, Line 2. See also 18.1
64. V. *Patikam* 7.8.
65. Cuntarar, VII, *Patikam* 36.1.
66. *Ibid.*, 10.

67. VII. 46. 4.
68. *Periya Purāṇam, 'Taṭuttātkoṇṭa Purāṇam'*, v. 274.
69. *Tiruviḷaiyātaṟpurāṇam*, (Parañcōti), Maturakkāṇṭam v. 1283, also *Ibid.*, I, *pat*. 5, v.70. Parañcōti refers to both Murukaṉ, as the bearer of the spear or *vēl* and also to CuntaraViṭaṅkar which is a double entendre meaning both the Viṭaṅka and the handsome Cuntarapāṇṭiaṉ, the Pāṇḍya ruler, the ruler of Madurai.
70. *Mucukundasahasranāmam*, invocation 485.
71. *S.I.I.*, Vol. II, 6.
72. *S.I.I.*, Vol. II, 1.
73. *Ibid.*, Also *S.I.I.*, Vol. II, 2 paras. 14-22.
74. *S.I.I.*, Vol. II, 7.
75. *S.I.I.*, Vol. II, 8.
76. Several inscriptions from Tiruvaiyāṟu refer to Dantiśakti viṭaṅki and the Tiruvaiyāṟu temple was named after her as lōkamahādēvīśvaramuṭaiyār temple.
77. *S.I.I.*, Vol. II, 14, 15, 16 and 17.
78. *ARE* 1922, No. 21. This comes from the Abhirāmēśvara temple at Tiruvāmāttūr.
79. See *Peruntamiḻ*, Madras, 1975, p. 245.
80. *ARE* 1904-05, Part II, para 12.
81. Barrett, Douglas, *Early Cōḻa Architecture and Sculpture*, p.92.
82. *Ibid.*
83. *ARE* 1908, No. 454. It is incomplete and records a gift of land for the reciters of *Tirumuṟai* in the *Tirukkaikoṭṭi* of the Tirukkāṟavācal temple. While demarcating the boundaries *inter alia* it refers to the Ātiviṭaṅka canal.
84. *S.I.I.*, Vol. XVII, No. 593 and 595 etc.
85. *S.I.I.*, Vol. XVII, No. 595.
86. *S.I.I.*, Vol. XVII, No. 624.
87. *S.I.I.*, Vol. XVII, No. 509. See also the *Vētāraṇiya Purāṇam*
88. 559 of *ARE* 1962-63 of the time of Rajadhiraja II.
89. 586 of *ARE* 1962-63 of Kulōttuṅga III's time. Another dance is also referred to in the Tiruvāymūr inscriptions called *Vaṭṭaṉaiyāṭal* (582 and 587 of *1962-63*).
90. L'Hernault, Francoise, *L'Iconographie de Subrahmaṇya au Tamiḻnad*, p. 265, where she suggests that though the Somāskanda was worshipped it was through the medium of the *liṅga*. See also Nagasamy, R., *The Art and Culture of Tamiḻnadu*, p. 114.
91. Soundararajan, K.V., "Cult in Pallava Times", *Trans. Archaeological Society of South India, 1962-65* and Srinivasan, K.R. *Cave Temples of the Pallavas*, p. 2 ff. See also Srinivasan, K.R., *Some Aspects of Religion as Revealed by Early Monuments and Literature of the South*, Madras, University of Madras, 1960, p. 61.
92. See Wirz, Von Paul, *Katirgāma, The Holiest Place in Ceylon*, Colombo, 1966.
93. Soundararajan, K.V., *Indian Temple Styles*, p. 105, where he states that "although *liṅgas* are found in most of the temples of Rājasiṁha, as we see them today there are strong grounds in favour of their being later insertions".
94. Lockwood, M., *op. cit.*, p. 46 ff.
95. L'Hernault, *op. cit.*, p. 266. English Summary of the nature of Somāskanda.
96. Nagasamy, R., *Tantric Cult in South India*, regards the 12th-13th centuries as the period of culmination of the various *śākta* doctrines.
97. Srinivasan, K.R., "Tirukkāmakōṭṭam" in *Proc. of All India Oriental Conference*, Nagpur.

98. Stein, Burton, "Devī Shrines and Folk Hinduism in Tamilnad", in Gerow and Lang (ed.), *Studies in the Language and Culture of South Asia*, pp. 76-8.
99. Brown, Norman, Introduction to *Saundaryalaharī*.
100. This view is based on the evidence of the text where the deity is twice invoked as 'Anapāya' coupled with the epigraphic evidence which testifies to the elaborate rites instituted by Kulōttuṅga II in the temple at Tiruvārūr and the fact that his epithet Anapāya was found in a Tiruvārūr epigraph and the *Periya Purāṇam* refers to the king only by this epithet.
101. See Nagasamy, R., *Art and Culture of Tamilnadu*, pp. 113-5, where he gives a number of reasons why he thinks that the Dakṣiṇamēruviṭaṅkar of the Thañjāvūr inscriptions is identical with the Thañjāvūr Somāskanda.
102. *Census of India, The Temples of Tamilnadu, 1961*, Sīrkāḻi Taluq, p. 6.
103. Ellappanāyaṉār *Tiruvārūrkkōvai*, v. 1. This work was composed around 1645 A.D.
104. Kumakuruparar, *Tiruvārūrnānmaṇimālai*, v.1. This is dated 1625 A.D. That Ārūran or its equivalent Tiruvārūruṭaiyar is Vītiviṭaṅkar can be inferred by the way they are invoked in the same breath in inscriptions such as S.I.I. XVII, 593. The *mūlabera* and the *vītiviṭaṅkar* are sometimes used as synonyms in epigraphs. Thus in 601 of S.I.I. XVII the deity is called *Vītiviṭaṅkapuṟṟiṭankoṇṭāṉ* and *Tiruvārūruṭaiya Śrī mūlasṭhānamuṭaiyār.*
105. Vikramacōḻa uses the epithet *Tyāgasamudra* (*E.I.*, Vol. VI, No. 21B and *S.I.I.* IV, p. 228-229. A *brahmadeya* by the name of *Tyāgasamudracaturvedi mangalam* is mentioned in 272 and 273 of 1907. Tyāgavallī is the name of the wife of Kulōttuṅga I and Kulōttuṅga II (S.I.I., Vol.III,72,line 5).
Cayankoṇṭāṉ's *Kaliṅkattupparaṇi*, X,vv.54-55 states that Tiyākavalli enjoyed equal power with the king. 85 of 1895 refers to Tiyākavalli, wife of Kulōttuṅga II. The Cavvēlimēṭu Sanskrit inscription of the 16th year of Kulōttuṅga II refers to an epithet of this king as *tiyākavarakara*. In all this the word Tyāga is used not in the Sanskrit sense of 'sacrifice' but in the Tamiḻ sense of the word signifying liberality, generosity, etc.
106. v.32, For the controversy regarding the dating of this work vide infra Ch.III. While Nagasamy, R., *The Tantric Cult of South India*, p.29 and Zvelebil, *History of Tamiḻ Literature*, pp.118-119 regard it as a genuine work of Oṭṭakkūttar, Mu. Arunachalam and Veḷḷaivāraṇar have expressed grave doubts as to its authenticity (Personal Communication). Veḷḷaivāraṇar 14.5.82 and Mu. Arunachalam 4.8.82. See also Mu. Arunachalam, *Tamiḻ Ilakkiya Varalāṟu*, 12th century.
107. The three kings were Vikrama coḻa (1118-36), Kulōttuṅga II (1133-50) and Rājarāja (1146-63).
108. *Mucukundasahasranāmam* is full of such associations, such as Om *Śrīvidyātmakarūpāya namaḥ* (v. 9) etc., *Vide Infra*, Ch. 6.
109. Winslow, Miron, *A Comprehensive Tamiḻ English Dictionary of High and Low Tamil*, Madras, P.R. Hunt, American Mission Press, 1962.
110. *Ibid*.
111. Veṅkatamakhin, *Caturdaṇḍiprakāśikā* v.1., Madras Music Academy, 1934. The translation is mine. The four *puruṣārthas* are generally taken to be *dharma, artha, kāma* and *mokṣa* - the first three refer to ethical conduct, prosperity and sensual enjoyment, all aspects of the *bhoga* or enjoyment form of the deity and the last

salvation.

112. Raman, K.V., *The Varadarājasvāmi Temple*, p.7
113. *Cil. Kaṭalāṭu*, 1.43, *Koṭukkoṭṭi,, Tuti, Ibid.*, lines 49-51.
114. This refers to the metaphysics and ontology of *ajapā* and *haṁsa*-vide infra, Ch.5
115. Mīnātcicuntaram Piḷḷai, *Tirunākaikkāroṇappurāṇam;* and the *Mucukunda-sahasranāmam*.
116. vv. 667-70.
117. v.337
118. See Ātmanāta Tēcikar, *Cōḻamaṇṭalacatakam*, v. 86. and U.Ve, Camināta Aiyar's introduction to *Tiyākarācalīlaikaḷ* and *Tiruvārūr ulā*. To this day, there are special rites conducted in the Tiruvārūr temple in the name of Karuṇākara Toṇṭaimān. See.Ch.6. A measure called Karuṇākaranāḻi is known from epigraphs in Vedāraṇyam.
119. *Mucukundasahasranāmam*, v. 54-63.
120. *S.I.I.*, Vol. I., Nos. 33 and 34.
121. Narayanan, Ramani, *South Indian Drawings and Paintings in the British Collection*, typescript. (Kindly lent to me by the author.)
122. For the Tyāgarāja mythology vide infra Ch.IV.
123. See *Cil. Kaṭalāṭu*, 11.54-55, for an early reference to this myth.
124. Sivaramamurti, C., *South Indian Paintings*, p.116.

Chapter Three

REGIONAL TOPOGRAPHY AND CULTIC GEOGRAPHY

During the course of this work several references have been made to the cultic geography, which marks it apart from all other features of the landscape. This is, in turn, closely connected with the Tyāgarāja mythology. The study of myths connected with the cult will however be reserved for the next chapter. The focus of this chapter will be on the networking tradition, as exemplified through the study of a regional cult.

The practice of grouping shrines into sacred clusters through the medium of myths and rituals is very common in the Tamil̲ Śaiva tradition. The largest and most general of such groupings is that of *pāṭal pe*r̲*r̲a talaṅkaḷ* and *vaippu talaṅkaḷ*, the former standing for all the temples believed to have been visited by the *Tēvāram* trio (Appar, Campantar and Cuntarar) in person where they are said to have composed hymns on the deity of the shrine; the *vaippu talaṅkaḷ*, on the other hand, are a group of temples which the three *nāyan̲mār* did not visit in person, nonetheless composed hymns on the deity of the place, which were then included within a general hymn of praise. There are two hundred and seventy-four *pāṭalper̲r̲atalaṅkaḷ* and two hundred and thirty-seven *vaippu talaṅkaḷ*. They are then grouped into smaller clusters on a geographical basis, such as those in Toṇṭaimaṇṭalam (32 temples), Col̲amaṇṭalam (190 temples) and Pāṇṭināṭu (14 temples), etc. Only five of the two hundred and seventy-four are situated in northern India. Thus, this is basically a Tamil̲ pilgrimage tradition, with the largest cluster being around the Kāvērī basin.[1] Some of the other well known groupings are the *aṭṭavīraṭṭāṇam,*[2] *saptasthalam,*[3] the five halls of Śiva's dance,[4] the shrines representing the Five elements,[5] the six Tāntric *cakras*[6] and on a Pan-Indian and in a modified form the regional grouping of the sixty-four Śakti *pīṭhas.*[7] The present thesis shall concentrate on one such grouping, the *saptaviṭaṅkatalaṅkaḷ*.

The reasons for such deliberate groupings become clear when the socio-religious dynamics of the period is borne in mind. The 7th-9th centuries A.D. was the period when several of these clusters were conceived. They were evolved at a time when the Tamil̲ concept of the Hindu faith was threatened by a non-Tamiḻ Jaina and Bauddha faith[8] and the *nāyaṉmār* acted as the chief agents in not only winning back the converts from these two faiths but also in actively propagating the new vigorous Tamil-Sanskritic,[9] Vedic-Āgamic,[10] Folk-Court syntheses of culture.

This could be accomplished only by linking up distant geographical zones with the central royally-sponsored faith system. This process was given a definite impetus by the Pallavas and conspicuously accelerated by the Cōḻas. In the absence of a unified ecclesiastic order, and not having even a fraternity of evangelical monks like the Buddhists and the Jains had, the Śaivas took recourse to creating a strong psychological bond between the *aṭiyār* (servants) of Śiva, and also between the deities of the different shrines. By this means there evolved a new feeling of community, to wean the people from the more organised Buddhist and Jaina faiths. The message was thus carried far and wide into the peripheral regions. It is only by understanding this phenomenon in such terms that the anger of Viraṉmīṇṭār at Cuntarar's ignoring the congregation of *aṭiyār* and going straight to offer his obeisance to the god of Tiruvārūr can be explained. Cuntarar's apologies finally result in his composing the famous *Tiruttoṇṭattokai* in praise of all the 62 devotees of Śiva.[11] Thus the canonical number of sixty-three saints (viz. the sixty-two *nāyaṉmār* plus himself) was the nearest approximation to the notion of the Buddhist *Sangha* and the Jaina *paḷḷi*. Hence the grouping of the shrines, like the grouping of the *aṭiyār* at Tiruvārūr and the concept of the holy three thousand of Tillai, (i.e. *Tillaivāḻ antaṇar* of *Periya Purāṇam*) acted as sacred networks of communication providing an identifiable bond in an otherwise nebulous faith system. Other groups of devotees also occur in the *Periya Purāṇam*.

Within the larger groups of believers there existed smaller units of 'faith system' which seems to have acted as important pressure groups propagating *bhakti* or intense personal devotion as an alternative to the ritualism of the Vedas and Āgamas. However, since the propagators of *bhakti* did not take an aggressive stand against any of the traditional forms and structures, their message was ambiguous and hence could not provide 'an alternative' in the strict sence of the term but settled weakly into offering a complementary ideology.

The Sapta Viṭaṅka

A listing of the *saptaviṭaṅka kṣetras* occurs in the *Tiruviḻācarukkam* chapter of the *Tiruvārūrppurāṇam.*[12] It is recorded as a couplet and the order of the sacred viṭaṅka shrines goes as follows:

Tirunākaikkāroṇam, i.e. modern Nāgapaṭṭaṇam, Kāṟāyil (Tirukkāṟavācal), Kōḷili (Tirukkuvaḷai), Maṟaivaṉam, i.e. Tirumaṟaikkāṭu or Vedāraṇyam, Naḷḷāṟu (Tirunaḷḷāṟu), Vāymūr (Tiruvāymūr), which, along with Tiruvārūr, form the sacred seven.[13] What is interesting in the above couplet is that Vāymūr is referred to as *caiṉiya* vāymūr. The word *caiṉiya* could be an adjective from the word *caina,* which could be a transliteration of the word Jaina or it could be derived from the Tamiḻ word *ceṉṉi,* meaning the Cōḻas. Tiruvārūr was a strong Jaina centre as we know from the *Periyapurāṇam.*[14] The above-mentioned stanza describes these seven sites as places where the Vedas and Āgamas were both followed and which were established by Vēlaracaṉ. It is again difficult to be precise about who is meant by this for the word *vēl* means a spear and *aracaṉ* a king. The *vēl* or spear is iconographically associated in particular with Murukaṉ, who is also called Vēlaṉ. The king Mucukuntaṉ, the progenitor of the Cōḻa race (and an ardent devotee of Murukaṉ, according to the *Kantapurāṇam* and the *Īṭṭi Eḻupatu*), is credited by the Tyāgarāja myths with bringing the Tyāgarāja image to the earth from the heavens. This could well be a reference to Mucukuntaṉ for the *Tiruvārūrppurāṇam,* whence the above couplet comes, was well aware of the standardised form of the Tyāgarāja myth.

The actual expression *saptaviṭaṅka* occurs in a popular saying, which runs: "*cīrār tiruvārūr tennākai naḷḷāṟu kārār maṟaikkāṭu kāṟāyil pēṟāna otta tiruvāymūruvanta tirukkōḷili catta viṭaṅka talam*".[15] When this popular ditty originated is difficult to tell but Mīnātcicuntaram Pillai quotes it in his notes to the *Tiruvārūr Ulā* (v. 25).[16] The *Tiruvārūr ulā* refers to *ēḻuñcōtiviṭaṅkamē* (v.25), the seven effulgent *viṭaṅkas.* Tradition has it that all these seven icons were fashioned as replicas at the same time by the divine architect Viśvakarmā and enshrined in different centres by Mucukuntaṉ. A few details about the *saptaviṭaṅka* sites are discussed below, mainly with an interest in comparing the common features which led to their being so combined and then to see the reasons for such bonds and the effects it had on the group of worshippers.

Tiruvārūr

This is the nucleus of the cult and was at one time one of the five centres of power under the Cōḻas[17] and was used by them as one of the towns where they were crowned.[18] It is a famous *pāṭalperra talam* and all the three members of the Tēvāram trio have devoted hymns not only to the deity of the Tyāgarāja temple but also to deities of two other shrines within the temple complex.

Appar nostalgically muses on the age of the temple and makes it seem as if it is even more ancient than Tillai.[19] The *Tiruttoṇṭattokai*, the hymn providing the canonical list of sixty three saints (including the composer), was composed by the saint Cuntarar in the *Tēvāciriyamaṇṭapam* at Tiruvārūr. Naminantiyaṭikaḷ, Taṇṭiyaṭikaḷ, Cēramāṉperumāḷ, Cōmacimāṟaṉār and Kaḻarciṅkanāyaṉār are some of the saints connected with the place and Kāṭavarkōṉ Aiyaṭikaḷ refers to Tiruvārūr in his *Kṣētraveṇpā*.[20]

The Tiruvārūr temple complex seems to have acted as the cultural model for the big Thañjāvūr temple of Rājarāja I, wherein he enshrined a *viṭaṅkar*[21] which shared with the *Āṭavallāṉ* of Chidambaram the status of a state cult. The last great Cōḻa monarch to play an important role in the affairs of this temple was Kulōttuṅga III in the early part of the 13th century A.D. It attracted Śaivas of all schools and was an important centre of the *Golaki maṭha* in the 13th and 14th centuries A.D. It was also an important Jaina dwelling place, which was attacked by the Śaivas, as is evident by the *Periyapurāṇam* account of the life of *Taṇṭiyaṭikaḷ*.[22] When precisely it became a Śrī-vidyā centre it is difficult to determine but in the 16th century it was already a renowned Śakti centre with focus on Kamalāmpikai, and the legends associate it with Murukaṉ as well.

Thus, Tiruvārūr, now a rapidly growing municipal town in the Tiruvārūr taluq of Thañjāvūr district (16 miles from Nāgapaṭṭaṇam town) must have been a great intellectual centre in the ancient and medieval periods. In the history of Carnatic music, Tiruvārūr occupies an important place as the three famous composers Tyāgarāja, Śyāmāśāstrī and Muttusvāmi Dīkṣita were all born in Tiruvārūr and the last-mentioned was an ardent devotee of Kamalāmpikai and a Śrī-vidyā *upāsaka* (initiate). He has composed several hymns on Tyāgarāja of Tiruvārūr as well.

The origins of this temple take it back to the folk cult of anthill worship for the presiding deity of the place is *Puṟṟiṭaṅkoṇṭāṉ* or

Valmīkanāthan. This was, in turn closely connected with the worship of snakes for the general belief was that serpents lived in anthills. The *liṅga* of precious stone is made of emerald and the *viṭaṅka* is called *vītiviṭaṅka*, as mentioned earlier. An *Ālaviṭaṅkar*[23] is referred to from a Satyavācakeśvara shrine at Tiruvārūr and described as an *utsavabera*. This refers to the present day Paravai-uṇ-Maṇṭali temple. All other Tyāgarāja centres consciously link themselves with Tiruvārūr; it is believed that Tyāgarāja specifically wanted to be enshrined in Tiruvārūr and his three hundred and sixty-four *līlais* (acts of divine sport) are believed to have been performed in this city and its environs.[24] Here there is a parallel with the *Tiruviḷaiyāṭals* of Cuntarēśvara in Madurai. Ideologically, there is a link with Chidambaram and the Naṭarāja cult.[25] The other focus of worship in this temple complex is the Hāṭakeśvara, which is regarded as a *nāgabila* or a subterranean cavern inhabited by snakes. That Hāṭakeśvara was an earlier cult than the Tyāgarāja is evident on a scrutiny of the *Tyāgarājalīlaikaḷ*. Thus, Hāṭakeśvara and Valmīka are the earliest layers of the belief system entempled at Tiruvārūr.

That the Tiruvārūr temple was a large temple even in the time of the *nāyaṉmār* becomes clear from Appar's reference to the size of the temple when he speaks of *añcaṇai vēlī ārūr* (53.7), which refers to the extent of the Kamalālaya tank, the *pūṅkōyil* and the lily tank, as encompassing five *vēlis* of land each. It was a part of Śaiva tradition of Tamiḻnāḍu to regard those born at Tiruvārūr as a special group, much like the three thousand of Tillai for Cuntaramūrti says, " I am the slave of all those born in Tiruvārūr" (*Tiruvārūr piṟantār ellōrkkum aṭiyēṉ*). The *Periyanpurāṇam* devotes a whole chapter (chapter XI. 4vv4158-59) to *Tiruvārūr piṟantār* or those born in Tiruvārūr.

After the fall of the Cōḻas, Tiruvārūr lost much of its prestige, caught as it was in a power struggle between the Hoysalas and Pāṇḍyas. After Rājendra II the power passed on to the Pāṇḍyas and with them the Śaiva centre gravitated away from the *Coḻamaṇṭalam*. It was with the rise of the Marāṭhās that it once more became a state cult in the 17th century A.D. during which period the God of Chidambaram took shelter for a while in Tiruvārūr.[26] In the interim period the cult was kept alive by the Tiruvārūr literati such as Maṟaiñāṉacampantar, author of *Kamalālayacciṟappu* (1547 A.D.), Campantamuṉivar, author of

Tiruvārūrppurāṅam (1592 A.D.), Ellappanāyaṉār, author of *Tiruvārūrkkōvai* and Kumarakuruparar, author of *Tiruvārūrnāṉmaṇimālai* and several others. *Maṭhas* and *Maṭhādhipatis* seemed to have been custodians of the literary tradition. Kumarakuruparar was a monastic recluse and founded a *Maṭha* in Kāśī (Vārāṇasī).

In the modern period, the princely state of Thañjāvūr, which was a generous donor to the temple, lost its regal status in 1800 and the ruler lost even his pension, when Dalhousie proclaimed the Doctrine of Lapse and annexed it to the East India Company's vast domains. Today, like most other temples in Tamiḻnāḍu it is under the management of the H.R.C.&E. Board aided by a complex web of thirteen endowments or *kaṭṭaḷais*.

For the many shrines in this vast temple complex the reader is referred to the Plan of the Temple, where, however, only the important shrines are marked.

Tirunākaikkāroṇam

This is situated in the present day town of Nāgapaṭṭaṉam on the seaboard, about ten miles south of Kāraikkāl, and is one of the major ports of this District. This was an ancient centre of trade and commerce and a renowned seat of Buddhism. Tirumaṅkai Āḻvār is said to have carried away a solid gold image of the Buddha from here and melted it down.[27] The Śailendras and the rulers of Keḍāram patronised the Buddhist monastery here.[28] It is a *pāṭal peṟṟa talam* and closely associated with the fisherman Saint Atipattanāyaṉār and the Saint Cuntaramūrtināyaṉār. The presiding deity is Kāyārohaṇasvāmī, a form of Śiva, particularly favoured by the Pāśupatas.[29] As the name Nāgapaṭṭaṇam, the city of *nāgas* (cobra), and the epithet *nāgābharaṇa* (one who is adorned with ornaments of snakes) of Gaṇeśa, enshrined in the temple, both indicate, it is a centre of serpent worship. The Somāskanda *utsavabera* here bears the name of Cuntaraviṭaṅkar and the *liṅga* of precious stone is made of garnet. Several inscriptions have come to light from here and some refer to the *viṭaṅka* form.[30] Here, as in Tiruvārūr, the goddess is regarded as being extremely powerful and Nīlāyatākṣī, the goddess of the site is often grouped with the Mīnākṣī of Madurai, Viśālākṣī of Kāśī and Kāmākṣī of Kāñcī, the most renowned *Śaktis*. At Tiruvārūr the goddess is Kamalāmpikai. Nāgapaṭṭaṇam was the entry port for vessels into

South India and was known to the Roman geographer, Ptolemy. Appar, in a hymn, consciously links the pilgrimage spots of Tirumaṟaikkāṭu, Vāymūr, Kīḻvēlūr and Oṟṟiyūr, with Nākaikārōṇam, by stating that the Lord of Kāroṇam manifested himself in these sacred spots. (VI. 22.3.). Whether Appar is enumerating the Pāśupata centres or simply, as is typical of the saint, forming yet another sacred network, it is difficult to say. That Nīlāyatākṣī, like Mīnākṣi was possibly the earlier deity is suggested in the *Tirunākaikāroṇappurāṇam* (19.1.147).

Tirukkāṟāyil

This is now a very small village about 16 kilometres south of Tiruvārūr and has a total population of about three thousand families. It was presumably a forest region in the time of the *nāyaṉmār* for it is variously called Kālāgaruvana, Panasāraṇya, Devādāruvana, etc. Inscriptions from the time of Rājarāja I have come to light from here.[31] In one of the inscriptions of this ruler reference is made to an Ātiviṭaṅkaṉ Canal and the Tyāgarāja here is called Ātiviṭaṅkaṉ.[32] From the myths in the *talapurāṇam* it seems likely that it was a *Kāpālika* centre.

Tirumaṟaikkāṭu (mod. *Vēdāraṇyam*)

This is situated on the south east coast of the Bay of Bengal on the Coromandel Coast about sixty kilometers from Tiruvārūr in a southerly direction. Tradition has it that the doors of the main temple which were shut by the Vedas could only be opened by the power of Appar's hymn and it was reshut by Ñāṉacampantar. The equal sanctity and efficacy of Tamiḻ and Sanskrit was thus dramatically emphasised through this myth. The images of Cuntarar and Paṟavai are placed just before the Tyāgarāja, exactly as in Tiruvārūr and Thañjāvūr and are in worship. Campantar and Cuntarar have together composed ten hymns on the deity enshrined here. Several Cōḻa, Pāṇḍya and Marāṭhā inscriptions have come to light from this place.[33] The presiding deity is Maṟaikkāṭēśvara and the Tyāgarāja is known as *puvaṉiviṭaṇkar*.[34] The site is also a renowned *śaktipīṭha* and is known as *Sundarīpīṭha*. The emerald *liṅga* is the *viṭaṅka* here. Appar, again, links the God of Tiruvārūr by referring to his manifestations at Maṟaikkāṭu and Vāymūr (VI.30.9.). Vēdāraṇyam is near a very ancient sacred spot, called Kōṭikkarai, possibly a pre-Vedic site of worship. Now it is an area full of salt pans and Mahatma Gandhi led his salt satyāgraha from here.

Tirunaḷḷāṟu

This is situated in the territory of Kāraikkāl. It is an ancient site, and Campantar has sung four hymns on the deity of the place, in one of which he refers to a contest with the Jains and his victory.[35] Appar and Cuntarar have also extolled the deity here. It was, like most of the shrines belonging to the sacred Tyāgarāja cluster, a site of Murukaṉ worship as well. Aruṇakirinātar has composed a hymn on the deity of Tirunaḷḷāṟu. The *viṭaṅka* is called Nakaraviṭaṅkar. The presiding deity was called Darbheśvara and is believed to be made of the *darbha* grass. The chief focus of worship has however shifted over the years and is now centred around the icon of the planet Saturn, which was originally regarded as the doorkeeper of the shrine. Śani or Saturn, who dwells according to Hindu astrology for two-and-a-half years in each *rāśi* (zodiac) and is a malevolent planet of suicides, is worshipped before one enters the inner *sanctum* of Śiva at Tirunaḷḷāṟu. Appar describes the deities of Maṟaikkāṭu and Naḷḷāṟu as dancers in *Patikams* 122.4 and 181.3 respectively.

Tiruvāymūr

This is 24 kilometres from Tiruvārūr in a south-westerly direction and about 3 kilometres east of Tirukkōḷili. This, like the other six, is a *pāṭal peṟṟa talam*, and both Appar and Campantar have composed hymns on the deity of the place. Appar, it is believed, was specially commanded by Śiva to come from Vēdāraṇyam to Tiruvāymūr (Appar, V.164.2) and Campantar followed him. Cēkkiḻār refers to this episode in the *Periyapurāṇam* (*Tirunāvukkaracu Purāṇam*, vv. 1574 & seq.). Apart from the statues of Appar and Campantar, Kāraikkāl Ammaiyāṟ is also worshipped here. The *viṭaṅka* form here is known as *Nīlaviṭaṅka* and is made of emerald. An inscription of Rājarāja I from this shrine refers to offerings to Atipattanāyaṉār and to Āḷuṭaipiḷḷaiyār (Tiruñāṉacampantar). Fifty-three inscriptions have come to light from here.[36] The expression Āṭal Viṭaṅkar occurs in an inscription of Kulōttuṅga III.[37] The dancing deity here is commonly referred to in epigraphs as Vaṭṭanaiyāṭal Uṭaiyār.[38] In all this there is also a mention of its being a processional image. 598 of *ARE* 1962-63 refers to a *Śrī-Pīṭha*. 45 of 53 inscriptions belong to the Cōḻa dynasty. What is specially significant is that the expression *vaṭṭanaiyāṭal* is used to describe the self-same deity by Ñāṉacampantar in v. 8 of his hymn on Tiruvārūr. (Tirumuṟai. *Tēv.* II, *pat.* 247, v.8). The dance of Tyāgarāja is the *kamalanaṭanam* and the procession moves in circles, which explains the prefix *vaṭṭa*. The word *vaṭṭa* signifies a circular motion in Tamiḻ.

As noticed earlier the *Tiruvārūrppurāṇam* describes it as *Caiṉiyavāymūr* 'the Vāymūr of Jainas', and the possibility that it was a Jaina centre and that is why the Lord 'commanded' Appar to come to this tiny settlement from Vēdāraṇyam to establish the Śaiva faith is a surmise that can be drawn, considering that Appar, like his more zealous contemporary Campantar was bent upon wiping out Jainism. God appearing in dreams to order the spread of the Śaiva faith, and the destruction of other so-called false doctrines was a well-known motif in Śaiva *bhakti* literature. Human actions were justified before the public and presumably the actors themselves believed in such a form of divine intervention. The Somāskanda image from Tiruvāymūr is an exquisitely chiselled Cōḻa bronze and conforms exactly to the Cōḻa bronze Somāskanda typology [39], though stylistically it looks more like a Pallava-Cōḻa transition piece.

Tirukkōḷili

This is about 19 kilometres to the South-East of Tiruvārūr and is now known as Tirukkuvḷai. The Tyāgarājasvāmi temple here is administered by the Tarumapuram Ātīṉam, which is a non-Brāhmaṇa *maṭha*, or monastic establishment. The presiding deity here is made of white clay and in concept is similar to the anthill deity of clay at Tiruvārūr. Four Tēvāram hymns are dedicated to the Lord of Kōḷili. Cuntaramūrti once requested Tyāgarāja to provide him with porters to carry the load of grain that was bestowed on him by divine grace at this site, to Tiruvārūr, in order to save his wife Paravai from starvation. There are nineteen inscriptions belonging to the later Cōḻas and Pāṇḍyas.[40] The ritual tradition of the place carries memories of Mucukuntaṉ and his *sahasranāmam* (referred throughout in this work as *Mucukunda-sahasranāmam* after its Sanskrit spelling of the name of the king) which is performed regularly during the *Vasantotsava*. The *viṭaṅka* here is known as Avaṉiviṭaṅkar.

Other Sites

Apart from this cultic network of seven sacred sites, there are several other sites which have become associated with the Tyāgarāja cult because of some specific links. Thus Tiruvoṟṟiyūr, in the suburbs of Madras (in the Saidapet taluq) seems to have become a cult centre mainly because of its links with Cuntarar. There are other centres like Tiruvāṉmiyūr, also in the suburbs of Madras, and Āccāḷpuram in the Śīrkāḻi taluq as well as Iṭakkal,[41] and Tirukkaccūr, near Singapperumāḷ (again in the suburbs of Madras). Of these, Tiruvoṟṟiyūr is the "closest in structure and myth" to Tiruvārūr.[42] The presiding deity here, as in Tiruvārūr, is an anthill deity. It is again, like Tiruvārūr, a renowned *Śakti-pīṭha* and has two Śakti centres, focussed around Vaṭivuṭaiyammaṉ and Vaṭṭappāṟai, like the Kamalāmpikai and Raudra Durgā or Eṟiñcakkoṟṟavai at Tiruvārūr.

The *Tiruvoṟṟiyūrppurāṇam,* composed in the 16th century A.D. by Ñāṉappirakācar, is conscious of a very close link between the two shrines. The *Tēvāram*-trio have glorified the deities of this temple and Cuntarar's life was closely connected with the site. He married his first wife Paṟavai at Tiruvārūr and the role of Tyāgarāja in acting as the go-between is an oft-repeated theme in the *Periyapurāṇam* and also finds mention in the hymns of the saint himself. He then proceeded to Tiruvoṟṟiyūr, where he fell in love with Caṅkili and the Lord Tyāgarāja played an important part in getting the two married and in subsequently making Cuntarar promise that he would never leave Caṅkili and hence Tiruvoṟṟiyūr. Later when he broke the promise due to an uncontrollable urge to see the Lord of Tiruvārūr, he was punished with blindness for his breach of promise. However, when Cuntarar reached Tiruvārūr, it was Tyāgarāja who laboured hard to work out a reconciliation between the husband and his estranged first wife. To this day the event of Cuntarar's promising Caṅkili that he would never leave her and hence Tiruvoṟṟiyūr is enacted as part of an annual ritual in the Tyāgarāja temple at Tiruvoṟṟiyūr. The scene is interesting and is an example of the rather unique devotee-god relationship between Cuntarar and Tyāgarāja.

The story goes that it was Tyāgarāja who appeared in Caṅkili's dream and asked her to take a promise from Cuntarar. When Cuntarar was approached with this demand, viz. that he would never part from Caṅkili, before she would agree to marry him, he hesitated to take such a major vow in the presence of Tyāgarāja. He decided on a plan. He asked Tyāgarāja temporarily to take shelter in the shade of the *makiḻam* (a precious flower) tree and promised Caṅkili that the vow would be taken in the inner shrine. Tyāgarāja outdid his devotee in cleverness and asked Caṅkili to impose the condition that the vow would have to be taken under the self-same *makiḻam* tree. This done, the saint was afflicted with blindness when he broke his promise, only finally to regain his sight in Tiruvārūr. Whatever be the symbolism involved in this myth, of equating blindness with ignorance and sight with spiritual awakening, in the realm of the religious topography of the cult the impact that the myth had was great and the two pilgrim-sites separated by over 300 kilometers were brought together into a network of sites by this most enigmatic of the Śaiva saints.[43]

Historically, Tiruvoṟṟiyūr was a famous temple under the later Pallavas and several of their grants as well as several Cōḻa inscriptions have come to light from this place.[44] The stone structure, however, as at Tiruvārūr, was built during the reign of Rājendra I.[45] Epigraphs (*ARE* 1912, Nos. 109, 129, 131, 220) refer to a Kāraṇai Viṭaṅkar which was presumably a corruption of Kāyārohaṇa, the epithet of the Pāśupata deity, enshrined also at Nākaikkārōṇam. Tiruvārūr and Tiruvoṟṟiyūr seem to have been connected through the *maṭha* establishments, private donors, myths, etc. Today the esoteric tradition of the viṭaṅkar and the veiling of the image has disappeared at Tiruvoṟṟiyūr, though the dance is still performed and the unique tradition of carrying the icon suspended on a bamboo pole is prevalent to this day. A special class of people called *śivatāṅkis* perform this function. Similarly, at Tiruvāṉmiyūr the Tyāgarāja performs eighteen kinds of dances on full-moon days before the Valmīkanātha, who is the presiding deity.

As remarked earlier, Appar connects several shrines together through the myths expounded in his hymns. In one of his hymns (VI.239.10) he refers to the route the deity of Ārūr is believed to have taken, and he refers to the icon dancing at Nallūr, riding a bull at Paḻaiyāṟu, standing at Ceṟṟūr, disappearing at Talaiyālaṅkāṭu, residing at Peruvēlur, spending a night at Pattīcuram, entering Maṇaṟkāl and walking through Taḷiccaṭṭāṅkuṭi and finally reaching Tiruvārūr.

Thus, these are connected with religious topography of the Tyāgarāja cult. The first place mentioned in the above itinerary, viz. Nallūr, could either be the Nallūr near Kumbakonam, which is a *pātalperra talam* and which has a *talapurāṇam* wherein the myth of *Vītiviṭaṅkatiyākar* resting for three days is recounted, or it could be Nallūrperumāṉam, (modern Āccāḷpuram in Śīrkāḻi taluq) where Campantar attained salvation. The former Nallūr was of special significance in the life of Appar, for it was here that he was converted from Jainism to Śaivism. The *Nallūrppurāṇam* (chapter 25, *Vītiviṭaṅkacarukkam*) recounts the story of Mucukuntaṉ but with a little variation. Having obtained the Somāskanda from Indra, Mucukuntaṉ is said to have brought it to Nallūr and placed it on a swing for three days, when the *devas* descended to give the swing a push. At the end of three days, on promptings from Tyāgarāja, the icon was enshrined in Tiruvārūr. Once again there is a conscious effort to group temples into inter-related sacred clusters thus providing a religous network.

Aruṇakirinātar refers to a Nallūr in the stanza *Caṅkaratiyākar vanturainallūr*, i.e., 'where Tiyākar rested for a while'. As this accords with the above myth, presumably both the hymnists were talking of a Nallūr near Kumbakonam. However, the deity of Āccāḷpuram is called Civalōkatiyākar, because of its being a sacred site associated with the life of Campantar; Aruṇakiri (who regarded Campantar as an incarnation of Murukaṉ) could well have sung of Āccāḷpuram.

Of the remaining sites mentioned in the itinerary of Tyāgarāja by Appar: a) Paḻaiyāṟu, according to the *Periyapurāṇam* (*Tirunāvukkaracu Purāṇam*, vv. 1561 & seq., esp. v. 1562) was a Jaina centre and Appar's hunger-strike prompted the king to reopen a Śaiva temple blocked by the Jainas. It was the ancient capital of the Cōḻas and renowned in Śaiva hagiography as the home of Amaranītināyaṉār. b) Paṭṭīcuram is near Kumbakonam, and the name of the deity, Paṭṭinātar, similar to that of the Lord of Pērūr, suggests pastoral origins, for the word *paṭṭi* means 'a cattle-pen', and the Lord Paṭṭinātar of Pērūr is also worshipped as an anthill. c) Tiruttalaiyaṉkāṭu, one and a half kilometers west of Tiruvārūr is dedicated to Naṭarāja and its *sthala* myth centres around the Dārukāvaṇa legend of Śiva going to the forests as a beggar (*bhikṣāṭana*). The deity is called *Āṭavallār*, 'adept at the dance'.

Thus, in conclusion, it is interesting to see what were the features which were common to the Tyāgarāja sites. First and foremost, all the myths carry memories of an imported Tyāgarāja, brought to earth by a king. Thus, this cult was superimposed on an earlier substratum represented in several of these temples by a cult of the anthill and consequently of serpent worship. Thus, all these cult centres were evolved out of a folk base which revered the snake, the anthill and the subterranean passage of *nāgabila*. These again are closely related to Murukan̲ worship and could well have been Murukan̲ centres in earlier times. In Tiruvārūr the Lord of this subterranean passage is called Hāṭakeśvara.

However, it must be remembered that the converse is not true; not all sites connected with anthill-worship and subterranean deites are directly related to Tyāgarāja. An obvious case that comes to mind is that of Kāñcī, which has a tradition of subterranean passage worship but none of Tyāgarāja. Several Valmīka shrines are known from all over Tamil̲nāḍu, such as On̲pattavēli, etc., which do not have Tyāgarāja associations.

All the Tyāgarāja cult centres were also seats of the goddess cult. The Tiruvārūr and Tiruvor̲r̲iyūr temples have a strong cult of *ugradevatās* (fierce goddesses). The Vaṭṭappār̲aiyamman̲ shrine at Tiruvor̲r̲iyūr according to Dhaky (Vol. I, pp. 255-256, *op.cit.*) was initially a *saptamātṛkā* shrine. The ritual traditions strongly link the Tyāgarāja temple at Tiruvārūr to the *piṭāriyamman̲* temple at the same place. The *saptamātṛkā* panel in Tiruvārūr appears to be the oldest sculpture in the temple complex, and appears to be of 'Pallava' origins. Thus, by the evidence drawn from myths and architectural designs, as well as from ritual practices, it seems clear that these shrines were probably connected with an ancient goddess cult which, as we shall see, was revived and adapted into the Śiva faith by the 13th century A.D. when all the major Śaiva temples of Tamil̲nāḍu had their own *Kāmakkōṭṭams* or shrines for the goddess. This, as pointed out by Eschmann in the context of Orissa, seems to have been the manner in which several regional beliefs were drawn into the orbit of Śaivism.[46]

All the Tyāgarāja temples discussed above were visited by the *nāyan̲mār*, particularly Appar and Cuntarar, and many of them are connected closely with lives of one or both saints. Most of these temples were also in areas which were strongholds of

Jainism or, as in the case of Nāgapaṭṭaṇam, Buddhism, and as such were of special interest to the Śaiva evangelisers.[47] The *saptaviṭaṅkatalaṅkaḷ* were all in Cōḻamaṇṭalam and received large grants from the Cōḻas starting from Rājarāja I. Most of the land grants to these temples were made in the 10th-11th centuries A.D. as pointed out by Noboru Karashima.[48] This lends strong support to the view that Tyāgarāja could well have been a territorial emblem of the Cōḻas.

Thus, the Somāskanda, which was the *leit motif* of Pallava sacred art and presumably the emblem of their sovereignty (possibly to begin with a territorial symbol of the Cōḻas) was expanded or readopted by the Imperial Cōḻas and under Rājarāja I the cults of the *Āṭavallāṉ* and the *Viṭaṅkar* were elevated into state cults. Once the state temple of Thañjāvūr was built, Tiruvārūr lost some of its importance.[49] Nevertheless, it remained a major sacred node in the Cōḻa religio-political network,[50] for this dynasty divided its royal patronage between selected sites favoured as pilgrimage centres.[51] The rationality behind it was either that they were traditional centres of folk cults or because they lay on key trade routes, in some of the richest agricultural lands of Tamiḻnāḍu. During the reigns of Rājarāja I and Rājendra I, the cult of the *Viṭaṅkaṉ* and *Āṭavallāṉ* seem to have enjoyed equal favour, but gradually the *Āṭavallāṉ* became the most revered symbol, as it was presumably a better medium through which to express the *Śaiva Siddhānta* philosophy and was perhaps aesthetically more pleasing.

The Naṭarāja in the Ānandatāṇḍava pose and the bronze Somāskandas make their appearance at about the same period, viz. the 9th-10th centuries A.D. The Tillai three thousand, now called the Potu Dīkṣitars, presumably because of their more cohesive organisational structure, made the Āṭavallāṉ the chief vehicle of expressing the Śaiva faith of Tamiḻnāḍu. Both the Tyāgarāja and the Naṭarāja have a strong Vaiṣṇavite substratum and tradition has it that Kulōttuṅga II flung the image of Gōvindarāja of Chidambaram into the sea.[52] Like most temple cults in Tamiḻnāḍu both these cults are deeply tinged with Tāntrism. The Dīkṣitars now point to the Chidambara-*rahasyam* or the esoteric truth of Chidambaram as a *cakra*—the *sammelana cakra*,[53] which is in essence the worship of a *yantra*. Thus, all Śaiva temples were sooner or later absorbed into the *Smārta-Śākta* brand of Tāntrism. The *ajapā yantram*, to be discussed in Chapter V, along with the worship of the *akṣarapīṭha* (the seat of the letters of the alphabet) to which a separate shrine is dedicated within the Tiruvārūr complex, is a clear indication of the predominance of Tāntric concepts in Tiruvārūr.

The presiding *liṅga* itself in all these *Śaivite* temples seems to betray strong chthonic traits. They are all named primarily after the geographical area, such as Tiruvoṟṟiyūruṭaiyār Mahātēvar or Maṟaikkāṭēśvarar, etc., and seem to symbolise territorial gods. Like the ancestral tablets of the Chinese, the Cham *kūṭs*, etc., they seem to have a strong root in the soil, and command a local loyalty. The Somāskanda, in the form of Tyāgarāja, expressed a shift of emphasis from the soil to the ruler. It was hence a palladium of sovereignty. The *Viṭaṅka*, then, as the subtle *Sūkṣmaśarīra*, was treated as the universalistic *kuṇḍalinī*. Thus, the realm, the ruler and the cosmos are blended into one, and the temple becomes both the transcendental and immanent abode of Godhead.

NOTES

1. See George Spencer, 'The Sacred Geography of the Śaivite Hymns' *Numen*, 17 (1970), pp.232-44; especially the map showing the sacred clusters and their locations.
2. The eight are: Tirukkaṇṭyūr (plucking off Brahmā's head), Tirukkōvalūr (annihilation of Andhakāsura), Tiruvatikai (burning of the three cities), a favourite metaphor for the *Siddhāntins*, who regard the three cities as the three *malas*, Tiruppariyilūr (plucking of Takkaṉ = Dakṣa), Tiruviṟkuṭi (killing of Calantarācura = Jalāndharāsura), Vaḻuvur (destruction of Kajācura=Gajāsura), Tirukkuṟukai (burning of Maṉmataṉ=Manmatha), and Tiṟukkaṭayūr, where in order to save Mārkaṇṭēyaṉ=Mārkaṇḍeya from death, Śiva kicked Yama, the god of Death.
3. The *Saptasthalam* are linked by the annual celebration of a common festival commemorating the wedding of Ṛṣabhadeva. The seven *kṣetras* are as follows:
   Tiruvaiyāṟu, which is the main focal point, Tiruppaḻanam, Tillaittāṉam, (Tillaisthāna) Tiruppūnturutti, Tiruccōṟṟutturai, Tiruvētikūṭi and Tirukkaṇṭiyūr. See Andre Beteille's description of this festival in 'Social Organisations of temples in Thañjāvūr Village'. *H.R.*, Vol. V., No.1, pp.74-92.
4. The Five Halls are:
   Ponna-ampalam, the Golden Hall - Chidambaram.
   Rajata-ampalam, the Silver Hall - Madurai.
   Tamra-ampalam, the Copper Hall - Tirunelveli.
   Irattina-ampalam, the Jewelled Hall - Tiruvalāṅkāṭu.

Citra ampalam, the Painted Hall - Kuṟṟālam.

5. The Five Elements are *Pṛthivī* - Earth - at Kāñci or Tiruvārūr, *Apās* or water - Tiruvāṉaikkaā *Tejas* or Fire - Tiruvaṇṇāmalai, *Vāyu* or Wind - Kālahasti, and *Ākāśa* or Ether (Space) - Chidambaram.
6. The *Cakras* and their hypostatisation are: *Mūlādhāra* - Tiruvārūr or Kāñcī; *Svādhiṣṭhāna* - Tiruvāṉaikkā; Maṇipūraka - Ṭiruvaṇṇāmalai; *Anāhata* - Kāḷahasti; *Ājñā* - Chidambaram and *Sahasrāra* - Kāśī. These equations vary from text to text and thus Madurai often claims to be Dvādaśānta, or the point closest to *sahasrāra*, etc. Note the close relation between *Cakras* and Elements referred to in note 5 above.
7. For a detailed discussion of the sites associated with the Śakti tradition and regarded as *Śākti pīṭhas* see D.C. Sircar, *The Śāktapīṭhas*. The list of 64 varies from region to region and the southern tradition again incorporates several sites in Southern India unknown to the northern tradition. For a brief look into the southern tradition see A.V. Jeyachundrun, *Śakti*, Madurai, 1966.
8. *Vide Supra* , Chapter II, for the derogatory terms used against the Jainas and Bauddhas as people who spoke through their noses an alien speech, etc.
9. The Tamil-Sanskrit synthesis is expressed by expressions such as *"muttamiḻum nāṉmaṟaiyum āṉāṉ kaṇṭāy"* (Behold him who is pure Tamiḻ and the four Vedas) and *"Vaṭamoḻiyum tentamiḻum maṟaikaḷnāṉkum āṉavaṉ kāṇ"* (Behold him who is the northern tongue and the southern Tamiḻ and the four vedas, Appar VI.301) or *"centamiḻōṭu āriyaṉai ccīriyaṉai"* (The one who has combined with pure Tamiḻ Aryan Tongue) etc. Several examples are cited by Vēnkaṭacāmi in *Camaṇamum Tamiḻum*, (in Tamiḻ) p. 60.
10. The Vedic-Āgamic synthesis is expressed several times by Cēkkiḻār, *"Vētaneṟi taḻaittōṅka miku caivatturaiviḷaṅka"*, (*Periyapurāṇam* Tiruñāna'cam, V.1); *"Caivaneṟi vaitikattiṉ tarumaneṟiyōṭum taḻāippa"*, etc. (Periyapurāṇam, Iṭaṅkaḻi, V.5, n.1).
11. Viraṉmīṇṭār is said to have been deeply affronted and practically excommunicated not only Cuntarar but the lord whom Cuntarar worshipped. See Chapter VI for some of the interesting additions and embellishments to the myth. Cuntarar, in order to appease Viraṉmīṇṭār composed the eulogy of the 62 saints preceding him. This is recorded by Cēkkiḻār, in the section called *Tiruttoṇṭatokaippurāṇam* in the *Periyapurāṇam*. Cuntarar's extolling the *aṭiyār* as a group as if they were a corporate Tamiḻ Śaiva group is interesting in a cultural and social context. Only Tirumūlar in the list was a non-Tamilian and even he, though from the north had entered into the body of a Tamilian cowherd, and was thus truly Tamiḻ.
12. *Tiruvārūrppurāṅam*, 'Tiruviḻāccarukkam', v.14, p.104.
13. The couplet runs:
    "Nākai Kāṟāyal Kōḷili Nakara nalaṉkeḻu Maṟaivaṉa
    Naḷḷāṟikaīvaṉpuri caiṉiya Vāymūrām ippati yāriṉum
    tollaiyākamam pakarnta vīti vali maṟṟaiyār uvakai mūrti kaṭamaiyum avakai vēḷaracaṉ
    arppaṇam purintu maliviḻāveṭuttāṉaṉmāto"
14. Examples are provided in the *Taṇṭiyaṭikaḷ purāṇam* (sp. v.26 and v.27) and *Naminantiyaṭikaḷ purāṇam* in the *Periyapurāṇam*. The former refers to the destruction of Jaina monasteries to enlarge the Kamalālaya tank within the Tiruvārūr temple complex. See also T.V. Mahalingam, ed., *Mackenzie Manuscripts*, No. 69, p.298.
15. The couplet *"cīrār ... cattaviṭaṅkaḷ"* appears in the written form in *Peruntokai*,

pāṭal 89, which is a collection of famous sayings and passages. *Kantapurāṇam* 6. 23 117-119 lists the seven *Viṭaṅka kṣētras* as Nākai, Naḷḷāṟu, Kaṟāyal, Kōḷariyūr, Vāymiyūr, and Tirumaṟaikkāṭu, apart from the chief one, Tiruvārūr. The place names, however, are not mentioned in the *Sivarahasyakhaṇḍa*, which only gives the information that six other images were enshrined in six other villages (see *SRRH* 5-6, 1-62; 5.7. 1-64). See also *Tirunaḷḷāṟuppurāṇam*, pp. 1-2; *Vētāraṇiya Māhāmyam*, 94. 1-59; Parañcōti Muṉivar *Vētāraṇiya Purāṇam* 8. 1-42; *Vētāraṉiya Purāṇam* of Akōratēvar, 18. 1-51.

16. U. Vē Cāmināta Aiyar, Notes to Antakavi Vīrarākava's *Tiruvārūr Ulā*, v. 25.
17. *Ibid*. p. V.
18. *Ibid*.
19. Appar, patikam, VI. 34.
20. Aiyaṭḷikaḷkāṭavarkōṇ, *Kṣētraveṇpā*, v. 4.
21. See above *Viṭaṅka* in Epigraphy. Also Catāciva Paṇṭārattār, *Piṟkāla Colavaralāṟu* for the influence of Tiruvārūr on the Thañjāvūr temple.
22. The '*Taṇṭiyaṭikaḷ Purāṇam*' in the *Periyapurāṇam* refers to a dream of the Cōḻa king in which the deity Tyāgarāja asked him to go to the rescue of Taṇṭiyaṭikaḷ and drive out the Jainas, who were obstructing his work of digging the temple tank wider.
23. 578 of 1904, S 11 Vol. XVII, No.624.
24. Tradition persisted in attributing *līlais* to Tyāgarāja, a belief corroborated by the *Mucukundasahasranāmam*. Tiricirapuram Mīṉātcicuntaram Piḷḷai collected thirteen of them in the 1840s and Piccāṇṭārkōyil Irācakōpāla Piḷḷai published all the 365 in the 1950s. This work has been discussed in detail in Chapter VI. These stories make the Tyāgarāja a palladium of Cōḻa royalty much in the fashion of the *tiruviḷaiyāṭals* which make the deity Cuntarēśvara the proprietor of Madurai, along with his consort Mīnākṣī.
25. See S. Vīrasamy Patthar, *The Temple and its Significance*, p. 125, for a comparison between Tiruvārūr and Chidambaram.
26. Two copper plates recently deciphered by the Dept. of Archaelogy, Thañjāvūr Tamiḻ University, have corroborated this. Personal Communication, 1983. The details of publication, if it has been published are not known to the author. B.G.L. Swamy had discussed this in his work *Chidambaram*. The ritual tradition of Tiruvārūr has preserved memories of this and to this day the Chidambaram Dīkṣitārs collect money from the the Tyāgarājaswāmi Devasthānam. An inscription from the thousand pillared hall in Chidambaram is also believed to refer to this.
27. Information recorded in *Guruparamparā*, a Vaiṣṇavite account of Vaiṣṇava matters and its activities etc., cited by K.A.N. Sastri *Cōḻas*, p. 107.
28. The Leyden Grant, *E.I.* XXII refers to Rājarāja's grant of Āṉaimaṅkalam village to the Cūḍāmaṇivihāra, built by the Śailendra king.
29. The term Kārōṇa is an abbreviation of Kāyārohaṇa meaning 'descent into the body' and refers to the myth of Lakulīśa, founder of a branch of Pāśupatas.
30. *A.R.E. 1957 B* 150-169; *A.R.E. 1958* A.7; This is a copper plate; 164 pf *A.R.E. 1956* refers to Nākai Aḻakar and it specifies that it refers to Aḻakaviṭaṅkapperumāḷ; 150 of 1956. 164 of *A.R.E.* 1956-57 records the gift of a jewel set with precious stones such as *paccai, māṇikkam*, etc., to the deity represented in the silver image of Nākai Aḻakar by the agent of the king of Śrī Vijayam. Nāgapaṭṭaṇam is called Cōḻakulavaḷḷipaṭṭaṇam and that gives an idea of the importance of the port to the Cōḻas. In 150 of 1956-57 the

Aḻakaviṭaṅkapperumāḷ is clearly distinguished from the *Tirukkāroṇamuṭaiyār*.

31. 451-4 of *A.R.E. 1908*; three of these refer to Rājarāja I, the fourth belongs to Rājendra's time.
32. 454 of *A.R.E 1908*.
33. *S.I.I XVII*, 445-545, mainly Cōḻa from Āditya I to Rājendra III. Thus, one hundred inscriptions have come to light from this temple.
34. 509 of *S.I.I. XVII*, 443 of *XVII* of the 15th year of Rājarāja I = 999-1000 A.D. Also of Parantaka I (*S.I.I. XVIII*, 517).
35. Campantar, the 'green hymn' or *paccai patikam* refers to the magical survival of Campantar's hymn from fire while the Jain hymns were burnt.
36. *A.R.E. 1960-61*, 298-309; *A.R.E., 1962-63*, 579-620.
37. *A.R.E. 1962-63*, 586.
38. *A.R.E. 1961*. Nos. 302 and 306 and *A.R.E. 1962-63*,Nos. 582 and 587.
39. L'Hernault, *op.cit.*, Pl. 30.
40. *A.R.E. 1951*, B 246-69. (Total number of inscriptions = 23; of these 19 belong to Cōḻa and 7 to Pāṇṭiya).
41. 491 of 1916 refers to Tiruvampikai Īśuramuṭaiyanāyaṉār at *Iṭaikkal* alias *Teṉtiruvārūr*. 492 of 1916 in modern Tamiḻ registers the name of a certain Kāḷiṅgaṉ, who is said to have celebrated the *Paṅkuṉi utsavam* in seven *veṇpā* verses of god Ampiki Īśuramuṭaiyār at Teṉtiruvārūr and constructed a chariot and a flag-staff. 501 of 1916 again refers to the same person as constructing according to Āgamic injunctions a big *gōpura* and *maṇṭapa* as well as jewelled car and the circuit wall for the Tyāga temple at Teṉ Tiru Ārūr. This expression '*Teṉtiruvārūr* ' occurs several times in inscriptions and according to the commentator of the *Periyapurāṇam*, C.K.Cuppiramaṇimutaliyār, the term '*Teṉ Tiru Ārūr*' refers to present-day Tiruvārūr and the areas of the Tyāgarājasvāmi temple while *vaṭa* or northern is the nearby hamlet. He has pointed out that this differentiation is registered even in modern land registers. See *Tiruttoṇṭarpurāṇam*, Vol. I, p. 631.
42. See Shulman, *Tamiḻ Temple Myths*, p. 381, n. 55.
43. The temples of Tiruvārūr and Tiruvoṟṟiyūr and the deities enshrined therein played a crucial part in the life of Cuntarar in his later years as well, when he lost his eyesight. This, according to the myth, was the result of divine punishment for breaking his vow and leaving Tiruvoṟṟiyūr and his wife Caṅkili, whom he had vowed never to part from; he is believed to have regained the sight in one eye in Kāñcī and the other in Tiruvārūr.
44. *A.R.E. 1912* from 98 to 208, a total of 151 inscriptions, a great majority being Cōḻa.
45. *A.R.E. 1912*, No.126, *S.I.I.*, IV, 553.
46. Eschmann, Kulke and others, *The Cult of Jagannāth and the Regional Tradition of Orissa*, p.79-99.
47. *Mackenzie Mss.* No.69, p.298, lists the Jain villages belonging to the Cōḻa country. Among them are Tiruvārūr, Vēdāraṇyam and Nāgapaṭṭaṇam. The list was composed in Śaka era 1798, i.e. 1846 A.D., obviously recording earlier history drawn from both oral and written sources.
48. Dr. N. Subrahmanian Felicitation, *Home to Historians*, pp.167-73.
49. Forty-four dancers were transferred from Tiruvārūr temples to Thañjāvūr by Rājarāja I, *S.I.I.*, II,66. This shows the shift of importance.
50. Spencer, George W., 'Religious Networks and Royal Influence in 11th century South India', *Journal of the Economic and Social History of the Orient*, Vol.11-

12, 968 ff. He views the Bṛhadīśvara temple as a "means of bridging together court and countryside in a politico-economic symbiosis".

51. Kulke, Herman and others, *The Cult of Jagannāth and the Regional Tradition of Orissa*, p. 199, f.n. 2.
52. There are several references to the removal of the Gōvindarāja image from Chidambaram by Kulōttuṅga II, such as *Takkayākapparaṇi*, vv.777; 808-10; *Kulōttuṅkaṉ Cōḻaṉulā* II. v. 69-106, especially vv.77-8; *Rājarājacoḻan ulā* II 58-66, and 65-6; *Kulōttuṅkacōḻaṉ Piḷḷaittamiḻ, pāyiram* 87; and 363 of 1907. *Kōyil Oḻuku* refers to the monarch as *Kirimikaṇṭa Colan*. The Vaiṣṇava substratum has been discussed in Chapters III and IV.
53. The main contention of the Chidambaram priests is that the worship at Chidambaram was Vedic and not even Āgamic, let alone Nigamic. The Sammēlana is a Cakra of Śiva and Devī. This could well be the Someśvara of the *Rauravāgama*. More detailed analysis of this *yantra* is likely to throw light on several aspects of the Naṭarāja Cult.

Chapter Four

THE TYĀGARĀJA ORIGIN MYTH

The Tyāgarāja cult and the myths surrounding it are so closely connected that it is impossible to study the one without the other. This chapter will focus on one particular aspect of the Tyāgarāja mythology, viz. the origin myth. In order to avoid repetition, other myths and legends which grew around this deity will be studied in sections dealing with religious syntheses, social adaptations and the close relationship between the cult and the state.

The Tyāgarāja origin myths, like most of this class of myths, is multi-layered and for the sake of clarity the various strata in its growth shall be traced bearing the following categories in mind, i.e. the origin; the period of ornamentation and variations; and the arrival of a standardised form.

The origin in an iconic and conceptual sense can be traced back to c.a. 7th century A.D. as seen in the last chapter. The period of ornamentation, elaboration and variety of renderings of the myth can be placed between the 7th and 16th centuries A.D. for it was at the last mentioned date that the *Sthalapurāṇa* (Tamil *talapurāṇam*) of Tiruvārūr appeared in the written form.

In the course of this study attempts will also be made to investigate the relationship between the Tyāgarāja and the other main foci of worship in the cult centres. Two examples, viz. the Tyāgarāja of Tiruvārūr and of Tiruvoṟṟiyūr would be studied at greater depth and treated as a typology for this study.

At Tiruvārūr the Tyāgarāja cult was comparatively a later arrival, much like the Naṭarāja at Chidambaram. The cult of the anthill[1] and presumably even that of the Hāṭakeśvara[2] preceded the introduction of the Tyāgarāja. The worship of the anthill is a well known feature of folk or village religion in South India.[3] Anthill worship, by the time of recorded history was no longer confined to the south for it was fairly prevalent in Northern India as well. In the South the worship of anthills and of the serpents inhabiting them was associated with both Śiva and Murukaṉ.[4] As Shulman has pointed out there are some oft-repeated motifs in the *talapurāṇam*, and one of the recurrent ones is that of the deity revealing its presence as a consequence of being wounded, albeit unknowingly, by a devotee. The most frequent sequence of events is one in which a cow or a horse or a man unknowingly hits a mound of earth or an anthill and it pours out blood, thereby revealing the *liṅga* beneath.[5] The Valmīkanātha or the Purriṭaṅkoṇṭāṉ of Tiruvārūr, however is not associated with any such direct violence to the *liṅga* but with the beheading of Viṣṇu and the theme of the great sacrifice at Kurukṣetra. This, however belongs to the stage of ornamentation and of the introduction of variations in the myth.

Connected very often with the cult of the snake and the anthill is that of subterranean caverns and passages which lead into the netherworld.[6] In Tiruvārūr the Hāṭakeśvara is regarded as a *nāgabila* or the passage leading to the netherworld. At Tiruvoṟṟiyūr too tradition persists in the existence of an underground passage connecting the anthill *liṅga* to the *atti* (fig tree) outside.[7] The anthill, a Pre-Āryan folk symbol, was adopted by the Sanskritists and as Shulman has pointed out the anthill in its Sanskritic classical form of religion assumed the connotation of the *yajña* or sacrifice, which is essential for creation. "The serpent dwelling in the anthill is the fiery seed of creation", "the locus of the *vastu*, the remnant of the sacrifice that produces new life".[8] At Tiruvārūr Murukaṉ is worshipped in his composite form of the Tyāgarāja, and the serpent and the anthill are as mentioned earlier connected intimately with Murukaṉ.

The Tyāgarāja origin myth too, at least in its earlier stages, centres around Murukaṉ. Shulman, however, holds quite the opposite view. He suggests that with the revival of the Murukaṉ cult in the 15th century the Murukaṉ cultic myth makers "capitalised on the Tyāgarāja popularity.[9] This does not bear close scrutiny since both the *Īṭṭiyeḻupatu* and the *Mucukundasahasranāmam* refer to the Murukaṉ connection. The latter is aware of both the traditions and makes no attempt to favour one or the other or even regard them as being at variance. The image is a Somāskanda and so the attributes, qualities and myths woven around Murukaṉ are transferred with ease to Śiva. The Vītiviṭaṅkaṉ, to my mind, was originally Murukaṉ, with the word *viṭaṅka* being equivalent to *Muruku*, 'beauty', and the *Tēvāram* singers transferred it to Somāskanda and in the process enhanced the position of Śiva in the trinity. Shulman also suggests the possibility that the Murukaṉ myth could be regarded as "a final assertion of Murukaṉ's identify with Skanda of Purānic tradition".[10] If this were so, it is easy to ascribe the period of its origin to the age of the Pallavas who were keen in working out a Sanskrit-Tamiḻ as well as a Śiva, Viṣṇu, Kumāra synthesis. This process of religious and cultural synthesis was best represented iconically by the composite Somāskanda and since it was a successful royal attempt at integration and hence acted as a source of prestige, it soon became a palladium of their sovereignty. Thus, the Tyāgarāja was superimposed and then synthesised with an ancient primitive cult of anthills and subterranean passages.

The origin myth carries distinct memories of the Tyāgarāja being brought to earth by a Cōḻa king. The concept of the processional *vītiviṭaṅka* (Tyāgarāja) was familiar to Appar and the icon itself made its debut in the 7th-8th centuries A.D. It was first patronised by the Pallavas. The connection between the Cōḻas and the image, however, has a long history. The Vītiviṭaṅkaṉ of the *Tēvāram* singers was certainly a Śiva symbol. However, the *Kanta Purāṇam, Sivarahasyakhaṇḍa* and the *Iṭṭiyeḻupatu* record his Murukaṉ associations. The *talapurāṇas* again revert to the Śiva symbol. The *Mucukundasahasranāmam* treats it as a Śiva-Śakti symbol. In this maze of symbols it is difficult to arrange them in any evolutionary order.

The Origin

In the *Cilappatikāram*[11] there are references to a mortal king guarding the heavens. Indra, we are told, appointed a *bhūta* to help this mortal king in guarding his celestial abode. When the demons engulfed the heavens with cloud of darkness the guardian *bhūta* swallowed it and the king was thus able to ward off the demons (Pukārkkāṇṭam, 7-13). Aṭiyārkkunallār, the commentator, states that the king guarded the heavens when Indra went to rescue the *amṛta* (ambrosia) stolen by the demons. The reference to this king occurs in three places in the above mentioned work. In the *Intiraviḻavūreṭutta kātai* of the *Pukārk kāṇṭam* [12] the story of the *bhūta* accomplice of the king, whom the commentary identifies with Mucukuntaṉ, is told in passing. The king's guarding the city of Indra is again referred to in *Kaṭalāṭukātai* of the same *Kāṇṭam.*[13] The commentary again identifies him with Mucukuntaṉ. This stanza, i.e. vv.14-17 further informs us that as a reward for his guarding the heavens he was given the five halls. The incident is beautifully captured in an *ammāṉaivari* in the *vañcikkāṇṭam, vāḻttukkātai,*[14] in which the king is referred to as a Cōḻa. Thus it is in the time of Aṭiyārkkunallār, the commentator that the name Mucukuntaṉ is associated with this Cōḻa guardian of Indra's quarters and the receiver of the five halls. Aṭiyārkkunallār is generally placed in the 12th-13th centuries A.D. Cayaṅkontār, of the same period reiterates the story and calls the Cōḻa hero Mucukuntaṉ.[15]

It is only in the *Īṭṭiyeḻupatu* of Oṭṭakkūttar that the first clear outlines of the Tyāgarāja origin myth begin to appear. On stylistic grounds Mu. Arunachalam and Veḷḷaivāraṇar regard this to be of such inferior literary merit that they believe that it was composed in the 18th century, when according to Mu. Arunachalam it was popular for books to be written extolling Veḷḷālas, Ceṭṭiyārs and other caste-groups.[16] On a close examination of the content, and reference to the names of some of the feudatories and certain geographical zones and placing it in the context of the importance of the Kaikkōḷar community in the 13th century epigraphs, it seems very highly probable that it was an authentic work of Oṭṭakkūttar, albeit of an inferior standard. As far as our present purpose is concerned, suffice it to say that Oṭṭakkūttar does refer to the origin myth in his other works as well. K.A.N. Sastri,[17] R.Nagasamy,[18] Kamil Zvelebil[19] and several other historians regard it as an authentic work. Zvelebil's dating is based on stylistic grounds as well.

The *Īṭṭiyeḻupatu*[20] is a poem in praise of the *ceṅkuntars*. Ceṅkuntars are a class of weavers known in epigraphs as *kaikkōḷars* (*Kai* is hand and *kol* is loom and so they were the handloom weavers), who played a very important part in temple administration as well as in military affairs. *Kaikkōḷars* are known to have been granted *ruttirapati* lands and were referred to by the title of *sēnāpati* or commanders-in-chief [21] and seemed to have sat on temple councils settling disputes.[22] Even the 9th century A.D. lexicon, the *Tivākaram,* refers to *Ceṅkuntarpaṭai* or army of *ceṅkuntars.* Oṭṭakkūttaṉ[23] belonged to this community and is said to have composed this poem of seventy three stanzas and two hundred and ninety two verses on constant entreaties from the weaver community.[24] A later work called the *Cenkuṅtar pirapantattiraṭṭu* was edited by Capāpati Mutaliār and published in 1926. They had constantly made a bid as a group for social mobility. *ARE 34 of 1957-58* of 13th century proclaims after much deliberation that ten thousand weavers (here called d*evāṅga'*, the weavers were called *cōḻiya cāliyar, kaikkōḷar* and *dēvāṅgas*) could wear the sacred thread. This is similar to the *rathakāras* or chariot makers, who too were given permission to wear the sacred thread (see Chapter 7). The *Kaikkōḷars* are referred to as *Ēkāṅgavīras* in *ARE No.5 and No.7 of 1943-44* who fought till death for ruler and realm. Thus there is a strong tradition of weavers following the martial arts and being worshippers of Murukaṉ.

The Tyāgarāja origin myth is introduced in v.32 of the *Īṭṭiyeḻupatu* where it is stated that Mucukuntaṉ, because of the succesful completion of his penances in his previous birth (*muntai nōṉpiṉāl*), won the favour of Lord Murukaṉ. The Lord bestowed on Mucukuntaṉ his nine personal warrior bodyguards, who were his own brothers, and sent them down to the earth as the protectors of the realm. With the aid of these nine brave men (*nava vīras*) Mucukuntaṉ conquered the world and earned the title 'King of Kings'. Mucukuntaṉ's capital city is given as Karūr. The nine warriors, the work tells us, took human forms, married Cōḻa princesses and settled in Cōḻa lands. Mucukuntaṉ himself married the daughter of the chief warrior Vīrabāhu and established a dynasty (v. 34). The link with the main story is provided by the fact that Ottakkūttaṉ, the poet, is presented as a scion of the family of the chief of the *ceṅkuntars,* who was one of the nine warriors of Murukaṉ. It was this warrior weaver and confidant of the king who is credited with bringing the Tyāgarāja to the earth.

Details are provided about the icon and its mythical origins. It was, the poet assures us, the self-same image which was enshrined in the bosom of Tirumāl, as he lay in the cosmic ocean attended upon by Lakṣmī (v. 33), and the very same one which was bestowed on Indra (*Ākaṇṭalaṉ*). This image was brought to earth by the Ceṅkuntaṉ chief for the benefit of his royal master Mucukuntaṉ.[25] It provides further information on the rule of Mucukuntaṉ, for we are told that a deluge in the form of floods and submarine fire swept through the earth and Mucukuntaṉ and the nine warriors had to take temporary shelter in Heaven. Mucukuntaṉ prayed to Śiva and the Lord asked him to marry the daughter of Vīrabāhu, the chief of the nine warriors and establish a new dynasty. He gladly obeyed and then embarked on consolidating his position by defeating the king of Kerala, Srī Lankā (*Īḷam*), etc. The political implications of the myth are extremely interesting and will be discussed in Chapter 9. Stylistically what is interesting here is that the legends are juxtaposed in such a manner whereby a close parallel is drawn between Mucukuntan̲ and the Cōḻa monarch Kulōttuṅga II and the chief of the Ceṅkuntars and the poet-author of the work Oṭṭakkūttan̲. That the royal patron of the poet was Kulōttuṅga II is made explicit in a verse which runs *"pāṭum pulavar paṇikoṇṭa kūttan̲ pātāmpuyattai cūṭum kulōttuṇka Cōḻan en̲r̲ēyen̲n̲ai colluvarē"*, added as a separate verse (*tan̲icceyyuḷ*) and referring to the praises heaped on our poet by Kulottuṅkan (Kulōttuṅga)[26]. That this Kulottuṅkan̲ was the second Kulōttuṅga has to be inferred from the fact that Oṭṭakkūttar is believed to have been the court-poet of three successive Cōḻa monarchs, Vikrama Cōḻa, Kulōttuṅga II and Rājarāja, on the three of whom he composed the *Mūvar ulā*.

Thus, in the *Īṭṭiyeḻupatu* the Tyāgarāja myth connects Viṣṇu, Indra, Mucukuntan̲ and the Ceṅkuntar chief. In the *Irācarācacōḻan̲ulā* (v. 140) of the same poet, we get the information that Mucukuntan̲ guarded the heavens on Indra's request and brought back the divine damsels to earth.[27] Here, no mention is made of the Tyāgarāja and the bringing of it to the earth. In *Kulōttuṅkkacōḻanulā* again of the same poet, a reference is made to Mucukuntan̲'s guarding the heavens till the arrival of Murukan̲ and, having sleeplessly guarded the gods, won the boon of uninterrupted sleep.[28] Here one can see that Kṛṣṇa of the *Bhāgavata Purāṇa* and *Harivaṁśa* has been substituted by Murukan̲. Here too, he is credited with having brought the heavenly damsels to earth. In all this, the myth is strongly tinged with the Murukan̲ cult. The *Mucukundasahasranāmam* v.376-7 refer to this Murukan̲ affiliation in the Tyāgarāja myth, in the following terms: "*Om navavīra samupēta Mucukunda suvanditāya namaḥ*". The aspect of the myth dealing with image being enshrined in the heart of Viṣṇu was hinted at by Appar (IV.4.9) when he described the deity as "*paiyañcuṭarviṭu nākapaḷḷikoḷvān̲ uḷḷattān̲ai*", 'the Lord who resides in the heart of one who lies on a five-hooded serpent', referring to the concept of Anantaśāyin Viṣṇu. Other than this one reference, there is very little information in the *Tēvāram* on the myths specially connected with Tyāgarāja. Nowadays the

Śūra Saṁhāra festival connected with Kārttikeya (to celebrate the destruction of a demon called Cūrapatuma<u>n</u> in Tami<u>l</u> and Śūra Padma in Sanskrit) is performed only by the Kaikkōḷar community, thus bringing back echoes of this myth.

Elaborations and Variants of the Myth

The *Kantapurāṇam* and the two *talapurāṇas* from Tiruvārūr give the two standard variants of the myth. The *Kantapurāṇam* looks at it from the Murukaṉ cultic point of view, while the two *talapurāṇas* give it a stronger Śaivite bias. The *Kantapurāṇam* has proved to be again a very difficult work to date, and "the most widely differing dates have been suggested... ranging from the 8th to the 17th or even 18th centuries A.D."[29] Mu. Arunachalam places him between *Vīracōḻiyam* and Aruṇakirinātar, i.e.c.a. 1070 to 1400 A.D.[30] K.A.N. Sastri places the author in 1625 A.D. As Zvelebil has pointed out three poets of the 17th century A.D. refer to the work and so that seems to be the safe *terminus ad quem*.[31]

The *Kantapurāṇam* is a work of ten thousand three hundred and forty-five stanzas by Kacciyappamuṉivar, an ardent devotee of Murukaṉ and a *Śivācārya* (a Śaiva priest) at the Kumarakkōṭṭam (the shrine of Kumara or Murukaṉ) at Kāñcīpuram. Kacciyappar also describes Mucukuntaṉ's great devotion to Murukaṉ and he is said to have attended the wedding of Skanda to Teyvayāṉai, the daughter of Indra, a mythical event localised at Tirupparaṅkuṉṟam.[32] He is said to have observed the *Kārttikkai ṣaṣṭi* and other fasts for Murukaṉ on the advice of Vasiṣtha. He is said to have meditated on Murukaṉ and when the god appeared asked that one of the Lord's attendants be bestowed on him. The invincible nine warriors bestowed by the generous Marukaṉ became the protectors of Mucukuntaṉ's realm. Mucukuntaṉ married the daughter of Vīrabāhu, Citrāvali, and founded a dynasty. Several minor incidents recording the whims of Vīrabāhu's daughter are recorded in the *Kantapurāṇam* (6.23; 41-44) and in *Kaliṅkkattupparaṇi* (6.192) and appear in an identical version in the *Īṭṭiyeḻupatu*. Was Kacciyappar copying Oṭṭakkūttar or was a spurious Oṭṭakkūttar using the *Kantapurāṇam* information? Judging from the abundance of quasi-historical details and the repetitions of some of the stories in other works of Oṭṭakkūttar, I personally feel inclined to place the *Īṭṭiyeḻupatu* among the minor works of Oṭṭakkūttar.

The marriage of Mucukuntaṉ to the daughter of Vīrabāhu and

his founding a new dynasty as the result of this union have a close parallel with the founding of the second line of Cōḻas by Kulōttuṅga I, who became the monarch by virtue of marrying the daughter of Rājarāja I and he took special pride in his Cōḻa link. He also needed the legitimisation of his power. This shall be dealt with at some length in Chapter 9.

Coming back to the *Kantapurāṇam*, the *Kantaviruttapaṭalam* describes the whole elaborated and ornamented origin myth of Tyāgarāja. Viṣṇu enshrined the icon in his heart and its gentle sway, following the rhythmic breathing of the deity, formed the motionless dance of Tyāgarāja. The icon was bestowed on Indra, who subsequently, in an effort to evade his promise to Mucukuntaṉ, (he had promised to give Mucukuntaṉ whatever he asked for and the mortal king asked for the Somāskanda-Tyāgarāja) made six replicas of the image and asked the Cōḻa king to choose the right one. This the mortal king promptly did with divine help, and Mucukuntaṉ thus received all the seven Tyāgarāja icons. It further refers to the seven villages in which the seven images were enshrined.[33]

Standardised Form of the Myth

It is in the 16th century *talapurāṇas* that the final stages of the embellishments are added and the myth acquires a standardised form. The *Kamalālaya ciṟappu* is the earlier of the two *talapurāṇas* and it was composed by Chidambaram Kaṅkaṭṭi Śrimaṟaiñānaca-mpantanāyaṉār of the Kukanamaccivāya *maṭam* of Chidambaram in 1469 Cālivākana Era, (i.e. Śaka Era) i.e. 1547 A.D. The date is given in the *pāyiraccarukkaṃ* (v. 25). The work consists of 1066 verses in twenty-four chapters. The Tyāgarāja myth as contained in the Somāskanda *carukkam* runs as follows:

Viṣṇu desired a son, and so performed severe penance and meditated on the *liṅga* of Śiva. Śiva appeared with Umā by his side and blessed him with a son. The goddess, however felt slighted as Viṣṇu had not offered her worship and in her boiling rage (*Kotittiṭu Umai*) at being ignored (*ennai matittilai*) pronounced a curse that the son thus born would instantly die (*kāṇ uṉ putalvaṉ vatai paṭuvāṉ*). Viṣṇu, realizing his folly, decided to meditate on Śiva, Umā and their son Skanda, all seated on the same platform, and asked Viśvakarmā, the divine craftsman to fashion such an icon depicting Śiva, three-eyed with a buck in his upper left hand

and an axe in his upper right with the lower left and right hands in *vara* and *abhaya mudrās* respectively. He was to be accompanied by Devī and Kumāra between them. Iconographically these attributes appeared only in the Cōḻa bronzes on a regular basis though a stone sculpture with these attributes has come from the Kailāśanātha at Kāñcīpuram, as seen in chapter II.

He then appeased Devī by explaining that there was no Śiva without Devī and *vice versa* and, thus appeased, she modified the curse by which the child of Viṣṇu though burnt by Śiva, would continue to live in a bodiless form. Thus the myth of *Kāmadahana* or burning of Kāma, the God of love, was woven into this. Tamiḻ myths were clearly reworkings of the Sanskrit myths and adapted to suit their specific requirements.[34]

While Viṣṇu was meditating on this icon the heavens were threatened by the demon Kāliyan, and Indra asked Viṣṇu for the efficacious emblem of Somāskanda. Thus armed, Indra defeated the *asura* only to be attacked by yet another demon called Valan̲. This time Indra entreated Mucukuntan̲ to help him, and the Cōḻa king vanquished the enemy; promised by Indra that he could ask for anything in return, Mucukuntan̲ asked for Tyāgarāja. Indra sent him to Viṣṇu to obtain his permission, which he did and duly enshrined it to the south of the anthill-deity, *Pur̲r̲iṭaṅkoṇṭān̲ irukkum poruḷin̲ ten̲pāl*, at Tiruvārūr. He is said to have installed it in the month of Māci in the *hasta nakṣatra* (referring to a zodiacal position). The chapter then describes the rites and rituals such as the *Paṅkun̲i Uttiram*, etc. and dwells at length on the efficacy of these rites and in the dangers incurred by a slipshod performance of the rituals.[35]

The other *talapurāṇam* on Tiruvārūr was written by Campanta Mun̲ivar, the disciple of Nirampavaḻakiya Tēcikar in the year 1592 A.D. He is believed to have belonged to the Tarumapura *Ātīn̲am*. This work consists of 111 chapters and 2929 verses. Three of these chapters refer to the Tyāgarāja myth. Mucukuntan̲'s fight with the demons is graphically described and so also his life in heaven prior to his being born as a mortal. He is believed to have been a monkey in the heavens and inadvertently dropped *vilva* leaves on Śiva and Umā. As a reward for this act of piety, he was made the king of the Cōḻas. Mucukuntan̲ is presented as the culture-hero of the Tamiḻs. He drove out hunger and disease and was an epitome of wisdom, courage and devotion.

In this chapter the son of Viṣṇu is explicity equated with Kāma and the theme of Śiva's dance, to be studied in the next chapter, is introduced for the first time with all the eschatological and soteriological implications. From this time on, this motif becomes the salient feature of the cult. The soft undulations of Viṣṇu's breath form the dance of Somāskanda, the *ajapā naṭanam*. That the icon is regarded as the immanent form of the deity and not just an emblem becomes clear when Viṣṇu, as stated in the *Tiruvārūrppurāṇam* requests Śiva, Devī and Skanda to descend and imbue the icon with their presence for the sake of the welfare of the world (*inta ulakam muḻuvatum uytal vēṇṭum*).

The basic pattern of the story in the two *Purāṇas*, apart from the theme of dance in the *Tiruvārūrppurāṇam*, is the same. The theme of dance finds mention in a very general manner in the *Tēvāram* hymns on *Vītiviṭaṅkan* or Ārūraṉ as Tyāgarāja was called. Appar addresses him as *'āṭuvāy nī naṭṭam'* and Campantar refers to the dance particularly of the Lord of Tiruvāymūr.[36] Another major difference between the two *talapurāṇas* is that the subterfuge of Indra and his making six replicas of the image are not mentioned in the *Kamalālayacciṟappu*. In the *Tiruvārūrppurāṇam*, the spot is much emphasised for the Somāskanda Tyāgarāja wants to be enshrined at Tiruvārūr: *eṉṉai Tiruvārūrukkku Koṇṭu cel; pūcaṉai cey*.[37] This theme is further emphasised in the *Tiruvārūrulā*, where Brahmā is said to have weighed the earth of every shrine against the weight of the icon and found that it was Tiruvārūr which weighed more and hence the icon was enshrined there.[38] In the fifty years between the two *talapurāṇas* a great deal of elaboration and embellishment had been added. It must be remembered, however, that Indra's subterfuge and the story of the seven images was known to the *Kanta Purāṇam* and *Śivarahasyakhaṇḍa*. The 17th century *Vētāraṇīyappurāṇam* of Parañcōti muṉivar basically keeps to the Mucukuntaṉ myth (ch.8, 1-42) and so does the *Vētāraṇiya Māhātmiyam* of Akōratēvar (18: 1-51). Other works which refer to the Mucukuntaṉ theme are *Tirumūrtimālai* 12-13 (91-108), *Tiruppērūrtalappurāṇam* 16 (1-54,171-26), *Tiruvāṉmiyūrpurāṇam*, 6, *Kāciyāraṇiyamāhātmiyam* (Kāciyāraṇya is Ālaṅkuṭi), *Nallurppurāṇam* and the *Tiruvoṟṟiyūrppurāṇam*. The earliest legends had a preponderently Murukaṉ base; in the *Tēvāram* hymns, however, the Śiva-*utsavabera* aspect is much emphasised but with the constant reminder that Śiva is with Śakti by his side.[39] In the *talapurāṇas*, both in relation to the story of *Purriṭaṅkoṇṭāṉ* and the Tyāgarāja, the area is regarded as the realm of Śakti and the curse on Viṣṇu is pronounced by Śakti since she feels relegated to an inferior position *vis a vis* Śiva. This, when studied in the context of some of the sculptures in the Tiruvārūr temple and other Tyāgarāja shrines and juxtaposed against the Comācimārāṉār episode [40] provides interesting information on the remarkable maze of syntheses that finally resulted in the Tyāgarāja cult.

Turning to another enigmatic source in Sanskrit, the *Śivarahasyaskhaṇḍa* of the *Skandamahāpurāṇa,* we find that it furnishes us with some interesting glimpses of the Somāskanda Tyāgarāja origin myth. The Tamil *Kantapurāṇam* claims to belong to the *Skandapurāṇam.*[41] Filliozat [42] and Zvelebil[43] have speculated on the possibility of the *Kantapurāṇam* being earlier than the *Śivarahasyakhaṇḍa,* the substance of which bears the closest similarity to the Tamiḻ work. The dating of the *Skandapurāṇam,* which again has a North Indian and a South Indian recension[44] has proved to be an impossible task. It is a monumental work and there is a popular saying in Tamiḻ that if there is any fantastic yarn to be found, the place to look for it would be in the Skandapurāṇa! Tradition ascribes it to Vyāsa. The *Śivarahasyakhaṇḍa* is a section of the part entitled *Śaṅkarasaṁhitā* and is by itself a thirteen thousand *śloka* work.[45]

The *Mucukuntarājacaritram* is recited in the sixth chapter of the *Devakhaṇḍa* of the *Śivarahasyakhaṇḍa.* The *Śivarahasyakhaṇḍa* tells the story of Mucukuntaṉ's pre-mortal existence in heaven as a monkey, his winning the boon to be born a great king; his induction into the rituals of Skanda worship by Vasiṣṭha; his attending the marriage of Murukaṉ, asking that the nine warriors be bestowed on him and the subsequent marriage to the daugther of Vīrabāhu, etc. It combines the myths of the two *talapurāṇas* with it and the story of Tyāgarāja being worshipped by Viṣṇu, then Indra and subsequently its being brought to earth by Mucukuntaṉ. Additional information is provided in v. 41 where we are told that Viṣṇu, in order to atone for his parting with the image went to Chidambaram and worshipped Naṭarāja there and then came to Kamalālaya. Indra (vv. 44-6) describes the image as having Skanda between Umā and Śiva. Mucukuntaṉ, after obtaining Viṣṇu's permission, decides to bring it to earth; Indra tries to trick him with six replicas. He chooses the right one, and enshrines it in Tiruvārūr and the replicas nearby. The work does not give the names of the other *kṣetras*. It, however, provides an interesting myth, which to this day forms part of the ritual of the Tyāgarājasvāmi temple, and that is that Indra had to expiate for the sin of subterfuge and so took birth as a *caṇḍāla* in Tiruvārūr and propitiated the Somāskanda by playing the musical instruments and after a considerable period of time returned to the heavens, thus cleansed (vv. 55-9). The first volume of the *Śivarahasyakhaṇḍa* concludes with the episode of Mucukuntaṉ and the finale is when the king and the nine warriors, having fulfilled their duties pray to the god Murukaṉ and are taken to the heavens after handing over the kingdom to their successors. In chapter 90 of the *Upadeśakhaṇḍa*, the Somāskanda, as seen earlier, is regarded as one of the forms of Śiva, which was to be worshipped by those desiring a son.[46]

Thus, either Kacciyappar has closely followed the *Śivarahasyakhaṇḍa*, or the Sanskrit work may be a later translation of the Tamil *Kantapurāṇam*. Shulman gives a number of reasons why he believes that the *Śivarahasyakhaṇḍa* is older than the *Kantapurāṇam*. To summarize Shulman's views: (1) the *Kantapurāṇam* is unitary in compositional style while the *Śivarahasyakhaṇḍa* is composite. (2). *Śivarahasyakhaṇḍa* is shorter, *Kantapurāṇam* is much more elaborate. (3) The Tiruvārūr-Mucukuntaṉ Tyāgarāja cycle is followed by the marriage of Murukaṉ and Vaḷḷi. This appears at the end of the 6th Kāṇṭam. In *Śivarahasyakhaṇḍa* it is after the wedding of Skanda that the story of Mucukuntaṉ is introduced. This is in accordance with the wishes of the assembly of sages who request the *Suta* to tell them more about the king Mucukuntaṉ. In the *Kantapurāṇam* the Mucukuntaṉ story is introduced abruptly after the Dakṣa episode and is an independent unit.[47] (SRKH 5.6. 1-62, 5.7. 1-64 give the story of Mucukuntaṉ and the seven images, KP 6.23. 49-123.)

A manuscript in the Saraswati Mahal Library at Thañjāvūr has a compendium of myths on the Tyāgarāja of Tiruvārūr called *Tyāgarājamāhātmyam*.[48] The extracts are claimed to be from the following works:

(1) *Śiva Purāṇa*, which the mss. describes as being the *Uparibhāga* of the *Sanatkumārasamhitā*
(2) *Skandapurāṇa*, *Sūtasamhitā Yajñavaibhavakhaṇḍa*
(3) *Bhaviṣyat Purāṇa*, the *Uparibhāga* of *Śivakṣetrakhaṇḍa*, entitled

Pārijātavanamāhātmya.

(4) *Śrīmat Hālāsyamāhātmyam* of the *Skandapurāṇa.*[49]

(5) *Nagarakhaṇḍa* of the *Skandapurāṇa.*

(6) *Śivarahasyakhaṇḍa* in the *Saṅkarasaṁhitā,* in the *Devakhaṇḍa.*[50]

(7) In the same work as (6) above in the *Sapta Brahmakaivartaka* section dealing with the *Vedāraṇyamāhātmyam.*

(8) Again in the same work dealing with *Nāgapaṭṭaṇamāhātmyam.*

(9) In the same work yet again under *kālāgarumāhātmyam* (Kālāgaru is the Sanskrit form of Tirukkāṟāyil).

(10) The *Śiva Purāṇa, Ēkādaśarudrasaṁhitā, kṣetra khaṇḍa* chapter 55, entitled *Kālāgaruvanamāhātmyam.* There are however minor variations in the two works of the same name and dealing with the same theme.

(11) *Padma Purāṇa,* the fifth *khaṇḍa* entitled *mantrasiddhikṣetra* under *Bhaktavatsaḷamāhātmyam, Lakṣmīvivāha.*

(12) *Śiva Purāṇa, Sītārāmeśvara māhātmyam,* chapter 5. This collection was made, according to the compendium by Paramahaṁsa Parivrājaka Ācārya Abhinava Nārāyaṇendra Sarasvatī and is basically a collection from ten works.

The rites and rituals conducted within the Tyāgarāja temple are described in the first work mentioned above. As it deals with the Nāgapaṭṭaṇam myth, it refers to Cuntara Viṭaṅka and classifies each of the *Viṭaṅkas* as belonging to a specific aeon of time. Thus, for example, a king called Cālicuka, is said to have established it in Kāyārōhaṇam during the second aeon of creation. In the third aeon they established the *viṭaṅka* at Vēdāraṇyam, in the fourth at Naḷḷāṟu, in the fifth at Kālāgaru and the sixth and seventh are given as Kōḷili and Vāymūr. It further introduces Vyāghrapāda and Patañjali and the theme of the dance of knowledge symbolised by the *Pañcākṣara* (the five sacred syllables being *na maḥ Śi vā* and *ya,* constituting the obeisance *namaḥ Śivāya,* I salute Śiva, which is the sacred greeting of the Śivabhakti schools) and performed by the *viṭaṅka* of the place. It then dwells on the theme of the dance. In the same work reference is made to the *Kāśī Khaṇḍa.* The work suddenly describes an Ambikeśvara icon in the form of a dialogue between Śiva and Pārvatī, much in the fashion of the Tantras, as follows: "Where you are Ambikā, there I am Ambikeśvara and the icon here is with the six- faced son between the two of us". This is interesting, as an epigraph from Iṭakkal refers to a deity called Īcuramuṭaiya Ampikēśvara from Teṉ Tiruvārūr and the temple is called the Tyāgarāja temple.[51] The Sanskrit work then proceeds to say: "If the trio are seen by mortals, Oh! Umā, they would surely conceive a progeny".

From here the author of the anthology refers to the *Nagarakhaṇḍa* where a question is posed as to the purpose of the dance of Somāskanda. The esoteric discussion that follows shall be discussed elsewhere. The *Kāśīkhaṇḍa* and the *Nagara Khaṇḍa* are both from the *Yajñavaibhavakhaṇḍa* of the *Sūta Saṁhitā* belonging to the *Skanda Purāṇa*. Thus these are both included in (2) of the list. Much of the other references deal either with the rituals connected with the cult or with the cultic dance.

The theme of *Mucukunda* as narrated in the *Śivarahasyakhaṇḍa* agrees *verbatim* with the published version edited by Anantarama Dīkṣitar quoted above, and also with the manuscript version in the India Office Library, London. The myth occurs in the seventh chapter of the *Deva Khaṇḍam* of the *Śivarahasyakhaṇḍa* and runs through sixty four *slōkas*.

In the *Brahmavaivarta* cited above, the main focus is on Vedāraṇyam but the Tyāgarāja myth is repeated and Kamalālaya is accepted as being the primary centre of the cult where the genuine image was enshrined. Vedāraṇyam and Nākaikkāroṇam seem to be the most important centres next to Tiruvārūr. The same format is basically repeated in the other *māhātmyas* of the *viṭaṅka kṣetras*. In the *Padma Purāṇa* version, the focus is shifted to extolling Devī as Kamalā and the spouse of Viṣṇu.

By the time of the *Kantapurāṇam* and the *talapurāṇas* of the *viṭaṅka kṣētras* were written down, the myth basically appeared in three variant forms. Mucukuntaṉ was the hero in all three, but was regarded as a Murukaṉ worshipper in one set of myths and a Śiva-worshipper in another set with the third set emphasising the Śakti aspect. *Padma Purāṇa* version gives more importance to the Viṣṇu and Kamalā aspect of the myth. This is also evident in the *Tiruvoṟṟiyūr purāṇa*. The story of Toṇṭaimāṉ and the founding of Tiruvoṟṟiyūr, as related in the *Skanda Purāṇam* assumes a Vaiṣṇava garb.[52] Tiruvoṟṟiyūr Ñāṉapirakācar claims to have obtained his knowledge of the sacred myths of Tiruvoṟṟiyūr from the *Skanda Purāṇa, Nagarakhaṇḍa*. On studying this work, it can be seen that the only myth that occurs here dealing with Toṇṭaimāṉ refers to the origin of Tirupati and is clothed in Vaiṣṇava terms. So we have to infer that not only were northern Sanskrit myths reworked into Tamiḻ ones, but Vaiṣṇava myths were also transformed into Śaiva myths and motifs were borrowed from one pilgrim literature to another with ease.

This brings us to the discussion of the connection between Viṣṇu, Kamalā and Somāskanda. That a strong Vaiṣṇavite base was present in the Tyāgarāja myths is obvious, specially if we remember the Mucukunda-Kṛṣṇa association in the *Mahābhārata*[53] and the *Bhāgavata*.[54] Shulman has discussed this Vaiṣṇava substratum at some length.[55] What is interesting is that the *Skanda Purāṇa* also introduces the motif of the *valmīka* or anthill but associates it with Viṣṇu and Toṇṭaimāṉ's founding Nārāyaṇapuri (Tamiḻ Tirupati).

Thus, by a study of the origin myth of the Tyāgarāja it becomes clear that the Tyāgarāja is a highly syncretistic concept connected with Murukaṉ, Śiva, Umā, Viṣṇu and Kamalā and the last aspect gets emphasised in the Tāntric cult of Tyāgarāja. This synthesis will be taken up for discussion in the next chapter.

The *Tiruvoṟṟiyūrpurāṇam* connects the founding of the temple with the interesting personality of a Toṇṭaimāṉ. Many Toṇṭaimāṉs[56] are known from Tamiḻ myths. Thus in the *Viṣṇu Khaṇḍa* of the *Skanda Purāṇa* (11.1.9.56) a king by the name of Toṇṭaimāṉ is the founder of Nārāyaṇapurī and this is connected with a *Valmīka* or anthill. Toṇṭaimāṉ is said to have accidentally hit an anthill and Viṣṇu revealed himself in his boar *avatāra*. This story also occurs in the *Padmapurāṇa* (ch.6). Another Toṇṭaimāṉ, connected with an anthill is known from several sources. He is often connected with a prince and a *nāga* princess.[57] The *Mackenzie mss.* has several stories of an illegitimate son of Kulōttuṅga I called Toṇṭaimāṉ, who was asked by the king to give half of his merit away and when he refused to do so the king beheaded him, but the head got stuck to the throne of Tyāgarāja and could be detached only after several people were sacrified.[58] The *Tiruvārūr Ulā* refers to one Karuṇākara Toṇṭaimāṉ, and the name of this devotee became an epithet of Tyāgarāja.[59]

The *Tiruvoṟṟiyūrppurāṇam* makes a point of linking the Tyāgarāja of Tiruvoṟṟiyūr with that of Tiruvārūr. The dance, we are told, is the very same dance, as the dance of Tiruvārūr and the Tyāgarāja of Tiruvārūr sends people to Tiruvoṟṟiyūr to look for the centre stone to his pendant.[60] Kumarakuruparar in his *Tiruvārūr Nānmaṇimālai* vv. 31-35 repeats the whole myth of Viṣṇu's worshipping the Somāskanda icon, Indra's asking for it and Mucukuntaṉ receiving it from Indra. *"Ticai ticai yuruṭṭum tikiriyāṉ cenṟa Mucukuntaṉukku muṉṉiṉṟāṅkuppoṉṉulakiḻintu puviyilttōṉṟi maṉṉuyirkkiṉṉaruḷ Vaḻaṅkutum yāmeṇa mēvara vaḻankumāṉ".*

The theme is repeated by all other writers. Mīnātcicuntaram Piḷḷai in his *Kaṭavuḷ Vāḻttu* of *Tiyākarājalīlaīkaḷ* (v.18) describes the myth. He repeats it in his invocation to Mucukuntacakravarti as well. Thus, it became standardised.

Thus, while the Somāskanda *viṭaṅka* tradition of the *utsavabera* can be traced to the 7th-8th centuries, the Tyāgarāja cult myth in its full fledged Mucukunta association appears in the recorded form from the 12th century A.D. and the seven clusters appear from the 14th century A.D., making their appearance in the *Kantapurāṇam*. The *Mucukundasahasranāmam* does not mention this.

Under Ekoji and Shahājī of the Marāṭhā royal family the Tyāgarāja cult, once more became a state cult as is obvious from Tyāgarāja being referred to in the *padas* of Shahājī as *Kamanīya Śahakula daiva*. However, no major innovations were made in the myth, except for one more embellishment that when Viṣṇu was worshipping Tyāgarāja with 1,000 flowers, there was one flower short and so he plucked his eye and offered it to the deity. Tyāgarāja, pleased, appeared before Viṣṇu and asked him to take the form of a prince of the Bhonsle family and Viṣṇu took the form of Shahāji. This is recounted in the *Viṣṇusaharājavilāsam*.[61] This again is a reworking of the *Kāñcīpurāṇam* myth. The devotee plucking his own eye and offering it to the deity is a motif that occurs in the Kaṇṇappanāyaṉārpurāṇam of the *Periyapurāṇam* as well.

Though no tangible variation was introduced in the myth during the era of the Marāṭhās, there was nevertheless, a change in the texture of the *bhakti* cult. Tyāgarāja became a Smārta-Srī-Vidyā (a Tāntric school worshipping Devī as predominant) symbol and thereby assumed a very ecclectic personality. This becomes particularly evident in the *Tyāgēśa Padas* of the Marāṭhā ruler Shahājī. Bhāskararāya, the renowned Śrī-Vidyā philosopher, had a great impact on the religious scene of the time. He was the recipient of the *brahmadeya* of Bhāskararāyapuram, and in his work the *Navaratnamālāmañjūṣā* he introduces strong Śākta traits in the iconology of the Tyāgarāja (See ch.V).

NOTES

1. For the cult of the Anthill at Tiruvārūr see. *Tiruvārūrppūrāṇam*, 6.1-112; *Kamalālayacciṟappu*, 4. 148-211. Valmīka, as a *liṅga* of Tiruvārūr is mentioned in Viśvakarma*vaśtuśāstra*, Sarasvati Mahal Series No. 85, p. 80, 7-10.
2. *Kamalālayacciṟappu*, 13. 535 refers to the Āṭakēśurar shrine (Hāṭakeśvara) as *pātālālayam* (a subterranean shrine), where he appears in the form of a *liṅga*. Very little else is said of this *mūrti*. The shrine of Hāṭakeśvara is now a small shrine, which the priests believe is a *nāgabila*, a *biladvāra*, i.e. a subterranean cave inhabited by snakes. The *Hāṭakeśvara Māhātmyam* occurs in *Skandapurāṅam*, 6.1. 4-68, where the myth of *Hāṭakeśvara* is told. The *Skandapurāṇa*, however, does not place it in Tiruvārūr but in an area called Nagna Haradeśa. This is another example of shifting the *locus sanctus* from the north to the south and the "Southern reworking of a classical northern myth". See Shulman, David Dean *Hindu Temple Myths*, Chapter I. Here, it must be remembered that there are, as stated in the main body of this chapter, two Sanskrit versions of the *Purāṇa*, the northern and the southern. Hāṭakeśvara occurs several times in the northern versions of the *Skandapurāṇa* as well as in the 6th and 7th chapters of the *Nagarakhaṇḍa* (VI.1. 32, IV. 1.65, VI.110,4, and in the following chapter in VII. 1. 319.48). A.B.L. Awasthi identifies the area called Nagna Haradeśa in the *Purāṇa* with Vadnagar in Gujarat. VI.62.2 refers to the sacred forest of Hāṭakeśvarakṣetra in Ānartadeśa and Awasthi identifies it with areas near Ahmedabad. Muthusvāmi Dīkṣitar has a composition called *Hāṭakeśvara saṁrakṣa mām*, in *rāga* Bilahari, see Raṅgarāmānuja Ayyaṅkār, *Śrī Kiruti maṇimālai*, Vol.5, pp. 356-9. Thus, apart from the differences between Sanskrit and Tamil recensions, there is also a difference between a northern Sanskrit and a southern Sanskrit tradition. However, the story in both the recensions is the same and deals with Śiva's casting off his *liṅga* after being cursed by the *ṛṣis* of Dārukāvana and this *liṅga* is said to have fallen in a cavern, whereto the deities hastened and finally the Lord was appeased and his *liṅga* worshipped by the other gods. He agrees to take back his *liṅga* after he learns that Satī has been reborn as Umā and so he would be joined to his spouse. In *Tiyāgarājalīlaikaḷ* Hāṭakeśvara appears as an old man in contradistinction to the young Tyāgarāja, whenever they are present in one story (Līlai 55).
3. Several *talapurāṇas* refer to the link between the site and the anthill-deity. Tadpatri, Mahānandi and several other sites in Andhra Pradesh are connected with the anthill myths. See N. Ramesan, *Temples and Legends of Andhra Pradesh*, p. 47 and pp. 52-53. *Tiruppērurttalapurāṇam*, 8.1-85. For further references see Shulman, *op.cit.*, p. 119. See also *Tirumullaivāyiṟpurāṇam* and *Tiruppērūrttalapurāṇam* for anthill deities. At Tirukkaḷaccēri near Tranquebar the Nāganātha Śiva temple is covered by an anthill and daily worship is offered by placing milk in front of the *liṅgam* to be sucked by what is believed to be a real serpent; cited by R. Kalyānacuntaramaiyar, 'South Indian Serpent Lore', *Quarterly Journal Of The Mythic Society*, Vol. 21-22, p. 426. The god of Tiruveṟumpūr, near Tirucciṟappaḷḷi, is called Eṟumpīśvarar or the ant-god. Here it is not the anthill but the ant itself that becomes the deity. W.T. Elmore, *Dravidian Gods in Modern Hinduism*, pp. 82, 994, 100, etc. and H. Whitehead, *The village Gods of South India*, pp.82 ff point out the popularity of the cult in South India. See Vogel, *Indian Serpent Lore*, pp. 14-30. He sums up by saying

"up to the present day the anthill performs as it were, the functions of a natural altar in the popular cult of the serpent" (p. 30). In front of the Indian Institute of Technology in Madras there is currently a huge anthill in worship.

4. Several examples of anthill and Murukaṉ associations are seen in Karnāṭaka State. There is a place called Subraḥmaṇyam at Bisleghati village in South Kanara district, where a colossal anthill is worshipped as Subrahmayya (Murukaṉ). There are no other iconic or aniconic representations in the shrine. There is another temple nearby dedicated to Ādi Subrahmaṇya and tradition has it that a subterranean *nāgabila* connects the two shrines and a live serpent is believed to inhabit the cavern. The earth from this anthill is given as a prescribed antidote for several illnesses. In the environs of this temple and in several parts of South Kanara when a serpent dies it is cremated with all due rites, including eleven *brahmacārins* officiating as priests and an eleven day period of pollution is observed. Such rites commonly called *Sarpa Vandana* are performed, however, only when the serpent dies in one's own farm or household, not if it is found dead by the roadside. This is interesting as it betrays the chthonic territorial and fertility aspects of the cult. The serpent in such cases is covered by a shroud and given all honours given to a human being.
5. See Shulman, *op.cit.*, p. 119 and note 2 above.
6. See Vogel, *op.cit.*, pp. 29.30.
7. This is the popular belief expressed by the priests. Similar stories of subterranean passages come from Kāñcī and Chidambaram. The sage Patañjali is said to have come to Chidambaram through a *nāgabila*.
8. Shulman, David Dean, *op.cit.*, pp. 130-131.
9. Shulman, David Dean, *The Mythology of the Tamil Śaiva Talapurāṇam*, Ph.D. thesis, Unversity of London, School of Oriental and African Studies, 1976, p. 26.
10. *Ibid.*, p. 25.
11. The edition quoted throughout this chapter is that of U. Ve Cāminātaiyar, Madras, 1927 with the *arumpatavurai* and the commentary of Aṭiyārkkunallār.
12. v. 65 "*Veṟṟivēṉ maṉṉav kūṟṟakai. . . kāvaṟ pūkakkai kaṭaikkeḻu pīṭikai*".
13. vv. 14-17.
14. v. 16
15. *Kaliṅkattupparaṇi*, VIII. 189, "*poruturaittalai pukuntu mucukuntaṉimaiyōr*".
16. Mu. Arunachalam, *Tamiḻ-Iḷakkiya Varalāṟu*, 12th century, p. 436 and in personal communication, 14.5.82. Veḷḷaivāraṇar, personal communication, Thañjāvūr, December 1982.
17. K.A.N. Sastri, *Colas*, 2.1. pp. 522-3 (1937 ed.)
18. Nagasamy, R., *Tantric Cult of South India.*, p. 29.
19. Zvelebil, *History of Tamil Literature*, p. 189 and personal communication, 21.08.1982, at Utrecht.
20. The verse numbers refer to the edition *Kūttaṉ Tamiḻ*, Kaviyaracar Oṭṭakkūttar, *Īṭṭiyeḻupatu* with notes by Kā. Kōvintan, Madras, 1957.
21. Eg. 635 of *ARE*, 1916.
22. Eg. 212 of *ARE*, 1912.
23. His real name was Kūttan. The word Oṭṭa was prefixed to his name because of a legendary incident that is believed to have taken place in his life. He was approached by the Ceṅkuntars to compose a work on their ancestors. Kūttan, reluctant to sing in praise of his own family, put forth a stiff con-

dition that if the weavers were prepared to offer the heads of their first born he would compose a panegyric on the community. To his surprise the request was met with and seated on a throne of skulls he composed the present work, *Īṭṭiyeḻupatu*. He then prayed to Sarasvatī and the heads joined to the bodies of the respective owners and since the word *oṭṭa* can mean both a 'bet' and 'joining together' both these meanings were suggested as explanations for this rather unusual name. The myth occurs in *pāyiram* of the *Īṭṭiyeḻupatu* according to *Peruntokai* 1481 and 1482. This *pāyiram* was found separately and is not attached to the work in any of the published versions.

24. The above mentioned legend occurs only in late works. See 23 above.
25. v. 33. The verse in question reads as follows: V*iṇṭu mārpatt iṭaiyirutti vēlaikkouri paṇimāṟa paṇṭu pūcitt iruṅkālai yākaṇṭalaṉ pōy pāṟkaṭaliṉ vaṇtuḷāy māyaṉai vaṇaṅki vāniṟ paḻiccuntiyakaraimēṟ kkoṇṭupōntu pāriṉ mucukuntaṟkutavum ceṅkuntaṉ.*
26. See introduction to the above work
27. vv. 140 *viṇṇāṭu kāttu Mucukuntaṉ mīṇṭanāḷ*
maṇṇāṭu kaṇṭa maṭantaiyarum...
28. In this work the name Mucukuntaṉ is not specifically referred to but that a king is said to have protected the heavens and brought back heavenly damsels to the earth, see v.1, lines 7-8:
"tuyil kāttaṟamakaḷir coṟkulaikāt tumpar yeyil kātta nēmi iṟraiyōṉ".
The reference to his sleeplessly guarding the heavens occurs several times. *Kampa Rāmāyaṇa Kulamuṟai* 6. *Īrācarācacōḻaṉulā* 19, 20. *Vikkirama Cōḻanulā*, 12. *Kaliṅkattupparaṇi*, 189 (see above). This reference to winning the boon of sleep is known in Sanskritic sources as well. *Bhāgavata Purāṇa*, 10.5. 23-4, *Harivaṁśa*, 2. 58 43-76, *Mbh. Udyoga Parva* Ch. 132 *śloka* 197. In all these, he is associated with Kṛṣṇa and wins the boon of sleep. He is depicted as a *gandharva* and this fact is stated in the *Tiruppērūrpurāṇam* as well. Interestingly enough at Karūr, the capital of Mucukuntaṉ, there is a Viṣṇu temple called Śri Abhayapradāna Raṅganātha temple, which has the Mucukuntaṉ tradition. Information from *Census of India*, 1961, Vol. IX, p. 148.
29. Zvelebil, *Tiru Murukaṉ*, p. 57.
30. Mu. Arunachalam, *op.cit.*, 14th century, p. 80
31. Zvelebil, *op.cit.*, p. 59.
32. *Śivarahasyakhaṇḍa* 5.1. 27-29 localises the event at Tirupparaṅkuṉṟam.
33. *Kantavṛtapaṭalam*, vv. 13-123. It is 6.23. 117-9 in the whole *Kantavṛttapaṭalam*. Later the *Tirunaḷḷāṟu Purāṇam* mentions the seven, pp. 1-2. *Vētāraṇiya Māhātmyam* 94, 1-59. *Vētāraṇiya Purāṇam* of Akōratēvar 18. 1-51. *Vētāraṇiya Purāṇam* of Parañcōti, 8. 1-42. The names of the seven places are not given in the *Śivarahasyakhaṇḍa*, though it states that the seven images were enshrined in seven places.
34. This motif occurs in a modified form in the story of the burning of Nakkīrar for his impiety in questioning the subject matter of the poem vouchsafed to Tarumi. For a reference to this myth see Parañcōti Muṉivar, *Tiruviḷaiyāṭaṟpurāṇam Paṭalam* 52.
35. *Kamalālayaciṟappu*, 9. 384-93.
36. Campantar, *"āṭal muḻavam atira kkaṇṭēṉ*
....
Vāymūraṭikaḷai nāṉkkaṇṭavārē
37. *Tiruvārūrppurāṇam.*

38. This theme also occurs in the *Kamalālayacirappu*, vv. 4. 140 and *Tiruvārūrulā*, vv. 132. The theme of Brahmā's weighing the earth and Tiruvārūr being the heaviest is represented in a panel relief in the maṇṭapa to the north of the Tyāgarāja shrine.
39. This Śiva-Śakti merger into one deity has been referred to several times in the *Tēvāram*.
40. Vide Infra, Ch.IV for details of the episode, which basically traces the conflict between Vedic religion and the left-handed Tāntric beliefs.
41. *Kantapurāṇam, pāyiram,* 56.
42. Filliozat, *Introduction a la legende de Skanda*. He suggests the 12th century as the date of the Tamil *Kantapurāṇam*.
43. Zvelebil, *Tiru Murukan*, pp. 59-65.
44. The northern version has been critically examined by Awasthi in his *Studies in the Skanda Purāṇa*. The northern text was published in Bombay, Venkateśvara Steam Press, 1867, Br.Lib.Cat. 14018 e. 14 in seven parts. A Bengali translation was published from Calcutta in 1959 (Br.Lib.14018 ee 4). Zvelebil refers to a Delhi edition. The southern recension is available in the printed form and is edited by Anantarāma Dīkṣitar, *Śrī Skandamahāpurāṇa, Śivarahasyakhaṇḍa,* 3 vols (Salem, n.d.), India Office Library, London has a mss. form of this work, San. IO 1431 and San. IO 238.
45. Introduction by Anantarāma Dīkṣitar, see note 44 above.
46. Chapter 11.
47. Shulman regards the *Kantapurāṇam* as a later work. Shulman, Ph.D. thesis 1975, London University, p. 22.
48. Saraswati Mahal Library, Thañjāvūr, Ms. no.1848/9621.
49. This is the *Purāṇa* that deals with the *tiruviḷaiyāṭals* of Cuntarēśvarar of Madurai.
50. This version tallies word for word with the printed version referred to above and the mss. in the India Office Library quoted above.
51. The inscription from Iṭakkal has been referred to in Chapter III and in a footnote, it occurs in *A.R.E. 491 of 1916.*
52. *Skanda Purāṇa* II. 1.9.53. *Toṇḍamāna nāmaka nṛpa vṛttānta*. It is Śrī Śeṣācala (Viṣṇu in Tirupati), who blessed him that in his next life he would be a king, *Skanda Purāṇa*, II, 1.10.96 and 101. The story of an anthill over which a cow offers its milk is introduced. In a dream the king sees all this and also the Lord scattering *pallava* (tender leaves), hence the name Pallava of the ruling dynasty. *Padma Purāṇa*, ch. 6, v. 6 ff also recounts the Toṇṭaimāṉ and the anthill-episode with the revelation of Viṣṇu. This section is entitled *Vēṅkaṭācalamāhātmya*. There is also a Hindi translation of this work by Hanumānadatta Joshi. Toṇṭaimāṉ is also mentioned in *Tirumullaivāyil Purāṇam*. In Veṅkateśa *Aṣṭottaram*, Viṣṇu is addressed as '*Kārttikēyavapurdhārṇe namaḥ*'. Both Viṣṇu and Kumāra share the epithet Perumāḷ and Arunakirinātar often equates Bālagopāla with Kumāra. In the *Viṣṇu sahasranāmam* also they are equated and in *Bh.Gītā* Kṛṣṇa says "Among the commanders of hosts I am Skanda". In the popular pilgrimage site of Subrahmaṇya, devotees flock to worship the anthill Murukaṉ and as a penance rite, roll on the hard earth for nearly two miles chanting as they roll, "Govinda, Govinda, Annadāna Subbayya", which is an interesting synthesis of Govinda (Viṣṇu) and Subbayya (Subrahmaṇya).
53. *Mahābhārata*, 12. 75 and 3-20. See note 28 above.

54. *Bhāgavata*, see note 22 above.
55. Shulman 'On the Pre-History of the Tyāgarāja Śiva at Tiruvārūr', *Art and Archaeology Research Papers* 13 (1978), pp. 55-8. Note also the link between Toṇṭaimāṉ, an epithet of Tyāgarāja, and the Viṣṇuite association of the man of this name. See notes 56 and 57 below.
56. There is a *Caṅkam* hero by this name who is believed to have had his capital at Kāñcī and led the *perumpāṇāṟṟuppaṭai*. The *Perumpāṇāṟṟuppaṭai*, one of the *Pattuppāṭṭu* or Tamil idyls describes an Ilantiraiyan Toṇṭaimāṉ as an epitome of virtue and a worshipper of Viṣṇu. See Irākavaiyaṅkār, Ra., Ed. *Perumpāṇāṟṟuppaṭai*, 2nd. Ed., Annamalai, 1958. See *Naccinārkkiṉiyar*, 29. There are songs of Toṇṭaimāṉ in *Puṟanāṉūṟu* 185; *Naṟṟiṇai*, 94, 99, 106. Another cycle of legends connects the king of Nākapaṭṭaṇam with an ancestor who entered the *nāga* kingdom through a *biladvāra* and cohabited with a Nāga princess. The child born of this union was called Toṇṭaimāṉ. A Toṇṭaimāṉ Iḷantiraiyaṉ is referred to as a ruler at Kāñcī and a subordinate of the Cōḻas at Pukār.
57. See. T.V. Mahaliṅgam, Ed., *Mackenzie Mss.*, mss.6 (p. 59), mss. 6 (p. 60), mss. 13 (p. 93), mss. 13 (p. 94), mss. 49 (p. 148), etc. In all these Toṇṭaimāṉ is an illegitimate son of Kulottuṅga I by a *nāga* woman and fights the *kuṟumpas*. Sec. 6 mss. 10 describes the *Kuṟumpas* as Jains and persecuted by a Śaiva king. The *Tiruvoṟṟiyūr Purāṇam* too refers to the Toṇṭaimāṉ who fought the *Kuṟumpas* and established the town of Tiruvoṟṟiyūr. The *Tiṟumullaivāyil Purāṇam* also has the story of a Toṇṭaimāṉ.
58. *Cōḻamaṇḍalaśatakam* v. 86. This is a work by Ātmanāta Tēcikar who lived around 1651-1728 A.D. The work has been edited by S. Cōmacuntara Tēcikar and published from Tranquebar in 1916.
59. *Tiruvārūrulā*, 245-246. A historical Karuṇākara Toṇṭaimāṉ is mentioned in *Kaliṅkattupparaṇi*, 11.366; 12.471; 13. 472. This Karuṇākara Toṇṭaimāṉ was the general of Kulōttuṅga I and defeated the king of Kaliṅga on behalf of the king. The canto 12 is devoted to a description of the battle between him and the Kaliṅga ruler.
60. *Tiruvoṟṟiyūrppurāṇam, Tiyākarājacarukkam*, 15, v.16.
61. *Viṣṇu saharāja vilāsam* by an unknown author. This was kindly brought to my attention by N. Visvanathan, Telugu Pandit, Saraswati Mahal Library. Several other works were composed on the deity Tyāgarāja during the Marāṭhā period such as *Tyāgēśa Kuṟavañci*, which was enacted during the Brahmotsava of the temple and here no new aspect of the myth is introduced except that he is made the object of love of the lady called Rājamōhinī. The *śṛṅgāra rasa* is in keeping with the *kuṟavañci* and *kōvai* traditions. Shahāji himself is credited with the composition of the *Pallaki Sēvā Prabandham* written in ornate Telugu. This was also performed in the Brahmotsavam and in order to perform this Shahāji endowed ten *vēlis* of land. This, according to the editor Sambamurthy was the first opera in South India and celebrates the love and subsequent marriage of Kamalampikai and Tyāgarāja. Muttusvāmi Dīkṣitar refers only to the traditional Mucukuntaṉ myth in a composition in rāga Kedāragaula which has:
Nīlotpalambikāyai namaste jagadambikāyai
Mūlādhārakṣetrasthitāyai Mucukundavarapradāyai
Mūlamantrātmikāyai Mulājñānaharaguruguhavaradāyai
Śrī Kiruti maṇimālai pt. II, Vol, III, p. 48. The Shahāji myth is an adaptation of the *Kāñcīpurāṇam* myth which is depicted iconically at Kāñcipuram. See

J. Filliozat, *Les Legendes Civaites de Kāñcīpuram*, Pondicherry 1964, Ch. 44, St. 9-10. See also P1. XXVI figs. 1 & 2. This *Kāñcīpuram* text is a Tamil translation (c.a. 18th century) of the Sanskrit *Kāñcīsthāna Māhātmya*.

Chapeter Five

THE TYĀGARĀJA ICONOLOGY—A STUDY OF THE ICON AS A SYMBOL

The metaphysics of the Tyāgarāja cult revolves around the theme of the esoteric dance, designated *ajapānaṭanam* and also referred to as the *haṃsanaṭanam, ajapātāṇḍavam* and *haṃsa tāṇḍavam*. It is the 'root symbol and makes no sense unless studied in its own doctrinal context and the general Hindu view of the world. Here the word 'symbol' has been used as "that which represents something other than itself to a knowing faculty". There is a basic difference between an image and a symbol. The image proceeds from another in its similitude, while the symbol is the means of leading the principle to the faculty and "substituting for it ....something more imperfect than it and dissimilar"[1]. Each type of iconic symbol exemplifies Thomas Aquinas' dictum that men apprehend intelligibles through sensibles. It is worth observing in this connection that the word *liṅga* means 'symbol' and not 'phallus', as commonly presumed, for it connotes several ideas such as, to give one example, the enlightened soul.

The object of this chapter is to study the iconology of the Tyāgarāja image, through the study of the focal symbol of this cult. The main interest is therefore on the symbolic function of the image and, as such, all discussions on the form and aesthetics of the icon have been studiously avoided and so also the controversies regarding the dating of the source materials used.

The Tyāgarāja image, as we have seen in the earlier chapters is a syncretistic ideograph which evolved as a result of the dynamic Tamiḻ response to the powerful stimulus of Sanskrit culture, imported by the rulers of Tamiḻnāḍu and sustained ritually by the upholders of the Vedic, Āgamic and Nigamic traditions, operating through the institutions of the *brahmadeya*, Temples, *maṭha* and *gurukula*, often generously endowed by royal patrons.

It therefore drew inspiration from the complex spiritual traditions of the Upaniṣads and the Āgamas with their different schools of interpretation. Yoga metaphysics, the Tamiḻ *bhakti* movement of the *nāyaṉmār*, the mystical *siddha* (Tamiḻ Cittar) ideas of Tirumūlar, the doctrinal commentaries, of the *Śaiva Siddhānta* and the *Trika* Schools of Śaivism, and from the canons of Śrī-*Vidyā*.

The Kashmir School of *Śivabhakti* focuses its attention on the spiritual devotion of the contemplative mind, concentrating on Śiva as the only Reality. The *sūtras* of the Kashmir *Trika* School served as the common source of Śaiva and Śākta cults and thus initiated a link between *Śrī-Vidyā* and the main Śaiva stream.[2] The Pan-Indian *Śrī-Vidyā* School received particular favour in Tamilnāḍu among the *Smārta* Brāhmaṇas. *Smārtas* are non-sectarian, inasmuch as they worship Viṣṇu, Śiva, Devī, Kumāra and Gaṇapati. They are commonly called *pañcopāsakas* or disciples of the five forms of worship: Vaiṣṇava, Śaiva, Śākta, Kaumāra and Gāṇāpatya. Tradition ascribes this synthesis to Śaṅkara, who further added the Saura or worship of the Sun God Sūrya to the five, thereby making it *ṣaṇmata* or the six forms of worship. Etymologically *Smārta* is derived from *Smṛti* and thus they are the followers of *Smṛti*. *Śrī-Vidyā* also has its following amongst the non-Brāhmaṇa population, though in a modified form with different emphases.

The Tyāgarāja cult further drew its inspiration from the grammarians' concept of the world as *Śabda Prapañca* and Truth as *Śabda Brahman*.

The icon, when taken out in procession, is accompanied by dance and music in which the assembled audience participates. Such community participation was associated with the worship of Murukaṉ (Kumāra) from Caṅkam times (e.g. Cilappatikāram: XXIV: 62). The emphasis on Tyāgarāja's anklet in these cultic dances is interesting for the *kaḻal* (anklet) and the *kiṇkiṇi* (the sound of the anklet) are often associated with martial dances by the Caṅkam poets (for Tyāgarāja and the motif of the anklet see ch.II).

A victorious hero returning from war was associated with tinkling anklets. Before proceeding to war, the warrior's anklets were worshipped. A ceremony called *kaḻalnilai* was performed to honour a steadfast soldier by adorning him with an anklet.[3]

The *Kantapurāṇam* also refers to tinkling anklets while describing scenes of war, such as in 1.18 which extols the bravery of Vīrapattiraṉ in his fight against Cūraptumaṉ. The tinkling anklets of Tyāgarāja is a recurrent ideological motif and the *bhakti* poet Cēramāṉ Perumāḷ, it is believed, would not eat his midday meal till he could hear the sound of the deity's anklets.

Thus, new meanings seem to have been added on, as if by collective fiat to old symbol-vehicles. The meaning of the symbol, as Turner states, is not absolutely fixed. He thus calls them "processual symbols".[4] The *haṁsa/ajapā* in this context is a host of symbols with several superimposed layers. One of the layers of the Tyāgarāja myth as seen in the last chapter, revolved around Viṣṇu. He desired a son; had displeased Devī by offering worship to Śiva alone, and in order to expiate for his sins and be rid of her curse on the unborn child, commissioned an image of Somāskanda to be made, and enshrined it in the inner recess of his heart. As Viṣṇu lay in the cosmic ocean meditating on this icon, his rhythmic 'inspiration' and 'expiration' (*ucchvāsa-niśvasa*) became the dance of Somāskanda Tyāgarāja. This forms the 'root metaphor', the idea by which the followers of this cult tried to explain the 'Real World'. This was the basis of their conceptual archetype of the essence of life. Yoga and Tantra metaphysics and *Śabdavāda* philospphy provided for most part the 'dominant symbol'[5] of this cult.

Each of the Tyāgarāja cult-centres has a specific form of dance-pattern set to a special beat and this can be witnessed at annual festivals when the cult-dance is re-enacted as part of the temple ritual. The dance patterns are as follows:

1. Tiruvārūr *Ajapānaṭaṉam* or *haṁsanaṭaṉam* by Vītiviṭaṅka Tyāgarāja.
2. Tirunākaikkāroṇam *Parāvarataraṅkanaṭaṉam* by Cuntara-viṭankar.
3. Tirumaṟaikkāṭu *Haṁsa* or *haṁsapātanaṭaṉam* by Puvaṉi-viṭaṅkar.
4. Tirukkōḷili *Piruṅka (Skt. Bhṛṅga) naṭaṉam* by Avaṉiviṭaṅkar.
5. Tirukkāṟāyil *Kukkuṭanaṭaṉm* by Ātiviṭaṅkar.
6. Tirunaḷḷāṟṟu *Uṉmatta naṭanam* by Nākaviṭaṅkar (alternative Nagaraviṭaṅkar)
7. Tiruvāymūr *Kamalanaṭaṉam* by Nīlaviṭaṅkar.

Of the other sites which claim to have their own dance-pattern, Tiruvoṟṟiyūr is the most important, with the *Padmanaṭaṉam,* which according to the *talapurāṇam* of the site is simply a continuation of the Tiruvārūr dance; for Viṣṇu is said to have become berserk with sorrow when the vision of dance vanished from his sight, and Tyāgarāja asked him to go to Tiruvoṟṟiyūr where he promised that he would perform the very same dance.[6] An interesting parallel to the *motif* is the dance story from Chidambaram. Viṣṇu's serpent raft Ādiśeṣa begged Śiva to be allowed to witness his cosmic Ānanda Tāṇḍava dance there. Śiva agreed provided Ādiśeṣa be born as Patañjali and in due course the serpent was reborn as the sage Patañjali (so called because he fell from the palm of his mother, who was terrified by his serpent body, for *'pata'* is 'fall' and 'anjali' is 'folded palms') and witnessed the dance.

The *Ajapā-Haṁsa* dance of Tiruvārūr provides the archetype for all other *saptaviṭaṅka* centres. The two concepts, i.e., *ajapā* and *haṁsa,* so intricately connected with the deity, though used as synonyms in most works on Tyāgarāja, are drawn from two different streams of thought. Here it is interesting to note that the word *ajapā* is in the feminine gender and it may not be without some significance for the concept is closely linked with that of *Śakti,* [7]and in fact Devī is given the name *ajapā* in some texts.

The *ajapā* tradition has deep psychological roots which lead into the subsoil of language and thought. By use of imagery, metaphor, personification, paradox and oxymoron the mystics try to convey the meaning of the Divine and man's relationship with the Divine. This they hoped to do through the medium of the 'speech world', which is the basic realm for all communication of determinate knowledge.

The Tyāgarāja iconology evolved around five discernible patterns of thought, in all of which the Divine was expressed through conscious or unconscious symbols, drawn from its phenomenal appearances. A particular symbol seems to have found special favour with one or the other of the mystical schools, which then became its special dogma. The five major ontological and soteriological symbols inherent in Tyāgarāja's dance are:

Prāṇa or 'vital breath';
Ajapā extended to mean 'the universality of the Life principle' as well as 'Primordial Sound';
Haṁsa, a mantra expressing *Ātmā-Brahman* identity;
Naṭaṇam or 'Dance as an expression of Primeval Vibration (*Spandana*) of life'; and

Ajapā and *Hamsa* expressed as geometrical patterns or power-diagrams, called *yantras*,[8] which are used as means of expressing in intelligible terms, experiences and notions of a purely noumenal nature.

The *modus operandi* was provided by the technique of *yoga* with its eight-fold aids[9] to realization and its ability to record minutely psychosomatic states and grade them as hierarchic levels of experience. The Tyāgarāja concept developed along the lines of *bhakti yoga* with its emphasis on complete love and surrender to God, as epitomised by the *nāyaṉmār*. The conjunction of *yoga* with *bhakti* is discernible for example in Cuntarar (See Tēvāram VII, 45., 9-10) where, while in search of God, he speaks of spiritual exercises in the yogic parlance of four fingers above the navel etc., and *yoga* is a focal point of Tirumūlar's *Tirumantiram*. Several forms of *yoga* such as *jñāna yoga* with its emphasis on introspective meditation and realization, the *forte* of the Śiva Advaitins, *laya yoga* as well as *haṭha yoga* with their stress on developing the hidden psychosomatic forces in man, favoured by the *Cittar*[10] (Skt. Siddha) and accepted generally by all Tāntrics, merged together in the iconological symbolism of the Tyāgarāja.

It must be remembered, however, that neither the term *ajapā* nor the term *hamsa* occur in Patañjali's *Yogasūtra*, nor even in the *bhāṣya* of Vyāsa. Terms like *Praṇava* (1.27) and *Prāṇa* (1.34) occur in the *Yoga Sūtras*. The former term is explained by later commentators as *'prāṇān avati*, protects the vital forces and *prāṇa* as (pra+aṇa) to breathe, (Latin, *anima*).[11]

All the above approaches to the Divine had one thing in common: belief that salvation was a state of union. However, on the precise nature of this union and the exact relationship between the individual and the Universal Soul there was considerable divergence of opinion. Despite the heterogenous origins of the Tyāgarāja iconology, certain basic assumptions are apparent, such as:

a) Primeval Reality is a Unity and as such superior to Multiplicity.
b) The ascent of the soul is directionally towards its state of pristine purity and unity.
c) 'Knowledge' that beyond the many in ONE is salvation.
d) Such soteriological knowledge can only be acquired by transcending the limitations of the human condition.

e) All phenomenological knowledge is limited, and it is by supra-rational insight that one can 'see' truth.
f) All empirical knowledge is interpenetrated with words and 'word forms', and it is only by transcending discursive speech that one can see Reality,[12] which is "completely silent, without noise, tone consonant or vowel".[13]

As a visual metaphor, as direct appeal to the sense of sight, Tyāgarāja seems unduly cryptic since the beholder is expected to see in his mind's eye a vibration and the personification of a metaphysical truth in an apparently solid, seated icon of a Divine Trinity of beings adorned in the splendour of royal regalia.

The icon, partly concealed, states diagramatically the belief that the ordinary mortal eye can see nothing beyond the phenomenal world and at that mundane level of religious experience the Tyāgarāja *is* a paradigmatic sovereign, filled with the quality of dynamic benevolence *(rajoguṇa)* and seen further as a loving father and husband, the model of domestic bliss. It is for the persistent seeker that the numinous experience with all its "mysterium fascinans"[14] is reserved. It is generally held to be dangerous for the uninitiated to dabble in the world of power, and the 'secrets' thereof, it is believed, must not be revealed without the proper supervision of a *guru.*[15] The icon, and hence its message, is covered by its own pleasing aesthetics, which delight the physical senses. For the true seer there is no need for the visual symbol and hence the icon is forever steeped in it's own mystery.[16]

If mysticism is the universal form of spiritual religion, magic is the form it acquires when put to use in the mundane sphere of existence, and no doubt magic and priestly craft played their part in the esotericism of the cult. Magic and superstition thus equated the representational and symbolising function of the image.[17]

In order to understand the five thought-patterns mentioned above, which converged in the Tyāgarāja cult, each one of them would have to be traced individually to its source.

Prāṇa

Prāṇa and *Vāyū* are terms that occur in the Upaniṣads, where they are equated with *ātman* and *Brahman* respectively.[18] Ātman and Brahman are both treated as synonyms;[19] In these works "the *ātman* stands for the known and the *Brahman* for the unknown, which can be known only by the *ātman* recognising itself as the *Brahman*".[20]

From the original meaning of 'breath' the word *Prāṇa* was extended to mean both 'the Life Principle' and 'the Comsic Principle'. "It gives Life, it *is* Life".[21] Elsewhere, we are told that when Primordial man asked himself the question "With the departure of what shall I myself depart and with the remaining of what shall I remain?[22] and upon realizing that the answer was *prāṇa* He created it". It was at once the empirical symbol of and at the same time the creation of, and hence dependent on, *Puruṣa*.[23]

That *prāṇa* was more than phenomenal life is made clear in the allegorical battle between the various psycho-sensory forces in which all except *prāṇa* succumb.[24] It gradually became identified with the illumined 'knowing' *ātman* (*prājñātman*).[25] Therefore while speaking of *prāṇa* or its plural *prāṇāḥ* one should be aware of the great diversity of meaning. Its meaning expands in concentric circles. At its simplest it can be the 'nostrils' or 'smell', then 'exhalation', then a collective for *prāṇa, apāṇa, udāna* and *samāna*, (the various yogic breath channels) and finally *ātman* and *Brahman*. The Collective *prāṇa* is expounded in the *Maitrāyaṇīya Upaniṣad* (2.6-7), where it describes how *Puruṣa* entered the unconscious beings in the following terms:

> "Thereupon having made himself as the wind he entered into them. He did not enter as one. Having divided himself into five...*Prāṇa* is breath that goes upward; *apāna* downward... and the *samāna* is one which places the more solid food elements in the *apāna* and conducts the less solid ones to every part of the body. The *udāna* is the one which pushes the eaten and drunk nourishment upward and downward. The *vyāna* is one which follows the course of the canals."[26]

The Equation Prāṇa = ātman

The earlier meaning of *prāṇa* as 'breath' got intermingled with the metaphysical postulate of *prāṇa* and the *Praśnopaniṣad* refers to the "two libations of expiration and inspiration"[27] and the *Kauṣītakī* to the "two sacrifices of inspiration and speech" (i.e. expiration).[28] The Brahmanic ritual of *Agnihotram* in which butter was offered as libation to the fire was completely interiorised into the *prāṇāgnihotram,*[29] wherein *prāṇa* is offered into the fire of *ātman*. However, quite often this simply refers to a rite in which food is offered twice a day within the sacrificer himself. The *Praśnopaniṣad* 4.3 refers to *Prāṇāgni* (*Prāṇāgnaya evaitasmin pure jāgrati*). The *Muktikopaniṣad* refers to *Prāṇāgnihotram*. The *Prāṇāgnihotropaniṣad*[30] prescribes an elaborate but totally interiorised ritual. Thus, in the Upaniṣads *prāṇa* is "life from the biological point of view, consciousness from the psychological point of view and *ātman* from the metaphysical point of view" and the *mahāvākyas* of the Upaniṣad equate this illumined ātman with Brahman.[31]

The various symbolic meanings of *prāṇa* in the Upaniṣads account for the definition of the word *ajapā* in the Sanskrit dictionaries, as the "mantra or formula called *haṁsa,* which consists of a number of inhalations and exhalations". This is the definition given in V.S. Apte's *Sanskrit-English Dictionary*. He elucidates a little more in his Sanskrit rendering where he quotes some passages, a few of whose origins can be traced to the *Dakṣiṇāmūrti Saṁhitā*[32] which focuses on the following symbolic association of the term *ajapā*:

1) the inhalation and expiration process (*śvāsa praśvāsayoḥ bahirgamanāgamanābhyām...*).
2) a chant with no form or syllabary to denote it by (*akṣarāṇiṣpādanarūpojapaḥ*).
3) The two syllables *ha* and *sa* stand for the process of inhalation and exhalation; the *prāṇa* resides in the Ātman called *haṁsa*

"Ucchavāse caiva niḥśvāse haṁsa ityakṣaradvayam
Tasmāt prāṇastu haṁsākhya ātmākāreṇa saṁsthitaḥ"
(*Dakṣiṇāmūrṭi Saṁhitā,* 7.3-4; Saraswati Bhavan Texts. No. 61 1937)

Apte also gives the masculine form *ajapaḥ* and describes it as "a Brāhmaṇa who does not properly repeat his prayers" and as "one who reads heretical books". In his *Shorter Students' Sanskrit-English Dictionary,* p. 7, he does not even mention the feminine form of the word and gives only the masculine form *ajapaḥ* as "a Brāhmaṇa who does not properly repeat his prayers" and as "one who reads heretical books". This is interesting inasmuch as the word seems somehow to have changed its connotation even if the original meaning was known to the purists. It may not be too far-fetched to argue that the term was associated gradually with those sects such as the Pāśupatas, *laya* and *haṭha yogins* of several eclectic schools and in the process one senses a certain value judgement on the part of the lexicographers from the more orthodox School.

The *Vācaspatyam* of Tārakanāth Tarkavācaspati (p. 89) repeats the information given in Apte's dictionary (i.e. the 2nd Ed. Revised & Enlarged, Bombay 1912). He then proceeds to give more meanings of the 'word' *ajapā* such as 'having traversed the navel it settles in the heart' (*hṛdaya*). There are six kinds of breath that constitute *prāṇa* and the sixth is recognized as synonymous with the *nāḍis* (nervous system). It is this that functions day and night and then it proceeds to discuss the number of breaths, etc. (See below.)

The *Śabdakalpadrumaḥ* of Rādhākānta Deva (Pt. I, p.18) gives an encyclopaedic reference to *ajapā* and describes in a nutshell the metaphysical postulates discussed below. Monier Williams gives the popular meanings and "the *mantra* or formula called *haṁsa* which consists *only* of a number of inhalations and exhalations" (italics mine).

G.A. Jacob in *A Concordance to the Principal Upaniṣads and Bhagavad Gītā* (p. 20) refers to only one text in the context of *ajapā* and that is the *Haṁsopaniṣad*. This work has been discussed below. He lists it under the caption '*Ajapopasaṁhāra*'. The concept of *haṁsa*, however, is treated more elaborately by Jacob and also by most lexicographers. Jacob gives copious references to the use of the term.

An interesting reference occurs in the *Śvetāśvatara Upaniṣad* 6.15. "There is only one *haṁsa* in the midst of the universe". To mention a few more examples: In *Maitrāyaṇī Upaniṣad*, 6.8. "*Ēṣa hi khalu ātmā..... haṁsaḥ*". In *Kṣurikopaniṣad* "*pāśāmś citvā yathā haṁsaḥ*" (like the *haṁsa* which has torn asunder all bondage); in "*Piṇḍa Upaniṣad*" "*haṁsas tyaktvā gato deham*" (having abandoned the body the haṁsa has gone - here it is the *ātmā*); *Mukti Upaniṣad*" 1.31 "*garbho Nārāyaṉo haṁsaḥ*" (in the womb of Nārāyaṇa is *haṁsa*). This could explain one of the iconic forms of Viṣṇu which is called Haṁsa. The *Nādabindopaniṣad* refers to *Haṁsayoga* (1.5).

The Encyclopaedic Dictionary of Sanskrit on Historical Principles,

Vol. II pt. 1, p. 735 provides copious references to *ajapā* drawn from both Advaita and Tantra literature. A very interesting inscription from Taxila in Kharoṣṭhi script on a gold plate refers to '*hasisa*' and '*hasase*' the Prākṛit form of 'haṁsa' (an unusual form) and Sten Konow translates the relevant passage as "(Gift) of Śira depositing a relic of the Lord in the *haṁsa* of her mother, the *haṁsa* of her father. Might it become its place when corporeal birth comes."[33]

The Yogic texts, several of which call themselves *Upaniṣads*, refer to five kinds of *prāṇa*.[34] Of these, two are important for the Tyāgarāja iconology, viz. *prāṇa* which causes expiration (*ucchvāsa*), and *apāna*, which causes inspiration (*niśvāsa*), for it is the *prāṇa* and *apāṇa* of Viṣṇu which cause the *haṁsa* or *ajapā naṭanam* of Tyāgarāja. The *Mucukundasahasranāmam*, which records the liturgical invocations to Tyāgarāja addresses him as "*Śvāsa niśvāsa kampitāya* (v. 216), 'the one who vibrates with inhalations and exhalations' and as 'the wise knower of the path of *prāṇa* and *apāna*" (*prāṇāpānāgamaprajñāya* - 623) and states in an invocation that the *Āgamas* and *Nigamas* are born out of his sport of expiration (*niśvāsalīlāsañjāta nigamāgamasantataye*).

The Grammarian's Equation of Prāṇa with Sound Patterns

The class of Yogic *Upaniṣads*,[35] referred to above, also introduces the experiments of auditory meditations, thereby linking *prāṇa* with sound-patterns. The grammarians[36] equate *prāṇa* and *apāna* with *bindu* and *nāda* for they see the world as a world of sound (*śabda prapañca*) and Reality as the Eternal Verbum (*Śabda Brahman*).[37] It is with this postulate in mind that the grammarians introduce *bindu* and *nāda* as stages in the unfolding of Reality. It is significant that the Tyāgarāja temple in Tiruvoṟṟiyūr has a *Vyākaraṇamaṇṭapa*, a pavilion for the teaching of grammar and the God is called Vyākaraṇadāṉapperumāḷ or the "Lord who has given grammar as his gift."

Śiva is said to have taught Pāṇini Sanskrit grammar. The general idea was that a thorough study of grammar would enable the student to use the correct words and thereby acquire virtue and avoid sin, and after gradually severing the knots of egotism he would find himself capable of attaining union with the highest Reality. (*Vākyapadīya I.* 132)

Several theistic myths equate Śiva with grammar and the

Tiruvoṟṟiyūr tala purāṇam equates Tyāgarāja with grammar. Another parallel to this comes from the *talapurāṇam* of Madurai: Śiva deputed Agastya to teach *Nakkīrar,* the self appointed President of the Caṅkam literary academy, grammar and rhetoric as a punishment for Nakkīrar's blasphemy in calling in question the subject matter of a poem Śiva vouchsafed to Tarumi. This poem is "preserved" as *Kuṟuntokai* v.2. (See Parañcōti, *Tiruviḷaiyāṭal purāṇam,* 54).

Haṁsa or the Interiorised Identity

The term *haṁsa* (=*aham saḥ:* I am He), in the form of its corollary *Soham* occurs for the first time in the *Bṛhadāraṇyaka Upaniṣad*[38] while discussing the self-confident awareness of Brahman. It states that Brahman, on not perceiving another, knew itself as *soham,* i.e., He is I, meaning that it was All. In the *Śukla Yajurveda* occurs the general expression *'haṁsaḥ śuciṣad'* (*haṃsa* is Pure). This occurs several times in the Vedas such as *Ṛgveda* 4.40.5; *Vājasanēyi Saṁhitā* 12.14; *Taittirīya Saṁhitā* 1.8.15; *Maitrāyaṇī saṁhitā* 2.6.12 etc.[39]

The *Haṁsopaniṣad* which belongs to the class of Yogic Upaniṣads[40] uses the term *haṁsa* several times in different ways, much like the Upaniṣadic use of the term *prāṇa.* This Upaniṣad has several recensions and the published version has the format of a Tantra, wherein the *Brahmavidyā,* which is knowledge of *haṁsa,* is expounded by Pārvatī and much secrecy is enjoined. Some of the manuscript recensions do not have this preamble.[41] The dance of Tyāgarāja is distinctly described as the *haṁsanaṭanam* and *ajapātāṇḍavam* in the liturgical text of the *Mucukunda-sahasranāmam,*[42] which was in all probability compiled in the period of Kulōttuṅga II (1133-60 A.D.). The same text also describes it as *ajapātāṇḍava* and *āsīnatāṇḍava.*[43]

Haṁsa in the *Haṁsopaniṣad,* as stated earlier, means several things - it is an all-permeating principle in the universe, "like fire in all kinds of wood and oil in all kinds of gingelly seeds" and this knowledge assures freedom from death.[44] In the 6th paragraph the author of the Upaniṣad suddenly introduces the concept of the six *cakras,*[45] "principal holistically organised centres of consciousness", and the seventh conceived as transcendental and situated at the cranium. The yogī's object is to rouse the *kuṇḍalinī,* the vast potential of psychic energy, to ascend through the above-mentioned psychic centres, which lie along the axis of the spine, and finally to unite with Śiva (Pure Consciousness) at the *Brahmarandhra* or the seventh transcendental *cakra*. At this stage individuation ceases and the *yogī* is formless. He is then the *paramahaṁsa*. In this passage *haṁsa* is equated with the *kuṇḍalinī* and with the enlightened ātman and *paramahaṁsa* with Brahman. The *Haṁsopaniṣad* is the first text, according to Deussen,[46] where the *cakras* are enumerated and equated with the six mystical and imaginary regions of the body - the regions of the stomach, loins, navel, heart, throat, the centre-point between the eyebrows. It becomes completely standardised in the later Tāntric texts.

The *Haṁsōpaniṣad* uses the term *haṁsa* to denote also the human dispositions to sloth, cruelty, virtue, etc., ideas expressed through the metaphor of a lotus at the centre of which is detachment.[47] Here the term is used to designate the unliberated *ātman*. The same metaphor is extended to cover the different states of the soul, i.e. waking, dreaming, dreamless sleep, and awareness. The fifth and transcendental state which is one of noumenal awareness is fully absorbed in *nāda* (Pure sound, Primal Sound)[48].

At this stage of complete union the *haṁsanāda* is a "glowing crystal extending from the *mūlādhāra* to the *Brahmarandhra*", signifying that the goal of *kuṇḍalinī* has been reached. So *haṁsa* is equated with *prāṇa*, Brahman and *kuṇḍalinī*. In the *Yōgaśikhopaniṣad* (6.35) the *haṁsa* is the ever-ascending *kuṇḍalinī* (*suṣumṇāyām yadā haṁsaḥ adha ūrdhvam pradhāvati*). This concept of *haṁsatāṇḍava* or the dance of *haṁsa* as symbolising the movement of *kuṇḍalinī* is well known to the priests of the Tyāgarāja temple who state categorically that the seven sacred sites dedicated originally to the Tyāgarāja cult (see Chapter III for the religious topography of the cult) are simply the seven *cakras*.

The terms *nāda* and *bindu* are used by several schools with varying nuances of meaning. Thus, in Śaiva Siddhānta, while talking of evolutes of *śuddhamāyā*, which being pure is operated on by Śiva, regards *śuddhamāyā* as *jñāna śakti* or pure knowledge alone, and from it evolutes *nāda*, which is *kriyā śakti* only and from there *bindu*, which is *jñāna* and *kriyā* in equal measure. *Śuddhamāyā* itself is called *bindu*. Stated in more general terms, speech at its purest, as the cause of all knowledge, as potential intelligence in all beings is *nāda*, sometimes qualified with the prefix *sūkṣmanāda* to make its subtle character explicit. As it begins its process of manifestation into gross speech (*varṇa*) the intermediary state is *bindu,* which is the cause of the evolution of the word (*śabda*) and its meaning (*artha*). This is accepted by most schools based on the Āgamas and by the *śabdavādins* or grammarians as well, though the Mīmāṁsakas and Śabdavādins interpret it in their context of the essence of the World as the Word. The *Mucukundasahasranāmam* v.272 invokes Tyāgarāja as *'bindunāda kalākḷpta sāṅgōpāṅgamanōhara.'* ("One who delights in accomplishing the interplay of *nāda* and *bindu*)"

Auditory Meditations, Sound and Ajapā-Haṁsa

The introduction of *nāda* here leads us on the experimental plane to auditory meditations and on the philosophical plane to *sphoṭavāda,*[49] which studies the metaphysical relation between word, its meaning and the object it signifies. In Śrī *Sundaramūrtyaṣṭottaraśatanāmāvali* v .62 Tyāgarāja of Tiruvārūr is addressed as *'Drāviḍavyākaraṇaguru'* i.e. 'the teacher of the Tamiḻ grammar'.

Auditory meditation and the concept of the Supreme Brahman as 'Om' led to the belief that the purely spiritual body can be regarded as *mantraśarīra* or body of sacred syllables. One of the symbols of Brahman in the Vedas is the sacrosanct *Gāyatrī* [50] and so *haṁsa* was conceived in the *Haṁsopaniṣad* and all other Yogic-Tāntric texts as a *mūlamantra,* i.e. root mantra and as a *Gāyatrī.*

Following the ritualistic tradition of the Vedas, the Gāyatrī was converted into an interiorised ritual of *nyāsa* by the Yogic Upaniṣads; this ritual has been succinctly described by Mookerji as "an empathy building method" [51] to expand the practitioner's awareness. By *nyāsa* the deities conceived as *māntrik* syllables were invoked into different parts of the body and the body, thus purified, assumed the form of divine Mantras. So *haṁsa* as *Gāyatrī* is *ajapāgāyatrī* (e.g. *Brahmavidyopaniṣad* v. 78 - *ajapānāmagāyatrī yogınām mōkṣadā sadā*). The *Mahābhārata* VI app. 3 (36), (BORI Edn.) states clearly *'gāyatrī sā parā jñēyā ajapā nāma viśrutā'*. The *Agnipurāṇa* (214.26) and *Skanda purāna* (IV. 41.158) state the same.[52] When split into its phonetic members it is used to condition the individual's psyche by the *nyāsa* rite. The phonetic members form the word *haṁsa* which is then *ajapā* (literally, "not pronounced")

Sonic consciousness leads the Yogī through several sound

zones till he reaches the state called *unmanī* and this is the state where *ajapā* has finally finished its soteriological function.[53]

The *Haṁsopaniṣad* mentions several sound zones of consciousness such as the hearing of bells, flute, lute, etc. and corresponding to these theYogī experiences physical symptoms such as shaking of the head, the producing of saliva, etc. The State of union is the most quiescent Om. The *Mucukundasahasranāmam* (V. 416) describes Tyāgarāja as the centre of *unmaṇī*. This is a key concept in yogic texts, though Patañjali himself does not describe this state. The *Ṣaṭcakranirūpaṇa* defines *unmaṇī* as *"yatra gatvā tu manaso manastvam naiva vidyate"*.[54] This is a late work and is dated 1577 A.D. It is in the eighth state of yogic experience that *parā vāk* or transcendental speech is envisaged and the body becomes Brahman. In trying to express the inexpressible even Om became merely a Brahman- word for

"Higher than the original syllable
Is the point, the echo higher than this;
The syllable vanishes with the sound,
The highest is silent." [55]

The Soteriology of Dance and the Concept of 'acapai' in the Tirumantiram

The Āgamas and, based on them, several doctrinal works in the Tamil̲ language delve into the metaphysics of sound. It is in the most abstruse work of Tirumūlar's i.e. *Tirumantiram,* that the term *acapai* occurs for the first time in Tamil̲. The *Tirumantiram* is Āgamic and Tāntric in its content (in fact it describes itself as an Āgama) and the fourth chapter or Tantra, as the chapters of this book are called, is entitled *acapai* (Tamil̲ for the Skt. *ajapā*); the word is nowhere used in the body of the text. It occurs only in the caption to the chapter. The author calls this chapter an exposition of *Śivayoga,* thus suggesting by inference that *Ajapā is Śivayoga.* The whole Tantra is very terse and abtruse but two themes stand out as predominant. The universe, considered as emanating from the Godhead of the Transcendental Śiva, represented by the 'one word', i.e. Om[56] expressed through the medium of his dance becomes the many - 'the giddy whirl' (*mayakkamē ur̲r̲atē*). This refers to the standard symbolism in Śaivite mysticism in which a = Śiva; u = Śakti and m = māyā (in *Śaiva Siddhānta*).[57] The non-theistic Sānkhya school visualises it slightly differently; a = Puruṣa; and m = Prakrti with u representing the stage of interaction. The Tāntric work *Śāradātilaka* 25.50-7 states this clearly *"haṁsau tau puṁprakṛtyākhyau ham pumān prakṛitistu saḥi ajapā kathitā tābhyām jīvo 'yam upatiṣṭhate* (*haṁ is Puruṣa, sa prakṛti* and *ajapā* is the interaction of the two to unfold life).

Coming back to Tirumūlar, he visualises the god Śiva as a body of letters, as a pattern of sounds in which numbers such as two, three, five,[58] eight, ten, seven thousand, and seven million etc., symbolize mystical number of syllables in the *mantras* used in Śiva worship and stand for special concepts. The whole chapter centres on the theme of the ontology, eschatology and soteriology of Śiva's Dance. God and the Universe are conceived of as *māntrik* formulae in an audial sense and an intricate geometrical pattern of *yantras* on a visual plane. His ultimate import is that Śiva in the final analysis is the culmination of all knowledge. In v. 874 he declares the Āgamas to be revelations of Śiva and thus his own brand of mysticism is based greatly on the Āgamas.

Tirumūlar regards the *kūttu* (dance) of Śiva [59] as the supravisual image of the *pañcākṣara* or *Na Maḥ Śi Vā Ya* mantra. The last verse of this section concludes:

"In One dances the Two, the One alone accompanying
In One dances the Three, the One Seven in harmony
By the One, dance the Four and the Nine
Thus in this world did (He) dance the Precious Dance.[60]

The numericals referred to here have a doctrinal significance, the One = Śiva; the "One alone accompanying" is Grace in the form of Śakti, seven is the seven worlds in Hindu cosmogony etc. Again in v. 879 and v. 880 of the *acapai* section he refers to the seven crores of mantras, all forms of Śiva but the root of all, by implication, is the *ajapā* mantra, for that is the title of the Chapter or Tantra.

The number seven crore is interesting—for in the Āgamas such as *Svacchandatantra* the belief is expressed that the human body has three and a half million pores and the breath goes in and out thereby making the pores breathe seven crore times and hence

Śiva is called *saptakoṭīśvara*, which takes us back again to the symbol of universal life. In Goa there is a temple of *saptakoṭīśvara*. The *Mucukundasahasranāmam* invokes Tyāgarāja as *Saptakoṭīśvara niṣevitāya* (v. 932)[61]

The 19th century *Tirunākaikkāroṇappurāṇam* by the veteran chronicler Mīṉātcicuntaram Piḷḷai refers to the dance of the deity as *uṟavi poḻi naṭam*. *Uṟavam* is 'knowledge' and *poḻi* is 'illumination' and hence it is a *jñānanaṭaṉam* or dance of knowledge. It is also described as the *Pañcākṣaranaṭaṉam* and *sūkṣma pañcākṣara*.[62] The *Tiruvoṟṟiyūr purāṇam* (another saptaviṭaṅka site) calls it *jñānanaṭaṉam*.

The *Uṇmai Viḷakkam* by Maṉavācakam Kaṭantār, believed to be one of the forty-nine disciples of Meykaṇṭār, states the relation between dance and the *pañcākṣara* and the dance which is described as the dance of soteriological wisdom. We are told that it scatters *māyā*, burns *karma* and stamps out *āṇava* (egotism) and by showering Grace engulfs the soul in an ocean of bliss.[63] This is the quintessence of *Śaiva Siddhānta*.

In the *acapai* section of the *Tirumantiram*, the concept of the corporeal body of Śiva is treated as a *mantraśarīra* or body of mantras.[64] Since all determinate knowledge, as mentioned earlier, is believed to be interpenetrated with sound and syllables, hence the *māṇikkakkūttu* in this mortal world is a dance of the *mantras*, the whirl of the sounds indicating all determinate knowledge.

When Divine Grace keeps tune, the resultant experience is almost a maddening exhilaration, which can be presented in an algebraic, geometric formula of the *tiruvampalacakram* with the syllables *a, i, u, e, om*, (5), and *am, krīm, am kṣam, am* (5) forming the root or seed syllables. The *acapai* section of the *Tirumantiram* expresses a state of yogic ecstasy typical of the *Cittar* (*Siddha*) tradition and not of the *haṭhayoga* tradition. There is a certain spontaneity, a sense of suddenness and ineffable joy that distinguishes it from the systematic and gradual schools of salvation.

It is in Tirumūlar that one can trace a very close parallel to some of the *Pratyabhijñā* works like *Śivastotrāvalī* of Utpaladeva. They share in the quality of intuitive personal flashes - there is not the element of laborious ritual or even of severe yoga practices. There is, to quote Gonda, a certain "Spontaneous *elan*".[65] Utpaladeva too was moved into a spiritual ecstasy by the dance of Śiva. The imageries of Śiva as the lover of Umā, the dancer, etc., are eulogised in a similar manner. There is something very similar in the texture of introspective mysticism - an absorption with the central essence of all existence.

It is interesting to see the close connection postulated by Tirumūlar between *acapai* and the *Tiruvampalacakkaram* or the *cakra* of Chidambaram. One can thus see the metaphysical proximity of the concept of *ajapānaṭana* Tyāgarāja and the Naṭarāja. Tirumūlar by entitling the section on Śivayoga and dance of Śiva as *acapai* and envisioning it in the form of the *Tiruvampalayantra* shows the close blending of the two concepts of Tyāgarāja and Naṭarāja.

The element of dance is crucial to the understanding of the *Tirumantiram*. It is rich in significance from the aesthetic, ethical and metaphysical points of view. Tirumūlar sees the dance of Śiva everywhere "When he danced the dance of illumined bliss, the Vedas danced, the Āgamas danced, the melodious sounds danced, the elements danced."[66]

From this mood of extrospective mysticism he switches over to one of introspection when he adds: " I searched and discovered the supreme dance of the *guru* within myself".[67] For Tirumūlar the dance of Śiva is a symbol of both extrospective and introspective mystical experience, of the wave of movement in the macro- and the microcosmos. Though the 4th Tantra is entitled *acapai*, it visualises a dramatic movement and thus is more in keeping with the iconology of Naṭarāja than the subtle *acapai* of Tyāgarāja, which is the gentle breath of Viṣṇu, but presumably *acapai* is regarded by Tirumūlar as the fundamentum of all movement.

Dance is so crucial to the understanding of Tamil̲ Śaivism that one could quote from numerous sources on the symbolism of this theme. The 12th century work *Uṇmaiviḷakkam* sums it all up by taxonomising the soteriological functions of the different attributes and features of the dancing Naṭarāja such as his left hand, his right leg etc.

It is thus in the *Tirumantiram* that for the first time *acapai* is equated with *mantraśāstra* and the dance of Śiva and thus, provides the iconology of Tyāgarāja. It is also here that for the first time in Tamil̲ literature the figure of 51 denoting the fifty-one letters of the alphabet is introduced (*iṇaiyār kal̲aliṇai aimpattonr̲ākum*, v. 878). This is a popular theme of *Tirumantiram* with the variant 50 introduced in some. This fifty-one is popular in Tāntric texts from the north as well and refers to the Sanskrit rather than the Tamiḻ syllabary scheme.

The *Trika* system of Kashmir is also called *Ṣaḍardha Śāstra* (lit. half of the six) and holds that Devanāgarī or the Śāradā alphabet represents the manifestation (*ābhāsa*) of ideas (Abhinavagupta, *Tantrāloka* 1.3) and this manifestation is graded in terms corresponding to the vowels. The first six vowels represent six stages—the three major ones and the three minor ones. The long vowels are born of the three short vowels. The three short vowels are the three *Śaktis* - *Cit, Icchā* and *jñāna* Śaktis, being Consciousness, Volition and Knowledge.

The Sanskritic scheme is also aware of fifty-one *śakti pīṭhas* or sites sacred to Devī and this explains the intimate symbological relationship between numbers, letters and *pīṭhas*.[68] Several *yantras* capturing the *ajapā-haṁsa* thought are symbolically represented by yantras with fifty-one letters.[69] The *ajapā yantra* is a 51 syllabled diagram. The fifty-one letters are visualised as fifty-one names of Śakti which are daily recited by Tāntric worshippers. The Śaktis are named after the initial sound of the syllabary such as *Amṛtā, Ākarṣiṇī, Īśānī, Umā*, etc. The *Dakṣiṇāmūrtisaṁhitā* mentions that a goddess should be envisaged by the *Sādhaka* as a body formed of the letters from *a* to *kṣa*. The *Kāmakalāvilāsa* of Puṇyānanda (v. 32) which is the most sacred work of the Śrī-Vidyā School equates the fifty-one letters with the *Śrī-Cakra*. But this is much later, presumably of the 15th century A.D. All Tyāgarāja icons are believed to be embossed with a Śri-cakra and hence the taboo on perceiving them. When exactly this was superimposed on the icon, it is difficult to tell.

The place of Tirumūlar in the canonical literature of *Śaiva Siddhānta* deserves special notice. His *Tirumantiram* is the earliest exposition of the metaphysical, moral and mystical aspects of *Śaiva Siddhānta*. Tirumūlar is aware of the close proximity and the subtle difference between the interpretation of the *mahāvākyas* as rendered by the Vedāntins and the Siddhāntins. Furthermore, he is acquainted with various shades of Tāntrism and Schools of Yoga and several schools of Śaivism, "but often he has juxtaposed them without making either an attempt to incorporate them into Śaiva Siddhānta or openly refuting them".[70] Thus, this work of three thousand verses is often very abstruse and defies systematic understanding. One thing that emerges clearly is that salvation is an interplay of Śiva's Grace on the pure soul of the individual. Thus, the doctrine expounded is one of salvation through surrender of self to Śiva by which Śiva's Grace will descend on the devotee. The point of unity when the ascending soul and the descending Grace meet is a state of ineffable ecstasy which Tirumūlar expresses through visual symbols and sounds. Tirumūlar, as pointed out by Zvelebil, is primarily a *Siddha*. The *Tirumantiram*, says Zvelebil "contains *in nuce* all or almost all the typical features of the Tamil̲ *Siddha* movement." [71]

The Third *Tantra* deals with eight *aṅgas* of Yoga and closely follows Patañjali's *Yogasūtras* II. 29. He also deals with the eight great powers or *mahā citti* (*Mahā Siddhi*). He asserts the importance of the human body to achieve all this. The body is the means to salvation, flawless and fully disciplined. For this he takes recourse to *Haṭhayoga*. To quote Zvelebil again, in *Tirumantiram* "As in later *Siddha* works, and in contrast to classical *bhakti* (devotional literature) there is almost total absence of any local cult of the deity". Zvelebil uses the term *henolocotheism* to describe the bhakti cult and its emphasis on the *locus sanctus*. [72]

Tirumūlar, who has had such a profound influence on the mystical aspects of this cult was a great integrator and brought together Upaniṣadic thought, Yogic methodology for Salvation and *bhakti,* all permeated by Tāntric thought. Zvelebil excellently summarises Tirumūlar's contribution to Tamil̲ by stating that he is "the Tamil̲ poet who, by expressing his mystic and occult experiences, lingering on the borderlines between speech and wordless thought, framed the Tamil̲ language to express the ineffable".[73] Tirumūlar has been placed anywhere between the 5th-9th centuries A.D.

The *Tamil̲ Lexicon,* interestingly enough, refers to both the audial aspect and the yogic psycho-somatic experimental angle, in its definition of the word *acapai* as "one-letter *mantiram,* meaning Om and the fire that traverses from the *mūlādhāra* to the *Brahmarandhra*". This is what is described as a crystal column in the *Haṁsopaniṣad,* when Śiva and *kuṇḍalinī* are united and the *haṁsa-nāda* is effulgent like a growing crystal extending from the *Mūlādhāra* to *Brahmarandhra. Laya yoga or kuṇḍalinī yoga* formed the *modus operandi* of realising the state of pristine oneness. It is this "resplendent column" that is worshipped as the *liṅga* of precious stone.

The Panṭāra Caṉṉiti of Tarumapuram Ātīṉam (The head of the Dharmapura monastic establishment) explained how the seven *viṭaṅka kṣetras* were the seven *cakras* and the *Sphaṭika liṅga* of Chidambaram and the *lingas* of these *kṣetras* were really the resplendent *Kuṇḍalinī* in the *Brahmarandhra*. Thus the *Viṭaṅka* of Tiruvārūr and the six other *viṭaṅka* sites as well as the crystal liṅga called Candramoulīśvara in Chidambaram all reflect according to the Tāntric school of thought the resplendent *kuṇḍalinī*.

The *acapai* chapter of *Tirumantiram* has to be studied in the context of Āgamic thought in general, with particular emphasis on their view of sound, word and its meaning. The Upaniṣadic seers in their quest for symbols to explain the mystery of Brahman hit upon *Vāk* as one of them. Thus, *Prāṇa = Brahman =Vāk* formula was elaborated by the Āgamas into a complex system of categorising the various stages of sound corresponding to the various states of realising the Unmanifested One in the Manifested Many. The Āgamic postulates were interpreted differently by the Vaiśeṣika, Nyāya, Sāṅkhya,Vedānta, Śabda-Brahma vāda and the Śaiva-Siddhānta.

Ajapā and the Evolution of the Speech World

The aspect of Āgamic thought that has relevance for us in the study of the doctrine of *ajapā* is the one that deals with the evolution of the Speech-world. The Āgamas categorise four stages in the descent of Reality (conceived as Soundless, or Transcendental Sound) or in the ascent of the individual soul towards Reality, depending on the angle of vision. Thus, there is a hierarchy in the levels of speech and corresponding to the each speech level there is the spiritual degree of bondage in the individual beings. In the ultimate liberation, which is reached through transcending all conceptual archetypes of sound there is no degree, no level. In the following classification the basic assumption is that all "determinate knowledge is interpenetrated with words" and conversely "determinacy in knowledge free from word association is impossible".[74]

The lowest level in the evolution of speech is the *vaikharī*, which connotes the spoken word in all its multifarious sound systems and in all its imperfections of expressing an idea. It is the basic stage of physical Verbalisation of an idea. At this state only approximate meanings of a word are conveyed. The actual act of articulation is performed by the ideo-motor force called *prāṇa*. *Prāṇa* is expiration=speech, as we have seen earlier in the Upaniṣads.

The level of speech preceding articulation is where the inner sound becomes assembled into internally differentiated letter sounds but still remains an inner sound or *dhvani*. This assembling is done by the breath called *udāna* and the stage is called *madhyam*. This is not empirically 'hearable' but is a concept. The differentiations are already present as covert patterns, overtly unexpressed. This is the link between fully-determinate and empirical knowledge and the indeterminate supra-rational perception. It is implicit speech and in that sense conjures before the individual patterns intended by the word.

The stage preceding this is designated *paśyantī*, where letter sound are present in their order but are undifferentiated. This is the potential state of speech and the most frequent analogy is that of the yoke of the egg of a peahen, which has all the potential of the many colours of the peahen but is itself a yellow blob. "It is", as described by K. Sivaraman, "the state of indeterminate awareness of determinate knowledge".[75]

A stage above this in the hierarchy is *parā vāk*, which literally translated would mean beyond speech, supra- or transcendental speech. This state is described by the term *nāda* in the *Haṁsopaniṣad*. The dance of Tyāgarāja is often described as *nādāntanaṭanam*, the dance transcending *nāda*. The dance of Naṭarāja is similarly described.

The word *nāda* is therefore used in some texts to denote the ultimate and in some the penultimate stage. The *parā vāk* or *nāda* (of the *Haṁsopaniṣad*) is ever-present in the individual as a general "condition of intelligibility", even when all other modifications have not evolved. It is the symbol of ultimate undifferentiated knowledge and thus is equated with *haṁsa* in the *Haṁsopaniṣad*. It is the very voice of intelligent life. The *Mucukundasahasranāmam* in v. 620 invokes Tyāgarāja as "*paśyantīmadhyamābhikhya vaikharyāśrita vigraha*" (having rendered *paśyantī* and *madhyamā* one who has assumed the image of *vaikharī*) and in 745 the deity is described as form of *nāda* at the end of the *suṣumnā*, i.e. when *prāṇa* has gone straight to the *brahmarandhra*. The *Haṭhayogapradīpikā* (iv. 14-16) describes in almost identical language how the *vāyu* must move in the *suṣumnā* and how the Yogin should restrain the *vāyu* in *suṣumnā*.

It is at this stage that there emerges a difference of opinion between the theistic and the abstract monistic schools of metaphysics of speech.[76] The abstract monists regard the word as the *a priori* condition for object, for *artha* or meaning is the appearance of *śabda* or word and *śabda* is the reality of *artha*. In that sense *parā vāk* is the fundamentum of speech, the ultimate, the Eternal *Verbum* the *Śabdabrahman*. The *Sphoṭa* doctrine enunciated by Audumbarāyaṇa and other ancient grammarians stresses the identity of the universe with the eternal sound called *sphoṭa* transcending letters, i.e. sounds. There is no reference to this doctrine in the *Sūtras* of Pāṇini and also in the *Vārttikas* of Kātyāyana.[77]

The theistic Siddhāntins cannot conceive of Śiva as Perfect, Eternal, unapproachable Principle; for the Siddhāntin Śiva is also a loving, caring figure of Grace and so *parā vāk* is equated with the Grace of Śiva, the *parigraha śakti*, who then evolves out of the material cause of *māyā* the various states of the speech world. Thus, while to the Vedāntin the world of appearances is a projection of the Supreme *śabda* and, hence, not real, to the Siddhāntin it is real. The grace of Śiva acting on *māyā* unfolds the undifferentiated One into the Differentiated Many. Thus, the *ajapā* or the *haṁsa* or the *nāda* or *parā vāk* is Śakti, loving and caring and the agent for the revelation of the One into the Many. That *one* is the "One-letter mantra" Om, and according to Tirumūlar, when it becomes two it is Śiva and Śakti and when the two act on *māyā* it is the "dizzying whirl", the Many.

The *Mucukundasahasranāmam* describes Tyāgarāja as *Śabda brahmarūpa* (437), *Śabdabrahmanaikarūpa sarvaśabdaikakāraṇa* (440) and as the "seed" (*bīja*) of *vāk*, called *kāmarāja* (Śrī-Vidyā terminology for Śiva and Śakti) and as the seed of *parā vāk* who manifests himself as three (*parā bīja trayābhidhāya*) and in v. 736 as the three luminaries of *śabda, artha* and *bhāva*, i.e. the link between Word, its Meaning and its Being (*bhāva*). The Tyāgarāja ideograph, thus looked at, represents Viṣṇu as *māyā śakti* as he is often described in Śākta literature and this *māyā* is acted upon by Śakti, whom Viṣṇu is forced to worship, and Śiva and so it is Śiva, Śakti and Māyā. In the Somāskanda, Skanda plays the role of Viṣṇu. The two deities are often henotheosised, for, in the *Bhagavadgītā* Kṛṣṇa says "Among the Commanders of hosts I am

Skanda". Skandadhāra is one of the *nāmāvalis* (list of names) of Viṣṇu in his *sahasranāma*. In *Veṅkaṭeśa aṣṭottaram* Venkaṭeśa is described as *Kārttikeyavapur dharaḥ*. Aruṇakiri and Toṇṭar Aṭippoṭi Āḻvār often equate the two. In the traditional Tamiḻ assigning of deities to the geographical realms, both Cēyōṉ (Murukaṉ) and Māyōṉ (Viṣṇu) are assigned the woody tracts. The final synthesis is of course with the worship of Devī as Kamalā. The *ajapāhaṁsa mantra* occurs in the *Pañcarātra* (a body of literature dealing with Viṣṇu worship) work *Lakṣmī Tantra* where *Ha* and *Sa* become Viṣṇu and Lakṣmī and Tārā and Buddha. Thus Kamalā as the *Mahāvidyā Mahāśakti* was the mode of Śiva Viṣṇu synthesis.

Other Pāñcarātra texts like *Āhirbudhnya Saṁhitā* and *Sanat Kumāra Saṁhitā* deal with the *ajapā-haṁsa* concept. The *Lakṣmī Tantra* states that the beginning and the end of the two essential liturgies, the *Puruṣa-Sūkta* and *Śrī-Sūkta* are the syllables *ha* and *saḥ*. Thus the *ajapā haṁsa* soteriological doctrines were pan-sectarian. Besides, it harmonized excellently ritual and doctrine, myth and symbol, philosophy and religious theism.

Thus, the breath of Viṣṇu, the *ucchvāsa, niśvāsa*, the *ajapā* and the haṁsa are all synthesised into one cultic doctrine, whereby *prāṇa*, the symbol of Brahman in the Upaniṣads and the ideomotor force that drives the inner sound into external verbalisation in the *Āgamas*, are both synthesised with the arousal of *kuṇḍalinī* and its recognising its full potential as *haṁsa* "I am He". Thus through Āgamic metaphysics and haṭha yoga techniques the circle of ideas is completed, coming back to the Upaniṣadic statement "I am Brahman." The elements of a theistic Siddhānta are evident in the metaphor of the *parigraha śakti* or *parā vāk* and the point of contact is the "fire" or the "line of crystal extending from the *mūlādhāra* to the *brahmarandhra*", the state of *unmanī*, the state of *ajapā*, the state of Om. Thus, the Śaivas, in tune with the concept of the Loving God, modified the *aham Brahmāsmi, Tat tvam asi* and *ayam ātmā Brahma* of the Upaniṣads into the *haṁsa*, whereby the statement "I am He" does not mean a total literal identity but "togetherness".[78] Thus, *ajapā* is the state of *unmanī*, the state of Grace for the Siddhāntin and union for the Tāntric and the experimental psycho-somatic state of bliss for the yogī, when he conceives of the world as a world of Sound or *Śabdaprapañca* and thereby reaches a state (*unmanī = ut+mana*, i.e. transcending the mental states) where Reality is beyond discursive speech.

Thus the *ajapā-haṁsa* was a free *mantra* - a process, a way of looking at *mokṣa* (liberation) a *mantra* and an *artha* which allowed it to be incorporated into any philosophical or theistic context. It was an ideal emblem of harmonising ritual prescriptions with theological and philosophical doctrines.

Spandana

The only other symbol not taken up for discussion in this complex *ajapā-haṁsa-nādānta naṭanam* iconology of the Tyāgarāja image is the concept of vibration itself. Wherein does the concept of dance fit? Tyāgarāja in the myth is enshrined in the heart of Viṣṇu and dances by his breath. The *Maitrāyaṇī Upaniṣad* (6.27 and 6.38)[79] tells us that Brahman resides in the heart wherein also reside the vital breaths. Furthermore, the Brahman emerges during the meditation of the yogī by literally pushing the heart to one side. The Āgamas describe the state of *parā vāk* as a "slight stir, a throb or vibration in Reality and the eternal self revelation of this reality is the Primal and original vibration".[80] This forms the central point of speculation of the Trika school.[81] "Reality", says Utpala, "reveals itself in the *heart* of the successful adept as an intense and vibrant energy" (1.6). The teachings of this school belong to the *rahasya sampradāya* or the esoteric school. The theatre of Tyāgarāja's dance is described as the *hṛtsabhā* or the 'hall of the heart' in contradistinction to the *cit sabhā* or the theatre of the mind where Naṭarāja is believed to dance. The *Kāñcīpurāṇam* describes the dance of Tyāgarāja as *takaravidyai* in contrast to *citākācavupācaṉai* (contemplation of the ether as consciousness) at Chidambaram. The former, i.e. Tyāgarāja is said to reside in the heart.

Thus, one can see the synthesis of Upaniṣadic Absolutism, theistic Āgamism and yogic experimentalism in the concept of the dance of Tyāgarāja. The ritual of dance itself is re-enacted every year at *Paṅkuṉi Uttiram* festival in a carnival-like atmosphere and much in the spirit of the dances attributed to Murukaṉ in the early Caṅkam literature.

Ajapā, Haṁsa and Śrī-vidyā

The *ajapā* and *haṁsa*, when adopted by the *Śrī-Vidyā* assume yet another set of sound symbolisms. *a* = *Śiva and ha* = *Śakti* and together they form the first and last letter of the Sanskrit syllabary.[82]

A + ha = Kāmakalā which is equated with *Śabdabrahman* and forms the prime *mantra* of *Śrī-Vidyā*. As we have seen *parā = śakti,* so the totality is in *śakti;* and *aham* or individuation is also in Her in the pristine form of Oneness. Thus *Kāmakalā = śabdabrahman =* the equation *aham saḥ = haṁsa*. The concept of *śabda* (sound) is very important in Śrī-Vidyā for the syllabary sounds are believed to be energy centres.

The Tāntric school of Śrī-Vidyā lays great stress on mantras and "there are Tāntric parallels of all *smārta* and *Paurāṇika* rites, complete in every detail".[83] Vedic mantras were often used for Tāntric rites. The different *Gāyatrī* mantras assigned to different deities are nothing but Tāntric incantations in which the *Gāyatrī* of the *Ṛg Veda* (III. 62.10) are incorporated. "The elaborate rules regarding the regulation of breath and the high importance attached to it in Yoga have scarcely any trace in the Vedas".[84] Here the term 'breath' signifies the physical process as in *prāṇāyāma* and not the *prāṇa*, as the metaphysical Principle.

Several Tāntric texts like the *Ghēraṇḍasaṁhitā, Haṭhayogapradīpikā, Dakṣiṇāmūrti Saṁhitā, Gorakṣaśatakam,* etc. deal with the theme of *ajapā, haṁsa* and the contents of these works form more or less a homogeneous branch of knowledge. Dating these works is an impossible task but most of them were known by the 12th century A.D. and even otherwise their content is very much a repetition of the statements made in the Yogic Upaniṣads and in the Haṭhayoga manuals or the *nātha saṁpradāya* literature such as the *Gorakṣa saṁhitā* of Guru Gorakṣa,[85] regarded as the founder of the Nāthas, a school of mystics who were popular all over Northern India specially in the Bengal region. It has been suggested that Tirumūlar, who was believed to have come from Kashmir and bore the surname Nātha was presumably of this lineage of *Siddhas*.[86]

One thing common to all these texts is the secrecy that is enjoined in initiating a disciple; the secrecy, however, is not of the mere word but of experience. A mantra, by itself, is just a sound unless taught by a *guru* who breathes into it the experiential sense and it is with the aid of the guru that the state of consciousness induced by the mantra can be realized.

The *Ajapākalpam*[87] is an anthology of several mss. dealing with the *ajapā* doctrine. The *ajapā* mantra, which is *haṁsa,* is treated as *citśakti* in her aspect of *ānanda* and in movement.

Every breath taken in and every breath let out is *ajapā,* for it is a spontaneous and subconscious affirmation of the life principle. When this almost unconscious instinctual act is consciouly realized it becomes *haṁ saḥ,* expressing the Divine unity of life. As we breathe, the *mantra* without being vocalised (*a+japā*), is being repeated continually and involuntarily. The indrawn breath (*pūraka*) and its subtle sound (*haṁ*) signifies one's self and the outgoing breath (*recaka*) with its sound *sa* (*saḥ*) i.e. He. Thus even as we are, we go on affirming the supreme identity. In the swing of breath the soul is in eternal rhythm in the ceaseless dance of ineffable bliss. That all sins are destroyed by the conscious realization of the *ajapā mantra* is stated in the *Sūtasayajña* (Ch. 7 st. 8, cited in *Ajapākalpam*).

It is believed that the unenlightened man does not realize that by his breath he is affirming this universal life principle and since he is ignorant of it he is unable to see salvation.[88] This is also repeated in *Gorakṣa śataka* v. 39. Thus one has to 'see' the universality of life - the One beyond the Many and that 'seeing' is a discipline, an exercise and finally an intuitive 'vision'.

In a twenty-four hour period, 60 *nāḍikās,* according to the traditional Hindu reckoning, between sunrise of one day to sunrise of the next, an individual inhales and exhales 21,600 times[89] and he should by training become aware that these are affirmations of universal principle of life and should thus dedicate his breaths in the following order:

600 breaths signifying *ajapā* is offered to Gaṇapti in *mūlādhāra*
6000 " " " " " " Brahmā in *svādhiṣṭhāna*
6000 " " " " " " Viṣṇu in *maṇipūraka*
6000 " " " " " " Rudra in *anāhata*
1000 " " " " " " Jīvātmā in *viśuddhi*
1000 " " " " " " Paramātmā in *ājñā*
1000 " " " " " " Guru in *sahasrāram*
These add up to 21, 600.

Interestingly enough, the roof of Chidambaram has 21,600 tiles and the explanation is that it denotes the breath-offerings to the realization of this identity. The way this figure of 21,600 is arrived at is interesting for in the yogic technique of *prāṇāyāma* the ingoing breath should be taken in at one count of time, be held at two counts of time, and again exhaled at one count of time, thereby making it a count of four and the whole process should last 4 seconds. Thus, for every minute there are 15 respiratory processes; so for one hour there are 15 x 60 = 900 and thus in a day there are 900 x 24 = 21,600 breaths. Western medical system reckons that a healthy human being will breathe in and out 18 breaths per minute. The *Cittars* in Tamil̲ tradition are also renowned for their knowledge of medicine. Their system is called *Cittavaitiyam.* Romarṣi is one of the *Cittar* doctors and his work *Romarṣijñān̲am* (v. 13) states that a man who has lived to be a hundred years old, breathes the ideal number of breaths, i.e. 21,600 per day. When the Yogin temporarily ceases to breathe, he reaches *samādhi*. Ajapā as a *Gāyatrī,* in combination with the *nyāsa* rite acts as an important aid in Tāntric meditation.[90]

Apart from the *ajapā* texts referred to above, the liturgical text the *Mucukundasahasranāmam* has several references to the Śrī-Vidyā aspect of the deity Tyāgarāja. Tyāgarāja is extolled as:

> Ōm Śrī-Vidyātmakarūpāya namaḥ (Inv. 9)
> Ōm Śrī-Pīṭhāntarnivāsine namaḥ (Inv. 10)
> Ōm Śrī-Vidyācchādita (cchādya?) hṛdayāya namaḥ (Inv.11)
> Ōm Śrī-Vidyā haṁsa saṁpuṭāya namaḥ (Inv. 12)
> Ōm Śrī-Vidyā paridhānākhyāya namaḥ (Inv. 13)
> Ōm Śrī mūlādhāranilayāya namaḥ (Inv. 20)
> Ōm Śrī nāḍi vidyā svarūpiṇe namaḥ (Inv. 37)
> Ōm Śrī Ambikāguhasamyutāya namaḥ (Inv. 38)
> Ōm Śrī-Vidyā japa priyāya namaḥ (Inv. 51)
> Ōm Śrī kalāṣoḍaśakṣastambhasahasrasthānamadhyakāya-namaḥ (Inv. 114).

Tyāgarāja and the Carnatic Music composer Muttusvāmi Dīkṣitar

Muttusvāmi Dīkṣitar, the renowned 19th century composer, from Tiruvārūr and a Tyāgarāja devotee describes the dance of Tyāgarāja as *"yogividita ajapānaṭana raṅgam"* (the Yogic determined ajapā dance) in his composition *Tyāgarāja pālayāśu mām in Gaula rāga* (Tyāgarāja protect me) and *"atilalita haṁsanaṭana"* (the extremely graceful haṁsa dance) in the song *Tyāgarāja virājatē* in *Aṭhāṇā rāga* where he addresses the deity as Vāgartha (the sound and its meaning) and as *"ajapānaṭana ānandavaibhavam bharaṇam"*(the glory of the joyous *ajapā* dance)[91] in a *naṭābharaṇa* compostition. In *Tyāgarājamahādhvajāroha* he describes the deity as one in the midst of *aṣṭāṇga yoga* - the eightfold path of Yoga, and again refers to *ajapānaṭanam*. In *Candraśekharam sadā bhaje-'ham* in *Mārgahindolam* he uses the number eight to depict different cult doctrines - as one who is fond of the eight instruments, as the giver of the eight *Siddhis*, the remover of the eight bondages and finally the dancer of joy. In a song addressed to Nīlōtpalāmpāḷ, the divine spouse of Tyāgarāja, he describes her as the *Kādi hādyādi manu viśvāsinīm*. *Kādi* and *hādi*, are two sound systems of mantras within the Śrī-Vidyā School. In the *Tyāgarāja Yoga Vaibhavam* in *Ānandabhairavī* he describes the deity as the voice of *nāda bindu* and describes the *Vaibhavam* (festive glory) of Tyāgarāja as ordained by the *Yogirāja* (Śiva as Yogī). He invokes Nīlōtpalāmpāl (Consort of Tyāgarāja) in a composition called *Nīlōtpalāmbām bhajare* in Rītigaula in which he describes her as "*Vītiviṭanka Tyāgarājāntaraṅgam*" (the close confidante of Tyāgarāja alias Vītiviṭanka.)

The *rāga haṁsadhvani* was composed for the first time by Rāmasvāmi Dīkṣitar, the father of Muttusvāmī, inspired by the music of the *kalhalas* (long trumpets), *suddhamattalam* (drum) and *tālam* or cymbals used to mark the time measure which are played as accompaniment to the *haṁsanaṭanam* of the Tyāgarāja of Tiruvārūr.[92]

Dīkṣitar was a Śrī-Vidyā *upāsaka* and took the name of Cidānandanātha as his initiation-name. His *Devī kīrttaṉai* are numerous and focus around two deities of Tiruvārūr, Kamalāmpāḷ and Nīlōtpalāmpāḷ, and Mayūrāmpāḷ of Mayūram for the special *navāvaraṇa* worship of Devī. He has also composed a number of songs based on the Lalitopākhyāna or special invocations to the Śrī-Vidyā deity Lalitā. He was well versed in the Śrī-Vidyā lore and his *Devī kīrttaṉai* are full of references to the tenets and beliefs of this school. In the *Kīrttaṉai* "Hāṭakeśvara" he describes the deity as being identical with Tyāgarāja and invokes him as '*niśvāsa haṁsa rūpa citravilāsa*'. Zvelebil labels this easy process of interchanging of deities as "henolocotheism".

Thus, the iconology of the Tyāgarāja image revolved chiefly around the two concepts of *ajapā* and *haṁsa*, both of which were predominantly tinged with Yoga metaphysics and Āgamic thought of both the Pratyabhijñā and the Śrī-Vidyā schools and the theory of grace, removal of the veil of ignorance and the Divine Dance of the Siddhāntin.

Other Literary References

One notices a change of emphasis in Kumarakurparar. He takes the name Tyāga in his *Tiruvārūrnāṉmaṇimālai* v. 13 and says that the name Tyāga is the apt epithet of the great giver, but the hand that gives (the *varamudrā* sporting hand) is the left hand and the left is Devī. Here the half-man-half-woman form or Ardhanārī is envisaged and the generosity is attributed to Devī. In v. 22 he discusses the theme of dance and says the great dance takes place at Ārūr and the poet puns on the word *(y) ār ūr* = *Ārūr,* i.e. whose city? and the answer is everybody's and in that sense the dance is a universal one. He treats the Somāskanda as the *Sat Cit Ānanda* emblem.[93] The fact that the Somāskanda had three components lent it a specially symbolic character for three is a very significant number in Hinduism.

The dance of Tyāgarāja is enacted as a rite during the annual festivals and the icon is suspended by a chord of banana fibre and so appears freely to move up and down when moved by the bearers. It is not taken in a palanquin like other deities. The idea is that the two poles are the two arteries *idā* and *piṅgalā* and the icon is tossed up and down re-enacting the *ajapā haṁsa* dance which symbolises the *kuṇḍalinī,* the *prāṇa* in the *suṣumnā.* One of the legends has it that when Tiruvārūr Ñāṉapirakācar was entering the temple in search of a guru the strap binding the icon snapped as the procession approached near where he was, and he immediately sang a song and it joined. A part of this hymn goes as follows:

> "Tuṇṭupaṭṭa acapā niruttam acaiyumpaṭi taṇṭicaiyum vakaiyaruḷvāy iṉṟu" (Quoted by Mu. Arunachalam, *Tamiḻ Ilakkiya Varalāṟu,* Sixteenth *nūṟṟāṇṭu,* pt. 11., p. 265). Ñāṉapirakācar is also credited with the *talapurāṇam* and also several songs on Tyāgarāja.

The Tamiḻ tradition passed on to Marāṭhī and the *Tyāgarājamāhātmyam* by Śrī Rāma Paṇḍita in the 18th century A.D. refers to the *haṁsa mantra svarūpa* (v. 46) and goes on to explain *ha,* as Śiva and *sa* as Śakti and the *bindu m* producing the nasal tone as Skanda (v. 48).

Conclusion

Thus, to conclude, the Tyāgarāja metaphysics is woven with the theme of dance and *mantra* and the two are in turn connected. All the *talapurāṇams* refer to this dance. The *Tirukkāṟāyil Purāṇam* asks the specific question, Why does Śiva dance? The answer is, for the welfare of the world (*viṭaṅka kapāla vana rahasya carukkam*). In the true style of the *talapurāṇam* the abstract is reduced to the concrete and the universal to the specific and the poet states that Śiva, the repository of the six *guṇas*, dances every evening at Tiruvārūr a very special kind of dance. The uniqueness lies in this, that the Lord dances in a seated position (*āsīnatāṇḍavam*). The world, we are told, functions because of this dance... The dance is the symbol of unsullied wisdom and uncontaminated happiness. Patañjali, we are told, was once intrigued by the thought that since life is multi-faceted there ought to be a variety of dances and as he pondered over this, a voice was heard and it proclaimed the intricacies of the dance in relation of spiritual knowledge. The voice explained "The dance is the union of Kāmeśvara and Kāmeśvarī" (Śiva and Śakti) and is a vision reserved for the devas and enlightened men. "It is at Tirukkāṟāyil that Patañjali in the company of Vyāghrapāda will be able to witness the thirty-two forms of dances (note again a 'Chidambaram motif': *ekapāda naṭanam* there too Vyāghrapāda and Patañjali witness Śiva's dance), including forms such as *kamalanaṭanam, ekapādanaṭanam, uttānanaṭanam* (dance of the submarine fire), *kukkuṭa naṭanam*, etc.

Thus the general theme of dance as associated with the Tamiḻ Murukaṉ and the Vedic Indra were blended into the dance of Tyāgarāja. The *Cilappatikāram* mentions a *tuṭipaṟai* performed to the accompaniment of a percussion instrument and performed by Murukaṉ. Aṭiyārkkunallār, the 12th -14th century commentator, states that when Cūrapatumaṉ hid himself after suffering defeat at the hands of Murukaṉ the victorious deity danced this form of dance *in a seated posture* using the sea-waves as his stage. The Nāṭukāṇkātai of the same work describes a static dance in most poetic terms. Thus old Tamiḻ idioms appear in a new garb in the dance of Tyāgarāja.

The *Lalitātriśatī Bhāṣya* attributed to Saṅkarācārya where he defines the form of *ajapā* as *ajapārūpeṇa prāṇa-apāna-nāmaka-candra sūrya-niyamane*. He thus equates the breath with the precept or rule (*niyamana*) of rhythmic movement of the Sun and Moon, the microcosmic with the macrocosmic. The *Mucukundasaharanāmam* constantly invokes this trinity as a form of the Sun, Moon and Agni.[94]

The actual terms *ajapā* and *haṁsa* etc., are traceable only from the 12th century A.D., that is if we ignore the evidence of Śaṅkara cited above, for several works are attributed to Śaṅkara, which we now know were definitely not written by him. The 12th century date is assuming that the *Mucukundasahasranāmam* was composed in this period, as I believe it was.

All 20th century *stotras* and songs are aware of the theme of Tyāgarāja's dance and describe it on very similar lines. Similar motifs are also 'shared' by the *Maturai Talapurāṇam* wherein Śiva, witnessed again by Vyāghrapāda and Patañjali, dances in the Silver Hall, Veḷḷiyambalam. (See Parañjotimunivar, *Tiruviḷaiyātaṟpurāṇam, Pāyiram* 6.) The *padas* composed by Shahāji and the *Tyageśa Kuṟavañci* as well as the *Pallaki Sēvā Prabandham* are full of references to *ajapā* and *haṁsa* in connection with the Tyāgarāja.

In the anthology *Tiruvoṟṟiyūr talamāṉmiya ttōttiraṅkaḷ* there is a song in praise of Ātipurītyāgar in which Skanda is envisaged as keeping the beat and Umā watching Ātipurī Tyāgar dance. (*Kārārum malaiyaṉār kaittālam ulavolippa vārārum tanattumaiyāḷ kaṇṭuvantu manam uruka cīrārum Ātipurittiyākar tiruvaṭi pōṟṟi*). A *Tiyākapaḷḷu* attributed to Ñāṉapirakācar describes the gentle swaying of Tyāgarāja. On almost similar lines there is a composition on Tiruvoṟṟiyūr Tyāgarāja by a Municāmi Mutaliyār, which begins with "*mānāṭa maḻuvāṭa*" (as the deer dances the axe sways). There is a great emphasis on the aspect of joy in Tyāgarāja's dance "*iṉpanaṭanavullācattiyākar*" I.V. Ponnayya Pillai in a more philosophic vein describes the dance thus:

"When the centre dances the peripheries dance
When the Mūlādhāra dances the universe vibrates"

He further refers to the dance as *palvariyīrāṟṟu*, a term reminiscent of *veṟikkūttu* associated with Murukaṉ in the *Cilappatikāram*. An anonymous poem dated 1924 describes graphically the *Paṅkuṉiyuttiram* festival and mentions the buffalo sacrifice at the Piṭārikōyil initiating the rites, and describes the dance of Tyāgarāja as he comes to the *vasantamaṇṭapam*. The poem ends charmingly by stating that though Queen Victoria's rule brought in the telephones and telegraphs there was no rule like that of Tyāgarāja.[95] These record in almost similar terms the metaphysical import of Tyāgarāja's dance.

The next chapter will study the personality of the cult deity in the general context of religious synthesis in the Śaiva fold in Tamiḷnāḍu. In the process an interesting manuscript of Bhāskararāya which deals both with the Goḷaki *maṭha* and the *ajapā-haṁsa* doctrine will be discussed.

NOTES

1. John of St. Thomas, *Logica II*, p. q. 21 . a.6, cited by Jose Perriera, in "Dance as a symbol" - a lecture delivered in Bombay, Oct. 1982
2. *Śrī-Vidyā* is fundamentally a worship of Śakti as Tripura, Lalitā, etc., through *Śrī-Vidyā mantra* and the *Śrī-Cakra*. It is a more dualistic and more Śakti oriented school than the *Trika*. The *Trika* system of Kashmir Śaivism is also known as *Pratyabhijñā* and *Anuttara*. It is monistic and hence rejects *Siddhānta* as dualistic. Its focal theme centres around '*Consciousness*'. It distinguishes itself from the Buddhist *Vijñānavāda* as also the *Śabdādvaita* (the notion that Sound=Brahman) of the *Vyākaraṇa* (Grammarian's) School. The Supreme Reality, which is Pure *Cit* is the personality of Śiva. This Pure Śiva *appears* (*Abhāsa*) as the universe. Hence they are called *Abhāsavādins*. They are also called *Pratibimbavādins* for believing that the universe is a reflection of the Lord. The Supreme Reality *Paratattva* appears as *parāpara* and *apara*. The *Abheda, Bhedābheda* and *Bheda* are all in one *Anuttara* Reality. It is a very eclectic School. A great deal of its doctrine conforms to the *Sadba Brahman* or Grammarians's School. See *Somānanda Śiva Dṛṣṭi*, Ch. II. *Vāk* is the heart of the Supreme Being and *a - kṣ* (the syllabary) are the embodiment of this Being. In this Being which is Cidānanda the three *Śaktis, Icchā, jñāna* and *Kriyā* lie dormant. Thus this *cit* Reality has the aspect of *Vimarśa* (Self Brooding) and this results in all the categories by which unlimited Bhairava becomes limited *jīva*. The *Mucukundasahasranāmam* uses several of the terms like *prakāśa, vācya, vimarśa, vācaka, spanda*, etc. Abhinavagupta of the 10th-11th centuries was one of the greatest philosophers of this School. Very little work has been done on this School of Śaivism. The two well known works are those of Pandey, K.C., *Abhinavagupta*, and Sastri, Gourinath, *Philosophy of Word and its Meaning*.
3. See Subrahmanian, N. *Pre Pallavan Tamil Index*, Madras, 1966.
4. Turner studies symbols in a processual context as something changing in significance for the set of believers because a new set of meanings have been added on either by a group of believers or sometimes even an individual follower. The connotation thenceforth takes on a new dimension. See Turner, Victor and Edith, *Image and Pilgrimage in Christian Culture*, pp. 242-50.
5. For "dominant symbol" see *Ibid.*, p. 243 where the authors discuss the "two

poles of meaning" in a dominant symbol, viz. "ideological" and "orectic", or pertaining to desire. The expression "root paradigm" is interpreted by the authors as something which represents the goals of man as a species; the general good over the individual welfare. "They go beyond the cognitive and even the moral to the existential domain and in so doing become clothed with allusiveness, implicitness and metaphor".

6. *Tiruvoṟṟiyūr Purāṇam*, Ch. II. *Vimalaṉār Naṭaṉam*. In Yatīndrasvāmī's prose rendering the chapter is entitled 'Tirunaṭaṉacarukkam'. Nandī makes it clear that the dance of Tiruvoṟṟiyūr is of the same order as the dance in Kailāsa (ñāṇatāṇṭava) and the one at Tillai (Ānantatāṇṭava), the difference being that it is done in a seated position (ācīnatāṇṭava) Ch. II, vv. 10-12.
7. This was kindly pointed out to me by Dr. T. Gelblum.
8. See Pl.X captioned *ajapā yantra.*
9. The eight yogīc aids are *Yama, Niyama, pratyāhāra, dhārana, dhyāṇā* and *samādhi* forming the six chief aids called *Ṣaḍanga* and it becomes eight when the two physical aids *āsana* and *prāṇāyāma* are added. These are discipline, restraint, withdrawal of the senses, aids to concentration, meditation, and the final stage of deep and devout meditation respectively. The two physical aids are sitting posture, including seats, and breathing exercises. Some *laya yoga* texts lay down nine *aṅgas*. For the eight *aṅgas* see Patañjali, *Yogasūtra* II. 29.
10. *Siddhas* seem to belong to two kinds, those that believe in an instant flash of wisdom like the 'Satori' of the Rinzai Zen and those that believe in slow developmental stages of spiritual evolution, more like the Soto School in Japanese Buddhism.
11. For *praṇava* and *prāṇa* and other terms in the *Yōgasūtra* see Das, Bhagwan, *Concordance to the Yogasūtra of Patañjali and Bhāṣya of Vyāsa.*
12. A similar view was held by Pseudo Dionysius who states that the higher we rise the more concise our language becomes and when one advances into the realm beyond the 'intelligibles' words and thoughts will cease altogether. Dionysius, Ed. p. 182 cited by Gombrich, E.H., *Symbolic Images*, p. 168.
13. *Amṛtā Nāda Upaniṣad*, 4.
14. Eliade, Mircea in *The Sacred and the Profane* pp. 9-10, characterises the essence of the experience of the sacred as one of mysterious fascination and "awe inspiring mystery" (*"mysterium tremendum"*)
15. The *guru* is an essential and central feature of the Tāntric system.
16. For dance *padas* or lyrics capturing this esoteric mood see Pāpavināśa Mutaliyār's 18th century compositions *'mukattai kāṭṭiya deyvam'* popularised by the Kalākśētra dance school at Aḍyār, Madras, and 'Perum nalla Tiyākar'.
17. See *Tirukkāṟāyiṟpurāṇam*, the chapters entitled *Viṭaṅka Kapāla vaṉa rahasya Carukkam* and *Tyāgarājarahasya Carukkam*, for the warnings on the dire consequences that would befall a curious beholder of the icon and lists numbers of legendary and semi-historical characters who faced disasters because of breaking this taboo on unveiling the icon.
18. For example *Br. Up*. 3. 7; 3.23; *Sat. Br*. x. 33; 5-8; *Ait. Br*. 8.28 where the cosmic force is equated with *vāyu* and the microcosmic with *prāṇa*.
19. Such as *Br. Up*. 1.4. 10; *Chānd. Up*. 6. 8. 7 ff. These are called the *'mahāvākyas'*, 'the great statements' in the *Upaniṣads*.
20. Transl. Deussen, Paul, *The Philosophy of the Upaniṣads*, p. 390 ff. The discussion on the nature of *prāṇa* in this section is largely based on Deussen's analysis.

21. *Chānd. Up.* 7.15 Deussen's translation. The italics are mine.
22. *Praśnopaniṣad,* 6. 3-4. transl. *ibid.*
23. Deussen, *op. cit.,* pp. 390 ff.
24.. *Br. Up.* 1.3; *Chānd. Up.* 1.2.
25. *Kauṣītakī Up* 3. 8. analysed by Deussen, *ibid.*
26. Transal. Van Buitenen, *The Maitrāyaṇīya Upaniṣad,* p. 127.
27. *Praśnopaniṣad* 4.4. Also *Br. Up.* 1.5.23.
28. *Kauṣītakī* 2.5.
29. For *Prāṇāgnihōtra* see Bodewitz, H.W., *Jaiminīya Brāhmaṇa I 1-65, Translation and Commentary with a Study of Agnihōtra and Prāṇagnihotra.* He classifies it as a *gṛhya* version of the *Śrauta Agnihotra* with no metaphysical content. An unpublished Manuscript RASB No. 5990 called itself the *Prāṇāgnihotra Tantra* and explains the ritual details of performing fire sacrifice to one's own breath.
30. *Prāṇāgnihotra Upaniṣad* is one of the Upaniṣads included in Deussen, Paul, *Sixty Upaniṣads of the Vedas.* Transl. Bedekar, V.M. and Palsule, G.M., See Part II p. 645 ff.
31. Ranade, R.D., *A Constructive Survey of the Upaniṣadic Philosophy.* The *Maitrāyaṇīya Upaniṣad* uses the word *prāṇa* in both the biological and metaphysical senses. See 2. 2/2.
32. Unfortunately, Apte does not clearly state his source. However, the passage in question can be traced to the *Dakṣiṇāmūrti Saṁhitā.*
33. Konow, Sten Ed., *Corpus Inscriptionum Indicarum,* Vol. II, pt. I. Ins. No. 31, pp. 83-86. Here *'hassa'* is presumably the unenlightened *ātman* waiting to be reborn. Professor Thomas interpreted it as "the embodied soul, 'jīva'". For problems of interpreting this enigmatic epigraph see *Ibid.,* p. 85. This inscription was kindly brought to my attention by Professor Bratindranath Mukherji of Calcutta University.
34. These are *prāṇa, apāna, Vyāna, Samāna* and *udāna.*
35. Deussen, *The Philosophy of the Upaniṣads,* p. 9, classifies the following Upaniṣads as 'Yogic": *Brahmavidyā, Kṣurikā, Cūlikā, Nādabindu, Brahmabindu, Amṛtabindu, Dhyānabindu, Tejōbindu, Yogaśikhā, Yogatattva* and *Haṁsa.* These apprehended the Brahman through auditory meditations and the sound *om.* Deussen's claim that all *Yogic Upaniṣads* are in poetry is not borne out by the fact that the *Haṁsopaniṣad* is partly in prose and partly in poetry. Most of these were appended to the *Atharva Veda* though the Haṁsa was appended to the *Śukla Yajur Veda.* Deussen has a further classification of Upaniṣads as *Sannyāsa Upaniṣads.* Many of these have long discourses on *haṁsa* and *paramahaṁsa.* The Advaitin *Sannyāsins* took the appellation of *Paramahaṁsa* before their monastic name.
36. See for example Lakṣmaṇa Deśikēndra's commentary on *Śāradātilaka* 1.7. *Nādabindū Sṛṣṭyōpayogāvasthārūpau* Also Sastri, Gourinath, *The Philosophy of Word and its Meaning,* where he discusses this idea in several chapters.
37. Bhartṛhari, *Vākyapadīya* II. 31. says that *Śabdatattva* is to the grammarian what Brahman is to the *Advaitin.* In *Vaiyākaraṇabhūṣaṇa* under *"Sphoṭa nirūpaṇa"* the author Koṇḍabhaṭṭa equates *Sphoṭa,* another term for *Śabdatattva,* with Brahman. (*Niṣkarṣe tu Brahmaiva Sphoṭaḥ*).
38. *Bṛ. Up.* 1.4.1 *'nānyad ātmano, paśyat so ham asmi iti agre vyāharat.'*
39. See Jacob, *op. cit.*
40. For anthologies of published Yogic Upaniṣads see editions by Raghoram,

Babu Siv Prasad, Narayaṇaswamy, K. and Ayyanagar, Srinivasa T.R. listed in the Bibliography.

41. Saraswati Mahal Library, Thañjāvūr, has two manuscripts of this Upaniṣad, both without the preamble.
42. Invocations 8, 36, 321, 510, 722, refer to *haṁsa*. 321 describes *haṁsamantra* as part of the six limbed yoga, i.e *Ṣaḍaṅga Yoga*. 722 links *haṁsa* with the speech world and it is equated with *akṣara* and *dhvani*.
43. Invocation 35 refers to *ajapātāṇḍava* 398 to *ajapānaṭana* at *Utsava* times. 499 and 570 refer to *Phālguna* (Tamil *Paṅkuṉi*) *Utsava* and the *ajapā* dance done in a seated position (*āsīna*).
44. *Haṁsopaniṣad*, para 5.
45. *Ibid.* 6.
46. Deussen, *The Philosophy of the Upaniṣads*, p.284, where he states "The name *brahmarandhra* is first found in *Haṁsa* 3 in connection with six mystical and imaginary regions of the body that occur there for the first time."
47. Para 8.
48. *Ibid.*, also *Nādabindopaniṣad*, 31-5.
49. The technical meaning of the word *sphoṭa* as used by the grammarian is a sentence conceived as an indivisible unit. In its metaphysical sense *sphoṭa* is the same as *Śabdatattva* and as stated by Bhartṛhari *Śabdatattva* to the grammarian is the same as Brahman to the Vedāntist. See *Vākyapadīya* II. 31.
50. The *Gāyatrī* is the first order of Vedic metres, consisting of three feet thrice repeated. Later a fourth foot was added and it symbolised the four stages of the soul and also Brahman and the four footed Brahman. The *Haṁsa Gāyatrī* is an attempt to link the spirit of the Tantra with the spiritual and ritual element of the Vedas as well as its metre.
51. Ajit Mookerjee, *The Tantras*.
52. *Agni Purāṇa* 214-26. "*ajapānāma gāyatrī Brahmā, Viṣṇu, Maheśvarī; ajapām japatē yastām punarjanma na vidyatē*"
53. "*Ajapopasamhāra iti abhidhīyate*" according to *Haṁsopaniṣad*.
54. See *Ṣaṭcakranirūpaṇa* in Avalon, Arthur, Ed. *Tāntric Texts*, Calcutta, London, 1913, p. 58.
55. *Dhyānabindu* 4; Translation Deussen, op.cit., *p.392.*, *Nādabindu* 48-9, where the verse in question runs: *niḥśabdam tatparam Brahma paramātma samīyate, nādo yāvat manas tāvat nādāntopi maṇonmaṇī.* Here the word *unmaṇī* is explained as a state beyond consciousness-*manaḥ* and that is synonymous with *nādānta*.)
56. *Tirumantiram*, v.865; Also *Pāśupatabrahmopaniṣad, 1. 19.* where it is stated "*haṁsapraṇavayor abhedaḥ*" - "there is no difference between *haṁsa and* praṇava".
57. This splitting of *om into* a, *u*, m and treating it in a symbolic manner is an ancient tradition. See *Māṇḍūkya Up.* 8-12; *Tirumantiram*, v.872. 773 depicts it as knowledge of two kinds - i.e. Śiva and Śakti. The imagery of the dizzy whirl is popular in *Śaiva Siddhānta* literature. See *Supakkam* 2. 53. "*māyai mayakkamum ceyyum aṉṟē*".
58. The five are *na, ma, śi, vā* and *ya*, standing for obeisance to Śiva but it is not the literal but the symbolic meaning that is important. For this see *Uṇmaivilakkam* 34-6; *Tirumantiram* v. 873. refers to the two syllabled letter *ha* and *sa* and treats them as symbols of Śiva and Śakti and he treats *om* and the *pañcākṣara* as an expansion of this cryptic formula. The eight are *na, ma,*

śi, vā, ya and *a, u* and *m*, which constitute *om*. This expands to fifty-one, the total number of syllables in Sanskrit.

59. See *Tirumantiram*, specially *Tantra 9* for Tirumūlar's exposition on the ontological and soteriological symbolism of Dance.
60. *Tirumantiram Tantra* 4. v. 893. Translation mine.
61. *Mucukundasahasranāmam*, Invocation No. 932.
62. *Tirunākaikkāroṇappurāṇam*, Invocation to Aḻaku Viṭaṅkar, St.10.
63. For co-relation between *pañcākṣara* as an audial symbol and a visual emblem see *Uṇmai Viḷakkam* v. 34. Also *Tiruvaruṭpayaṉ* 9.3 wherein the *pañcākṣara* is arranged in a hierarchic order as follows: *Śi* =Śiva, *vā* =Śakti, *ya* =ātman, *na=tirōdhāna*, and *ma* =*mala*. Thus, as the soul ascends casting off its *malas* (*āṇava, māyā* and *karma*) and its blinding veil (*tirōdhāna*) then it beholds Śiva and Śakti. Thus the *ātmā* is a kind of nexus between phenomenal existence symbolised by cosmic dance *ūna naṭaṉam* and the dance of redeeming wisdom "ñāṉanaṭaṉam". *(See also Uṇmaiviḷakkam,* v. 38 ff.)
64. *Tirumantiram* v. 880, "*Irukkinṟa mantiram Civaṉ tirumēṇi*". See also *Civañāṉacittiyār*, 12-4; *Uṇmaiviḷakkam*, 44-45.
65. Gonda, *Medieval Religious Literature- A History of Indian Literature*, Vol. II p.33.
66. *Tirumantiram*, v. 2683, "*Vētaṅkaḷāṭa miku Ākamamāṭa*".
67. vv. 2727, 2759 are some of the examples. Several of them refer to this for the guru is one of the focal points of this work.
68. See Pal, P., *Hindu Religion and Iconology*, pp. 147-8, where he studies the tradition of homologisation according to the tradition expounded in the *Tantrasāra* of *Āgamavāgīśa*, a 16th century work. For equating letters of the alphabet with Śakti see Aryan, K.C., *The Little Goddess*. He discusses the equation of the vowels with the *Saptamātṛkās* and the equation of the syllabary to the 5 elements, 5 senses, etc. See also Gonda, J., *Medieval Religion and Literature*, p. 33.
69. See Pl.X *Ajapā yantra.*
70. Sivaraman, K., *Śaivism in Philosophical Perspective*, pp. 224-226.
71. Zvelebil, K., *The Poets of the Powers*, p. 74.
72. *Ibid.*, p. 79.
73. Zvelebil, K.V., *The History of Tamil Literature*, p. 55.
74. Sivaraman, K., *op. cit.*, p. 226.
75. *Ibid.*
76. See Sastri, *op. cit.*, particularly pp. 71 ff. The later grammarians were influenced by the Śaiva School. In the *Mahārtha Mañjarī* cited by Sastri, *op. cit.*, p. 76 and also pp. 128-9, the different levels of speech are linked with different forms of Śakti. Thus *Vaikharī* is *Kriyā, madhyamā =jñāna, paśyantī = icchā* and *Sūkṣma* is a unifying state which unites all three, i.e. the state preceding differentiation.
77. Sambhasivasastri, K., Ed., *Sphoṭasiddhi*, Trivandrum 1927. Introduction p 2 for a definition of *Sphota* and its equation with *parā, paśyantī*, etc. The editor, Sambhasivasastri, believes that though Pāṇini has not explicitly mentioned it he knew of *Sphoṭavāda* since he refers to a man called Sphoṭāyana. He believes that Patañjali knew it.
78. See Pandey, K.C., Saiva Siddhānta and the Philosophy of Grammar' in *Bhāskarī*, Vol. III, p. xcvi, xcviii. Also Sivaraman, *op. cit.*
79. For Deussen's interpretation see *op. cit* p. 288; for a different view see Van Buitenen *op. cit* pp. 46-8.

80. See *Mahārthamañjarī*, p. 73 and *Paryanta Pañcāśikā* 54.7 wherein are mentioned the two forms of Śiva, i.e. *Vimarśa* and *prakāśa* and the two *Spandas*. This minor work of Abhinavagupta has been edited by V. Raghavan, Madras, 1951.
81. The name 'Trika', meaning 'of three' is given to the system because it sets out to explore various triads such as three groups of *āgamas*, viz. 1) Siddha, 2) Nāmaka, 3) Mālinī, the three stages of Reality, *parā, aparā* and *parāparā*, the three aspects of knowledge *abheda* (non-duality), *bhedābheda* ('Predominant Oneness') and *bheda* (Duality). Other triads are mentioned by Pandey, K.C., *op. cit.*
82. *Kāmakalāvilāsa* of Puṇyānanda v. 2. This is a very important text of the Śrī-Vidyā School.
83. See Sastri, Haraprasad *Catalogue of Sanskrit Manuscripts in the Royal Asiatic Society of Bengal*, Introduction.
84. *ibid*
85. *Gorakṣa Śataka*, v. 32 ff. In v.42 *haṁsa* is equated with *prāṇa*. v. 43 describes the 21600 *mantras* that all *jīvas* pronounce in one day. In v. 44 it states that it is the means of salvation for the Yogī and that meditating on it and resolved in it (*Saṁkalpa*) one could attain redemption from all sins.
86. Nagaswamy, R., *Tāntric Cult of South India.*
87. Irācakōpala Piḷḷai, Ed. *Ajapākalpam* is a compendium of five manuscripts gathered from the Adyar Manuscripts Library and Madras Oriental Library. He has listed the texts in his Introduction.
88. See Mukhopadhyaya, Govinda Gopāl, *'Ajapārahasyam'* in *Sarasvatī Suṣamā*, Vārāṇasī Sanskrit University journal, Śrāvaṇa 2022, where he refers to two kinds of *ajāpā* - *jāgrat* (conscious) and *ajāgrat* (unconscious). He cites Ātmānanda Sarasvatī who says that only those who are conscious realise that the universal rhythm of life is an unfolding of Śiva's desire to manifest into the many. The unenlightened do not realise this and therefore remain in the ignorant bondage of the empirical world.
89. This figure 21,600 is mentioned in several works, such as *Puraścaraikārṇava* 494.16. entitled *Ajapāsaṁkalpa Bālārcanapaddhati* 493.9. *Tantrarāja* Ch. 27, Bhāskararāya's *Navaratnamālāmañjūṣā* (an unpublished manuscript kindly brought to my attention by Paṇḍit Vaṭuknath Śāstrī, a disciple of the Bhāskararāya *paramparā*), *Dakṣiṇāmūrti Saṁitā Brahma Upadeśa* (Mss. No. B 7098, sup. 4486, Tanjore Saraswati Mahal Library) and Nirbhaya Das's *Gītagōvinda*. The last mentioned work is presumably a modern work in Hindi. A translation of this work with no more bibliographical details is published in *Suṣamā*. See note 88x above.
90. *Ibid., nyāsavidhi*. See also *Ajapā gāyatrī*, Saraswati Mahal Mss. No. D 15543-6904 where the *nyāsa* is equated with letters of the alphabet and introspective worship (*mānasa pūjā*). D 15540-6905 has minor variations.
91. For the lyrics see Iranka Rāmānuja Ayyaṅkār, Ed., *Śrī Kirutimaṇimālai*
92. See Raghavan, V., *Muttusvāmi-racita-kavyam* and the same author's Introduction to Vol. IV. of Irācakōpāla Piḷḷai, Ed., *Tiyākarācalīlaikaḷ*.
93. The three terms *sat, cit* and *ānanda* occurring together and referring to the nature of Brahman, though commonly attributed to Śaṅkara, was certainly used only in post-Śaṅkara literature and from then on became a standard form for Brahman.
94. See Gonda, J., *The Triad in Hinduism.*

95. See Bibliography for references to modern compositions. Most of the references are from J.R. Marr, *Tami<u>l</u> Catalogue of India Office Library* (in progress). The catalogue has cross references to gods, goddesses, sites, etc.

Chapter Six

RELIGIOUS SYNTHESIS—THE PATTERN, THE PROCESS AND THE AGENTS: A STUDY OF THE TYĀGARĀJA CULT IN THE TAMIḺ ŚAIVA CONTEXT

The Tyāgarāja Cult was, as we have seen in the previous chapter, a synthesis of several streams of thought. The specific iconology of the cult has been studied in the last chapter. Since several of the ideas that merged into the Tyāgarāja concept were not exclusive prerogatives of this cult but formed the general components of the Tamiḻ Śaiva faith as well, it will be necessary to place the Tyāgarāja ideology within the general context.

As temples and temple cults along with *maṭhas* or monasteries provided the main channels through which diverse attitudes were accommodated, a study of a regional cult like the Tyāgarāja not only enables one to identify the various strands, but also helps in understanding the manner in which they were allowed to coexist under an institutional umbrella. Some specific episodes like the Cōmācimāṟaṉār episode, are associated with the Tyāgarāja in a very special manner and have considerable significance.

Literary and epigraphic data form the basic source material for this study and attempts have been made to arrange them in as chronological a manner as possible.

The main schools of thought that shaped the tenets of this cult, as of most other Śaiva temple cults, were Vedic, Āgamic, Tāntric, or Nigamic, Yogic and Siddhāntic which were all fused together to be included in the general *Śaiva-smārta* framework. Each of these and the impact it had on the cult and on the system will be studied separately.

Vedic

To this day the reciting of the Vedas, the performance of *homa* rites, the chanting of the *Puruṣa-Sūktam*, (RV. 10. 90. 1-16), *Śrī-Sūktam*, *Rudra-camakam*, (*Rudram-Kṛṣṇa Yajur Veda*, *Tait. Saṁ*. IV. 5 *Camakam- Kṛṣṇa Yajur Veda Taitt. Saṁ*. IV.7) etc., are a part of the rites of temple worship.

Every day and at all special temple services verses from the four Vedas are chanted. The Vedic priests perform all the *homa* (sacrifice) rites and they chant from the *ardhamaṇṭapa*, i.e. the hall outside the *garbhagṛha*. They are not allowed inside the *garbhagṛha*, the right of entry being reserved only for the Śaiva *kurukkaḷ*. The latter are Ādi Śaiva Brāhmaṇas who have received *Śaiva Dīkṣā*. These *Dīkṣās*, or initiation-rites, belong to the Āgamic tradition. The much-revered *sannyāsins* or recluses and monks are normally allowed to worship only from the *mukhamaṇṭapa*. Exceptions to this rule are in temples like Kāñcī, where the worship is done by the pontiff of the Śankara *maṭha*. Thus the two traditions, Vedic and Āgamic, though blended, are still separable into two realms. The philosophical realm of the *nirguṇa Brahman* with *sannyāsa* as an ideal model belongs predominantly to the Vedic conceptual archetype, while the world-affirming and icon-worshipping religion of the temples has a different set of paradigms. In the temple 'this-worldly' aspects are generally emphasised and the *kurukkaḷ* aids in the general well being of the realm and the monarch. In that sense he is hierarchically superior to the Vedic priest who sits at the *ardhamaṇṭapa* and chants hymns from the Vedas and performs the *homa* and looks after the 'higher', spiritual planes. This is so only within the temple.

Apart from acting, so to speak, as complementary and somewhat subsidiary to priests in temples, the Vedic scholars seem to have had the major job of teaching and performing the Vedic sacrifices in their own houses. *Bhaṭṭavṛttis* or specific honorariums to teach Vedas and other allied subjects were regularly recorded in Pallava and Cōḻa epigraphs.[1] The more general endowments of lands to Brāhmaṇas were variously called *brahmadeya*, *caturvedimaṅgalam* and *agrahāram*[2] and were held in communal ownership. Making such endowments was regarded as the moral duty of the king. Individual donors vied with royal patrons to provide for the feeding of the Brāhmaṇas well versed in the Vedas. The hierarchic status of the *kurukkaḷ vis a vis* that of the *Vaidikas* has been studied by Fuller in the context of the Madurai temple.[3] The *Periya Purāṇam* refers to schools where Vedas were taught as *Kiṭai* (*maṟai payilum Kiṭai*).[4]

In the *Tēvāram* literature, to which period one can trace the genesis of the Tyāgarāja cult, several references are made to the

Vedas which are collectively called *maṟai* in Tamiḻ. Śiva is often described as the spirit of the Vedas (*kuṟaiya maṟaiyam...pirān)*[5] and as the essence of the Vedas (*Arumaṟai pporūḷē*),[6] as the teacher of the Vedas (*ceḻumaṟai pakarnta paṭṭaṉe*)[7] or as the expert reciter of the Vedas (*tiruntanāṉmaṟai pāṭavallāṉ*).[8]

The word Veda in its Sanskrit form is also used: e.g. *Vedattin poruḷāṉāy*, 'you became the substance of the Vedas' (VII. 86.1.) or *Veda mutalāṉāy*, 'you became the first among the Vedas' (VII. 40.10) or simply by referring to Śiva as the *vedin* or *Maṟaiyaṉ* or *Maṟaiyavaṉ*. Campantar has several references to this Vedic association of Śiva. Vedic rites are approvingly commented upon and the Vedic scholars are called 'blessed' (*puṇṇiya nāṉ maṟaiyōr*).[9] The *Periya Purāṇam* also refers to god as the object of the Vedas (e.g.v. 141). Thus, at the time when the Tyāgarāja cult was evolved, i.e. around the 7th century a.d., the traditional Tamiḻ attitude of respect for Vedic study and its upholders, the Brāhmaṇas, was maintained and incorporated into temple worship both directly and indirectly through invocations such as those mentioned above. This respect is expressed in several early works such as *Kalittokai* (v. 52). *Tolkāppiyam* (*Poruḷ*, 26; *Akat.* 125)[10] etc. The six main functions of the Brāhmaṇas according to Nacciṉārkkiṉiyar, who commented on the *Tolkāppiyam (Cūttiram* 27) are:

1) The study of the Vedas,
2) Teaching of the Vedas,
3) Performing sacrifices for themselves and
4) for others,
5) making gifts and
6) receiving gifts.

Ñāṉacampantar speaks in a derogatory manner of the Jains because they condemned *inter alia* the Vedas and Vedāṅgas (*Vēta vēḷviyai nintaṉai ceytalāl*).[11] He goes so far as to say that they are the great sinners who do not observe the Vedic practices.[12] Appar says in a more neutral manner that the Vedas are for the Brāhmaṇas while the *pañcākṣara* is for the other Śaivas.[13] This is a significant statement inasmuch as Appar, unlike the other two *Tēvāram* hymnists, was a Veḷḷāḷa and also because the dance of the Tyāgarāja and Naṭarāja are regarded as the *pañcākṣaranaṭaṉam* and so, by this definition of Appar, the *Pañcākṣara* ought to have been a purely egalitarian cult. On this point more will be said in the next chapter. Suffice it to say that if Tyāgarāja was viewed as the model *Vedin* then there was a sharp dichotomy inherent in the cult as the vast majority of the populace were not allowed to read the Vedas nor even to learn Sanskrit, and bhakti, which at one level was an attempt to transcend such limitations, seems at another to have strengthened them.

The *Mucukundasahasranāmam* (v. 865) invokes Tyāgarāja as "the only expert in the path of the *Vedas*" (*Vedamārgaikanipuṇāya*) and "one immersed in the ways of the Vedas" (*vaidikācārasaṁpannāya*) (v. 867). The *Śrī Sundaramūrti aṣṭōttara śata nāmāvali* invokes Tyāgarāja (104, 105) as *Vedaśāstraviśārada* (expert in the knowledge of the Vedas) and *vaidikācārasaṁpanna*, a term referred to above. The *Tyāgarājanāmāvali* (760) invokes him as '*Vedapravaṇa*', (761) '*Vedaguhya*', the personification of the esoteric wisdom of the Vedas, '*Vedavid*', or expert in the Vedas and simply as '*vedin*'. The *Tyāgarāja aṣṭakam* describes him as *Vedaśekhara*, *Vedaturaṅga*, etc. Cuntarar in his famous *Tiruttoṇṭatokai*, v. 11, addresses Tyāgarāja, i.e. Ārūraṉ, as *maṟaināvaṉ*, one whose speech (literally tongue) is the Veda. Only Tirumular limits the validity of the Vedas with the statement that only the worshippers of Śiva could qualify for real knowledge, (vv. 80-83.)

Thus, the religion of the *nāyaṉmār* was in no way a revolt against Vedic beliefs, which were accepted as the basis of spiritual life. The very nature of Vedic faith made it elitist, for not everyone could perform Vedic rituals. However, the *nāyaṉmār* at the same time were insisting that the individual by means of sublime faith or *bhakti* could attain the Divine. Their modality of action, as pointed out by Ishwaran, was "temple building and Sanskritisation" but they also created a "Tamiḻ linguistic consciousness" cutting across political divisions.[14] More will be said of this later.

The Āgamas

The Āgamas were a little more inclusive than the Vedas. They were a body of literature respected by the *nāyaṉmār*. The close relationship between Āgama and Śiva is mentioned several times. Campantar addresses Śiva as *Āgamacelvar*[15], 'expert in Āgamas or the wealth of the Āgamas'. He explains in a hymn why Dakṣa's sacrifice was destroyed by Śiva. It was because Dakṣa did not know the Tantras and so did not know how to worship Śiva (*Tantiram aṟiyā Takkaṉ*, IV. 65.5.). Strictly speaking the word *Tantra* is used for Śākta literature and Āgama for Śaiva but they are quite often interchanged. Tirumūlar regards the Āgamas as authoritative scripture but in him one sees a conflict between Brāhmaṇas and Śaivas.[16]

The Pallava king Narasiṁhavarman II proudly assumed titles such as *Āgamapramāṇa* and *Āgamaśīla* testifying to his expertise in the Āgamas. Appar uses the term *nūl vaḻi, uraicei nūl vaḻi* and *niyamaneṟi* to describe the path of the *Āgamas*. Campantar uses the Sanskrit word *Āgama* often besides using terms such as *āyntanaṟkalvi* and *nūl vaḻi*. Parameśvaravarman I, while recording an endowment of land mentions the complete sequence of worship as enjoined in the Āgamas such as *pūjā, snapāna, kusuma, gandha, dhūpa, dīpa, havis, upahāra, bali, śaṅkha, patākā*, etc.[17]

The reason for this long digression on the mention of the Āgamas by the *nāyaṉmār* is two-fold. Firstly, they were closely connected with temples and temple cults and all three of them have sung on the Tyāgarāja cult centres. Apart from that the Āgamas, from the above evidence were definitely known in Tamiḻnāḍu by the 7th century A.D. and the Pallava rulers patronised the Āgamic faith. Lastly, the rites and rituals of the Tiruvārūr and other Tyāgarāja temples, the performance of which are crucial to the cult, were based as all temple rites are, on the Āgamas.

There are six daily rites in the Tiruvārūr temple. The first or *Tiruvaṉantal* begins with the Cokkanātar (the symbolic feet of Tyāgarāja, made of silver) being brought from the chamber of Nīlōtpalāmpāḷ (where he is taken the previous night), to his own shrine. Milk-offerings are then made to Tyāgarāja and the *prasāda* is distributed to the devotees assembled. Simultaneously, an offering of lights (*dīparātaṉai*) is made to the Valmīkanātha.

The mid morning *kālaicanti* has the ritual ablution (*abhiṣeka*) for all the *liṅgas* and offerings to the two main deities. At twelve o'clock the *abhiṣeka* is done to the *marakata Viṭaṅkar* (the emerald linga) in the Tyāgarāja shrine. Offerings are made to the Tyāgarāja icon. It is interesting to see that no daily *abhiṣekas* are done for the Tyāgarāja. Only a fragrant paste called *puṉuku* (*Tyāgavinoda* is the Sanskrit name by which it is known) is applied, as it is for Viṣṇu icons, confirming the Vaiṣṇava substratum of Tyāgarāja beliefs. *Abhiṣeka* is particularly imperative in Śiva worship for he is regarded as *abhiṣeka priya* or one who loves ritual ablutions. Valmīkanātha, being by tradition, an anthill, no *abhiṣeka* is done for him either. This tradition is followed in Tiruvoṟṟiyūr, Tirukkōḷili and other anthill sites.

The *Cāyarakṣai* or evening service, also called the *Tiruvantikkāppu,* is the most important daily rite in this shrine. The music of the drum called *śuddha mattalam* and the wind instrument called the *pārināyaṉam* and the dances of the *tēvaraṭiyār*[18] were the highlights of the ritual and it was believed that even the gods attended the *Cāyarakṣai* in Tiruvārūr.[19] With the abolition of the Devadāsī system, it is only the *śuddha mattalam, pañcamukha vādyam* (Pl.XI) and *pārināyaṉam* that one can hear today.

The late evening *iraṇṭāṅkālam* ritual is also accompanied by *abhiṣekas* to the *marakata liṅga* (the emerald *Viṭaṅkar*) and the last rite of the day *ardhayāmam* is when Cokkanātar is brought in a palanquin to the *Palliyaṟai* (bed chamber) and after the *ūñcalāṭṭu* rite of swinging the icons the temple gates are closed for the night. Standard Āgamic rites are followed in all the temples with minor local variations.

The annual rites for Tyāgarāja include *Aippaci, Viṣu puṇyakāla, Mārkaḻi Tiruvātirai, paṅkuṉi uttiram* and *Tai Saṅkrānti.*

The *Paṅkuṉi utsavam* (March-April) is the Brahmotsavam and is celebrated with all Āgamic injunctions. It was the call of this *utsava* that brought Cuntarar to Tiruvārūr from Tiruvoṟṟiyūr. The Mārkaḻi Tiruviḷā festival is the theme of a *patikam* of Appar sung to Campantar which brought both of them to Tiruvārūr. The two special *arccaṉai* or invocation rites for Tyāgarāja are the Mucukunda and the Mukunda *sahasranāmams.* These two, particularly the former, shed important light on the belief-system of this cult. The *Mukundasahasranāmam* has not yet been published and the present author is still in the stage of transcribing the liturgical incantations. Suffice it to say at this juncture that this incantation reveals even more clearly the Vaiṣṇava substratum of the cult, for above all Mukunda is another name of Viṣṇu.

Having seen how both the Vedas and the Āgamas were observed by the temples dedicated to the Tyāgarāja cult it is imperative to see the basic differences between the Vedas and the Āgamas.

In the philosophical plane, the Vedas, more precisely the *Vedānta*, relies exclusively on soteriological knowledge: knowledge is *sui generis*, it is salvation. In the Āgamas, *will* is accepted as more fundamental than *Knowledge*. In the Vedas the Real and the Unreal are distinctly separated. The Āgamas do not regard anything as unreal, though the *Trika* system of Kashmir Śaivism based on Āgamas interprets Reality on the more Vedantic assumptions of regarding the world as a reflection of Śiva. *Śivādvaita* developed on both Vedic and Āgamic patterns.

On a ritualistic plane the Vedic rituals are in the nature of sacrifices to the gods, while the Āgamas worship the iconic forms. The Vedic altar needs no shrines, no images. The Āgamic emphasis is on *pūjā*, or worship not on sacrifice or *yajña*. Some schools of Vedic thought may be non-theistic, while theism is a prerequisite for Āgamic religion. The Āgamic God, by the very fact of his being enshrined, is pinned to a particular locale and assumes the character of a territorial deity.

Yantras and other symbols such as *mudrās* play an important part in Āgamic rituals while the Vedas have no place for such practices. Yoga is the *modus operandi* predominantly of Āgamic thought. The worship of Śakti, very much a part of Āgamic philosophy and much elaborated by the Tantras was not a part of Vedic thought. In a sociological sense the Vedas were more exclusive and reserved for only the upper *varṇas*, while the Āgamas with their more egalitarian *Dīkṣā* or initiation rites had an allotted ritual place, even if hierarchic, for most members of the religious community.

Despite such major variances, the theologians have tried to reconcile the two. Tirumūlar in his *Tirumantiram* regarded both as integral (*Tirumantiram* v. 2397). Tāyumāṉavar expresses the same idea through a metaphor: he likens the Vedas to a path and the Āgamas to a horse.

Both the Vedas and Āgamas are regarded as divine revelations. There are twenty-eight Śivāgamas and each is divided into four parts, the first, *caryā*, lays down rites for *pūjā*; the second, *kriyā*, dwells on the different kinds of initiations, the "dos" and "dont's" of temple building, *liṅga* making, icon making, chariot making, the right time, place, etc., for such activities. The third or *yōgapāda* concentrates on yoga. The last section or the *jñānapāda* refers to the metaphysical postulates which are an exposition largely of *Śaiva Siddhānta* with its categories of *pati, paśu* and *pāśa*, the Lord, the individual soul and the bondage, terms to be presently discussed. The Āgamas claim to presuppose and indeed to transcreate the Veda as independent revelations. Thus, we get in the *Civañāṉacittiyār* (VII. 15) that the Vedas are general and meant for those of the world while the Āgamas are special and revealed for the benefit of the *Śaktinipātas* or worshippers of Śakti and they contain truths not found in the Vedas and hence, while all other books are *pūrvapakṣa* the Śaivāgamas alone are *Siddhāntas* or complete works. There are Āgamas which belong to the heterodox *Kaula* tradition as well.

Some later works such as those of Appayyā Dīkṣitar question the belief that the Vedas and Āgamas are the same. He cites many passages from the *Mahābhārata* and the *Purāṇas* to refute the view of Śrīkaṇṭha that Āgamic traditions were the same as Vedic. The Āgamic literature is characterised by him as pseudo-scripture (*moha śāstra*) in his commentary on *Śrīkaṇṭhabhāṣya* (2.2.42), and as a conspiracy of the Grace of Śiva and Viṣṇu directed against the Vedic path (*Brahmasūtra* 2.2.42).

That there was a certain tension between the Vedas and Āgamas becomes clear on reading works like the *Vāstuśāstra Upaniṣad* attributed to Pippalāda, who is also believed to have written the *Praśnopaniṣad*. The author is very categorical and assertive about image worship. His tone implies that he is defending his views in the face of a controversy. He refers to the icon maker (*sthāpaka*) as *Śilpahotṛ* and *Vāstuhotṛ* and the Vedic priest who questions him addresses him reverentially as *Vāstukarmāṅgāvātāra* and *Ṣoḍasakalāpuruṣa* or perfect in the 16 arts. It is interesting that a work on art should be called an *Upaniṣad* and as stated by the editor Alice Boner it is the first text on *Śilpa* to be called an *Upaniṣad*. It tries to reconcile Vedāntic metaphysics with Āgamic concepts of the sacred form. The terms *prāṇa* and *rāyī* are used in the text. The former term has been discussed in the previous chapter; the latter i.e. *rāyī* has been used in the sense of "crystallisation of this life force into sensible elements, primordial materialisation, the first product having form in which the working of *prāṇa* is apprehended, realized and reflected".[20]

The Āgamic speculations on the world of sound and its evolution have already been discussed at length in the context of Tyāgarāja metaphysics, where it was seen how much the philosophical categories of the cult were drawn on Āgamic assumptions. The bridge lies in regarding form, like *vāk*, "as the creative word and its means of expression as equivalent to written or spoken word".

The ritual section of the Āgamas decrees that entry into the *sanctum sanctorum* is the prerogative of the *Ādiśaivas* (*kurukkaḷ*) who are Brāhmaṇas initiated into the Śaiva faith. The temple, as upholder of this directive, was faced with several problems, which were of a sociological nature, and hence will be taken up for discussion in the next chapter.

Tiruvārūr has been described in most of the works including late 16th century works such as the *Tiruvārūrkkōvai* as the land where the sound of the Vedas and Āgamas constantly echoed (v. 135 and 43). The Thañjāvūr district is to this day a strong bastion of both Vedic and Āgamic traditions.

The Bhakti Movement

Chronologically the next movement which largely shaped the Tyāgarāja cult was the religion of the *nāyaṉmār*, popularly called the *bhakti* movement.[21] This movement was particularly powerful in the period between the 7th and 9th centuries a.d. After Cuntarar the *bhakti* movement lost much of its freshness. Individual followers were there to carry on the tradition but it had certainly lost its momentum. Three distinct modes of *bhakti* are visible on a close scrutiny of the hymns. One expresses an attitude of humble adoration as seen in the hymns of Appar and called *dāsa mārga*, the second an intellectual and personal approach of Campantar characterised as *putra mārga* with an accent on filial piety associated with the relationship of a son to his father and lastly the absolute familiarity between two friends (*sakhāmārga*) as exemplified in the behaviour of Cuntarar. These three paths are discussed by Tirumūlar.[22] Several *nāyaṉmār* are connected with the Tyāgarāja cult centres.

The salient features of this movement are its tremendous and unquestioning faith, its untiring evangelical zeal, its feeling of *communitas vis a vis* the Śaiva *aṭiyār*[23] and correspondingly its bigoted despising of the faith of the Jains and the Buddhists.[24] The relationship between God and the devotee is direct and intense and hence transcends all intellectualisation or ritual communication. It was a romantic movement expressed through powerful

Tamil̲ lyrics, thereby providing itself with its own distinct personality. It is in this mood of intense devotion that Tirumūlar exhorts the devotees to

> "abandon the reading of the *śāstras*
> Look within for a second, with firm and steadfast gaze
> The fetters of rebirth will fast be removed."[25]

Or again in the same vein Appar says "What use are these discussions on the dogmas, these *stotras* and hymns of praise? Know that Śiva is the saviour and you are saved".[26] The feeling of *communitas* finds expression in Appar when he says "Though they suffer from leprosy, though they are *pulaiyas* who eat beef, if they are Śaiva devotees they are gods we worship".[27]

On the purely ethical level the Tamil̲ bhakti movement adopts an almost antinomian stance. Though none of the *nāyan̲mār* explicitly related to the Tyāgarāja cult expresse the extreme forms of behaviour such as, for exmple, attributed to the *bhairava* in *Cir̲uttoṇṭa nāyanār Purāṇam,* nevertheless forms of behaviour which would be considered horrendous in the normal walk of life are attributed to some of the saints connected with this cult. Cer̲uttuṅai and Kal̲ar̲ciṅkar are associated with the Ar̲aner̲i shrine at Tiruvārūr. Cer̲uttuṇai, in a pique of rage cuts off the nose of the queen for having sniffed at a flower to be offered to the deity. On hearing of the sacrilegious act Kal̲ar̲ciṅkar adds his share of punishment on the unfortunate woman and cuts off one of her hands as well.[28]

Taṇṭiyaṭikaḷ, mocked by the Jains has his revenge on them, after being miraculously aided by Śiva. The blind *aṭiyār* recovers his sight while the Jainas lose theirs. Here, at least an element of poetic justice is introduced inasmuch as the Jainas are said to have tormented the blind *aṭiyār* earlier on in the myth.[29] Naminanti drives out the Jains after performing the miracle of lighting the temple lamps with water and hence winning the bet.[30] Appar approvingly refers to this myth in a hymn on Tiruvārūr (4.102.2). As for the enigmatic Cōmācimār̲an̲ār, more will be said in connection with the *kaula* faith.

On a more palpable level, the *bhakti* protagonists emphasised pilgrimages, wearing of the sacred ash, pronouncing the sacred five syllables (*na, ma, śi, vā,* and *ya*) and singing in an ecstatic spirit of surrender to the will of God. Typical of this spirit of melting devotion is the song of Māṇikkavācakar:

> "Oh to sink in bliss
> Mingling forever, mingling with thy grace
> melting and with soul pulsating in rhythmic dance
> in grace grant the bliss of sweet union.
> Myself, mine I know no more
> Day and night's recurrence I know not
> Thou art my all, my comfort thou
> My trepidations thou
> my good and evil thou art
> None other have I"[31]

Thus, at first glance, it seems that the religion of the *nāyaṉmār* fostered an ectypal behaviour pattern, flouting the rules of institutionalised religion and orthodox framework with their paraphernalia of priesthood, mantra chants and learned scriptures. The emphasis seems to have been on intuitive faith. Poet saints from various castes gathered at Tiruvārūr and spread the message throughout the region now called Tamilnāḍu.

However, during the Pallava and Cōḻa period the theologians carefully developed the cult of *bhakti* into a bond of synthesis of Vedic and Epic theology and Purāṇic mythology by channelling its influence on heterodoxy, to serve their own cause, and tended in course of time to merge it into the orthodox fold. "Bhakti became a vehicle for the socialisation of cultural values".[32] Thus, the social effects of the teachings of the *nāyaṉmār* was quite limited when considering Tamiḻ society at large, but amongst the saints themselves few caste restrictions were observed. Thus Nantanār's life is full of discrepancies between his earthly life as a *paṟaiyaṉ* and the purity of his heart and intensity of his devotion to the Lord Śiva. Even in death Nantanār could not escape his position as a *Paṟaiyaṉ*. It was when a new body was given to him that he could enter the temple.

The synthesis was so complete on the emotional plane that with total disregard for logical formulation it could be said that "The *Veda* is the cow, its milk is the true Āgama, the Tamiḻ sung by the four is the *ghee* extracted from it and the purity of the work of Meykaṇṭār is the fine taste of the ghee".[33]

The Tyāgarāja cult was intimately connected with the cult of the *nāyaṉmār* and in fact Cuntarar was almost the *alter ego* of Tyāgarāja[34] much in the same way as the Pāṇṭiyaṉ princess Taṭātakai was the *alter ego* of Mīnākṣī of Madurai. Cuntarar instituted or rather gave an official format to the existing cult of the *bhaktas* whereby the community of Śiva worshippers were collectively sanctified. The *Tiruttoṇṭattokai* with its refrain "*aṭiyārkkum aṭiyēṉ*"[35] (I am the slave of the slaves) became the central affirmation of the Śaiva saints, providing the psychological framework for the institutionalising of the movement.

In fact the spread of the cult into Tiruvoṟṟiyūr and its environs seems to have been because of this saint. The most popular episodes in the 'life' of the deity at Tiruvoṟṟiyūr are connected with his cheating Cuntarar and making him take a vow that he would never part from his wife Caṅkili and hence leave Tiruvoṟṟiyūr. The narrative is full of tricks and countertricks played between the deity and his devotee. The focal point of the myth is its strong emphasis on the territoriality of the deity. Cuntarar vows not to leave Tiruvoṟṟiyūr and when he breaks his promise, he becomes blind. The Lord of Tiruvoṟṟiyūr and Tiruvārūr are one and the same at one level of religious experience but on the other level of pilgrim tradition the Lord of Tiruvoṟṟiyūr is affronted because Cuntarar abandons him and goes back to Tiruvārūr.[36] This event is celebrated to this day in the Tyāgarāja temple at Tiruvoṟṟiyūr. The *Periya Purāṇam* attributes a semi-divine status to Cuntarar and thus, by the 12th century A.D. itself, Cuntarar was not only canonised but deified as the principal figure in the propagation of the cult of Ārūraṉ. (Tyāgarāja, Lord of Ārūr)

The *Mucukundasahasranāmam*, the special liturgy for Tyāgarāja, refers several times to the close link between Tyāgarāja and the *nāyaṉmār*, particularly Cuntarar, in 19 verses (253-271) and gives a great deal of biographical data on the life of Cuntarar. Tyāgarāja is said to be specially pleased with the twenty-one Drāviḍa (Tamiḻ) songs. The number twenty-one is interesting for it refers to the hymns of Appar, who has composed twenty-two on Tiruvārūr, but one on the Aṟaneṟi shrine and hence only twenty-one were composed on Valmīkanātha-Tyāgarāja, i.e. on the Mūlattāṉar (the liṅga) and the Ārūraṉ (Tyāgarāja).[37]

Tyāgarāja not only has a special partiality for Cuntarar but also for Paravai, in whose song he is said to delight.[38] The role of the deity as the messenger between Cuntarar and Paravai is faithfully echoed in an invocation where the deity is addressed as *Parava dautya kovidāya*.[39] Ñāṉacampantar and Māṇikkavācakar (vv. 264 and 265) are also referred to, and the deity is said to rejoice in their lyrics. It refers among the other *nāyaṉmār* to the steadfast devotion of Viraṉmīṇṭar (called Vīramuṇḍa)[40] and to the strange episode in the life of Somayājimāṟaṉar, (Tamiḻ Cōmācimāṟaṉār) to be discussed in the concluding section of this chapter.

Epigraphical evidence also points to the cult of the *nāyaṉmār* in several temples of Tamiḻnāḍu. Tiruvārūr and Thañjāvūr have the icon of Cuntaramurtināyaṉār facing the Tyāgarāja icon (see Pl. XV) Epigraphs found at the *sapta viṭaṅka kṣetras* and other Tyāgarāja shrines have several references to the images of *nāyaṉmār*, the singing of the *Tēvāram*, etc. An inscription refers to the *Śrī-Purānam*[41] of Āḷuṭaiyanampi being recited in the temple at Tiruvoṟṟiyūr in the presence of the king Rājādhirāja II. This work, we are told was read aloud as an accompaniment to a procession in which the deity was taken from the *sanctum sanctorum* and placed under the *makiḻam* tree. This is an enactment of the crucial episode in Cuntarar's life referred to above.

Interestingly enough, an inscription of Rājādhirāja from Tiruvoṟṟiyūr refers to a service and lighting of lamps before Mānikkavācakar, who is described as chief of the *āṇṭār* and depicted with folded hands. The interest lies in the fact that very few references to Māṇikkavācakar are found in inscriptions. Installation of the images of the 63 *nāyaṉmār* in Tiruvārūr and Tiruvoṟṟiyūr and the instituting of their worship seems to have been known from fairly early times, for as early as the 10th century an inscription from Tiruvoṟṟiyūr refers to the singing of the *Tēvāram*.[42] It has since then been a continuous tradition. It is to this period that the Sanskrit-Tamiḻ synthesis must be traced. It is a ritual imperative in Tamiḻnāḍu Śaiva temples that both the Sanskrit *arccaṉai* and the Tamiḻ *Tēvāram* be simultaneously recited before the deity at important services for the day.

Thus, whereas Jainism and Buddhism challenged the orthodoxy, the *bhakti* movement of the *nāyaṉmār* and *āḻvār*, though apparently ectypal, was simply cathecting the normative symbols of traditional religion. All ritual symbols have, as pointed out by Turner, both a 'normative' and an 'orectic' component - the former with stated norms, ideals and values - the latter with cathecting these ideals.[43] The cult of the *nāyaṉmār* was institutionalised and thus the main stream of tradition was left untouched.

The Tāntric School

The primary focus of the *bhakti* religion was Śiva, but considerable importance was given to Śakti. The hymns were always addressed to Śiva, with Śakti by his side or with Śakti as part of him. Expressions such as *Umaipaṅkan, Umaipākaṉ, peṇ āṇ āya pirāṉ, maṅkai orupṉkaṉ,* denoting her constant presence are used in almost all the hymns. Cuntarar is deeply moved to see Śiva alone at a place called Kōṭi and he repeatedly questions him as to why he is alone. The pain is reflected in the questions *"Yēṉtāṉ taṉiyē iruntāyē empirāṉē", 'ettāl taṉiyē iruntāy empirāṉē?*[44]

Thus the *bhakti* cult, much like the *Trika* system of Kashmir, was already a bridge between Śaivism and Śāktism. The development of Śrī-Vidyā in the Tyāgarāja cult was therefore a logical continuation of a thought-process. The Āgaṃas cater to the needs of three major divisions, of Śaivism, viz. *Vāma* (including *Kāpālika, Kālāmukha* etc.), *Dakṣiṇa* (Kashmir Śaivism) and *Śaivasiddhānta* with its claim to the twenty-eight Āgamas. So the development of *Śrī-Vidyā* can be traced from Āgamic thought which had been further synthesised with *kuṇḍalinī yoga,* and a more complex scheme of mantras and *sādhana*. The *Śrī-Vidyā* mantra, of which the *pañcadaśī* is regarded as most effective, is divided into three parts or *kūṭas* as follows:

ka ye yī la hrīm
ha sa ka ha la hrīm
sa ka la hrīm.

Each of these syllables symbolises a Śrī-Vidyā postulate[45] to the devotee. The *Śrī-cakra* is the paramount *yantra*[46] and the sacred scriptures are the *tantras*. The guru's role is much emphasised.

One of the traditional preceptors of this School is the sage Durvāsa. He is also regarded as the preceptor of the *Trika* system of Kashmir as well as the *goḷaki maṭha,* of which we shall have more to say presently. Durvāsa figures prominently in the Tiruvārūr oral traditions. The Śivācāryas of this temple are called *nāyiṉārs* and they claim this title from Durvāsa who as the *krodhabhaṭṭāraka* (the angry one) was capable of destroying people with a look (nayana). An image of Durvāsa is enshrined in the Paravaiuṇ maṇṭaḷi shrine in the Tyāgarāja complex.

Cuntarar addresses a hymn to Turvāya (Tamiḻ for Durvāsa) before this shrine. A Durvasa shrine was walled in because of the fears of the people that his displeasure was the cause of some of the tragedies in the town. The *periya maṭham*[47] was believed to have been a Durvāsa *maṭham*. This tradition finds confirmation in the legends inscribed as labels under the murals in the Tiruvārūr temple. There the equation is made explicit. (See Pl.XII)

The *Mucukundasahasranāmam*, which is a treasure house of traditions regarding the Tyāgarāja cult refers to Durvāsa several times. In invocation 357, it groups Durvāsa in the same category as Mucukunda, the founder of the Tyāgarāja cult and says that the shrine was established by Mucukunda and Durvāsa. In v. 358 it refers to the Āgama *pūjā* instituted by Durvāsa. It further specifies that the Āgamas were *Svatantra Āgamas*, a term which generally refers to Āgamas like the Rudra Yāmala etc. belonging to the Bhairava tradition favoured by the Śāktas. In the *Tyāgarāja aṣṭakam* Tyāgarāja is addressed as *kopajanmānipūjita* (worshipped by the 'born-angry', i.e. Durvāsa).

That this Tāntric faith was both of the orthodox and unorthodox variety has been remarked earlier. A sculpture depicting *yoni pūjā* is carved on a pillar on a *maṇṭapa* adjoining the Tyāgarāja shrine. (Pl.XIII) This is not a unique example. Other such examples have come from Bheraghat in Madhya Pradesh[48] and Tārācuram[49] in Thañjāvūr district.

While the *nāyaṉmār* movement with its emphasis on Tamiḻ and *bhakti* and its apparent disregard for the orthodox trimmings of religion was easily assimilated into the Vedic Āgamic fold there were other trends in the Śaivite faith which proved a little less easy to accommodate. To this class would belong the following schools: *Kāpālikas, Kālamukhas, Somasiddhāntins, Mahāvratins, Māheśvaras* and their Sacred Networks.

The Kāpālikas, Kālamukhas, Pāśupatas and Sacred Networks

The Tyāgarāja cult and the temples belonging to this cult were strong centres at one time or the other of most of the above-mentioned sects. A *maṭha* which finds frequent mention in the epigraphs of the temples connected with this cult is the *Golaki maṭha* also called *Bhikṣā maṭha* which was, as we shall presently see, a Pāśupata *maṭha*. It must, however, be reiterated that none of these sects or *maṭha* connections were exclusive to the Tyāgarāja cult. These networks were shared with other Śaiva temple complexes subscribing to similar eclectic notions.

That Tiruvārūr was a centre of several of these sects is made clear in a hymn by Appar where he refers to the *māvratis* (*mahāvratis*), *antaṇar* (Brāhmaṇas), *Śaivas*, *Pāśupatas*, *Kāpālikas* and others as worshipping the Lord of Ārūr. In the inscriptions the two name *mahāvrati* and *kālamukha* occur, particularly the former, which occurs several times in the epigraphs from Tiruvārūr and Tiruvoṟṟiyūr. The God of Tiruvoṟṟiyūr is called *Kāraṇai Viṭaṅkar*, much in the same manner as the Lord of Kumbhakonam is called Kuṭantaikkārōṇam in the *Periya Purāṇam* (1556, 2364, 3810, 3831, 3832, etc.) and the *Tēvāram* (Campantar called it either Kārōṇam or Kuṭantaikkārōṇam) and the Lord of Nāgapaṭṭaṇam is called Nākaikkārōṇam. The word *kārōṇam* is an abbreviation of *kāyārohaṇa*, which is a term used in Pāśupata literature to mean the ascent of Lakulīsa Kāyā=body; ārohan-to rise to the body of Śiva. Lakulīsa is a founder of one of the Pāśupata sects. The *Tēvāram* hymnists clearly allude to the deities of these places as *kāyārohaṇa* or *kārōṇa*. Other important Pāśupata centres in Tamiḻnāḍu were Kāñcī, Mayilāpur and Koṭumpālūr. Rudra Paśupati Nāyaṉār, a Pāśupata, according to the *Periya Purāṇam*, stood up to his neck in a pond and recited the *Rudra mantra* (vv. 1035-38).

The term *mahāvrati* or *mahāvratikaḷ* is also of frequent occurrence, both in epigraphs and literature. The physical appearance of a *mahāvartin* is provided in the *Mānakkañcāranāyaṉār Purāṇam*. He wears three stripes of sacred ash, hair clip of bones, beads of bones, and a cluster of hair as his sacred thread. He further wears a *yogapaṭṭikā* (a belt that is normally used to support a yogī, when he sits in meditation) on his shoulder and a loin-cloth with a small piece hanging loose (vv. 886-891).

In addition to these terms the Tiruvoṟṟiyūr epigraph gives the name of a sect called the *Somasiddhāntin* while an inscription from Tiruvārūr refers to *Maheśvara* as well. It is interesting to take these terms one by one and note their significance in the development of Śaiva theology in Tamiḻnāḍu as propagated through the institution of temples and temple cults.

Mahāvratins

The ancient lexicons *Tivākaram* and *Cūṭāmaṇi* group the *māviratiṉs* (Tam. for *mahāvratin*) with *pairava* (Tam. for *Bhairava*), *Vāma*, *kālamukaṉ* (Tam. for *Kālamukha,*) *Pāśupata* and *Śaiva*. They are grouped under the heterodox orders *'Uṭcamayam'*. Tirumūlar mentions *Pāśupata, Kāpālika, Bhairava, Mahāvrati* and *Vāma*.

Lorenzen, Bhandarkar, Pathak, Karmarkar[50] and other scholars have dealt at great length with these sects. As Lorenzen has ably pointed out in the introduction to his work the term sect used in the Hindu context is more a concept, and lacks the clarity of, for example, a Christian sect in its definition. It is structurally much more amorphous. The *mahāvratas* have been equated both with the *Kāpālikas* and the *Kālamukhas*. Several sources equate the *Mahāvratins* with the Kāpālikas.

Pathak, basing his opinion on some texts concludes that *Mahāvratikas* were identical with *Kāpālikas*. However, he adds, that because of certain common practices they were sometimes confused with *Kālānanas*[51] (another name for *Kālamukhas*).

Lorenzen has gone to great pains to trace sources where the *Mahāvrati* is distinguished from the *Kāpālika* and where quite often he is equated with the *Kālamukha.*[52]

Tirūmular specifically distinguishes them and in his list of sects that he mentions, the term *Kālamukha* is absent and hence, it can be inferred that he has substituted it with *Mahāvrati*. *Civañāṉacittiyār*, a 13th century commentary on the *Civañāṉapōtam* of Meykaṇṭatēvar also treats it in a similar manner. The *mahāvratis* according to him hope to attain beatitude by *caryā* (rituals) alone. Hoisington, while commenting on the *Civapirakācam* of Umāpati says that the *Mahāvrati*, Great Hermits (which is the literal translation of the expression) "have the following creed: "Souls are from eternity united with the three *malam* ... and by removing the three *malam* at the proper time by *Dīkṣā* and by cherishing great desire and acting as the excellent *śāstrin* requires they will, at the dissolution of their bodies, remain in possession of only *ñāṉacatti*. This is the *mōṭcham* of the *mahāvrati*".[53] Here "*mōṭcham*" is the Skt. *moksa*.

The *Yogasūtra* of Patañjali (II. 30-31) states that the following five categories, when practised without exception being made for status, place, time, etc., are collectively known as the great vow or *mahāvrata*. The five in question are: *ahimsā*, *satya*, *asteya* (non-theft), *brahmacarya* and *aparigraha* (non-acceptance of what is needed for more than bodily subsistence) is known as the great vow of *Mahāvrata*. Thus Patañjali gives a highly ethical colouring to the term while the earlier writer referred to above interprets it in a metaphysical and doctrinal manner.

Inscriptional references to the *Mahāvratis* of *koḍiya maṭha* at Belagave speak of the study of *yogaśāstras* and the fact that at least a branch of these *Pāśupatas* insisted on the ethical and the mystical aspects of the yoga school becomes evident when we see that Kauṇḍinya's commentary on the *Pāśupatasūtra* devotes nineteen pages to the discussion of *yamas* and *niyamas* of the yogī.

In the *śrauta* section of the Vedas, which are basically functional manuals for priests with each *sūtra* following its own *Brāhmaṇa* text, we get some very interesting description of the term *Mahāvrata* or the Great Observance. Chitrabhanu Sen in his *Vedic Index* provides the following description of the *Mahāvrata* rite: "the name of a rite, which takes place on the last but one day of the *gavāmayana sattra*. Among other usual offering of Soma cups, a *mahāvratiya* cup is offered accompanied with a *Sāman* called *Mahāvrata* (whence the name of the rite)". He describes the offering of an animal sacrifice, the unusual arrangement of the sitting plan of the officiants, the strange backdrop of a Brāhmaṇa and a śūdra hurling insults at the performers and a mimetic battle which takes place between an *ārya* and a *śūdra*, a *brahmacārī* and a harlot while a man and a woman perform the ritual act of copulation.[54]

The name Caturānanapaṇḍita (described as a *Mahāvratin*) occurs several times in the epigraphs at Tiruvoṟṟiyūr.[55] Furthermore, the epigraphs tell us that it was this pontiff, who lived during the reign of Rajendra I, who caused an apsidal shrine to be built within the Tiruvoṟṟiyūr temple complex. The description of the shrine as apsidal in shape would lead us to conclude that it is the Ātipurīśvara-Tyāgarāja complex that is referred to.[56]

As the name Caturānanapaṇḍita occurs in epigraphs stretched over a long period of time (957 A.D. - 1171-72 A.D.) it is logical to conclude that it was a pontifical name and that all succeeding generations of the heads of the monastic establishment were known as Caturānanapaṇḍita. This tradition is common in the monastic traditions of South India and all *maṭhādīpatis* of Tarumapuram *ātīnam* for example are known as Śrī-la Śrī-

Tiruñāṉacampantar. Inscription number *181 of ARE 1912* of 969 A.D. describes Caturānana as *mahāvratin*. In line 9 it states that he took the great vow to protect his monastery (*āpta vrata tat rakṣāt tam mahāvrataḥ*). This monastery, run by the *mahāvrati* Caturānana, was obviously very influential. The founder, a Caturānana bearing the personal name of Vallabha, was a general of the Cōḻa Rājāditya and belonged to the order of Nirañjana guru and bore the office of Dharma around 957-88.[57] This *maṭha* was large enough to attract donations from merchant of Mānyakheṭa (modern Malkhed in central India.)

The other important epigraph in this connection is that of the time of Rājendracōḻa and refers to the building of the Tyāgarāja temple at Tiruvoṟṟiyūr. An epigraph of Rājarāja I registers a gift of gold by Caturānana to celebrate the birthday of the king in the temple. Here he is clearly described as the owner (?) of Tiruvoṟṟiyūr *tirumayāṉam* and *maṭham*;[58] *mayāṉam* here stands for the cremation ground and so he is described as being in charge of that as well. An inscription dated in the 9th year of Rājādhirājadeva II (1171-1172 A.D.) mentions his status as the head of the temple monastery and refers to his contemporary a certain Vāgīśa Bhaṭṭa who is described as the expounder of *Soma Siddhānta*.[59] He is also described as *vārīśa*,[60] head of a *vāriyam*, which K.A.N. Sastri takes to be an executive committee functioning under the *sabhā*.[61] Kampaṉ in his *Rāmāyaṇa* refers to this *Caturāṉaṉa maṭha*.[62]

It is interesting to see that the *Tiruvoṟṟiyūr Purāṇam*[63] credits a certain Toṇṭaimāṉ with bringing 500 Brāhmaṇa *Mahāvratins* from the banks of the Ganges and installing them in the temple he built. He is furthermore credited with the setting up of an image of Śiva in the form of a teacher of the *mahāvratins*. That the *mahāvratins* were not Bhairavas is made clear by the fact that Toṇṭaimāṉ defeated two fierce *kuṟumba* chiefs who were equipped with the *Bhairava mantra*. He fought them with the innocuous looking *darbha* grass after worshipping Maheśvara. Today there is an image of Śiva as a teacher in the temple and it goes by the name of Gaulīśa,[64] which is generally believed to be a corruption of the term Lakulīśa, the founder of the *Pāśupata* order. The 18th century work *Sarvadevavilāsa*, recently edited by V. Raghavan, describes the icon as Tryambaka[65] and interestingly enough Tryambaka is a form of Śiva popularly worshipped by the

Kālamukhas.

An inscription of Parāntaka I from Tiruvoṟṟiyūr records a gift of fifty *kaḻaṉju* of gold for feeding two *mahāvratins.*[66] An inscription of Kulōttuṅga III (1190-91 A.D.) is dated in his 13th regnal year and comes from Tiruvārūr, and mentions a *mahāvrati* Bādarāyana[67] as the custodian of some land endowments and the supervisor of the temple. This arrangement, we are told, was approved by the deity at the instance of the *tiruvāykēḷvi* while the icon was taken out in procession in the *āṭṭattu vēli* on the *taipūcam* festival. Thus, it seems in all likelihood that the deity referred to was Tyāgarāja in procession. The land endowments were made to the Piḷḷaiyār (Gaṇeśa) temple at Tiruvārūr. Thus *mahāvrati* Bāradāyana had a special relationship with the Tyāgarāja cult; his appointment was approved by Vītiviṭaṅkar (Tyāgarāja) himself.

A Pāṇḍyan inscription from Paḷḷimaṭam refers to a *mahāvratikaḷmaṭam* and one from Jambai refers to a *Mahāvratin* Lakulīśvara Paṇḍita.[68] The Koṭumpālur inscription of the reign of Parāntaka II (956-73 A.D.) refers to a Mallikārjuna as a great Vedic scholar and to his *Kālamukha* teacher, a Vidyārāśi as a 'storehouse of penance' (*taporāśi*). The ascetics are described as *Asitavaktra*[69], which is the same as *Kālamukha.*

Kālamukha temples existed in Tamiḻnāḍu in the Chingleput, North Arcot, Thanjavur and Tiruchirapalli districts, all of which refer to responsible positions being accepted by Kālamukha ascetics. Large numbers of inscriptions, all mainly from the Karnāṭaka region of the 11th, 12th and early 13th centuries A.D. record donations made to these *Kālamukha maṭhas.*[70] They reveal two major divisions of the order and both seem to be highly learned and disciplined, for the inscription states that those who break the codes of behaviour, including the rule of celibacy, will be driven out by the king, the chief officer and a council of twelve.[71] A record of 1162 A.D. refers to the *Koḍiya maṭha* of this order and describes their intellectual activities which included commentaries on grammatical works and on the six systems of philosophy, on *Lakula Siddhānta* and the *Yogaśāstras*, the eighteen *Purāṇas*, law books, dramas, comedies, etc., and the *maṭha* is further described as a place where charity was provided for the needy.[72] Tiruvoṟṟiyūr seems to have prided itself (as seen in the previous chapter) as a centre for the teaching of grammar, for the deity is referred to as *Vyākaraṇadānapperumāḷ* and a *Vyākaraṇa maṇṭapa* features regularly in epigraphs.

The *Mahāvratin* seem, therefore, as pointed out by Lorenzen on the basis of the Caturānana inscription [73] and other epigraphs more closely related to the *Kālamukhas* with their eclectic pursuit of learning and seem to have taken responsible positions in the management of temple and monastic affairs. They seem to have had a certain northern orientation inasmuch as their inscriptions come mainly from Karnāṭaka and even further north of Tamiḻnāḍu. That most of these southern temples, particularly Tiruvoṟṟiyūr, had a great deal of contact with the north regularly is evident from epigraphical sources. Donors from Kashmir, Āryāvarta, Virāṭa, etc.,[74] are constantly referred to. The fact that the *Tiruvoṟṟiyūr Purāṇam* states that the *Mahāvratis* came from the banks of the Ganges is interesting as Rājendracōḻa is credited with having brought Śaivācāryas from the bank of the Ganges and established them in various places in the Cōḻa country.[75] Furthermore, he is credited with endowing grain for the use of his preceptor and all his guru's pupils from Āryadeśa and Madhyadeśa as well.[76] That several of the *maṭhas* had connections with the parent organisation in Vārāṇasī seems to be evident from the study of epigraphs.[77]

The *Kālamukhas*, whom, following Lorenzen, we have identified with the *mahāvratis* were associated with the Pāśupatas. Rāmānuja has left us some idea of the doctrines of this sect. He groups the four *viz. Śaivas, Mahāvratas, Kāpālikas* and *Kālamukhas* as Pāśupata and then adds:

"All of these make an analysis of reality and about attainment of bliss in this world and the next, which are *opposed to the Vedas* (italics mine). They make a distinction between the instrumental and material cause and designate Pāśupati as the instrumental and not the material cause of this universe".[78]

This unsystematic grouping of all the four sects into one is not of much use. On the *Kālamukhas* he adds that they eat from the skull-bowl, besmearing the body with the ashes of a corpse, eating these ashes, bearing a staff (*laguḍa*), keeping a pot of wine and using this in the worship of gods. As Lorenzen has pointed out these are more in keeping with the *Kāpālika* rather than the *Kālamukha* rites.[79] Unfortunately no religious text of this school has survived and what we know is from hostile critics. The element of hostility would explain the atrocious descriptions of the Buddhists and Jainas in some of the texts and fortunately we have ample independent materials to study at least their beliefs.

Pāśupata

It seems certain that the *Kālamukhas* belonged to the *Pāśupata* order, which itself seems to have belonged to two categories, Vedic and non-Vedic. This explains the ambivalent attitude of the orthodox systems to the *Pāśupata* order. The *Smṛti Candrikā* (11. 310) *Ṣaṭtrimśanmata* states emphatically "A man should bathe with all his clothes on if he chances to touch the Bauddhas, the Pāśupatas, the Jainas, the Lokāyatikas, the *Kāpālikas* and those Brāhmaṇas who have taken up the duties not meant for them, but he who touches the *kāpālika* should perform *prāṇāyāma* in addition".[80]

The *Pāśupatas* do not seem to have conformed regularly to the *varṇāśramadharma*. The *Vāyu Purāṇa* describes them as having performed theistic yoga. *Pāśupata* ascetics are called *ūrdhvaretasaḥ Pāśupatas tapasvinaḥ*, referring to their ithyphallic characteristic, and their control over the outflow of semen, and again as *bhasmoddhūlitavigraha*, 'as one covered in dust and ashes'. Several texts denounce the Pāśupatas and group them with *Kāpālikas*, *Lokāyatas* (materialists) and Buddhists. The *Varāha Purāṇa* states that once Viṣṇu, upset by the number of mortals who entered heaven, requested Śiva to teach them *Nyāyasiddhānta* and *Pāśupata* in order to delude them and place them outside the path of the *Vedas*.[81] In the *Padmapurāṇa* the same story is told with the slight variation that Śiva describes a heretic as the wearer of bones and skulls besmeared in ash, etc., to which the astonished Pārvatī queries why does Śiva himself then wear such ornaments. In answer Śiva reiterates the theme mentioned above.[82] From the above references it would not be wrong to describe the *Pāśupatas* as 'sub-Vedic', if not 'anti-Vedic'. As O'Flaherty summarises in all these cases, the 'heresy' is a bridge between true religion and complete darkness, to purify them enough so that they can enter the waters of purification. "They need an orthodox heresy to break the ritual chain of impurity just as other sinners need a sacrifice prompted by the emotion of *bhakti* to break the logical chain of sin."[83]

The *Mahāvratas, Kālamukhas* and *Pāśupatas* seem very closely related to each other. There are instances when the *Pāśupata* is described as a Vedic sect. This might have evolved over the years when heterodox practices gradually became modified and assimilated into the orthodox fold. Upadhyaya is of the opinion that "primitive rituals as represented in the non-Vedic Pāśupata sect became a sort of instrument of protest against the elitist *varṇa* economy and the culture having it as its base."[84] Despite such a social situation the Brāhmaṇa theologians never desisted from transforming and modifying these sects and their rituals in order to accommodate them within the orthodox ideologies and ethical standards. In the course of this historical process the rituals of the *Pāśupatas* and *Vāmācāra* seem to have been performed by the Brāhmaṇas and Kṣatriyas. Thus in the *Kūrma Purāṇa* (1, 29. 25) the *Pāśupatas* are classified as Vedic. The Karmakāṇḍa stone inscription of Kumāragupta seems to refer to the Brāhmaṇas of Ayodhyā as *Pāśupata* clerics.[85] Thus, concludes Upadhyaya, "the Brāhmaṇa priests were instrumental in formulating a synthetic ritual."[86] The appellation Paṇḍita applied to Caturānana and the fact that the Kodumbālur inscription refers to the *Kālamukha* priest as a great Vedic scholar and the *Tiruvoṟṟiyūr Purāṇam* speaks of the five hundred *mahāvratikaḷ* as Brāhmaṇas all point to their Brāhmanic origins.

The inscriptions recorded in *E.C.* VII Sk. 114, 19 & 20 seem to connect the *Kālamukhas* with Kashmir. The donors of the Tiruvoṟṟiyūr temple also include people from Kashmir. The Tiruvoṟṟiyūr temple tradition ascribes the image of Gaulīśvara a form of (Lakulīśvara) to have come from the north. They claim it to be from Gauḍa and call the Lord Gauḍīśvara. The fact that several *Kālamukha* priests bore the name Kāśmīra Paṇḍita led A.V. Subbiah to feel that they originated in Kashmir.[87]

The general *Pāśupata* order of monks seems to have been *brahmacārins* for an inscription of this order, dated Saka 1506, i.e. 1584 A.D., has a long discussion on whether a householder *Pāśupata* can be appointed as the head of a *maṭha* and given the power of administration of the temple. The conclusion was that a *gṛhastha* (householder) could be appointed. So there were obviously no *gṛhastha Pāśupata* temple administrators and *maṭhādhipatis*. The Vēlakkuricci Maṭam (Skt. *maṭha*) of Tiruppukaḻūr, which is one of the trustees of the Tiruvārūr temple consist of *gṛhastha maṭhādhipati* and the Paṇṭāra Caṉṉiti (Skt. *sannidhi*) bears the title *ajapāpaṇṭāram*. Their existence is recorded in a 16th century epigraph from Tiruppukaḻūr. They seem earlier on to have had *Pāśupata* connections and were householders though the members of this order are now Śaiva Siddhāntins.

Very little is known of the actual philosophy of the *Pāśupatas*. In fact a lot more is known about their ritual. The *Saddarśana Saṁuccaya* of Haribhadra (pp. 11-12) describes the *Pāśupatas* as *Vaiśeśikas;* Śaṅkara too seems to have held this view as seen below. However, this does not seem to bear scrutiny.

The *Pāśupatas* were also called *Pañcārthikas* (*pañcārtha kulāmnāye viśvarūpo 'bhavad guruḥ*)[88]. The five categories are (1) Effect (*kārya*), (2) Cause (*kāraṇa*), (3) religious injunction (*vidhi*), (4) yoga, and (5) cessation of miseries (*duhkhānta*). The little idea that we can draw of Pāśupata doctrines is from the *Nakuliśa Pāśupata Darśanam*, which forms the 6th chapter of *Sarvadarśanasaṁgraha* of Sāyaṇa Mādhava. This school seems to have stressed greatly on the importance of *guru, gurubhakti*, etc. The means of attaining a state of freedom from sorrow is by knowledge (*jñāna*), austerity (*tapas*), constant association with god (*devanityatva*), fixedness (*sthiti*) and perfection (*siddhi*). *Mala* or the impurities are classified as false knowledge (*mithyājñāna*), demerit (*adharma*), cause of attachment (*sakti-hetu*), deviation (*cyuti*) and the animal instincts (*paśutva*). A combination of factors bring the freedom from these *malas* and they are doctrine and adherence to it, good conduct, meditation and repeating mantras (*japa*), the constant thought of Rudra and finally Grace or *prasāda*. It prescribes the places for observing these and describes the stages of progress as *vyakta* (marked by ashes, etc.), *avyakta* (learning the esoteric truths *vidyāgopanopadeśa*), *jaya* or victory over the senses, destruction of the fetters and finally, reaching *niṣṭhā* or complete cessation.

The *Pāśupata Sūtra* is believed to be quite an ancient text and the *Nakulīśa Pāśupata darśana* of Mādhavācārya in his *Sarvadarśanasaṁgraha* (14th century A.D.) is based on this and the commentary on *Pāśupata sūtra* attributed to Rasikara of the Gupta period.

The rites are described which include besmearing the body with ashes, laughing, singing, dancing, making peculiar sounds with the tongue and palate, etc. The other practices include *krathana* (pretending to sleep while awake), *mandana*, convulsions, walking as if the legs were disabled, making erotic gestures in the presence of beautiful women, indulging in unsocial and despicable acts, speaking absurd and senseless words, etc.[89] The Pāśupata, as O'Flaherty observes, was instructed to 'play the lecher' in order to stimulate slander, acquiring *tapas* by this means.[90]

Śaṅkarācārya, in his *Brahmasūtra Bhāṣya* (2.2.37) equates *Māheśvaras* with *Pāśupata* who, he says, maintain five categories - *pañcārthikas*, essentially a dualistic view. Śaṅkarācārya further associates the *Māheśvaras* with *Vaiśeṣikas* who teach "that the Lord is somehow the operative cause of the world" [91]

The only reason for this persistent attribution seems to be that the Vaiśeṣikas seem to have favoured the life of the householder to that of a renunciate.

Turning to the commentary of Kauṇḍinya on the *Pāśupatasūtra*[92] he states emphatically that liberation from sorrow, can, in the ultimate analysis be attained only by Grace - *'tasmāt prasādāt sa duḥkhāntaḥ prāpyate na tu jñāna-vairāgya-dharma-aiśvarya-tyāgamātrād iti arthaḥ'*. The person who is regarded as fit for receiving this discipline is a Brāhmaṇa with keen senses. It is forbidden for him to address women or Śūdras except under special circumstances and then he should purify himself by smearing himself with ashes, by *prāṇāyāma* and by reciting the *Rudragāyatrī*. The *Pāśupatas* were particularly powerful between the 10th and 14th centuries A.D.[93]

That the Pāśupatas also had an unseemly side to their personality seems to be evident from passages in the *Mahābhārata*, the *Vāyu Purāṇa*, etc. In the *Mahābhārata* Jarāsandha imprisons a hundred kings with the intention of sacrificing them to Pāśupati enshrined in Varaṇāvata. [94] The *Vāyu* (58-59) and the *Brahmāṇḍa* (11. 31. 59-60) state that in the Kali age when everything turns topsy turvy a number of strange things will happen such as some will consciously turn into *Kāpālikas*, while some will sell the Vedas and some the *tīrthas*. In short the moral order will be reduced to anarchy and chaos.

Somasiddhānta

An inscription *ARE403 of 1896* dated in the 9th year of Rājādhirājadeva II (i.e. 1171-72 A.D.) mentions Caturānana as the owner or manager of the Tiruvoṟṟiyūr temple, *maṭam* and the cremation grounds and casually refers to his contemporary Vāgīśa Bhaṭṭa who is described as the expounder of *Somasiddhānta*. This term *Somasiddhānta* occurs several times in literature and has quite often been identified with the *Kāpālika* cult.[95] Thus Śrī-Harṣa's *Naiṣadhacarita* contains a lengthy description of the goddess Sarasvatī in which the various parts of her body are said to be formed from different philosophical doctrines. Her face is described as *Somasiddhānta* (x. 87). The commentator Candupaṇḍita equates this with the *Kāpālika*[96] (*Somasiddhānta nāma Kāpālika darśana śāstram*, p. 427). Kṣīrasvāmin, as seen earlier equates *mahāvrati, Kapāli, Somasiddhānti* and *Tāntrika*. In *Īśāna Śiva Guru Paddhati* it is equated with *Tāntrika* belonging to the *Bala* school (III, p.6). Vīramitrodaya of Mitramiśra (I, p. 22) equates them with *Kāpālika*. Raghottama's commentary on Vātsyāyana's *Nyāyabhāṣya* includes *saumya* in a list of heretical doctrines (*ṣaḍ bahyāḥ siddhāntāḥ*)[97]. Several other sources identify it as a *Kāpālika* school but say very little about its beliefs.

The farcical play *Prabohacandrodaya* summarises the doctrines of the *Somasiddhāntin* in a highly derogatory manner.[98] This work was written by Kṛṣṇamiśra at the court of Kīrtivarman, the Chandella king of Jejakabhukti and possibly in Khajuraho. The play is an allegory of the deliverance of the human spirit from the mundane temptations of this world. The characters in the play are personified human traits. *Viṣṇu bhakti* at the onset stirs up discrimination and with the aid of the Upaniṣads, Faith, Sense and their friends, crushes Delusion, Lust, Greed etc. True Knowledge arises and realises its true identity with the godhead. The satire is against all non-Advaitins, be they Buddhists, Jainas or *Lokāyatas*. The *Kāpālika* character is called *Somasiddhāntin* and according to the commentator the deity worshipped is sa+Uma = Soma, i.e. Śiva and Śakti. The adept (*sādhaka*) indulges in drunkenness and gluttony and is all in all a caricature rather than a description.[99]

The *Mattavilāsaprahasana* attributed to Mahendravarman Pallava, the *Mālatī Mādhava*, the *Caṇḍakauśika* and the *Prabodhacandrodaya* are the works that refer to the *Kāpālikas*. In all of these they sport ornaments of bones, get drunk and behave in a most sensuous manner and justify it all as a philosophy of life. Such acts, say the Somasiddhāntin in Ānandarāya Makhin's *Vidyāpariṇayana*, are prescribed by the *Bhairavāgamas*.[100] Their association with *kuṇḍalinī yoga* is brought out in Bhavabhūti's *Mālatīmādhava* where references are made to the ten *nāḍis*, the six *cakras*, etc., while expounding their doctrine. The same work also presents the macabre aspects of their cult where a *kapālin* collects 108 skulls as part of a vow. *Amṛtodaya* of Gokulanātha (1639 A.D.) treats *Somasiddhānta* as a personal name (no doubt a personification) and attributes the materialist Cārvāka to be his close friend. Appaya Dīkṣita, in his commentary on *Śrikaṇṭhabhāṣya* (2.2.38) refers to Vedic Pāśupata as distinct from *Vāma, Pāśupata, Soma,* and *Laguḍam* as creeds not to be adopted and describes them as the great system of delusion (*mohaśāstra*).

Ānandagiri's *Śaṇkaravijayam* refers to the fierce encounter Śankara is said to have had with them. The inscriptions from Tiruvārūr and Tiruvoṟṟiyūr and other Tyāgarāja shrines refer to human sacrifices[101] which seem to have been prevalent from the Pallava times.[102] In fact, rumours have it that the last human sacrifice in Tiruvoṟṟiyūr took place in the 1930s. There is the general belief that the temple was known for secret rites of a macabre nature.

Thus, while a number of texts identify the *Somasidhānta* with *Kāpālika,* there are some works which suggest a close connection with specific *Tantras. Soma* in Sanskrit is a synonym for the moon (*Candra*) and there is an Āgama called *Candrakalāgama*. As pointed out by Lorenzen '*Candra*' is another epithet for a *Kapāli-Bhairava*. Cakravarti refers to *Candrajñānavidyā,* as forming "part of Tantra thelogy", and to its classification into an orthodox and a more heterodox school. The *Kāpālika* doctrines are expounded in the *Candrajñānatantra* and it claims to be worship of the sixteen deities or *nityas* who symbolise the sixteen syllables of the *ṣoḍaśīmantra,* which is the mainstay of the Śrī-Vidyā school.[103] In fact Lakshmīdhara mentions Śrī-Vidyā as more or less the respectable form of *Candrajñāna,* and states quite clearly that while *Śrī-Vidyā* draws its adherents from all castes, *Candrajñāna* attracts only the Śūdras and the lowest elements of society.[104] A similar ambivalence has been noticed earlier in the classification of *Pāśupatas* into *śrauta* and *aśrauta*. Thus temples and temple cults acted as agents in incorporating several heterodox sects by providing them with respectability and legitimacy and in turn institutionalising them by 'taming' them.

The *Siddha* tradition all over India places a great emphasis on *Soma* 'moon', as the centre of the *Sahasrāra* and frequently refers to the metaphor of nectar oozing from the moon. The Haṭhayogins regard the syllable *ṭha* as the sun and *tha* as the moon and it is their aspiration to unite the two. Thus the *Siddhas* of the *Nātha saṁpradāya* were greatly involved with the Soma-Sūrya-Agni trinity. This triad is frequently mentioned in Tyāgarāja liturgical texts.

From what we know of the Tyāgarāja cult, it seems very likely that the *Somasiddhānta,* which was presumably of *Kāpālika* origin, was gradually adopted by the more acceptable and official religion of the *Śrī-Vidyā,* which as we have repeatedly seen, was of great importance in the Tyāgarāja cultic centres. Both Ghurye and Mahalingam have pointed out how the more fierce forms of the *Kāpālika* traditions were softened and modified in the post-Śaṅkara era.[105] Memories of Śaṅkara taming fierce goddesses are current to this day and though not probably true historically at least express in the language of myths the impact of the *Advaitic* doctrine on the fierce Śaiva schools.[106] According to Nagasamy, stories regarding Śaṅkara's taming the bloodthirsty goodesses were known in writing only from the 16th century onwards.[107] The mystical symbolism of Sun, moon and Agni and Sun, moon and Rudra (as a synonym for Agni) are used several times in the *Mucukundasahasranāmam.* The sixteen digits of the moon (*kalā*) are often referred to in Tyāgarāja liturgical texts.

Mattamayūra and the Golaki Maṭha

A very important unpublished manuscript entitled *Śrī-nātha navaratnamālā Mañjūṣā* by Bhāskararāya, the renowned 18th century exponent of *Śrī-Vidyā,* was very kindly brought to the author's attention by Pandit Vatuknath Sastri Khiste of the Saṁpurnanand Sanskrit University, Vārāṇasī, and a member of the *guruparamparā* of Bhāskararāya. In this work Bhāskararāya discusses the metaphysics of *ajapā* with its usual equation with 21,600 breaths to which we have referred to in the previous chapter, and apportions them to the sixteen *nityās* amongst offering them to other deities. The first of the *nityās* is Lalitā, a key figure in the *dhyānaślokas* of the *Śrī-Vidyā* school. The *Nityāṣoḍaśikārṇavam,* a renowned Tāntric (Śrī-Vidyā)[108] work also refers to the sixteen *nityās.* It has usual *dhyāna ślokas* and refers to the offering of wine, in a cup, etc. Thus, a hybrid *Śrī-Vidyā Kāpālika* cult called *Candrajñāna* with the sixteen *nityās* as one of the focal points could well have been the basis of the Somasiddhānta. Tirumūlar, in the third *tantra* of the

Tirumantiram also expounds the doctrine called *Candrayoga*. Thus a Śākta-yoga form of worship of the 16 *nityās* was what was in vogue in the Tyāgarāja temple at Tiruvoṟṟiyūr.

The above work of Bhāskararāya lends another interesting clue to the puzzle of the *golaki maṭha*. The reason that this *maṭha* is of interest to someone studying the Tyāgarāja cult is that the southern headquarters of this establishment was in Tiruvārūr, as will be proved in the following discussion.

Bhāskararāya in his nine *ślokas* uses the refrain *Mattamayūra* as a metaphor for the guru. He states that just as a peacock unfolds its wings and displays its grandeur only at certain times, so also the guru unfolds the excellence of his esoteric wisdom only at certain times and only to the choice disciples.[109] What is interesting is that he uses the term *Mattamayūramārga*,[110] the path of the *mattamayūra* and following the *kaṭapayādi* system[111] of reckoning deduces that the expression *Mattamayūramārga* is equivalent to 21,600 for *mattamayūra*=21,565 and *mārga*=35, which are the number of *ajapās* or breaths that the average man according to the Yogic reckoning inhales and exhales in a twenty-four hour period. Having equated *mattamayūra* to the breaths he offers them to the different concepts as an act of meditation on abstract ideas which are visualised, such as to the *pūrṇamaṇḍalākṣara*, to the thiry-six *tattvas*, the sixteen *nityās*, the twelve *rāsis*, the nine *grahas*, etc.

The key phrase is the *mattamayūra*, a term, as we shall presently see, refers to a clan of Śaiva ascetics belonging to the *golaki maṭha*. That Bhāskararāya meant something more than simply to compare his guru to a peacock is evident. The work had a hidden meaning in the general *Śrī-Vidyā* context.

Mirashi has painstakingly collected all the data on this clan of ascetics who are said to have built monasteries, hospitals, schools and charitable institutions.[112] Their curriculum seems to have been very wide and eclectic including subjects such as grammar, literature, etc. Of the philosophical system of the *Golakis*, however, we know little. From Bhāskararāya's work we can gather that whatever school they belonged to they were certainly committed to some form of Śakti worship and accepted the approach of *haṭhayoga* and *layayoga*, for it is in this school that one gets repeated reference to the concept of *ajapā*.[113] The reference to yoginis, *nityās*, etc., lends definite emphasis to their affiliation with *Śrī-Vidyā*.

The *Golaki Maṭha* is referred to in several inscriptions from different parts of India, from present day Madhya Pradesh, Bengal, Andhra Pradesh and Tamilnāḍu. The Malkapuram inscription (94 of 1917) dated Saka 1183-1261 A.D. gives a wealth of information. It states that between Bhāgīrathī and Narmadā in the Dahala Maṇḍala was a *maṭha* called the *Golaki maṭha* founded by Durvāsa, and Yuvarāja, the Kākatīya king, gave three *lakhs* of villages to the preceptor of this *maṭha*, whose name was Sadbhāvaśaṁbhū. The exact location of the original *golaki maṭha* is a matter of speculation. The suggestions made are Bheraghat in Jabalpur (the *caunsat yoginī* temple), or the *caunsat yoginī* at Khajuraho. Another inscription of this order is the Gorgi inscription wherein we are told that the ascetic Prabhāva Śiva was from Malwa, where the peacocks were wild with joy (*mattamayūra*).[114] The ascetic is described as an adherent of the Siddhānta.[115] A branch of this clan was at Karkoni, somewhere in Central India. Others are known from Konkan. Most of the inscriptions of the *Mattamayūra* contain references to the Yogic practices of the *ācāryas*. These led to *siddhi* and the emancipated were known as *siddhas*. Kadambaguhā, the original habitat of the *Mattamayūra* is called the abode of the *siddhas*.

The Malkāpuram inscription states that one of the *ācāryas* of this *maṭha* was from Pūrvagrāma in the Rādhā country, identified with a part of Bengal. The royal disciples and patrons of this *ācārya* from Bengal were the Cōḻa, Malwa and Kalachuri kings. This *ācārya* is said to have given lands to sixty families of Drāviḍa Brāhmaṇas in a village called Mandaram to enable them to settle there. References are made to settling teachers of *Ṛg*, *Yajur* and *Sāma* Vedas, Logic, literature and the Āgamas. An interesting reference is made to the bringing of musicians and dancers from Kashmir.[116]

A macabre piece of information provided by this epigraph from Malkāpuram is that ten village guards, called *vīrabhadras*, who came from the Cōḻa country and wore matted locks and belonged to all the different castes were appointed as the guards of the village; they cut off their heads, scrotum or stomach for the protection of the village. Whether this refers to some grisly form of self-torture or is simply a poetic way of describing their valour is difficult to say.[117] However, references to ritual suicide in order to protect someone or a village have come to light from epigraphs from Tiruvārūr, Tiruvoṟṟiyūr etc. The *Tiruvoṟṟiyūr Purāṇam* also refers to the *vīrabhadra* guardians of the village who would cut off their heads etc., for the protection of the villages. There too they are said to have come from Cōḻadēśa. They definitely have a striking similarity to the *navavīras* who are said to have helped Mucukuntaṉ and brought the Tyāgarāja to earth.[118]

Thus, the *Golaki Saṁpradāya* had a strong following among the Tamiḻ peoples and sixty Drāviḍa Brāhmaṇas were given land, which again was to be guarded by the Cōḻa warriors. That it was a Pan-Indian organisation becomes evident from the Bangad copper plate wherein the *ācārya* of golaki maṭha is described as the royal guru of the Pāla king Mahīpāla. Here too we are told that *Saṁpradāya* originated from Durvāsa. This inscription[119] has an invocation to Śakti as *jaganmātā* and the temple where the monastery was situated was dedicated to Śiva and Bhavānī.

One of the epithets for the *Golaki maṭha* is *lakṣādhyāyi*, presumably because of the gift of three lakh of villages to the preceptor by the Kākatīya king. That in Tamiḻnāḍu, it was also known by the name *bhikṣā maṭha* (again presumably referring to the same charity) becomes evident from the statement in an epigraph (134 of *1924*) wherein the *bhikṣā maṭha* is equated with the *lakṣādhyāyi*. That it also had an alternative name the *kīḻai maṭha* or the southern *maṭha* is clear from another inscription from Madurai district[120] wherein *kīḻai maṭha* is equated with the *Golaki maṭha* at Tirupparaṅkuṉṟam. That the three were of the same order is explicity stated in 213 of *1924* of the Pāṇḍya dynasty dated Saka 1422 (1500 A.D.) which refers to *bhikṣāmaṭha* alias *lakṣādhyāyi* of the Golaki *santāna*. That the *kīḻai maṭha* was the southern branch seems plausible from an inscription from Pirāṉmalai wherein a gift is recorded for the *Dakṣiṇa Golaki maṭha* at Tiruvārūr.[121] Thus, Tiruvārūr seems to have been the southern headquarters of *kīḻaimaṭha*, which seems to be the Tamiḻ for *Dakṣiṇa Golaki maṭha*. 483 of *1920* from Puḻal of the 13th century refers to Vāgīśa of *kīḻai maṭha santāna* in Celva Tiruvārūr and residing at Perumpaṟṟappuliyūr, i.e. Chidambaram. The inscription is dated in the reign of Saṁbuvarāya. The same preceptor of the same order is mentioned in 169 of *1926*. That the origin of the *Golaki maṭha* was in the north seems to be suggested by 209 of *1924* from Pirāṉmalai which records the gift of tax-free land to a *maṭha* built by Īśāna Śiva Rāvalar, the disciple's disciple of Śrī Deśikendra of the *Golaki maṭha* and the *Lakṣādhyayi santāna* of the *Aryavarta* country. That Vārāṇasī was presumably the main centre is suggested in 111 of *1929-30* of the 36th year of Kulottuṅga from Tiruppāccūr which refers to Jñānaśiva Rāvalar of the Lakṣādhyāyi *santāna* of the *kolla maṭha* at Vārāṇasī. Another Rāvalar is referred to from the *Golaki maṭha* of Tiruvannamalai (1234 A.D.) (11 of *1935-36*). Yet another Rāvalar is said to belong to the Vārāṇasī *bhikṣā maṭha* (72 of *1930-31* from Pandanallūr).

Thus *bhikṣā, Lakṣādhyāyi* and *Golaki* refer to the same monastic order which was Pan-Indian with its ecclesiastic headquarters at Vārāṇasī by the 13th century and its southern regional headquarters at Celva Tiruvārūr (the term *Celva* Tiruvārūr has been discussed in chapter 7). Teachers from this monastic order were the royal preceptors of the Cōḻas,[122] the Kākatīyas, the Pālas and the rulers of Malwa. Their cult was a form of Śiva-Śakti worship (cf. Bangad Copper Plate). It is interesting to find a Vāgīśa in 169 of *1926* belonging to the *vaṭakīḻ* maṭha of Celva Tiruvārūr and belonging to the same period as the Vāgīśa of Tiruvoṟṟiyūr, the reader of *Somasiddhānta*. From the evidence in hand, it appears that a school of Yoga, Tantra and eclectic learning was sponsored by them.

The names of the *ācāryas* of *Golaki maṭha* are Īśānaśiva, Viśveśvara Śiva, etc., thus ending in Śiva or Śivācārya. The above mentioned *ācāryas* were trustees and treasurers of the Dēvikāpuram temple in North Arcot district (9352 of *1912* and 193 of *1924*); also 354, 365, 389, 390, of *1912*. Dēvikāpuram is still a monastic centre and Cattanāta Civācārya is the present head. The monastic heads here are the preceptors of certain sects of Pērichetti Śaiva merchants who are also the main patrons of the Tiruvoṟṟiyūr temple. They are also connected with the Jñānaśivācāryas of Mullindram (North Arcot dist.), who are the religious preceptors of the Tamiḻ speaking *Vāṇiyas* (oilmongers).

Hultsch in his report on *Sanskrit Manuscripts* II, mentions Jñānaśivācārya of *Golaki maṭha*. He refers to a Sanskrit work called *Snapanasārāvali*.[123] The predecessors of these Jñānacivācāryas are said to have been related to the famous Ḍanḍina family of Sanskrit poets of the Vijayanagara court.

In a record of Śaka 1507 (1585 A.D.) a certain Perumanāyaṉār Paṇṭāram of Accuṟṟamaṅkalam is referred to as belonging to the *bhikṣā maṭha* at Chidambaram (79 of *1911*). He is described as a pupil of Aghoraśiva. We know of an Aghōraśiva Paṇṭāram, who was closely connected with the management of both the Tiruvārūr and Chidambaram temples and was a trustee of these two temples. 16 and 17 of 1946-47 both engraved at Tiruvārūr mention gifts to the Tyāgarāja temple and to the Naṭarāja temple at Chidambaram respectively which were entrusted to Aghoraśiva. The inscriptions are dated in 1743 and 1719 A.D. respectively.

An interesting point noted by Swamy[124] is the change in the suffix or appellation; the head of the *maṭha* is no longer called an *ācārya* or a *paṇḍita* but Mutaliyār. 213 of 1924 and 636 of 1904 speak of Mutaliyārs of *Lakṣādhyāyi santāna;* Ēkāmradēva Mutaliyār is said to head a *Dakṣiṇa Golaki maṭha* at Celva Tiruvārūr (234 of 1912). Thus after the 12th and 13th centuries the *Golaki maṭha* seems to have been a *maṭha* headed by non-Brāhmaṇa community. The various *santānas* of the *Golaki maṭha* have been discussed by M. Rajamanikam.[125] Chidambaram seems to have been an important centre.

Whether the *Golaki maṭha* which, though preponderant in the Cōḻa period was still very strong in the period up to the 16th century A.D., had any connection with the Tarumapuram, Tiruvāvaṭāturai, etc., it is difficult to say. The Tarumapuram Ātīṉam was founded by a disciple of Kamalai Ñānappirakācar, an ardent devotee of Tyāgarāja and Naṭarāja. He was the son of Ceṭṭitteru Ñānappirakācar, 'the Ñānappirakācar of Ceṭṭi Street', thereby pointing out to his Ceṭṭiyār origin. Apart from education, their functions included the management of temples and to this day 27 temples are managed by them and an endowment called the *Rājaṉ kaṭṭalai* is still managed by them in vogue in the Tyāgarājasvāmi temple at Tiruvārūr. These later non-Brahmin *maṭhas* were mainly of the Śaiva Siddhānta school, tracing their philosophy to Meykaṇṭār, Umāpati Śivācārya, etc. More will be said of the caste composition of the *maṭhas* in the next chapter. The *Golaki-Bhikṣā-Lakṣādhyāyi maṭhas* seem to emphasise a great deal on yoga and this could be the school of philosophy which influenced the metaphysical concepts of the Tyāgarāja.

Śaiva Siddhānta

Śaiva Siddhānta conceives reality in three ultimate irreducible categories - *pati, paśu* and *pāśa*, God, the individual soul and the bondage of the soul, a freedom from which would make it realize

Pati. God wills and it is this WILL that creates and this creativity is itself a characteristic of God. His justice works in the form of *karma*. The individual self is from the very beginning tainted with *mala* and so cannot initiate the cognitive process. God as Being is Śiva and His Divine Will is Śakti. With the Grace of *pati* the individual soul can be made to cast its *mala* and perceive itself as Pure and illumined. There are variations in the interpretation of *Śaiva Siddhānta* doctrines ranging from a more dualistic to a more monistic interpretation. There are also differences as to whether ignorance or *āṇava* ever leaves the soul. It is there from the beginning and according to some is present even at the time of *mukti* - the only difference is that at the time of *mukti* it is powerless for it is covered like light covers darkness but the darkness is still there. The Siddhānta respects the Āgamic tradition and in fact is an intellectualisation of the *bhakti* movement. In order to fulfil his various acts of Grace to souls, God takes on forms. These are different from the bodies taken on by souls. The soul covered by *āṇava mala* needs bodies made of *māyā* (matter) but since Śiva is free of the *āṇava mala*, he has as his body *Śakti* (Civañānacittiyār 1, v. 41). God is able to assume forms at his own will. The body meted out by God to the soul is determined by *karma*. God can assume *ñānaśakti, kriyā śakti*, or *icchā śakti*.

The fact that the Tarumapuram *ātīnām*, a Siddhānta maṭam had its origins in Tiruvārūr and was and still is in close connection with many of the Tyāgarāja temples has left an indelible impression on this cult. In fact the Siddhānta is a school most close to the Śaivas of Tamiḻnāḍu and it is interesting to note that the earlier Non-Brāhmaṇa movements of this century like the Justice Party regarded the Śaiva Siddhānta as the rallying point of both Tamiḻ nationalism and the Non-Brāhmaṇa movement. It was only later that the Non-Brāhmaṇa movement developed an atheistic stance. The Veḷḷāḷas see themselves as carriers of Tamiḻ culture and the way of life and are the spiritual leaders of this school.

The visible iconic symbolism of the Siddhānta philosophy was the concept of the dancing Śiva and it stood for the five cosmic acts of Śiva as well as the five sacred syllables of the Śaivas.

Māheśvara and Śivayogis

Other expressions that occur in epigraphs denoting groups of

Śaiva schools are the terms Māheśvara and Śiva Yogīs (624 of *S.I.I.* Vol. 19). The present day *Vīra śaivas* describe themselves as *Māheśvaras* and the Śiva yogīs were possibly the *sannyāsins* dedicated to Śiva and in all probability not Brāhmaṇas. Mu. Arunacalam refers to an interesting case brought before the King Cēvappa Nāyaka in the Vijayanagara period when the Śaiva *sannyāsins* were regarded as inferior to the Brāhmaṇa *sannyāsins.* A Brāhmaṇa *sannyāsī* from Sūryanārāyaṇa kōyil *maṭha* belonging to the Śankara order of Brāhmaṇa monks propagated the equality of Śaiva *sannyāsī* with Brāhmaṇa monks and wrote treatises such as *Kriyā Dīpikā* and *Sannyāsa Paddhati* to give them the necessary ritualistic credentials. (Mu. Arunacalam, *Tamil̲ Iḷakkiya Varalāṟu*, 16th cen. part 2, p.239). Thus, corresponding to the *Śankaramaṭha* which was subscribed to by the Smārta Brāhmaṇas, with their emphasis on the Vedas and the *Smṛtis* there were also Śaiva *Sannyāsis* who were followers of the Āgamic tradition.

The Kauḷa Mārga and Cōmācimāṟaṉār Episode

Cuntarar, as mentioned earlier, is a crucial figure in the Tyāgarāja cult. There are some very interesting aspects in the personality of this saint which links him, in a manner of speaking, to the Tāntric faith. First and foremost he emerges from his own hymns (in which he provides a great deal of biographical information) and from Cēkkil̲ār's writings and other later writings as a this-wordly, life-affirming, sensuous character.

Iconographically he is represented in a semi—almost a regal attire.[126] The scriptural justification for this is provided by the fact that Tyāgarāja is said to have asked him to be in the garb of a bridegroom, about to be married, for it was Śiva, who in the first place, had stopped Cuntarar from getting married so that he may fulfil his life's mission of being a Śiva *aṭiyār* or slave of Śiva.[127]

Cuntarar's requests to the Lord Śiva are often very detailed and almost disarmingly sensuous for a saintly character. He asks the Lord of Nākaikkārōṇam and Lord of Tiruvārūr for money, gold, diamonds, silk, food, including things like *ghee.*[128] He asks the Lord of Kōḷili for grains and not content with getting it, asks for porters to carry it to his wife's house.[129]

On the emotional plane, he asks the Lord to help him reconcile his differences with his first wife Paravai, who refuses to accept her bigamous husband. Tyāgarāja acts as the messenger, not once but twice.[130]

This incident is mentioned *in passim* by the saint himself and finds mention in the *Mucukundasahasranāmam* as well.[131] His life at Tiruvoṟṟiyūr with his second wife, Caṅkili, is also full of divine intervention. He is addressed as *tampirāṉtōḻaṉ,* the friend of the Lord.

His asking Tyāgarāja to intervene with Paravai on his behalf was looked upon with great disfavour by Ēyarkōṉ Kalikkāmanāyaṉār, an *aṭiyār* who would rather die than be cured by Cuntarar, whom he considered a vile blasphemer[132] taking the name of God Tyāgarāja in vain.

Viraṉmīṇṭār was so annoyed by the saint's behaviour towards fellow devotees that he is believed to have left Tiruvārūr, when he heard that Cuntarar had been granted a secret vision of the Lord.[133] Thus Cuntaramūrti was probably the most controversial of the saints and his intuitive direct appeal to the Lord for the most wordly pleasures was not in keeping with the ascetic otherworldly devotionalism, characteristic of most of the other *nāyaṉmār*.

However to call him a proto-*Kaula* would probably be going too far for his only loyalty was to Śiva and if ever to Śakti, it was only as the consort of Śiva. He was pained to see the Lord accept *pali* (used both to denote sacrifice and alms) and his gentle faith was in no way connected with the more fierce elements of the Tāntrics, nor did his silken robes have any semblance to the *kauḷa* skull and bone attire.[134]

It is, however, in the Cōmācimāṟaṉār episode that his link to the *kauḷa* doctines becomes more evident. The story, to be presently investigated in detail, it must be remembered, is not mentioned in any of his hymns nor in the *Periya Purāṇam.* It would be interesting to trace the growth of this myth for it throws important light on the nature of the conflict between the Vedic and Tāntric faiths. For, while on one hand theologians were trying to reconcile the differences between the Vedic and Tāntric faiths and gloss over the differences by designating some forms of Tāntrism as Vedic, such as Vedic *Pāśupatas* or Vedic *Śrī-Vidyā*, etc., there were, as is clear from this myth, irreconcilable zones of dogma, and thus conflicts seem to have been inevitable.

Since temples and temple cults acted as major bridges over

zones of religious tension it is of great significance to note that conflict too was expressed through temple cults and temple myths. The temples, as upholders of the Vedas and more so of the Āgamas, were bastions of a structured faith, which as upholders of *bhakti* and some forms of Tantras they were committed to oppose. It is this dichotomy that finds expression in the myth.

Cōmācimāṟaṉār is referred to for the first time by Cuntarar in his *Tiruttoṇṭattokai*,[135] wherein he offers his obeisance to sixty-two saints and invokes each one by his name. It is in this context that he declares himself to be the slave of Cōmācimāṟaṉār, who is given the epithet Amparaṉ (V. 5. line 7), i.e., born in Ampar, which is the name of a village in the Nannilam taluq of Thañjāvūr district. This information is reiterated in Nampiyāṇṭār Nampi's *Tiruttoṇṭar Tiruvantāti*, where his friendship with Cuntarar and Paravai is stressed.[136]

The *Periya Purāṇam* describes him as a Brāhmaṇa well-versed in the Vedic lore and extols his generosity, hospitality and his steadfastness in the worship of Śiva.[137] He is said to have regarded any devotee of Śiva as his master, irrespective of his caste affiliations. This is significant as we shall presently see. Beyond this, Cēkkiḻār simply states that he regarded the pronouncement of *pañcākṣara* as his daily duty. Cuntarar in this work is exalted almost to a semi-divine status, for we are told that his feet were worshipped by the inhabitants of both the heavens and the earth. The link with Cōmācimāṟaṉār is provided by stating that he was blessed with the friendship of such a man and came to visit him in Tiruvārūr. He is said to have led a pure life and obtained salvation.

There are two works in Sanskrit called *Śiva Bhakta Vilāsa*. One is believed to have been expounded by the sage Agastya and was composed by a certain author by the name of Haradatta.[138] There is another Sanskrit work by the name *Śiva Bhakta Vilāsa* by an unknown author.[139] Both recount the life of Śaiva saints. The latter closely follows the *Periya Purāṇam* and both the above-mentioned Sanskrit works claim to be parts of the *Upapurāṇa* of the *Skanda Mahā Purāṇam*. Whilst I have included details of the published versions in my notes (f.n. 139 and 140), I have not been able to access either of these printed versions. The numbering of chapters and stanzas in this chapter is based on a manuscript edition available at the Thañjāvūr Saraswati Mahal Library. A copy of this mss. entitled *Śivabhaktavilāsa* was kindly copied out in entirety by Śrī-S. Swaminatha Sastrikal and Mrs. S.Rajalaksmi in November 1983 but without a catalogue number of the manuscript. The chapter dealing with the Somayāji episode concludes by stating that it is taken from the section entitled *Māra Somayāji kaivalya prāpti* (The attainment of salvation by Māra Somayāji) of the 66th chapter of the work entitled *Śivabhaktavilāsa*, which is a part of the *Śrī Skandapurāṇa* Chapter ten of this work gives the myths of the establishment of the Somāskanda icon and chapter twelve the Mucukunda episode. The Somayāji hagiography begins in Chapter 56, where it follows the usual *Periya Purāṇam* style of describing him as a great devotee. Then it continues on the Somayāji story in Chapter 66 and it is in this chapter that the episode recounted below is described in great detail. So the following numberings for the Sanskrit version come from Chapter 66 of the mss. recension. This mss. is in *nāgarī* script.

A Marāṭhi work based on the *Agastya Bhakta Vilāsa* was composed by one Virūpākṣa Kavi in 1827 A.D.[140] under the command of the Marāṭhā ruler, Sarfoji II. It is difficult to date the Sanskrit works with any degree of precision. The *Cennabasava Purāṇa*[141] and the *Arupattimūvarcaritam* in Kannaḍa are based on the *Agastya Bhakta Vilāsa*. These were certainly composed before the 15th century A.D. and record the story of Basava, the founder of the Lingāyats, and sketches as well the lives of the sixty-three *nāyaṉmār*. The author Śaṅkarādhyāya was familiar with the details of the story of the lives of the *nāyaṉmār* and as he is believed to have lived in the 14th century A.D., it is likely that these works were composed before the 14th century, somewhere between the 12th, when the *Periya Purāṇam* was composed, and the 14th centuries A.D. J.M. Nallaswami Pillai does not provide adequate reasons for his theory that they were composed before the 12th century A.D.[142] The Tārācuram frieze of the 12th century A.D. depicts Cōmācimāṟaṉār performing a Vedic sacrifice but is otherwise 'non-episodic'.[143]

It is in the *Agastya Bhakta Vilāsa* that the story of Somayājimāṟaṉār, as he is called, which is the Sanskrit rendering of Cōmācimāṟaṉār, is episodically presented. The basic information given in the *Periya Purāṇam* is reiterated in this work but it gives further details and adds an interesting new episode which provides the origin myth of the Madhyāhna Brāhmaṇa community.

Somayāji wins the friendship of Cuntarar (who is called Sundara in Sanskrit) whom he regards as a representative of Tyāgarāja and hence treats him with profound respect. Once Somayāji decides to perform a Vedic sacrifice and is seized with an inordinate desire to invite Tyāgarāja to be present in person and to offer him the *havis*. He requests Cuntarar to intercede on his behalf and persuade the deity to attend the sacrifice (Ch.66, st.35). Cuntarar promises to do so and approaches Tyāgarāja with this strange request. At first Cuntarar is reprimanded by Tyāgarāja for making such an unheard of promise to Somayāji (66.52). However, after considerable cajoling on the part of the saint, the deity accepts the invitation, but only after imposing the stern condition that he may present himself in any form *(kenāpi rūpeṇa)*, be it low, or high *(nikṛṣṭenottamena)* (66, st..59) The condition agreed upon, Somayāji proceeds with the preparation for the sacrifice.

Śiva, meanwhile, mentally substitutes the carcass of a calf for the Vedic altar (*yūpa*), and four dogs for the four Vedas, and satisfied with this picture in his mind, decides that he, along with his consort and two sons would don the form of *caṇḍālas* (*sarvasvarūpī sarveśaś cāṇḍālam rūpam asthitaḥ* - ibid. st. 82). Having so decided, he descends on the scene of the sacrifice in the most unwholesome attire.

The Marāṭhī version devotes 87 verses (Ch. 56) to Somayāji and the episode of the sacrifice begins in v. 26. and about 10 verses are devoted to describe the pandemonium.

The scene is presented with great *panache*. Śiva carries a bloody and foul-smelling carcass on his shoulder and his eyes are red and bloodshot with intoxication. He moves with the unsteady gait of a drunkard, his head rolling uncontrollably from side to side. Pārvatī presents hereself as the youthful Mātaṅgakanyā, her glance tipsy with drink (*madhughūrṇitalolākṣīm* v.58), as she sways into the hall carrying a pot of alcohol on her head and holding the hands of Gaṇeśa and Kumāra, who are dressed as the sons of Mātaṅga. She cheerily offers the Brāhmaṇas present a sip from her drink. The horrified Brāhmaṇas scatter helter skelter. This scene is painted on the lintel of the *yāgaśālā* (sacrificial hall) doorway in the Tyāgarājasvāmi temple complex at Tiruvārūr, in the 18th century Marāṭhā style,[144] and repeated in the Nīlōtpalāmpāḷ shrine. The latter painting seems to be of more recent origin and by the presence of Sarfoji II in several of them, they can be attributed to his reign (1798-1833 A.D.). The late 17th and early 18th century saw the revival of the Tyāgarāja cult under Shahāji II and several works were composed on the deity at that time.

Coming back to the myth, a bewildered Somayāji looks helplessly at Cuntarar who assures him by secret gestures unnoticed by others, that the form is verily that of Parameśvara. Somayāji duly completes the sacrifice, after honouring the caṇḍāla guests and offering them the *havis*. The Brāhmaṇas, who abused the caṇḍālas and demanded that they leave the sacrificial hall, themselves become caṇḍālas by their deeds (*Brāhmaṇāḥ karmacaṇḍālāḥ*, (Skt. Mss. ibid 66.98-99) , even if only for a period of time everyday, because they failed to recognise Parameśvara (*na viduḥ Parameśvaram, ibid*) in a Caṇḍāla. These details are given in the Agastya version.[145]

The Marāṭhi work closely follows the Agastya version, even to the extent of using identical phrases, such as '*madhughūrṇitalolākṣī* (ch. 65, v. 58). It is interesting to note that in the *Śrī-Lalitāsahasranāmam*, one of the epithets of Devī is *madhughūrṇitaraktākṣī*, 'one whose eyes are red with wine'.[146]

The use of the name Mātaṅga and Mātaṅginī is significant as these are names of Tāntric deities, who had tribal origins and were popular in the *kaula* form of worship. Mātaṅginī is the name of a goddess worshipped in South India by the Madigas. She is the daughter of Mātaṅga, a Caṇḍāla, who by his *tapas* (austerities) became a *muni* or sage. In the folk traditions Mātaṅgī is associated with the anthill, for it is when a king pierced her anthill home with a lance that Mātaṅgī emerged bleeding, with the heavens in her left, and Ādiśeśa in the right. [147] The *Tantrasāra* of Kṛṣṇānanda of Bengal describes her as a Pulinda girl, '*pulinda yuvati*,[148] Pulinda being the name of an East Indian tribe.' In Maharashtra to this day there is a caste called the *mātaṅga* who are scheduled castes.

The *Tantrasāra* of Abinavagupta says of the goddess Mātaṅgī "I remember again and again the dark Mātaṅgī swayed by her passion, her beauteous face heated and moist with the sweat of amorous play, bearing a necklace of *guñja* berries and clad with leaves.[149] She is one of the *dasamahāvidyās* [150] and her *dhyāna ślokas* giving iconographical descriptions occur in the *Vāmakeśvaratantra* i.e. the *Nitayāṣoḍaśikārṇavam*, and also in the *Mātaṅginītantra*.[151]

The *Tantrasāra* of Kṛṣṇānanda of Bengal states that Mātaṅginī should be worshipped in the cremation ground or at crossroads with fish, meat, etc., and should be worshipped in the presence of women. She is a nocturnal deity only to be worshipped at night.[152] Gopinath Rao describes her gentler form in which she is an allotrope of Sarasvatī.[153] He bases his description on the *Kāḷikā Purāṇa*.

An interesting piece of information on Mātaṅgānīśa and Mātaṅginī comes from Sumatra and is found in the Buddhist Tāntric inscription of Ādityavarman engraved on the pedestal of a statue of Amoghapāśa.[154] From what we know of the Buddhist Tāntric beliefs of Ādityavarman it is easy to connect these deites with the *kaula* order. Madurai Mīnākṣī is worshipped as Mātaṅgī. She is green in colour, carries a *vīṇā* (a stringed musical instrument) and has a green parrot. Since she is also the temporal ruler of a realm she is called Rājamātaṅgī and Rāja Śyāmalā. She is treated as the intellectual power of Śrī-Rājarājeśvarī, the focus of Śrī-Vidyā worship.

We thus see in the myth of Somayāji the classic situation of conflict between the Vedic and Tāntric schools of thought, as expressed by the *vāma mārga* (left hand path). In the myth, Cuntarar plays the role of the bridge between these two tension zones. One can clearly see that the Nigamas and Āgamas are being reconciled. In the earlier Āgamas there is no mention of Tripurasundarī, who becomes the focal point of the later Āgamas through the mediation of the Tantras.

In the Tyāgarāja myth Somayāji looks up to Cuntarar as if he were Tyāgarāja himself. It is Cuntarar, who recognises Tyāgarāja in the caṇḍāla form and so the whole episode is connected with extollation of Cuntarar as well. In the *Tiruttoṇṭattokai* Cuntarar hails Cōmācimāṟaṉār and refers to himself as the slave of this devotee but in the *Śivabhaktavilāsa* Cuntarar is definitely the senior partner in the friendship. The *Periya Purāṇam*, by describing the activities of Cuntarar in heaven, makes him a semi-divine character.[155] His unorthodox life style and his enigmatic personality, tinged with a certain amount of sensuousness makes him the ideal link between Vedic, Āgamic and Tāntric practices.

A point to note is that none of these works refer explicity to any curse of *caṇḍālahood* pronounced by Śiva on the Brāhmaṇas, who failed to recognise God in the *caṇḍāla* form. Yet, this curse is crucial to the origin myth of the *Madhyāhna Brāhmaṇas* or *Madhyāhna Paṟaiyas* as they are called. The only subtle suggestion is that those who failed to recognise god became *karma caṇḍālas,* i.e. *caṇḍālas* by their deed. The Marāṭhi version remarks in a sadly ironic tone that the Brāhmaṇas ran from the touch of Parameśvara for fear of caste pollution only to try and seek him in Sūrya (*tyācī sparśa śankāmaṇīm dharūṇa ....pāhtē jhālē tē Sūryātē.*)[156]

Tiricirapuram Mīnātchicuntaram Piḷḷai describes this episode in his *Tiruvampar Purāṇam.*[157] which he composed in 1869 and which was based on the oral traditions drawn from Ampar. The *Mucukundasahasranāmam* refers to the myth in four verses.[158] Tirukkaṭavūr is another site associated with this myth.[159]

The first cogent narrative of the myth of the present day Madhyāhna Brāhmaṇas providing a link with the cult celebrations at Ampar is given by F.R. Hemingway in the *Tanjore Gazetteer of 1915.*[160] The community of *Madhyāhna Brāhmaṇas* are both resentful and aware of this myth and its relation to the socio-religious status that they are accorded in the orthodox framework of Tamiḻ society.

The geographical focus of the myth, according to Hemingway, lies in the village of Kōyil Tirumalam, "five miles north-east of Naṉṉilam in a straight line" and which has a grand new temple endowed by the Nāṭṭukoṭṭai Ceṭṭis. Hemingway refers to the tradition of the enactment of a play as a part of the *Brahmotsava* celebrations of this temple; for, though the present structure is new, the temple site and its traditions are ancient. The dramatic repertoire of the play is provided by the following myth. As it is the first clear exposition of the myth, it is quoted verbatim:

"There is however, an old story connected with the place, which is enacted at the largely attended festival here and in many popular dramas. This relates that the god of the Tiruvārūr temple was entreated by a *pujāri* of this place to be present in the village at a sacrifice in his (the god's) honour. The deity consented at length, but gave warning that he would come in a very unwelcome shape. He appeared as a Paṟaiyaṉ with beef on his back and followed by the four Vedas in the form of dogs and took his part in the sacrifice, thus accoutred and attended. All the Brāhmaṇas who were present ran away, and the god was so incensed that he condemned them to be Paṟaiyaṉs for one hour in the day from noon till one p.m., ever afterwards. There is a class of Brāhmaṇas called Mid-day Paṟaiyaṉs who are found in several districts and a colony of whom reside at Sēdānipuram, five miles west of Naṉṉilam. It is believed throughout the Tanjore district that the 'mid day Paṟaiyaṉs' are the descendants of Brāhmaṇas, thus cursed by the god. They are supposed to expiate their defilement by staying outside their houses for an hour and a half every day at mid day and to bathe afterwards; and if they do this they are much respected. Few of them, however, observe this rule, and orthodox persons will not eat with them, because of their omission to remove their defilement. They call themselves the Prathamaśākhā".

I have not had the opportunity to visit Kōyil Tirumālam, Tiruvampar or Amparmākālam as it is now called, but found an excellent spokesman for the community in the very well-informed Kuñcitapādam and the following information is based on an interview with him on 29th November 1982 at Iñcikolla.

He gave the number of Brāhmaṇas at the sacrifice as eleven and these, he knew, were regarded as the progenitors of his community. He strongly resented the social stigma and stated that till just thirty years ago, i.e. till the 1950s, marriage alliances between the orthodox Brāhmaṇas and the members of this community were practically unknown. He referred to his discussions with the elder Śaṅkarācārya and quoted the Pontiff's views that the members of the community were legitimate, orthodox followers of the *Śukla Yajur Veda*. He further referred to his 'Letters to the Editor' in *The Hindu* sometime in 1942 on the subject. He made an educated guess that there would be about three to four hundred families belonging to this community in Thañjāvūr district and he constantly referred to them as the *Prathamaśākhins*, refusing to call them either *Madhyāhna Brāhmaṇas* or *Madhyāhna paṟaiyas*.

According to Mr. Kuñcitapādam, all the *Prathamaśākhins* belong to the White (*Śukla*)*Yajur Veda* and they follow the Vājasaneyi text in the *Madhyandina* recension. The majority of people in South India belong to the *Kṛṣṇa Yajur Veda*. The appellation 'white' as applied to the *Śukla Yajurvedins*, indicated their worship of the Sun according to our informant. Macdonell, on the other hand, believed that since the *Saṁhitā* of the *Vājasaneyi* recension consists "entirely of the verses and formulas to be recited at the Sacrifice, and is therefore clear (*śukla*), that is to say, separated from the explanatory matter", it is called *Śukla Yajur Veda*. In contradistinction, *mantras* and explanations all mixed together is called *Kṛṣṇa*.[161] Those portions of the *Śatapatha Brāhmaṇa*, which is the Brāhmaṇa of the *White Yajur Veda*, and where Yājñavalkya plays the role of the highest authority, seem to be of a different date and compiled in a different terrain from those in which Śāṇḍilya, i.e. Books VI-X is regarded as the highest authority. Macdonell believes that all the books except VI-X were composed in North Eastern India, and that Yājñavalkya was probably a native of Videha.[162]

"The *Vājasaneyi* school of the *White YajurVeda* evidently felt a sense of superiority in their sacrificial lore which grew up in these eastern countries. Blame is frequently expressed in the *Śatapatha Brāhmaṇa* of the Adhvaryu priests of the Caraka school. The later is meant as a comprehensive term embracing the three older schools of the *Black Yajur Veda*". Macdonell further points out that the school of the *Vājasaneyins* spread South East down the Ganges valley. The *Taittirīyas* of the *Black Yajur Veda* have been found "only to the south of the Narmadā". Each of the Vedas have their ascribed *Śākhās*. Thus Ṛg Veda has 21 śākhās, Yajur Veda 109, etc. These *Śākhās* are said to contain one Upaniṣad each.

All the above information is important insofar as the Madhyāhna Brāhmaṇas are *White Yajurvedins*, followers of the Yājñavalkāya-Vājasaneyā tradition and carry memories of a schism between the *Vājasaneyins* and the *Taittirīyas*.[163] This schism is again explained through the medium of a quaint myth. This myth was narrated by Mr. Kuñcitapādam.[164] It is believed that the Guru Vaiśaṁpāyana was once treating a king with a loathsome disease with medicines brewed after a proper worship of Sūrya. Once Yājñavalkya, the disciple of Vaiśaṁpāyana was asked to take the medicine to the king, which he did. The monarch, however, treated him with scant respect. The mortified Yājñavalkya refused to take the medicine a second time to the king, whereupon Vaiśaṁpāyana, infuriated with his disciple's audacity in disobeying his command, bade him vomit all that he had learnt from him. The proud Yājñavalkya promptly did so and the vomit was swallowed by the *Tittiri* birds, who were the originators of the *Taittirīya Saṁhitā*. Yājñavalkya, then prayed to the Sun God and obtained the unrevealed portion of the Vedas and this was the *Śukla Yajur Veda*. This myth is recorded in the *Bhāgavata* (12th book XII-6), *Vārāha Purāṇa* and other ancient works. Authors like Uvaṭa, Mahīdāsa (commentator on the *Caraṇa Vyūha Pariśiṣṭa*) have also reproduced the same account of the *Śukla Yajur Veda*. The details of the myth are recorded by Max Müller in *A History of Ancient Sanskrit Literature*.[165]

The strong emphasis on Sun worship was brought to my attention by Mr. K. Kuñcitapādam, who further added that the *Prathama śākhins* place the body of a dead person facing the Sun, while the *Kṛṣṇa Yjurvedins* place it facing south, the direction of Yama, the God of Death. This practice of facing the Sun, was, I believe, the practice followed in the Vedic sacrifice of *Puruṣamedha* performed as a part of the scarifice to the Sun God.

The special *Purāṇa* of the *Prathama Śākhins* is called the *Āditya Purāṇa*. A copy of a *Purāṇa* by this name in Mss. form is available in the Saraswati Mahal Library, Thanjavur, but it deals mainly with the glorification of Śiva. It is nevertheless interesting that their sacred text should be called the *Āditya Purāṇa* and that Śiva should be equated with Āditya or the Sun God. The fact that the *Madhyāhna Brāhmaṇas* called themselves *Prathamaśākhins* may, in all probability, connect them with the *Prātiśākhyas* of the *Vājasaneyi* school. *Prātiśākhyas* are phoneticogrammatical treatises. Thus, the Prathamaśākhās could well have been purists - Vedic purists. It is in the *Kātyāyana Prātiśākhya* of Śukla Yajur Veda (Vājaseneyi Saṁhita) that the term *Mādhyandina* is mentioned as a disciple of Yājñavalkya. This was probably corrupted to Madhyāhna, and integrated with the myth.

It is interesting to see that the Marāṭhī version of the *Agastya Bhakta Vilāsa* mocks the Brāhmaṇas at the sacrifice as those who ran away from the real Parameśvara to look for him in the Sun. The *Prathamaśākhins* are also found amongst the Vaiṣṇavas (the *Aiyaṇkārs* and even the *Mādhvas* in the areas of Srirangam and Kāñcīpuram and they are allowed to function as officiants in temple rites (Information source: Mr. Kuñcitapādam of Iñcikollai).

Thus in the origin myth of this community one traces a socio-religious conflict between the pure Vedic worshippers with their strong belief in the caste system and the more heterodox worshippers of Śiva on the one hand and on the other between the *Tattirīyas*, as a school, predominantly from the South and the *Vājasaneyins* from Central and Eastern India. These *Yajurvedins* of the White school were, as pointed out by Macdonell, ritual purists and presumably foreign migrants to Tamil soil from areas now belonging to Bengal, this term used in a geographical sense.

Thus, ethnic, social and doctrinal tensions seem to be portrayed in the myth of Somayājimāranār. The Tāntric and Āgamic schools claim to be followers of the Vedas as well, but quite often the discrepancies in the doctrines between the hierarchic Vedic and the ritually egalitarian Tāntric seem to have been unbridgeable and the orthodox Vedic Brāhmaṇas regarded the Tāntrics as outside the pale of Vedic civilisation. That the conflict was not merely social is obvious by the reference to the drunken state of the deities and their carrying the carcass of a calf, etc., all emblems of left handed Tāntrics, which were totally abhorrent to the orthodox Vedins.

Nevertheless, the social angle cannot be entirely ignored. The *caṇḍālahood* of the manifestation is specifically emphasised in the 18th century Marāṭhī version where Somayāji is specifically described as the friend of the *caṇḍāla*.[166]

The Tiruvārūr temple has several unique ways of coping with the large paṟaiya population in the neighbourhood and has worked out through the rituals of the cult a peculiar socio-religious status for them *vis-a-vis* the cult deity.[167] There is a class of paṟaiyas called the *Yāṉai ēṟum perum Paṟaiyaṉ* (Pl.XIV), who are given special ritual status in the temple. Their special role in the Tyāgarāja temple will be critically assessed in the next chapter in connection with the temple's role as a bridge between zones of social tension.

The 12th century A.D. was an important period in the history of religion in Tamilnāḍu. It was the age of the culmination of Tāntric beliefs and it was also the beginning of sectarian rivalries. It is generally believed that Kulōttuṅga II, who was an ardent Śaiva and a patron of the Tyāgarāja cult, was responsible for casting the image of Viṣṇu in Chidambaram into the sea. The Somayāji myth, by its being referred to in the *Mucukundasahasranāmam* has been placed by us in the 12th century. The fact that the *Periya Purāṇam* does not mention it does not invalidate the dating, for Cēkkiḻār chose only themes that were of interest to him.

Thus while an uneasy amalgamation of ideas was worked out through the medium of temples, cults and myths, there remained an undercurrent of tension on a religious plane between those who came from the subcultural groups and propagated fierce and erotic rites and those who were the upholders of the Vedic Āgamic faith. That the differing life styles often posed problems for the temples and temple myth makers is apparent when one looks at the different situations of conflict as expressed through myths. Here it is interesting to note that the members of the extreme orthodoxy were punished so as to enable the system to survive.

The Two Compendiums of Tyāgarāja's līlaikaḷ or Divine Sport

An important anthology of Tyāgarāja myths was edited by Irācakōpāla Piḷḷai and published as a four volume work called *Tiyākarājalīlaikaḷ*.[168] Several references will be made to this work in the next chapter. It records three hundred and sixty-two sports or *līlai* of the Lord Tyāgarāja in and around Tiruvārūr. Details of the dating of this work, and problems connected with the finding of the Mss. will be discussed in the next chapter. Here, only a few samples of the *līlais* which dictate the various philosophical attitudes of the Tyāgarāja devotees will be discussed. The myths will be analysed only from philosophical and doctrinal, not social, perspective. The following *līlai* numbers refer to the numbers in the four volume work edited by Irācakōpāla Piḷḷai. In this chapter no reference is made to the other work of the same name, i.e. *Tiyākarājalīlaikaḷ* but edited by Mīnātcicuntaram Piḷḷai, as most of the 13 myths recorded in this work are connected with the Cōḻa monarchy.

The conflict between the concept of Destiny and Grace and the assessment of which is more important, forms the subject matter of *līlai* 26. In the story Grace is declared to be all important.

Līlai 31 is interesting as an allegory of the conflict between asceticism and erotic aspects of Tāntrism. Śiva and Pārvatī come to Tiruvārūr to enact their *līlai* of conjugal love and Bhṛgu sees them in the act of copulation. Śiva, unperturbed continues caressing Pārvatī. Bhṛgu curses them. Śiva, then explains to the irate Pārvatī that even the gods are not immune to rules of propriety and if they behave improperly they would be reprimanded by the Vedas. It is the use of the word Veda that is interesting and makes the situation an allegorical confrontation between the Vedic and the Tāntric world. This motif of 'interruption of sexual activity' occurs several times in the *Purāṇas*. It was, as suggested by Wendy O'Flaherty, an attempt to find the right balance between eroticism and asceticism.[169]

Līlai 54 is enigmatic in its moral stance. A king mourns the death of his wife. The Brāhmaṇas, whom he has been holding in scorn for some time, advise the distraught king that there are only two alternatives open to him; either to lead a chaste pure life and meet her in heaven or take a prostitute from Kāñcī. This i.e. the mention of the prostitute, presumably refers to the *Vāmācāra mārga* of the *kauḷa* school. The king decides to follow the latter advice. Sometime later he is separated from his new spouse in a forest and prays to Tyāgarāja. The ex-prostitute of Kāñcī, i.e. the spouse of the king is restored to him by Tyāgarāja. The king thereupon builds temples, institutes rites and rituals in the temple at Tiruvārūr.

The eclectic nature of beliefs is nowhere more explicitly brought out than in the two following stories. In *Līlai* 77, six disciples from six different caste groups share a common *guru* and each proceeds on his own path. The śūdra states that since he does not know the Sanskrit scriptures he will reach Tyāgarāja merely through *bhakti* and he does so. On the other end of the spectrum of beliefs is *līlai* 22, where Kasyapa requests Tyāgarāja to explain the Vedic *śloka: apāma somam* and Tyāgarāja does so. The whole episode is simply an excuse for an exposition of Advaita philosophy.

In *Līlai* 324, a learned Brāhmaṇa is a pious devotee of Tyāgarāja. To test him, Tyāgarāja dons the garb of a foul-smelling man full of oozing sores. Others shun him. The Brāhmaṇa nurses him. When asked where he comes from, the old man simply says that he is of Tiruvārūr. The test over, Tyāgarāja reveals himself as the man and blesses the Brāhmaṇa with *sāyujya* or eternal proximity to Śiva, a very *Śaiva Siddhānta* term for salvation.

Līlai 331 is almost a modified version of the *Śibi Jātaka*. A deer takes shelter with a boy to escape from a pursuing tiger. The father of the boy offers the tiger his own life. Tyāgeśa appears and impressed with the father's courage and devotion, grants him salvation. In this, compassion towards fellow human beings is emphasised as being of paramount importance. Here it is important to remember that Śibi is regarded as one of the mythical progenitors of the Cōḻas.

Several *līlais* are in fact simply the assertion of the efficacy of cultic rites. Thus, 338 and 339 both tell us how the proper carrying out of the rites of *abhiṣeka*, and other rites would benefit the realm, procure the fertility of the soil, preserve the *varṇāśrama dharma*, the chastity of the women of the realm, the *yāga* of the Brāhmaṇas and the *tapas* of the *munis*. Here not only are we told the effects the rituals are said to have but also given an idea of what constituted a proper state of affairs, a right order of society.

There are situations where Tyāgarāja is called upon to uphold two doctrines at variance. In *līlai* 43, a man wants to dedicate his life to the worship of Tyāgarāja and hence refuses to get married and seeks the deity's help as his parents compel him to wed. The parents too appeal to Tyāgarāja. Tyāgarāja gets out of the sticky wicket by changing the bride into a man and the two then become *sannyāsin* and worship Tyāgarāja. Thus the deity's casting vote on whether *gṛhasthāśrama* or *sannyāsa* is dearer to Tyāgarāja is held in abeyance.

In *līlai* 44, attention is focussed on another tension area. A king wants a son and is advised to perform a human sacrifice. The king sends his messengers to find a volunteer. The impoverished parents of three sons agree to offer their second son. The boy willingly complies. The parents soon after realise the enormity of their crime and beg Tyāgarāja to do something. A Divine voice is heard proclaiming that the very gods who can grant a son can do so even without the *narabali* (human sacrifice). The king, pleased, frees the lad. This is obviously an adaptation of the Vedic myth of Śunaḥśepa and human sacrifice. Furthermore, it reflects the attempt at taming the fiercer elements in the faith.

Two themes occur repeatedly in these myths. One is that of *bhakti* and the other of Divine Grace, both central doctrines of the *Siddhānta* school. Tyāgarāja in the description of his *līlais* almost seeks out souls to bestow his grace on them. He blesses a prostitute (*Līlai* 52), a merchant (*Līlai* 61), a gambler (*Līlai* 62), a devout but poor Brāhmaṇa (*Līlai* 65), a king (*Līlai* 66), etc. They are all interspersed with doctrines on the efficacy of pilgrimages and pilgrim rites.

There are, however, some very strange stories which adopt a rather enigmatic moral stance. In *līlai* 76, for example, a newlywed couple are passing through a forest and they are attacked by a tiger. The man runs for his life and abandons the woman, who is saved by a brave passer-by. The woman falls in love with her saviour and wants to marry him. The man explains how it is improper for him to wed an already married woman. This, however, does not stop him from secretly meeting the woman. Suddenly the story ends with the statement that the king was pleased with this man, a devotee of Tyāgarāja. Obviously, an important but controversial moral problem had been enunciated but could not be absorbed within the framework of the "sacred", however broad that parameter may be. It was too "secular" and too socially sensitive to be synthesised.

Tyāgarāja, in these *līlais,* is presented as an infinitely human, understanding and compassionate 'person'. In *līlai* 81 for example, there is a debate between a *guru* and his disciple. Can versatility in the Śāstras destroy *kāma* (lust, eroticism, etc.)? The *guru* states that it does not necessarily have to be so. The disciple, disappointed at the guru's attitude, leaves him in a fit of intellectual arrogance. Tyāgarāja sends a beautiful woman on a thunderous night. She is forced to take refuge in the same room as the disciple. The hot-blooded disciple realises his folly and apologises to the *guru,* and the eternal conflict between life affirmation and life renunciation goes on in the Hindu debate.

The usual pattern of the myths is that Tyāgarāja takes human form to correct an erring soul, be it to wipe out pride, anger or greed or simply to reward the truly pious after their piety has been put to the test. He manifests himself as a servant, even as a mid-wife to alleviate the sufferings of a calving cow (*Līlai* 239). This again is a well-known motif. The god Tāyumāṉavar of Tirucci is said to have acted as a midwife, a myth which offers explanation of his name (one who became even the mother), i.e. looked after the daughter in labour.

Līlai 141 depicts a fickle man, good at one moment and wickedly avaricious the next. It is interesting to see the reason for the fickleness. We are told, that since he was born in Tiruvārūr he was inherently good and it was due to the residual impressions of his previous lives that he was fickle. His friend tells him that the only way to overcome this is to steal something from Tyāgarāja, get caught and in full vigour to pray to the deity and that should rid him of his greed. He does as he is told, and when caught, clings to the feet of Tyāgarāja so firmly that the soldiers are unable to separate him from the deity, and thus enlightened he drops the unseemly side of his personality. This is one of the explanations of Tāntric attitudes that in order to get rid of temptation, get at its heart.

Some of the *līlais* ask deep penetrating questions but offer such naive answers that it is interesting to see the mind function at two different levels. This moving between levels is typical of this genre of pilgrim literature. Thus, in *līlai* 225, a group of Brāhmaṇas are distressed to note that despite all their efforts they cannot avoid being quarrelsome and difficult in their relationships amongst themselves. They pose the problem to the minister who says that only Tyāgarāja can explain the mystery. Tyāgarāja explains that it is because of sins in previous lives that they cannot live in human amity and in order to expiate their sins they are asked to bathe in the Kamalālaya (the holy tank in the temple complex). Having done so they live in harmony.

No scepticism was tolerated as is evident from *līlai* 241. A minister of the king of Kerala advises his royal master not to spend so much money on rites and rituals of Tyāgarāja for the treasury would be impoverished. Promptly the minister is afflicted with blindness and his wife entreats lord Tyāgarāja on his behalf, bathes in the Kamalālaya and all is well.

In *līlai* 271 the concept of ego-centredness is dealt with. A Brāhmaṇa, who piously follows the call of his profession, is restless and worries about the bringing up of his children and feeding the family etc. Tyāgarāja decides to lead the whole family into a dense forest and nobody knows the way out. The Brāhmaṇa realizing his total helplessness prays to god and is finally redeemed. At the moment of quest, truth dawns on him that he is not the Prime Mover and his *ajñāna* or ignorance and his restlessness vanish. The enlightenment in these stories is usually presented as sudden and instantaneous, almost akin to the Zen *satori*, a metamorphosis, a change of perspective and vision. This however, occurs only by the Grace of Tyāgarāja.

Other concepts that are explored are those of the divine *maṇḍala*, the divine dance, etc. In *līlai* 218, we are told that the Cōḻa king, in order to test the honesty of his subjects, once proclaimed that a diamond ring had been found and the genuine claimant would not only get the ring but also half the kingdom. Despite this temptation, the honest men of the realm did not want to put in a false claim. Nevertheless, it attracted a merchant from Kaliṅga and he came to claim it. However, he would not claim it within the divine *maṇḍala* of Tiruvārūr, sacred to Tyāgarāja. He therefore persuaded the king's men to bring the jewels outside the boundaries of Tiruvārūr and then claimed it as his own. Meanwhile Tyāgarāja, to enlighten him, played a trick. Everytime he looked at the ring with greed it looked to him like a snarling serpent; everytime he looked at it with Tyāgarāja in his mind it became once again the brilliantly dazzling diamond. Cured of his greed the merchant returned the jewel and became an ardent devotee of Tyāgarāja.

Dance as a *līlai*, as a mode of revelation of True Knowledge is mentioned several times. To give one example, in *līlai* 296 the Tyāgarāja dances the Ānandatāṇḍava of Chidambaram to please a hunter devotee. Thus Tyāgarāja's *ajapānaṭanam* got gradually fused with the *Ānandatāṇḍava* of Chidambaram and the two became identical in the minds of the devotees.

The *Tiyākarājalīlaikaḷ* is an attempt at popularising philosophical and ethical systems through the medium of myths. Typically a story is told, an event is believed to have occurred, a divine voice is believed to have been heard, a divine presence revealed, the tension in the situation is alleviated and at the end of every myth there occurs the refrain, i.e."the 'event' was reported throughout the realm". The circulation of the myth was important for on it depended the survival of the cult. The cultic network for disseminating the beliefs was a crucial element.

Another cultural remnant, as it were, from the earlier period, which finds expression in the *Tiyākarājalīlaikaḷ* is the story of conflict between Śaivas, Bauddhas and Jainas. This, by the time these *līlais* were written down, had surely become a cultural motif, for Buddhism as a force was a spent one. It therefore records an early oral tradition. Tyāgarāja becomes the culture hero of the Tamiḻ Śaivas. In the *līlais* portraying this conflict there is no attempt at any rapprochement. In *līlai* 114 for example, the devotees of Tyāgarāja approach him and mourn that in the very city of the Lord, the heretics were winning converts and they implored him to do something about it. He promptly blinds the Bauddhas and they leave the place.

In this context George Spencer has pointed out how in the workings of the Tamiḻ myths the conflict between Śaivas and the Bauddhas or the Jainas is always fought out in the presence of a king.[170] The royal person is a vital factor for it was state patronage that was in question. In this bid the Bauddhas and Jainas lost in South India and the Śaivas won and under the Cōḻas Śaivism became the royal cult, though under Vijayanagara and the Nāyakas it gave way, to some extent, to Vaiṣṇavism. Stories from the life of Ñāṉacampantar at Madurai make the point obvious.

Thus, religious synthesis was attempted only within the Hindu fold. No compromises were possible with the Buddhists and the Jainas, but many of their doctrines were absorbed into the Śaiva and Vaiṣṇava faith and many of the stories in the *Tiyākarājalīlaikaḷ* read like Buddhist parables. It is only now in contemporary Neo-Hinduism that conscious attempts are being made to incorporate the Buddhists, Jainas, Sikhs etc. to present a unified cultural front as a strategy to mobilise the masses by means of a religio-cultural nationalism.

The system, in order to survive, had to have popular appeal and the temple and temple cults and the myths acted as cultural integrators. Several beliefs, once considered outlandish and outside the pale of Vedic-Āgamic fold were brought into it by smoothing out some of the rough edges and providing their practices with a philosophical base. Rival beliefs were neutralised by persecution on the one hand and imitation on the other.

In order to assess the significance of temples as socio-cultural integrators, the study would have to extend further to the field of the impact that they had on the believers and on society at large and also to institutions other than but akin to temples through which such an integration was accomplished. This would be attempted in the next chapter.

CONCLUSION

To sum up, temples were based on the concept of the Āgamas which were fashioned to propitiate icons entempled in specific localities and regions. Thus temple worship fostered a regional unity and a regional consciousness. The Āgama, though drawn from the stream of beliefs centering around territorial and chthonic deities, were merged in some form with the more universalistic Vedic beliefs.

The Bhakti movement, which seemed apparently to challenge the structured Vedic-Āgamic faith, was soon marshalled to support the system it set out to challenge. It, however brought

Tamilnāḍu into the Sanskritic fold and established a religious system in which two distinct streams were brought together and coalesced. That the synthesis was partial is clear from the fact that the *ōtuvār*, who is the custodian of the *Tirumuṟai*, the bible of the Tamiḻ bhakti school, and the *Śivācārya*, who is the custodian of the Sanskrit Āgamic thought, to this day stand as two parallel movements. The former sings his Tamiḻ hymns of praise standing at the doorway of the *garbhagṛha* or sanctum sanctorum, the latter offers direct worship to the icon, inside the *garbhagṛha*. Thus, the *ōtuvār* was definitely assigned an inferior but indispensable role in the hierarchy. For a temple rite to be efficacious chants drawn from both streams as well as officiants drawn from both the Sanskritic and Tamiḻ fold were essential.

That the Āgamic and Vedic streams were also two distinct streams is clear from the fact that the Vedic *purohita* has his *homa* in the *ardha manṭapa*. It is the prerogative only of the Śivācārya to worship the deity. The Vedas, in the general sense, may be higher in the hierarchy but the Āgamic priest was the closest to the deity, once it was entempled. He officiated in the rites of the chthonic, territorial, and regional deity who was the immediate protector of the ruler and his regional realm. The Vedic *hotṛ* was the more distant even if more universalistic symbol. This distinction becomes even more obvious when we notice temples like Tiruvoṟṟiyūr where Śaiva priests, Śākta priests, *Smārta kurukkaḷ*, *Uvacar* and *Ādiśaiva kurukkaḷs* along with special Nambūdiris (Brāhmaṇa priests from Kerala) form the ritual personnel of the temple. The last mentioned group are believed to have been introduced into Tamiḻnāḍu by Śaṅkara. They represent special group interests as well.

The worship of the goddess and the concomitant development of Tāntric worship with its Yogic leanings had a profound impact on temple cults and the Tyāgarāja himself was converted into the esoteric *Śrī-cakra* emblem. That an ambivalent relationship persisted with the *kauḷamārgas* is evident from several myths and ritual practices. The fact that Hinduism survived as a system is, however, mainly due to the attempts of the temples and temple cults which acted as cultural arbitrators between several belief systems belonging to disparate levels of civilisation, and provided the institutional framework within which the orthodox and heterodox could hold a discourse.

NOTES

1. 185 of 1912 *from Tiruvoṟṟiyūr for example records a* Bhaṭṭavṛtti. *Eṇṇāyiram records several. These were different from specific money endowments for feeding Brāhmaṇas well versed in the Vedas and even from the* Brahmadeya *which were communal lands for Brāhmaṇas in general.* Bhaṭṭavṛtti *were different as they were special grants for teachers. Shahāji in the 18th century endowed the village of Shahājipuram for 49 scholars, each with their own individual property. This was legally a* Bhaṭṭavṛtti *not a* Brahmadeya.
2. The main types of elee mosynary teṇure were three: Brahmadeya, Devadāna and Ekabhoga. Sometimes Devadāna and Brahmadeya were combined, e.g. 127 of 1925; 388 of 1913. The sabhā of the Brahmadeyas required as electoral qualifications expertise in the Vedas and śāstras as recorded in the *Uttaramērūr* epigraph. There were also examples of ekabhoga brahmadeya, that is sole proprietorship by Brāhmaṇas recorded in the Anbil Plates of Cuntara Cōlā (E.I. *X.V, p. 60).*
3. See Fuller, C.J., *Servants of the Goddess,* Sp., pp. 36-8.
4. *Periya Purāṇam* vv. 81, 1063, 1208, 1222, 1286, and 2525.
5. *Tirumuṟai, VII. 10. 1.*
6. *Tirumuṟai, VII. 69. 2.*
7. *Ibid., VII. 69. 9.*
8. *Ibid., VII. 57. 10.*
9. *Ibid., VII. 89. 7. Refs. in notes 5-9 above are to hymns by Cuntarar.*
10. Cited by Narayana Ayyar, C.V., *Origin and Early History of Śaivism in South India,* pp. 108-10.
11. Tirumuṟai, III. 108. 1.
12. *Ibid.,* III. 108. 3. Hymn 108 is full of references to the Anti- Vedic nature of Jaina beliefs. This was sung at Tiruvālavāy (Madurai). Also hymns *47 and 53* sung at *Tiruvālavāy and Tiruvāṉaikkā.* Also *III.297, III.305, III.366 etc.*
13. Tirumuṟai, *IV. 11. 5.*
14. Ishwaran, K., *'Bhakti Tradition and Modernisation' in Lele, Jayant (ed.),* Tradition and Modernity in Bhakti Movements, *E.J. Brill, Leyden, 1981, p. 75.*
15. Tirumuṟai, *III. 57. 10. sung at Oṟṟiyūr (Tiruvoṟṟiyūr).*
16. *Tirumūlar* in his 2nd Tantra places a great stress on temple worship and *vv 516-19* (Tantra 2, *19.3.)* of Tirumantiram states *"If* pūjā *were not performed well in the temple, rains will decrease, the fighting power of the king will also diminish. If a Brāhmaṇa who is not well-versed in the Āgamas but is a Brāhmaṇa only by name is appointed an* arcaka, *the king will suffer from diseases and famine will occur in the land". The Āgamas are regarded as emanating from Śiva and hence feeding a few ash-smeared Māhēśvaras is regarded as better than food given to a crore of Brāhmaṇas who perform sacrifice.*
17. See Nagasamy, R., *"Śiva worship as gleaned from Appar's Devaram" in* Śaiva Siddhānta, 1, 1966, pp. 49-61.
18. Before the abolition of the Devadāsī system sacred dance items were performed called the Kavuttuvams beginning with jatis and followed by sāhitya. See Seetha, S., Tanjore as a Seat of Music, *Madras, 1981, pp. 516-18.*
19. The cāyarakṣai *of Tiruvārūr* and the ardhayāmam *of Cidambaram* are regarded as aesthetically most pleasing and ritually most efficacious.
20. *See Boner, Alice (ed.)* Vāstuśāstra Upaniṣad *The Essence of Form in Sacred Art,* Vārāṇasī, 1981 - Introduction.

21. *Bhāgavatamāhātmyam*, 1: 45-50, Bhakti is personified and says "Born in Drāviḍa I grew up in Karnāṭaka and became old in Mahārāṣṭra and Gujrat ...", and then goes on to conclude that she was rejuvenated in Vrindāvan; cited by Dhavamony, Mariasusai, Love of God according to Śaiva Siddhanta, p. 102.
22. *Tirumantiram*, st. 1484 ff refers to the three mārgas for the first time.
23. *Ibid.*, v. 1861. See *note 16* above for his loyalty to the aṭiyār.
24. Devotion to *Śaiva aṭiyārs* and contempt and intolerance toward the Jainas and Buddhists are characteristic traits of all the *nāyaṉmār*. Cuntarar's composition of the *Tiruttoṇṭattokai*, offering his obeisance to each one of the *aṭiyār*, by naming every one is one example of the respect shown to the institution of saints. An even more important example of institutionalised reverence towards *Śivabhaktas* is provided by the outrage expressed by *Viṟanmīṇṭār* when he felt that Cuntarar had slighted the congregation of *aṭiyār* assembled at the *Tēvāciriyamaṇṭapam* at Tiruvārūr. His rage seems all the more strange when we bear in mind that the only crime of Cuntarar was that he went staight to the sanctum sanctorum without offering his obeisance to the august body assembled in the temple. His direct approach to God was circumspect. The Periya Purāṇam approvingly narrates the biographies of several *nāyaṉmār* who would die, murder, surrender everything, rather than insult a *Śaiva aṭiyār*. Thus it was not a personal bond but was a cult or sect-loyalty that was demanded. For the attitudes of the *nāyaṉmār* against the Jainas, including having them impaled, see Subrahmanya Aiyar, K.V., *'Origin and decline of Buddhism and Jainism in South India'*. Indian Antiquary, Vol. 40. 1911, pp. 218 ff; Also Chengalvaraya Pillai, *V.S.,Tēvāram Oḷi Neṟi, Appar, Campantar and Cuntarar* pp. 190-95, 189-98, 154-55 respectively.
25. *Tirumantiram 1604*. A similar idea is expressed by Appar. *See Tev. V. 60.* See also *Periya Purāṇam, Tirunāvukkaracu Purāṇam, v. 3.* "What will you do with your castes and creed?" asks Appar, "or even your scriptures", for if you just prayed to Śiva you will be saved.
26. Appar, *Tirumuṟai*, VI. 74. 4.
27. Appar, VI. *Taṉiṭiruttāṇṭakam* v. 10.
28. *Periya Purāṇam, Kaḻarciṅka n. Purāṇam* vv. 3. ff Sp. vv. 6. & 10.
29. *Periya Purāṇam, Taṇṭiyaṭikaḷ Purāṇam*, Sp. vv. 10, 19, 21.
30. *Periya Purāṇam, Naminantiyatikal n. Purāṇam* sp. vv. 10-154.
31. *Māṇikkavācakar*, trans. G.U. Pope.
32. Upadhyaya, G.P., *Brāhmaṇas in Ancient India*, p. 89.
33. Sastri, K.A.N., *Cōḻas*, Vol. II, Pt. I., p. 539.
34. *Periya Purāṇam, Tirumalai Carukkam* refers to Cuntarar's life in *Kailāsa* before being born a mortal. The Sanskrit work *Śivabhakta vilāsa* has a very long section, Chs. 3-13 that describes his 'life' on *Kailāsa* as *Hālāla Sundara*, born of the image of *Śiva*, and officiating as one of his attendants.
35. VII. 39 beginning with *"Tillai vāḻ antaṇar tam aṭiyārkkum aṭiyēṉ"* and following with salutation to the whole group of *ātiyār* whose slave Cuntarar claims to be.
36. *VII. 89. 9 and VII. 35.2* both refer to this autobiographical detail. See appendix A.
37. Tiruvārūr Ratna Tēcikar pointed out the significance of the figure 21 to me. Personal communication February 1984.
38. *Mucukundasahasranāmam*, vv. pp. 260-1.
39. *Ibid.*, v. 262. See appendix A.

40. *Ibid.*, v. 267.
41. *ARE 1911*, No.471, See also S.I.I., Vol. V., 1358. This was in 9th year of Rājādhirāja II's reign i.e.1175 A.D. "when the deity Patampakka Nāyakka tēvar was taken underneath the makiḻam tree on the 6th day of the Paṅkuṉi Uttiram festival".
42. E.I. XXVII, pp. 292-303.
43. Turner, V. and Turner, Edith, *Image and Pilgrimage in Christian Culture. p.29*
44. Tirumuṟai, VII.32, especially line 8.
45. For details see Pūrṇānanda's *Kāmakalāvilāsa*. Also *Lalitā Sahasranāma, Saundaryalaharī, Yoginīhṛdaya, Varivasyārahasya* and other Tāntric texts of the *Śrī-Vidyā Kula.*
46. The *Śrī-Cakra* is the primary symbol of *Śrī-Vidyā*. The first forty-one stanzas of the *Saundaryalaharī* relate to the formation of the *Śrī-Cakra.* For the stages in the drawing of the *Śrī-Cakra* see Pandit S. Subrahmanya Sastri and T.R. Srinivasa Ayyangar (ed.), *Saundarya Laharī*, Introduction, p.2.
47. This was a functioning maṭha till recently and was situated in the East bank of the Kamalālaya.
48. See Devangana Desai, *The Erotic Sculptures of India*, p.18
49. See Nagasaṁy, R., *in South Indian Studies, Vol.I, pp.134-5,* he links it with descriptions in *Takkayākkapparaṇi.* The Tārācuram icon is housed in a modern shrine but is a Cōḻa piece. It is now worshipped as Cakrāyī.
50. See Bibliography. For reference to Mahāvratin see Pathak, V., History of Śaiva Sects in Northern India, p.21
51. Pathak,V. op.cit p.21 Fleet, J.F.(ed.and trans), *'Sanskrit and Old Kanarese Inscriptions', Indian Antiquary 1880, pp.123-5.* This records the grant of the village of Baḷegram for the rite of *guggula pūjā* in the temple of Kapāleśvara and for the benefit of the great ascetics *(mahāvrātis)* who live in the temple. The two works written during the Vijayanagara rule, *Madhurāvijaya* (IV 4.11) and *Vemabhūpālacarita (1.8)* refer to the *gugguladhūpa* in all *Śiva* temples. Whether this had anything to do with the *guggulapūjā* which was a rite of self torture, it is difficult to say.
52. Lorenzen, David, *The Kāpālikas and Kālamukhas*, p. 83 ff.
53. Hoisington, Civapirakācam of Umāpati, in *The Journal of the American Oriental Society*, IV., 1854.
54. Sen, Chitrabhanu, *Vedic Index*.
55. *181 of 1912* of the 20th year of Kannaradeva, i.e. the Rāṣṭrakūṭa king Kṛṣṇa III who came to the throne in 939 a.d. So this epigraph belongs to 959 a.d. *739 and 735 of 1905* seem to record events in Caturānana's earlier life when he was a civilian in Grāmam. For this earlier account see *E.I. XXVII*, pp. 292-303. His monastic career at Tiruvoṟṟiyūr dates from 957 a.d. as recorded in 177 of *ARE 1912. S.I.I.* Vol. V., 1354, which is 104 of *ARE 1912* refers to him in the reign of Rājendra I (dated 1043 a.d.). 126 of *ARE 1912* is not dated but refers to the building of the temple at Tiruvoṟṟiyūr at the bidding of Caturānana in the reign of Rājendra I. This is 553 of *S.I.I.*, Vol. IV. *S.I.I.*, Vol. V, 1356 which refers to Caturānana belongs to the reign of Kulōttuṅga I (1077 a.d.). *371 of 1911 (403 of 1896), 206 of 1912* of the time of Rājādhirāja II (1171-72 a.d.) describes Caturānana as the head of the *maṭha* and a contemporary of Vāgīṣa Bhaṭṭa, an expounder of *Somasiddhānta*.
56. *126 of ARE 1912* (*S.I.I.*, Vol. IV, 553).
57. 177 of *ARE 1912* - *'bibhrāṇe Caturānane maṭhapatau dharmyām dhuram'*.

58. *S.I.I.*, Vol. V. 1354; *104 of 1912*.
59. 371 of *ARE 1911; 206 of 1912*.
60. 206 of *ARE 1912*, *'vārīśaścaturānano maṭhapatiḥ sthityartham ālekhayet'*.
61. Sastri, K.A.N., *Cōḻas*, Vol. II, pt. I, pp. 281-5.
62. Raghava Aiyangar, R., 'Life and Work of Kambaṉ', *Tamiḻ*, Vol. III, cited by Sastri, K.A.N., *Cōḻas*, (2nd ed.), p. 672. Rangacharya, *Topographical List*, p. 434, inscription number 973.
63. *Tiruvoṟṟiyūr Purāṇam*, Canto 12.
64. Rao, T.A.G. *Elements of Hindu Iconography* - photograph facing p. 285.
65. Raghavan,V., ed. *Sarvadvavilāsa*, p. 71.
66. 168 of *ARE 1912*.
67. 550 of *ARE 1904*; 595 of *S.I.I.* XVII of the time of Kulottuṅga *III*.
68. *S.I.I.*, XI, no 88 comes from Paḷḷimaṭam, Ramnad district, and refers to *Mahāvratikal* "attached to the Sundara Pāṇḍiya Īśvara Kōyil and belongs to the 11th century a.d." 100 of *ARE 1906* comes from Jambai and the fact that the head of the *maṭha* is called *mahāvrati* Lakulīśvara establishes a close link with the Lakulīśvara Pāśupatas.
69. Sastri, K.A.N., *Cōḻas*, 2nd Ed., p. 648.
70. *E.I.*, Vol. V. (1898-99), pp. 213-65. Also *ARE 1915*, Reports Past I, Para. 25, p. 88. 443 of *1914*, *E.C.* VII, Skt. 106 dated 1098 a.d. Several Simha Parisad records have come from Andhra Pradesh.
71. The two orders are the *Siṁha Pariṣad* and the *Śakti Pariṣad*. 443 of *1914* says "Of those who enjoy the fruits of the charity given both to gods and ascetics the latter must punish the wicked, if there be any in the congregation and drive them out of the monastery. This monastery will always be for ascetics who follow a strict discipline (*niṣṭhā*). Such ascetics as go astray giving up *brahmacarya* must be expelled by the ruling king, chief officer and a council of 12 great men of Moringeri and replaced by better teachers of the same school".
72. Lorenzen, David, *op. cit.*, p. 150 ff. Also *J.B.B.R.A.S.*, X, 167-298.
73. The Caturānana inscriptions provide a clue and a Kannada inscription from Belagave, Shimoga district. *E.C.* VII, Skt. 106 refers to a Caturānana Paṇḍita, the chief priest of the Tripurāntaka temple which was Kālamukha temple. The Kālamukha heads had names ending in Paṇḍita. An inscription from Chinnatāmbūlam in Bellary district refers to the guru Kālamukha Ācārya Nirañjana Paṇḍita and is published in *S.I.I.*, Vol. IX, pt. I, 133 and 218. Caturānana, according to Tiruvoṟṟiyūr Epigraphs, followed a certain Nirañjanaguru.
74. *ARE 1912*, 127, 132, 138, 155, etc.
75. Ananta Śaṁbhu in his gloss on *Siddhāntasārāvali* of Trilocanaśiva says that Rājendra Cōla on reaching the Ganges and having bathed there discovered the many learned men and brought them back to the land of the Cōḻas, in his own country (*svarājyā sthāpayāmāsa*). See *Journal of Oriental Research*, VII, p. 200.
76. See Sastri, *Cōḻas*, p. 484. As Mahīpala was his adversary the teachers could well belong to the Golaki *maṭha*.
77. One of the most important monastic networks with Vārāṇasī as its headquarters was the *Golaki maṭha* (q.v).
78. Rāmānuja *Śrī-Bhāṣya* 2.2.35-37, cited by Lorenzen, op.cit p. 4.
79. *ibid*, p. 4.
80. Cited by O'Flaherty, Wendy, *The Origin of Evil in Hindu Mythology*.

81. Sastri Hrishikesh, *Varaha Purāṇa*, 70, 29-42, cited by O'Flaherty, Wendy, *op. cit.*, p. 250.
82. *Padma Purāṇa*, 6, 263; 1-91 cited *ibid*
83. O'Flaherty, Wendy, *op. cit.*, p. 151.
84. Upadhyaya, Govinda Prasad, *Brahmins in Ancient India*, p. 87.
85. Upadhyaya, op. cit., p. 239, states that with the rise of powerful dynasties the Brāhmaṇas attempted to ally with the monarchy and the kings welcomed them because of their yeoman service to the process of "detribalisation of the primitive social strata, which extended the power of the king over them".
86. Upadhyaya, *op. cit.*, 87.
87. Mahalingam, T.V., 'The Pāśupatas in South India', *J.I.H.*, Vol. 27, pp. 43-53. See also *Memoirs of the Epigraphical Report 1936-37*, pt. II. para. 79.
88. *Hara, Minoru. See note 89 below.*
89. Hara Minoru, 'Nakulīśa Pāśupata Darśanam' in *Indo Iranian Journal*, Vol. II, (1957-58), pp. 8-32 describes the rites under the two headings 'upahāra' and 'dvāra'. These include laughing (*ahaha*=wild laugh), singing, *nṛtya, huddukāra* (making strange sounds with tongue in the palate), *namaskāra*, and as *dvāra* or preliminary practice, *krathana* (fainting), *spandana* (trembling), *mandana* (stumbling), *sṛṅgāraṇa* (erotic gestures), etc. See Dasgupta, S.N., *History of Indian Philosophy*, Vol V., pp. 13 ff. and O'Flaherty, Wendy, op. cit., pp. 182 ff.
90. O'Flaherty, *ibid*.
91. Cited by Lorenzen, *op. cit.* p.83
92. *Pāśupata Sūtra Commentrary*, p. 6
93. Dasgupta, S.N., *op.cit.*, p. 132.
94. Thus, there seems to have been both a *śrauta* and *aśrauta Pāśupata*, an orthodox and a heterodox school. *Kūrma Purāṇa* (XVI. 1) states "By me was first composed for the attainment of liberation *Śrauta Pāśupata*, which is excellent, subtle and secret, the essence of Vedas. The learned who are devoted to the Veda should meditate on Śiva Pāśupata. This is Pāśupata Yoga to be practised by seekers of liberation. By me have also been spoken *Pāśupata,Soma,Lakula* and *Bhairava* opposed to Veda.
    They should not be practised." Karmarkar, A.P., *The Vrātya or Dravidian Systems*, pp. 219-20.
95. Chakaravarti Chintaharan, 'The Soma or Saumya Sect of the Śaivas', *I.H.Q.*, 1932. pp. 221-23; Also Handiqui (Ed), *Naiṣadhacarita*, pp. 640-44. The Śaiva Āgamas also refer to the Somasiddhāntins. "They are a bridge between Pāśupata and Śākta cults" according to K.A.N. Sastri, *The Cultural History of India*, Vol. 2, p. 29.
96. *Vāman Pāśupatam Somam lāṅgalam caiva bhairavam na sevyam etat kathitam Vedabhyam tathetarat'*. Cited by Chakravarti, *op. cit.*, p. 221. see also note 100.
97. Cited by Pathak, *op. cit.*, p. 24.
98. Handiqui, *op. cit.*, p. 640 ff.
99. The following disconnected facts can be gleaned from this work:
    a) The Somasiddhāntin is a votary of Mahābhairava.
    b) Drinks wine from a skull cup (3.13).
    c) Is a mahāsiddha with magical powers (3.22)
    d) Philosphically he believes that the world, though full of diversities is identical with Śiva (*janāmitho bhinnā abhinnamīśvarāt*).
    e) The liberated soul assumes the form of Śiva and sports with its beautiful mistress like Śiva does with Pārvatī (3.16).

100. Act IV. vv. 32 ff. This work was composed in the first half of the 17th century A.D. and describes a drunken *Kāpālika Somasiddhāntin* who offers human sacrifice to Mahābhairava and the deity pleased grants him a form similar to the divine (4.29) and unrestricted sensual pleasures. The Somasiddhāntin says that though they accept the Vedas, the orthodox revile them for their practices which are based on the *Bhairava Āgamas.*
101. *138 of 1912* from Tiruvoṟṟiyūr of Rājendra I's time refers to the endowment of 90 sheep for a lamp by a certain Kaṅkaikoṇṭacōḻaṉ of Tiruvārūr for the merit of a certain man who stabbed himself and died in order to relieve the distress of the owner. There are several examples of such ritual suicides.
102. Suicides are depicted in the sculptures of Mahābalipuram, e.g. Mahiṣāsuramardinī Cave which shows a man offering his head to Durgā. Also at Pullamaṅkai, etc. Goldsmiths were offered as sacrifices at Kaṇṇaki altars. This is referred to by Induchūdan while describing the present day mimic rites at the Caranganore temple. Induchūdan, *The Secret Chamber.* See also Karmarkar, *op.cit.*, p. 214. See Obeysekere, *The Pattiṇi Cult.*
103. For its description and its division into *hādi* and *kādi* schools see *Brahmāṇḍa Purāṇa,* 4. 39. 9-10.
104. Lakṣmīdhara, *Commentary on Saundaryalaharī,* Govt. Oriental Mss. Series, p. 82.
105. Ghurye, G.S., *Indian Sādhus,* p. 128.
106. Śaṅkara, according to the folk ballad *Kōvalaṉkatai* is said to have thrown the fierce goddess Vaṭṭappāṟaiyammaṉ into a well and covered her with a slab of stone and a stone is still pointed out by the priests as being the one. *Śaṅkaravijaya* refers to similar stories. C. Krishnamurthy in his unpublished thesis *The Tiruvoṟṟiyūr Temple* Madras University, refers to several similar legends connected with Vaṭṭappāṟai and the *saumya rūpa* or the benign form of Śiva. See also Mahalingam, *op. cit.*, p. 51
107. Nagaśaṁy, R.*Tāntric Cult of South India,* p.2
108. Ed. Dvivedi, V.V., *Nityāṣoḍaśikārṇava,* where he points out that the text is a part of what is called the *Vāmakeśvaratantra* which is really a ghost title and no such work has been found. See note 151 below.
109. A typical example is v. 1 itself; *"hamsaḥ so'ham mantramāyasvāsani kāryai gāyatrimajñuṣu sarveṣapinaddha tadrayah san avirbhūdvasanaya yastam sanmārgam mattamayūram gurumīḍe"*
110. v.6 where he recommends that the breaths be offered to the different categories. He also tries to explain in terms of the *mattamayūra* phraseology and the reasons for its being 21,600.
111. The *kaṭapayādi system* is also used in Carnatic music in the classification of the *melakartā/ragas.* It is a system of reckoning by which ka, kha, ga, gha and ṅa are equated with 1, 2, 3, 4 and 5 respectively; then ca becomes 5, cha 6 , and so on; the next series begins with ṭa, ṭha, ḍ, ḍh, ṇa being 1, 2, 3, 4, 5 and ta,tha,etc. being 6, 7, etc. pa, pha, ba, bha and ma are again 1, 2, 3, 4 and 5 while ya, ra, la, va again revert back to 1, 2, 3 and 4. Thus, na, jna, etc. do not have any corresponding numerals. The *Kaṭapayādi Sankhyā* would hence be like this:

1	*2*	*3*	*4*	*5*	*6*	*7*	*8*	*9*	*nil*
k	*kh*	*g*	*gh*	*ṅ*	*c*	*ch*	*j*	*jh*	*ñ*
ṭ	*ṭh*	*ḍ*	*ḍh*	*ṇ*	*t*	*th*	*d*	*dh*	*n*
p	*ph*	*b*	*bh*	*m*					
y	*r*	*l*	*v*	*ś*	*ṣ*	*s*			

In our case ma = 5, tta = 6, ma = 5, yū = 1 and ra = 2; so *mattamayūra* = 5 6 5 1 2; this when transposed becomes 21,565 and *mārga* = 5 3, which again is 35 and adding the two = 21,600. The order in the list of 72 *Melakartās* is worked in this way. Thus Mecakalyāṇi would be 65 in the list by transposing the numbers. *259 of ARE 1927* from Paṭṭīśvaram records the chronogram in the *Kaṭapaya* system. This record is dated Śaka 1574. Another record dated Śaka 1514 used the *Kaṭapaya* chronogram. (578 of *South Indian Temple Inscriptions,* Vol.2, 570.

112. See. *I.H.Q.*, Vol.26 (1950); *C.I.I.*, Vol. IV, 150-61.
113. See Chapter V.
114. *E.I.*, Vol. I, No. 46.
115. Ibid.
116. See Reports, *A.R.E. 1917*, para 34.
117. *A.R.E. 1915-16*; Reports 44 ff; *A.R.E. 1917*, Reports, para 36; *A.R.E. 1913*, Report p. 100 and *A.R.E. 1916*, para 16 refer to Koṅguvīras who used to cut off their heads and tongues in a *maṇṭapa* specially erected for that purpose in the Śrī-Śaila temple.
118. See Chapter IV.
119. D.C. Sircar discusses this inscription in his work *Śilālekha tāmra śāsanādir prasanga* (in Bengali). One of the preceptors is said to have instituted *Ṣōḍaśamahādānam* and another is said to have brought Bengali Brahmins to settle in the *Golaki maṭha* in Andhra Pradesh and given them 2,400 acres of land.
120. Rangacharya, V., *Inscriptions of Madras Presidency*, Vol. II, Madurai district, No. *403.*
121. *234 of 1912* refers to Ēkāmradēvar of *Dakṣiṇa Gōlaki maṭha. 504 of 1910* refers to a guru who emigrated from *Kṛṣṇa Golaki maṭha* at Tiruvārūr.
122. The Cōḻa royal preceptors all bear names ending in Śiva and the names of 108 of them are inscribed as labels in the Tārācuram temple.
123. Cited in *ARE 1913*, P. 121, para 55
124. Swamy, B.G.L. *Chidambaram p. 29*
125. Rajamanikam M.A., *The Development of Śaivism in South India*, p. 223 ff. *ARE 1929-30*, P. 77.
126. *See Pl.XV.*
127. *Periya Purāṇam, Taṭuttāṭkoṇṭapurāṇam* v. 127. Cuntarar refers to this incident in several hymns such as vii. 17.5 and 10, also vii. 62.5., vii. 59.10; vii.5.10; vii. 45.1., etc.
128. vii. 46 vv. 1, 2, 4, 5, 7, 8, 9, 10, 11.
129. vii. 20 vv. 1, 3, 4, 5, 6, 7, 8, 10.
130. vii. 68.8 and 84.9.
131. *Mucukundasahasranāmam* v. 262.
132. *Periya Purāṇam, Ēyarkōṉkalikkāmanāyaṉār Purāṇam*, v.323-374. Also *Tirumuṟai* vii. 55. 3. refers to the illness of kalikāmanāyaṉār.
133. *Periya Purāṇam*, 2.6. *Viraṉmīṇṭanāyaṉārpurāṇam.*
134. There are a number of references to this word *pali* in Cuntarar's hymns such as 6, 15, 18, 32, 43, 46, 57, 63, 49, 98, etc. In most cases it refers to Śiva's begging for food. It is an allusion to the *piccāṇṭār (Skt.Bhikṣāṇḍār)* aspect of Śiva and hence closely connected with the dance theme.
135. *Tirumuṟai*, vii. 39.
136. *IX. 33 and 39.*

137. *Periya Purāṇam*, VI.6. *Cōmācimāṟaṉārppurāṇam.*
138. Raja Sastri, S. (ed.), *Śiva Bhakta Vilāsa*, Vani Bhusan Press, 1907. This is in Grantha script and consists of 103 chapters. I have not been able to access this work.
139. Mahāmahopādhyāya Sastri, Krishna (ed.) *Śiva Bhakta Vilāsa*, Madras Law Journal Press, 1931. This is in *nāgarī* characters. I have not been able to get this work. The references in the body of my chapter are to the manuscript recension. The manuscriptologists assured me that the printed version follows the exact numberings of this particular manuscript recension.
140. Srinivasa Chari, V. (ed.), *Śivabhakta Vilāsa*, Madras, Govt. Oriental Series, No. 57, 1952.This has 79 chapters and is the Marāṭhī version of the Sanskrit work. The mss. version in the Thañjāvūr library has been closely followed in this Marāṭhī version.
141. The *Cenna basava Purāṇa* is considered a part of the *Bhaviṣya Purāṇa* and ascribed to Śaṅkarādhyāya of Kāñcī. (14th century A.D.) Śrīpati Paṇḍita, the Vīraśaiva commentator on Brahma sūtra, knew of and regarded the *Basava Purāṇa* as authoritative literature. For details see Sakhare, M.R., *History and Philosophy of Lingayat Religion*, Belgaun, 1942. Also *The Cultural Heritage of India*, Vol. IV, pp. 99-101.
142. Nallaswami Pillai, J.M. (trans.), *St. Sekkilar's Periya Purāṇam*, Introduction.
143. Veḷḷaivāraṇaṉ, *Pannirut Tirumuṟai*, Vol. III. For the most recent account of the friezes see Marr, J.A.R., 'The Periyapurāṇam Friezes at Tārācuram: episodes in the lives of the Tamiḻ Śaiva Saints', Bul. S.O.A.S., Vol. XLII, part 2, 1979.
144. *See Pls. XVII and XVIII*
145. Chapter 56, lines 59-100. The version followed here is the Mss. entitled *Śivabhakta Vilāsa* in the Saraswati Mahal Library.
146. *Sl. 432.*
147. Elmore, W.T., *Dravidian Gods in Modern Hinduism*, p. 94.
148. Rasik Mohan Chatterji (ed.), Kṛṣṇānanda Āgamavāgīśa's *Tantrasāra*, Calcutta, Basumati Press, 1929. For a study of the iconology of Tantrasāra see Pratāpāditya Pal, *Religion and Iconology according to the Tantrasāra*, Los Angeles, Vicitra Press 1981.
149. Pandit Mukund Ram Sastri (ed.), Abhinava Gupta's *Tantrasāra*, Kashmir Series of Texts and Studies, Srinagar, 1918. Abhinavagupta was the first one to openly accept his faith in the *Vāma Kauḷa Mārga.* His earlier gurus were consciously suppressing their Kauḷa origins and presenting themselves as the orthodox *Smārta* school. Thus the author Somāskanda never refers to any kauḷāgamas or rites. After Abhinavagupta, Kashmir Śaivism and *Śrī-Vidyā* became very closely related. O. Sanderson, personal communication, Oxford, 1984.
150. This is a collective term for a list of ten goddesses. The number sometimes varies for the *Mālinī Vijaya* describes twelve *Mahāvidyās.*
151. *Vāmakeśvaratantra* is a ghost title. Two works called the *Nityāṣōḍaśikārṇavam* and *Yoginīhṛdaya* are two parts which are commonly known as *Vāmakeśvaratantra.* See Vrij Vallabh Dvivedi, *Yogatantragranthamālā*, Vārāṇasī, 1968. See also Teun Goudrian and Sanjukta Gupta, *Hindu Tāntric and Śākta Literature*, Gonda, Jan (ed.). *A History of Indian Literature*, Vol. II., Otto Harrasowitz, Weisbaden, 1981.
152. See Pal, *op. cit.*, p. 89.
153. Rao, T.A.G., *Elements of Hindu Iconography*, Vol. I, pt. 2, p. 372.

154. *Verspreide Geschriften*, Vol. VII, pp. 163 ff. For a discussion of this phase of Tāntric Buddhism in Indonesia see 'Het Buddhisme op Java en Sumatra in zijn laatste bloeiperiode', *T.B.G.*, 1924, PP. 522-79. Also Ghose, Rajeshwari, *Śaivism in Indonesia in the Hindu Javanese period*, unpublished M A. thesis, University of Hong Kong, 1966, pp. 376-80.
155. *Periya Purāṇam, Tirumalai Carukkam* narrates the story of how Cuntarar was born out of the reflection of Śiva in a mirror and fell in love with two of the female attendants of Pārvatī and hence appeared in a human form with the two heavenly damsels as his mortal wives.
156. *v. 67-68.*
157. Mīnāṭchicuntaram Piḷḷai, *Tiruvampar Purāṇam*, Chapter 13.
158. *Mucukundasahasranāmam*, vv. 716-19.
159. *Tirukkaṭavūr Purāṇam*, cited by Taṇṭapāṇi Tēcikar, *Tiruvārūr*.p.5
160. Hemingway, F.R., *Tanjore Gazeteer*, 1915, pp. 237-8.
161. Macdonell, A., *A History of Sanskrit Literature*, pp. 174-84 and 211-7.
162. Macdonell, *op. cit.*, pp. 215 and 176. Macdonell also believes that the *White YajurVeda* was later than all the recensions of the Black (p. 179).
163. *Baudhāyana Śrauta Sūtra*, XLV, IX-XIV.
164. *Personal Communication.*
165. For a detailed discussion on the myth see Venkatarama Sharma, Critical Studies on Kātyāyana's *Śukla Yajurveda Prātiśākhya*, Madras, University of Madras, 1935, p.91.
166. *'Ha Māracaṇḍālache maitra', v. 74. (Mara was a friend of the caṇḍālas)*
167. See *Vide Infra*, Ch. 7.
168. Piccāṇṭārkōyil Irācakōpāla Piḷḷai *Tiyākarājalīlaikaḷ* (4 vols.,) Śrī-Rangam, Vani Vilas Press, 1955-64.
169. Wendy O'Flaherty - *Śiva, the Erotic Ascetic*, pp. 302-10
170. Vide *Infra*, Ch. IX.

Chapter Seven

THE TYĀGARĀJA CULT, ITS INSTITUTIONAL FRAMEWORK AND SOCIAL RAMIFICATIONS

This chapter is the study of one aspect of social relationship in Tamiḻnāḍu which was regulated to some extent by religious institutions such as the temples and the *maṭhas*. Historically Hinduism has been very closely related to the Indian social system in which the institution of caste has played a major role. Theological ideas and social structure mutually acted on each other to produce a complex rubric of Hindu society.

The ritual framework for the Tyāgarāja worship was provided, as we have seen, by the *Āgamas* with their emphasis on temple-centred locotheistic manifestations of the sacred. The transcendental reference point was provided by the *ajapā* and *haṁsa* concepts. This doctrine provided the supra-empirical view of a larger totality. Thus, while the *Āgamas* defined the normative patterns, and *ajapā-haṁsa* the supra-ethical supra-rational texture of religious experience described by Otto as "*Mysterium tremendum et fascinosum*",[1] *bhakti* provided the charismatic element.

If one were to follow Weber's line of reasoning, all charismatic elements are outside the natural order. Hence they introduce elements of instability and innovation, and are strategic elements in social change.[2] As by their very nature charismatic phenomena are unstable and temporary, they can survive only by being formalized or by becoming transformed and then "incorporated into the routine institutionalised structures of society".[3] This is precisely what happened with the spontaneous and creative movement of *bhakti* as expressed by the *nāyaṉmār*. The nature of this charismatic movement and the process of its incorporation into institutionalised temple religion has formed the focal point of the first section of this chapter.

Tiruvārūr was one of the main foci of Tamiḻ Śaiva bhakti movement. Tiruvārūr and Chidambaram were the two most famous temples during the time of the *Tēvāram* authors. The saints invoked in the *Tiruttoṇṭattokai* were a religious collective defined by the fact of a shared ideology. Bhakti, it is true, provided a critique of the social order but only *inter alia,* for it's true involvement was with what concerns humanity ultimately: the encounter so to speak with a beyond and in this encounter caste was irrelevant. Thus the *nāyanmār* did not take it upon themselves to advocate the overthrow or even a reformation of the social system. And so they could carry on a religious discourse within the parameters or rules set by temples. The temples, as institutions, serving the adaptive needs of society on the other hand were primarily concerned with the process which Weber calls the "routinization of Charisma"[4] .

This "routinization" is clearly articulated in the narrative of the *Periya Purāṇam* and in the *Tiyākarājalīlaikaḷ*. The nature of orthodoxy, heterodoxy and dissent are all reflected in these myths.[5] Thus the deity often sets out to take the burden of suffering of the poor underdog of society on himself but without a murmur of protest against the social system that gave rise to such a situation in the first place! This is because social differences belong to 'connate religion' and bhakti to 'subjective religion'.

In the second part of this chapter, the caste and ritual status of the temple personnel will be analyzed. Another related area of enquiry, i.e. the rise of Śaiva *Veḷḷāṭa maṭhas* which came into prominence in the 13th century A.D., will be taken up for discussion in the next chapter. This signalled the corporative upward mobility in a social and ritual sense of a large community of non-Brāhmaṇas who, as trustees and managers of vast temple estates, became important leaders of the community. Their socio-religious status was legitimized by the Āgamic priestly Brāhmaṇas through the ritual of *mariyātai* or temple honours. The relationship between members of the cult community and their leaders was again freshly worked out. Thus with land, class and ritual status enhanced, the upper class 'Non-Brāhmaṇas' became an important social force.

For the study of specific myths relating to the issues of caste, *bhakti* and the deity Tyāgarāja, the *Tiyākarājalīlaikaḷ*[6] briefly discussed in the last chapter, has proved to be an invaluable source of information. Tradition has for a long time credited the Tyāgarāja of Tiruvārūr with performing 364 *līlais* or divine sports in and around Tiruvārūr and this work purports to be a collation of these *līlaikaḷ*. The authorship of the work has also been traditionally attributed to Kamalai Ñaṉappirakācar a native of Tiruvārūr and revered as the *guru's guru* of the author of the *Tiruvārūrppurāṇam*. He is said to have composed this work originally in Sanskrit. That Ñaṉappirakācar himself was a great devotee of Tyāgarāja seems evident from the vast corpus of literary references connecting him with the deity and the temple.[7] He is also believed to have composed the *Tiyākarājakaḻineṭil*, which is a collection of ten poems on Tyāgarāja in which he refers to several of the deity's attributes such as his tinkling anklets, his throne called the *Vīracōḻiyam*, the special evening rite of *Tiruvāntikkāppu*, the Tamiḻ of the *Tēvāram* trio, the *ajapā* dance, and the reading of *Māṇikkavācakar* in the month of Mārkaḻi Tiruvatirai. He even refers to the little window in the deity's shrine, *tiruccāḷara vāyil*, and the great festival of *Paṅkuṉi Uttiram*,[8] etc. The little window is specially mentioned in several texts since the *garbhagṛha* according to canonical injunctions, has no windows.[9]

Kamalai Ñaṉappirakācar's life was closely connected with Tiruvārūr. It is said that he was the son of Ceṭṭitteru Ñaṉappirakācar and a descendant of the family belonging to Cīrkāḻi Ciṟṟampalam aṭikaḷ lineage of *gurus*. It is believed that he was desperately looking for a teacher to initiate him into the Śaiva lore. In a dream, God suggested that he should go to Tiruvārūr and, as he entered the temple, the icon was being taken out in procession. The rope carrying the icon snapped, and he, in that moment of anguish sang a devotional hymn and the rope instantly became whole again.[10] Ñaṉappirakācar was the guru of Ñāṉacampantar, the founder of Tarumapuram *ātīṉam*, one of the major trustees of the temple to the present day.

With such strong Tiruvārūr connections there seems to be little reason to doubt the tradition that ascribes to him the authorship of the *Tiyākarājalīlaikaḷ*. However, despite the efforts of devotees the manuscript had evaded discovery until Piccāṇṭārkōyil Irācakōpāla Piḷḷai found it in the 1950s. The Late V.I. Cōmacuntara Mutaliyār of Vaṭapātimaṅkalam, who was both a devotee and a trustee of the temple and closely connected with the Tyāgarāja temple, published the *Tiruvārūrppurāṇam* in Tamiḻ in 1895. In the preface of this work he announced that fourteen other works on Tyāgarāja would be published, and gave their titles; one of the titles was that of *Tiyākarājalīlaikaḷ*. What became of the manuscripts and press copies is not known. In 1928 Dr.U.Ve. Cāminata Aiyar published the *Tiyākarājalīlaikaḷ* by Tiricirapuram Mīṉātcicuntaram Piḷḷai which describes only 13 *līlais* of the deity. According to this work, the *Tiyākarācalīlaikaḷ* is said to have been narrated in the *Nagara Khaṇḍa* of the *Skandapurāṇa*. However, the *Nagara Khaṇḍa* that is available to us in print does not contain this list of *līlaikaḷ*. The *Mucukundasahasranāmam*, to which several references have been made earlier, addresses Tyāgarāja as "*Ṣaṣṭitriśatasaṅkhyāta līlākalpita vigraha*",[11] " the form which sported 360 *līlais*". Here the number given is 360 and not 364. It was the persistent efforts of Irācakōpāla Piḷḷai that finally unearthed this work. He states in the introduction to the work that he found the Tamiḻ manuscript in the Vani Vilas Press. All efforts of the present author to trace the people who were earlier custodians of this manuscript have so far failed.[12]

As explained by the editor in the preface to the work, the *līlaikaḷ* (Tamiḻ plural for līlai=sport) fall into three sets; the first, a series of 50 designated *Tēva līlaikaḷ* were published in 1962 and deal mainly with the founding of the town of Tiruvārūr, the establishment of the temple, and the fight between the gods and the demons. The second as well as the third part describe the *līlaikaḷ* performed in the *uttarāyaṇa*, or the latter part of the year. The fourth volume relates the *līlaikaḷ* numbering from 212 to 362. The actual narratives end with the 362nd *līlai* and the last two though numbered 363 and 364 simply speak of the benefits accruing to the devotees from listening to these *līlais*.

The only other deity who has a codified number of *līlaikaḷ* is Cuntarēcuvarar of Madurai. The *Hālāsyamāhātmyam* and the two works which go by the name of *Tiruviḷaiyāṭaṟpurāṇam*, one a 13th century and another a 17th century work of the same name, record 64 *līlaikaḷ* of Cuntarēcuvarar of Madurai,[13] which link him totemistically with the Pāṇḍyas. The connection between Tyāgarāja and the Cōḻas, as recorded in this work, will be discussed in the next chapter. Here only those *līlaikaḷ* which have a bearing on the caste system will be dealt with.

Another important method of enquiry pursued in this chapter, has been to trace the caste composition of the present day hereditary office holders of the temple. Their accounts of the myths, history and role of ritual offices throw interesting light on the classes of people who were integrated into the societal fold through the medium of temple-cults and ritual. Important informants were: the *yāṉaiyēṟumperumpaṟaiyaṉ* (Pl.XIV). P.R. Tilakammā, a descendant of the hereditary family of *Tēvaraṭiyār* (Sanskrit *Devadāsīs*) attached to the Tyāgarāja temple, the *uvacaṉ*, who is a hereditary *pūcāri* of the Piṭāriyammaṉ temple and the hereditary drummer in the Tyāgarāja temple at Tiruvārūr, the *ōtuvārs*[14] and the *kurukkaḷ* who believe that their families have been in the service of the temple "from times immemorial",[15] and operators of the *kaṭṭaḷais*, or specific endowments which can, with reasonable certainty, be traced back in several cases to the 16th, 17th and 18th centuries A.D.[16] The Vēḷākkuṟicci *maṭam* and the Tarumapuram ātīṉam claim to have been in charge of these *kaṭṭaḷais* from the 16th and 17th centuries A.D. respectively. They own large properties which were donated by kings or wealthy people in the past. Some of these donations have been corroborated by inscriptional sources. Precise dating of this oral history would be impossible, but land tenure registers of the 19th century recognize their legal claims to land endowments.

Two interesting epigraphs provide information on the Tyāgarāja temple as a mediator in caste disputes. Particularly interesting is a 12th century epigraph from Tiruvārūr.[17] Several inscriptions from Tyāgarāja cult-centres, and from other temples as well, record the importance of a class of people called the *kaikkōḷars* who are given the honorific title *kaikkōḷamutalis*.[18]

The Temple as a regulator of Tamiḻ Society: Recent Studies

The socio-economic importance of the institution of the temple has been studied by several recent historians such as George Spencer and Burton Stein. Temple money-lending and livestock distribution has formed the interesting subject-matter of one of Spencer's articles wherein he analyzes the data provided by the 11th century Cōḻa epigraphs of the Thañjāvūr temple and thus traces the link between the temple and agrarian society.[19] Burton Stein has studied the role of the temple under the following two categories:

1) as links between towns and the rural hinterlands, and
2) as bridges over social and cultural stress-points which were forged through the *bhakti* cult.[20]

The growth of *sampradāyas* or lineages of monastic establishments is another interesting link between temples and society at large, for the *maṭhas* drew their supporters from different segments of society, depending on their own caste composition and, at the same time, were also managers of temple properties.

Arjun Appadorai and Carol Breckenridge have studied the relationship between donor, deity and congregation and emphasized the principles governing the allocation of *mariyātai* or 'honours', thereby making the temple the legitimizer of social positions.[21] Appadorai has, therefore, defined a South Indian Hindu Temple as a place and a process, whereby there is a "continuous flow of transactions between worshippers and deity, in which resources and services are gifted to the deity and are returned by the deity to the worshippers in the form of 'shares' demarcated by certain kinds of honours".[22] The temple thus provides an "arena in which social relations in the broader societal context can be tested, contested and refined".[23] Viewed thus, states the author, the temple has a "metasocial" or "reflective" quality.

Appadorai particularly stresses the role of the deity as sovereign ruler, "not so much of a domain as of a redistributive process".[24] He then traces the psycho-sociological results of this economic transaction between donor (*upayakāra*) and deity and the process of redistribution (*viṉiyōkam*), by which 'shares' of the donations are recycled to the donor himself, the staff of the temple and to the congregation. It contributed to, in the words of the author, a spirit of "unity and centricity", codified the corporate structure and thus sustained it in a social sense.[25]

The reciprocal model clearly defined the donor's privileges expressed through his receiving the *parivaṭṭam* or sacred silk vestments, *prasādam*, or 'leftovers of the food offered to the deity" (hence blessed) and other forms of tangible and intangible *mariyātai*, 'honours'. Baker and Washbrook have studied the political uses of such *mariyātai* and social recognition for aspirants for power thus drawing the temple into modern day regional politics.[26]

This vast pooling of economic resources and the meticulous distribution of goods and honours to the donors and congregation was fully developed only in Vijayanagara times. Appadorai concentrates on the 'colonial' period but also studies the 'honours system' in the context of present day social structure.

The present study revealed that, in the period up to the 13th century A.D., there was a noticeable miasmatic development within Tamil̲ society and the different social challenges were met by attempts at accommodating some forces of change. By the 13th century A.D., organized Veḷḷāḷa *maṭhas*, designed very much after the fashion of the Brāhmaṇa *maṭhas*, organized the so-called upper caste non-Brāhmaṇa, and gradually the attempt to accommodate what were regarded as the lower castes into a cohesive social unit was abandoned. Concomitant with this, the lower castes of society were increasingly alienated from the 'higher' temple and its cults. When the *harijans* gained entry into these exclusive temples by means of legislation, the temple as a vehicle of social cohesion had already failed, and the entry was no more than a modern-day egalitarian humān rights issue for them.[27] The Tamil̲ religio-cultural scene was dominated, as a modern historian using strong partisan vocabulary described it, by "the clerical order of the Brāhmaṇas and the aristocratic elite of the Dravidians" (Rajayya, in a public lecture in Madras, Dec. 1981).

Recently, however there is a tremendous resurgence of temple worship and pilgrimage, with special emphasis on building a pan-Indian Hindu identity by underplaying pluralism and stressing homogeneity. This new wave calls itself 'Hindutva', possibly to distinguish itself from both the more orthodox and heterodox kinds. It is organized efficiently and addresses a new set of religio-political concerns through a network of institutions under the broad organizational umbrella of groups such as the Vishva Hindu Parisad, Rashtriya Svayam Sevak Sangh etc.

This process of decline in the accommodating process of Tamil̲ society was neither sudden nor uniform through all regions of Tamil̲nāḍu. As late as the 18th century the Cētupatis of Ramnād belonging to the Mar̲avar community were assimilated into the higher echelons through their patronage of the Rāmēśvaram temple in particular, and temples all over southern Tamil̲nāḍu in general.

Again, the above statement must not be taken to mean that in the period before the 13th century A.D. there was a harmonious pattern of society which was later abandoned. What becomes clear, however, is that the earlier process of integration which was characterized by a certain vigour and a certain proselytizing zeal, gradually gave way to orthodox rigidity and Tamiḻ society slowly crystallized into disparate and polarised 'ethnocentric' groups.[28]

The Nāyaṉmār and Social Challenges

The 9th century A.D. *Tiruttoṇṭattokai* of Cuntarar composed in Tiruvārūr Temple contains eleven stanzas beginning with the famous line "I am the servant of the servants of the Brāhmaṇas of *Tillai*", after which he proceeds to introduce the saints with just a word or two to indicate their identity. Thus Tirunīlakaṇṭa is called the 'potter', but Cuntarar does not prefix any caste-affiliations to the other sixty-one saints (the total number invoked by Cuntarar being sixty-two). Nampiyāṇṭār Nampi gives the caste-affiliations of some of the *nāyaṉmār* with a brief biography of each of the saints in his *Tiruttoṇṭartiruvantāti*. It is Cēkkiḻār of the 12th century A.D. who provides detailed hagiographies of the sixty-three saints. Thus, our picture of the castes at the time of the *nāyaṉmār* is drawn from the 12th century poet's point of view.

In Cēkkiḻār's list of sixty-three saints, which he bases on Cuntarar's list, there are 12 Brāhmaṇas, 6 Vaiśyas or Vaṇikars, 4 Ādiśaiva Brāhmaṇas, 13 Veḷḷāḷas, 11 Kings and princes, and among the Śūdras he enumerates : 1 washerman, 1 fisherman, 1 cowherd, 1 toddy-tapper, 1 hunter, 1 *Pāṇar* or minstrel and 1 *Pulaiyaṉ* or untouchable, thus presenting a wide spectrum of caste groups. No caste is mentioned for six of them. Several of these *nāyaṉmār* were closely associated with the temple at Tiruvārūr.[29] It is worth noting that the biggest single group is that of the Śaiva Veḷḷāḷa. The vast majority moreover came from the upper caste groups. Only 7 of them came from really lowly origins.

The following pages will concentrate on the lives of those of the *nāyaṉmār* connected with the Tyāgarāja, as recorded by Cēkkiḻār, and on specific episodes in their lives, which throw light on the areas of social tension, to see how these contrary pulls were reconciled through the medium of the selfsame narratives. Thus, we shall see how Cēkkiḻār presents the problem and the solution. In discussing the matter of chronology we enter a rather complicated area. It is extremely difficult to be sure whether Cēkkiḻār reflects the conditions prevalent in his own time, i.e. the 12th century A.D., or those in the time of the *nāyaṉmār*. Besides, the dating of the *nāyaṉmār* is itself a matter of heated controversy among Tamilologists, while a consensus on the date of Cēkkiḻār has been arrived upon only in recent times. For the purpose of this thesis the most generally accepted dates of 7th century A.D. for Appar and Campantar, 9th century A.D. for Cuntarar, and 12th century A.D. for Cēkkiḻār are adopted.

Naminantiyaṭikaḷ was a Brāhmaṇa of Ēmappērūr and a devotee of Śiva at Tiruvārūr. He was appointed manager of a temple by the Cōḻa monarch. He had to participate in the *Paṅkuṉi Uttiram* procession when the deity was taken out to the neighbouring village of Tirumanāḻi. His public duty thus conflicted with his concept of 'ritual purity', which he was wont to maintain as a practising Brāhmaṇa. His domestic rites could not be performed in the state of ritual pollution which he had incurred in consequence of his commingling with the masses at the procession. Having ordered the purificatory bath-water to be prepared, he took a short nap. The issue presented itself in his dream and Tyāgarāja (Vītiviṭaṅkapperumāḷ) admonished him for forgetting that all those born in Tiruvārūr were Śiva *gaṇas* and thus there was no question of being polluted by their touch.[30] Several interesting conclusions emerge from this myth, a discussion of which will be reserved for a later section, after briefly tracing some more narratives of Cēkkiḻār.

Tirunīlakaṇṭar was a lowly *Pāṇar*, a travelling minstrel by caste, who thus could not enter into the precincts of the temple. However, on two occasions, the god Śiva, pleased with his playing on the *Yāḻ, (lute)*[31] made a special concession for him; once in Madurai, Śiva as Cokkanātar, appeared to the priests in a dream and asked that the *Pāṇar* be brought to his presence. In Tiruvārūr, however, the Lord Tyāgarāja was obliged to open a side gate, i.e. the northern gate, to let the *Pāṇar* in.[32] Another interesting story is recounted of the same *yāḻ* player and his sister the *viṟali* or songstress. It is said that they both accompanied Campantar to the house of the Brāhmaṇa *aṭiyār* Tirunīlanakkanāyaṉār. The host hesitated to accommodate the two *aṭiyār*, but persuaded by Campantar, decided to open his house, and the two slept by the side of the sacrificial pit, the *homakuṇḍa*. At night a great miracle took place. The *homakuṇḍa* blazed forth of its own accord, convincing the host of the power of devotion over the mechanistic rules of caste.[33]

Classic examples of this dichotomy between the egalitarian fraternity of Śaiva *aṭiyār* and the hierarchic caste-structure of

Hindu society are depicted in the hagiographies of Nantaṉ and Kaṇṇappaṉ. The huge Nandi, that blocked the view of Nantaṉ, the untouchable *pulaiyar*, moved just a little on command of the deity of Tiruppuṉkūr to enable the devotee to behold the form of the Lord.[34] When the same devotee implored the Lord of Chidambaram for a 'Vision' of his divine form, the deity appeared to Nantaṉ in a dream and commanded him to enter a purificatory fire. Nantaṉ emerged with a purified golden form in front of all the priests present and, thus ritually cleansed, entered the temple and became one with the Lord of Tillai.[35] Such stories occur in the context of other *bhaktas* too later all over India. Thus, the Lord of Uḍipi, Śrī Kṛṣna, opens a window to let Kanakadāsa behold him. Viṭṭhaldev secretly 'carries' Chōkhmēla into the *sanctum sanctorum* which was far more 'revolutionary' an act than any recorded in the legends of Tamiḻnāḍu.

Several interesting facets of the social divisions and the mechanism of social control emerge from a study of these 'narratives'. A social confrontation was defused by subterfuge. The Lord of Tiruppuṉkūr moved the Nandi to enable Nantaṉ to behold the deity; the Lord of Tiruvārūr opened a special gate for the *Pāṇar*; the Lord of Tillai suggested a purificatory rite to Nantaṉ before he could enter the temple gates. The God himself was powerless to throw open the doors of the temple directly.

The *nāyaṉmār* too flouted the conventions but only in an indirect manner. There was no open rebellion and so no open solution was warranted. This reserve in dealing with the question of temple entry is particularly significant in the context of the antinomian behaviour-pattern of the *aṭiyār*. The community of saints considered devotion to Śiva as above the ethical norms of society and what would have been censored as the most antisocial and unethical conduct at normal times, were applauded when done in the name of *bhakti*.[36] However,this did not include forceful entry into temple precincts. When it came to the fundamental question of right of access to the inner precincts of a temple, the answer was couched in the most ambiguous codes of behaviour.

In the previous chapter, we have noticed the ambivalent attitude of the *nāyaṉmār* to the Vedas and the Āgamas. While on one hand they accepted the Vedas and Āgamas as the norms of civilized behaviour, yet *bhakti*, which often contradicted these norms, was applauded as the supreme means of salvation. Such conflicts between *dharma per se* and *svadharma* or duties to one's station in life were often encountered. The *nāyaṉmār* had evolved a community of Śaiva saints and within this community all caste rules were ignored. It was as if the Śaiva *aṭiyār* had wielded themselves into a separate distinct group and once entry into this group was assured then caste had no meaning. They were, however, not concerned with an overall general reorganizing of society. Caste was transcended by *bhakti* and in that sense for those that did not transcend it the fetters remained.

The system was thus maintained and individual confrontations were diffused by accommodating the particular individual or accepting one's particular situation without drawing a general rule. By means of myths and rituals individual patterns of deviant behaviour were sanctioned without an overall challenge to the system itself. Thus, the Nandi could be moved, the 'Tiruvārūr Born' could be categorised as semi-divine for the purposes of ritual processions, but not in an overall societal context. The discourse between the individual nāyaṉār and the deity Tyāgarāja was a free one, without the social parameters infringing on it, and a safe outlet was hence ensured for the overwhelming need for *communitas* of the Śaiva *aṭiyārs*, without unduly hampering the modality of structure. The deviant behaviour, by being 'canonised', by being imprisoned in the bronze icons could be neutralised without any major change to the system. Literally and metaphorically, the Tamiḻs opened the peepholes while keeping the main doors shut! Thus *nāyaṉmār* were charismatic leaders of an egalitarian religion but were also supporters at least in principle, of Vedas and Āgamas, with all their social ramifications, and it is their ambiguous attitude which made it easier for *bhakti* to be 'routinized' into the Āgamic faith system.

The system required that the strict rules of exact positioning of the various castes *vis a vis* the temple, as expounded in the Āgamas be followed. Thus, the reciters of Veda were physically positioned in the *ardhamaṇḍapa,* the sacrificers, sages and ascetics in the *mukhamaṇḍapa;* kings and people belonging to Vaiśya caste in the *dvāramaṇḍapa;* the people belonging to the *śūdra* caste who have obtained *samayadīkṣā* in the *nṛttamaṇḍapa* and the people belonging to other castes in the entrance near the *gōpura* (*Suprabhedāgama, Kriyāpāda*) and the warning that abandoning one's allotted place will incur the wrath of Śiva and the punishment for which crime will be nothing short of hell (Somakaṇṭha, *Ālayapraveśavidhi*) did not leave much scope for the gates to be open but several other complex devices were invented by the proponents of *bhakti* to bring the disparate groups together. The deity himself could be polluted by contact with the 'impure' such as those not conforming to the Vedic rules, mountaineers, heretics, those who have committed heinous sins, women who have lived with men other than their husbands, liquor sellers, those born of intercaste unions, etc., and in such cases the deity itself will have to be reconsecrated. (*Kāraṇāgama Ārōhaṇavidhipaṭala*). This was built into the legal system. In 1908 the famous Kumudi temple case ruled that it was illegal for Nāṭārs to enter into a temple as it was a contravention of Āgamic regulations. Cuvāminātha Kurukkaḻ has published a succinct account of Āgama rules and regulations in a short pamphlet entitled *What is the Āgama?*, Madras, The South India Archaka Association, n.d.

It must be remembered that the *aṭiyār* flourished during very difficult times for Tamiḻ Hindu society. The Jainas and the Buddhists, the former most probably with the royal support of the Kalabhras, had established the two faiths in Tamiḻnāḍu. 'Hindu' society felt that it needed to face the challenge. The intense competition against these two faiths, which finds mention, particularly in the hymns of Appar and Campantar, necessitated to a great extent the imitation of some 'popular' elements of the two rival faiths.

Hinduism has always shown a remarkable capacity for generating within itself religious movements which served to meet the challenge of other faiths, even if only for temporary periods of time.[37] This is achieved either by conscious imitation or by means of emphasising those elements of Hinduism most in tune with the challenging creeds. Thus egalitarianism and an organised fraternity of monks with an evangelical zeal were the two strong points in the sociology of Buddhism and Jainism and these two aspects were at least ideologically accommodated into the two branches of devotionalism of Tamiḻnāḍu, *viz* Śaiva and Vaiṣṇava.[38] The accommodation was made on the terms of the Āgamic faith system in controlled doses. The *nāyaṉmār* themselves became objects of worship inside the temples, into the portals of which some of them failed to get entry while leading their mortal lives.

A classic example of such an attitude of relativism is given by Iravati Karve in her description of the pilgrimage procession to the shrine of Viṭṭhaldēv at Paṇḍharpur.[39] Women in *dolies*, (palanquins) segregated on caste basis, sang songs of Chōkhāmēla, bemoaning the lot of the Pariahs (the *mahārs*), and the superficiality of the caste system. A typical stanza would run: "The river is twisting, but its water isn't twisted. Why be fooled by outward appearances?". So anti-caste songs were sung with ease in caste segregated *dolies*.

The *nāyṉmār* connected with Tiruvārūr, such as Taṇṭiyaṭikaḷ and Naminantiyaṭikaḷ, were active antagonists of the Jainas according to the *Periya Purāṇam*. Naminanti once went to a Jaina household to ask for butter to light the lamps in the temple. The Jainas mocked at him and asked him to use water instead of butter to demonstrate the efficacy of his faith. The saint promptly appealed to Tyāgarāja who advised him to fetch the waters of the holy tank and light the lamps. He obeyed and the lamps began to burn brilliantly. This miracle, according to the hagiography, weaned several people from the Jaina faith.[40]

Taṇṭiyaṭikaḷ was born blind and once when he was groping around digging a tank in the temple, the Jainas teased him about his infirmity. Infuriated, he challenged them by asking them what they would do if he regained his vision and they lost theirs. They promised to leave Tiruvārūr.[41] Taṇṭi prayed to Tyāgarāja who asked him to appeal to the Cōḷa monarch to be the witness of such a miracle. In the presence of the king, the miracle took place and the Jainas had to leave the town. Though one cannot fail to notice the element of a parable here with 'vision' and 'blindness' used as metaphors for spiritual enlightenment and spiritual darkness, yet the antagonism is also marked in another level, divine intervention coupled with royal patronage.

In the Mackenzie Mss.[42] there occurs a list of villages which were Jaina strongholds; both Tiruvārūr and Nākapaṭṭaṇam are included in the list. Appar and Campantar were, according to the *Periya Purāṇam* involved in a protracted war against the Jainas. Thus, it is not very unlikely that in order to combat the Jainas several aspects of religous beliefs of the Jainas were incorporated in the Śaiva faith. The *bhakti* heroes were constantly intervening on behalf of the threatened Hindu community against the politically or socially powerful "heretics." Campantar is said to have defeated the Jainas in an argument at Madurai and had them impaled (*Periya Purāṇam* (6.1.648-856). This is also depicted in the Tārācuram friezes. (see Marr, J.A.R. *Periya Purāṇam* frieze at Tārācuram', Pl. iv.)

The rather egalitarian stance of the *nāyaṉmār* is reflected in the marriage between Cuntarar, a Brāhmaṇa, and Paravainācciyār, a *Ruttirakaṉṉikai* (Sanskrit *Rudragaṇikā*) or a dancing girl, in the temple of Tiruvārūr. His second wife Caṅkili was also of a lower caste of Veḷḷāḷas.(vv. 277-282 and vv.3361 & 3362)

The Tiyākarājalīlaikaḷ and other Myths

Turning away from the life of the *nāyaṉmār* to the other interesting source of information, the *Tiyākarājalīlaikaḷ*, which records a series of episodes recounting Tyāgarāja's showering of grace on a lowly-born devotee, but in all this we see the deity handling the situation very carefully and without upsetting the Āgamic order. The general paradigm is enunciated in *līlai* 77. There are six disciples of a *guru*, each coming from a different caste. They follow their *svadharma*; the Brāhmaṇa follows the Vedic code; the *śūdra* confesses his igonorance of the written word and follows the path of devotion; but they all receive a vision of Tyāgarāja. The didactic portion of the myth concludes by stating specifically that *Tyāgeśa* is for all castes.

Here no situation of conflict is envisaged. Each follows his allotted path and thus in no way upsets the clearcut 'parallel growth'. In *līlai* 93 , Tyāgarāja appears to a distraught *śūdra* who is about to take his own life for he feels that, being born a *śūdra*, he has no chance of seeing the deity in this life and hence concludes that such a life is purposeless. The God explains to him that all men are equal in his eyes and the wise and the good shall attain him.

It is in *līlai* 105 that a more tricky situation is portrayed. A *śūdra* garland-maker is a devout worshipper of Tyāgarāja and offers the first garland of the day to the deity as a part of his regular offering. Following the taboos regarding temple entry, the garlandmaker dutifully leaves a garland hanging on the branches of a tree at the entrance to the temple. The deity accepts the offering and wears the garland. A priest is intrigued with the extra garland round the deity's neck every morning and reports the matter to the Cōḻa king. Investigation reveals the garlandmaker as the culprit. The king thereupon orders all the flowers in the area to be confiscated and the poor garland-maker decides to offer himself and makes preparations to hang himself on the branches of the same tree. Tyāgarāja makes the tree bloom and the regular garland is offered as usual. The king, realising the devotion of the *śūdra* garland-maker, announces his piety to the village. He is acclaimed by all the villagers and given the right to make a garland every morning, which an officer of the king collects and offers to the deity. The point to note here is that the garland-maker is given social recognition, and makes contact with royalty, but is still not allowed to enter the temple directly and garland the deity. All the fuss detracts the attention from the crucial questions. Nowhere are we told that the deity, pleased with his devotion, allowed him to enter the temple. The same ambivalence one encountered in the attitudes of the *nāyaṉmār* is noticeable here too.

Līlai 106 seems to have be a more cryptic version of the Sōmayājin episode.[43] A Brāhmaṇa was performing a Vedic *yajña* and a *caṇḍāla* walked in. Pandemonium broke loose amongst the Brāhmaṇas present. The sacrificer invoked Tyāgarāja and continued the sacrifice after giving the due honours of a guest to the *caṇḍāla*. In the midst of all the din, the voice of Tyāgarāja was heard announcing that the *caṇḍāla* was God himself and He had donned the form to test the devotion of the Brāhmaṇa, and the voice further assured those present that particular sacrifice had not been polluted.

This *caṇḍāla* theme must have been a very important one in the minds of the Tyāgarāja worshippers for in the list of names of Tyāgarāja, the *Tyāgarājanāmāvali*, he is invoked as *"Om Caṇḍāmśave namaḥ"* - Obeisance to him in the guise of a Caṇḍāla (Invocation 320.)[44] In the *Sundaramūrtyaṣṭottaram*, the *nāyaṉār* is lauded as a boon granter to Sōmayājin, referring no doubt to the Sōmayājin episode discussed in the last chapter, wherein Cuntarar requests Tyāgarāja to be present at Sōmayājin's sacrifice and the deity attends the *yajña* in the form of a *caṇḍāla*. The *Mucukundasahasranāmam*, as referred to in the previous chapter, describes this event in five of its invocations. Invocation 716 specifically addresses him as *"Umāskandādisahita mahācaṇḍālaveṣabhṛt"*, 'The Lord, who along with Umā and Skanda appeared in the form of a *caṇḍāla'*. This myth must have played an important part in the cult for it is painted at least three times in the temple at Tiruvārūr[45] and occurs as a part of the cultic celebrations at Tiruvamparmākālam.[46] The Mātaṅgas, referred to in the Sōmayājin myth, as seen in Chapter VI, were known as *Caṇḍālas* in Buddhist literature and both Ucchiṣṭa Mātaṅgī and Ucchiṣṭa Cāṇḍalī are known in Śākta *Tantras* and are equated as synonyms. The Madigas who worship Mātaṅginī are also numerically a large untouchable caste; they are classified as Cakkiliyars (leather working untouchables) in Andhra Pradesh (Govt. of India Schedule for backward castes and Tribes, State Govt. of Andhra Pradesh, 1980)

The theme of the *caṇḍāla* is again voiced in *līlai* 143. The temple entry is again the point in question. A *caṇḍāla* shoemaker wants to make an offering of a pair of slippers to Tyāgarāja but his lowly birth precludes him from entry into the temple to judge the size of the foot of the icon. The cobbler dozes off in a despondent mood leaving his leather canvas unattended. The deity leaves his footprint on the leather and the cobbler, jubilant at this act of divine grace, makes the icon a pair of slippers. The next day the priests are horrified to find a pair of leather slippers on the feet of the icon. Leather, in the Hindu concept, it must be remembered, is polluting and as such even devotees are not allowed to enter temples with shoes on. A divine voice proclaimed that the offering was particularly pleasing to the deity as it was offered with love. The *caṇḍāla's* devotion was publicly acclaimed and the episode officially circulated through the village. The *caṇḍāla* was given a special social recognition. The fact that he was a shoemaker makes him a man of the *cakkiliyar* caste. Michael Moffatt describes how they were regarded as lower than the Harijans because of their use of the carcass of dead animals as raw materials of their profession.[47]

Quite out of keeping with the general mood of this work is *līlai* 177. A dog, having partaken of the leftovers of a Brāhmanic *yajña* is born a man and becomes a minister. Tyāgarāja then begins to extol the virtues of the Brāhmaṇas and describes them as primal gods and prescribes piety towards Brāhmaṇas as a cure for all obstacles.

Līlai 195 seems to be a modified version of the Nantaṉ myth.

A *caṇḍāla* decides to immolate himself out of sheer disgust at having a polluted body because of which he cannot behold the deity in the temple. Tyāgarāja intervenes and commands him to look at the *liṅga* in front of him. When he does, he beholds the image of Tyāgarāja. Thus the vision itself is never denied to the devotee. It is only the entry to the temple. The former belongs to the spiritual universe, the latter to the social world. Stories of this nature are not restricted only to the Śaiva faith. Kṛṣṇa at Uḍipi as we have seen earlier is said to have given *darśan* to his *bhakta* Kanakadāsa through a window in the west.[48]

This collection of stories seems to take special pride in the fact that the grace of Tyāgarāja descends even on the most lowly born. In *līlai* 194 a brave *śūdra* devotee of Śiva stops an old Śiva temple from collapsing by temporarily holding the pillars, much in the fashion of Samson in the Old Testament. The *līlai* sounds incomplete for we are simply told that the temple was then renovated by the king.

Svadharma, or one's individual sense of duty, is often a point of discussion.[49] In *līlai* 186 a Vaiśya is said to have abandoned his *varṇadharma* and become a hunter and accidentally killed a Brāhmaṇa. He was born a demon in his next birth. Here it is not made clear as to which is the more heinous crime, the slaying of the Brāhmaṇa or the abandoning of one's caste-dharma.

In another story, a Brāhmaṇa, once told that he would become a king, wonders how that would be possible as it would go against his caste rules. Finally, however, his fears are calmed as the king asks him to take over the government for a few months, while he remains incognito for reasons of state policy. As Wendy O'Flaherty has pointed out, "The Hindus distinguish two categories of duty: *Svadharma* and *Sanātana dharma,* relative and absolute and she traces a continual conflict between the two in the period after the advent of Buddhism and Upaniṣadic thought. (Cf. note 49). Bhakti, however superceded both *Svadharma* and *Sanātana dharma,* and hence the congregation of *bhaktas* were unconcerned with either.

Līlai 210 presents a strange love-hate relationship between a Brāhmaṇa and another man of a lower caste. The low-caste man constantly sniggered at the Brāhmaṇa's profession, whilst he remained his friend on a non-religious plane. Once the poor Brāhmaṇa fainted out of sheer exhaustion brought on by starvation. His friend chanced to pass by and hurried to get him food. On the way he met a Muslim carrying meat. The temptation to test the Brāhmaṇa's vow of vegetarianism overcame his love for the man and he fed the Brāhmaṇa the meat. Faced with an alternative of death by starvation, the Brāhmaṇa accepted the meat after duly offering his salutation to Tyāgarāja.

Days passed by and the Brāhmaṇa restored to health, went to the temple to offer his prayers. The priests stopped him and accused him of having willingly partaken of animal flesh. The Brāhmaṇa prayed to Tyāgarāja who made a miracle come to pass. For, wheresoever the Brāhmaṇa set foot, the place turned to gold. It is interesting to observe the emphasis placed on vegetarianism, which was certainly a late development, and the fact that a Muslim is mentioned possibly contains clue to the dating of this compilation of myths. It was in the 14th century A.D. that Muslims became an important social factor in Tamil̲nāḍu. The Tyāgarāja temple at Tiruvor̲r̲iyūr has an inscription dated 1344 A.D. (203 of *ARE* of *1912*) which refers to the trustees of the temple hiding temple property underground to protect it from the Muslim marauders. If in fact these legends were put into writing in the 16th century, i.e. if they can be attributed to Ñān̲appirakācar, the Muslims were by then a very important social factor in Tamil̲nāḍu. Again a meat-eating ostracised person, by birth a Brāhmaṇa, was allowed to enter the temple precincts by the intervention of Tyāgarāja, but such a mode of intervention was unavailable to the deity in the case of a Caṇḍāla devotee, even if he were to become a vegetarian.

Līlai 229 preaches the social order as envisaged by the cultic leaders. The *kali age*, our present aeon of time, according to traditional Hindu reckoning, is an age wherein immorality and impiety reign supreme, and Tyāgarāja describes the nature of sins and the kind of hells the sinners would inhabit. Adulterers, thieves, those fallen from their castes, those who propagate heresies, those who censure the Śaiva devotees, the Vedic Brāhmaṇas who drink, killers of cows, infants and Brāhmaṇas are condemned to different kinds of hells. The intermixing of castes is considered a crime at par with the killing of infants or Brāhmaṇas. No attempt is made at any hierarchic classification of sins.

Līlai 230 is a highly contrived one in which it is easy to spot the hand of the orthodox Brāhmaṇa. Once a group of pilgrims were on their way to Kāśī and were lost in a forest. A divine voice was heard proclaiming that only those with deep faith in Tyāgarāja and those that are Brāhmaṇas can cross the forest. Furthermore, those that question the authority of either will perish by their own fears. The *kṣatriyas* and others on hearing this resorted to respecting the Brāhmaṇas.

A quaint case is presented in *līlai* 235 by a Brāhmaṇa who was once, he claimed, chased by wild animals and forced to take shelter in the house of a *caṇḍāla*. He approached the ritual expert to find out if his action warranted any expiatory rites. While a debate on the issue was in progress the voice of Tyāgarāja was heard which absolved the Brāhmaṇa of any sin explaining that in such dire circumstances his taking refuge in a *caṇḍāla* household was not a sin.

Thus one can see in these myths the dichotomy between universal grace and "systems maintenance"[50] For, while the deity or the saints are sympathetic to the cause of the social underdog, the cause is narrowed to an individual predicament and not stated in social or collective terms. Thus in *līlai* 307 it is strongly emphasised that Tyāgarāja is perfectly impartial and does not adhere to caste regulations. He is the God of the rich and the poor, the Brāhmaṇa and the low caste. The *nāyaṉmār* also tried hard to carry that message of the god Śiva as being the bestower of Grace on all castes. At the same time the *nāyaṉmār* were upholders of the Āgamic system of temple worship and the legends woven around the entempled Tyāgarāja assert the supreme role of the Brāhmaṇa and the necessity for respect to the laws of the Brāhmaṇas.

Coming back to the *Tiyākarājalīlaikaḷ*, *līlai* 299 works out a conscious reversal of roles. A hypocritical Brāhmaṇa confronts Tyāgarāja who appears in the guise of a hunter. This hunter imagery often occurs in the Tyāgarāja myths, presumably indicating the Murukaṉ substratum in the composition of Tyāgarāja, for Murukan in Tamiḻnāḍu, as the husband of the huntress gypsy Vaḷḷi, is an image of the divine. The Brāhmaṇa boasts to the hunter that he can alter people's minds to which the hunter replies that he, on the other hand, can grant that which people do not even consciously seek, meaning presumbaly spiritual advancement. So saying he converts the unholy Brāhmaṇa to the right path, and the latter instantly accepts the hunter as his *guru*.

This again is a local reworking of the Kirātārjunīya myth of the Mahābhārata. Unfortunately, the *līlai* ends here for it is incomplete and it would have been interesting to have seen what the hunter had as his message.

Thus, in all these stories, as well as in the *Periya Purāṇam*, one can trace the uneasy relationship that existed between the structure of caste and the rather ambiguous protest movement originating from *bhakti*. Both the organisation and the theme of protest were rather amorphous and thus the system adapted to these changes. "Within a rigid conception of the caste system, any modernising change would have to terminate that system; given an adaptive caste system, change can be accommodated within it".[51] Thus individual protests were accommodated and protesters canonised as a means to give the ideas of protest a legitimate but controlled outlet.

It is this compromising aspect of the *Periya Purāṇam* that must have angered E.V. Ramasvami Naicker, the founder of Drāviḍa Kaḻakam, when he burnt both the *Rāmāyaṇa* and the *Periya Purāṇam* in the same bonfire to rid himself of the "Āryan Brāhmaṇas" and the "Draviḍian clerics."

The Cōmācimāṟanār episode (described in the last chapter) where Lord Śiva appears at a Vedic Sacrifice as a *caṇḍāla*, with his wife and son dressed similarly,[52] definitely has a social content. The Brāhmaṇas present at the *yajña* refused to recognise the possibility of divinity in *caṇḍālas*.

In this context it is interesting to note that K.G. Ñāṉāmbāḷ records a case dated 2.2.1951 in which a Vaṭama Brāhmaṇa from Thañjāvūr district asks the Śaṅkarācārāya, then at Kumbakonam for religious sanction to get his daughter married to a Madhyāhna Brāhmaṇa boy. He states: "I am a Brāhmaṇa Vaḍama. My native place is M. in Thañjāvūr district. I want to give my daughter in marriage to a boy of Śukla Yajurvarṇa. (i.e. the community with the supposed curse). I request you kindly to let me know whether it can be done". The reply was clear cut, dated 23.2.1951. "It is against the *Śāstras*".[53]

Thus the Cōmācimāṟanār mythical episode, had social ramifications. Yet in the myth there is no open confrontation and no open resolution to the problem. Somayājin, or for that matter Cuntarar, was no social reformer, ready for a break with the traditional system, and the issue was handled in a typically conciliatory manner. That particular Somayāga of Somayājin māṛanāyaṉār was not polluted; those particular Brāhmaṇaṣ who failed to recognise Parameśvara were ostracised; and Parameśvara was given the epithet in the *Mucukundasahasranāmam* of one who had the *caṇḍāla* as an aspect. However, sacrifices *per se* were still pollutable by *caṇḍāla* presence and Brāhmaṇas *per se* followed their 'ethnocentric notions' [54] of purity as a part of their *Varṇāśrama dharma* and their *Svadharma*. The particular was differentiated from the general, and the solution was to a specific challenge which was neutralised by accepting the possibility of Parameśvara appearing as the *caṇḍāla* and punishing those who refused to adapt so that the larger system could flourish.

A single accommodation did not necessitate the proclamation or adherence to a general social formula applicable in all cases. A *caṇḍāla* shoemaker, a low caste garland maker, a hunter *kaṇṇappaṉ*, a *pulaiya Nantaṉ*, a *Pāṇar*-Tirunīlakaṇṭarṉ, a *cāṇār*- (toddy-brewer) Ēṇṇāti, and a host of other individuals could be accorded honours, could be canonised and enshrined in bronze icons in temples, which, in many cases, they could not enter when they were bodily alive. The adaptive mechanism was necessary by which individuals could be accommodated without having to accept the norm of corporate mobility for social classes. Nantaṉ longed to see the Lord enshrined at Chidambaram. He did not question the authority of the *Dīkṣitars* to stop his entry into the temple. Yet, his fame had spread far and wide. He was the epitome of devotion and fully qualified for the status of an *aṭiyār*, (slave of Śiva). Denying his entry into the divine presence (even though it could be accomplished only by subterfuge) would stifle the system which, bereft of its adaptability, would soon be moribund. Corporate mobility and recognising the principle of corporate mobility were quite different for, that would entail far-reaching changes which would then alter the social, religious and legal framework. That necessity was not found till the 20th century and the caste system is now in the process of adapting to this massive challenge, the outcome of which will not become fully apparent till at least fifty years from now. Marc Galanter cites legal instances of compensation being provided to the temple for conducting purificatory rites when untouchables entered the temple. In 1908 the Privy Council had declared that the presence of Cāṇārs was "repugnant to the religious principles of the Hindu worshippers of Śiva as well as to the sentiments and customs of the caste Hindu worshippers". Those that entered were punished.[55]

It is only in this manner one can explain the ambiguity in both the *Periya Purāṇam* and the myths collected in the *Tiyākarājalīlaikaḷ* which present very serious situations of social conflict and conclude by the most naive answers. A Brāhmaṇa partakes of animal flesh; another takes refuge in a *caṇḍāla* household; another commingles with fellow pilgrims at the Paṅkuṉi Uttiram festival; a lowly born *Pāṇar* travels with the Brāhmaṇa Campantar and sleeps in a Brāhmaṇa household, that too next to the sacrosanct sacrificial pit; etc. Each of these persons could claim a place in the social structure, even a much revered one, but only for himself, and herein lay the strength and weakness of the caste system, as far as its survival was concerned. The mode of behaviour, the means to attain the chances to practise that mode of behaviour, the exclusivity of the model, the intricacies of the paradigm, the social power it wielded, none were ever in question and, as far as these fundamental assumptions were not in jeopardy, mobility presented no threat to the system. In this manner, all these confrontations and the concomitant adjustments were, to use the expression of Barnett, "systems maintaining".[56]

The system did not allow extreme orthodoxy of behaviour unless it was approved by the whole caste. Thus an individual or group of individuals who tried to assert their orthodox views without corporate sanction were often, ironically and paradoxically enough, ostracised by the very community whose norms they tried to uphold in the first place. Thus the orthodox Brāhmaṇas in the Somayājin episode were simply following orthodox notions of pollutions but, since it was not the mode approved by the leaders at the time, they suffered ostracisation.

A similar incident in the modern context is reported by Barnett. A Kārkātta Veḷḷāḷa, who carried the orthodox mores of his community to the extreme, refused to invite a prominent Veḷḷāḷa leader to his daughter's marriage because he ate with outcastes. However, the Kārkātta Veḷḷāḷa community as a body, which was the official upholder of the community's purity refused to attend the wedding unless this prominent man was invited.[57] Thus orthodox pressure of ostracising a marriage was put to counter extreme orthodoxy which could bring into question the survival of the system.

The difference in the attitude of the story teller becomes obvious when we compare the hagiography of Nantaṉār as recorded in the *Periya Purāṇam* with the play of Gōpāla Kṛṣṇa Bhāratī in the 19th century portraying the same theme, *viz.* Nantaṉ's ostracisation as a Paṟaiyaṉ (See *Nantaṉar Carittirakkirttanai,* an opera). Gōpāla Kṛṣṇa Bhāratī fumes with moral indignation at society's attitude towards the devotee Paṟaiyaṉ, while the author of the *Periya Purāṇam* simply extols Nantaṉ's piety.

The Age of Experiments and Synthesis

The 12th-13th centuries A.D., the age when the *Periya Purāṇam* was composed was also a period when several important religious transformations were taking place in Tamiḻnāḍu. The village goddesses were absorbed into the Āgamic temple culture, as seen in the building of separate *Kāmakkōṭṭams,*[58] in Śiva temple complexes. The earlier *saptamātṛkā* and *Jyeṣṭhā* temples were discarded by the 11th century A.D., and replaced by Umā Parameśvarī of the Āgamic faith. The Vaṭṭappāṟaiyammaṉ shrine at Tiruvoṟṟiyūr, for example, architecturally betrays its *saptamātṛkā* origins with its long rectangular *maṇṭapa* and a sacrificial altar in front of the *ardhamaṇṭapa.* Several distinct architectural features of this shrine have been noticed by Meister and Dhaky who conclude that the "present Devī shrine overlies basal courses of its own earlier structure".[59] Tradition links Vaṭṭappāṟai with Kaṇṇaki.

Burton Stein has pointed out how from 1350 A.D. onwards there was an increase in the number of Ammaṉ shrines and conversely a decline in the number of Śiva temples.[60] Thus, the process of integrating Ammaṉ shrines seems to have been accelerated in the 14th century. Gradually the Ammaṉ began to occupy a predominant position in some of the cultic temples of Tyāgarāja, as at Tiruvoṟṟiyūr, Tiruvārūr and Nākapaṭṭaṇam. In all the three above-mentioned temples Devī worship is of great importance; the Nākapaṭṭaṇam temple is popularly known only as the Nīlāyatākṣī temple and the Tiruvoṟṟiyūr as Vaṭivuṭaiyammaṉ temple. Tyāgarāja of Tiruvārūr shares the place of honour with Kamalāmpikai.

Another interesting phenomenon noticeable in Tamiḻnāḍu is the bifurcation of the goddess into a peaceful golden spouse of the Lord and a dark fierce local goddess in some cases, and in others an independent one commanding at any rate veneration in her own right.[61] In some instances the process is 'linear': the fierce Taṭātakai becomes the meek Mīnākṣī at Madurai, but annually her warlike nature is reasserted during the *Navarātri* festival. In the case of village goddesses the lines sometimes get blurred. The village goddess is often transformed temporarily into Pārvatī by getting her married to Śiva. The 'tāḷi' in these cases is usually tied by the Brāhmaṇa priest.

In the ritual field a symbiotic relationship was evolved during this period between the functions of the *pucāri* or priest officiating at the *Piṭāriyammaṉkōyil* (the temple of the folk goddess) who is usually an *uvacaṉ* by caste, and the rites of the main Āgamic temple.

This period also witnessed the rise of very strong Veḷḷāḷa Śaiva *maṭhas*, the precursors of the 16th century *ātīṉams* and *Siddhānta maṭhas*. This bid for socio-religious and economic recognition was the culmination of a historical process whereby the Veḷḷāḷas had been, for a long time, symbiotically linked with the Brāhmaṇas and the local rulers as well. Their organised bid definitely resulted in their being accepted into the upper strata of society, both in a social and a ritual sense. The link of these Veḷḷāḷa *maṭhas* to the temple organisations will be discussed in the next chapter.

This was also the period when the kings, particularly the Cōḻas and later the Pāṇḍyas, evolved a very systematic and organised state-sponsored religion expressed through the medium of the temple, and this led to elaboration of temple rites and the increased participation in the temple of large sections of the people. Several temple edicts of this period bear witness to a unique formula by which the resident deity of the temple issued edicts and thus directly intervened in secular matters of property and the like.[62]

The increased importance of the temple as an institution was reflected in the distribution of royal patronage, for, by the 13th century A.D., there was a decrease in the grants of *brahmadeya* lands and a concomitant increase in the *devadāna* lands.[63] Temples were expanding their clientele and hence qualified for increased royal patronage.

The following pages will explore the important sections of Tamiḻ society that were connected with the Tyāgarāja temples, particularly the Tiruvārūr temple, and study the mechanisms by which they were absorbed and the special 'honours' or *mariyātai* that they received. It will also study the regulation of the various castes connected with the temple as described in the temple inscriptions. The specific changes in ritual in the times of the Vijayanagara, Nāyaka and Marāṭhā rule, and the impact of colonial rule on Tamil̠ Caste organisation and temple administration have only been very briefly hinted at as they open up a wide new vista of investigation and deserve an independent study.

Particularly interesting examples of integration into the Āgamic system through the Tyāgarāja cult are provided by the cases of the *uvacan̠*, the *par̠aiyan̠*, the *Tēvaraṭiyār*, and the *vil̠uppar̠aiyan̠*. These will be taken up for individual discussion.

THE RITUAL OFFICIANTS, THEIR CASTE COMPOSITION, AND THEIR STATUS IN THE MARIYĀTAI SCHEME

The Uvacan̠

In early Tamil̠ literature the religious rites are described as being carried out by the lowest castes, such as the Par̠aiyan̠s, the Pāṇan̠s, the Tuṭiyan̠s and the Vēlan̠s. The low status of these castes and their religious duties, which made them handlers of dangerous power, are intimately connected. They lit the cremation fire and worshipped the memorial stone which was believed to contain the spirit of a dead hero. They played a special instrument which was believed to have sacred power.[64] These concepts persisted in the Tamil̠ mind and were accommodated into the " higher" Sanskritic religion assuming different forms. This would explain the special role of the *Uvacan̠* and the *yān̠aiyēr̠umperumpar̠aiyan̠* in the Tyāgarāja temple. The former is a more widely known ritual specialist and many *Uvacan̠* are connected by ritual ties to the 'main' temple.

The Uvacan̠'s role in the Tiruvārūr Temple

The *piṭārikōyil amman̠ pūcāri* (the priest at the temple of the folk deity *piṭāri* at Tiruvārūr) is an *Uvacan̠* by caste. He is ritually linked with the Tyāgarāja temple by a sacred thread called *kāppu* which is tied round his wrist. It is only after this ritual tie is established and all other worship to the *piṭāri* is complete, that the Brahmotsava (or annual temple festival) can commence in the Tyāgarāja temple. This is true of Tiruvor̠r̠iyūr as well where a bull used to be sacrificed to Vaṭṭapār̠ai until recent times. The place would then be cleansed and the rites begun in the Ātipurīśvara and Tyāgarāja temples.

This tradition finds mention in the Āgamas, and Candraśekhara Kurukkaḷ at the Tyāgarāja temple quoted the popular saying "*Paraśaivasya Karmāṅgam balipatrapradhānkam*", i.e. 'the rites of the Paraśaivas 'bali' receive precedence'. The term *paraśaiva* to denote this class of priest i.e. the *Uvacaṉ* is more commonly used in the Kāñcīpuram area. However, they are referred to thus in Tiruvārūr. The term paraśaiva occurs in several commentaries on the Āgamas such as that of Sadyojāta Śivācārya's commentary on *Kāmikāgama* (South India Arcaka Association, Madras 1974, p.303) and the *Kriyākarmajyoti* by Aghoraśivācārya (South Indian Arcaka Association, Madras) gives a comprehensive account of castes and their rights.

The *Uvacaṉ* is also the hereditary musician of the Tiruvārūr temple and plays on the *śuddhamattalam* and *pañcamukhavādyam*. (See Pl XI). The latter instrument was considered to be unique to the Tiruvārūr temple, although there are a few imitations in other temples now. He is thus also called the Muṭṭukkārar, and the *mattalam* or drum played at *cāyarakṣai* or evening temple rite is called *paṇikkoṭṭu*. On his assuming office he is invested with three cords of sacred thread taken from the Tyāgarāja icon.

Thurston describes the *ōcchaṉs* or *Uvacaṉs* as a class of temple priests who officiate in *piṭāri* and other Ammaṉ (goddess) shrines and wear the sacred thread only when within the temple. Their insignia are the *uṭukkai* or hour-glass shaped drum and the *cilampu* or hollow brass ring filled with bits of brass, which rattles when it is shaken. Thurston also says that in the Chingelput district many *naṭṭuvaṉs* or dance masters belong to the *Uvacaṉ* class. He further traces the word *Uvacaṉ* to *occhaṉ*, which he traces to the Tamiḻ word *ōcai*, meaning 'sound' in reference to the usual mode of invoking the *grāma devatās* by beating on a drum and singing their praises.[65] Several inscriptions refer to a tax on *Uvacaṉ*. This class of priest is variously called *arcaka, Umaiarcaka, Tēvar, mutaliyār, vaḷḷappaṟaiyaṉ, kampaṉ*, etc.[66] Collectively they are known as *Paraśaivas*. Brāhmaṇa *kurukkaḷ* officiate at their marriages. The inscriptions from Tiruvoṟṟiyūr also refer to special taxes on *Uvacaṉs*.

That the tradition of linking people from lower class communities with the major Śiva temples continues well into very recent times can be seen by a study of the Baramahal Records, where several *paṇṭārams* of Ammaṉ temples became custodians of *kaṭṭaḷais* or endowments to Śiva temples.[67] There are upper caste and lower caste *paṇṭārams*. The upper caste *paṇṭārams*, according to Thurston, are usually from *Cōḻiya* Veḷḷāḷa community and are householders. The celibate scholar-mendicant *paṇṭārams* are the custodians of Tamiḻ culture and call themselves *tampirāṉ* or *Tēcikar*, which is an honorific title meaning *guru* or teacher and etymologically could also mean of the *tēcam* (Skt. deśa,) i.e. native of the place in contradistinction to 'imported' Śiva *gurus*. The lower caste Paṇṭārams are often *Uvacaṉs*.

In the Paṅkuṉi Uttiram festival which lasts for fifty-one days in the Tyāgarāja temple at Tiruvārūr (incidentally the number 51 is believed to be sacred as it signifies the syllabary in the Sanskrit language), ten days are allotted to the worship of *piṭāriyammaṉ*, with whose worship the Brahmotsavam begins, followed by five days of worship offered to Aiyaṉār and then the remaining thirty-six days are reserved for Valmīkanātha and Tyāgarāja. Thus the first fifteen days are devoted to placating the deities drawn from the sphere of what may be loosely termed 'folk tradition', which was predominantly pre-Āgamic, though many of the present day rites are based on the Āgamas. The Paṅkuṉi festival is referred to in Caṅkam literature. *Naṟṟiṇai* 234 mentions Urantai with its Paṅkuṉi festival and Vañci (Karuvūr) with its Uḷḷi festival. The Paṅkuṉi festival seems to have been connected with the Cōḻas from Caṅkam times. Thus Āgamic modes of worship seem to have been superimposed on an earlier base.

In Tiruvoṟṟiyūr, till 1936 the Vaṭṭappāṟaiyammaṉ was worshipped on a specified day in the year by an *Uvacaṉ*, and a bull was sacrificed. There was a direct door leading to the shrine. The *Kurukkaḷ* were not involved in the rites. After the rite was complete the temple was ritually cleansed with *mantras* and *samprokṣaṇam* and it was then that the Brāhmaṇa *kurukkaḷ* took over the normal duties.[68] Piṭāriyammaṉ of Tiruvārūr or Vaṭṭappāṟai of Tiruvoṟṟiyūr belong to what may be termed the village goddess, genre and share a chthonic character and a persistent association with fertility of the soil. It was true, by such ritual means, that sub-caste peasant tutelary deities and their ritual personnel were amalgamated religiously into the Āgamic fold and socially into the caste system.

The Uttaramērūr temple inscription provides an early example of such integration. Uttaramērūr land was a Brahmadeya, that is, a land collectively owned by Brāhmaṇas. The temple inscriptions, however, refer to grants made by the *sabhā* (a committee consisting of Brāhmaṇa representatives) for worship in temples dedicated to *saptamātṛkās* (the seven mothers), particularly to Jyēṣṭhā (goddess of poverty and misfortune but in some later works fully assimilated as one of the Śaktis), and even more significantly to the *piṭāriyār*, and to "the white one," Maturai Vīraṉ.[69]

Thus the Brāhmaṇas, serving as Śaivite clerics, besides transforming these gods, secured for themselves the patronage of heterogeneous sections of the society. A parallel occurs at Madurai where the village goddess Cellaṭṭammā receives a special *abhiṣeka* at the Mīṇākṣī temple and is ceremonially wed to Cuntarēśvarar (Skt. Sundareśvara)[70], the form of Śiva at Madurai.

The Yāṉaiyēṟumperumpaṟaiyaṉ

In the Paṅkuṉi Uttiram and other annual rites many people from various walks of life are ritually connected to the cultic deity and in return are given the *mariyātai* and a share of the offerings. The *yāṉaiyēṟumperumpaṟaiyaṉ* is an interesting institution. The following is the origin myth recounted by the present *yāṉaiyēṟumperumpaṟaiyaṉ*.[71]

"There was a watchman called Kaṇkuttikkavirāyaṉ who was asked to guard the lands of the temple. A white elephant from the temple came repeatedly and devoured all the sugarcane. The king, believing the watchman to be careless, warned him that if he failed to catch the marauding beast within a week he would be executed. The clever wife of the downcast watchman set a trap and, as luck would have it, the elephant fell into it. The watchman, determined not to let the beast escape clung tightly and flew heavenward. He thus managed to enter heaven where the gods were embarrassed by their uninvited guest. Indra, the king of Heaven promised to grant the watchman anything as long as he would agree to leave the heavens. The watchman desired only one thing—the Tyāgarāja icon. Indra tried to trick him by presenting him with seven identicial icons i.e. the *Sapta Viṭaṇkar* and he was asked to choose the right one. With divine intervention he chose the right one, for Tyāgarāja revealed a sign above the genuine icon. The sign was that of a tiny grasshopper '*piḷḷaippūcci*".

The watchman brought the icon back to earth along with the white umbrella, the conch and the mirror.

Since the watchman had forgotten to put his trust in Tyāgarāja, at the time of crisis (i.e.when the king threatened to execute him) he was cursed to become a *caṇḍāla*. Kaṇkuttikkavirāyaṉ protested against the harshness of his punishment. Tyāgarāja promised to recognise his great service in bringing the deity to earth, and in recognition of this, promised him that every year before the Brahmotsavam begins, the *caṇḍāla* would be ritually married in the temple and only after this event was complete could the rites of the temple begin.[72] This assured the *caṇḍāla* his place in the parish. The recurrence of a 'bringing the image to earth' motif by a person of a lower caste in this Tiruvārūr story is worth noting.

To this day, a complete wedding ceremony is repeated every year in the *maṇṭapa* behind the flagstaff of the Tyāgarāja temple. A *tāḷi*—the insignia of a married woman is brought, and the wedding of the couple takes place in the presence of Āticaṇṭikēcuvara (Skt. Adi Caṇḍikeśvara) icon. The *yāṉaiyēṟumperumpaṟaiyaṉ* is brought with all honours accorded to a king. Musicians and drummers follow him, and a white umbrella, a symbol of sovereignty,[73] is held over his head. He is then presented with the *Tyāgaparivaṭṭam*, 'mantle of Tyāgarāja' which is ceremonially tied around his head like a turban. He is then presented with a *vēṣṭi* (lower garment), nine *kalams* of paddy and other gifts. The office of the *yāṉaiyēṟumperumpaṟaiyaṉ* is a hereditary one and passes to the eldest son. The present officiant remembers the time they owned five *vēḷis* of land which was given to them by the temple. He recounts how his father, who had fallen on bad times, sold the land.

The version of the story given by the *yāṉaiyēṟumperumpaṟaiyaṉ* is slightly different from the official version given by the priests and recounted in literature. The priestly version runs as follows: Indra, aided by the mortal king Mucukuntaṉ, defeated the demons. He promised to give his ally anything he asked for. Indra was thinking only of his mundane possessions, wealth, elephant, etc., and had momentarily forgotten his most cherished possession, the Tyāgarāja. He was, as seen in the chapter on the origin myth, forced to part with the icon. It was (according to this version of the myth), Indra who for his momentary lapse of *bhakti* was cursed to be born a *caṇḍāla*, and the annual wedding rite celebrates the wedding of Indra and Indrāṇī in their form of *caṇḍālas*. Indra finally prays at Chidambaram to expiate for his sin. His mortal offspring are the hereditary office bearers called the *yāṉaiyēṟumperupaṟaiyaṉ*. The title indicated his role as the rider of the elephant and in the Paṅkuṉi Uttiram festival it is this *paṟaiyaṉ* who sits in front of the icon on the back of the elephant.[74] This must have been unique for this finds special entry in general encyclopaedias like the *Apitāna Cintāmaṇi*. The point of interest here is that the *paṟaiyaṉ* was allowed till the *dhvajastambha* into the temple. As a *paraiyan* he would not have qualified for entry into the temple precincts.

The *caṇḍāla*, as can be seen from these myths, was in some sense a pivotal point of social tension and by according him a ritual status, and incorporating him into the *mariyātai* scheme he was enfolded within the system. He was the paramount Indra but with a curse, the curse of *caṇḍāla*hood, thus combining in himself a high ritual status with a low social status. Thus, the *yāṉaiyēṟumperumpaṟaiyaṉ* rides by the icon on an elephant's back, and thereby makes Tyāgarāja his tutelary deity and establishes a link with the higher gods.

Moffatt records the rites associated with the worship of a village goddess by the Harijans. He records how the village goddess is transformed by the ritual actions of the community from a "predominantly low, hot and angry being into a higher beneficient being". Corresponding to the states of the goddess "she is ritually serviced by the Harijan Pūjāri, the Vaḷḷuvar purōhita and the Brāhmaṇa priest who actually ties the *tāli* on the neck of the goddess."

It is interesting to note in this context that according to a recent demographical survey, a high percentage of the agrarian population in the Thañjāvūr district are *paṟias* and *paḷḷas*, jointly called Āti Tirāviṭa. The highest proportion is in the Nākapaṭṭaṇam taluq (where Tiruvārūr used to be situated, for it is presently in Tiruvārūr taluq).[75] In Nākapaṭṭaṇam taluq the percentage of *pariahs* in the agricultural labour sector is as high as 82% as compared with 60% for the whole district.[76] The Thañjāvūr district has also the largest number of temples, with the figure standing at close to 1,500, and more than half of these are of Śaiva denomination. Interestingly enough the district also has the largest Brāhmaṇa population in Tamilnāḍu, constituting 6% of the total population, whereas the average for the State is 3%. This geographical area, thus, had the right mix to work out a symbiotic relationship between the higher and lower caste members of the cult. What is interesting is the persistence of the belief that the Tyāgarāja was brought to the earth not by a Brāhmaṇa but by a man of a lower caste, either a *pariah* or a Ceṅkuntar (weaver) accompanying Mucukuntaṉ. As Thañjāvūr is the rice bowl of Tamiḻnāḍu and grows one quarter of the total paddy of the State, the cooperation of 82% of the agricultural labour force was sought through different myths and rituals.

That such ritual accommodation to people belonging to low castes was made from time to time in other parts of India also is evident by a study of cults like the Jagannātha where the Śabara tribe plays an important part. In fact there is so much similarity in the mythological origins of the Tyāgarāja and Jagannātha that it would be a fruitful field of enquiry to make a comparative study. The Jagannātha is connected with a king Indradyumna, the Tyāgarāja with a Mucukunda. Both are trinities and symbolically stand for all the qualities of the triad. Like the *viṭaṅka* at Tiruvārūr, there is the Sudarśana emblem at Puri. The Śabara mythico-ritual traditions[77] have their parallel in the pariah traditions of Tiruvārūr temple.

Eschmann in her study on the 'Hinduisation of Tribal Deities in Orissa' has pointed out how the Liṅgarāja temple in Bhubaneswar, which is believed to house a *svayambhū liṅga* is serviced by two classes of priests: "Brāhmaṇas and a class called Baḍus who are ranked as śūdras and said to be of tribal origins". They are, she observes, "not only priests in this important temple; their duties bring them in the most intimate contact with the deity as his personal attendants. Only Baḍus are allowed to bathe the Liṅgarāja and to adorn him at the times of festivals and again only they are allowed to carry the processional image during religious processional rites. Without them, it is said, the god cannot 'move one step'. The Baḍus are of course not allowed any contact with the *bhoga* or food offerings to the deity and have to leave the *garbhagṛha* when food is offered to the god by a special class of Brāhmin attendants.[78]

Considering the very close relationship between the Cōḻas and the Cōḻagaṅgas it is significant to see the similarities between the two regional traditions. That such accommodations were made elsewhere for other 'predominant' communities becomes evident from the Nākapaṭṭaṅam temple where the *'mariyātai'* is accorded to the fishermen and their 'patron saint' Eripatta Nāyaṉār of *Periya Purāṇam* fame.

The Tēvaraṭiyārs

The other community to be very closely linked with the temple through the *mariyātai* scheme socially and ritually is the *Tēvaraṭiyār*. They are traditionally a community of performing artists, whose lives and talents were dedicated to the service of the deity. Hart traces the existence of this class of dancing women, who were also courtesans, to a very early period of Tamiḻ history.[79] Their exact role in society still needs to be investigated. They seem to have had some ritual function, for which reason they lived in a separate part of the city, and ultimately came to be associated with temples.

Tiruvārūr, a traditional centre of dance and music, had a large body of dancers associated with the temple, as can be inferred from the inscriptions of Rājarāja.[80] Tyāgarāja is invoked in a most touching manner in some of the hymns in which he is beseeched to protect the asesthetic sensibilities of the devotee,[81] for he, like the Naṭarāja, is regarded as the personification of the Arts.[82]

A descendant of one of the *Tēvaraṭiyār* families connected with the worship of Tyāgarāja of Tiruvārūr, and at present a lecturer in Tiruvaiyāṟu College, provided the information given below regarding the *mariyātai* that was and is still offered to her family in the temple. She was also the main informant regarding the links between several of the myths connected with the family of dancers and present day rituals in the temple.[83] Tilakammā claims to be from the *Icai* Veḷḷāḷa community and was married to a Brāhmaṇa. The *Tēvaraṭiyār* are regarded by Thurston as a caste by themselves. He points out how many people who belong to this community affix the terms Piḷḷai and Mutali to their names. These surnames are usually used by the Veḷḷāḷa and Kaikkōḷa (weavers) communities "from which most of the *dāsīs* are recruited".[84]

The above informant, P.R. Tilakammā and the elderly *pārināyaṉam* player, V. Natesan,[85] recounted how the institution of the *Tēvaraṭiyār* was constituted at Tiruvārūr. There were two distinct groups of dancers, one dedicated to Tyāgarāja and the other to Kamalāmpāḷ. Those dedicated to Tyāgarāja came, according to Tilakkamā, from the *koṇṭi* family, to which she claims to belong. Interesting myths connect this family with the deity, as we shall presently see.

Latchappa, another *nāgasvaram* player at the temple, recounted the tradition as told him by his father, by which he identified three groups of *dāsīs* who performed before the Tyāgarāja. They were the Rājadāsīs, who are believed to "have performed dances even before the Brāhmaṇas took over the temple", the *naṭana dāsīs*, who danced before the deity and the *ca<u>nn</u>iti dāsīs* who sang at the performances. Apart from these he corroborated Tilakammā's account of the other two categories viz. the Tyāgarāja *dāsīs* and the Kamalāmpāḷ *dāsīs*.

The two *nāgasvaram* players gave a graphic description of the dance that was performed at Cāyārakṣai, which commenced from the first *prākāra* to the accompaniment of the *mṛdaṅga*. Pure dance or *nṛtta* was danced from the Rājanārāyaṇa *maṇṭapa* to the Gaṇeśa shrine.[86] While the *ci<u>nn</u>amu<u>r</u>ai dāsīs* (again another set of classification based on age, this term denoting those under 50) danced, the *periyamu<u>r</u>ai* (the older women, over 50 years of age), dressed in white with their hair tied in a 'Śiva knot' sang. On important occasions when the Tyāgarāja was taken to the Vasantamaṇṭapam, then *jatisvaram*, *varṇam*, *padam* and *tillānā* were danced before the deity. Whilst the order of the dances performed, as recounted by the *nāgasvaram* players, was possibly a 19th century innovation,[87] the basic rules of the ritual seem to have been known from early times, for Cō<u>l</u>a inscriptions refer to Vītiviṭaṅka (Tyāgarāja) sitting in the *Tēvaciriyamaṇṭapam* (Skt. *Devāsrayamaṇḍapam*) and watching the dance of *Talaikōli* or the chief dancer.[88] Their importance in the ritual is made evident by the Tiruvo<u>rr</u>iyūr record, which recounts a prolonged dispute between the dancers and the temple authorities. The dancers, in protest against their working conditions and dissatisfied with the allocation of functions assigned to them went on strike.[89] Three different epigraphs record the nature of disputes and the methods by which they were finally settled.[90] The *nāgasvaram* player at the Tiruvārūr temple belonged to the *mēḷakkāra<u>n</u>* caste. According to him most *dēvadāsīs* also belonged to this sub caste.

Tilakammā, as mentioned earlier, comes from the family called Koṇṭi, who were exclusively dedicated to Tyāgarāja. The family name is interesting, for Appar in one of his hymns, refers to it and uses it as an epithet for Nīlōtpalampāḷ, the consort of Tyāgarāja.[91] The *Tēvaraṭiyār* are ritually wed to the deity and the *kurukkaḷ* ties the *tāḷi* round their necks on behalf of the deity. Tilakammā recounted the event with great emotion and narrated how in traditional society, the *Tēvaraṭiyār* relinquished their status as dancers at the age of forty, when they symbolically took off their nose-ring and took to wearing only white garments, and were engaged in singing and teaching the next generation of singers and dancers. Thus the epithet *'koṇṭi'* used for the consort of Tyāgarāja was aptly applied to the family dedicated to serving the deity as his spouses.

The word *'koṇṭi'* is provided with several meanings in the *Tamiḻ Lexicon*.[92] The two most relevant in the present context are 'one who is stubborn' and 'one captured in war as booty'. That *Tēvaraṭiyār* were often recruited from the ranks of women war captives makes the latter meaning a plausibility. Tilakammā believes that it was their resolute will to serve Tyāgarāja, a resolution tantamount to stubbornness, that gave rise to the expression *'koṇṭi'*. It is in this context that Appar uses it to refer to Nīlōtpalāmpāḷ. *Paṭṭinappālai* (VV. 246-49) uses the term *koṇṭimakaḷir* in the sense of captive women who performed menial duties in the temple. Thus the concept of *"koṇṭi"* women engaged in ritual worship can be traced to Caṅkam literature.

Tilakammā recounted the details of the special *mariyātai* that was given to her family by the Tiruvārūr temple authorities. She is the last of the line to have been thus dedicated, for the institution of *Tēvaraṭiyār* was declared illegal by Act of Parliament.[93]

When a lady belonging to the family of *Tēvaraṭiyār* of Tyāgarāja died, her body was brought before the *gōpuram* of the shrine and the *kurukkaḷ* duly honoured it by placing a garland of red water-lilies taken from the icon and sprinkling the body with the holy water taken from the shrine. These were the last *rājamariyātai* performed for the devoted dancer. While alive she received the usual honours of *parivaṭṭam* (a piece of cloth taken from the icon) and *prasādam* (food blessed by the deity). They were, in the past, endowed with land, money and other essential commodities.

Tilakammā recounts the story often told in her family of how her grandmother Kamalāmpāḷ was once stopped from entering the temple as the *kurukkaḷs* put a rival claimant as being the real representative of the *'konṭi'* family and worthy of receiving the *mariyātai*. Kamalāmpāḷ, disguised as a Brāhmaṇa woman, wearing the nine yard saree, entered the temple precints without being detected, and danced in such a professional manner that her claims were soon upheld by the audience present.[94]

Several interesting myths are known about the Tyāgarāja *Tēvaraṭiyār* and some of them, like the famous episode in Māṇikkanācciyār's life, are painted on the walls of the Nīlōtpalāmpāḷ temple.[95] Furthermore, a separate temple called the Māṇikkanācciyārkoyīl is dedicated to this saintly courtesan.

The Tiruvārūr dancers claimed their descent from Paravainācciyar, the first wife of Cuntarar who was a *Rudragaṇikā* (a dancer at the shrine of Śiva). Several temple dancers bore the name Paravai and a famous woman by that name was a companion of Rājendra I and accompanied him in his royal chariot to the Tiruvārūr temple and lit a temple lamp. The spot where they stood and worshipped was given a special importance and the epigraphs tell us that a big temple lamp was installed there to mark the occasion.[96] Paravaiyār, the wife of Cuntarar was already given a semi-divine status in the *Periya Purāṇam* for she was none other than the divine attendant of Pārvatī in heaven and was sent to earth so that she might marry the saint Cuntarar. To this day the icons of Cuntarar and Paravaiyār receive worship in the temple at Tiruvārūr.[97]

The myth of the courtesan Māṇikkanācciyār is recounted in the *Tiyākarājalīlaikaḷ*,[98] without however mentioning her by name. She is believed to have been a great dancer and a staunch devotee of Tyāgarāja. Once, the deity appeared to her in the guise of a poor old man, but an ardent devotee of Tyāgarāja sporting all the external insignia of the *aṭiyār* or slave of Śiva. She received her guest with great hospitality and, when he asked her to spend the night with him, she readily agreed simply because he was an *aṭiyār*, though all he could offer her in return was a rosary. The old man, at the end of a night's amorous dalliance, died. Māṇikkanācciyār, felt a spiritual union with the *aṭiyār* as a Śaiva devotee and ascended the funeral pyre of the old man, thereby fulfilling the vows of a *satī*. She is a much-venerated figure and has been elevated almost to the status of a saint. The noble harlot is a persistent motif in Indian literature.

Another story narrated by Tilakammā centred around yet

another ancestor called Koṇṭiyammā. The lady was asked to attend the chariot festival by the king. Being of a reserved temperament and an ardent devotee of Tyāgarāja she shunned all public exposure and so refused to attend. The chariot came in front of her house and stopped. Not all the efforts of the people present could make it budge an inch. This motif of the stuck chariot appears repeatedly in Tamil temple myths as pointed out by Shulman.[99] The king sent her a further request and, suspecting the king's motives, Koṇṭiyammā said that if what the king said were true and if the Tyāgarāja would not move without her offering ritual worship, then she would come outside; but, if all this be untrue, then with her first touch of the chariot she would cast off her mortal frame and be joined with Tyāgarāja. The story then goes on to tell how she touched the chariot and fell dead and thus obtained her *mokṣa*. This myth, according to Tilakammā is the origin of the temple ritual by which the *Tēvaraṭiyār* have to perform worship before the chariot can start. The late Tyāgarāja Mutaliyār of Vaṭapātimaṅkalam and a hereditary trustee of the Tyāgarāja temple invited Tilakammā to officiate in this ritual when the *Tēr*, 'chariot', festival was resumed after a long period of lapse in the mid-sixties. This was inaugurated with the patronage of Mr. Karunanidhi, the then Chief Minister of Tamilnāḍu, who strangely enough is a self-proclaimed atheist. The sociopolitical impact of the chariot festival was not lost on this astute politician.[100]

The caste and the constitution of the community of *Tēvaraṭiyār* from whom many of the *naṭṭuvaṉārs* or dance-masters originate is not homogeneous. The informants referred to above all regarded themselves as *Icai* Veḷḷāḷas as mentioned earlier. Fuller has pointed out how this caste name is a relatively modern coinage and was formally adopted at a caste conference in 1947.[101] Tilakammā's husband was a Brāhmaṇa and her family tradition had it that her great-grandmother bore the children of Muttusvāmi Dīkṣita, the great composer.[102] It was their training and initiation that qualified a person to be a temple dancer, not her caste.

From inscriptional sources it seems that, while some *Tēvaraṭiyār* were sold to the temple and branded with the marks of the temple, others offered themselves voluntarily and some seemed to have married and settled down, in the manner of Paravaiyār marrying Cuntarar. Inscription 147 of 1912 records the name of a dancer, Caturaṉ Caturī who was not only married, but seemed to have been wealthy enough to bequeath land to the temple. Monier Williams in his *Brahmanism and Hinduism* (cited by Thurston) writes that some Devadāsīs amassed huge fortunes and many spent it on works of piety. He adds, "Here and there Indian bridges and other useful public works owe their existence to the liberality of the frail sisterhood". The fact that the dancers all traced their geneology through the maternal line leads to the assumption that several of them were born out of wedlock.

At Tiruvoṟṟiyūr, the chief trustee explained how in former times the dancing girls were divided into two classes, *Valaṅkai* and *Iṭaṅkai* (right and left-handed castes) and the former danced before Tyāgarāja, the latter before Vaṭivuṭaiyammaṉ. Thurston[103] records how when a Kaikkōḷadāsī dies no *pūjā* is performed in the temple till the corpse is disposed of as the idol being her husband has to observe the rites of pollution. Incidentally, the term *kaikōl* in the above phrase refers to the weaver community. Devadāsīs were the only women who could adopt girls on their own right. Thus their caste, ritual and legal status seem to have varied and whether this was simply determined by the power of the patron, it is difficult to tell. While some dancers seem to have been oppressed workers as is evident from the strike at Tiruvoṟṟiyūr referred to above, others seem to have been powerful royal paramours and yet others high class courtesans. Some seem to have had only the choice of ritual suicide to avoid the unwanted attention of a royal paramour, as is reflected in the myth of Koṇṭiyammā.

The Viḻuppaṟaiyaṉs

The other community of people who held special *mariyātai* rights in the Tiruvārūr temple were the *Viḻuppaṟaiyaṉs*, also called *viḻpperumār*. They belong to a hereditary family connected with the Paṅkuṉi Utsavam and they are the repositories of the secret technique of rituals of tying the banana fibre cords to the pole and suspending the deity in such a manner as to enable the icon to imitate the *ajapā* dance. Mr. Dakṣiṇāmūrti is the present recipient of the honour and the following account was provided by him:[104]

"The important officials in the temple are the *nāyiṉār* (the Śivācārya, i.e. *kurukkaḷ*), *Paramarāyar* (people involved with the decoration of the icon, not its worship), *ōtuvār* (the singer of the

Tēvāram) and the *Vilupperumār* (*Viluppar̲aiyan̲s*.)

Even about fifty years ago only the *Vilupperumārs* were allowed to carry the icon in processions. They had to be strong for no change of hands was allowed till the prescribed pauses. They carried the poles bearing the icon on their shoulders and initiated the movement of the *ajapānaṭanam* to the accompaniment of eighteen kinds of instruments and the *tompai* dance." Dakṣiṇāmūrti recollected how his grandfather Cāmināta Piḷḷai once rescued the icon from a great fire. They regard their community as specially appointed watchmen of the Tyāgarāja icon. They received no salaries, but the *arcan̲ai* (money) during the procession was shared by the *Paramarāyar* and *vilupperumār*. During the procession they (i.e. the *vilupperumār*) were entrusted with the safekeeping of all the ornaments and jewellery.

As in the case of the *Tēvaraṭiyār*, they were also given special last rites. The bodies of dead members of the community were brought to the eastern *gopuram* and it was after the dead man was honoured with sandal paste, rose water and *vibhūti* (sacred ash) and covered with the *parivaṭṭam* taken from the icon, that the corpse was taken to the cremation-ground.

Tradition has it that Tyāgarāja had twelve thousand *aṭiyār* and hence the *Tēr̲* had to be dragged by twelve thousand people, two thousand on each side of the hexagonal chariot. Dakṣiṇāmūrti explained the symbolism of the chariot as the Mēru, the four horses as the four Vedas, the charioteer as Brahmā and the 64 pillars supporting the roof of the chariot as the 64 arts, and the six wheels as the six systems of philosophy. The symbolism of the chariot is explained in exactly the same manner in the *Mucukundasahasranāmam*. Late Mutaliyār, the grandfather of the present trustee of the *ulturai kaṭṭaḷai* (one of the trusts) is said to have slept by the side of the chariot on the floor along with the *Vilupperumār* for the whole duration of the festival. Thus these ritual officiants were given considerable ritual status by the temple administrators.

The term *Viluppar̲aiyan̲*, as they are often called, is an intriguing expression. It is popularly explained by the belief that since the icon, which was tossed up and down in the performance of the *ajapānaṭanam*, fell on the shoulders of the carriers they were called *Viluppar̲aiyan̲s* (after the Tamil word *vilu*, meaning 'to fall'. They are the *ajapā* dancers inasmuch as they are the people responsible for the movement.

What makes the name *Vil̲uppar̲aiyan̲* intriguing is that it occurs several times in inscriptions from Tiruvārūr. In the second regnal year of Rājādhirāja II (i.e. 1164 or 1168 A.D.), a donor by the name of Paḻaiyan̲ūruṭaiyān Vētavan̲amuṭaiyān̲ Ammai Appan̲ alias Rājarāja Vil̲uppar̲aiyan̲ of Men̲malai Paḻaiyan̲ūrnāṭu in Jayaṅkoṇṭa Cōl̲amaṇṭalam donated some land to the temple. This land had been bought from a *mūvāyirattil oruvan̲*, (lit.one of the three thousand), a collective number usually used to represent the priests of Chidambaram) and hence possibly refers to one of the three thousand of the Dīkṣita community from Chidambaram.[105] The same donor with the same epithet is mentioned in several other inscriptions.[106] That a relative of the donor of the above epigraphs was a well-known figure in the court of Rājarāja II and, in fact, was responsible for restoring him to power in troubled times is clear from other inscriptions.[107] The donor himself is known from several epigraphs from Vedāraṇyam, Tiruvālaṅkāṭu, Tiruvalañcuḻi and Paṭṭīcuram. Vil̲uppar̲aiyan̲ is a title bestowed by the king.

Noboru Karashima records the names of several donors to temples bearing the title *Vil̲uppar̲aiyan̲*. They came from Toṇṭaimaṇṭalam (Tiruvor̲r̲iyūr), Cōl̲amaṇṭalam (several) and Pāṇṭimaṇṭalam. It is therefore tempting to conclude that the community that regards itself as the custodian of the Tyāgarāja, the watchman of the deity, and now connected only by ritual ties to the deity, could well have descended from a family of title holders in the 12th century A.D. The connection between Cōl̲a royalty and the Tyāgarāja was a very intimate one as we shall see in the next chapter. If this ancestry of the *Vil̲uppar̲aiyan̲s* of Vētavan̲am could be established, then, on a sociological plane, it would seem that there were families of certain feudatory groups such as the *Vil̲uppar̲aiyan̲* who held power in court and were connected to the state cult by ritual ties. The family of Dakṣiṇāmūrti regard themselves as belonging to a separate caste but most akin to the Tēcikar (Veḷḷāḷas), though they share *arcanai* rights with *Paramarāyar*. The family of Dakṣiṇāmūrti live in the Piṭārikōyil street and he believes that there are less than fifty members of this community living in Tiruvārūr and nearby areas.

Interestingly enough the Vedāraṇyam *kurukkaḷ* also recounted the connection between Tyāgarāja and the *Vil̲uppar̲aiyan̲s*. The *parivaṭṭam* and *prasādam* were regularly given to them on all festive occasions. *Prasādams* were given in the form of twenty or thirty huge balls of rice called *paṭṭaicātam,* and all other offerings to the temple were distributed to them. While going through the '*Rājan kaṭṭaḷai tiṭṭam*', or list[108] of expenditure incurred by this particular trust, an interesting item recorded was the price of cloth which was offered as *Parivaṭṭam* to the *Viḻupparaiyan̲* for the *rahasyam* (secret). It reads: "*-ivarahasyam paṭi kūli*", Rs. 30 per metre and so total Rs. 217.00, and the quality of cloth was recorded as *kucumpamal,* a kind of muslin cloth. This item was recorded in 1970 as part of the expenditure of the *Ārudrā darśanam* rites. It was difficult to obtain other sheets of the account book from the trust officials.

In 1970, when the *Tēr* or chariot was revived after a number of years, it was equipped with iron axles, automatic brakes, tractor wheels and other modern innovations and so pulling the *tēr* was no longer a herculean task! The icon, however, which is believed to weigh over 200 lbs was still carried on the shoulders of the carriers. Dakṣiṇāmūrti is the only one of the *Viḻupparaiyan̲* family still associated with the secret of tying the banana fibre (*pullatantu*) and suspending the icon. The people who carried it in 1970 came from all communities and were volunteers. The *tēr* has again been suspended for some time due to internal disputes.

At Tiruvor̲r̲iyūr the band of people who carry the Tyāgarāja icon are called Civantāṅki and they came from the *Kaikkōḷar* (weaver) community and until the 1930s were the only people who could carry the icon in procession. One is to presume that the *Kaikkōḷar* were an important people in the environs of this particular temple as they sit on councils, deliberate and pass judgements with other representatives. Noboru Karashima has pointed out how the title *viḻuppa* was added to *araiyan (aracan)* = ruler. These were feudal titles bestowed by the Cōḻa monarch. In Vēdāraṇyam, as seen earlier, one finds mention of Viḻupparaiyan̲s—both in inscriptions and from contemporary informants.

It would be impossible to study in one chapter the various classes of participants in temple rituals who were given a socio-religious standing by the temple and amalgamated into the Āgamic system through the ritual of "mariyātai" or honours. The study is, therefore, in this respect restricted to only a limited but representative sampling.

The Ōtuvār, Brahmarāyar and Nāyiṉār

There are two *ōtuvār* at present in the temple maintained by Uḷtuṟai and Rājaṉ Kaṭṭaḷais. The *ōtuvār,* involved with the singing of *Tēvāram,* belong to the *Tēcikar* community and are regarded as a special section of the *Veḷḷāḷa* community. They are also called the *paṇṭārāms;* and more will be said of this community in connection with the study of the role of *Veḷḷāḷa maṭhas.* In the present context it is interesting to trace the development of the institution of *Tēvāram* singers as recorded in inscriptions. The earliest reference to the *Tēvāram* is in an inscription of the 9th century A.D., although some scholars take the term *Tēvāram* in the epigraph to denote *pūjā* generally and not the singing of the hymns of the three Śaiva saints. Images of the saints were regularly consecrated from the 10th century A.D. and became almost a regular feature of temple worship by the 13th century A.D.[109]

Today in the Tiruvārūr temple during the *paktakaṭci* (Skt. *bhaktakākṣi*) festival which is celebrated to honour the saints the *Kārkāṭa Veḷḷāḷas* play an important role. The procession (*puṟappāṭu*) of the saints is managed by the *kārkāṭa Veḷḷāḷas* and the cost (*ubhayaṁ*) is borne by the stallholders of *Vijayapuram,* the market area of Tiruvārūr.

In the Tiruvārūr temple the *kurukkaḷ* services consist of two classes of rights: *pūjā* rights and *sthānam* rights. *Pūjā* rights involve attending to the worship ceremonies and rituals conducted in the temple. These are the prerogatives of the *nāyiṉār*. There are two *nāyiṉār* in the temple. They perform the ritual ablutions (*abhiṣeka*), offer praises (*arcaṉai*) and food offering (*prasādam*). There are assistant *nāyiṉār,* young men who cannot perform all functions because they are bachelors. When the *Tirumukham* is written, which is an invitation, or more precisely, an announcement of the dates of the festivals, the special honour goes to the 'writer' who is called *Tamiḻ moḻi paṇṭāram.* The invitation itself is an interesting document. It begins in Sanskrit with *Śubhamastu* (May it be auspicious) and the *Jagat traya nirvāṇa dhāraṇa kāraṇa tat idam śāsanam,* etc. 'for the well-being of the three worlds is this proclamation issued'. After the initial introduction the invitation is in Tamiḻ. What is further interesting is that it is the saint Cuntarar, the alter ego of Tyāgarāja in whose name the invitations are issued. It is issued in the name of Śambh Ālāla Sundara the saint Cuntarar) the Vaṉtoṇṭar (the friend) and the *tānamahēcuvara* (deity or the administrators of the deity's needs) in Tamiḻ.

The *sthānam* rights lie with the *Paramarāyars*(Brahmarāyars). They have the key to the doors. The *Paramarāyar* are assistants to the *nāyiṉār* in the worship of the deity. Their main function is to decorate the deity and give the *nāyiṉār* the objects needed for worship. Each of the above rights has an office and specified initiation-rites attached to it. They were originally intended to be purely hereditary offices but such a practice is no longer feasible as the younger members of the priestly family are increasingly branching off to the cities in quest of more lucrative fields of employment.

Both the *nāyiṉār* and the *brahmarāyar* are Śivācāryas or those Brāhmaṇas who are initiated into Śaiva rites. They are according to the Āgamas descended from the five sages Kauśika, Bharadvāja, Gotama, Agastya and Durvāsa, who were believed to have been initiated by the five faces of Śiva. Thus only Śivācāryas belonging to these five lineages are allowed to officiate at the Tiruvārūr temple. Since some texts replace Gotama with Atri, members of the Ātreya *gotra* are also permitted to act as officiants. The *'Nityārcanavidhi'* of the *Kāraṇāgama* defines the five kinds of Śaivas as follows:

"Anādi Śiva is the Lord Śiva himself; Ādi Śaivas are the Śiva Brāhmaṇas; Mahāśaivas are the other Brāhmaṇas (i.e. not belonging to the above *gotras*); Anu Śaivas are *kṣatriyas* and Avāntara Śaivas are *Śūdras*". The Ādi Śaivas, according to this text were appointed by Ādi Śiva to perform worship for the well-being of others (the community, etc., i.e. *parārthapūjā*). Others can, with proper initiation perform *ātmārtha pūjā*, i.e. for individual well-being as distinguished from collective well-being. Thus even Brāhmaṇas belonging to other *gotras* were not allowed to do *pūjā* for the general weal according to the *Āgamas*. *Parārthapūjā*, i.e. *pūjā* for common well-being is defined as *pūjā* to a *liṅga* installed in a temple or a *svayambhu liṅga*, while *ātmārtha* is defined as worship to the *liṅga* given by a guru. Detailed codes of the geographical limits of the temple to which each caste could enter are worked out in the *Āgamas*, where even the kings are allowed to enter only up to the *ardhamaṇṭapa* or the hall just at the entrance of the *garbhagṛha*.[110]

There are five *Paramarāyar* and four *Nāyiṉār* families in Tiruvārūr at the time of writing. Many of the *Paramarāyar* have had no Dīkṣā rites. The *nāyiṉār* are not allowed to work in any other Śaiva temples. They are related in a special manner to the Tyāgarāja. Thus there is a kind of guild monopoly, geocentricity and caste requirement which characterises the constitution of the priests in this temple. Both their economic plight and their social status have plummetted down over the years as the temple clientele is dwindling.

Kaikkōḷar

The professional association of the weaving community with the temple is defined by their weaving the Tyaga *parivaṭṭam* or the sacred cloth covering the conical object to the right of the Śiva image in the Tyāgarāja trinity. There was a very significant ritual performed in Tiruvārūr in the past, which has now been discontinued for over ten years, during which the innermost *prākāra* of the shrine was covered with sheets of cotton cloth and after due worship was offered to the deity, the cloth was distributed amongst the ritual officiants which included the donor *Kaikkōḷar*. This rite was called the *niṟaipaḷi* and the Rājaṉkaṭṭaḷai in 1970 spent Rs. 40 on this, while the other *kaṭṭaḷais* contributed an equal amount, totalling Rs.460.00. This again is recorded in the *'tiṭṭam'* list of the Rājaṉkaṭṭaḷai. Money was paid as coolie wages to the people who carried the cloth, laid it, cut it and distributed it,[111] while the actual cloth was distributed as a temple honour.

The *kaikkōḷar* are also called *ceṅkuntar* and in the chapter on Tyāgarāja mythology we have seen how the icon is believed to have been brought to earth by the *ceṅkuntar* chief, who was the commander of the army of the king, Muckunataṉ. This event, as we have seen, was commemorated by Oṭṭakkūttar in the *Ittiyeḻupatu*. Thus, besides being weavers they were also involved in leading armies and sitting in investigatory councils on temple disputes.

The Paṭṭunūlkārars, of Gujrati extraction, from Saurāṣṭra were obviously a later wave of migrants. The process of integrating new arrivals into the traditional fold is an interesting subject for study. When the Saurāṣṭra Brāhmaṇas arrived in large numbers in Tamilnāḍu they were integrated into the Tamiḻ fold by providing the Tamil̲ deity Aiyan̲ar or Śāstā with a Saurāṣṭran weaver bride. To this day the Saurāṣṭra Brāhmaṇa weavers offer dowry in several Aiyan̲ar shrines on festival days.

The Tiruvor̲r̲iyūr epigraph records a temple investigation into the conduct of *Tēvaraṭiyār* and *iṣṭapāṭṭāliyār*, and the council that sat to decide the issues consisted of the head of the *bhikṣā maṭha*, the *tānattār* or trustees, the *vīracōl̲an̲ukkār* and the *kaikkōḷar*.[112]

The *kaikkōḷar* and *ceṅkuntar* are now officially classified as belonging to the backward community by the Government of Tamil̲nāḍu. Thus, they too, like the Rathākaras or chariot makers seem to have slid down the social scale when the caste system was organized on a more orthodox mould in the Vijayanagara and Nāyaka time.

The *Viracōl̲an̲ukkār* seem to have been a class of soldiers and are referred to in inscriptions from Tiruvārūr, Tiruvor̲r̲iyūr, Vedāraṇyam, etc.[113] They are referred to fondly as *nam makkaḷ* or 'our people' by Vītiviṭaṅkar[114] who is also said to have granted land to the dramatist who composed an eulogy on them.[115] The dramatist was called Pūṅkōyil Nampi and so seems to have been himself connected with *pūṅkōyil* (the Tamil̲ texts often refer to the Tyāgarāja shrine by this name). The *Vīracōl̲anukkār* may then well be connected with the myth of the nine soldiers given by Murukan̲ to Mucukuntan̲, credited with bringing Tyāgarāja to the earth, and that could well account for their being referred to as *nam makkaḷ* (our sons or our people). The Tiruppōrūr temple in the suburbs of Madras has images of the nine warriors on its pillars. An inscription from Vedāraṇyam refers to a throne called the Vīracōl̲an, which was given as a gift to the temple by Vīracōl̲an̲ukkan̲.[116] Thus Parāntaka I, who bore the title Vīracōl̲an̲, seems to have had a regiment of bodyguards who helped him to establish Cōl̲a rule and they are closely connected with the Tyāgarāja icon. This theme will be explored in a subsequent chapter.

Thus we see that a study of the myths and the ritual manifestation of the cult worship reveal a particular typology. The cult, as is evident, provided a substantial social bond and defined the relationship and hierarchy of the believers. There is, we have seen, an extremely intricate interplay between individual mystic experience in religion and the various forms of institutional expression and both these aspects define the parameters of this cult.

In the next chapter we shall explore the administrative structure of the Tyāgarāja temple of Tiruvārūr and study the rise of Śaiva Veḷḷāḷa *maṭhas,* which played an important part in the management of the vast estates of the temple. Several members of the ritual personnel such as the cooks, who are *Smārta* brāhmaṇas and other functionaries, like the water carriers, lamp-lighters, etc., are not discussed since they had no special *mariyātai* in the temple. Their roles were thus simply functional with no special ritual status attached to them.

NOTES

1. Otto, Rudolf, *The Idea of the Holy,* trans. J.W. Harvey, London, O.U.P., 1970. The holy was referred to by Otto as the 'numinous' and was characterised by something esoteric and was beyond ethical and rational considerations.
2. Weber, Max, *The Theory of Social and Economic Organization,* New York, O.U.P., 1947, pp. 358-60.
3. See O'Dea, F. and Aviad, Janet, *The Sociology of Religion,* New Jersey, Prentice Hall, 1983, p.25.
4. Weber, *op. cit., passim.*
5. See Eisenstadt, S.N., Kahane, R. and Shulman, D., (ed.), *Orthodoxy, Heterodoxy and Dissent in India,* Mouton, Berlin, New York, Amsterdam 1984, for an interesting collection of papers which analyses the impact of dissent and heterodox movements on the Hindu-Buddhist institutional framework of culture. Of particular interest are Eisenstadt's paper on 'Dissent, heterodoxy and civilization dynamics', pp. 1-9, and Shulman's 'The Enemy Within Idealism and Dissent in South Indian Hinduism', pp. 11-55.
6. Mīṉāṭcicuntaram Piḷḷai, *Tiyākarājalīlaikaḷ,* Madras, 1928 contains only 13 *līlais.* The author was the official Tamiḻ scholar (*vidvān*) of the Tiruvāvaṭuturai ātīṉam and composed this work in 1845. He states in the introduction that despite all his efforts he could not trace the rest of the *līlais.* Piccāṇṭārkōyil Irācakōpāla Piḷḷai (ed.), *Tiyākarājalīlaikaḷ,* in 4 vols., Sri Rangam, Vāṇī Vilās Press, 1952-64 contains 362 *līlais* and is a modern Tamiḻ prose version of what is originally believed to have been a Sanskrit work.
7. See Tarumai Citamparanāta Muṉivar, *Ñāṉa Pirakāca Māṉmiyam,* unpublished Mss. in Tarumapuram collection. For the literary references to this eminent member of the Tiruvārūr literati see Cōmacuntara Tēcikar, *Tamiḻ Pulavar Varalāṟu,* 16th century, Madras, 1936.
8. Cited by Mu. Arunacalam, *Tamiḻ Ilakkiya Varalāṟu, Patiṉārām nūṟṟāṇṭu,* (16th century) pp. 280-81. The refrain in these ten verses goes *'arava kiṇkiṇi kāl kaṭṭi ariyācaṉattirukkum karuṇānitiyai yārūriṟ kaṇṭār piṟavi kāṇārē', Ibid.,* p. 281.
9. This is unusual, for the main deity is always worshipped in the *garbhagṛha* with no windows to let in light. The Tyāgarāja icon is actually in the *ardhamaṇṭapa* and has definitely been so from the 16th century as can be seen from literary references. The main *sanctum,* which is rectangular in shape is locked and there is a persistent speculation amongst local people and scholars

that it once housed a reclining image of Viṣṇu. If this were so, it could possibly have been removed during the reign of Kulōttuṅka II, when a strong sectarian bias was noticeable and Kulōttuṅka is said to have cast the image of Govindarāja at Tillai into the sea. *Vide Infra* p. 113. f.n. 51.

10. "— *tuṇṭupaṭṭa acapā niruttam acaiyumpati tanticaiyum vakaiyaruḷvāy iṉṟu*". See Cōmacuntara Tecikar, *op. cit.* p. 29. *Ñāṉa Pirakāca Māṉmiyam* and *Guru Ñāṉacampantarcaritra caṅkirakam* describe this incident and also describe the *guru bhakti* of Ñāṉacampantar, the founder of Tarumapuram ātīṉam towards his *guru* Kamalai Ñāṉapirakācar of Tiruvārūr. These works provide interesting information on several episodes in the life of Kamalai Ñāṉapirakācar. On returning from Kāśī he is said to have composed the *Tiyākarāja Paḷḷu* and it is believed that this Paḷḷu provided the lyrics for dances by the *rudrakaṇikai* during the *Āvaṇi pavitrōtsava.* Cited by Mu. Aruṇācalam, *op. cit.*, p. 267. For the Paḷḷu itself see Ātmanātha Tēcikar, *Cōḻamaṇṭalacatakam*, Ed. S. Cōmacuntara Tēcikar, Tranquabar, 1916, p. 84.
11. *Mucukundasahasranāmam*, Inv. 996.
12. I have tried to trace the original manuscript but with no success. The Vāṇī Vilās Press referred me to a certain Śrī Veṅkaṭarāma Śāstrikāḷ of Ammāḷ Agrahāram, Tiruvaiyāṟu, who was the proof reader of the mss. He informed me that he had proof-read the Tamiḻ prose version, which was contained in a closely written paper mss., which looked according to our informant "about a hundred years old" and which claimed to be a copy of a Sanskrit original. This could well have been the press copy of the Late V.I. Parivaṭṭam Mutaliyār referred to earlier. Veṇkaṭarāmaśāstrikāḷ could remember nothing else except that Irācakōpāla Piḷḷai was very excited about the find and spent a huge sum of money in trying to publish it and that publication was held up several times because of his inability to raise the necessary funds. The subject matter of the stories contained in this work and the general treatment of the subject make it almost certain that it is an authentic work. The Tamiḻ scholar Veḷḷaivāraṇar, on looking at the work believed it to be an authentic work on the basis of its stylistic organisation and content. What is intriguing, however, is that the most well known *līlais*, like his acting as a messenger of love for Cuntarar, his secret vision granted to Cuntarar when he incurred the wrath of Viraṉmīṇṭār and stories of this nature do not find mention in this large collection. It seems to have been composed with the clear aim of extolling Cōḷa royalty and the explicit purpose of winning converts for the cult from all sections of the populace, given the constraints of the caste system. It has a strong *Śaiva Siddhānta* tinge and I believe that it is a genuine work written like the *Tiruviḷaiyāṭal Purāṇam* from an earlier, presumably 12th - 13th century version, now lost. The present version is hence a prose rendering of a Tamiḻ work of the 16th century which was based on oral tradition and presumably an earlier text. The *nāyaṉmār* by then had ceased to have any immediate relevance. It is hence a much later tradition that is recorded. It seems most likely to have been composed in the troubled times of Kulōttuṅka III when every need was felt for legitimising a tottering royalty.
13. Perumpaṟṟappuliyūr Nampi, *Tiruvālavāyuṭaiyār Tiruviḷaiyāṭaṟ Purāṇam* composed in the 13th century and Parañcōti, *Tiruviḷaiyāṭaṟ Purāṇam.* An annotated edition of this work was published in Madurai, 1973. Parañcōti also wrote the *Vētāraṇṇiya Māhātmyam.* Present day Vedāraṇyam is one of the Tyāgarāja cultic centres.

14. Personal interviews during several visits to Tiruvārūr between October 1981 and August 1983.
15. The Śivācāryas of the Tiruvārūr temple claim descent from Durvāsa and trace the origin of their title *nāyiṉār* to the eye of Durvāsa, the *krodhabhaṭṭāraka*. Durvāsa is claimed to be the founder of both the Trika system of Kashmir and the Śrī-Vidyā. Thus, these *kurukkaḷ* could well be the descendants of the followers of the Golaki maṭha, again belonging to the Durvāsa *sampradāya* or lineage which had a strong centre in Tiruvārūr.
16. Regarding Akōrapaṇṭāram, one of the trustees, and a member of the Vēlakuricci maṭha, see *ARE 1946-47*, 16 and 18. These Copper Plates were in the possession of Thañjāvūr Tamiḻ University, Dept. of Epigraphy in December 1982. The first mention of this is in the *Tanjore Gazeteer*, Vol. II, p. 257. Also v. 84 of *Cōḻamaṇṭalacatakam*. For dating of Velakkuriccimaṭha see *ARE* 1927-28, No.77, dated Śaka 1581 = 1659.
17. *SII* XVII, No. 603 and *ARE* 1908, No. 479. See Derrett, J.D.M., 'Two Epigraphs on Rathakāras and Kammāḷas', *K.A. Nilakantha Sastri 80th Birthday Felicitation Volume*, Madras, 1971, pp. 32-35. Also reprinted in Derrett, J.D.M., *Essays in Classical and Modern Hindu Law*, Vol. I., London, E.J. Brill, 1976.
18. Sastri, K.A.N., *Cōḻas*, pp. 454 and 456. He believes that it is only in modern usage that the term *kaikkōḷar* has assumed the meaning of weavers and that in Cōḻa times it was used to refer to a regiment. However, like in other broad caste groups of artisans there seems to have been several professional occupational groups included within the large caste group. The armed wing of the *kaikkōḷars* could well have belonged to the *Iṭaṅkai* or left handed groups, who clashed so often with the right handed or *valankai* castes.
19. Spencer, George W., 'Religious Network and Royal Influence in 11th Century South India'. *Journal of the Economic and Social History of the Orient*, Vol. 11-12, 1968-69 and 'Temple Money Lending and Livestock Redistribution in Early Tanjore'. *Indian Economic and Social History Review*, Vol. V., 1968, pp. 277-93. See also Cohn, Bernard S. and Marriott, Mckim, 'Networks and Centres in the Integration of Indian Civilisation', *Journal of Social Research*, Vol. I, No. 1, 1958, pp. 1-8.
20. Stein, Burton, 'Temples in Tamiḻ Country 1300-1750 A.D.', *Indian Economic and Social History Review*, Vol. IV, 1977, pp. 11-47. For other works of the author see Bibliography.
21. Arjun, Appadorai, 'Kings Sects and Temples', *Indian Economic and Social History Review*, Vol. XIV, No. 1, 1977, pp. 47-73. This article has also been reproduced in Stein, Burton (ed.), *South Indian Temples*. This is a chapter of his doctoral thesis, which has since been published as *Worship and Conflict in South India in the Colonial Period - The Pārthāsarathi Temple, a Case Study*, Cambridge University Press, 1981. Breckenridge, Carol Appadorai, *The Minaksi Cuntaresvara Temple - Worship and Endowments in South India, 1833 - 1925*. (Unpublished Ph.D. thesis, Madison, Wisconsin, U.S.A., 1976).
22. Appadorai, *op. cit.*, p. 18. Also Appadorai and Breckenridge, Carol, 'The South Indian Temple: Authority, Honour and Redistribution', *Contributions of Indian Sociology*, New Series, December 1976.
23. Appadorai, *op. cit.*, p. 18.
24. *Ibid.*
25. *Ibid.*
26. Baker, C.J. and Washbrook, D.A., *South India: Political Institutions and Political*

Changes, 1880-1940. See also Washbrook, D.A., *The Emergence of Provincial Politics*, sections under the heading 'Temples'. Also Baker, C.J., 'Temples and Political Development' in Baker and Washbrook, *Political Institutions*.

27. Between 1939-45 Harijan entry into temples was a major issue. Virulent protests led by the Sanātanists who belonged to the All India Varṇāśrama Svarājya Saṅgha followed C.Rajagopalachari's accompanying two Harijans into the Mīnākṣī temple at Madurai. Many of the priests quit unless purificatory rites were performed. It was finally in 1945 that the Harijan Entry Act was passed. See Lee Hardgrave, R.L., *Political Participation and Primordial Solidarity: The Nadaras of Tamilandu* and Kothari, R. (e.d.), *Caste in Indian Politics*.
28. The term 'ethnocentric' has been used in the sociological sense of the term as in *Encyclopaedia of Social Sciences*. See note 54 below.
29. The lives of Cuntaramūrtināyaṉār, Sōmayājimāṟanār, Naminantiyaṭikaḷ, Taṇṭiyaṭikaḷ, Viraṉmīṇṭār, Ēyarkōṉ, Kalikkāmanāyaṉār, Ceṟuttuṇai and Kaḻarciṅkar are directly associated with Tiruvārūr. Major incidents in the lives of saints like Tirunīlakaṇṭaryāḻppāṇar are also connected with the Tiruvārūr temple. The geographical focus of Cēkkiḻār's *Periya Purāṇam* is at Tiruvārūr and the author devotes a whole chapter to Tiruvārūrppiṟantār or those born at Tiruvārūr.
30. See *Periya Purāṇam* 5.7/ v.v. 1866-1897 *Naminantiyaṭikaḷ n. Purāṇam* v. 21-32, especially 27 and 29. v. 27 runs: *'mēṉmai viḷaṅkum Tiruvārūr vīti viṭaṅkapperumāl tam mana vanpar pūcaṉaikku varuvārpōl vantaruḷi ñāṉa maṟaiyō yārūriṟ piṟantārellā namkaṉaṅkaḷ'*.
31. *yāḻ*, lute. Possibly, at that period, a bow-harp. The matter is yet undecided.
32. *Periya Purāṇam*, XII, V (69) *Tirunīlakaṇṭaryāḻppāṇanāyaṉār Purāṇam*, V 2, 3 and 8. v.8 runs: *vāyil vēru vaṭa ticaiyil vakuppap pukuntu vaṇaṅkinār'*. (He entered through the gap in the Northern gate).
33. For the life of this saint see also *op. cit.*, V. Vi, *Tirunīlanakkanāyaṉār Purāṇam*, specially vv. 30 and 31. In verse 30 Campantar requests his host to give his Pāṇar friend a place to stay. In 31 the poet describes the Vedi igniting itself. See also, *Tiruñāṉacampantanāyaṉār Purāṇam*. The Pāṇars to this day are included in the list of backward classes in Tamiḻnāḍu. In Kanyākumāri district and Shencottah taluq of Tirunelveli district the community is included in the list of scheduled castes.
34. *op. cit.*, IV. IV./ 1041 - 77 *Tirunāḷaippōvār Nāyaṉār Purāṇam*, specially v. 17. Nantaṉ used to make drums, etc., needed for Śiva worship. It is clearly stated that he stood outside the temple when he supplied these objects of worship (*kōyilkaḷiṟriruvāyiṟ puṟa niṉṟu*) (v. 15, line 2). In stanza 17, it is made clear that by his grace the Lord made the Nanti move aside so that the saint may behold the deity (*poṟēṟṟai viḷaṅkavaruḷ purintaruḷi pulappaṭuttār*). The topographical layout of the temple is also indicated here, with the Nandi in an axial arrangement with the main icon.
35. *Ibid*. The 19th century social and economic protest movement and its ideals are woven into Gopalakrishna Bhāratī's reworking of the legend in his opera *Nantaṉcaritram*. Though the theme is identical the difference in treatment is significant. The latter was a social outcry, the former an expression of interiorized faith.
36. There is a certain fanatical obedience to the call of 'Śiva' and an unquestioning compliance to the request of anyone they conceived as an *aṭiyār*.

Iyarpakaināyanār gave his wife to Śiva, who appeared in the garb of a libertine but with the marks of a devotee, (*tūrttavēṭam*); Mānakkañcāranāyanār gave his daughter's tresses, Caṇṭikēśvara cut off his father's leg in a pique of rage at being disturbed in his worship of Śiva, Kalarciṅkanāyanār cut off his wife's hand after Ceruttuṇai had cut off her nose, for sniffing at a flower offered to Śiva, Kōṭpulināyanār killed his family members including the babe in arms to punish their stealing grain meant for the temple and that too at the time of a famine, while Ciruttoṇṭanāyanār offered the cooked meat of his son to the Bhairava devotee. All this could be done in the name of the community of *aṭiyārs*. The community and the faith was the prime determinant. However the doors of the temple could not be thrown open by an aṭiyār for another of a lower caste.

37. Thus, when faced with challenges from Christianity there grew the Arya Samaj and Brahma Samaj movements.
38. Apart from the castelessness of the Jainas they too believed in sixty three saints and followed a work called the *Śrī-Purāṇa*, which was a hagiography of these saints. It is interesting to notice that the Tiruvorriyūr epigraph mentions the name Śrī-Purāṇa of Āḷuṭaiyanampi, as being recited by a certain Vāgīśvara Paṇḍita. This Śrī-Purāṇa has been identified by scholars with Cuntarar's *Tiruttoṇṭattokai*. Thus, there seems to have been a great deal of conscious borrowing not only in the concept of the egalitarian brotherhood of believers (the Śaiva counterpart of the Jaina paḷḷi) but also in details of the standardisation of the number of saints, etc. The cult of the Vaiṣṇava Āḻvārs too in a similar manner adopted the egalitarianism of the Jainas, at least as an acceptable and desirable ideal.
39. Karve, Iravati, 'On the Road', *Journal of Asian Studies*, XXII, 1, 1962, pp. 13-29.
40. *Periya Purāṇam*, V. 7, *Naminantiyaṭikaḷ Purāṇam*, specially, v.10.
41. *Ibid.*, VI, 4 (31), *Tantiyaṭikaḷnāyanār Purāṇam.*
42. Mahalingam, T.V. (e.d) *Mackenzie Manuscripts.*
43. For a detailed account of the Sōmayājin episode *vide infra*, Chapter VI.
44. Caṇḍālas were according to Manu the product of a hypogamous marriage of the most unequal type as between a śūdra male and a Brāhmaṇa female. He is described as the 'lowest of men'. Their dwellings had to be outside the village. (Manu 10. 51-53).
45. This is painted on the lintel of the yāgaśālai, the inner west wall of the Nīlōtpalāmpāḷ *sannidhi* and the dado of the *maṇṭapa* adjoining the Tyāgarāja-Valmīkanātha shrines. See Pls.
46. Tiruvamparmākālam, where the cultic festival is held, has, I am told, a large frieze of this episode. For the celebrations at Amparmākālam and Hemingway's account of it *vide infra*, Chapter VI.
47. See Moffatt, Michael, *An Untouchable Community in South India: Structure and Concensus*, Princeton, 1979, pp. 140-42.
48. It was J.R. Marr who drew my attention to this myth.
49. See O'Flaherty, Wendy, 'The Clash between Relative and Absolute Duty; The Dharma of Demons' in O'Flaherty, Wendy and Derrett, J. Duncan (ed.). *The Concept of Duty in South Asia*, Vikas Publishing House, Pub. Ltd., S.O.A.S., 1978.
50. Barnett, S.A., 'Approaches to Changes in Caste Ideology in South India' in Stein, Burton (ed.), *Essays on South India*, pp. 154 and 167 ff. Also the same author, 'Blood symbolism and Urban kinship Network's in Keiser, L. (ed.),

Urban Socio-Cultural Systems.

51. *Ibid.* p. 154
52. *Vide Infra,* Chapter Vi.
53. Gnanambal, K., *Religious Institutions and Caste Panchayats in South India,* Calcutta, 1973.p. 50
54. *Encyclopaedia of Social Sciences,*Vol. V. defines the term ethnocentric in a sociological sense as "View of things in which one's own group is the centre of everything and others are scaled and rated with reference to it". Again this term emotionally finds expression in "sympathetic awareness and approval of one's own fellows and their ways as per contra in a feeling of fear, suspicion and contempt towards outsiders and their ways".
55. Galanter, Marc, 'The Religious Aspect of Caste' in Smith, D.E. (ed.), *South Asian Politics and Religion.* See also Hardgrave, *op. cit.,* p. 114.
56. Barnett, *op. cit.,* p. 167.
57. *Ibid.*
58. Śrīnivāsaṉ, K.R., 'Thirukkāmakkōṭṭam; *Proceedings of the All India Oriental Conference, 13th Session, Nagpur,* 1946, III, 50-56.
59. Meister, Michael W. and Dhaky, M.A. *Encyclopaedia of Indian Temple Architecture - South India, Lower Drāviḍa Dēśa,* p. 255.
60. Stein, Burton, 'Temples in Tamiḻ Country,1300-1750 A.D.', *Indian Economic and Social History Review,* Vol. IV, 1977, pp. 11-47.
61. Shulman, David Dean, *Tamiḻ Temple Myths,* p. 267.
62. *SII,* Vol. V., no. 456; *SII* XVII, No. 595; Other such inscriptions are known from Viṣṇu and Śiva temples. Sethuraman, N., 'The Deity Speaks' in Nagasamy, R. (ed.), *South Indian Studies,* Vol. I.
63. Stein, Burton, 'Integration of the Agrarian System of South India', in Frykenberg, R.E. (ed.), *Land Control and Social Structure in Indian History,* Madison, 1969.
64. Hart III, George, 'Ancient Tamiḻ Literature - Its Scholarly Past and Future', in Stein, Burton (ed.), *Essays on South India,* pp. 41-63.
65. Thurston, Edgar and Rangachari, K., *Castes and Tribes of Southern India,* Madras, 1909. See under *Ocan.*
66. *Archakas, Tēvars, Kampaṉs,* etc., are registered as Backward Classes in the Tamiḻnāḍu Government List.
67. The Baramahal Records are cited by Stein, Burton, *Peasant, State and Society in Medieval South India,* p. 466.
68. See Krishnamurti, C., *The Tiruvoṟṟiyūr Temple - A Study* (unpublished Ph.D. thesis, University of Madras, 1951). He refers to the tradition of getting only 'Namboodris'from Kerala to officiate in the Tripurasundarī shrine. There is also the myth of connecting the Vaṭṭappāṟiammaṉ here with Kaṇṇaki. This Kaṇṇaki connection could also be one of the causes of the human sacrifices, etc. that are said to have taken place here. The Bhagavatī Temple at Caranganore still has the symbolic ritual of the sacrifice of goldsmiths as symbolising the revenge of the wronged Kaṇṇaki. Thus Kaṇṇaki got mixed with Kālī or Bhagavatī. For the ritual of the sacrifice of the goldsmiths at the Bharaṇi rites see Induchudan, V.I., *The Secret Chamber.* Krishnamurti, *op. cit.,* p. 135 refers to the sacrifices to Vaṭṭappāṟai and the role of the 'osar' (uvacar). He also refers to the myth of Śaṇkara setting up a nude Kālabhairava in front of the Vaṭṭappāṟai and how her sense of modesty kept her from coming out (p. 126). That the Kaṇṇaki cult must have been very popular in Tamiḻnāḍu in the Cōḻa times is obvious from its great following in Sri Lanka, where it

became known as the Paṭṭini cult. See also Jagadisa Ayyar, P.V., *South Indian Shrines*, Madras Times Publishing Company, 1920. The prevalence of these myths was independently confirmed by the trustee and the Kurukkaḷ. See the recent study on *The Paṭṭini cult* by G. Obeysekere.

69. For Uttaramērūr inscriptions see *190 of 1923*. The Sabhā laid down the qualifications and tenure for the Archaka in the temple of Tiruppulivaṉamuṭaiyār. See *SII* VI, No. 295 (*ARE* 192, Nos. 240, 241).
70. This was brought to my attention by C.J. Fuller.
71. Personal communication, July 1983. See Pl.XIV for a photograph of Mr. Kaṅkātaran, his wife and son in ritual attire.
72. Oral communication, July 1983.
73. The seven emblems of royalthy such as Elephant, wheel, queen, Prime Minister, royal parasol, throne, etc., are carved on a stele from Jaggayapeta belonging to the 2nd-1st centuries B.C., now in the Madras Museum. The white parasol was the insignia of royalty in many parts of South East Asia as well.
74. The importance of his role on the back of an elephant in front of the Tyāgarāja icon tallies with the *yāṉaiyēṟumperumpaṟaiyaṉ's* narrative wherein the elephant's role is of great importance.
75. Dietrich, Gabriele, *Religion and People's Organization in East Thañjāvūr*, Madras, 1977, p. 88.
76. See Beteille, A., 'Agrarian Relations in Tanjore District', in *Studies in Agrarian Social Structure*, pp. 142-50, especially p. 165.
77. See Mishra, K.C., *The Cult of Jagannath*, Calcutta, Firma K.L.M., 1971.
78. Eschmana, A., 'Hinduisation of tribal Deities in Orissa', in *The Cult of Jagannath and the Regional Tradition of Orissa*, p. 97.
79. Hart, *op. cit.*, p. 45.
80. *SII* Vol. II, No. 66.
81. A typical example is provided by the *Tyāgarājakavacam*, (Thañjāvūr Saraswati Mahal Library Mss. No. d 22265 B. 12466), where the devotee entreats the Lord to protect his sense of hearing, etc.... and then says "Please protect my aesthetic sensibilities to appreciate music (*sundara saṅgīta rasanam pātu me aniśam*). Three great composers of Carnatic music were born in Tiruvārūr, *viz.* Śyāma Śāstrī, Muttusvāmi Dīkṣitar and Tyāgarāja.
82. The *Mucukundasahasranāmam* also refers to him as the *kaḷānidhi*, the storehouse of the arts.
83. Personal communication, December 1982.
84. Thurston, *op. cit.*, Vol. II, p. 127.
85. Notes from personal interviews corroborated by those collected by Saskia Kersenbohm-Story in Debember 1977. Typescript kindly lent to me by the author.
86. Personal communication, Tiruvārūr, 1982.
87. The format of the present day Bharatanāṭyam performance of starting with an Alārippu and ending with a Tillānā was codified by the Tanjore school in the 19th century A.D. Individual dance numbers were known but the repertoire, conceived as a narration by a solo dancer, within the the naṭṭuvanār tradition was evolved by the four brothers from Thañjāvūr, Chiṉṉayya, Poṉṉayya, Vaṭivēlu and Śivāṉandam.
88. *SII* XVII, No. 593.
89. *ARE* 1912, Nos. 208 and 212, (Saka 1265-66 = 1343-44 A.D.).
90. *ARE* Pt. III (Records), 1913, paras. 51 and 67.

91. Appar, *V. 7. 7.* (*kaṇṭu kaṇṭivaḷ kātalit taṉpatāy koṇṭi yāyiṉa vāreṉkōtaiyē*). The *mariyātais* given to Tilakammā are called *Koṇṭi parivaṭṭam* and what she offers to the deity before the icon starts on the chariot procession is called *koṇṭinaivedyam* which is when Tilakammā goes to the *caṉṉititterumaṇṭapam* where a *naṭapāvāṭai* (the equivalent of the red carpet) is spread and she dances the *puṣpāñjali*.
92. See *Madras University Tamiḻ Lexicon*.
93. The Devadāsī system was abolished in 1947 (Madras Devadāsīs Prevention of Dedication Act 31 of 1947.) It was in the 1930s that people like Rukmini Devi Arundel revived Bharatanāṭyam and made it respectable for girls from traditional Hindu families to learn and perform.
94. It is this selfsame Kamalam (great great grandmother of Tilakkaṁmā) who offered to sell all her ornaments to redeem Muthusvāmi Dīkṣitar from penury but he would not hear of it and was confident that God would provide. He composed a Telegu varṇa in Tōḍi (*Rūpamu jūchi*) and another in Śrirañjanī *dāru nī sati*) for her to dance. The former was on Tyāgarāja and the latter on Valmīkanātha. See *Kalki*, Deepavali Number 1966, pp. 65-68 and Raghvan, V., *Śrī Muthusvāmi Dīkṣita Kāvyam*, Madras, 1980 (a posthumous publication). According to Tilakammā, Kamalam was the only dancer who could dance to the *Simhatāla* of 108 beats. She was trained by her mother, Ñāṉāmpāḷ.
95. There is a Māṇickanāccīārkōyil in the north street. It is in the same street as the ancestral house of the koṇṭi family, and is still called *koṇṭivīṭu* or house of Koṇṭi by the locals.
96. *ARE* 1919, No. 680 (*uṭaiyār Śrī Rājendra Cōḻa Tēvarum anukkaiyār paravai naṅkaiyārum niṟkumiṭam teriyum kuttuvinḷakkonṟum.*) Tiruvārūr remained a renowned centre of temple dancing even under the Vijayanagara kings as borne out by the accounts of foreign travellers. See Mahalingam, T.V., *Administration and Social Life under Vijayanagara*,p. 269.
97. Recently, in the summer of 1982, the Paravai icon was stolen and so Cuntarar, at the time of writing this stands alone waiting for a new image to be installed. see P1 XV.
98. *Līlai* No.264. There are several references to dancers in this collection of stories. *līlai* 354 a Rudragaṇikā prays to Tyāgarāja and he teaches her divine music as an accompaniment to his divine dance.
99. Shulman, *op.cit.*, p.53. He refers to the myth which recounts how a chariot refused to move at Kāñcī till the sacrifice of a pregnant woman with her first child was completed. He gives another example from Tillai kāḷi temple myths.
100. It appeared from the general tone of Mr. Karunanidhi's conversation (Personal interview February 1984) that the religous sentiments of the people of Tamiḻnāḍu is something that one has to recognise as a reality and such community gatherings were an important platform for expressing political viewpoints. He, however, criticised the attitude of Mr. M.G. Ramachandran's government towards religious leaders like Śaṅkarācārya, who were in his opinion still clinging to outdated beliefs in the Varṇāśramadharma. It is interesting to note that the chariot festival at Tiruvārūr was given great publicity and a poem was composed on it and on Karunanidhi's involvement in it. However, he took pains to point out that he, along with Velu Rajan, the son of the Justice Party leader, P.T. Rajan, had suggested that no temple *parivaṭṭams* should be offered to ministers and other political personages. This, according to Mr. Karunanidhi was one of the issues of dispute with the

"MGR" government.

101. Fuller, C.J., *Servants of the Goddess: The Priests of a South Indian Temple*, Cambridge University Press, 1984, p. 189, footnote 27.
102. Personal communication, Tiruvārūr, August 1983.
103. Thurston, *op. cit.*, Vol. II, p. 139.
104. Personal communication, January 1984.
105. *SII* XVII, No. 583.
106. *SII*, No. 94 refers to a Viḻuppaṟaiyaṉ as one of the donors in the Thañjāvūr inscription. *SII* XVII, 578, 587, 585 are other epigraphs from Tiruvārūr which refer to a Pallavarāyaṉ Vētavaṉamuṭaiyāṉammaiy Appaṉ alias Rājāraja Viḻuppaṟaiyaṉ. Two Pallavarāyaṉs are mentioned in the reign of Rājarāja II. Kaṅkaikuḷattur Tiruccirrampalamuṭaiyāṉ Perumānampi was the trusted lieutenant of Rājarāja II and helped the queen and heir apparent after Rājarāja's death. The Viḻuppaṟaiyaṉ of the Tiruvārūr inscriptions came into prominence after Rājādhirāja's accession and has made several grants to temples. See also *ARE* 1908-90, pt. II, p. 104 for a Pallavarāyan who built a *maṭha* of brick in Celva Tiruvārūr headed by a Netradeva. (Also 477 of Appendix B) The epigraphists regard this as an an important non-Brāhmaṇa *maṭha* (*ARE* 1913, Reports, p. 112) See *ARE* 1904, 538 and *ARE* 1925, 261.
107. The Pallavarāyaṉpēṭṭai inscription records the role of the two feudatories, the two Pallavarāyars in the Pāṇḍyan civil war. The elder Pallavarāyar died soon after his royal master. It is the Vētavaṉamuṭaiyāṉ who distributed the lands of the former among his relatives. See Sastri, K.A.N., *Cōḻas*, p. 373.
108. The only inventory that I could lay my hands on was the one prepared in 1970. The recent ones were regarded as confidential and *ātīṉam* property.
109. Swamy, B.G.L., 'The Four Śaivite Samayācāryas of the Tamiḻ Country in Epigraphy', in *JIH* Vol. 50, April 1972, pp. 95-129.
110. Cuvāmināthakurukkaḷ, *What is the Āgama?*, Madras, The South Indian Archaka Association (n.d.).
111. Information acquired from the Rājaṉ kaṭṭaḷai tiṭṭam.
112. *ARE* 1912, no. 212.
113. *SII* XVII, No, 446 from Vedāraṇyam refers to a member of Vīracōḻaṉukkāra, who donated 1,500 *Kācu* of ghee for lighting lamps before Tirumaṟaikkāṭuṭaiyār Interestingly enough this ghee was to be measured by *karuṇākaraṉ nāḻi*. Karuṇākaraṉ toṇṭaimāṉ was a renowned devotee of Tyāgarāja. It is dated in the 29th regnal year of Kulōttuṅka III, i.e. 1207-8 A.D. *SII* XVII, No. 446 also refers to this body. In *ARE* 1912, No.212 from Tiruvoṟṟiyūr they are present in the committee for investigation into the complaints of the *Tēvaraṭiyār*.
114. *SII* XVII, No. 593 from Tiruvārūr.
115. *Ibid.* In this Tyāgarāja is said to have honoured the playwright who presumably composed a panegyric on the Vīracōḻanukkār. This close connection between this body and the Tyāgarāja and the fact that both Parāntaka I and Vīrarājendra bore the epithet Vīracōḻa makes it very tempting to equate one of the two rulers with the myth of the Tyāgarāja being brought to earth by Mucukuntaṉ with the aid of nine warriors. The fact that Parantaka consolidated his hold and in that sense established the Cōḻa suzerainty makes it highly likely that he could have been instrumental in establishing the identity between the Pallava Somāskanda, which, as we have seen earlier was regarded by the rulers as a palladium of their royalty, and the Tyāgarāja, who was converted into the Cōḻa emblem of royal power. That the Mucukuntaṉ

myth and the Tyāgarāja are closely connected with the principle of legitimising Cōḻa rule becomes evident by a study of the *Tyāgarājalīlaikaḷ*. *Vide Infra* Chapter IX for a study of Tyāgarāja as the palladium of Cōḻa royalty.

116. *SII*, XVII, 466.

Chapter Eight

KAṬṬAḶAI MAṬHAS, TEMPLES AND CULTS AS REGULATORS OF SOCIAL STATUS

Veḷḷāḷa Maṭhas and Temple Trusteeships

In the preceding chapter, the nature of orthodoxy and the characteristics of the *bhakti* brotherhood were defined in as far as they had a bearing on the Tyāgarāja cult and the Tiruvārūr temple complex. We have seen that the Śaiva *bhaktas* had a highly well defined conception of fellowship *within the body* and insisted upon the principle of egalitarianism, but that in their relationship to the organized structure of religion outside the body, they adopted an ambivalent attitude.

We also noticed the pattern of elaborate temple rites which involved communal participation of its members who were of various castes and were given special *'mariyātai'* or 'honour' within the temple. It was by such means that temples acted as regulators of socio-sacral status.

This chapter will be dealing mainly with the administrative structure of the the temple and the management of temple finances and see how they impacted on the ordering of social status. An interesting inscription has come from the Tyāgarāja temple at Tiruvārūr. It deals with the status of chariot makers and artisans, as determined by the temple committee. Therefore it seemed appropriate to include its study within this chapter.

There were changes in forms of temple worship by the time of the later Cōḻas, as many new rituals were added. Under the royal patronage of the Pāṇḍyas and Vijayanagara kings, offerings of food and its distribution assumed great importance. By the 13th century, large tracts of land were dedicated to temples, either as general endowments or special endowments called *kaṭṭaḷais*. As the agrarian and mercantile population increased their support of the institution, the temple had to adjust to the general trends in society. With the increased accumulation of wealth in the hands of agricultural Veḷḷāḷas and merchants there was felt a need to assign to them a higher-ritual and social status and temples and *maṭhas* proved to be formal agents of recognising such upward mobility. This process of instituting new rituals and legitimising new status groups was a continuous one.

Today with increased availability of cash among the urban middle class Hindus, rituals which were considered expensive about 20 years ago, such as the *Mucukundasahasranāmam*, (which at today's cost is about Rs. 2,000), and hence fell into disuse, have been revived. Oversea migrants from Tiruvārūr have also contributed to the revival of such rites. Two performances of this rite within the period of four weeks of my stay in Tiruvārūr in January 1983 and both sponsored by local migrants to the United States indicate the tenacity of the cult on the one hand and indicate on the other the new emerging structures of patronage.

One peculiarity of the Tiruvārūr temple is that it has no general endowments but its internal economy is based on a curious system of specific endowments constituted over the period of time for carrying out the different objects and performing the various services in the institution. These specific endowments are popularly called *kaṭṭaḷais*. There are thirteen such *kaṭṭaḷais*. A *kaṭṭaḷai* is a special endowment for specific services or religious charity in the temple. *Ardhayāma Kaṭṭaḷai* or endowment for midnight service is an instance of the former and *Aṉṉadāna Kaṭṭaḷai* or an endowment for distributing food *gratis* to the poor is an example of the latter. This system, in recent times, led to constant disputes between the various *kaṭṭaḷais*, mainly due to internal rivalry. Several legal suits dealt with the responsibility of general maintenance of the temple, particularly with the bearing of the expenses.

Under Hindu Law an icon, or rather the deity as symbolised in the icon, is a juristic person capable of possessing rights and owning porperty. Thus in law, all property was owned by the deity, and managed by *tāṉattārs*, who acted as trustees. Sometimes an individual was made a trustee[1], but in the later period when large land endowments were made, trusteeship was invested in an institution.[2]

The Tāṉattār, Maṭhādhipatis and present trustees

The term *tāṉattār* occurs several times in the temple epigraphs of Tamilnāḍu. They were the administrators, who seem to have been of many kinds. There are names of individuals who acted as trustees of endowed property. There were also religious groups, some of whom were simply termed as *māhēśvaras*.[3] Monastic organisations or *Maṭhas*[4] are also mentioned as trustees and they administered temple properties and saw that worship was properly conducted.

To study the caste composition of these trustees from inscriptions is a difficult task as the castes are not always clearly stated. As such, the method of investigation followed here is to look at the present day trusteeship pattern in the management of the Tyāgarājasvāmi temple at Tiruvārūr, and then try to trace the histories of these trusts. Though a general principle of governing temple trusts seems to have been followed, the actual rights and obligations varied considerably from one temple to another. The following study deals only with the temples at Tiruvārūr and Tiruvoṟṟiyūr.

As far as the eclecticism of castes in the management of temples is concerned, the Tiruvārūr temple, far from being unique, is a typical example of temple administration practices in general in Tamiḻnāḍu. The *kaṭṭaḷais* at Tiruvārūr are as follows:-

1. The *Uḷtuṟaī kaṭṭaḷai* is in charge of internal administration and its powers are mainly with regard to the management of festivals and *pūjās*. Considering that there are 55 major shrines (*Caṉṉitis*) and several minor ones the responsibility of ritual management vested in this *kaṭṭaḷai* and in the *Rājaṉ kaṭṭaḷai* is enormous. Until 1981 the hereditary trustee was V.S. Tiyākarāja Mutaliyār, after whose death trusteeship passed on to his son, V.I. Cōmacuntara Mutaliyār. In the 1930s, it was under a joint trusteeship of Tiyākarāja Mutaliyār and C.Vaittiyaliṅka Mutaliyār, the head of the Vēḷakkuṟicci *maṭha* (q.v). Tiyākarāja Mutaliyār comes from the Toṇṭai-maṇṭalam Veḷḷāḷa community, thus belonging to the upper class Veḷḷāḷa group.
2. The *Rājaṉ Kaṭṭaḷai* is under the trusteeship of the Tarumapuram *ātīṉam*, a *Śaiva Siddhānta* pontificate and monastery.
3. and 4. The *Vītiviṭaṅkar* and *Cētupati kaṭṭaḷais* are also managed by the Tarumapuram *ātīṉam*.
5. *Aṉṉadāṉa kaṭṭaḷai* administers large landed properties, mostly donated by the Bhonsle rulers of Thañjāvūr for the performance of specific functions in the Tyāgarāja temple and the

Naṭarāja temple at Chidambaram. There is a legal difference between the way that this particular *kaṭṭaḷai* is constituted and the manner in which other *kaṭṭaḷais* are organised. The lands are trust property of the *Vēḷakkuṟicci maṭha* and not specific endowments of the Tyāgarājasvāmi temple. The properties of this *kaṭṭaḷai* were granted by the Marāṭhā rulers as *iṉāms* to Tyāgarāja *paṇṭāram* for the specific purpose of feeding the Brāhmaṇas in the *choultries* or pilgrim hostels, associated with both the Tyāgarāja and Naṭarāja Temples.

The *Vēḷakkuṟicci maṭha* consists of married clerics who assume the epithet *ajapā* before their name, signifying their connection with the Tyāgarāja, and wear white instead of the usual saffron robes of monks. In the paintings on the Tēvāciriya maṇṭapam there is the figure of a *paṇṭāram* or head of a *maṭha* wearing white and receiving *mariyātai* or honour from the temple officiants at a Tyāgarāja procession. This pontiff in white is further described in the written caption beneath the painted panel as the *paṇṭāram* of the *periya maṭha* or the big *maṭha*. It seems fairly logical to equate the above mentioned *periya maṭha* with *vēḷakkuṟicci maṭha*, whose pontiff is called a *paṇṭāram* and is attired in white (not saffron) as he is a householder and not a monk. (See Plate XII)

6. The *Abhiṣēkakaṭṭaḷai* is also operated by the *Vēḷakkuṟicci maṭha* and was created for the specific rite of *abhiṣēka* or ritual ablution to the deities as the name signifies.
7. The *Tiruccāntukaṭṭaḷai* was established to provide the deity with the special paste made of saffron, rose water, sandalwood, *vibhūti* (sacred ash) camphor, etc. This is managed by a family belonging to the Veḷḷāḷa caste in Putukkōṭṭai.
8. *Ardhayāmakaṭṭaḷai* was for the management of midnight services under the trusteeship of a *Tēcikar*.
9. *Kaṟpūrakaṭṭaḷai* was to supply all the requirements of camphor.
10. *Pālāyikaṭṭaḷai* was established by a young virgin widow of Telugu origin. She was 8 years of age when widowed. This is an unusual *kaṭṭaḷai*. This was managed by non-Brāhmaṇa virgin widows who could name others in similar predicament as successors.
11. *Parivaṭṭakaṭṭaḷai* was for paying for the cloth, which, as a mantle of the deity, was a symbol of honour, when bestowed

on a devotee.

12. *Śukravārakaṭṭaḷai* was for special services on Fridays.
13. *Viṣu puṇyakaṭṭaḷai* was for providing for special festivals like *Cittirai, Āṭi, Aippaci, Tei, Tulā*, etc. [5]

Other smaller *kaṭṭaḷais* like the *toṇṭaimāṉ kaṭṭaḷai* are later endowments by the Toṇṭaimāṉs of Putukkōṭṭai State, feudatories of the *Cētupatis*, who also enjoy special *mariyātai* rights in the temple.

Of the above mentioned *kaṭṭaḷais* the more important ones are the *Uḷturaī, Rājaṉ* and *Abhiṣēka kaṭṭaḷais* under the trusteeship of the Mutaliyār family, the *Tarumapuram ātīṉam* and the *Vēlakkuṟicci maṭam* respectively. Another *maṭha* involved in this complex scheme is Mōccākkuḷam *maṭham* in Nākapaṭṭaṇam Taluq, about eight miles from Tiruvārūr. All three of the trusteeships are in the hands of people who are not Brāhmaṇas or under organisations which do not exclusively cater to the Brāhmaṇas. In fact both the above *maṭhas* draw their following mainly from the non-Brāhmaṇa section of the populace, chiefly from the general group of Veḷḷāḷas. Only *kaṭṭaḷais* numbered 9, 11 and 13 in the above list were managed by a Brāhmaṇa family at Tiruvārūr, and Number 12 was managed by a priest.

Literary and inscriptional references to the two *maṭhas* and their role as managers of large temple estates can be traced from the 16th centuay A.D. onwards. An inscription from Tiruppukaḷūr (77 of 1927 - 28) dated in *Śaka* year 1581 refers to the repairs to the temple being completed by a certain Aruṇācalatampirāṉ, a disciple of Mahātēva Paṇṭāram of *Vēlakkuṟicci maṭam.* An icon by the name Rājarājaviṭaṅkar is also referred to from the same place, i.e Tiruppukaḷūr in Tirunelveli district. Legends from the *Periya Purāṇam* locate the episode of Cuntarar getting gold from Śiva at this site. The gold was to be used to celeberate the *Paṅkuṅi uttiram* festival at Tiruvārūr. Thus the Rājarājaviṭaṅkar is likely to be a Tyāgarāja icon presumably installed by Rājarāja as the name would suggest.

As for the Tarumapuram *ātīṉam*, the guru of the founder was from Tiruvārūr. An inscription of 1560 A.D. of Sadāśiva Rāya of the Vijayanagara dynasty refers to his appointing a certain Ñāṉapirakāca *paṇṭāram* in charge of certain temples. He is most probably the same as Ñāṉacampantar, the founder of *Tarumapuram ātīṉam*. At present twenty-seven temples are managed by the *ātīṉam*. Of the Sapta-viṭaṅka Tyāgarāja temples, Tirunaḷḷāṟu and Tirukkuvaḷai are under *ātīṉam* control. Tirukkāṟavācal is under the hereditary control of a *Ceṭṭiyār* family and Tiruvoṟṟiyūr under the hereditary trusteeship of a member of the *Pēri Ceṭṭi* community, whose chief business is connected with processing and sale of edible oil.

Several of the Tyāgarāja temples, and in fact several Śaiva temples in Tamilnāḍu, are under the trusteeship of *Śaiva Siddhānta maṭhas* run by members of the *Veḷḷāḷa* community. Since the *Veḷḷāḷas* are the one major example of a whole mega-caste moving socially upwards and assuming religious roles which were traditionally the prerogative of the Brāhmaṇas, it would be worthwile to study their *maṭha*-organisations in greater detail, especially in their composition and social role as assimilators of different segments of society.

The second tier in the caste system of Tamilnāḍu is constituted by the blanket group called Veḷḷāḷas, who are structurally diverse and heterogenous. There are high caste and low caste Veḷḷāḷas. Furthermore, there is a hierarchy based on the geographical region of their origin. This tier consists of Mutaliyārs, Ceṭṭis, Veḷḷāḷas of various regions and of several endogamous sub-groups, and several other occupation/caste groups.

The religious role of the Veḷḷāḷas can presumably be traced back to the 13th century A.D. when the first non-Brāhmaṇa disciples of Meykaṇṭār, the great exponent of *Śaiva Siddhānta* and author of the treatise *Civañāṉapōtam*, established their *maṭhas*. Meykaṇṭār's main aim in life was to spread the *Śaiva Siddhānta* gospel through a line of disciples who stood in personal relationship to their preceptors. The disciples were mainly recluses and bore the epithet *tampirāṉ*, while the guru was called *paṇṭāracaṉṉiti*.

These *maṭhas* commanded respect from all communities though several of the *paṇṭāracaṉṉiti* and *tampirāṇs* were Veḷḷāḷas. Both Meykaṇṭār and another renowned guru of this lineage, Ñaṉacampantar, were *kārkātta Veḷḷāḷas* and are believed to have come from the Pāṇḍya country. The members of these *maṭhas* were strict vegetarians and were, in their modes of behaviour very much akin to the Brāhmaṇa *maṭhas* although they tended to use Tamil instead of Sanskrit, and held the *Āgamas* rather than the Vedas as primary authority.[6]

The Veḷḷāḷas regard themselves as the custodians and propagators of Tamiḻ culture. They held a special status *vis a vis* the Brāhmaṇas, for they were educated, rich, and had acquired a high social recognition. According to Chidambaram Piḷḷai[7] it was during the British rule in the 18th and 19th centuries A.D. that the Brāhmaṇas managed to entrench themselves into a privileged position with regard to Veḷḷāḷas who were classified as *Śūdras*, a nomenclature which they resented.

Under the Nāyakas of Thañjāvūr, (1532-1765) particulary under the Prime Ministership of Gōvinda Dīkṣita, (1550-60) Tamiḻ learning and Veḷḷāḷa *maṭhas* received great patronage. Govind Dīkṣita himself translated the *Tiruvaiyāṟu Māhātmyam* into Tamiḻ. His son Vēṇkaṭamakhin, as seen in Chapter II, was a worshipper of Tyāgarāja of Tiruvārūr. Thus *Śaiva Siddhānta* under the guidance of Advaita scholars like Govinda Dīkṣita and Appayya Dīkṣita became philosophically more monistic. Socially the prestige of Śaiva Siddhānta enabled the Veḷḷāḷa *maṭhas*, to acquire a higher status. They also further enhanced their status by becoming trustees of temples.

Thurston traces various occupational groups within the Paṇṭāram community such as landlords, priests and *tampirāṉs* or celibate monks.[8] It was from among the *tampirāṉs* that the *paṇṭāracaṉṉitis* arose. They controlled many temples particulary in Thañjāvūr district.

Rājās and *Zamindārs* endowed the temple with landed properties, which were managed by the *maṭhas* in the form of *kaṭṭaḷais*. By mid 19th century from which period we have documentary evidence, the Tiruvāvaṭatutṟai ātīṉam, in the Māyavaram taluq, owned twenty-five thousand acres of land in Tirunelveli district, 1,000 acres in Madurai district and 3,000 acres in the Thañjāvūr district.[9] Tarumapuram had an endowment of 2,500 acres in Thañjāvūr. In addition *tampirāṉs* from these two *ātīṉams* were responsible for the management of thousands of acres of temple lands and other endowments in the Madras area and elsewhere. It is only the vegetarian castes among the Non-Brāhmaṇas who take *Śivadīkṣā* or Śaiva initiation.

Thus, ironically, the *tampirāṉs*, whose initiation vow required them to renounce land and women, found themselves with the management of huge properties. Of all the *kaṭṭaḷais* at the Tiruvārūr temple, the *Rājaṉ kaṭṭaḷai* is the largest. The Tarumapuram *Paṇṭāra Caṉṉiti* and his representative Palaṉiyappaṉ Tampirāṉ were responsible for the *Rājan̲ kaṭṭaḷai* in 1848, as is clear from a legal document, which further states that this *kaṭṭaḷai* was the third richest in the temple and had an income of Rs. 5,024 p.a.[10] A certain Vaittiyaliṅka Paṇṭāracan̲n̲iti, the head of Tiruppukaḷūr *maṭha* (i.e.Vēḷakkur̲icci *maṭha*) controlled an income of Rs. 7,613 p.a. as the trustee of the *Abhiṣēka kaṭṭaḷai* and Rs. 4,829 p.a. as the trustee of the *An̲n̲adān̲a kaṭṭaḷai.* The two *maṭhas* thus owned in 1848 , about 47% of the total income of all endowments in the temple and, as the operator of two trusts, it made the *paṇṭāracan̲n̲iti* of the Tiruppukaḷūr *maṭha* the richest[11].

Tiruppukaḷūr is in Nan̲n̲ilam taluq about 10 miles from Tiruvārūr. Other trustees in the temple were, according to the 1848 Law Report, two Brāhmanas, one *sannyāsi* and one *paṇṭāram.* The lands held by these *kaṭṭaḷais* are now, as from 1946, under the control of the government. The *Abhiṣēka kaṭṭaḷai* at that date held 561 acres of wet lands (Nañcai) and 769 acres of dry lands (*puñcai*), while *An̲n̲adān̲a kaṭṭaḷai* held 134 acres of wet lands and 187 acres of dry lands. *Ardhayāma kaṭṭaḷai* held 134 acres of wet lands and 118 acres of dry lands. All these were managed by non-Brāhmaṇa Śaiva *maṭhas.*

The Tarumapuram *ātīn̲am* again, as the operator of *Rājan̲, Vītiviṭaṅkan̲* and *Cētupati kaṭṭaḷai,* owned 2,774.30 acres of land prior to 1947. The other ten *kaṭṭaḷais* owned 5053.10 acres of land making the total land ownership of all 13 *kaṭṭaḷais* amount to 7,827.40 acres (figures provided by Hindu Religious Charities and Endowment Board, commonly known as HRC&E). At present due to government land laws the total land held is only 1942.87 acres.

The corporate mobility of the Veḷḷāḷa community into places in the ritual sphere reserved for Brāhmaṇas, seems to have met with some opposition as early as the 13th century A.D. An inscription of the Cōḻa king Kulōttuṅga III refers to a *kukai īti kalakam,* i.e. destruction of *kukais,* or monastic establishments. It also refers in the same context to a certain Tiruccir̲r̲ampala Mutaliyār, a Śaiva devotee who went to Tiruviṭaimarutūr and established a monastery at the request of the local inhabitants. This *maṭha* was used for feeding pilgrims but in the 22nd year of Kulōttuṅga it was destroyed by order of the king. This has been interpreted by the epigraphists, and by M. Rajamanickam who approvingly quotes their views[12] to mean a clash between

Brahmanical and non-Brahmanical monasteries. No adequate reasons are provided by either of the above writers for their stated views. In the absence of reasons, it is to be presumed that the crucial word in this context is *mutaliyār*, which is used to describe the monk Tiruccirrampalam, and is usually a caste suffix, of a group of Veḷḷāḷas mainly involved in agriculture.

Several references are made in the epigraphs beginning from the 13th century A.D. to *Maṭhādhipatis* who bear the suffix Mutaliyār to their names. A Tiruccirrampala Mutaliyār is repeatedly mentioned as the head of a *kīḻai maṭha* and the Tirutturaippūṇṭi epigraph provides the added information that the *maṭha* was situated in Celva Tiruvārūr. His predecessor Vāgīśvara Mutaliyār is also described as the pontiff at Celva Tiruvārūr.[13] Thus the *kīḻai maṭha* of the Gōḻaki Cantāna seem to have been headed by a community of *mutaliyārs*. Another Mutaliyār *maṭha* was the Ācārakiyāṉ Tirumaṭham.[14]

While it seems extremely logical to agree with Rajamanickam when he states that Mutaliyār *maṭhas* sprang up suddenly at several places in the 13th century in consequence of the spread of the Meykaṇṭa doctrines, and it is tempting to equate all of them with the Meykaṇṭa *paramparā*, it must be borne in mind that it was also the tradition in Tamiḻnāḍu to use the term *mutaliyār* in the sense of 'owner' and also as an honorific title irrespective of caste affiliations. An inscription from Tiruvorriyūr, for example, refers to the deity as '*mutaliyār pāṭi āṭuvār*. (the Lord who dances and sings; owner=Lord of)[15] The deity is also called *tampirāṉār*,[16] again often a caste name. The *Tillai Ulā* refers to Naṭarāja by the term *Mutaliyār* and so do the *Ekāmranātaṉ Ulā* and the *Tiruvāṉaikkā Ulā* of Kāḻamēkapulavar.[17] The variant *Mutali* is used by Cēkkiḻār in *Periya Purāṇam, Kaṇṇappa nāyaṉārppurāṇam*.

Expressions in the inscriptions which refer to *kīḻaimaṭattu mutaliyār* or *bhikṣāmaṭattu mutaliyār* seem to denote 'heads' or 'owners' rather than names of caste groups. 88 of 1946-47 dated in the 29th year of Tirupuvaṉa Cakravartiṉ Rājēndra Cōḻadēva registers a gift of land by a *sabhā* to Kaṇakacapāpati Tēcikar residing at Kīḻaikaṭṭu which is described as being a seat of the *ācāryas* of the Lakṣādhyāyi *Cantāṉa of* the *maṭha* of Patāñjalitēvar situated at Perumparrappuliyūr (= Citamparam, mod. Chidambaram). Here it becomes evident that Kaṇakacapāpati was a *Tēcikar*, a common Veḷḷāḷa designation. The *ōtuvār* at

Tiruvārūr and several other temples call themselves *Tēcikar*.

The *Kīlaikaṭṭu maṭam* referred to above seems to have been a branch of a Pāṇḍyan monastic organisation but seems to have been associated in Tamiḻnāḍu with Tēcikars. *169 of 1926* refers to Vāgīśapperumāḷ of Vaṭakīḻmaṭam of Celva Tiruvārūr. *209 of 1924* refers to a Iśāṉa Śiva Rāvalar of the Gōḷaki Vaṁśa of Lakṣādhyāyi *Cantāṉa*. 56 of 1914 refers to Vāmaśiva Mutaliyār of Celva Tiruvārūr. 652 of 1916 from Sermadevi refers to a gift of land to a Puṟṟapavaḷa Cira Mutaliyār of Kīḻaimaṭha cantāṉam. Another Rāvalar of Lakṣādhyāyi Cantāṉam of the Kolla *maṭha* at Vārāṇasi is referred to in *111 of 1929-30*. *164 of 1935-36* refers to a Rājēndrattu Mutaliyār Civappirakācar, a Bhikṣāmaṭha mutaliyār. 129 of *ARE* 1908 from Tirupputtūr refers to an *Ācāra maḷakiyāṉ Tirumaṭam* headed by Mutaliyārs at Celva Tiruvārūr. This is dated in the time of the Pāṇḍyan king Māṟavarmaṉ (c.a. 1236 A.D.). Thus Tiruvārūr seems to have been either the branch headquarters or simply one of the seats of several mutaliyār *maṭhas* by the 13th century A.D. Most of these *maṭhas* bear the name of *nāyaṉmār* and seem to be interlinked through a large system of lineages as is very much in vogue in the present day. Whenever a *maṭha* is headed by a Brāhmaṇa or a group of Brāhmaṇas they are generally given the apellation Śivabrāhmaṇas and frequently their *gotra* as well. From the absence of such specifications in the case of the Tiruvārūr *maṭha*s, it seems fairly safe to conclude that the Śaiva Siddhānta monasteries here used the term "Mutaliyār" to refer to a caste group.

In the 16th century several monastic establishments claim descent from Meykaṇṭār. This suggests a second wave of increased monastic participation by non-Brāhmaṇa *maṭhas*. 203 of 1912 refers to a *ceṭṭikaḷ maṭam*. Rajamanickam quotes from the *Caṉātaṉācāriyārcarittiram* wherein it is stated that Meykaṇṭār was born to establish the true Śaiva faith and to dispel much of the religious confusion caused by the many works popular at the time such as the commentaries or *bhāṣyas* of Nīlakaṇṭha, Śaṅkara, Rāmānuja, Madhva, etc. He also refers to two epigraphs (206 and 207 of 1936 37) of the Nāyaka period which record the name of a *maṭha* at Villiyaṉūr as *Meykaṇṭacantatimaṭha* and hence he concludes that most of these *maṭhas* must have belonged to the same lineage.

Turaiaraṅkacāmi (also spelt Dorai Rangasami) in fact suggests an earlier date for the rise of institutionalised non-brāhmaṇa *maṭhas*. According to him, the 63 saints of the *Tiruttoṇṭattokai* were the originators of Tamil̲ Śaiva maṭhas.[18] In the *Tillai Ulā*, a work often assigned to the 12th century A.D., there is a reference to the *Nār̲patteṇṇāyiravar* ("the 48 thousand") as the assembly at the *Tēvāciriyamaṇṭapam*. The description which goes *'tappuraikkil nātaṉaiyum piṉṉeṉum* Cōl̲arājaum *nār̲patteṇṇāyiravar cōtit tirunīr̲r̲u ttoṇṭarum'* is given in the context of Vir̲aṉmīṇṭanāyaṉār episode where Vir̲aṉmīṇṭār is described as excommunicating Cuntarar from the 'group' for the latter's lack of courtesy.[19] Cuntarar's sin was that he entered the shrine of the deity before greeting the assembled forty-eight thousand devotees (Nār̲patteṇṇāyiravar) in the Tēvāciriyamaṇṭapam.

This *nār̲patteṇṇāyiravar* became the name of a *maṭha* and frequent reference is made to this expression either to denote a group or as a part of the name of a person or the name of a street etc.[20] Interestingly enough the same phrase is applied to describe the immigrant community of *Veḷḷāḷas* into *Toṇṭaimaṇṭalam*. Oral tradition has it that forty-eight thousand Veḷḷāḷas are said to have been brought to *Toṇṭaimaṇṭalam* and settled there after cleansing the place of *Kur̲umbas*, etc. The tradition, however is silent about the place from where they were brought. *The Archaeological Survey Reports* for 1909 refer to a *maṭha* by the name of *Nār̲patt eṇṇāyiram* at Tiruvāṉaikkā which was taken over by the Brāhmaṇas and converted into an *Advaita Śaṅkaramaṭha*.[21] This link is interesting as the Tiruvārūr collective of 48 thousand were Tyāgarāja worshippers and it confirms my view (see ch.9) that the Tyāgarāja was a Cōl̲amaṇṭalam territorial symbol implanted into *Toṇṭaimaṇṭalam* by the Pallavas.

That these *maṭhas* and the teacher monks therein were not only educated in Tamil̲ but also in Sanskrit is evident from the nature of their doctrinal treatises. As to the question how they learnt Sanskrit, Burton Stein cites the epigraphist Krishnan and states that special grants called *kāṇimur̲r̲aṭṭu* were made for non-Brāhmaṇas to learn Sanskrit.[22] If this be true then a definite effort was made to accommodate groups that made a consistent bid to enter the ritual zones reserved for the Brāhmaṇas, when backed by their wealth and power as landlords.

The non-brāhmaṇa *santānas* then, to quote Burton Stein, were "the crucial intermediaries between the priesthood and worshippers of local sub-caste temples and the great temple centres of the Tamil̲ country".[23] The medieval period marked the proliferation of non-*brāhmaṇa maṭhas* and at the same time a marked increase in the number of structural shrines.

The Vijayanagara dynasty established an overlordship over several new tributary chiefs who, in their bid to establish their sway over the different geographical regions and different sections of the population, began a process of supporting those sectarian leaders who could act as the mediators between central temples and the peripheral regions. Temples and Brahmadeyas were still the core institutions and there was great mobility for the Brāhmaṇa specialists who added prestige to any court.

The Vijayanagara period also marked the time when elaborate rites were introduced into the temple and the time when several important sectarian leaders came into prominence.[24] At the same time large scale land endowments overshadowed the endowments of sheep, grains, ornaments etc.[25], thereby providing for a greater concentration of power.[26] The rise of vast landed estates and the religious connection between the landlords and the big temples gave the temple a new socio-economic dimension. There was a shift of patronage from Cōl̲a-Pāṇḍya domain temples to Tirupati, Śrīraṅgam and other large Vaiṣṇava temples generously endowed by the new rulers.

The 16th and 17th centuries proved to be the period of the rise of several important monasteries and monastic leaders. A good deal of discussion also seems to have taken place regarding the nature and organization of Hindu society. It was a matter of prime importance, for the Hindus felt threatened by the rapid spread of Islam in South India, and the Vijayanagara monarchs claimed to have been appointed by god to wipe out the atrocities committed by the Turkas (general term to denote all Muslims)[27].

The Tiruvārūr Temple and Arbitration Courts

Tiruvārūr as an ancient temple and a seat of the Tamil̲ Śaiva *bhakti* movement must have had to deal with several caste claims. However, there is only one documented record of a caste case and verdict recorded in an inscription from the temple here. This inscription which appears in *ARE 1904* (No. 558) in brief and is recorded in detail in *SII XVII* (No. 606), dwells at length on the rights and obligations of mixed castes. A body of scholars was summoned to pass judgement on a case and they assembled at the Tiruvārūr temple and discussed earlier judgements by different schools of Hindu jurists. There was an awareness of major discrepancies. The Assembly then arrived at a consensual decision. All this presupposes a fairly serious confrontational situation.

Such religio-legal disputes are today taken to secular courts of law, where again the ancient scriptures are analyzed and weighed against the demands of the secular state, making it complex and messy. A case that immediately comes to mind is that of Cuvāminātakurukkaḷ, the President of the South Indian Arcaka Association, who sued the Tamiḻnāḍu Government in the Supreme Court for trying to abolish the *sole* right of *Śivācāryas* to act as priests in the Śiva temples. The Central Government after duly referring to the ancient scriptures to determine the rights and obligations of *Śivācāryas*, nevertheless, passed a legislation abolishing the hereditary nature of the profession thereby opening it to all castes. Their judgement was based on the constitutional rights of a citizen for fair and equal employment. The Arcaka Association, needless to say felt wronged. The President of the Association, when interviewed by the present author not only quoted from several Āgamas justifying his stand but also felt that secularism affected only the majority community of the Hindus in such a negative manner. This is one of the rallying cries of the contemporary 'Hindutva' movement as well.

The Tiruvārūr epigraph presupposes a similar scenario in a different context, for it deals not with the rights of the *ācāryas* but with those of the artisan community.[28] Its religio-legal focus is on the role of *rathakāras* (makers of the temple chariot) and *kammāḷas* (workers in metal etc.). It quotes the *Smṛti* texts of Gautama, Yājñavalkya and Maskara, as well as the *Brāhmaṇas, Purāṇas, Vaiṣṇava Pāñcarātra* and *Vaikhānasa*, to determine the social position of those born out of *anulōma* (where the husband is of a higher caste than his wife) and *pratilōma* (where the wife is of a higher caste than her husband) unions. It is interesting to see that there is a literary parallel to this epigraphic account which is recorded in the *Vaiśya vaṁsa Sudhākara* wherein too reference is made to the settling of a dispute between the same two caste groups.[29]

With the increased temple building activity, the *rathakāras* were in great demand and accumulated some wealth. Added to this was the increasing ritual importance given to *ratha* festivals. The *ratha* was also constantly being invested with new symbolic meanings, adding to its spiritual grandeur. All this may have prompted the makers of the ratha to bid for a higher socio-economic and ritual status.

The Āḻittēr or the *ratha* called Āḻi at Tiruvārūr was famous and Appar has referred to it in his hymns. The chariot festival at Tiruvārūr is one of the best known in Tamiḻnāḍu and hence it is but natural that this dispute was brought before a council meeting at Tiruvārūr. The artisans associated with the rathakāras in turn made their bid to pass off as rathakāras and demanded hereditary rights, monopolies, etc. K.A.N. Sastri refers to this kind of demand as of frequent occurrence in South India.[30] As for the *kammāḷas*, some are untouchables while some are of higher social status. The key issue in this document revolves around who could be invested with the sacred thread.

As the dispute was crucial to the *varṇāśramadharma* it was passed over to be arbitrated by the Brāhmaṇs who were learned paṇḍits in the Śāstras. The Tiruvārūr arbitration committee quoted from several sacred texts, some of which are now lost. Several architectural manuals were also consulted. It opened by stating the well known dictum that a marriage between a *kṣatriya* man and *vaiśya* woman was an *anulōma* union, and a boy born of such a union had the right to be invested with the sacred thread in a regular *upanayanam* ceremony.

The main concern of this august body was to allot the various occupations of icon-making, chariot-making, building the actual temple, i.e., that of being an architect, a stone mason, a carpenter, a blacksmith, etc., and to determine the caste status and caste rights of such people. Thus for example the progeny of a *kṣatriya* father and a *vaiśya* mother was allowed to follow the occupation of icon-making and *vāstuvidyā* (planning) and other occupations connected with the iconography and layout of a temple. The present day icon-makers from Swāmimalai come mainly from the *Viśvakarma kammāḷa* community, although legally anyone is allowed to follow the profession now.

A child (a male child) born of a *vaiśya* father and a *śūdra* mother became a carpenter. Children born of *pratilōma* unions of *vaiśya* and *śūdra* or *kṣatriya* and *vaiśya* were assigned the profession of weaving (208 of 1919). The weavers and carpenters were not allowed to be invested with the sacred thread. Thus, the *rathakāras* and *kammāḷas* belonged to two distinct groups-one born of the *anulōma* union of *Kṣatriya* and *vaiśya* and another out of a similar union of *vaiśya* and *śūdra* parents. Those others born of a variety of *pratilōma* unions were assigned professions which did not involve direct contact with the icon or the interior of the temple. This is a very simple account of a complex document.

A *rathakāra* for example is defined by Yājñavalkya as born of *mahiṣya* male and *karaṇī* female. A *mahiṣya*, again, is defined by the same author as the product of an *anulōma* wedding between a *kṣatriya* and a *vaiśya*. Being *anulōma* he is twice born though of a mixed caste. He is not a *śūdra*. He just makes it, to enable him to study the Vedas and be invested with the sacred thread. Yājñavalkya, therefore, assigns a high status to *rathakāras* born of *anulōma* marriages.

It is an interesting document and needs to be further investigated by one knowledgeable in the *Smṛtis* to see how faithfully it has adhered to the numerous texts it quotes. An excellent but very brief study of this epigraph has been published by Duncan Derrett.[31] The epigraphs referred to above come from Tiruvārūr (SII XVII, No. 603) and from Uyyakoṇṭāṉ Tirumalai (*ARE* 1908,478,499) respectively.

Derrett quotes from several of the now existing texts. We have already seen the view of Yājñavalkya; Mitākṣara and other sources agree that a *rathakāra* is an *anulōmaja* of *kṣatriya* and *vaiśya* origins and is entitled to *upanayana*. His livelihood, however, is to be based on the study of horses, foundation and consecration of temples and the business of chariots, carpentry and building in general (*vāstu*).

The more orthodox Jaimini denies them the right to *Upanayana*, but only gives them the right to tending the fire (*ādhāra*). Mitramiśra allots *rathakāras* the right to *Upanayana*. The question raised by Derrett is could they teach like the Brāhmaṇa if they could wear the sacred thread and light the Vedic fire? He refers to the incidence of two *kammāḷas* being given the honorific title *ācārya* in an inscription (*ARE 189 of 1925*). Alice Boner refers to the sculptor being called a guru and the sculpture manual an Upaniṣad.[32]

Derrett has pointed out how interestingly enough the epigraph abstains from quoting Baudhāyana who is unflattering to the *rathakāras* and calls them *śūdras*. So here one can see the Tiruvārūr conference at the Tyāgarāja temple trying to arrive at a workable compromise. Derrett also feels that the inscriptional quote of Yājñavalkya "sounds suspicious", for though he traces one part of the quote to the original text mentioned, i.e., regarding their origin, the verse which follows it (and gives the *rathakāras* full right to wear the sacred thread, perform sacrificial acts, and lay Vedic fires) seems to be an interpolation. Here again one sees the *rathakāras* successfully making their bid.

In para 12 of the epigraph (603 of *SII* Vol. XVII) the *rathakāras'* pedigree is further elevated. They are born of an *anulōma* union between *anulōmajas* (children of *anulōma* marriages) of a higher order, *viz. karaṇa* female and *ambaṣṭha* male.

Other texts are also quoted which give the *rathakāras* a right to *Upanayana* but not the other Vedic prerogatives. The *Vaikhānasa* (Āgamas dedicated to Viṣṇu) are the most strict and call them *śūdras* and restrict their livelihood to feeding horses, training horses, etc. They are regarded as children of *sūtas* (charioteers) who themselves are born of a brāhmaṇa wife and a *kṣatriya* husband and hence a union of a *pratilōma* order. Thus the upper caste *anulōmas* fared well. The *Pratilōmas* were assigned a low place and worse still, were the illicit unions of *pratilōmas*.

Thus the Tyāgarāja temple at Tiruvārūr was one of the regional focal points of social arbitration. The Tamil̲ work *Cātinūl*, to be discussed later in this chapter, was also composed in Tiruvārūr by a literati of the place and deals with the *anulōma* and *pratilōma* unions in the Tamil̲ country and their status.

During the Pāṇḍyan and Vijayanagara periods such social confrontations became more frequent. Social status was tested and contested through the institution of the temple. One such endemic confrontation model was presented in battles between *Iṭaṅkai* and *Valaṅkai* groups.[33]

Another epigraph (309 of 1916) dated *Śaka* 1545, i.e., 1623 A.D. comes from Vēḷakkur̲icci. It is a *maṭha* of this place, which as we have seen earlier, administers considerable lands of the Tyāgarāja temple as trustees for specific endownments. It records the decree of the temple priest of the Ericca Uṭaiyān̲ temple at Vēḷakkur̲icci in Muḷḷināṭu, issued on the orders of Viśvanātha

Nāyaka, that five subdivisions of *kammāḷas* be prohibited from communal fellowship. This was, in all probability, the result of some communal tensions caused by the above-mentioned subdivisions. The *Kammāḷas* or artisans thus seem to have been and still are of heterogeneous mix. The *kammāḷas* of Tiruvoṟṟiyūr were provided land tax-free and the stone masons, carpenters, sculptors, etc. seem to have all been housed in one street called interestingly enough the *nāṟpatteṇṇāyiram* street (the street of the 48 thousand). It denotes the Śaiva collective of saints from Tiruvārūr. The *kammāḷas* seem to have made a bid to a higher ritual status like some other branches of the Veḷḷāḷas but met with less success than some of their brethren.

In the list of communities issued by the Tamiḻnāḍu government graded as belonging to the forward or backward communities, the *kammāḷas* are sub divided and listed as *viśvakarmās*, *viśvakammāḷa*, and include *taṭṭāṉs* (goldsmiths), *kammāṉ*, *karumāṉ* or *kollar* (stone masons), *taccar* (carpenters), *kaltaccars* (lit. carpenters in stone, meaning sculptors) and *kammāḷaviśvabrāhmaṇa* who are icon makers. They all belong to the backward communities.

Returning to the Tiruvārūr epigraph, which is engraved on the wall of the Tyāgarāja shrine, the conference that met to discuss the societal rights and obligations of the *anulōma* and *pratilōma kammāḷas* was constituted of the Hindu elite and the names of its members are suffixed with epithets such as *'Somayājī'*, *'Vājapeyī*, etc. to signify their having completed these Vedic sacrifices. The directly unaffected and hence supposedly 'impartial' interpreters of the law were obviouly chosen to deliberate and the Brāhmaṇas came out as the social arbiters in disputes amongst non-brāhmaṇa aspirants to social status.

Communal Tensions and their Resolutions

One of the most important communal sectors in which social tensions were ubiquitous was, as mentioned earlier, that of the community which was bifurcated into an *iṭaṅkai* (left hand) and *valaṅkai* (right hand) groups. Clashes between these two groups are recorded regularly from the time of Kulōttuṅga I, i.e., 11th cen. A.D. (31 of *ARE* 1936-37 and *Reports*, para 27). Interestingly enough a North Indian origin is given to the *iṭaṅkai* in an inscription of the time of Kulōttuṅga III (489 of *ARE* 1912, and *ARE* 1913, PARA 39) where 98 castes are included in the *iṭaṅkai* group.

The term *valaṅkai* occurs as the name of a regiment of the Cōḻa army. The *niyānaṉ ciṟuntāṉattu valaṅkai vēlaikkāra paṭaikaḷilar* were attached by the royal order of Rājarāja I to the image of Dakṣiṇamēru Viṭaṅkar set up by Rājarāja I with a *brahamadēya* grant for meeting expenses of service to this Dakṣiṇamēru Viṭaṅkar, i.e.,Tyāgarāja (*SII* II,15 and 16). There is no way of determining to which caste group these servants or *vēlaikkārar* belonged (*SII* Vol. II, Ins. 14, 15, 16, 17, 18 and 19). It could well be that these were the *anulōma* and *pratilōma* groups discussed above. Some weaver groups seem to have taken up martial duties for there is a reference to *Kaikkōḷapperumpaṭai* (the great army of the *Kaikkōḷar*) in an inscription (253 of (253 of *ARE* 1909), and to *vāḷpeṟṟakaikkōḷar* or the *kaikkōḷar* who were bestowed with swords, etc.[34] They were, as seen earlier, given *rudrapati* lands, i.e., fiefs for military service by the Cōḻa kings, but this martial character was hardly in keeping with their professed occupation of being weavers. Thus, it may have been that there arose a difference between the *iṭaṅkai* and *valankai* (martial) groups of *kaikkōḷar*. The *kaikkōḷars* claim close connection with the Tyāgarāja cult.

That the rise of the *Veḷḷāḷa maṭhas* to positions commanding socio-religious prestige was also not entirely smooth appears from some of the conflicts that they encountered with the more orthodox Brāhmaṇa ascetic orders. Mu. Arunacalam refers to the conflict between the *sannyāsins* of Sūryanārāyaṇarkōyil, who were Brāhmaṇas and wore the safforn robes and the other Śaiva *sannyāsins* who wore white. The former regarded the latter with contempt and derogatorily called them the 'little ones' in contra distinction to their own *maṭha* which was called *periya maṭha*. This confrontation was brought to the attention of the Vijayanagara monarch who referred the issue to a panel of *sannyāsins* of both camps. It was finally accepted that non-Brāhmaṇa Śaivas were also entitled to sannyāsahood, and two books *Kriyā Dīkṣā* and *Śaiva Sannyāsa Paddhati* were written in Sanskrit explaining the Śiva Dīkṣā. Thus, at one stroke, the two prestigious behaviour patterns of the Brāhmaṇas, i.e. becoming *sannyāsins* and using Sanskrit as their vehicle of expression, were adopted by the non-Brāhmaṇa Śaiva *sannyāsins* wishing to rise in the socio-religious hierarchy of their times. The Nāyakas, a Telegu people ruling as conquerors over Tamiḻs, were extremely keen on marshalling the support particularly of the agricultural class, the Veḷḷāḷas. This confrontation and this bridging over the social tension took place in the reign of the Vijayanagara king Sadāśiva Rāya (1543-73) and at a time when his vassal Cevvappa Nāyaka (1572-1614) was ruling in Thañjāvūr.[35] Here this incident can be interpreted to mean that while the Meykaṇṭār lineage continued to command the respect of the members of the non-Brāhmaṇa community, the Brāhmaṇa still looked down on them. This must have been a socially irksome situation and was brought out into the open in the Nāyaka period. In this context we may recollect that a *paṇṭāram* wearing white and claiming to belong to a *Periya maṭha* is painted on the walls of the Tēvāciriya maṇṭapam. Was he trying to refute the derogatory appellation of 'small' by assuming the grand prefix "*periya*" or big? (Pl.XII).

The *Brāhmaṇa Sūryanārāyaṇakōyil maṭha* passed gradually into the hand of *Kārkātta Veḷḷāḷas* by the end of the 16th century A.D. Śivāgrayōgin, a Brāhmaṇa, was the author of the *Śaiva Sannyāsa Paddhati*, supporting the rights of the non-brāhmaṇa Śaivas to *sannyāsa*hood. In this work he discusses among other things, yōga, *pañcākṣara* and interestingly enough the *ajapā mantra*, (Ch. 4), which is crucial to the understanding of the Tyāgarāja cult. His immediate successor to the pontificate was a Brāhmaṇa but, after that, the *maṭha* was taken over by Tirumānturai *paṇṭāra caṉṉiti* who was succeeded by Cokkaliṅka Tēcikar, both of whom were *Kārkātta Veḷḷāḷas*. This transfer took place between 1640 and 1680 A.D.[36] Thus the upward mobility in class and power gradually assured upward caste mobility and inclusion into the "principal locus of power".[37]

From the 12th century A.D. onwards, with the rise of religious thinkers such as Meykaṇṭār, Aruḷnandi Śivācārya, Kantāṭai Maṟaiñāṉacampantar and Umāpati Śivācārya, Śaivism was transformed into a distinctly Tamiḻ and Siddhāntic faith system which, in a philosophical sense, inaugurated a new syncretistic phase of *advaita* and *siddhānta*,[38] and in a sociological sense marked the elevation of the *veḷḷāḷa* community into the upper echelons of the non-*brāhmaṇa* society, with their leaders being drawn into the circles of the intellectual elite.

Meykaṇṭār himself was a *veḷḷāḷa* but his immediate disciple Aruḷnandi was a Brāhmaṇa *Śivācārya*. Aruḷnandi's disciple Maṟaiñāṉacampantar was again a *veḷḷāla* but he attracted Umāpati, who was not only a Brāhmaṇa but a Potu *Dīkṣita* (the select priests of Naṭarāja temple) of Chidambaram. Stories related about the life of Umāpati bear traces of the early animosity that the Śaiva *maṭha* faced from the orthodox Brāhmaṇas. One of the stories related is about Umāpati who, as a *Potu Dīkṣita*, was once being carried in a palanquin with torch bearers going in front of him. It was a bright afternoon. Maṟaiñāṉa was standing by the road talking to a disciple, who asked his master as to the identity of the man in the palanquin to which Maṟaiñāṉa answered that he was a blind man who needed the aid of torch-bearers even to see by daylight. The philosophical content hidden in this apparently innocuous remark shook Umāpati to the core. He then and there decided to follow Maṟaiñāṉacampantar as his guru.

Once Maṟaiñāṉacampantar was walking through the streets occupied by *kaikkōḷar* (weavers) and he approached a woman and asked for food. She gave him *kañci*, the rice broth brewed for starching the yarn and the high caste Veḷḷāḷa teacher drank it with no thought of adhering to the prescribed caste rules, for the *kaikkōḷar* was of a much inferior caste. Seeing his guru act thus, Umāpati, a Brāhmaṇa unflinchingly accepted the broth that trickled from his guru's folded palm. News of this incident spread quickly and the next day, when Umāpati tried to enter the Naṭarāja temple at Chidambaram to offer his usual worship, the priests refused to let him enter. He sadly withdrew to the riverside. When the self-righteous priests entered the shrine they found both Naṭarāja and his consort Śivakāmī missing. They then heard a divine voice which said that since Umāpati was excommunicated from the temple the Lord too had decided to move away.[39]

This is an interesting legend inasmuch as the deity at Tiruvārūr is portrayed in the myths as coming out of the temple to give his devotee "darshan" but never forcing the priests to accept a devotee who has broken the temple rules, into the temple. The difference in paradigm is obvious for Umāpati was an initiated Brāhmaṇa with traditional right of worship, while the devotees of Śiva at Tiruvārūr often came from lowly castes.

Thus the *Sanātanācāryas*, as these early *Śaiva Siddhānta* teachers are called, started an egalitarian movement but it too soon lost its vigour, like the earlier *bhakti* movement. It assured, however, the corporate mobility of one section of the populace, *viz.* the upper echelons of Veḷḷāḷas. The *Veḷḷāḷas*, along with other upper-class non-Brāhmaṇas, imitated the cultural pattern of the

Brāhmaṇas and acquired for themselves and their followers a higher place in the system, but closed the doors for the other lower caste aspirants, thereby becoming the supporters of a neo-orthodox movement.

Barnett quotes an instance when a *Kārkātta Veḷḷāḷa*, in the 1950s called a meeting in his house to protest against Brāhmaṇa domination; only then did he realize that he could not include all the castes, for by the conventions to which he subscribed, several castes could not cross his threshold.[40] This is a classic example of demanding equal status for oneself with one's superiors but denying it to one's perceived inferiors.

Looking at it from another perspective, it is the easy manner in which a Hindu shifts his philosophical position between a transcendental equality and immanent inequality that is often baffling. He can adjust to the *nirguṇa-saguṇa*—the absolute equality versus the relative inequality, the Brāhmaṇa-Māyā shift, and thereby find what appears to him as a way of rationalizing social inequality. This explains the attitude of the pilgrim of Paṇḍharpur described by Karve and referred to earlier.[41]

The 13th and 14th centuries, however, were still the period when the newly founded *maṭhas* were enthusiastically preaching an egalitarian creed. Meykaṇṭār's disciples opened several *maṭhas*. Thus, the Kāñcī Ñāṉapirakācarmaṭam traces its lineage to Umāpati through Maccuceṭṭiyār and his disciple Civappirakācar, the last mentioned two being *Kārkātta Veḷḷāḷas*. Ceppāṟaimaṭam of Tiruvaiyāṟu is a *maṭha* consisting of *gṛhasthas*, and claims descent from the same Maccuceṭṭi. In the region of Tiruvārūr and its environs there were sectarian leaders like Śivāgrayōgin, who established a *maṭha* richly endowed by the Nāyaka monarch at Tiruvīḻimiḻalai in the 16th century.

The same period witnessed the rise of Kamalaiñāṉapirakācar, who was guru of the founder of Tarumapuram ātīṉam and, as we have seen earlier, a devotee of Tyāgarāja. He traces his lineage to Ciṟṟampalavaṭikaḷ.

Kamalaiñāṉappirakācar's work, the *Cātinūl*, describes the origin of pure castes and mixed castes born of both *anulōma* and *pratilōma* unions, and those of indeterminate origins. It also discusses those born out of secret wedlock, and means by which one could move up or down the social or caste ladder. An interesting mention is made of the caste called *ṭiṇṭima* and the author traces them to an *anulōma* union between a very learned Vedic scholar and a cultured lady, but of inferior caste standing. The respect with which he sings of this group is particularly significant when we remember that several courtiers and poets of the Vijayanagara dynasty in the 16th century were people belonging to the *Ṭiṇṭima* caste.

The *Cātinūl*, according to my informant the Late Mu. Arunachalam, a renowned Tamil̲ scholar, was published in 1875 by Madras Art Trust. I could not lay my hands on this published edition, which was according to Arunachalam jointly edited by Mayilai Cantiracēkara Nāṭṭār and Tiruvallikkēṇi Caṇmuka Kirāmaṇiyār. This work is however available in the Mss. form in U.Ve Cāmināta Iyer Library at Tiruvāṉmiyūr.

Obviously caste issues in and around the environs of Tiruvārūr must have prompted this eminent Veḷḷāḷa scholar *paṇṭāram* to write this religio-juridical treatise. The biography of this householder *paṇṭāram* was according to Arunachalam recorded in an unpublished manuscript called *Ñāṉapirakāca māṉmiyam* by Tarumai Citamparanāta muṉivar. According to this biography Ñāṉapirakācar was a member of the Tirukkayilāya order of monks who were householders and donned white robes.

Thus, the movement of establishing *Veḷḷāḷa maṭhas*, begun in the 13th century, gained momentum in the 16th century, several *maṭhas* claiming descent from Meykaṇṭār and lineage from Nanti or calling themselves the Tirukkayilāya *paramparai* operated in Tamil̲nāḍu and a *Brāhmaṇa-Veḷḷāḷa* alliance slowly evolved. According to Burton Stein there was a 'conspiracy' between *brāhmaṇas* and *Veḷḷāḷas*, or *satśūdras* as he chooses to call them (although the expression is rarely used by Tamil̲ speaking peoples). A symbiotic relationship grew which can, according to him, be traced back to Pallava times, but which gradually strengthened with time.[42]

The *Veḷḷāḷas* made a corporate bid for upward mobility and by a process of imitating the *Brāhmaṇas* by becoming vegetarians, abandoning animal sacrifice, and acquiring a working knowledge of Sanskrit, though still expressing themselves in Tamil̲, they became cultural mediators between Āgamic temple religion and Tamil folk cults.[43] These *maṭhas* continued to flourish and in 1957-58, 126 *maṭhas* are recorded as functioning in Tamil̲nāḍu.[44]

With the emergence of a few of these communities into prominence the lowest segments of society were pushed further down and in course of time the *yāṉaiyērumperumpaṟaiyaṉ* and *Viḻuppaṟaiyaṉ*, etc., became simply ritual ornamentation for the cult and lost all their emotive and charismatic content. It was no longer a vehicle of social absorption, as it must have been during the period of its inception. The Paṟaiyas and other low caste communities, the *kaikkōḷar*, etc., lost touch with the higher Āgamic faith and an increased polarity began to develop between the Āgamic temples, with their strictly enforced codes of ritual purity and the folk cults.

Several socio-religious changes are noticeable in the recent three decades or so. There is a definite shift of political power from Brāhmaṇas to the *Veḷḷāḷa* and *Kaḷḷa* castes in the Thañjāvūr district, and other sub-groups in other districts.[45]

Certain ideological shifts are also noticeable in monastic establishments like that of the Śaṅkara maṭha which was till recently the bastion of Brāhmaṇa orthodoxy. It is now trying to conduct *Āgama* classes not only for Ādi Śaiva Brāhmaṇas but also for non-Brāhmaṇa priests - the Pāraśaivas. Śaṅkarācārya is performing a number of *kumbhābhiṣēkams* and is actively involved in the renovation of temples. The cooperation between the Government and Śaṅkarācārya on religious matters has been discussed by Fuller.[46] More *kumbhābhiṣēkams* are performed now than ever before.[47] The Tyāgarāja temple had its *kumbhābhiṣēkam* in 1985.

The Government is also using the temples to propagate the new egalitarian stand by organising what are called *camapantipōcaṉam* whereby the temple is obliged to feed people from all castes sitting and eating together on certain festive occasions. Tiruvārūr temple was directed to hold this feast during the *Paṅkuṉi Uttiram*. This is the government's effort to break the taboo of commensurability and has a dramatic impact as large crowds assemble in the temple grounds for a free meal amongst other things. The Press coverage gets the message across. This process of injecting new ideals is what Pressler calls the 'spiritualization' of the temple.[48]

Other noticeable changes are in the replacement of Sanskrit *arccaṉais* with Tamiḻ in several smaller temples.

With the coming to power of Tirāviṭa ideology, there was a short period of atheistic radicalism. E.V. Ramasami Naicker had for a time toyed with Buddhism as an alternative philosophy to promote egalitarianism but later discarded it. Ambedkar felt that the only way caste consciousness could be wiped out in Hindu society was by mass conversion to Buddhism. The Dalit movement in Mahārāshtra, like the Tirāviṭa movement in Tamiḻnāḍu, was looking for the right idiom of protest.

Soon however, in Tamiḻnāḍu the earlier radicalism was gradually replaced by Tamiḻ religiosity which was seen as a complementary ideology to Tamiḻ consciousness. Temples have become major contributors to quasi government sponsored Tamiḻ conferences. In 1968 Murukaṉ temples of Paḻaṉi and Swāmimalai contributed Rs. twenty thousand.[49] Some temples are recording enormous increases in their income. The Tyāgarāja temple is a Class III temple according to the HRC&E Board and has an income of less than Rs. Sixty thousand per year.

On a pan- Indian front, temples are once more being recruited by organizations such as the Vishva Hindu Parishad to act as vehicles of conveying a pan-caste, pan-Indian Hindu ideology termed 'Hindutva' to the masses. The political agenda is to solidify the Hindu vote. The Tyāgarāja cult is, as yet, little involved in the new wave and as such it falls outside the purview of this book. Suffice it to say that sections of Hindus feel threatened by what they see as special privileges to the minorities guaranteed by a secular state and their expressed reactions bear echoes of similar statements expressed in the Vijayanagara epigraphs, when the slogan "Hinduism in danger" was first expressed. The Vijayanagara rulers too took recourse to temples, cults, myths and rituals to counter the perceived threat. Tamiḻnāḍu's official ideology had been somewhat anti-north and anti-Hindi but in recent times the VHP-RSS combine have made major inroads even in the Tamiḻ belt.

Coming back to the Tiruvārūr temple, it was embroiled in disputes between temple trustees[50] and constant litigation along with lack of patronage and loss of charismatic leadership accounted for the decline in the popularity of the cult. It had also, by too strongly identifying itself with the 'orthodox', lost its appeal. More egalitarian deities like Ayyappaṉ were coming into prominence.

One thing that emerges clearly from this study is that while Veḷḷāḷas took over power and śūdras of a lower order found a niche in the institution of the temple, the paṟaiyas were left out until Gandhi inaugurated the *Harijan* movement on religious patterns, and the D.K. and D.M.K. adopted a confrontation model in order to integrate the *pariah* into Tamil̲ society. The process is too close to our times for a dispassionate conclusion to be drawn on the success or failure of the present integrative process. It is nevertheless interesting to find that in 1968 a few *pariahs* were made temple trustees in Tamil̲nāḍu. One of the things that the VHP-RSS combine is trying to do is to revitalize Hinduism minus its caste structure and the new "Hindutva" (Hinduism as defined by the RSS-VHP-BJP) rites were inaugurated by *caṇḍālas* or untouchables.

Temple Donors and their Caste Affiliations

Before concluding this chapter it will be worthwhile to analyze the list of donors as provided in the inscriptions from Tiruvārūr and study them by juxtaposing the data against present day list of donors at the Tiruvor̲r̲iyūr temple and see the trends as far as the caste compositions and status roles of the donors are concerned.

Most of the donors of the Tiruvārūr temple were either kings, courtiers or administrative officials and royal title holders. Donors often tended to add the name of the deity to their name. The name Pur̲r̲iṭaṅkoṇṭān̲ (the anthill deity of Tiruvārūr), seems to have been very popular both in Cōl̲amaṇṭalam and Toṇṭaimaṇṭalam and was borne by Brāhmaṇas and Śūdras alike.[51] Whole regiments like the Cōl̲ēndraciṅka both receive land from the king and donate land to the temple (e.g.558 of *SII* Vol. XVII).

Exact caste affiliations except for Brāhmaṇas are difficult to determine. Several Śaiva Brāhmaṇas donated cattle or money and the council called the *nakarattār* is also on record as having made collective contributions. 578 of *SII* XVII records the names of several *Cirēṭṭis*, who belong to the present day *ceṭṭiyār* community, among its donors.

A Veḷḷāḷa bearing the title Pallavarāyan̲ appears as a very important and powerful donor in the Tiruvārūr epigraphs (582,584,585 of *SII* Vol. XVII). More will be said of this chieftain in the next chapter.

Two Kaṭikaimārāyan̲s (Ghaṭikāmahārājas or heads of Sanskrit schools called *Ghaṭikās*) are recorded as donors and mediators between temple and court (590 and 593 of *SII*, Vol. XVII). These *madhyasthas* seem to have been important local personages and their role will be discussed in the next chapter.

A study of present day *Ubhayakāra* or donor list from Tiruvoṟṟiyūr temple, which preserves a better record than Tiruvārūr, reveals an underlying continuity in the patron-client relationship within the temple system. Let us look at one example, which is quite typical of the process of putting together a temple festival:

The *Aruḷmiku Tiyākarāca cuvāmi tirukkōyil* at Tiruvoṟṟiyūr issued a *Mācipperuviḻā* (festival) brochure with details of the festivities to be held between 17.2.83 and 28.2.83 and the following information is taken from the brochure. As it is typical of festivities in Tyāgarāja temples, it is indicative of the modern kind of patronage for temple upkeep and conducting of religious rites. It also serves as a kind of commercial advertisement for the donors' businesses. Thus at one stroke it serves several purposes and combines in an ingenious manner traditional religious rites with modern media methods of advertising goods and services.

The Convenor of the festival was a certain S. Kōḷappaṉ who was interestingly enough closely connected with Vaṭapaḻaniyāṇṭavar Kōyil, a well-known Murukaṉ pilgrimage site.

The following programme is a copy of the temple brochure:

Days	*Rituals*	*Ubhayakāra* (donor)
Pre-festival day Preliminaries (morning)	Vināyaka Utsava	M.S. Pacciyappa Mutaliyār, Proprietor, Manōnmaṇi Press, Madras.
Day 1.	Hoisting of temple flag Tyāgarāja procession	C.T. Pāḻaṉivēlu of Śrī Dēvi & Co. & Proprietor Sri Vēnkaṭēśvara Theatre, Tiruvoṟṟiyūr.
Day 2. a.m.	Procession	Brāhmaṇa lady (anonymous)
Day 2. p.m.	Procession	Kuppuswāmy Ceṭṭiyār, Hereditary trustee, Tiruvoṟṟiyūr temple and Rattinavēlu Ceṭṭiyār, H.R.C. & E.Board, Madras.
Day 3. a.m.	Granting boon to Mucukuntaṉ and procession of Candraśēkhara, a representative icon of Tyāgarāja	Community of Ironmongers Rājappa Cheṭṭy St. Madras

Day 3. p.m	Tyāgarāja procession Dance	Same as above.
Day 4. a.m.	Granting boon to Ādiśeṣa	Banana sellers of Koṭṭavācalcāvaṭi, Madras.
Day 4. p.m.	Procession of Candraśēkhara	T.P. Rājamānikkam Cheṭṭiyār,a herbalist (with address).
Day 5. a.m.	Boon to Brahmā	People who rent out cooking utensils, (address, Madras 7).
Day 5. p.m.	Candraśēkhara procession	Pañcanāta Ceṭṭiyār and family.
Day 5. late night	Procession of Tyāgarāja	Coconut sellers
Day 6. a.m.	Dance and procession of Tyāgarāja	Mānikka Mutaliyār, flower gardener
Day 6. p.m.	"	P.S.Ātipuricantira Mutaliyār P.S.Ananta Kiruṭṭina Mutaliyār and Tirumati (Mrs) Tirucantiram wife of Rājamānikkam of 76, Piṭāriyār Kōvil Street, Madras 1 P.S:Teyvacikāmaṇi Mutaliyār
Day 7. a.m.	*Utsava* or rites of worship of Candraśēkhara	Māṅkāṭu Ellappa Ceṭṭiyār Estate, Madras
Day 7. p.m.	Taking Candraśēkhara back from the pavillion to the temple.	Śri Kalyāṇa Perumāl, a Dēvasthānam (Temple Management Board) member.
Day 7. p.m. (2nd event)	Utsava of Tyāgarāja	T.G. Rājaṣanmukham, Landlord, Kālāḍipēṭṭai, Tiruvoṟṟiyūr.
Day 7. (night)	Taking Tyāgarāja in procession	Same as above.
Day 8. a.m.	The *vimocana* of Indra from the curse of Caṇḍālahood (ref.ch.IV for myth)	T.G.Rājaṣanmukham Piḷḷai, Landlord Same as above.
Day 8. p.m.	Procession of Tyāgarāja	Same as above.
Day 9. a.m.	Celebration of marriage between Śiva and Pārvatī (manifested as Vaṭivuṭaiyammaṉ, the dēvī of the temple)	T.V. Mahalinga Sastri Tiruvoṟṟiyūr.

Day 9. a.m	Marriage of Cuntarar and Caṅkili & *Makiḻaṭicēvai* (under the makiḻa tree; See Ch.IV. for myth)	Same as above.
Day 9. p.m	Ṛṣabhārūḍhar procession, (The icon of Śiva on the *Nañdi* taken out in procession) Abhiṣēka for Naṭarāja and Tyāgarāja Procession.	"Oṟṟiyūrānaṭimai" (Slave of the Lord) Cūḷai and the Śrī Tyāgarāja Bhaktajanasabhā (Assembly of Tyāgarāja Worshippers of Madras) & Tiruvoṟṟiyūr & P.L.D. Rājēndran and Bros, Ever Silver and Aluminium Traders, 3/4 Evening Bazaar, Madras
Day 10. (Whole day)	Blessing of all the Dēvas, Immersion and Cleansing of the processional icons in the sea	T.Celvarāja Mutaliyār and Kalyāṇacuntara Mutaliyār.

The above is not a complete list but an indicative one. In all, 18 dances of Tyāgarāja were performed before the final end of the festivities. This involved payments for decorating and carrying the icon supended on poles (as at Tiruvārūr) and eighteen clothiers undertook to provide the necessary funds.

The above record shows in fact traditional form of putting a religious festival together. So apart from permanent endowments i.e. *kaṭṭaḷais*, there were temporary endowments like the above for individual rites in a particular festival. The main subscribers as can be seen from the list above are and probably were in the historic past traders, artisans, landlords, a few Śiva brāhmaṇas or ritual officiants in the temple itself. A large majority of them in this case comes from the Ceṭṭiyār and Mutaliyār community. The trustee himself is from the Bēriceṭṭi community, traditionally in the oil-milling industry. Small contributions by pious devotees like the *bhajanasamāja* or groups of believers are also part of the whole financial scene. The brochure ends with a request for funds for renovation purposes. The most recent patrons have come from overseas non-resident Indians, commonly abbreviated as NRIs.

It is interesting to see how myth, philosophy, *bhakti*, devotion and advertisement of firms, shops, etc., all crowd into the brochure. Ironmongers from Rajapettai street, Madras, Sri Venkatesvara Theatre, 2 Ellaiyammaṉ Koyil Street, Tiruvoṟṟiyūr, etc. stand alongside Tyāgarāja bestowing a boon on king Mucukuntaṉ and Indra expiating the sin of his parting with the icon, and along with all this takes place the metaphysically infused dance of Tyāgarāja, here called the *padma* dance, which is a continuation of the *haṁsa* and *ajapā* of Tiruvārūr, signifying the universality of life principle, the unravelling of Truth, the stages of revelation and the Brahman-Ātman identity in a theistic context. It is difficult to draw a line between commercialism and piety, advertisement and *bhakti,* metaphysics and religion, the sacred and the profane.

The reason for analysing the donor list of Tiruvoṟṟiyūr, rather than Tiruvārūr is that while the former one was published the latter donor list seems very complicated and is involved with the economic and 'political' power-groups involved in the administration of the temple. The Uḷtuṟai trustee is embroiled in a battle with the Tarumapuram ātīṉam. Rumours were on that the Uḷtuṟai trustee, whose family since the late 19th century have accumulated a great deal of power and prestige in the temple, do not 'allow' other rival donors to contribute money.

Leaving aside rumours of personality clashes which may or may not be true, the very structure of the Tiruvārūr *Kaṭṭaḷais* made the conflict inevitable. Thus for example the sweeping of the innermost *prākāram* or enclosure is the responsibility of the *Uḷtuṟai kaṭṭaḷai,* of the 2nd enclosure is a joint responsibility of 4 *kaṭṭaḷais,* while the removal of the garbage is the responsibility of *abhiṣēka* and Rājaṉ *Kaṭṭaḷai.* One *Kaṭṭaḷai* removes 1/3 and the other 2/3 of the heap. At the *Paṅkuṉi* festival the ritual ablution of the icons and the ritual offerings is the reponsibility of *Abhiśēka Kaṭṭaḷai.* Looking after the silver vessels used in these rites of the deities is the responsibilty of Rājaṉ Kaṭṭaḷai; 1 pole for the procession is provided by one *Kaṭṭaḷai,* the other by another, while the rope for fastening is provided by a third. All these are needed for the dance of Tyāgarāja. Though much rationalization has been achieved in the management, the structure of this particular temple administration is highly complex and very conducive for prolonged litigation!

The above study of donor list from Tiruvārūr epigraphs and the present day list of *Ubhayakāras* of Tiruvoṟṟiyūr, and the

Kaṭṭaḷais system in Tiruvārūr all lead however to the conclusion that the temple as an institution in Tamiḻnāḍu, though sanctified by the Śaiva brāhmaṇas and the following of the Āgamas was mainly the institution *par excellence* for the upper strata of non-brāhmaṇa society, who were exempted from traditional Brahmanic functions of learning and teaching. They however could find a legitimate outlet through temple patronage for their aspirations to be regarded as leaders and elites of society. The Brāhmaṇa presence had legitimized their positions and sacralized the wealth. *Dharma* and *artha* were wed in the temples of Tamiḻnāḍu and the holders of *artha* (wealth) were admitted into the realm of the *dharma* (religion - culture) - thus ritually and socially accepted as the upper echelons of the *dhārmic* conscious Hindu society.

The 'orthodox' Brāhmaṇas of both Śaiva and Vaiṣṇava tradition were not, strictly speaking, tied in allegiance to the locus centred temples. They could lead their spiritual existence with their domestic and *śrauta* rites without feeling the need of a temple. The Paṟaiyas were excluded from any participation in the big temples. Hence the temple became increasingly an institution for a special section of people who were neither Brāhmaṇa nor Paṟaiya.

NOTES

1. For example 595 of *S.I.I. XVII* refers to Mahāvratī Pāratāyaṇa (Bādaryaṇa) as the trustee. In the 16th century Akōracivapaṇṭāram was one of the trustees of both Tiruvārūr and Chidambaram
2. Institutions, which acted as trustees were of various kinds. 601 of *S.I.I. XVII* for example refers to *Śiva brāhmaṇar Nāṟpatteṇmar*. There are several inscriptional references to *sabhās* acting as trustees.
3. For the term *Māhēśvaras* see Chapter 6.
4. Bhikṣā *maṭha* or Gōḷaki *maṭha* were the *tāṉattārs* (trustees) at Tiruvoṟṟiyyūr. The southern branch of this establishment had its headquarters in Tiruvārūr. From the 16th century, the Śaiva Siddhānta *maṭhas* became popularly associated with temple management.
5. The history of the *kaṭṭaḷais* and the purposes for which they were constituted in the Tiruvārūr temple are recorded in three decisions of the High Court of Madras. See *Vythilingappandara sannadhi* v. *Somasundara Mudaliar*, ILR 17 Mad. 199., *Gnāṉasmabandha* v. *Vythiliṅga Mudaliar*, LTR 18, LW 27 and *Ātmanātha Chettiar* v *Bālāyee Ammāḷ*, ILR 27, lw 32.
6. They did not reject the Vedas but regarded them as the initial teachings (*pūrvapakṣa*) and the Āgamas as the final teaching (*Siddhānta*).

7. Piḷḷai, Chidambaram, *Temple Entry*, p. 130.
8. Thurston, E. and Rangachari, K.J., *Castes and Tribes of Southern India*, See under '*Paṇṭāram*'.
9. Oddie, G.A., 'The Character, Role and Significance of Non-Brāhmaṇa Śaiva Cults in Tanjore District in the 19th Century', paper presented to *The 7th European Conference on Modern South Asian Studies*, London, School of Oriental and African Studies, 1981.
10. *Ibid.*
11. Ibid.
12. Rajamanikkam, M.,*The Development of Śaivism in Tamiḻnāḍu* and also 'The Tamiḻ Śaiva Maṭhas under the Cōḻas (A.D. 900-1000)' in Chari, C.I.K. (ed.), *Essays in Philosophy presented to T.M.P Mahadevan on his Fiftieth Birthday*, Madras 1962, especially, pp. 221-22.
13. *ARE 1912*, No. 207 refers to Tiruccirrampala Mutaliyār as the successor of Vāgīśvara Mutaliyār. *ARE 1912*, No. 215 and *South Indian Inscriptions*, No.254 also refer to the pontiff and place him at Celva Tiruvārūr.
14. M. Rajamanikkam, see note 12 above.
15. *ARE 1912*, No. 213.
16. *ARE 1912*, No. 223.
17. *Tillai Ulā*, 138-39. *Ēkāmranātaṉ Ulā*, 14, *Tiruvāṉaikkā Ulā*, 159. cited by Arunachalam, Mu. *Tamiḻ Ilakkiya Varalāṟu* (in Tamil) 14th cen. p.131.
18. Dorai Rangasamy, M.A. (Turaiyaraṅkacāmi), 'The *Tiruttoṇṭattokai* of Ārūrar' in the *Journal of Madras University*, 1957, pp. 75-84.
19. Mu Arunachalam -*Tamiḻ Ilakkiya Varalāṟu* 12th century, part2, pp. 804-5.
20. *S.I.I. XVII*, NO.601.
21. *ARE 1908*, Nos. 486 and 487 are inscribed on the walls of the Śaṅkara Maṭha at Tiruvaṉaikkāval and describe the priests there as direct disciples of Tiruccāṟṟimuṟṟattu Mutaliyār maṭha and its pontiff Namaccivāya Tēvar. A person of the same name is also believed to have established the Tiruvāvaṭaturai maṭha in the Thañjāvūr district.
22. Stein, Burton, *Peasant, State and Society in Medieval South India*, p.46. see also 'Temples in Tamil Country, 1300-1750 A.D.', *I.E.H.R.*, Vol.XIV, 1977, pp.11-47.
23. Stein, Burton 'Agarian Integration in South India' in Frykenberg, (ed.), *Land Control and Social Structure*, p. 179 ff.
24. Examples in the context of this cult would be Kamalai Ñāṉappirakācar, Maṟaiñāṉacampantar, author of *Tirvārūrppurāṇam* etc. In fact the Meykaṇṭār lineage seems to have been in the forefront only from the 14th and 15th centuries A.D. Maṟaiñāṉacampantar is referred to in *ARE 1936*, Part II, Para 86, who was alive 1484 A.D. and was a sectarian leader. Meykaṇṭār is referred to in an insription of about 1232 A.D. (*ARE 1920*), pt. II, and *1936*, pt. I, para 86).
25. Stein, Burton, has analyzed it particularly in the context of the Tirupati Temple. See his article, 'Temples in Tamiḻ Country'. (See Bibliography)
26. See Appadorai, Arjun, *Worship and Conflict under Colonial Rule: a South Indian Case* for his treatment of Kings, Sects and temples.
27. Gaṅgādēvi's *Madhurāvijayam* contrasts the atmosphere of the *agrahāras* before and after Muslim conquest. The antithetical juxtaposition is dramatic - Vedic scarifices contrasted with stench of beef, etc. This was written by a Vijayanagara queen, the wife of Kampanna. See *ARE 1928*, para 33. For inscriptional references to this Hindu model see *ARE 1916*, Pt. II, para 33 and *ARE 1916* No. 64. For description of this Hindu model and its occurrences in literature see Hari

Rao, V.N., *A History of Trichinopoly and Śrīraṅgam*, Ph.D. thesis, University of Madras, 1948, pp. 299-307.

28. See Derrett, Duncan, 'Two Epigraphs on Rathakāras and Kammāḷas' in *K.A. Nilakaṇṭha Śāstrī Eightieth Birthday Felicitation Volume*, Madras 1971, pp. 32-5. A reprint appears in the author's collection of articles entitled *Essays in Classical and Modern Hindu law*, Vol. I, Leiden, E.J. Brill, 1976. See *ARE 1916*, Pt. II, para 45.
29. This work is cited by Raghavan, V. *A Volume Presented to Sir Denison*, Bombay 1939, pp. 234-40 and Kane, P.V., *History of Dharmaśāstra* III Poona, 1946, p. 252 n. and in Sastri, K.A.N., *Cōḻas*, 2nd Ed., p. 549.
30. See Sastri, K.A.N. *Cōḻas* (1937 Ed), Vol. II,pt. I, 324, 355, and Vol. II,pt. II, 603, 659 and 779. P. 779 refers to Ālaṅkuṭi ins. which praises the *rathakāras*.
31. See note 28 above.
32. Boner, Alice, *Vāstusūtra Upaniṣad: The essence of form in Sacred Art*, Delhi, 1982.
33. Several people have discussed this very elusive problem of *Iṭaṅkai* and *Valaṅkai* conflicts. See Beck, Brenda, "The Right-left Division of South Indian Society", *Journal of Asian Studies*, Vol. XXIX, No.4, August 1970, pp. 779-98 and in *Peasant Society in Konku*, pp.74 ff. Srīnivasa Aiyaṅgar, M., *Tamiḻ Studies*, Madras, 1914, pp. 95-109. Srinivasachari, C.S., 'The Origin of the Right and Left Hand caste Division', *Journal of the Andhra Historical Research Society*, Vol.IV, Pts. 1 & 2 (July, October 1929), p. 80. See also Stein, Burton, ' Integration of the Agrarian System..',pp. 191-92. (See bibliography for full details.) see also Appadorai, Arjun, *Right and Left hand Castes in South* India, *I.E.S.H.R.*, Vol. II, NOs. II and III, June-Sept 1974, pp. 216-59. Also Hanumanthan, K.R., *Untouchability in Tamiḻaham*, unpublished Ph.D. thesis, University of Madurai, 1981.
34. Sastrī, K.A.N., *Cōḻas*, pp. 454, 457. *ARE 1926*. Nos. 69-72. There are instances of a major strike by *kaikkōḷars* (*ARE 1910*, Pt. II, para 53) and several regiments were named after the kings' surnames (*ARE 1919*, Pt. II, para 10, and *ARE 1910*, Pt. II, para 28) showing the close link between kings and *ceṅkuntars* (*kaikkōḷars*). That there was a close link between *ceṅkuntars*, Tyāgarāja and the kings is evident from the *Īṭṭiyeḻupatu* (see chapter IV). The 9 warriors of Murukaṉ referred to in the *Mucukundasahasranāmam* were, *kaikkōḷars*, according to oral traditions.
35. See Anavarata Vinayakam Pillai, Ed., *Civaneṟippirakācam of Civākrayōki*, Introd., pp. vii-ix.
36. Arunachalam, Mu., *Tamiḻ Ilakkiya Varalāṟu*, 14th century, pp. 133 and 143, cites the *Caṉātanācārya Purāṇa Caṅkirakam* as the source for all these legends. See also *ibid*, 16th Century, pt.II, pp. 254-8. Much of the information on the 16th century Tamiḻ literati was very kindly brought to my attention by Arunachalam himself (Oral communication Dec. 1980 at Gāndhigrām).
37. Beteille, A., *Caste, Class and Power....*, p.8.
38. Sivaraman, K., *Śaivism in Philosophical Perspective* p. 129.
39. See note 36 above.
40. Barnett, S.A., "Approaches to Changes in caste Ideology in South India", in Stein, Burton (ed.), *Essays on South India.*
41. See Karve, Iravati, 'On the Road', in JASII,XXII, 1 (1962), pp. 13-27. See Zelliot, Eleanor, 'Chokhmalla and Ēknath' in Lele Jayant Ed., *Tradition and Modernity in Bhakti Movements*, p.139.
42. Stein, Burton, 'Brāhmaṇa and Peasant in Early South Indian History', in *Adyār Library Bulletin*, Vol. 31-32, 1967-68 (V. Rāghavan Felicitation Volume). For

information in English on Kamalai Ñāṉappirakācar see Zvelebil, K.V. *Tamiḻ Literature* pp. 207-8.

43. *Ibid.*, See also by the same author, 'Social Mobility and South Indian Hindu Sects', in Silverberg. J. (ed.), *Social Mobility of Caste Systems in India*. His main contentions:
    1) There was individual mobility, very little corporate mobility.
    2) Śūdras were assimilated into the temple pattern but not Paṟaiyas.
44. Mutaliyar, C., *State and Religious Endowments in Madras*, p.324.
45. Beteille, A., *op.cit.*, p.8.
46. Fuller, C.J., *Servants of the Goddess ...*, p. 148.
47. See Kennedy, R., 'Status Control of Temples in Tamiḻnāḍu', in *I.E.S.H.R.*, II, 2-3; pp.260-90.
48. See Presler, Franklin, 'The Legitimation of Religious policy in Tamiḻnāḍu', in Smith, Bardwell, (ed.), *Religion and Legitimation of Power*, pp. 106-23.Refer especially to p.132.
49. Kenney, R., *Op.cit.* It must be remembered that 20 thousand acres of land were owned by temples in East Thañjāvūr alone. See Dietrich, Gabrielle, *Religion and People's Organization in East Thañjāvūr*, Madras, C.L.S., 1977. p. 56.
50. The Tarumapuram ātīṉam and the *Uḷturaī Kaṭṭaḷai* have a court case going on for years. The Government has also another case against the *Uḷturaī Kaṭṭaḷai*. For earlier court cases see note 5 above.
51. See Karashima, Noboru, *Concordance of Cōḻa Names*.

Chapter Nine

TYĀGARĀJA AS CULT TYPOLOGY AND LEGITIMIZATION OF POWER

Temple cults in India often operated on two levels in the process of integrating society and linking the political and socio-religious systems. Herman Kulke aptly categorizes these processes as 'vertical' and 'horizontal' legitimation. Furthermore, he sees temple cults as having the ability to "unite the various sub-regional nuclear areas of the multicentred empire through a regional loyalty".[1] Kulke bases his study on the cult of Jagannātha and the regional tradition of Orissa. Kulke's taxonomy has been used here with some modifications made to suit the specific regional traditions of Tamilnāḍu.

The main difference between the Orissan and Tamil traditions is, as suggested by Kulke himself, that while the rulers of Orissa concentrated on the centre of Puri, the Pallavas and following them the Cōlas divided their royal patronage between their official state temple and famous places of pilgrimage sanctioned by tradition.[2] Besides, like the Khmer kings of Cambodia, the Cōla kings, (most conspicuously Rājarāja I and his illustrious son Rājēndra I) tended to shift their political capitals and to match the political shift of power, they built new state temples.

Another distinguishing regional feature is that despite the political vicissitudes, the Naṭarāja temple at Chidambaram remained a major focal point of Tamil Śaivism as a whole. The Pāṇḍyas of Madurai seem to have been a little more monolithic than the Cōlas in their loyalty to the Cuntarēśvara-Mīṉākṣī cult, though with them too Chidambaram retained its special place of sanctity.

When we compare the Somāskanda, later called Tyāgarāja, with the Jagannātha of Orissa; we see that unlike the latter, the former was a brand new Brahmanic cult which was synthesized with local cults; it was not the revival of a 'lost' autochthonous cult quite in the same manner as the Jagannātha. The only exception to this argument will be if we take the *Viṭaṅka* (vide infra ch.2) to have been an ancient chthonic Cōḻa territorial emblem, which by being united with the Somāskanda concept was once more revived.

In South India, the Pallavas, inasmuch as they were the 'innovators' of a new religio-political system effectively channelled the *cathecting* force of *bhakti* to establish a network of religious institutions, with possible political ramifications.

Now to briefly define the terms used:

Vertical Legitimation

By vertically integrating several beliefs of the more ancient strata of people and enfolding them in the Vedic and/or Āgamic fold, temples and temple cults brought together people in various stages of civilization with their own 'sub-cultural' symbols of the sacred under one umbrella. The temples in this sense played the role of cultural 'brokers' as they "stood guard over the crucial junctures of synopses of relationships which connect the local system to the larger whole".[3]

In the case of Jagannātha, Kulke has shown how "autochthonous pre-Brahmanic and only partly Hinduized sub-regional deities with their strong 'territoriality' were incorporated into the Jagannātha triad and helped in the "formation and stabilization of political power in Orissa".[4]

Thus legitimation acted on two planes - religious and political. Having settled on a cult to patronize, the kings usually manoeuvred it to suit their own special requirements. Kulke draws a parallel with the Cōḻa King Kulōttuṅga I (1070-1118 A.D.) who perpetuated the Tillai three thousand myth by incorporating priests from Veṅgi, his original homeland into this sacred group of three thousand and hence legitimized his royal and their priestly power[5]. Interesting examples of such legitimation at crucial political junctures in Cōḻa history come from Tiruvārūr and Thañjāvūr.

In a cultural context this process of integration has been variously styled "Sanskritization",[6] merger of "Great and Little Traditions",[7] or a constant interchange between "universal" and "parochial" traditions[8] or simply "Hinduization"[9] in order to emphasize its general character.

A classic example of defining this cultural process is preserved in the oral tradition of Burma. King Anawaratha is believed to have accommodated the thirty seven delightfully impish looking Nāṭs in the Shwezigon Pagōda at Pagan by saying, "Men will not come for the sake of the new religion. Let them for their old gods and gradually they will be won over".[10]

The typologies of such absorption have been studied by Eschmann. She classifies them into the 'Śākta', 'Śaiva' and 'Vaiṣṇava'.[11] All three typologies occur in the Tiruvārūr tradition. To state it briefly, the anthill (Valmīka) as the abode of serpents was a symbol of fertility and the Somāskanda is worshipped for the sake of progeny. Viṣṇu worships the triad for a son (vide infra ch. 4). The subterranean passage, the *nāgabila*, the snake pit becomes *Hāṭakēśvara*.[12] At Tiruvoṟṟiyūr Kaṇṇaki becomes Vaṭṭappāṟaiyammaṉ, somewhat quietened by being entempled with Śiva and Pārvatī but still retaining memories of her fierce bloodthirsty personality of the avengeress.[13] She was Kaṇṇaki merged into Kālī as at Koṭuṅkōlūr and other places in Kēraḷa.[14] The chthonic anthill at Tiruvārūr, as a liṅga became 'Nirguṇa' (transcedental) Śiva to be represented by the 'Saguṇa' (immanent) Tyāgarāja, who by acquiring almost the status of the principal deity, had in turn to be represented by a precious *liṅga* of emerald - the *Viṭaṅka* - (a Cōḻa territorial emblem?) and by a processional image - the *Candraśēkhara*.[15] The serpent god is ancient in several cities and forms the 'root paradigm' of most *sthalapurāṇas*. Shulman refers to the *paripāṭal* myth in which Ādiśēṣa, the serpent raft of Viṣṇu is said to have determined the boundaries of the city of Madurai.[16] The snake god and the anthill concepts are recurrent motifs and occur for example in the specific context of the Tyāgarāja cult not only in Tiruvārūr but also at Tiruvoṟṟiyūr (Paṭampakkanātar) and at Tiruvāṉmiyūr (Puṟṟiṭaṅkoṇṭāṉ).[17]

The process of vertical integration was accelerated all over India in the post-Buddhist times.[18] In South India a marked acceleration of this process is noticeable under the Pallavas and the agents of acculturation were the *nāyaṉmār* and *āḻvār*. The reasons for this are not hard to seek. The Pallava king Mahēndravarman and the Pāṇḍya king Neṭumāṟan were both Jainas and in the period before the rise of the Pallavas, the Kalabhras also seem to have been Jainas.[19] Buddhists too made their headway in Nākappaṭṭaṇam and other centres. Jainism was a far more important force in the Tamiḻ context. Tiruvārūr,

Tirunaḷḷāṟu, Tiruvāymūr, Vedāraṇyam, Nākappaṭṭaṇam, to mention just a few, have all once been major Jaina centres. Nearer Madras, Mylapore was an important centre. Elsewhere in the vicinity Jaina centres have been discovered at Pulal, Viḷḷivākkam, Kuṉṉattūr and Māṅkāṭu.[20]

The Cōḻamaṇṭalam never seems to have completely yielded to Jainism and it was here that several of the Śaiva shrines belonging to the early *bhakti* period were situated.[21] It is also significant to note that the Pāṇḍyan queen, who invited Ñāṉacampantar to spread Śaivism in the Pāṇḍyan lands was a Cōḻa princess. In the Kāñcī inscription of the Pallava king Paramēśvaravarman I, the god Śiva is portrayed as being particularly concerned about his seeing the land of the Cōḻas and the Kāverī river. He is in love with the Kāverī river.[22]

The Nāyaṉmār thus set out from the nucleus area of the Cōḻanāṭu and the the Naṭunāṭu area and travelled to the nooks and corners of Tamiḻnāḍu, spreading the gospel of Śaivism, and incorporating the local belief systems, the local saints and the local deities into the Āgamic Śaiva fold and thus acted as important agents of vertical legitimization.[23] The names of the deities like Puṟṟiṭaṅkoṇṭāṉ were Sanskritized into Valmīkanātha and assumed as personal names not only by members of the lower castes but by Brāhmaṇas as well.

More will be said of this process of vertical integration in the course of the chapter.

Horizontal Legitimation

The term 'horizontal' legitimation is used to describe the process of horizontal integration whereby the regional state and its monarch were brought into a pan-Indian world of royal *dharma* and accepted as *dhārmic* brethren by co-monarchs. The Pallavas seem to have been conscious of this and made deliberate attempts to define the role of kingship in *dhārmic* terms. The Pallava concept of kingship has been excellently analyzed by Dirks.[24] Three kingly traditions or rather three models on which the king could base his royal power and which people would recognize as paradigms of royalty have been suggested by Burton Stein.[25].

Legitimation

Berger defines the term 'legitimation' as "socially objectivated knowledge that seems to explain and justify the social order" and sanction social reality. He adds that "it would be a serious mistake to mistake legitimation with theoretical ideation" for what passes as "Knowledge in society is by no means identical with the body of ideas existing in the society". Ideas operate in the realm of a few intellectuals and legitimation is a process in operation amongst the general mass of people and "most legitimation consequently is pre-theoretical in character"[26] and belongs to what Larsen calls the "praxis" dimension of religion belonging to the "pre-reflexive" sphere of beliefs.[27] This process of legitimation operates through the medium of myths, miracles, pageantry and rituals of magico-religious character. Thus, this chapter is basically concerned with what Larsen describes as an "essentialist" approach as distinguished from an "isms" approach to religious issues.[28]

The Pallava Model of Sovereignty in its Religio-Political Context

The Somāskanda made its debut in the 7th century A.D. in Pallava times. The Vītiviṭaṅka finds mention for the first time in the *Tēvāram*. It appears as if the concept of the Somāskanda Vītiviṭanka could well have originated in Cōḻamaṇṭalam and found its earliest iconic expression (at least earliest icon made of non-perishable material) in Toṇṭaimaṇṭalam. The Cōḻamaṇṭalam was the most "Hindu" (in contradistinction to patronage of Jainism elsewhere in Tamiḻnāḍu) at the time of the early Pallavas. Appar converted Mahēndravarmaṉ and Campantar Neṭumāṟa Pāṇṭiyaṉ. The icon, judging from extant samples seems to have been fashioned in and travelled from Toṇṭaimaṇṭalam, for the earliest occurrence is at Mahābalipuram and Kāñcīpuram,[29] both in Toṇṭaimaṇṭalam. However, by tradition the Somāskanda is always associated with Cōḻa territory, though it was associated with Pallava monarchy, at a time when they were the overlords of the Cōḻas.

During the period of Pallava and Pāṇḍya supremacy the Cōḻas, though not a major power, were never totally forgotten. Pallava and Pāṇḍyan epigraphs constantly refer to Cōḻa princes. So it seems likely that somehow a tenuous Cōḻa connection was maintained and the princes of this family seemed to have been hovering around the Trichinopoly-Thañjāvūr area playing a subordinate role to whoever was most powerful at the time. The term 'Cōḻa' in this case denotes a territory and a 'realm' with a regional chief rather than an imperial dynasty. Here it must be remembered that the Cōḻa lineage goes back a long way with their being mentioned in the 3rd cen. B.C. Aśōkan epigraphs and the area of Toṇṭaimaṇṭalam is said to have been under Cōḻa rule from the time of Karikāla's northern expedition. Toṇṭaimaṇṭalam was known to the early Caṅkam Cōḻas as Ōymānāṭṭu.

Hart, Dirks and Burton Stein have analysed the Pallava model of Kingship. Hart points out how the Pre-Pallavan Tamiḻ kings had evolved a state polity based on personal loyalty and feudal vassalage. He believes that such a system did not provide them with the opportunity to acquire extensive power like their north Indian contemporaries, the Guptas, and they seemed to have made a conscious switch of policy and handed over the control of nuclear areas to non-militaristic groups who had a vested interest in the kind of stability which a powerful king could provide. The Pallavas, thus, according to Hart, following the Gupta example, presented themselves as upholders of orthodoxy in order to dramatize the new nature of their rule and to break away from the old system.[30] Hart's views seem to be substantiated by the proliferation of *brahmadeyas* and *devadānas* under Pallava rule and these were lavishly supported by royal and courtly munificence.

The Pallavas were innovators. There was a great difference between Caṅkam culture and that of the Imperial Pallavas. It has often been pointed out by Tamiḻ culturalists how the secular minded, commercially worldly Tamiḻs of the Caṅkam age were transformed into those given to devotion and other worldliness. Temples became more prominent than marts and religious architecture prevailed over secular structures.[31] The Tamiḻ word 'kōyil', originally a palace of kings, became the abode of the gods. The Tamiḻ word *Iṟai* denoted chiefs and later gods. The religious fervour with which the king was approached and royal manner in which the Āgamic deity was treated established a ritual parallel and hence set the legitimation process at work. Kulacēkara āḻvār was therefore not being merely obsequious when he stated that to behold the king is verily like beholding the Lord Viṣṇu humself (*Tiruvuṭai maṉṉaṉaik kāṇil Tirumālaik kaṇṭār pōl).*

Mahendravarman (c.a. 600-630 A.D.) proudly proclaims the

building of stone temples and from his time on, regular stone temples were constructed to house icons in whom the spirit of the deities was believed to inhere. The icon was metaphorically and symbolically invested with life, *prāṇa pratiṣṭhā*, and the Āgamas emerge during this period to define codes of temple worship. The nāyaṉmār speak of the Āgamas.[32] The Kuṭumiyāṉmalai inscription refers to them.[33] Rājasiṁha calls himself *Āgamapramāṇa* in his epigraphs.

The choice of Somāskanda as the *leitmotif* of Pallava sacred art is significant. Sculpture manuals, as seen earlier, emphasize the 'kingly' quality of the icon (vide infra ch.II). The Śiva in this triad is not the ascetic Yogī or the beggar of souls, nor the quiescent teacher of knowledge, or a cosmic dancer, but Śiva the man, the father and the king, this-worldly and responsible, kingly and paternal. He was a *bhogamūrti*, a life-affirming deity, whose worship assured the continuity of the human race. His association with fertility is one of the root paradigms of the cult.[34]

Apart from expressing through a symbol the concept of the fecundity of man and the fertility of the soil, the triad of deities also expressed the continuity of royalty, for the three figures could symbolically represent the king, queen and the heir apparent. This symbolism was a recurrent theme in South East Asian iconography. Śiva, Umā, Agastya (or Bhaṭṭāraguru) and Gaṇēśa installed in the four cells of the Śiva temple at Lara Jongrang in the Prambanam valley seem to signify such a grouping. Portrait sculptures in Indonesia represented both king and deity and the cosmological implications were pronounced in town planning particularly of the royal capital.[35] These were Indic forms of expression and were transplanted into South East Asian soil, presumably from South India.

Dirks identifies two major phases in development of the idea of kingship under the Pallavas. The earliest Prākṛt charters envisage kingship in terms of Brāhmanical sacrifice and the figure of the king as the Vedic sacrificer. Between 400 and 550 A.D. the Sanskrit charters, though mentioning Brāhmanic sacrifices, exhibit a slight change of emphasis and the sovereign is shown sharing power, even if in a very limited manner, with Brāhmaṇas and Sabhās. Chronologically this is what is called the period of the Kālabhāra interregnum. This period is followed around 550 A.D. by increased participation of local executors *(ājñāpatis)* who are called Lords or Īśvara.[36]

The second phase, according to Dirks, begins with the accession of Nandivarman II in 731 A.D. The times were troubled and wars with Cāḷukyas and Pāṇḍyas was a recurrent feature. Dirks traces a change in the pattern of kingship at this time from a king/army dominated kingship to one in which the sovereign was perceived as sharing power among locally influential chieftains. The local chief often acts as a petitioner of religious grants (*vijñāpati*) and as a kind of semi-independent executioner.[37]

This was furthermore the period when, according to Dirks, gift giving, which was an act of generosity on the part of the monarch, assumed such an important place in the socio-religious and political structure that it became not only a characteristic but a prerequisite of legitimate monarchy and *dāna* became the sacred duty of the king.[38]

Brahmadeyas and temples became the vehicles through which this kingly charity could be expressed and institutionalized, and in return kingship itself legitimized. Gift to temples became a part of the economic, social and religious obligation of the monarch. Gradually the stone icon assumed a very special personality and stood in the language of Appadorai as a symbol of a "set of moral and economic transactions".[39] Spirituality of gift giving was mixed with self interest leading very often to its being "conceived of as a contract" whereby by the "profane sustains the sacred and the sacred rewards the profane".[40]

Burton Stein, as noted earlier, traces three models of kingship in the Pallava-Cōḻa times. They are the heroic ideal as portrayed in the bardic literature of the *Caṅkam* poets, the moral kingship which he believes was fully espoused in the Jaina and Buddhist literature (and to a lesser degree in Hindu literature, though it was present even in the early bardic tradition) and finally, the ritual kingship.[41]

Dirks notices changes in the inscriptional expression of Pallava kings which indicate the incorporation of lesser chiefs into Pallava sovereignty. New idioms of incorporative kingship evolved and, according to Burton Stein, "In this process, earlier formulas of Brahamnical kingship were set aside". "The concept of *dāna* and the king as prestator was but one of these idioms, others were drawn from the earlier kingly tradition and still others from the Jaina tradition".[42] The donor of the land, money or cattle is identified in the later Pallava epigraphs and the person honoured. Thus begins the nucleus of the 'honour' system by which several people were incorporated into the temple institution and into the orbit of ritual kingship.[43]

This process of incorporation seems to have started probably a little earlier than Nandivarman II's reign. Of the major aids to royalty in their task of incorporating local leadership under the loose hegemony of Pallava sovereignty were the *nāyaṉmār* and *āḻvār*. As the primary concern of this work is with the Śaiva Tyāgarāja cult we shall confine ourselves to the work of the *nāyaṉmār* in this process of incorporation.

The Nāyaṉmār and the Pallava Process of 'Incorporative Kingship'

Royal patronage was a key issue in the battle between the Jainas and Śaivas. The religious confrontation was always in royal presence. To quote just a few examples: Mahēndravarman's conversion was a great triumph for Appar.[44] *Taṇṭiyaṭikaḷ's* gaining his sight back took place in the royal presence. The king's presence was crucial to the myth. The deity appeared not only to *Taṇṭiyaṭikaḷ* in a dream but also to the Cōḻa monarch.[45] The miracle convinced the king and consequently the Jainas were driven out of Tiruvārūr. Neṭumāṟaṉ's body was burning with fever and the 'miraculous' cure by *Campantar* won him the royal favour and resulted in the persecution of Jainas, and their impalement is enacted as a part of the cultic ritual in the Madurai temple complex every year.[46] The neo-convert Pāṇḍyan monarch wanted to follow *Campantar* everywhere but was advised by the saint to protect Śaivism in *Pāṇṭināṭu*.

The espousing of this temple-oriented 'heno-locotheistic' brand of Śaivism fitted excellently with the concept of *dāna* as a major motif in the Pallava paradigm of ritual kingship. As pointed out by Dirks, the concept of *dāna* completely displaces the element of sacrifice in the Pallava records during the reign of Nandivarman Pallavamalla in the 8th century and thereafter.[47] Thus a symbiotic relationship existed between the *bhakti* religion of the *nāyaṉmār* and *āḻvār* and the ritual kingship paradigm of the Imperial Pallavas.

This court-temple symbiosis took interesting turns in the 13th century A.D. as expressed through the Pāṇḍyan myths and a century earlier as revealed in the Tiruvārūr epigraphs and Tyāgarāja myths localized in Tiruvārūr and its environs. The *Tiruviḷaiyāṭal Purāṇam* was composed by Perumparṟappuliyūr Nampi in the 13th century A.D. when the Pāṇḍyas were making an important re-entry into the political arena.[48] Having Mīṉākṣī as Taṭātakai, a Pāṇḍyan princess and Cuntara Pāṇṭiyaṉ as the royal and divine consort was helpful in both 'vertical' and 'horizontal' legitimation of power. Mīṉākṣī was obviously the earlier inhabitant of Madurai and she was incorporated into the 'Śākta', 'Śaiva' typology and brought into the fold of Āgamic-Paurāṇika brand of Śaivism. The superimposition of royalty on divinity led to a situation whereby Mīṉākṣī and Cuntarēśvara were virtually treated as owners and proprietors of Madurai with the Pāṇḍyas acting as their representatives. A need to resuscitate the myths was again felt in the 17th century A.D. when Parañcōti gave a face-lift to the compendium of myths to meet the requirements of Tirumala Nāyaka. Much of the ritual paraphernalia of the Mīṉākṣī cult was introduced during this period.[49]

A significant reference as far as the Tyāgarāja cult is concerned is that in v. 91 of the 'Maturai Kāṇṭam' of the *Tiruviḷaiyāṭal Purāṇam* of Parañcōti; it is the Somāskanda form (i.e. Cuntarar, Aṅkayaṟ Kaṇṇi and Murukaṉ) which is regarded as the ruler of the Pāṇḍyan lands. The *Utsavabēra* of Cuntarēśvarar is a Somāskanda. Thus the 'root paradigm' of sovereignty is maintained, specially through this iconic symbol.

The Tyāgarāja-royalty emblem is remembered in myths as a Cōḻa emblem of royalty. It was the Cōḻa Mucukuntaṉ who brought the image to earth and instituted its worship. It can be inferred from the Tiruccirāppaḷḷi inscription of Guṇabhāṟa, a Cōḻa territorial emblem.

As pointed out by Burton Stein the Tamiḻnāḍu traditions knew of a territorial tripartite division under the three monarchs - the Cōḻa, the Cēra and the Pāṇḍya. This was "deep-rooted in the Tamiḻ political and cultural consciousness".[50] The Pallavas were in that sense intruders and had to "accommodate the ancient *kṣatra* of the Tamiḻ chiefs to the *dhārmic* pretensions of the Pallavas".[51] It seems, therefore, highly likely that the Somāskanda, a Cōḻa territorial concept, was incorporated into the ritual kingship tradition of the Pallavas. The period would have to be taken back by two generations before Nandivarman II, i.e., to the period of Rājasiṁha (680-700 A.D.) when the Somāskandas became a regular feature of Pallava sacred art.

This view is further strengthened by the fact that Appar eulogizes the Vītiviṭaṅkar[52] presumably a few years before the extant iconic Somāskanda form makes its debut in the Toṇṭaimaṇṭalam. Thus the concept seems to have been Cōḻa, though giving it form in imperishable material was a Pallava innovation and the icon was, as we know it today, a product of Toṇṭaimaṇṭalam. The Cōḻas, when they overthrew the Pallavas, adopted it as their state deity, thereby combining in the symbol a link between the realm and the ruler. The term Cōḻa here is used in the terriorial sense, for when Appar composed his hymns, Cōḻamaṇṭalam was under Pallava rule, probably under the Muttūrāyar chiefs. Interestingly enough a number of *nāyaṉmār* belonged to Pallava royal families. The *Periya Purāṇam* describes Aiyaṭikaḷ Kāṭavarkōṉ as a Pallava king (Aiyaṭikaḷ Kāṭavarkoṉ purāṇam v. 1-7). A village called Aiyaṭimaṅgalam is situated near Tiruvārūr. He was a devotee of Śiva at Ārūr and Oṟṟiyūr as he mentions in his *Kṣētraveṇpā*. A certain Pallava Siṁhavarman is said to have decorated the Chidambaram temple with gold (*Kōyil Purāṇam* and *Citampara Māṉmiyam*) and he has been identified with Siṁhavarman III. Kaḻaṟciṅkar was a Pallava king. Seventeen of the sixty-three saints were kings or chiefs or directly connected with royal power as commanders-in-chief. Thus there was a close connection between kings and saints.[53]

Sacred Clusters

The *nāyaṉmār,* in particular Appar and Campantar and later Cuntarar, travelled from place to place cathecting the old Śaiva faith in the region. A new charismatic leadership was provided. A typical scenario was something as follows: Appar invites Campantar to witness the Mārkaḻi Tiruvāttirai at Tiruvārūr; then they perform miracles together at Vētāraṇṇiyam (Vēdāraṇyam) and Appar, directed by the Lord, goes to Tiruvāymūr and Campantar follows him to witness the divine dance. At Paḻaiyāṟai Appar is grieved to see the temple blocked by Jainas and refuses to eat unless the Cōḻa king reinstitutes the *pūjā* to Śiva and the king not only does what Appar asks him to do but also drives out the Jainas.

The two saints instituted the worship of brother saints. Thus

Appar installed the worship of Naminanti at Tiruvārūr. A deliberate attempt to establish a religious network is clearly discernible in the *modus operandi* of the *Tēvāram* writers. Sacred clusters were deliberately fostered which were linked either through mythical incidents in the life of the deity or actual incidents in the life of the saint in question, often converted into a 'miracle' to serve the thaumaturgical requirements of religion. Tiruvārūr and Tyāgarāja form one of the nodal points of this network. The route of Tyāgarāja on his descent from heaven is mapped out by Appar as seen in Chapter III while discussing the Religious Topography of the Cult. The *līlais* of Śiva as recounted in the *Periya Purāṇam* link several sites such as Tiruvoṟṟiyūr, Tirukkuvaḷai, etc., and the *līlais* of *Tiyākarājalīlaikaḷ* tend to link even more distant areas with the Tiruvārūr node.[54] 'Sacred clusters',[55] thus seem to take the place of more monolithic loyalty structures such as that of Jagannātha envisaged as the ruler of Orissa.

A note of warning. This argument must not be interpreted to mean that cultic geography coincided with political boundaries. It must be remembered that the loyalty of the *nāyaṉmār* was not strictly confined to the deity of their own realm. Cēramāṉ Perumāḷ for example made the deity of Tiruvārūr in Cōḻamaṇṭalam his main deity and wrote the *Tiruvārūrmummaṇikkōvai.* He was a Cēra king. Thus all that the nāyaṉmār seems to have done was to provide networking facilities for the patron monarchs.

The kings installed *liṅgas* and called them very often by their own names. Often only the *praśasti* of the king was engraved on temple walls. The *liṅga,* donated by a powerful chief, bore his name. Rites called *Sandhis* were initiated in the name of the royal donor or one of his loyal chiefs who, by stating the regnal year of the king and his *meykīrtti* or eulogies, was restating his loyalty. These were some of the ways by which this incorporative kingship flourished.

The sites in the Tyāgarāja sacred cluster were important only in the South Indian pilgrimage tradition. The *Rāmāyaṇa* and the *Mahābhārata* do not mention them as part of the pan-Indian pilgrim tradition. Thus for the first time, attempts were made under the *nāyaṉmār* to link the gods of these South Indian sites with the northern Sanskritic Āgamic tradition. This process was noticed by Kulke in his study of the *Cidambara māhātmyam* and in his study of the Jagannātha cult. The *nāyaṉmār,* by calling Śiva both the 'Āriyan' and the 'Tamilan' and by extolling the Vedas and the Tamil songs of the saints were making a pioneering attempt at drawing the Sanskritic tradition into the Tamil fold and giving the Tamil tradition a pan-Indian acceptability.

This process of 'horizontal legitimation' was greatly accelerated under the Cōlas when myths and legends multiplied around the entempled icons. The Ānantatāṇṭava, in the southern city of Chidambaram was the 'same dance' as performed at Dārukāvana and the Tamil place names were Sanskritized. Puliyūr became Chidambaram; Tiruvārūr was variously called Śrīpuram, Camatkārapuram, Kamalālaya, etc. The Cōla effort at pan-Indian legitimation culminated in Rājēndra bringing the waters of the Ganges and establishing a new capital around the enshrined sacred waters. The Pallavas were the earliest South Indian rulers who assumed Sanskritic names and titles and joined them to Tamil titles.[56]

From the time of Mahēndravarman inscriptions became bilingual. The Tamil portion of the document followed the Sanskrit portion and could well be taken as an official document in itself.

Tyāgarāja Cultic Centres and the Pallavas

If we were to move further from the generic cult of Somāskanda to the specific cult of the Tyāgarāja-Viṭaṅka traditions (vide infra chapter II and V) then we get the picture of the Tyāgarāja cult being a pre-eminently Imperial Cōla sponsored one. For, of all the early Tyāgarāja shrines, it is only at Tiruvorriyūr that Gaṅga Pallava records have come to light.[57] Even here the icon Kāraṇai Viṭaṅkar, i.e. the Tyāgarāja appears only in Cōla inscriptions.

At Tiruvārūr the earliest record is from the Acalēśvara shrine and is dated in the reign of a Rājakēsarin (578 of *ARE* 1904; *SII* Vol. XVV. 291) and is a 12th century copy of an earlier epigraph. The shrine itself, i.e., the Acalēśvara, was built of stone by Cempiyan Mātēvi either during the last years of Uttamacōla's reign (970-88 A.D.) or in the early years of Rājarāja I. Thus the 'Rājakēsarin' inscription referred to above must be earlier than this and could be assigned to Āditya I (871-907 A.D.).[58] As the site was well known from earlier times the shrines were presumably either of mud or brick. The possibility that it was made of earth (mud) seems very likely since the earliest *liṅga* was a *purru* (an anthill) and according to the Āgamas, the structure often matched the substance of which the main icon was constituted. Other *Saptaviṭaṅka* shrines also have epigraphs only from Cōḻa times.

The icons at Tiruvoṟṟiyūr bear the names of Pallava kings and of persons generally termed 'feudatories' but who were in reality traditional local chieftains 'incorporated' into the ritual kingship of the Pallavas. The deities belonging to this class were Viṭelviṭukīśvara, Cōḻamāḷīśvara (a temple by the name Cōḻīśvara was built during the reign of Āditya I), Kampīśvaramuṭaiyār and Ariñjīśvaramuṭaiyār, the last two being names of Pallava kings and the first two of chieftains.[59]

A study of the donor list shows the mistress of Vānakōvarāyar (most probably of the chieftaincy controlled by the Bāṇas) donating land (158 of *ARE 1912*); another mistress of the same chief again deposits money with the same committee called the Amṛtagaṇa. These two epigraphs are dated in the reign of Aparājitavarman, who ruled from 885 A.D. The wife of Viṭelviṭukīśvara Iḷaṅkōvalar of Koṭumpāḷūr again deposits money with the residents of Maṇali. The Koṭumpāḷūr chiefs were other important political figures in Pallava times. Donors from Cōḻanāṭu are referred to and a *liṅga* by the name of Cōḻamāḷīśvara as seen above is worshipped. These chiefs would probably be the Cōḻa chiefs of Uṟaiyūr and Paḻaiyāṟai, who, as we noticed earlier, never completely disappeared from the scene. This Cōḻanāṭu or Cōḻamaṇṭalam traditionally was a small area comprising modern day Thañjāvūr and Tiruccirāppalli districts.The reigning queens have also made their donations to the temple (162 and 163 of *ARE* 1912). Central Government officers, presumably bearing the title Pallavarāyar, are also recorded as having made endowments to the temple.

A few inscriptions from this temple dated in the reigns of Vijaya Kampavarman (a later Pallava King) and the Rāṣṭrakūṭa king, Kṛṣṇa III and Kannaradēva refer to ascetics, who were, as is evident from the epigraphs, much venerated and important personages. The two names recorded are Nirañjana Guru and Caturānana Paṇḍita. In an epigraph of Vijayakampavarman, Nirañjana Guru is referred to as Tiruvoṟṟiyūr Uṭaiyār (owner of, belonger of Tiruvoṟṟiyūr) and in another inscription (181 of ARE *1912*) the same religeuse is given the Sanskrit title Ādhigrāmapati, Ādhigrāma being another name for Tiruvoṟṟiyūr. He has a *maṭha* in the temple and a deity is named after him as Nirañjanīśvara

Mahādeva. Thus, apart from so-called 'feudatory' chiefs, the Tiruvoṟṟiyūr temple was also the centre of religious *maṭhas*. Caturānana Paṇḍita was connected both with the Rāṣṭrakūta and Cōḻa powers in Toṇṭaimaṇṭalam. The *maṭha* of which he was the head seems to have been an organization under pontiffs who assumed the title Caturānana.

Tyāgarāja and the Cōḻas

The earliest Cōḻa inscriptions from Tiruvārūr and Vēdāraṇyam go back to the time of Āditya I (c.a. 871-907 A.D.) and Parāntaka I (907-955 A.D.). Over a dozen inscriptions of Parāntaka I's time have come from Vēdāraṇyam. It was, as seen earlier, Cempiyaṉ Mahādēvi who built the Aṟaneṟi shrine of Tiruvārūr. A record of Rājarāja dated in his 7th year also comes from Tiruvārūr. Thus the earliest epigraphic links of the Cōḻas with Tyāgarāja centres date from Āditya I.

The Cōḻa policy was in the main a continuation of the Pallava policy and several nuclear institutions grew up all over the kingdom. There was a particular concentration of sacred networks in the Cōḻamaṇṭalam. The Cōḻa *praśastis* starting from Rājarāja I became elaborate and were carved on the temples, thus making the royal presence felt. Literate men were involved in the writing of these *praśastis* and they "expressed the symbols by which particularistic loyalties, interests and affiliations of powerful local persons were merged as segmentary state within a spatial zone of legitimate overlordship". [60]

The temple under the Cōḻas greatly expanded its influence and merchants, artists, peasants, landlords, officials and local personages legitimized their social status *inter alia* through the temples.

Rājarāja I and Dakṣiṇamēruviṭaṅkar

In the 9th century A.D. when Cuntarar wrote his *Tiruttoṇṭattokai* Tiruvārūr and Chidambaram were the two capitals of Śaivism. So when Rājarāja built his state temple at Thañjāvūr he tried to sanctify it by entempling the two most sacred emblems of Śaivism of the period, the Āṭavallāṉ and the Vitaṅkaṉ. He enshrined them both in Thañjāvūr which was the royal capital of the Cōḻas from Vijayālaya's time (c.a. 850-871 A.D.). Rājarāja made it into an ecclesiastical capital as well. The sacral royal presence was made dramatically visible through his grandiose temple which he named

Rājrarājeśvaram after himself (*SII* Vol. II. 91). He also called it Śivapādaśekhara (*SII* Vol. II .91) after one of his own epithets. The king was definitely using the temple to make a political statement.

Before entering a discussion on the nature of 'ritual' or 'Sacral Kingship' of the Cōḻas, it is essential to establish the identity of the Dakṣiṇamēruviṭaṅkar, Mahāmēruviṭaṅkar and Tañjaiviṭaṅkar mentioned in Rājarāja's inscriptions. Throughout the arguments put forward in Chapter II the *Viṭaṅkas* have been taken to be symbolic of the Tyāgarāja as in Tiruvārūr where he is most certainly the Vītiviṭaṅka Somāskanda-Tyāgarāja.

The facts gleaned from the Thañjāvūr epigraphs are as follows:

1) Rājarāja I set up several *pañcaloha* (an alloy of 5 metals) images, prominent among these were Āṭavallāṉ Dakṣiṇamēruviṭaṅkar, Tañjaiviṭaṅkar and Mahāmēruviṭaṅkar.
2) Kuntavi, the king's sister, gave generous grants to these images, particularly the Dakṣiṇamēruviṭaṅkar and set up images of the consorts of these deities.
3) The consorts of all of them are grouped under the common nomenclature Umā Paramēśvarī.
4) The Dakṣiṇamēruviṭaṅkar and Āṭavallāṉ and their consorts were processional images.
5) They were extremely important deities, for apart from the king and his much revered sister, seven other queens of Rājarāja donated to these images and their consorts.

Krishna Sastri, while editing the inscriptions of Rājarāja I, remarks that the name Dakṣiṇamēruviṭaṅkar is easily explained by referring to a hymn in the *Tiruvicaippā* in which *Mēru Viṭaṅkar* occurs as the god at Chidambaram. Thus he equates Dakṣiṇamēru with Āṭavallāṉ.[61]

There are several objections to this identity. Firstly the two Āṭavallāṉ and Dakṣiṇamēruviṭaṅkar are definetely mentioned as two separate deities, two separate icons with no aliases linking them. Two measurements of weight are named after these two deities. Thus they cannot be identical.

Conspicuously while all other icons are described, the term *Viṭaṅka* is left undescribed. Thus it stands very much to reason that the Viṭaṅka, like in Tiruvārūr was the 'sign' or 'symbol' by which Somāskanda was represented. Naṭarāja and Somāskanda-Tyāgarāja are both conceptually dance icons symbolizing the dance of knowledge. Thus, on a philosophic plane there is a great deal of identity but iconically they were different and the Somāskanda *also* represented other earthly mundane concerns, such as fecundity of the earth and fertility of man and the royal protection of the State. It stands to reason that a king like Rājarāja who was evolving a royal temple was definitely going to include the 'royal' deity, i.e. Somāskanda, known for its *rajōguṇa,* which as a palladium of Pallava sovereignty occurs over and over again in Pallava sacred art. The Cōḻas were the successors of the Pallavas. They had come to the throne after overthrowing the Pallavas, their erstwhile overlords. Thus to incorporate their iconic *leitmotif,* modify it into a bronze processional icon and endow it with all the wealth of the Cōḻa empire seems a very logical process. We have also felt that the Somāskanda was originally a Cōḻa territorial motif, used by the Pallavas and if that were accepted, then the motif was restated and elaborated under the Imperial Cōḻas, where it became a symbol of the ruler and the realm..

The fact that Somāskanda is nowhere clearly described in Rājarāja's inscriptions and the fact that Somāskanda with all the esoteric tradition of the Tyāgarāja is an important icon in the Thañjāvūr temple makes it most likely that the cultic taboos against its being exposed to ordinary mortal eyes had already developed in Rājarāja's time itself. Its essence was captured in a *Viṭaṅka* - a *liṅga* - and so could not be described. Shāhāji in his *Tyāgēśapadas* equates Tyāgarāja with Bṛhadīśvara and invokes them as the ruler of Tañjai or as a friend of the ruler of Tañjai.[62] The Marāṭhās claimed to be the successors of the Cōḻas and upholders of Cōḻa tradition.

Today Somāskandas are ritual imperatives in all Śaiva temples of Tamiḻnāḍu. Tiruvārūr was a famous pilgrim centre, closely connected with the *Tēvāram* trio, particularly Cuntarar. Rājarāja is believed to have codified (rediscovered) the *Tevāram*[63] and so had very close links with Tiruvārūr. In fact the *Tirumuṟaikaṇṭapurāṇam* of Umāpati Civācārya, which though a 14th century work obviously records an earlier oral tradition, tells us that Rājarāja, on hearing a few verses of the *Tēvāram* sung by a passerby was so impressed that he marshalled the help of the saintly Nampiyāṇṭār Nampi in his quest for the original manuscript. Here it must be remembered that Nampi Āṇṭār Nampi was the composer of the *Tiruttoṇṭattokai*, recording the names of the 63 saints. After several vicissitudes and with considerable divine help Rājarāja traced the mss. in a room at the Chidambaram temple and after persuading the priests to part with it had the text codified and its musical notes (*paṇ*) systematised. Besides he was a worshipper at Tiruvārūr and there are several ritual parallels between Tiruvārūr and Thañjāvūr.[64]

Going back to Krishna Sastri's identification of the Candramaulīśvara emblem of Chidambaram - the liṅga symbolising Naṭarāja, with the Mēruviṭaṅkar of Rājarāja's inscriptions, it stands to reason that Dakṣiṇamēruviṭaṅkar or Viṭaṅka of Southern Mēru (i.e, Tiruvārūr, which is to the south of Chidambaram) should symbolise Tyāgarāja. The southern aspect of Tiruvārūr's geography often gets mentioned and we have references to 'southern' branches of maṭhas being at Tiruvārūr.

Architecturally Tyāgarāja temples have a separate shrine for the Somāskanda, facing east like the *mūlabera*, presumably to show its ritual equality with the *mūlabera*. Both Thañjāvūr and Tiruvārūr have such Tyāgarāja shrines. The close connection between Cōḻa royalty and the Tyāgarāja as evinced in the inscriptions of Vikramacōḻa and his successors, (qv) and as portrayed in the *Tiyākarājalīlaikaḷ* as well as in the legends of Maṉunīti and Mucukuntaṉ, makes it amply clear that Tyāgarāja was one of the family deities of the Cōḻas. Shāhāji in his *padas* addresses Tyāgarāja as "*Rājabimbānane Cōḻarāja kuladevate Rājarājasakhā Tyāgarāja Tañjeśa dayite*" ('one who is in the image of a king, the family deity of the Cōḻas, the friend of Rājarāja, Tyāgarāja, the friend of the Lord of Tañjai').[65] This is a Marāṭhī *pada* (lyric) in the Mōhana *rāga* beginning "*Ānandavalli a tām abhaya majhāde*". It deals in brief with all the mythological assumptions of the Tyāgarāja cult. True enough Shāhāji was invoking his Cōḻa lineage for his own purposes of legitimization of Marāṭhā power but in so doing he is obviously referring to a well known traditional motif - the association of Tyāgarāja with the Cōḻa family, for there is no point in his referring to something which his audience could not easily understand.

In another poem entitled *Bṛhadīśvara Māhātmya Varṇanena* Shāhāji sings a long praise of the temple (and the deity) of

Bṛhadīśvara which owned land, wealth, cattle, and was according to the poet, colossal and reached up to the stars. He concludes by greeting the deity as "*janahita Tyāgabṛhadīśa*"[66] ('the beneficiary of the people', the Tyāgabṛhadīśa) thereby linking the Tyāgarāja with the Bṛhadīsa.

The Viṭaṅkar tradition is closely associated with the Somāskanda in Tiruvārūr and given the religious climate of the time and Rājarāja's veneration of Cuntarar and the *Tēvāram*, the Dakṣiṇamēruviṭaṅkar seems to be almost without doubt the Tyāgarāja. The Tyāgarājaviṭaṅka is in all Tyāgarāja temples supposed to represent the *mūlabera*. Hence the Dakṣiṇamēruviṭaṅkar Tyāgarāja was Bṛhadīśvara in the ritual sense in which Shāhāji used it.

Rājarāja seemed to have had a special preference for Cuntarar of all the *Tēvāram* saints. While this could be explained by the fact that Cuntarar was closest to Rājarāja in matter of time, the fact that Cuntarar as represented in his hagiographies, as following the *Sakhāmārga* and hence a 'friend' of the Tyāgarāja may have dictated Rājarāja's choice. Cuntarar was almost an "equal" of Tyāgarāja since the deity conferred on him the special privilege of being a friend. So by analogy Rājarāja too by his special association with Cuntarar was not merely a royal devotee but a semi-divine friend of the deity.

The Cōḻa paintings in the temple of Thañjāvūr of Rājarāja's time portray the life of Cuntarar. The Northern wall depicts episodes from the life of Cuntarar. These murals can be divided into three parts. The first scene in the series depicts the '*taṭuttāṭkoṇṭa*' episode where Śiva appears as an old man and claims Cuntarar as his bonded slave.[67] Epigraphists claim that on the bundle of palm leaves (the legal document on the basis of which Śiva claims Cuntarar as his slave) they have been able to decipher the phrase '*Ippaṭi nāṉaṟivēṉ*' (Thus do I know (it))[68]

Just above this panel describing the *taṭuttāṭkoṇṭa* scene is the episode of Cuntarar and Cēramāṉ on their way to Kailāsa. Cuntarar is seated on the white elephant and on his right Cēramāṉ Perumāḷ gallops on his white horse. Just above this is the scene in Kailāsa. Śiva is portrayed in Yōgāsana seated on a tigerskin mat and Nandī stands in supplication. They are surrounded by a host of sages, *apsaras*, etc. Śiva is portrayed in red and the sages in blue.[69]

The images of the three *nāyaṉmār* of *Tēvāram* fame were installed in the temple (*SII* Vol. II pt. II, Nos. 38 and 41) and so was an image of Paravai nācciyār the wife of Cuntarar from Tiruvārūr. They were set up by a local chief and *mūvēntavēlan̠* and endowed by several *nakarattārs*.

Thus Chidambaram, from where the Cōl̠a king is believed to have recovered the Tēvāram and Tiruvārūr where the *Tēvāram* saints were lauded as a group by Cuntaramūrtināyan̠ār provided the sanctity for Thañjāvūr.[70] The temple priests in Thañjāvūr talk of a tradition of Rājarāja as a devotee of Tyāgarāja of Tiruvārūr and of the special ritual links between the two temples.[71]

Rājrarāja and the Cōl̠a State Cult

With a grand concept of relationship between temple and State Rājarāja built his state temple in a place with least ecclesiastical ties. We know from inscriptions that the temple was completed in his twenty fifth year, which is c.a. 1010 A.D. Thañjāvūr was not a *pātalper̠r̠a talam* (a temple visited and sacralised by the nāyan̠mār) and had no special sanctity to it and so there were no priests or traditions that could offer an alternative power structure. The King of Kings commanded personnel from other temples to serve the deity of Thañjāvūr.

The great temple was easily the richest temple of the time. The king himself had presented to it large amounts of land, money and other treasures by the 29th year of his reign. Much of it was booty that he had acquired in war. Over 500 pounds of gold and well over 600 pounds of silver were presented to the temple by the twenty-ninth year of the monarch. He endowed the temple with lands spread over several areas in his domain and also in what is now Śrī Laṅka. The annual income from the lands set apart for the temple is estimated at 116,000 kalams of paddy. Four hundred women dancers and servants were transferred to the Thañjāvūr temple from other temples throughout his domains and they were each given a house and a *vēli* of land. Two separate streets (*taḷiccēri*) were reserved for the temple dancers. Forty-four of them came from Tiruvārūr, several from the seven Tyāgarāja cultic sites and others from temples made sacred by the nāyan̠mār's visit. Thus, at one stroke Rājarāja was trying to combine the grandeur of this worldly conquest with the sacredness of the entempled godhead.

Two hundred and twelve men including goldsmiths, tailors,

musicians, dance masters, etc., were settled as part of the temple personnel. Performing artists of the northern and southern styles of rendering music were part of this large entourage. Fifty members recited the *Tiruppatiyam* (the *Tēvāram* and the hymns of Māṇikkavācakar). Their wages and other conditions of employment were laid down and they held office on a hereditary basis.[72] The vast majority of donors to the temple at Thañjāvūr came either directly from the royal family or from the families of royal officers. The huge cash endowments were lent to village assemblies or other such bodies at rates of interest fixed in cash or kind.

A *Valaṅkai vēlaikkārarppaṭai* (a regiment of soldiers belonging to the right handed order) were assigned to guard the Dakṣiṇamēruviṭaṅkar,[73] the icon with which we are primarily concerned here. Rājarāja mentions thirty-one regiments in his inscriptions of which thirteen belonged to the right hand order. Interestingly enough no left hand order is specifically mentioned. At Tiruvoṟṟiyūr, it was the *devadāsīs* who were divided into a right handed and left handed groups with the former performing before Tyāgarāja and the latter before Vaṭivuṭaiyammaṉ.[74] One wonders whether to begin with, at any rate, any such association existed with regard to the soldiers and guardianship of icons as well, for we know that the subsequent relationship of the *iṭaṅkai* with the *valaṅkai* groups was extremely hostile with actual bloody clashes taking place.

The mechanism of linking various sections of society to the temple in what was not merely an economic but also a religious and social tie can be seen by a study of the epigraphs of the time. Thus an inscription (*SII* Vol II, pt II 24) records two deposits of money by officers of Rājarāja I in favour of the Presiding Deity, Rājarājēśvara and the Dakṣiṇamēruviṭaṅkar. The first deposit was lent out to a bazaar to provide seeds and *campaka* buds to be used in the bath water of the deities. An identical requirement was met by the villagers to whom the second sum of money was lent out. They were cultivators and agreed to provide *khuskhus* roots (roots of the poppy plant) to be used as before for scenting the bath water. Thus both the endowment and the usage of the commodities given as interest were used in the cultic rite of ritual ablutions to the Dakṣiṇamēruviṭaṅkar and the way in which the two, i.e. Rājarajēśvara and Dakṣiṇamēruviṭaṅkar are mentioned separately definitely precludes their being the one and same icon.

Stein has analysed the socio-political and economic role of the temple in Cōḻa and Vijayanagara time in several works.[75] His main contention is that the Cōḻa state was not a centralized state and lacked the necessary bureaucratic apparatus to control the peripheral regions. Thus the 'sacral' or 'ritual' kingship was made to function through several nuclear institutions such as the temples, the *ūr*, the *sabhā*, the *nāṭu*, the *periyanāṭu* etc.[76]

He distinguishes, however, between the central power of the Cōḻas which extended around Thañjāvūr and the Cōḻamaṇḍalam area from the peripheral region. The power of the centre must have operated in decreasing intensity corresponding to the distance from the capital.

Temples endowed by monarchs like Rājarāja undertook cultivation of arable land either directly or indirectly as financiers and opened up virgin lands for cultivation, participated in animal husbandry again—both by direct and indirect means, and the king, as observed by Spencer, "expanded the regulatory activities of royal adminstration through the auditing of temple accounts".[77]

Rājarāja I gave a definitive direction under his royal initative to the temple and his edicts laid the normative standards for temple state relationships. As we have seen, both money and livestock passed through the hands of the temple to villagers and shepherds in return for specified perpetual services and thereby a continuous link was maintained.[78] Villages gave to the court and the court gave to the Villages "a share in the plunder of neighbouring Kings"[79] through the medium of the temple. The transactions were clearly marked by a three-way traffic. Thus a vested interest group was evolved which had all to gain by keeping king, court and temple.

The Āgamic concept of a deity rooted to a spot and the territoriality of most of the village deities provided the necessary doctrinal and traditional backing without which the very *raison d'etre* was lost. The Āgamic rituals which were continuously enlarged by the endowing monarchs added to the sense of awe and grandeur. Since a sense of great antiquity and a feeling of revelation of the deity's presence at particular spot was central to the religious texture of 'locohenotheism', Rājarāja embarked on the venture of importing antiquity from Tiruvārūr and a sense of the sacrosanct from Chidambaram in building his state cult in Thañjāvūr. He had overlooked the essential quality of religious mystique and the colossal concept somehow failed to survive the monarch. The feeling was most pithily expressed by the present *Kurukkaḷ* at the Tyāgarāja shrine at Thañjāvūr who said, when asked about the Viṭaṅka tradition, that Thañjāvūr temple being *merely* a royal temple had no particular divine credentials[80] for Tamiḻ Śaivism. Today the architectural marvel is maintained by the Archaeological Department. Ritually it has none of the religious essence of Chidambaram, Madurai or Rāmēśvaram for the Śaiva mind.

While this does seem to provide a logical explanation for the decline in the sanctity of Thañjāvūr, the same reasoning does not hold good for the decline of Tiruvārūr with it's hoary antiquity. The reasons there were more temporal. On the pragmatic level it seems that the Thañjāvūr temple too declined because Rājēndra I, presumably to vie with his father in his quest for glory, abandoned this as his state temple and created his own vision of the magnificent at Kaṅkaikoṅṭacōḻapuram (Gaṅgaikoṇṭacōḻapuram).

Rājēndra I and the State Cult

Nagaswamy in his monograph, *Gaṅgaikoṇḍacōḻapuram*, has pointed out several interesting facts about the foundation of this royal city. It was "unheard of even as a village when Rājēndra I came to the throne".[81] The author then muses over the question as to why, despite the fact that Thañjāvūr served the military and administrative purpose of the Cōḻas admirably, Rājēndra I within a few years of the erection of the Bṛhadīśvara temple and the death of his father shifted his capital to Gaṅgaikoṇḍacōḻapuram. He suggests, rather half–heartedly, that it could be simply a question of an auspicious site. There seems to be, however, something more than the personal idiosyncracy of a king or his megalomania. A close parallel that comes to mind is that of the Khmer kings who constantly changed their cpaitals and built new royal capitals to signify the change. For them it was a means of opening up new lands and establishing new lines of communication.[82] The royal temples were the central foci of the regions in which they were situated and thus the creation of a new temple presented great economic and social possibilities. Even in more recent times examples of such expansion are not wanting. The prime minister of Mysore state made a deliberate decision to expand the Cāmuṇḍeśvarī temple and add a new dimension to the cult in order to attract more pilgrims and thereby give a fillip to the rather sluggish economy of the region.[83] Another example is that of the popularization of Śabarimalai by the rulers of Travancore. They were aided in this by the political conditions of the times when Justice Party leaders like P.T. Rajan decided Aiyappaṉ to be a symbol of their brand of egalitarianism and non-casteism.

Following the above analogies it seems likely that Rājēndra in building Gaṅgaikoṇṭacōḻapuram decided to open up peripheral areas in order to integrate them with the central system. What is an enigma however is that he should have transferred most of the lands donated to the Thañjāvūr temple by Rājarāja to his new state temple within twenty-five years of the original gift. It seems that Rājendra wanted to start his own state cult and also break away from the power of the ritual personnel entrenched in Thañjāvūr. A new royal emblem was needed to make his brand of the royal cult visible. This temple like many others bore the name of its imperial patron, for one of Rājendra's epithets was Gaṅkaikoṇṭa and inscriptions from the temple give great prominence to his conquest of pūrvadeśa, *kaṅkai* and Kaṭāram (*pūrvadēcamum kaṅkaiyum, kaṭāramum Koṇṭaruḷiṉa ayyar*).[84]

With the death of Rājendra this temple too lost the status of being the 'main' attraction and others such as Tribhuvanam detracted the attention of the people and with the fall of the Cōḻas the Gaṅgaikoṇṭacōḻapuram temple lost its royal character, though the Pāṇḍyan king, Jaṭāvarmaṉ Cuntara Paṇṭiyaṉ, who overthrew the Cōḻas made his 'sacral' presence felf thereby establishing a special rite called Cuntarapāṇṭiyaṉ canti after his name. The inscription tells us that this was to be a daily rite for the regular performance of which the new king endowed the temple with lands.[85]

The Somāskanda at Gaṅgaikoṇṭacōḻapuram is, according to Nagaswamy, by far the largest bronze icon in a South Indian temple. The main icon here as in Thañjāvūr was called Bṛhadīśvara. That Rājendra was commemorating his great victory in Northern India by establishing this temple is obvious. A quaint inscription from a dilapidated *maṇṭapa* in the Gaṅgaikoṇṭa temple states that "the Cōḻa king was amazed on beholding the lime fruit which had been placed in the Ganges at Benaras floating here in the lion well" (*Vārāṇaciyil Kaṅkaiyōrattil akappaṭṭu irunta elumiccam paḻam. . .*).[86]

The whole idea of celebrating the bringing of the waters of the river Ganges was symbolic and was a gesture to show that he had taken his rightful place among the kings of Āryāvarta as well. This is a classic example of 'horizontal legitimation' - the culmination of a process begun in the age of the Pallavas and the *nāyaṉmār*.

To sum up the argument, Rājarāja and Rājēndra had installed the cult of the Tyāgarāja in their respective state temples. Rājarāja had richly endowed the Viṭaṅka form of Tyāgarāja called the Dakṣiṇamēruviṭaṅkar and Rājēndra had built a separate shrine for a huge Somāskanda.

Vīracōḻaṉukkār

The Tyāgarāja cult of Tiruvārūr seems to have assumed a focal position in the Cōḻa times as a royal cult only from the time of Rājarāja I when it was transported to the Great Temple at Thañjāvūr. However, a class of people known as Vīracōḻaṉukkār seem to have been very important in the Tyāgarāja temples. The earliest occurrence of this expression is from an inscription in the Tyāgarāja temple at Vēdāraṇyam belonging to the period of Parāntaka I and dated in years corresponding to 936-37 A.D. Vīracōḻaṉukkār occurs as the name of a regiment in the Thañjāvūr inscription of Rājarāja I (*SII* Vol. II, 66). At Tiruvārūr Tyāgarāja (Vītiviṭaṅkar) himself honours a playwright who is said to have written a drama entitled *Vīracōḻanukkavijayam*. Thus this regiment seems to have been associated with a king bearing the epithet Vīracōḻa. The fact that Vītiviṭaṅkar himself confers the honour is significant. The class of edicts in which the deity himself speaks will be taken up for discussion further on. Thus, the Tyāgarāja cult was presumably connected with a regiment of soldiers as well, which leads us to the myth of Mucukuntaṉ and the nine *vīras* who claim to have brought the Tyāgarāja to earth. The myth and its resuscitation by Oṭṭakkūttar will be discussed in connection with the political crisis and the later Cōḻa monarchy. The term Vīracōḻanukkār continues to occur in an epigraph from Vēdāraṇyam of the time of Kulōttuṅga III (446 of *SII, XVII*).

Rājēndra I and Tyāgarāja

Rājendra too, like other Cōḻa emperors, continued to patronize several shrines though he reserved his special munificence for his state temple. Rājendra I made special gifts to the Vītiviṭaṅka of Tiruvārūr for bathing the deity with scented water on his father's birthday as well as on his own (674 of *ARE* 1919). The images of Rājendra I and his lady friend, Paravai Aṉukkiyār, were set up in the temple and offerings were made to them (679 of *ARE* 1919). Naṅkai Paravai (Paravai Aṉukkiyār) donated twenty thousand six hundred and forty-three kaḻañju of gold to gild the *Śikhara.* She also plated the doors of the shrine and the pillars of the *maṇṭapa* for which she further contributed forty two thousand *palams* of copper (680 of ARE 1919). Considering the value of land at that period of time, says Ponnusamy, this donation of gold and copper for purposes of gilding various parts of the shrine was equal in value to several villages put together.[87] Not content with these generous endowments, the lady also gave twenty-eight huge brass lamps which weighed fifteen thousand five hundred and seventy-nine *palams* in total, built a *maṇṭapam* and called it after her royal paramour Rājēndracōḻan maṇṭapam (679 of *ARE* 1919). She was also responsible for converting the brick structure of Tyāgarāja shrine into stone just as Cempiyaṉ Mahādēvī had converted the Aṟaneṟi shrine in the same temple complex. Paravai installed two images and donated a large number of gold, pearl, ruby and diamond ornaments. Ponnusamy has pointed out how her munificence far exceeded that of any individual donor inculding the large land donations of Kulōttunga II.[88]

It was during the reign of Rājādhirāja I that regular offerings were made to the images of Rājendra and Paravai (679 of *ARE* 1919). The Paravai Īśvarmuṭaiyār temple at Paravaiyāvaram also records the fact that offerings were made to the two above-mentioned images (320 of *ARE* 1917).

The fact that the lady's name was Paravai and that she was a dancing girl and a royal favourite all point to the fact that she was a *tēvaraṭiyār* of Tyāgarāja and presumably belonged to the family of Paravainācciyār, the first wife of Cuntaramūrti Nāyaṉār. Icons of Cuntaramūrti and Paravai are placed directly facing the Tyāgarāja image both at Tiruvārūr and Thañjāvūr.[89] There are several images of Cuntarar and Paravai which belong to this period, the most beautiful ones are those from the temple at Chidambaram and the bronze from Tiruvālaṅkāṭu, now in the Tanjore Art gallery.

An inscription of Kulōttuṅga II records the installation of an image of Cuntarar and another of Paravai (269 of 1901, 485 of *SII* VII) and states that worship was offered to both of them. That Rājendra I and Paravai were both devotees of Tyāgarāja is clear from the very rich endownments made by Rājendracōḻa to the deity Vītiviṭaṅkar (680 of 1919) and even more so by the incident related in the aforementioned epigraph wherein we are told that in the 20th year of Rājendra the monarch and his lady arrived in a chariot at the temple and offered their worship at the Tyāgarāja shrine. The spot where the two devotees stood was regarded as very special and a brass lamp was set up at that very spot to commemorate the royal visit. Thus the Tyāgagarāja which had evolved as a cult in Tiruvārūr was patronized presumably by Parāntaka I and certainly by Rājarāja I and Rājendra I.

Rājendra I also built another shrine to Tyāgarāja at Tiruvoṟṟiyūr at the request of Caturānana Paṇḍita. The deity installed here went by the name of Kāraṇai Viṭaṅkar, Kāraṇai being the name of a village (165 of 1912),[90] presumably another name of Tiruvoṟṟiyūr itself. It is significant to note that he built both the Tyāgarāja shrines in stone, one at Tiruvārūr and another at Tiruvoṟṟiyūr for these two were sites intimately connected with the life of Cuntarar.

An image by the name of Cōḻarāja (Pl.XIX) is used in worship at Tiruvārūr to this day. It belongs to the Cōḻa school of art and is a beautiful 11th century bronze image and could stylistically well belong to the Rājēndra period. Candraśēkhara kurukkaḷ of the Tiruvārūr temple recounted how Vijayadaśamī was celebrated in the Tiruvārūr temple till recently.[91] The *Tēvaraṭiyār* from *Konṭi vamcam* spread the cloth through the *prākāra*. The Cōḻa Mahārāja image was taken out in procession very early in the morning between 4 and 6 a.m. The auspiciousness of this early hour is related to the Mahābhārata story wherein it is said that the Pañca pāṇdavas had hidden their weapons and were desperately trying to find them. It was at this early hour of dawn that they finally succeeded in finding them. Vijayadaśamī is an enactment of the theme of the *Mahābhārata* war as well as the successful slaying of the bull faced demon Mahiṣa by Mahiṣāsuramardinī. It is in fact symbolic of royal and divine victory.

The two-armed image of the Cōḻarāja which is portrayed in the posture of carrying a bow and ready to pick an arrow from the quiver, takes part in a mimic tableau in which the arrow is shot and it is believed to drop at Kiṭāraṅkoṇṭāṉ. Kiṭāraṅkoṇṭāṉ was presumably the ancient boundary of Tiruvārūr. The extent of Tiruvārūr is traditionally described as *pañcakrōśa* (1 *krosa* = 10 miles) and the traditional extent presumably of the *kūṟṟam* or *nāṭu* was 50 miles. The tank, the courtyard, etc., of the temple are each believed to be 5 *vēḷis* respectively, a reference to which is made by Appar. Thus the procession of the Cōḻamahārāja is brought to the ancient boundary of the city and banana trees are planted and a cloth is tied to the old trees and a trunk is felled and taken back to the temple. The felled tree or *kaṭimaram* is an ancient symbol of both the king and the territoriality of the realm, and it is interesting to see this idea expressed in ritual. In *ARE* 1924-25, Pt. I, p. 81 a reference is made to another bronze image of Cōḻarāja with the legend "Rājarājacōḻa of the big temple"[92] in modern Tamiḻ characters inscribed on its pedestal. This is a genuine Cōḻa image though the inscription is modern.

The *pañcakrōśa* concept could well be a 'sacral' motif for Vārāṇasī is believed to be *pañcakrōśa* and Tīruvārūr's claim to be the same may be based on imitation of this motif and not necessarily reflect the extent of the city.

That Rājarāja's image along with that of his chief queen was installed in the Thañjāvūr temple is recorded in an epigraph from the temple. His sister installed the images of her parents and the Rājaguru Īśānaśiva Paṇḍita set up his own image.[93] The royal, the powerful and the divine were thus housed under one roof much in the spirit of the tombstones of famous men in the churches of Europe, a custom believed to have originated with the Crusades. In Thañjāvūr too the Cōḻamahārāja image was used as an *utasavamūrti* leading religious processions. The Tiruvārūr icon of Rājarāja is today housed along with the *utsavaberas* but in a special *maṇṭapa*. Rājendra and Paravai are in a small shrine near the Hāṭakēśvara. The Larger Leyden Grant captures this royalty—divinity mood with its benediction "As long as Śiva and Devī are together in Kailāsa and as long as Hari is in *yoganidrā* on the serpent couch, as long as the sole luminary (i.e., Sun) dispels universal darkness. . .so long may the Cōḻa lineage protect the whole world".

The Cōḻa Connection in the other Saptaviṭaṅka Kṣētras

Six temples, apart from Tiruvārūr are, as seen in chapter III, grouped together as *saptaviṭaṅka kṣetras*. Others like Tiruvoṟṟiyūr are linked with them through *sthalapurāṇas* or pilgrim literature and hagiographies of the *nāyaṉmār*. A brief look at the epigraphical data available on some of these temples and others with Tyāgarāja-Viṭaṅka associations would help to show how the Viṭaṅka tradition gained particular momentum under Rājarāja I and Rājendra. The epigraphs record the time when these temples were either originally built or converted into stone shrines.

The concept of Tyāgarāja of Tiruvārūr was, as seen earlier, brought to Thañjāvūr by Rājarāja I. His chief queen built her own temple at Tiruvaiyāṟu and had the *Viṭaṅkar* image enshrined. An inscription of the 24th year of Rājarāja I records elaborate gifts made by the queen to Lōka Mahādēvīśvarar (the main icon) and the *Ulōka Vītiviṭaṅka tēvar*, the processional icon. It is interesting that the presiding deity is called Lōkamahādēvīśvarar (the Lord of Lōkamahādēvī) for Lōkamahādēvī is the name of the queen. She bears the epithet Taṇṭi Śakti Viṭaṅki as well (*SII* Vol. V. No. 521). This was the queen's temple in much the same manner as the Rājarājeśvarar was the King's temple. The state cult was expanding in clusters of temples connected through a religious network.[94]

Of the Saptaviṭaṅka shrines Nākappaṭṭaṇam has a number of epigraphs of the time of Rājarāja I, Rājēndra I, Rājarāja II and Kulōttuṅga III. Rājendra I donated jewels to Nāgai aḻakar[95] (who seems to be identical with Nākai Viṭaṅkar for *aḻakar* and *Viṭaṅkar* share the same meaning of the beautiful (vide infra ch.II).

The present shrine of Tyāgarāja seems to have been erected somewhere in Kulōttuṅga III's time when we also note a reference to Aḻakaviṭaṅkapperumāḷ (*ARE 150 of 1956-57*). An interesting feature to note is that behind the *liṅga* of Kāyārohaṇa there is a sculpture of Somāskanda surrounded by *ṛṣis* or sages, reminiscent of the arrangement in Pallave temples. Balasubramanyan traces a parallel at the Vijayālaya Cōḻīśvaram temple at Vikkaṇampūṇṭi and Tiruvīḻimiḻalai.[96] The Viṭaṅkar shrine there is to the south of the main shrine.

Tirukkāṟavācal (Tirukkāṟāyil) supplied dancers and women workers to Rājarājēśvaram. A few Rājarāja epigraphs have come to light. (*451, 453, 414 of 1908*).

Tirunaḷḷāṟu inscriptions take us to the time of Rājendra I for an epigraph of Rājādhirāja I refers to gifts of his father to the temple. In the north-west of the second *prākāra* there is a shrine of Tyāgarāja possibly of the later Cōḻa period for the inscriptions are of the time of Rājendra III. There is a Viṣṇu temple in the courtyard, north-west of the Śiva temple.[97]

Tirukkuvaḷai has inscriptions from Rājendra I's time, and there seems to have been a close connection between this and Tirumaṟaikkāṭu or Vedāraṇyam.

A chief named Tirumaṟaikkāṭṭuṭaiyāṉ stops flooding of the village and receives temple *mariyātai* during the Pāṇḍyan rule (265 of 1950-51).

Tiruvāymūr has late Cōḻa and Pāṇḍyan inscriptions starting from Kulōttuṅga II though the beautiful Somāskanda bronze seems to be an early Cōḻa piece.[98]

Tirumaṟaikkāṭu or Vedāraṇyam has inscriptions from Parāntaka I's reign though the Rājakēsarivarman inscriptions have been assigned to Āditya I by S.R. Balasubramanian.[99] There is a Rājarāja(I)(?) record from the Tyāgarāja temple here.

Thus, most of the extant Tyāgarāja shrines built of stone seem to be from the time of Rājarāja or Rājēndra I. However, these shrines must have existed earlier, presumably constructed of more easily perishable material. Such a conclusion is warranted by the fact that Tēvāram saints have sung the glory of the deities enshrined in these places. They became state sponsored 'official' pilgrim sites from the 10th and 11th centuries A.D. Following upon the models of Tiruvārūr and Thañjāvūr, several temples added a Tyāgarāja shrine. The tradition of grouping them together as *saptaviṭaṅka* is possibly to be traced to the post-Rājēndra period. Dhaky's statement (vide infra chapter II, footnote 4) that the Tyāgarāja shrines belong to phase III of Cōḻa Art seems to be assigning it a slightly later date than is warranted by epigraphic evidence. Phase II (from late 10th and early 11th century) seems more likely.

The Later Cōḻas and the Revival of Tyāgarāja Myths

In chapter III, the origin-myth of the Tyāgarāja was traced only from the point of view of studying the development of ideas that culminated in the Mucukuntaṉ myth. The aim of this section is to see the manner in which myths occur in 12th century literature and epigraphs and are used for political ends. The works to be discussed inculde *Īṭṭiyeḻupatu, Caṅkaracōḻanulā, Periya Purāṇam* and *Tiyākarājalīlaikaḷ*.

Ottakkūttan is believed to be the author of both the *Īṭṭiyeḻupatu* and *Cankaracōḻaṉula*.[100] He was the court poet of Vikramacōḻa, Rājarāja II and Kulōttuṅga II. Epigraphs of Vikramacōḻa, Rājarāja II and Kulōttuṅga II also shed light on the relationship between the Cōḻa monarchy and the Tyāgarāja cult.

Here it must be remembered that the later Cōḻas, several of whom are called Kulōttuṅga or the Star of the lineage , had only partial claim to Cōḻa lineage. As mentioned earlier Kulōttuṅga I was a Cōḻa only from his maternal side, his father being a Cālukya. His mother, maternal grandmother and wife were Cōḻa princesses. He was brought up in Gaṅgaikoṇḍacōḻapuram and it is all these facts that provided him some legitimacy when he ascended the Cōḻa throne in the very end of the 11th century after Rājendra's son met with a premature end.

In the history of the later Cōḻas beginning with Vikramacōḻa, (1118-35), the successor of Kulōttuṅga I, several interesting phenomena begin to appear. Firstly, there is an unusual epigraph which describes in elaborate details an ancient myth - the Maṉunīti myth - to be presently discussed. It then establishes the "historicity" of the myth by making a certain person the descendant of Maṉunīti's chief minister and endows this descendant with land. Two other inscriptions dated in the regnal years of this monarch portray the deity Vītiviṭaṅkaṉ making grants. The deity, as the ruler, issues edicts in the first person. Thirdly, an inscription from Pallavarāyaṉpēṭṭai recounts some problems regarding the heir to the throne; a grandson of Vikramacōḻa is *chosen* as king and the same process is repeated before Rājādhirāja II is *chosen* to become king. With natural succession broken twice, the need to legitimize the rule of two kings Kulōttuṅga II and Rājādhirāja II was immediate and urgent.

When we juxtapose the above information drawn from epigraphs with the series of myths woven around members of the royal family who were real historical personages, several problems of chronology and identification present themselves. The myths of significance in this connection revolve around a Caṅkaracōḻan (alias Caṅkara cēvakaṉ), son of Caṅkamahārāja, who was himself never crowned but acted as indispensable helper to the throne. A 12th century epigraph refers mysteriously to an anonymous *prāṇa upakārī* - a 'life saver'. It stands to reason to equate the two.

Again during the rule of Rājarāja II in the middle of the 12th century a succession problem seems to have arisen. The two princes of the king seem to have been in mortal danger. These princes, aged one and two, were rescued and kept alive by a certain Pallavarāyaṉ Perunampi and one of them was finally anointed king and became Rājādhirāja II (1163/66- 1179/82), while nothing is known of the other brother. This brother could well be the "life-saver" who helped him and is by inference compared in the Maṉunīti epigraph to the minister of Maṉunīti, famed for his loyalty. It is the period when the deity "speaks" and issues edicts on its own name.

The minister of Rājarāja II plays an important part in protecting the princes and fighting in the Pāṇḍyan civil war on behalf of the Cōḻa candidate. In fact he is succeeded, presumably by a close relative who continues the work of protecting the Cōḻa monarchy. Thus the oft repeated legends of the uncrowned father Caṅkamahārāja and his uncrowned son Caṅkaracōḻan were most probably based on these troubled times and it would be interesting to try and fathom some of the mysteries. Before entering into a serious discussion on the characters in the myths and trying to fit them into the historical situation, a brief look into the background of the political history of the later Cōḻas may not be out of context, as it is essential for understanding some of the complexities of the problem. The following chart gives the genealogy of the 'Cālukya-Cōḻas', i.e., beginning from Kulōttuṅga I who ascended the Cōḻa throne by virtue of his mother being a Cōḻa princess. His mother Ammaṅkatēvi was the daughter of Rājēndra I. His father was an Eastern Cālukya prince. Thus his succession was "irregular" and could well have been considered as usurpation in certain sectors.

1. Kukōttuṅga I (1071-1122) (Rājakesarī)
2. Vikrama Cōḻa (1118-1135) (Parakēsarī)
(Maṉunīti myth expounded)

3 Kulōttuṅga II*
called Etirilāpperumāḷ — A daughter or son
or Etirilipperumāḷ — Niṟaiyuṭaiyapperumāṉ
(Presumably *chosen*, not natural heir)

4 Rājarāja II 5.
(Parakesarī) (1146-1173)
(His prime minister protects the two princes)

5. Rājādhirāja II *
(1163/66-79-82)
(Rājakesarī)

6. Kulōttuṅga III (1178-1217/18)
(Parakesarī)

7 Rājarāja III (1216-60)
(Rājakesarī)

8 Rājendra III (1246-79)

The two asterisks represent breaks in the natural line of succession.These two monarchs seem to have been *chosen*.

The relationship between Rājādhirāja II and Kulōttuṅga III is also not clear.

A Brief Outline of Later Cōḻa History

With Rājendra I's death the Cōḻa empire had to contend with repeated wars with Lankā (present day Śrī Lankā) and also with the Cāḷukyas. Added to it all, the Cōḻa king Rājādhirāja I (1018-54), successor of Rājendra I (1012-44) died in battle. His brother Rājendra II (1052-64) was crowned on the battlefield. Another brother Vīrarājendra continued the battle and fought with the Cāḷukyas, Gaṅgas, Nolambas, Kāṭavas and Vaidumbas. Several relatives, friends and regional chiefs are mentioned in his records.

Corresponding to the political problems, one hears of lavish gifts to Chidambaram temple and equally lavish munificence to Brāhmaṇas. The attempts at consolidating power bases are evident. Rājendra II's son and successor Adhirājendra (1067/68-1071) was killed by rebels. He was the last in the direct line and was succeeded by the Cōḻa-Cāḷukya line as seen in the chart above. This change was a watershed in Cōḻa history.

A prophecy in *Divyasūricaritra* , which is the Vaiṣṇava counterpart of the *Periya Purāṇam* states that the Cōḻa dynasty would end because of its persecution of the Vaiṣṇava philosopher

Rāmānuja. Kulōttuṅga II is known to have persecuted the Vaiṣṇavas. The above work further attributes the fall of the Cōḻas to a curse pronounced by God Śiva of Tiruvārūr[101]. This shows that in spite of frequent changes of capital the Tyāgarāja of Tiruvārūr was somehow connected with the Cōḻa territory and the ruling family in a special manner. It also provides an indirect evidence to the persistent rumour that the Tiruvārūr temple complex had a Viṣṇu icon within it which was in fact housed in the rectangular *grabhagṛha,* blocked for centuries. For as we have seen in chapter 2 the present location of the main focal points of worship in the temple, the Valmīkanātha (a *liṅga*) and the Tyāgarāja are not strictly speaking housed in the *grabhagṛha.* The tower or *vimāna* does not rise over it but over the rectangular room. The water chute is also connected to the rectangular room and there is a reference in epigraph to ritual personnel belonging to the Viṣṇu temple. The myth of Tyāgarāja has a strong Vaiṣṇava base.

Works like *Vikramāṅkadēvacarita* of Bilhaṇa portray a state of chaos and allude to Kulōttuṅga I at least indirectly as an usurper.[102] While Cōḻa sources agree with the description of the chaotic conditions, they regard Kulōttuṅga as the redeemer. Added to internal dissensions there were constant problems with Lankā. The period could do with legitimising myths and the Hiraṇyavarman myth of Chidambaram, as stated by Kulke was in all probability a deified biography of Kulōttuṅga I.[103]

The important event in the reigns of Kulōttuṅga I and Vikramacōḻa was the Kaliṅga war against Anantavarman Cōḍagaṅga. This event and its hero, the general Karuṇākara Toṇṭaimāṉ have formed the subject matter of Cayaṅkoṇṭāṉ's *Kaliṅkattupparaṇi.*

Vikramacōḻa's reign is important in connection with the Tyāgarāja cult from several points of view. Firstly, his court poet Oṭṭakkūttaṉ while discussing the Mucukuntaṉ myth, refers to floods, submarine fire and utter chaos and the Cōḻa king is forced to go to heaven and bring damsels from heaven and set up a *new* empire (emphasis mine). This description seems to be an allegorical reflection of the political state of affairs in the Cōḻa dominions on the eve of Kulōttuṅga's accession and during the reign of Vikramacōḻa. A break and a new ruler, claiming the right to the throne because of his mother and wife being Cōḻa princesses is reflected in the *Īṭṭiyeḻupatu* myths of Tyāgarāja being brought to earth by a king who married a heavenly damsel and brought back several *damsels* to the earth and set up a *new* empire. The floods and famine are historical events that took place in Vikramacōḻa's reign.[104]

This period covering the reigns of Kulōttuṅga I to Kulōttuṅga III, i.e. 11th - 13th centuries A.D. was a period of myth-making to legitimize Cōḻa rule. While floods and wars raged, Vikramacōḻa was desperately appeasing the deities Naṭarāja[105] and Tyāgarāja. In one of his inscriptions he claims to have "covered with fine gold the enclosures ......where his family god practises the *tāṇṭavam*".[106]

Two inscriptions of the time of this monarch (579 and 583 of *SII* XXIII) register grants of *agrahāras* made for securing strength of arms to the king, made by his feudatories, the Telegu Cōḻa chiefs, Beṭṭarāssa and Poṭṭāpicōḻa. It is interesting that peaceful *Agrahāras* (Brāhmaṇa settlements) were created for securing strength. It defines the notion of 'incorporative' or 'sacred' kingship and clearly states the process of legitimation and consolidation of power.

Vikramacōḻa's rule was marked by the rise of a number of regional chiefs called *'maṇṭalikas'*. The most important one was Karuṇākara Toṇṭaimāṉ, but there were others and inscriptions provide a long and impressive list. These chiefs were 'incorporated' into Cōḻa kingship. Vikrama's relationship with Tiruvārūr temple will have to be seen in this political context.

His successor, Kulōttuṅga II seems to have had his share of problems. First and foremost there seems to have been a problem of succession to the throne and secondly problems with the Vaiṣṇavas.[107] The two seem to have been linked. He had close ties with Tiruvārūr. His rule is important as he was the greatest patron of the Śaiva faith and exhibited a fanatical zeal in spreading it. [108] He was the patron of the poet Cēkkiḻār[109] and a devotee of Tyāgarāja.[110]

Under Rājarāja II (1146-73) feudatories were becoming increasingly powerful. His successor, Rājādhirāja II (1163/66-1179/82) was embroiled in a Pāṇḍyan civil war, complicated further by Laṅkan involvement in the struggle. Comparable to the heroic loyalty of Karuṇākara Toṇṭaimāṉ and others in the Kaliṅga war, a certain Pallavarāyaṉ emerges as the loyal general of the Cōḻa monarchy at this stage. The General seems to have been very powerful, almost a kind of 'kingmaker'. Pallavarāyars, Kāṭavarāyars, Campuvarāyars (Śambhuvarāyars) and others were almost semi-independent feudatories during this period. The close link between politics and Śaivism can be noticed when the Ceylonese General is described as a 'Śivadrohin' (a traitor against Śiva) and the war, it is claimed was won "through the prayers, sacrifice and worship of Svāmidēvar or Umāpatidēvar".[111]

N. Subramanian characterizes the history of the Cōḻa period from the time of Vikramacōḻa as marked by "increase in the number of hereditary chieftaincies", which led to the "drama of disintegreation".[112]

Kulōttuṅga III continued the prolonged war with the Pāṇḍyans and defeated the Koṅkus and occupied Karūr, an event given great prominence in his inscriptions. A city called Karūr figured prominently in the account of Cōḻa kings of the Caṅkam period but that Karūr was presumably the city by that name near Tirucciṟāppaḷḷi, much further north. However, famine, Pāṇḍyan invasion and increased power of feudatories could not be checked and around 1279 A.D. after Rājendra III, the Cōḻas succumbed to Pāṇḍyan pressure and became a part of their empire.

Rājarāja II and Kulōttuṅga III

Rājarāja II, the successor of Kulōttuṅga II and his successor Kulōttuṅga III continued the Cōḻa tradition and built their own state temples at Tārācuram (mod.Dārāsuram) around 1150 A.D. (with the icon named after himself) and Tiruppuvaṉam, (Tribhuvanam, completed in the year 1212 A.D.) respectively, the place and the icon being named after his epithet meaning "conqueror of the three worlds".

The Succession Issue

A name of great importance in the succession issue seems to be that of a certain Pallavarāyaṉ. He is referred to in the Pallavarāyaṉpēṭṭai inscription[113] and in four inscriptions from Tiruvārūr, i.e. 582, 583, 585 and 587 of *SII*, Vol. XVII, belonging to the reigns of Rājādhirāja II and Kulōttuṅga III.

The donor in each of these cases is a Paḷaiyanūruṭaiyāṉ Vētavaṉamuṭaiyāṉ Ammaiyappaṉ, alias Rājarāja Viḻuppaṟaiyaṉ. He assumes the additional title of Pallavarāyaṉ in inscription nos.

585 and 587 referred to above. He describes the queens of Rājādhirāja and one of them is described as a Yādava, i.e. of Hoysāla stock, and this information is corroborated by the *Kulōttuṅkacōḻaṉulā*.[114] The inscription under discussion further states that she ruled from the ancillary capitals[115] of Uṟaiyūr, Pērūrākai and Maturāpuri, a rather unusual tradition in Cōḻa history.

Venkatasubba Ayyar edited the Pallavarāyaṉpeṭṭai inscription (*ARE* 433 of 1924 in *E.I.XXI.*). This is closely related to the above epigraphs in content. Nilakantha Sastri and T.N. Subramanian analysed it in *E.I.* XXXI (pp. 223-228). Another study under rather esoteric circumstances was undertaken by N. Sethuraman.[116] Rājādhirāja II's accesion and the circumstances under which he ascended the throne form the main subject matter of this inscription.

The Pallavarāyaṉ mentioned in this inscription is said to have crowned Rājādhirāja II, the son of Rājarāja II. It states that two princes of Rājarāja II, aged one and two years were in some danger and were kept hidden by Pallavarāyaṉ. The queens were also protected by this General, who is referred to in this and several other inscriptions such as the Aṟappākkam inscription (20 of *ARE* 1899 and 465 of 1905) as having been the successful military leader against the Paṇḍyaṇs and the Ceylonese. Thus he seems to have been in many ways the protector of the Cōḻa monarchy in critical times.

The Pallavarāyaṉpēṭṭai inscription states that Rājarāja II had no one fit to succeed him and so he appointed a successor, i.e. Rājādhirāja II. A council was called to approve this arrangement. At this point the inscription introduces, like a flashback in movies, a parallel situation in the past in Cōḻa history, presumably to justify this appointment by citing a precedent. Subramaniaṉ and Sastri have analysed this section and come to conclusions at variance with those of Sethuraman.

The parallel situation described in the inscription is said to have arisen in the reign of Vikaramacōḻa, when the monarch, realizing that there was no one fit to succeed him, appointed his grandson, Etirilāpperumāḷ, the son of Neṟiyuṭaiyapperumāḷ. Pallavarāyaṉ, convinced of the proper precedent, anointed Rājādhirāja II as the new king. Sastri and Subramanian thus read two breaks in succession. Sethuraman believes that the portion regarding Vikramacōḻa has been misread and that there is only one break. From the transcript (*EI* Vol. XXXI) it seems that there were certainly *two* such incidents.

Sastri and Subramanian then very soundly argue the reasons why this Etirilāpperumāl, the successor of Vikramacōḻa, should be identified with Kulōttuṅga II. For details, I refer the reader to their ariticle, but what is of interest in this context is that Kulōttuṅga II also traces his lineage to the Hoysālas and from the above interpretation of Sastri and Subramanian it appears that one of Kulōttuṅga I's wives was a Hoysāla princess. The fact that the Hoysāla princesses are mentioned with such regularity makes them an important political factor. What is of relevance here is that Kulōttuṅga I, Kulōttuṅga II and Rājādhirāja II were all in need of legitimization of their powers as they do not seem to have been natural successors to the Cōḻa monarchy.

Thus two characters remain a mystery in this whole sequence of events. Why does the Pallavarāyaṉpēṭṭai inscription mention *two* sons aged one and two ? One became Rājādhirāja II, but what happend to the other one ? The second question is who was the father of Etirilāpperumāḷ ? His grandfather was Vikramacōḻa. He is described as the son of Neṟiyutaipperumāṉ, but what happened to this person ? Subramanian and Sastri regard this person to be a woman and the daughter of Vikramacōḻa.

In the world of Tamiḻ myths there is an uncrowned and saintly man called Caṅkaracōḻan or Caṅkara-cēvakaṉ who helps the Cōḻa rule and prays to Tyāgarāja to come and assume the mantle of government to tide over the problems and the deity agrees. Thus this uncrowned hero is very important in legitimizing the monarchy at a moment of crisis. This is told in the *Tiyākarājalīlaikaḷ* of *Mīnātcicuntaram Piḷḷai* (*Līlai I* vv. 3-31, pp. 77-81 and *Līlai 3*). He is one of the sons of Caṅkama Mahārāja who was also not crowned.

Caṅkama Mahārāja is referred to in *Kulōttuṅkakkōvai* and one of his sons is called Caṅkaracōḻan. The *Caṅkaracōḻaṉulā*, a work attributed to Oṭṭakkūttaṉ[117] also refers to Caṅkaracōḻan. In the *Viṉāyakarkāppu* v. 272 of this work it is stated that the *ulā* is composed on the Tamiḻ hero Caṅkaracōḻa Cēvakaṉ. This work has been published contrary to Zvelebil's statement that the work was never found.[118] It describes the Cōḻa genealogy (both legendary and historical) and accords with the genealogy given in the *Vikramacōḻaṉulā* of Oṭṭakkūttaṉ until the time of Kulōttuṅga

II.[119] After this there is a discrepancy. *Caṅkaracōlaṉulā* refers to Caṅkama Mahārāja and his three sons Nallamāṉ (v.32) Kumāra Kulōttuṅga (referred to as Kumāra Makītaraṉ in v. 37, who was crowned) and Caṅkaracōlan, (*Kāppu* 272), also called Caṅkara rācaṉ (v. 38, 115) and Caṅkara Vēntaṉ (v.114) and simply as Caṅkaraṉ (v. 235, 337 & 338) who was not crowned but was a great helper. This Caṅkaracōlan must have been after Rājarāja II for v. 26 refers to Rājarāja II and the story of Caṅkaracōlan appears after that.[120]

Kumāra Makītaraṉ (Sanskrit Mahīdhara) referred to above has been identified with Kulōttuṅga III (1178-1218). That Kulōttuṅga III was the son of Caṅkamaṉ and brother of Kumāra Kulōttuṅgaṉ is corroborated by *Kulōttuṅkaṉkōvai* (cited in Introduction to *Caṅkara Rājēndra Cōlan Ulā*, p. 6). Some historians such as Irāmacantira Tītcitar are of the opinion that Neṟiyuṭaipperumāṉ was a man and is to be identified with Caṅkara Cōlan. (See *Mūnṟām Kulōttuṅga Cōlan*, Madras 1941, p.34)

The *Tiyākarājalīlaikaḷ* of Mīnātcicuntaram Piḷḷai, as we have seen earlier, refers to a Caṅkara Cēvaka Cōlan.[121] He is said to have handed the kingdom to his son and retired. He was from Kāñcī. He requested Tyāgarāja to come and rule, which he did. *Līlai* 3 describes his rule.

A reference occurs, as mentioned earlier to a 'life saver' in an inscription from Tiruvārūr (591 of *SII*, Vol. XVII). This last inscription refers to the deity Vītiviṭaṅka, i.e., Tyāgarāja of Tiruvārūr giving land to a certain *'pirāṇaupakārī* and the only information we have on this 'life-saver' is that he was a *Cōlēntiraciṅkam* (the lion of the Cōla lineage). This inscription exasperatingly enough does not give the name of the monarch, only his regnal year, which is Year 2. The record has been paleographically dated in the 12th century A.D. The only lead we have is the name Cōlēntiraciṅka, for we know that a whole regiment was called Cōlēntiraciṅka Vēlaikkāraṉ and that lands were given to this regiment by Vikramacōla (*SII* Vol. XVII, No. 588).

The epithet Cōlēntiraciṅka was assumed by Rājarāja I and Tirunaḷḷāṟu was referred to in inscriptions as *Cōlēntirciṅka Caturvētimaṅkalam*. Thus, this *'pirāṇaupakārī'* was possibly also the military commander of an important regiment and claimed a very special relationship with Tyāgarāja.

Thus, we can see that in troubled times unknown heroes, one

a prince of royal descent and another a prime minister, saved the Cōḻa monarchy. The prince is embellished in myths and is presumably the one with the epithet of the 'life-saver' in the epigraphs and Tyāgarāja is said to have bestowed honours on him. The other a general, has also been eulogised in epigraphs and myths and more will be said of him presently.

A strange trend can be noticed in the 12th century in the epigraphs from Tiruvārūr. A set of inscriptions, which for want of a better term, can be classified as 'Deity's inscriptions' suddenly became popular in Tiruvārūr. While such inscriptions were not completely unknown, for example Cuntara Pāṇṭiyaṉ requests Viṣṇu to grant lands to Nācciyār (Viṣṇu's local spouse) (343 of *ARE* 1960-61), they were very uncommon in Tamiḻnāḍu.

Maṉunīti Myth and Vikramacōḻa

The most important one of these so-called deity's edicts is 163 of *ARE* 1894 (*SII* Vol. V. No 455) of the time of Vikramacōḻa and records in detail the whole of the Maṉunīti episode. It must be borne in mind that this inscription belongs to the reign of Vikramacōḻa and in that sense predates the composition of the *Periya Purāṇam*, which is believed to have been composed during the time of Kulōttuṅga II and describes this myth at Tiruvārūr.

Two significant approaches are noticeable in the epigraph. Firstly, the whole myth of Maṉunīti is told in all its details almost making it appear as if the myth in its complete form was only then presented for the first time. Secondly, Maṉunīti is presented as a real historical character whose family lineage is known and can easily be traced for grants of land are made to a descendant of the prime minister of King Maṉunīti. The epigraph is a classic example of legitimation. The whole episode of Maṉunīti is narrated *by the deity Vītiviṭaṅkaṉ* while seated in the Tēvāciriya Maṇṭapam. It is the deity who orders the restoration of a palace site which once belonged to the minister of Maṉunīti to his (i.e. the said minister's) descendant, Paḻaiyūruṭaiyāṉ Candracēkaraṉ who was also known as Ātiviṭaṅkaṉ. Another inscription 545 of 1904 (*SII*, Vol. XVII, No. 590) also records the Maṉunīti episode and the donee. [122]

The Antecedents of the Maṉunīti Myth

The Maṉunīti legend had a long antecedent much like the

Mucukuntaṉ one. Even as early as the time when Vijayālaya and Āditya, the founders of the Imperial Cōḻa line, consolidated their hold over Koṅgudēśa and the whole delta of the Kāvērī river, they felt the need to acquire a pedigree. One way of doing it was to link themselves with the Cōḻas of the Cankam period who had themselves claimed to be descendants of the Sun (*Maṇimēkalai* 1.9; *Cilappatikāram* 7. 27, *Pukārkkāṇṭam* XXXIX 11 1-2) and laid their claims to be recognised as *kṣatriyas* (*Maṇimēkalai* (I II 1-9). Though the nucleus of the Maṉunīti myth occurs in *Maṇimēkalai*, II, 10-12) the name Maṉu itself is not used.

To briefly provide the outline of the Maṉunīti myth, a righteous king by the name of Maṉu, on hearing that his son had accidentally killed a calf by running over it while driving his chariot, listens to the appeal for justice by the aggrieved mother cow. He then orders his prime-minister to execute the heir-apparent in a similar manner by mowing him down under the royal chariot. The prime minister rather than carry out the royal order commits suicide and the king carries out the punishment himself. However, all ends well as Tyāgarāja restores the dead prince and prime minister to life.

In *Cilappatikāram* (23:58, and in 29: Ammāṉaivari, 17) the king is referred to as the protector of the complainant cow (*kārṟvai muṟai ceyta kāvalaṉ*). In *Maturaikkāṇṭam* 20.53-56 of the same work, Kaṇṇaki, while singing the praise of the city of Pukār, says that it is in this city that the episode of the killing of the prince at the wheels of the chariot took place (*arumpeṟṟapputalvaṉai āḻiyiṉ maṭittōṉ*.) In *Maṇimēkalai* I, II 1-9 the king is referred to as one who killed his own son (*makaṉai maṟai ceyta maṉṉaṉ*). Reference to this episode is found in several works such as the *Vikramacōḻanulā*, *Irācarācacōḻanulā* (st. 3) *Kuṟaḷ* etc. and is even used in popular proverbs. So this became the motif of the *dharmic* or righteous king.

The elaboration of the narrative, whereby the cow rings the bell, the king comes out, etc. is not mentioned in these early works. In *Maṇimēkalai*, the episode is again mentioned in passing when Udayakumāraṉ commits a mistake and dies. The father in his lamentations refers to the noble traditions of their family and mentions the Maṉunīti episode. In the *Cilappatikāram*, the emphasis is on the cow, in the *Maṇimēkalai* on the prince.

While the name Maṉu occurs several times in the epigraphs

and literature, nowhere is this story told. After the lapse of centuries the story surfaces again in the 12th century A.D. with all its elaborations and ornamentations. The *Kaliṅkattupparaṇi,* the *Mūvarulā* of Oṭṭakkūttaṉ in 1.4, 2.2 and 3.3 all emphasise on the king and the prince and describe the king as one who drove the chariot over his son (*āvin ceyal mutal taṉ makaṉ mītu tērūrtal*). It is the commentator who equates the actor of these deeds with Maṉu and his son. The story, complete with all its embellishments, occurs in the *Periya Purāṇam* which is generally held to have been composed in the time of Kulōttuṅga II.

The inscription under discussion is older than the *Periya Purāṇam* and paragraph 4, lines 4 to 6 describe Maṉu as Cūriyaputtiraṉ (son of Sun God) and narrates how a calf was once accidentally killed by his son, the crown prince. The calf was caught between the wheels of the prince's chariot and died. The mother cow rang the bell of justice. The minister, whose name is given as Ubhayakulamallaṉ was asked to attend to the matter by the king. He reported that a cow was ringing the bell of justice.

The king personally attended to the matter and on being told by the cow that its calf had been crushed to death at the prince's wheels he decided to have his son killed by similar means to atone for the death of the calf. The name of the prince is given as Priyavarttaṉaṉ. The king commanded the minister to drive the chariot over the prince. The minister rather than commit such a crime dashed his head to the ground and died. The king thereupon drove the chariot himself. At that juncture says Vītiviṭaṅkaṉ, (for the whole episode is recounted by the deity), "we bestowed our grace and restored the calf, the minister and the son of Maṉu to life" and Maṉu filled with joy took the calf back to the cow..., performed *abhiṣēka* and made Cūriyaṉ, the son of Ubhayakulamallaṉ as his minister, and bestowed him with his son's palace... and the king with Ubhayakulamallaṉ retired to do *tapasyā* and now the person belonging to the lineage (Vamśa) of Ubhayakulamallaṉ... etc." and thus links the present to the past. The minister descendant is endowed with land by Vītivitaṅkaṉ (*nam kāṅikkaiyāka taṉtōm* - "we bestowed it as our gift"). The *'nam'* meaning the deity - narrator and bestower of grace, Vītiviṭaṅkar Tyāgarāja.

According to this inscription the donee's name was Paḻaiyūruṭaiyāṉ and his epithet Tiyākacamuttira (Tyāgasamudra) whilst his wife's name was Tiyākapatākā. Paḻaiyūr was one of the king's many ancillary capitals. According to the inscription Maṉu, and by inference the king at the time of the inscription, (Vikramacōḻa) retired with his minister. Other inscriptions testify to this inasmuch as Kulōttuṅga II was chosen heir-apparent in 1133 A.D. and it was only in 1135 A.D. when his predecessor died that he became a full-fledged king. In this context it stands to reason to attribute the epigraph mentioned above, giving only the regnal year 2, and referring to the "*pirāṇa upakāri*", to Vikramacōḻa. Then the so-called descendant of Ubhayakulamallaṉ could well be the '*pirāna upakāri*' (life-saver).

In the context of all that has been said of the Etirilipperumāḷ episode it seems likely that there was some irregularity in succession and the minister had obviously helped a great deal to smoothen matters and thus there was a great need to legitimize and stabilize Kulōttuṅga II's rule. So a joint rule (with his predecessor retiring to the forests) was worked out and succession legitimized through resuscitation of myths. The minister and his son were rewarded. In fact kingship and ministerial powers were both legitimized at one stroke. The religio-political shrine dedicated to Maṉunīti (Pl. XX) at Tiruvārūr could well belong to this period. Only the basement and some of the pillars of the structure are original. The Vimāṉam and vaulted roof of the porch are recent additions.

This legend is further developed by Cēkkiḻār where he tells the story in fifty-three staṉzas (*Periya Purāṇam* I, 103-56) and the much embellished version served the cause of Śaiva evangelism, patronised by Kulōttuṅga II. V. 50 of *Tirunakaracciṟappu* of Cēkkiḻār adds that the Lord who redeemed the calf, minister and prince to life was the Lord of Pūṅkōyil, i.e. Tyāgarāja. Thus it is in the 12th century that the Śaiva element of Grace and restoration of the dead to life is added. The story of Maṉunīti does not occur in the *Tēvarām* but assumes an important place in the literature and epigraphy of the Cōḻas in the 12th century A.D.

The Śaiva slant to the story given by the author of the *Periya Purāṇam* stayed as the main feature of this legend in the minds of the people. In a 17th century work called *Mukkūṭaṟpaḷḷu* (v. 165) one finds the Vaiṣṇava contempt (*ēcal*) for the Śaivas expressed through the medium of this myth, and the Śaiva repartee using the same medium. The editor of the work also refers to an *ammāṉai*, while elucidating this verse (i.e 165) which also has this light hearted rebuff on the Maṉunīti episode. (*Īcaṉ Pacuvāki yemaṉ oru Kaṉṟāki vīcupukaḻ Ārūriṉ Vītīvantārammāṉai*). An excellent edition of this *paḷḷu* by Mu. Arunachalam (Madras, 1949) provides a valuable introduction.

The Vaiṣṇava chides the Śaiva and says, "Your Lord came as the cow and Yama came as the calf (i.e. the calf was killed) - can the cow now give milk ? To this the Śaiva replies, the calf was once kicked by the cow and could only then give milk". The whole diatribe is clothed in metaphors. In the first instance, the calf is killed and so is equated with Yama, the god of death. In the second instance the cow, as Śiva, kicks the calf who is Yama and thereby preserves the life of Mārkaṇḍēya, another well known myth of Śiva saving his devotee Mārkaṇḍēya from Yama. The whole episode is placed at Tiruvārūr in this *Ammāṉai* and *Paḷḷu.* Milk is the metaphor for life sustenance. This legend travelled to Sri Lanka and Thailand, where it underwent further transformations.

Myths, Epigraphs and Cōḻa Kings

It is interesting to see that inscriptions in which the deity speaks and epigraphs recording detailed myths as well as literary revival of myths should occur at a period when a usurpation of royal power has taken place. Thus, Kulōttuṅga I had no direct claim to the Cōḻa throne and the second in line to the usurper is left with no direct male descendant. In succession, the subjects had to accept two breaks in the royal line. The anti-Vaiṣṇavism of the king too could have something to do with this. The Vaiṣṇava priests at Chidambaram and presumably at Tiruvārūr may have supported an alternative candidate. The desperate urgency of making Śaivism the royal faith is evident in Kulōttuṅga's policies. He has the *Periya Purāṇam* written , persecutes the Vaiṣṇavas; donates to Tiruvārūr and Chidamabaram lavishly, assumes the Śaiva epithet Anapāya and institutes special rites at Tiruvārūr.

Apart from the two epigraphs discussed above, two other epigraphs from Tiruvārūr employ the technique of the deity speaking, acting and making decisions. A record dated in the 13th regnal year of Kulōttuṅga III (1178-1218 A.D.) describes a land gift to the temple of the deity Piḷḷaiyār and this endowment is made in the first person by the deity Vītivitaṅkaṉ in much the same manner as the last mentioned epigraph. Furthermore Piḷḷaiyār is referred to "as our son" thereby making it doubly clear that it was Vītivitaṅkaṉ who was issuing the edict (550 of 1904; *SII* Vol. XVII No. 595), for in Hindu mythology Piḷḷaiyār or Gaṇapati is the son of Śiva.

The deity of Tiruvārūr called Pūrvārūrvāsi in the above epigraph (the inhabitant of ancient Ārūr) orders the redistribution of uncultivated lands and bestows them on the people who were serving in the temple. The monarch is referred to endearingly by the deity as "our friend" (*nam tōḻaṉ tirupuvaṉa vīraṉukku irupattunālāvatu mutal* i.e. in the 24th regnal year of "our friend" Tribhuvanavīra, an epithet of Kulōttuṅga III).

Kulōttuṅga II enlarged the temple ritual at Tiruvārūr for he claims in an inscription to have instituted fifty-six festivals and records meticulously the details of food to be offered, the amounts of ingredients to be used and registers endowments in cash and kind to meet these requirements. The Mārkaḻi Tiruvātirai and Paṅkuṉi Uttiram were the big festivals and in both these the Tyāgarāja icon was taken out in procession. Images of Campantar and Appar were set up and worship offered. The king calls himself 'Anapāya' an epithet of Śiva and "a bee at the lotus feet of Naṭēśa at Citamparam"(Chidambaram). He has left by far the largest record at the Tiruvārūr temple. The epigraph also records his renaming a village Aṉapāyanallūr after joining two villages together and donating them to the temple to meet the expenses of the rites instituted by him. It is this record that enabled historians to identify 'Anapāya' the royal patron of Cēkkiḻār with Kulōttuṅga II.

The *Mucukundasahasranāmam* invokes Tyāgarāja distinctly as Anapāya Mahīpāla (Inv. 318) and Anapāya Pureśa (Inv. 340) and describes the deity as "Rājaveśadhārī" (one who dons the robe of a king). The *Tiyākarājalīlaikaḷ* of Mīnātcicuntaram Piḷḷai relates how on the request of Caṅkara Cēvakaṉ, Tyāgarāja donned the robe of a mortal king and ruled the Cōḻa dominions. The elaborateness of the rituals instituted by Kulōttuṅga II coupled with the use of the epithet Anapāya in the *Sahasranāma* makes it clear that the rite of the *Mucukundasahasranāmam* was also instituted by this king.

The war against Kaliṅga was regarded as an epoch making event in Cōḻa history which prompted Cayaṅkoṇṭāṉ to write the

Kaliṅkattupparaṇi. Ottakkūttar is also believed to have written a *paraṇi* on the Kaliṅga war which is now lost to us.

Apart from the monarch the other individual on whom praise is lavished in the *paraṇi* is Karuṇākara Toṇṭaimāṉ, the commander-in-chief of Cōḻa army. It has been mentioned earlier that Karuṇākara Toṇṭaimāṉ is one of the epithets of Tyāgarāja. Soon myths began to grow around the General and the cultic deity. One such myth is recorded in the *Cōḻamaṇṭalacatakam* of Ātma Tēcikar,[123] wherein we are told that Karuṇākara Toṇṭaimāṉ refused to part with half of his merits at the command of the king and was consequently beheaded by the king. His head, we are told, got stuck to the throne of Tyāgarāja and could only be extricated after a *śīrṣamālā* (a garland of heads) was offered to Tyāgarāja, a veiled allusion perhaps to many other heads rolling. The merits were in the first place acquired by Karuṇākara Toṇṭaimāṉ because of his acts of piety in richly endowing the temples of Śiva.

Whether this is just a folk tale or whether it preserves memories of the rise of a great chief, his victories in a major war and his piety which fully qualified him to challenge his erstwhile suzerain and so had to be dealt with sternly by the monarch, is a matter of speculation. That Karuṇākaraṉ was a very importaṉt personage becomes evident by the fact that a unit of measurement called the Karuṇākaranāḻi is mentioned in an inscription from Vedāraṇyam (*SII* XVII, 416). An inscription of Kulōttuṅga II dated in his twelfth regnal year also refers to a *devadāna* village by the name of Karuṇākaranallūr (597 of *SII* Vol. XVII; 552 of 1904). A Karuṇākara *canti* was performed in the Tiruvārūr temple till recently and the endowment came from the family of the Toṇṭaimāṉ of Putukkōṭṭai state. The Toṇṭaimāṉs of Pudukottai state, as it was called under the British, were the overlords of the Cētupatis and they presumably claimed descent from the hero of the Kaliṅga war.

The Kaliṅga war and the strengthening of temple cults in Tiruvārūr and Chidambaram,when juxtaposed against the rise of Jagannātha cult in Puri at about the same time are probably more significant than have hitherto been recognised. Herman Kulke suggests this line of reasoning when he says Anantavarman chose to develop the Vaiṣṇavite cult at Purī at a time when the Cōḻa king Kulōttuṅga II (1133-50) "as a fanatic Śaiva had by an exceptional act of intolerance forcibly removed the famous image of Viṣṇu from the renowned Śiva temple at Chidambaram and had it thrown into the sea".[124] It may, says Kulke, have been "mutually influenced". For the Jagannātha cult under the Sōmavaṁśins had remained only a subsidiary *rāṣṭradēvatā*; it was Cōḍagaṅga who through his "royal patronage" elevated Puruṣōttama clearly to an Imperial level.[125] He further proves his point by stating that the Jagannātha temple reached the same height as the Bṛhadīśvara Śiva temple of his Southern Cōḻa rivals at Taṉjore (216 ft) which till then had been the grandest in the whole of India. In order to strengthen his imperial claim, Cōḍagaṅga, at the same time took up the imperial title of a *Cakravartin*, "which had become in South India almost an imperial privilege of Cōḍagaṅga's relatives and rivals on the Cōḻa throne".[126] It is further significant that until the period of Cōḍagaṅga the god Śiva Madhukeśvara at Kaliṅganagara seems to have been the State deity of the Gaṅgas. It was only under Anaṅgabhīma III (1211-38) that the god Puruṣōttama, Lord of Puri became the official State deity of the Gaṅgas. Thus in the context of the horrors of the Kaliṅga war, as described in the *Paraṇi* dealing with the event, this shift is understandable and makes sense.

Thus the idea of making the deity the real ruler in Orissa seems to have been suggested by the Cōḻas. There is suddenly this cluster of five edicts from Tiruvārūr in which the deity issues orders, interferes in transference of property and relates at great length the story of Maṉunīti and links it to the land donation.

The close parallel between political events in the state and rituals as well as myths in and about the temple is striking. An inscription speaks of a mysterious '*pirāṇa upakāri*', 'life-saver' and a myth of Caṅkaracēvakaṉ appears and at his request the deity Tyāgarāja assumes the mantle of the monarch to tide over temporal problems. Like pieces in a jigsaw puzzle they all fit in to form a coherent picture. The *Mucukundasahasranāmam* emphasises this 'Rājavēśadhārī' (donning the robes of a monarch) aspect and the recorded *Līlais* of Tyāgarāja completely endorse them. The migration of the idea to Kaliṅga is clearly seen. In 1216 Anaṅgabhīma III called himself a 'deputy' and 'the son' of Puruṣōttama, Rudra and Durgā. The fact that they, like the Somāskanda form a divine triad is not without significance. This is also the period when art motifs begin to migrate from Tamilṉāḍu to Orissa. The wheel and the horse-drawn *maṇṭapas* of Dārāsuram find an echo, albeit a magnificently eloquent one, at Kōṇārak. The Kaliṅga episode was a bloody one but does not seem to have left long-lasting political effects.

The political conditions, as we have seen, were troubled on the foreign and domestic front and the Cōḻa kings were expected to cope with an alarming array of problems. Vikramāditya VI, the western Cālukya complains that the "hostile Cōḻa does not come to the battlefield".[127] The last years of Vikramacōḻa were difficult ones when Vikramacōḻa took over the power of the State and "the land of Veṅgi at once fell into anarchy". Floods, succession problems, rising power of chiefs and foreign wars must have undermined the prestige of the king, who, through patronage of the age-old nuclear institutions was desperately trying to capture the imaginations of the people and bind them into a congregation of believers with him as the head.

Traditional sacred sites like Tiruvārūr and Chidambaram and personal royal temples like Dārāsuram and Tribhuvanam of the later Cōḻas were distributive zones of royal munificence. It was of paramount importance to keep the 'towns' in line and Tiruvārūr, always described as Celva Tiruvārūr, was a prosperous centre renowned for its sanctity. The Tyāgarāja was an ideal cultic medium for he was 'known' to have walked the streets of Tiruvārūr begging for love on behalf of Cuntarar. The personality of the deity matched the requirements.

Interestingly enough the first 'deity speaks' class of edicts from Tiruvārūr belongs to the difficult period of Kulōttuṅga I when even the partisan work *Kaliṅkattupparaṇi* hints at the state of anarchy and the rise of conspiracies which finally led to the rise of Kulōttuṅga I. All these presumably account for the rise of myths that he was a Śūdra, and that he was the father of the illegitimate Toṇṭaimān who later carved a viceroyalty for himself in the Toṇṭaimaṇṭalam.[128]

Thus it is not surprising that under Vikramacōḻa great efforts are made at legitimation of power. Apart from land grants etc. mentioned earlier, an inscription (*SII* Vol. XVII, 593 and 548 of 1904) records simply a grant to a playwright and yet the grant is made by Vītivitaṅkaṉ. It records the deity as addressing the playwright Pūṅkōyil Nampi as *'nam makkaḷ, 'our son'*. The dramatist is stated to have written a work called *Vīraṉukkavijayam* in honour of Vīracōḻanukkār. The deity is said to have issued the grant while watching a dance performace by Pūṇkōyil Nāyakkattalaikōḷili at the Tēvāciriya Maṇṭapam. Pūṅkōyil is the name of the temple of Tyāgarāja and the dancer as well as the playwright were obviously connected with the temple as the prefixes to their names indicate.

The Vīracōḻanukkār was a regiment of soldiers as we know from the Thañjāvūr inscriptions of Rājarāja I and the Vedāraṇyam inscriptions of Parāntaka I (466 of *SII* Vol. XVII). That they were a very important regiment becomes evident from a street being named after them in Rājarāja's time. So a play on the exploits of some loyal supporters of the king was staged in the temple and the deity was pleased to grant land to the playwright.

A Vīracōḻa Iḷaṅkōvalar, a chieftain and a donor is referred to in an inscription from Tiruvoṟṟiyūr (131 of 1912). He is recorded as donating land to Kāraṇai Viṭaṅkar. The Vīracōḻanukkār get referred to periodically in Cōḻa epigraphs until the time of Kulōttuṅga III. For example, 446 of *SII* Vol. XVII from Vedāraṇyam refers to a gift by Vīracōḻanukkār and interestingly enough the gift is a throne called the Vīracōḻiyam. Tyāgarāja of Tiruvārūr is believed to sit on a throne by that name.

Brave warriors were commemorated as deities in *naṭukals* or hero stones in ancient Tamiḻ tradition and a modified version of this motif keeps appearing in Cōḻa temple records. 578 of *SII* Vol. XVII of Kulōttuṅga I's time refers to an endowment made by the merchants (*nakarattārs*) several of whose names end in Śreṣṭhī and they endow money for the performance of a ritual connected with brave dead soldiers. The inscription is damaged and details are missing.

To conclude this part of the discussion, the Cōḻas evolved a State religion - Śaivism—but unlike the kings of Orissa, they extended royal patronage to various religious centres and their own special royal temples. Each king seems to have felt this urge to build his own royal temple. Portrait sculptures of kings, queens and even royal gurus were enshrined in these temples. Ritual services were often conducted on their names and special services on their birthdays, etc. Plays and performances eulogising the royal family and entourage were staged in temples. Important examples are the *Rājarājēśvaranāṭakam* at Thañjāvūr (*SII* Vol. II, No. 67), *Kulōttuṅgacōḻacarittiram* by Tirunārāyaṇabhaṭṭa and

Vīraṇukkavijayam already mentioned. In case of the second of the above mentioned plays the *sabhā* of the place was *ordered* by the king to gift land to the playwright and ordered to judge the merit of the play, while in the last example the deity himself did the rewarding. Apart from this, the *meykīrti* or eulogies of the king were recorded on the walls of the temple.

The Cōlarāja, as we have seen, was both a portrait sculpture and an icon and was taken out in procession and preceded the other icons as the forward guard - the protector of the other icons - the defender of *dharma*.

Before concluding the discussion of the role of Cōlas *vis-a-vis* temple cults it would be interesting to analyse briefly the salient features of the myths that grew at this time centring around king and deity. The Maṇunīti myth has already been explored. The *Iṭṭiyelupaṭu* and the *Tiyākarājalīlaikaḷ* will now be taken up for discussion.

The *Iṭṭiyelupaṭu*[129] was composed in praise of the Ceṅkuntars or Kaikkōḷars (weavers), who also took up arms. The poet Oṭṭakkūttaṉ belonged to the family of Ceṅkuntars. A close parallel is drawn between the king and his Ceṅkuntar confidants on one hand and Murukaṉ on the other. The *vēl* or lance of Murukaṉ is described as the lance of Ceṅkuntar. The king Mucukuntaṉ with the aid of his *navavīras* or nine warriors helped Indra and brought the Tyāgarāja to the earth.

Semi-historical information is provided from v. 24 onwards where the exploits of Ceṅkuntars and the monarch, Mucukuntaṉ are described. In v. 25 their patronage of Śaivism is emphasized. Leaving aside Mucukuntaṉ's exploits in heaven, etc., the historical portions recount his attack on Kuṭanāṭu which was the land of the Cēras in Malayāḷa country (present day Kerala). V.36 refers to the attack on Ceylon with the aid of Cuppaṉ of Tiruchendūr, a Murukaṉ pilgrim-site, which is about 64 kms. south-west of Tirunelveli.

V.37 refers interestingly enough to a struggle between the rulers of Bengal and Gūrjaras (Kūrcara) on one hand and the ruler of Maccanāṭu on the other. The tripartite struggle between Pālas, Gūrjara Pratīhāras and Rāṣṭrakūtas was one that lasted the whole of the 11th century A.D. These legends simply bear memories of such historic situations of conflict and convert them into mythic motifs. Maccanāṭu could refer to the Pāṇḍyas with their fish emblem. The Cōḻa monarch is said to have interevened and established order. V. 38 refers to the quelling of a rebellion nearer home at Tiruviṭaimarutūr. The battle against the king of Vaṅga is described in V. 39 in typical *paraṇi* (battle poetry) spirit, describing the havoc caused on the battlefield. V. 40 refers to the victory against Kaliṅga. V 44 refers to victories over Pāṇḍyas. The names of a few loyal chieftains called Ceṅkuntars are given. V. 49 describes the chief of Paḻuvūr, Nārāyaṇaṉ, the chief of Kāncī Taṉiyaṉ, so called because he fought the enemies alone. Kulōttuṅga II was callled 'taṉiyar' which is also an epithet of Śiva. Tiruvoṟṟiyūr Uṭaiyāṉ, the chief of Tiruvoṟṟiyūr, who endowed the temple to maintain a flower garden, the king of Kaḷattūr Puṟṟiṭaṅkoṇṭāṉ who, on the request from Aṅga country attacked Kaliṅga and won, Paḷḷikoṇṭāṉ of Chidambaram (the name is also the epithet of Gōvindarāja of the place), the chieftain of Kaṇṭiyūr, the chief of Mutukuṉṟu, the chief of Tañcai (Thañjāvūr) and their victories, etc. are mentioned. It is possible to trace some of these chieftaincies.

The *Īṭṭiyeḻupatu* presents a picture of the Cōḻa empire as one of a loosely knit confederation of principalities. The main aim of this work was to sing the praise of the community of Ceṅkuntars and to glorify Tyāgarāja and Mucukuntaṉ but it does, as seen above, refer to the Kaliṅga war, war aganst Pāṇḍyas, Lankā etc., thereby making it a semi-historical romance.

These could well refer to Vikramacōḻa's reign, when the poet composed this work. The invasion of Vaṅga could well be an echo of Rājēndra's conquest. The floods and submarine fire- the recalling of Mucukuntaṉ to heaven and the starting of a *new* dynasty on earth by marrying Citravēli are referred to in *Īṭṭiyeḻupatu* and narrated in *Kanta Purāṇam*. Thus one could probably trace a close analogy between the historical Kulōttuṅga I and the mythical Mucukuntaṉ, starting a *new* dynasty and from Vikrama's epigraphs from Tiruvārūr we know that the king was keen in linking himself with the deity of Tiruvārūr. It may be worth a historian's effort to identify the chieftaincies mentioned in the work to understand the nature of Cōḻa polity in the 12th century.

The controversy over whether *Īṭṭiyeḻupatu* is a genuine work of Oṭṭakkūttar or whether it was written by a 17th- 18th century author bearing the name has been discussed in Chapter III. The *Kanta Purāṇam* version of the Mucukuntaṉ myth refers to floods and subamarine fire - chaos and confusion and Mucukuntaṉ's coming back to establish a *new* empire. This could well be a reference to the reign of Kulōttuṅga I and/or Vikramacōḻa. There was chaos before the accession of the former and floods during the rule of the latter.

The Cōḻa Monarchy and Tiyākarājalīlaikaḷ

The *Tiyākarājalīlaikaḷ* which has been referred to several times in earlier chapters identifies Tyāgarāja with the Cōḻas much in the fashion of the *Tiruviḷaiyāṭaṟpurāṇam* which identifies Taṭātakai, the Pāṇḍyan princess with Mīṉākṣī. The oral traditions seem to have evolved in the 12th century. The following are a few examples from the *Tiyākarājalīlaikaḷ* edited by Irācakōpāla Piḷḷai, (not to be confused with the work of the same name composed by Mīnātcicuntaram Piḷḷai):

Līlai 1 [130] begins with Śiva's asking Viśvakarmā to proceed to Tiruvārūr and build a town with the Valmīka temple as its centre and the palace in the North East with ten streets and twelve lanes. The people were astonished to see this beautiful city rise in the midst of a dense forest.

Līlai 3 describes how Śiva appeared as Tyāgarāja and people hailed him as the *kulateyvam* (the family deity) of Cōḻanāṭu. *Līlai* 8 describes Tyāgarāja asking the elephant Airāvata to garland the right future king of Cōḻanāṭu. This is necessitated because the land is without a king. Airāvata crowns a sage, who is of solar race. In *Līlai* 53 a family which is illegitimately deprived of its wealth is desperate for justice but the Cōḻa king is deep in meditation. Tyāgarāja dons the robe of the monarch and dispenses justice.

In *Līlai* 70 the Cōḻa king Vikrama is an enemy of Sakuṇa Pāṇḍya. The Pāṇḍyaṉ tries to use magic to kill the royal heir-apparent but fails due to Tyāgarāja's intervention. In *Līlai* 102 a Cōḻa general is portrayed referring to Tyāgarāja as his friend. When the Pāṇḍyaṉs attack he askes 'his friend' for help and Tyāgarāja comes as a youth and drives out the Pāṇḍyaṉs. This is a recurrent theme. In *Līlai* 113 the Pāṇḍyan invasion is checked by the deity.

In *Līlai* 120 the Tyāgarāja appears as a physician and cures the wounded Cōḻa king, while in *Līlai* 121 a child king of Cōḻavamśa is looked after by Tyāgarāja in the form of a caretaker cum nursemaid. *Līlai* 191 preserves memories of religious conflict for it recounts how once when the Cōḻa king was defeated and imprisoned, the Bauddhas and Jainas established their sway. The kings of Karnāṭaka and Magadha occupied Cōḻa lands. Tyāgarāja caused insects, snakes and animals of various species to attack the Jainas and spare the Śaivas and the invaders were driven out and the king rescued. Here the Cōḻa king and the Śaiva faith are equated. In *Līlai* 248 we are told that a swordsman once challenged the Cōḻa king for a combat. The king was hurt in the left shoulder and the combat ended in a draw. The *kurukkaḷs* were amazed to find blood pouring out of the left shoulder of Tyāgarāja. The fencer too realized the folly of his challenge and bequeathed all his wealth to Tyāgarāja. In *Līlai* 322 the celestial women are said to have played on the Vīṇā everyday to Tyāgarāja and so were blessed to be born as mortals and wed Cōḻa kings! The last *Līlai*, 364, simply states the efficacy of listening to the *Līlaikaḷ* and *inter alia* reiterates Tyāgarāja's grace to Āticōḻaṉ.

Thus a close connection between the deity and the king was evolved through the medium of myths. Kings visited Tyāgarāja shrines and attended festivals. Vikramacōḻa witnessed the Chidambaram-tirunāḷ festival from the Tēvāciriya Maṇṭapam (164 of *ARE* 1895) at Tiruvārūr. Rājādhirāja II took part in the festival of Paṅkuṉi Uttiram which was celebrated at Tiruvoṟṟiyūr (371 of 1911). Kulōttuṅga III stayed in the Rājarāja maṇṭapa at Tiruvoṟṟiyūr temple and observed the *Āṉi* festival (368 of 1911). Rājarāja III took part in the *Āvaṇittirunāḷ* that took place at Tiruvoṟṟiyūr. Thus the Tyāgarāja temples seem to have been popular centres for royal participation. The Paṅkuṉi Uttiram festival, according to *Akanāṉūṟu* was a Cōḻa festival from Caṅkam times, and was held at Uṟantai, the Cōḻa capital. Similarly Āvṇiyaviṭṭam seems to have been originally a Pāṇḍyan ritual performed at Madurai (cf. *Iṟaiyanār Akapporuḷ* - Cūttiram 16) and Uḷḷi a Cēra festival held at Karuvūr (cf. *Akanāṉūṟu* 38).

In 1250 Rājarāja III, the last of the Imperial Cōḻas, was taken a prisoner by Kōpperuñciṅkaṉ.

Pāṇḍyan Rule

The Pāṇḍyaṉs were the traditional founders and patrons of the Caṅkams or literary academics and are known to have been an ancient royal family. They, however, seem to have been overthrown by the Kalabhras. Nevertheless, they survived to reemerge as a great power in the 13th century. The 12th century sees them emerge under the tutelage of the Cōḻas. Till 1218 they paid tribute to the Cōḻa king Kulōttuṅga III. The latter half of the 13th century saw them aggressively asserting themselves and this period has come to be known as "the age of the Second Pāṇḍyan Empire". In the 7th century A.D. Campantar converted a Pāṇḍyan king to Śaivism and Māṉikkavācakar was also closely associated with the Pāṇḍyan royalty.

It was with the fall of the Cōḻas, that they once more came to the forefront. As far as the Tyāgarāja cult is concerned, several Pāṇḍyan inscriptions have come from the *Saptaviṭaṅka kṣētras*. Temples were generously endowed by the monarchs and patronised by the villages (e.g. see *ARE* 1912, pt. II, para. 36, *ARE* 1924 No. 109). Tēvaraṭiyārs were specially honoured (*ARE* 1924 pt. ii, para 26). Mortgage of temple lands was considered treason against Śiva and against the King (*Ibid*). Temple inscriptions also record social tensions and conflicts, such as between *ceṭṭis* and oilmongers (432 of 1913), between temple priests or *bhaṭṭars* regarding their rights for officiating in temple services (571 of 1920 and 108 of 1916). Sectarian rivalries and conflicts between Vaiṣṇavas and Śaivas are also on record (387 of 1906).

Jāṭavarmaṉ Cuntarapāṇṭiyaṉ (1251-68 A.D.) was a great conqueror and he performed the ancient ritual of Vīrābhiṣeka and Vijayābhiṣēka at Puliyūr, i.e. Chidambaram (131 of *SII* Vol. XXIII). He instituted the *Cuntarapāṇṭiyaṉcanti* in both Gaṅgaikoṇṭacōḻapuram and Tiruvoṟṟiyūr. The Pāṇḍyan power was rudely shaken by the invasion of Malik Khafur in 1310-11 A.D. and by a continuous civil war.

The tutelary deity of the Pāṇḍyans was Mīṉākṣī of Madurai and it was during this period that Perumpaṟṟappuliyūr Nampi put into writing the sixty-four *Līlais* of the Lord Śiva in and around Madurai. He mentions only seven kings, while Parañcōti of the 17th century who wrote another edition of the *Tiruviḷaiyāṭalppurāṇam* mentions 74 kings in unbroken succession.

Several *maṭhas* came into prominence during this period. The Gōḷaki maṭha and the Mutaliyār maṭhas have been discussed in the last chapter. To reiterate just a few important details, *maṭātipati* Ēkāmratēva Mutaliyār of Dakṣiṇa Gōḷaki maṭha at Celva Tiruvārūr comes into prominence at this time (234 of 1924 from Pirāṉmalai in Rāmanāthapuram district) and receives land endowments from the residents of Puḻal, near Tiruvoṟṟiyūr (483 of 1920). This itself reveals the wide geographical area in which this maṭha operated. Records from Sērmādēvi and Tirunelvēli speak of Pāṇḍyan endowments to the *Kīḻaimaṭha* (southern) branch of the Gōḷaki santāṉa, which had its head quarters in Tiruvārūr.

The sectarian leaders of this maṭha who began playing an important role under the Cōḻas seem to have furthered their influence in the 14th century A.D. They continued to exist until the 16th and 17th centuries but their height of power was in the 14th, when they were linked with a series of branches extending all over Tamiḻnāḍu and Āndhra country.

The sectarian leaders seem to have been extremely mobile at the period. The Gōḷaki maṭha with its northern headquarters at Vārāṇasī and southern at Tiruvārūr with a strong base at Dēvikāpuram and Chidambaram seem to have sent their representatives to sort out problems as is evidenced by the Tiruvoṟṟiyūr epigraph in which a dispute about the female workers in the temple and their job allocations was settled by a committee consisting of the Gōḷaki maṭha leaders from Vārāṇasī, Chidambaram and the local leaders (*ARE* 1912, 212). The inscription in fact refers to the Pāṇḍyan monarch, Cuntara Pāṇṭiyaṉ in rather uncomplimentary terms. Under his 'feudatory' chief we are told that the dancers and other female officials in the temple decreased. The state of affairs was restored by the new feudatories, the Sambuvarāyaṉs.

The Pāṇḍyaṉs, harassed by civil war and Muslim invasion, do not seem to have left a very strong impression on the northern borders of their kingdom which comprised the ancient Cōḻamaṇṭalam. Their direct influence on the cult of Tyāgarāja is very limited.

The Vijayanagara (c.a. 1336-1565-contd. till 1649) Nāyaka Period (of Taṉjore-c.a 1532-1765 A.D.)

The Vijayanagara Empire which was founded around 1365 claimed to have one particular religio-political objective, *viz.* to stem the tide of Islam and consequent upon this to restore Hindu *dharma* and temple worship which had been interrupted by the iconoclastic invaders. This formula found expression in the typically ornate style of medieval epigraphs in the following manner: "In the Kali age evil having greatly increased *dharma* seeing that it was impossible for it to move about went to the creator and said 'With only one leg left how can I travel about in the troubles of the Kali age?'". The inscription goes on to state that the Creator on hearing this sent the faithful ... etc. Harihara I to restore *dharma* (*EC* Vol. VIII, Sorab 375).

Thus it was on the basis of this set religio-political formula that the Telegu warriors of Vijayanagara consolidated their hold over the Tamil̲ country. Their administrative policy finds clear mention in another epigraph from the Ramnad district in which it is stated that "Kampanna Oḍeyār destroyed the Mohammedans, established orderly Government throughout the country and appointed many *nāyakan̲mār* (officials) for inspection and supervision in order that worship in the temples might be revived and conducted regularly as of old". (*ARE* 34 of 1916.)

Gaṅgādēvī, wife of Kampana, wrote the play *Madhurāvijayam*. In Canto viii she describes how a mysterious lady appeared in Kampana's dreams and having bemoaned the state of affairs under the Turukkas (Muslims) gave him the *Sword of the Pāṇṭiyan̲* family, not directly but through Agastya, the culture hero of the Tamil̲s, in order to restore order. The importance lies in Vijayanagara claiming to be at one stroke the legal successor of the Pāṇṭiyan̲ rulers and the upholders of Tamil̲. Until 1565 the empire held its sway and even after the Battle of Talaikkoṭṭai (1565) a shadowy empire lingered on until 1676 under fleeting Nāyaka leaders.

Burton Stein has drawn our attention to the nature of agrarian integration in South India during the *three* periods, *viz*. Pallava-Cōl̲a, Vijayanagara and Early British. To briefly sum up his arguments:

During the Cōl̲a period 'nuclear' institutions such as *brahmadēyas*, temples, *periyanāṭu*, etc., functioned on a corporate basis and were integrated into the 'segmentary' state.[131] These 'nuclear' areas were densely concentrated in rich riverine valleys such as the Kāvērī and hence the Thañjāvūr area, the area of primary concern in this discussion. Spencer's article on the sacred geography of the Tamil̲ Śaivite saints comes to a similar conclusion by a study of the distribution of temple clusters. The largest ring of clusters is in the Thañjāvūr area with 160 *pāṭalperr̲atalaṅkaḷ*, followed by South Arcot (31) and Chingleput (20).[132]

A change is noticeable in the second phase of agrarian integration,[133] i.e. in the Vijayanagara period. They introduced the *nāyaṅkara* system by which the land was given to the *nāyakas* of the king. The term *nāyaka* acquired its caste connotation at a later stage. They were given land and in return they paid a fixed annual financial contribution and were obliged to maintain troops and help the king in wars. Thus a more contractual obligation is noticeable in Vijayanagar times and this governs the relationship between kings and chiefs. The *nāyakaship* which was personal in the early years of Vijayanagara rule become gradually hereditary as the centre weakened. So it was a tributary system arranged among warriors.

Thañjāvūr and Madurai were two of the importaṉt *nāyakaship* in Tamiḻnāḍu and they were constaṉtly fighting between themselves. Cevappa Nāyaka and Raghunātha Nāyaka were two of the well-known rulers of 16th century Thañjāvūr.

Since this was a period of warlordism, competitiveness was the hallmark of the age. "The warrior overlords attempted to control some institutions, such as village assemblies and local artisan and merchant groups, and to eliminate others, such as the older nuclear-area assemblies and itinerant guilds, since they were dangerous to their ambitions. Urbanisation of three basic kinds - military, economic and religious - accompanied the development of these warrior-dominated regions and gave them a quality quite different from the other regions." [134]

It is the religious kind of urbanisation that is our primary concern here.The role of these religious centres is clearly traced and emphasised by Appadorai[135] and Baliga.[136] The Nāyakas, like the Cōḻas, believed that the temple was the very bedrock upon which the whole Indian civilisation rested.

Thus temples and sectarian leaders became very importaṉt as legitimisers of the Telegu warrior rule in Tamiḻ country. The role of "kings, sects and temples" between 1350 and 1700 has been excellently analysed by Appadorai in the context of South Indian Śrī-Vaiṣṇavism. This was the more important sectarian context for the later Vijayanagara and Nāyaka rulers were predominantly Vaiṣṇava and this was a period of setback of the Śaivas to some extent. Of the Śaiva temples, Chidambaram seems to have presented a strong opposition to Vaiṣṇava predominance but failed.

That an ideological battle was fought between Śaivas and Vaiṣṇavas for royal patronage is evident from several myths and from several records of historical events.[137] This period marked the rise of intense sectarianism not only between the Vaiṣṇavas and Śaivas but also between the Teṉkalai and Vaṭakalai Vaiṣṇavas over control of the temples. The role of royal patronage, the shift of emphasis from Śrī-Rangam to Tirupati and the local temple politics in the Pārthasārathi Temple at Triplicane, Madras, form the subject matter of Appadorai's analysis of "kings, sects and temples". Open debates between rival schools, the victory of one, and the subsequent royal patronage extended to the victor, were traditional methods employed in this contest and several examples of such confrontation are recorded.[138]

In the Śaiva-Smārta context the Gōḷaki maṭha, referred to earlier in this chapter and discussed in the previous chapter, played an important role until 1600.[139] Several maṭhas claiming to belong to the Meykaṇṭār lineage and drawing their adherents mainly from the Veḷḷāḷa community also came into prominence as seen in the last chapter. A Ñāṉappirakāca paṇṭāram was, as seen in the previous chapter, appointed a trustee of both Tiruvārūr and Chidambaram and was probably the founder of Tarumapuram ātīṉam. The Rājaṉkaṭṭalai, one of the important endowments at the Tiruvārūr temple, is in the hands of the Tarumapuram ātīṉam and they claim to have had this right from the 16th century. The pontiff of this maṭha also built the superstructures of the Gōpuras of Chidambaram, Kālahastī and Tiruvaṇṇāmalai. During the reign of Dēvarāya II, Lakkaṇṇa Dannanāyaka Uṭiyār's general Nāgarassa, son of Siddarassa, erected a gōpura at Tiruvārūr for the merit of Dannanāyaka (611 of *SII, Vol. XVII* dated 1440 A.D.). A Kannaḍa version of the above epigraph, which in its original Tamiḻ is also engraved on the wall (612 of *SII* Vol. XVII). An inscription of Vīrappūpatiuṭaiyāṉ (1429 A.D.) refers to donations by king and merchants to the temple.

A number of sectarian leaders rose during this period. It was characterised by a new wave of henolocotheism. *Sthalapurāṇas* were the most popular brand of sacred literature and it is between the 16th and 18th centuries that most *sthalapurāṇas* were put down into writing. Almost all major shrines in the Tamiḻ region acquired a *sthalapurāṇa* of their own. Patronage to temples was thus a major means by which the Telegu warrior chiefs legitimised their power in Tamiḻnāḍu, particularly in the wake of Muslim invasion. This desire to be accepted is evident from the Vijayanagara myth of the Pāṇṭiyaṉ sword sent through Agastya and bestowed on the Vijayanagara monarch. Temple rituals were enlarged and this brought in more money to the temple coffers and temple honours became the crucial medium through which temple politics and royal patronage expressed themselves. Unofficial caste organisations mushroomed under the 'moral leadership' of sectarian leaders who worked in turn with the administration.

It was an age of social upheaval. The Telugu rulers brought with them large groups of warriors who had to be rewarded with land and given social status through the temple and maṭhas. Caste mobility and social rank mobility were constantly being legitimised by temple and sectarian leaders. The case of *Veḷḷāḷa sannyāsins* asking the Vijayanagara emperor to mediate in their favour has been discussed in the previous chapter. Such regulatory activities of society brought king, court, temple and maṭhas into close symbiotic relationship. During the 16th and 17th centuries when *Varṇāśrama dharma* became the keystone of the policies under Vijayanagara and Nāyaka domination caste hierarchies had to be restated. *Samayācāryas* or *dāsaris*, as pointed out by T.V. Mahalingam, were a kind of ecclessiastic department and no religious ceremony or marriage could be performed without their permission. [140] The Reḍḍis of Rēṇukoṇḍa and Bōḍipet, for example, had certain honours conferred on them by the sectarian leader Tātācarya (who was asked to arbitrate by the king) and they in return promised to pay certain fixed amounts of money into the Tirupati temple. [141]

Conflicts between Veḷḷāḷas and Veḷḷaninaṭṭārs, between Iṭaṉkai and Valaṅkai, between Maṟavas and Nāṭṭārs, all emerged into the forefront.[142] Caste groups seemed to make recommendations to kings which the kings seemed to approve. The decisions and the conflicts that in the first place led to the decisions, were both inscribed on temple walls, thereby making the temple a witness to the social legislation and arbitration.[143]

Tiruvoṟṟiyūr temple has two very interesting examples of social legislation. One with regard to taxation, which belonged to the Vijayanagara period and the other with regard to the women servants in the temple. The dispute was over the assigning of duties to the *paṭiyillār* and *iṣṭabhattāliyārs*. The latter case dragged on from the time of the Sambuvarāyars and was finally settled by a committee consisting of the *bhikṣā* maṭha head, the *kaikkōḷars*, officials of the state, the *nāttārs*, etc.[144] Thus religious and quasi-religious (civic, administrative) groups seem to have participated in discussions, which often took place in temple halls.

Under the Nāyakas of Thañjāvūr Śaivism received patronage at court levels due mainly to the chief minister, Govinda Dīkṣita, who was a Śaiva. His son Veṅkaṭamakhin wrote the *Caturdaṇḍiprakāśikā* which opens with an invocation to Tyāgarāja of Tiruvārūr.

To sum up, political and religious centres had shifted further north and it was the maṭhas, both Smārta and Śaiva, that kept the Tyāgarāja tradition alive. Another important feature of the Vijayanagara period seems to have been the resurgence of folk religion - sacrifices of goats, buffalos, etc., and inflicting tortures on one's self as an act of piety are recorded by foreign writers. Most of these were in village temples of the mother-goddess and seem to have received royal patronage.

The Marāṭhās and Tyāgarāja

The last of the Nāyakas of Thañjāvūr, Vijayarāghava, was involved in an incessant battle with the Nāyaka ruler of Madurai and just before his surrender he blew up his harem consisting of 700 wives and 15,300 concubines.

In this war between the Nāyaka families of Madurai and Thañjāvūr, the ruler of Bijapur was invited to intercede and he sent Veṅkōji alias Ēkōji to restore order. The Marāṭhā, after restoring order, is believed to have had a vision of god who told him not to return. Thus, prompted by divine command, he laid the foundations of the Marāṭhā state of Thañjāvūr.[145]

The Marāṭhās came in not only as aliens but as emissaries and agents of the Muslim state of Bijapur. Of the many rulers of this principality, Shāhāji (1684-1710) and one of his successors Sarfōji II (1798-1833) are the best known. Thañjāvūr was a dependent principality which paid tribute to the Nawab of Carnatic. A historian of this period pays tribute to the Marāṭhās by stating the "Politically dependent Thañjāvūr held intellectual hegemony over South India".[146]

The nature of this "intellectual hegemony" was expressed

through the Marāṭhā patronage of Sanskrit and Telegu and to some extent Marāṭhī literature: worship in and restoration of temples and upholding the traditional *dharma*. The Tyāgarāja cult became once more elevated to a state cult under Shāhāji.

Shāhāji was a prolific writer. The Bhonsles, to which family the ruler belonged, claimed Cōḻa descent. He presumably envisaged himself as a Second Rājarāja I and built up the Tyāgarāja cult to the status of a royal cult.

Shāhāji was fluent in five languages - Sanskrit, Telegu, Tamiḻ Marāṭhī and Hindi. He was also a great patron of the arts. An *agrahāram* called Shāhājirājapuram was given to forty-six authors among whom were grammarians, poets, playwrights, etc.

A huge corpus of literature grew around the Tyāgarāja of Tiruvārūr and several paintings of the deity were also undertaken in the traditional Thañjāvūr style.[147] Religious literature in the form of *Sthalapurāṇas*, plays and commentaries on philosophical works were produced in large numbers. Bhāskararāya wrote his commentary on *Nityāṣodaśikārṇava*. Several Advaita gurus came into prominence. Bhāskarāraya's unpublished *mss*. the *Śrī-Navaratnamālā Mañjūṣā* has been discussed in Chapter V, in the context of Tyāgarāja metaphysics.

The religion at court belonged to that genre which blended eroticism with *bhakti*. Shāhāji is credited with composing the *Tyāgēśa kuṟavañci* which was performed both at Tiruvārūr and Thañjāvūr temples till recently. It deals with the theme of the love of a lady, Rājamōhinī, for Lord Tyāgarāja. Serfōji, one of the successors of Shāhāji, had endowed ten *vēlis* of land for enacting this play at Tiruvārūr.

Another popular play of this period was the *Shāhēndra Vilāsa*[148] in which the king was equated with Viṣṇu through the means of a myth. The story of Viṣṇu plucking off one of his own eyes to offer Śiva in lieu of the one flower that was missing in his daily offerings, occurs originally, I believe in the *Kanta Purāṇam*. This story is linked to the birth of Shāhāji in the above mentioned play. Śiva, according to this play was so pleased with Viṣṇu's devotion that he asked him to be born as Shāhāji to redeem the suffering of the people. The *Kanta Purāṇam* episode is carved in one of the pillars in the maṇṭapa of the Kailasanātha temple at Kāñcīpuram. (Oral Communication, N. Visvanathan, Telegu Pandit, Saraswati Mahal Library, Thañjāvūr, Dec.1982)

Furthermore, a Marāṭhī version of *Tyāgarāja Māhātmyam* was composed by Rāmapaṇḍita. A *Yakṣagaṇa libretto* called *Tyāgarāja Vilāsam* is also attributed to Shāhāji and deals mostly with the life of Cuntarar. He also wrote a number of *padas* called the *Tyāgeśa Padas* in *rakti* and *ghana rāgas* on themes of *bhakti* 'devotion', *śṛṅgāra* 'love' and *vairāgya* 'renunciation'. He wrote in Sanskrit, Marāṭhī and Telegu.[149] Tyāgarāja is often described in these as *Sāhakuladaiva* and *Rājarājamitra*, the family deity of Sāhā = Shāhāji and 'friend of Rājarāja', king of kings. The latter epithet was obviously intended as a double entendre as it was also the personal name of the great Cōḻa monarch, whose successors the Bhonsles claimed to be. Other epithets for the deity were '*bhonsala sāhakula Dēva*', the deity of the Bhonsle family. Almost all his *padas* either begin or end with Tyāgeśa. This is such a persistent symbol that it has been regarded as his *Cinmudrā* or pseudonym.

Shāhāji renovated the Tiruvārūr temple and made several endowments to the temple and many of the temple honours are still given to the present prince. In the plays that Shāhāji wrote or had performed, the opening invocation is often addressed to Tyāgarāja "*Makaṉīya Tyāgēśanukku Maṅgalam.*" Tradition has it that the mid-day service of Tyāgarāja of Tiruvārūr had to be complete before Shāhāji would have his lunch.

Under the Marāṭhas several plays were written emphasising the theme of love - love for the deity and love for the monarch ran on parallel lines. *Śarabhēndra Bhūpala Kuṟavañci* by Koṭṭayiṉ Civakkoḻuntu Tēcikar was also presented in the Tiruvārūr temple and land endowments were made for its enactment. This deals with Serfoji's (Śarabhēndra of the play) passionate love for a woman whom he finally weds. All along there is a parallel theme which describes the greatness of Bṛhadīśvara and Bhavāṉi Candramaulīśvarī, the family deity of the Marāṭhās. The prevalence of Tāntric cults at this period may have something to do with the generally erotic tone of literature of the period. Another amatory play *Śṛṅgāramañjari Shahājīyam* also describes Shāhāji's love for a woman and this too was enacted in a temple at Tiruvaiyāṟu.[150] This work was by Periyappa Kavi.

Thus, the 'intellectual' era of Marāṭhā rule was at the same time a period of stagnation. But for occasional sparks like the music of the Tiruvārūr trio, Śhyāmā Śāstrī, Muttusvāmi Dīkṣitar and Tyāgarāja and the treatises of Bhāskararāya, the whole civilization lacked vigour and settled down with well worn-out cliches. The oft-repeated process of legitimation was very much at work - the Marāṭhā king came closest to calling himself Tyāgarāja. He was a Cōḻa and hence worshipper of Tyāgarāja. Empty boasts of conquest were added in works like *Sāharājavilāsa* which claims that the king conquered all areas up to Vārāṇasī.

The Nāyaka-Marāṭha period witnessed however the rise of great composers of music as well as renowned musicologists. Violin and clarinet were introduced into Carnatic music. The 72 *mēlakartās* were codified. Kṣētra Kīrtanas were composed. Muttusvāmi Dīkṣita composed songs on Tyāgarāja. It must be to this period that we trace the development of Tyāgarāja as the great aesthete. Prayers to him implore him among other things to protect the aesthetic sensibilities of the devotee! 'Preserve my love of music', pleads the devotee. [151]

In 1787 the British took over Thañjāvūr. In 1800 the last Mahārājā handed over his protectorate in lieu of a decent pension. In 1848 he lost even the pension under the Doctrine of Lapse introduced by Dalhousie.

Hemmed in by Muslim powers, the Marāṭhās defined *dharma* in very conservative terms. *Varṇāśrama dharma* and the position of temples as status arbitrators were perpetuated.

The British Period

With the disappearance of the Marāṭhās, the Tiruvārūr-Thañjāvūr area lost its religio-political importance. Under the British rule the population migrated towards the cities of Madras, Madurai, Salem, Coimbatore, etc. The patron-client, legitimiser-legitimised, pattern of relationship between king and temple was no longer valid. The British Government did not look to traditional institutions like the temple for legitimation. The Government was totally alienated from the culture of its subjects, had to innovate administrative means to control the vast wealth of temple and maṭhas.

The British, unlike their Muslim predecessors remained foreigners. They were 'expatriates' with a country to go back to with no interest in the system of kings, sects and temples. Even Muslim Nawabs of Carnatic often endowed land and arbitrated in temple disputes. [152] In 1817 for a brief period the British Government tried to play the role of a traditional government and in fact took over the management of the temples including that of Tiruvārūr. But in 1863 they abandoned this policy.

The British wanted to leave the local scene undisturbed. They accepted the native elite consisting of Brāhmaṇas and Upper Caste leaders of society who were sectarian heads and managers of temples. With the development of the British bureaucracy they were involved in the handling and control of the revenue of the temple but were very reluctant, unlike the Hindu master, to arbitrate in temple disputes. Thus, the 'trustees' of the temples and the Brāhmaṇa and other upper caste managers were given a free play to do what they pleased. Temple politics and rivalry for acquiring the post of a trustee became intense.[153]

With the separation of 'executive' and 'judicial' powers, the courts were filled with trustee disputes. Several temples were asked to choose their trustees in which prominent men of the area were asked to make decision. It was in one such decision-making session in the 1860s that the landlord family of Vaṭapātimaṅgalam acquired the trusteeship of the Uḷtuṟai kaṭṭaḷai of the Tiruvārūr temple. There was a long legal battle against the Tiruppukaḷūr maṭha. There were also prolonged legal battles against a Christian missionary to whom temple lands had been sold by one of the trustees.

The late 19th and early 20th centuries saw a series of court cases with regard to different *kaṭṭaḷais* of the temple. Even today long lists of court cases are pending in the High Court of Madras and in the taluq court at Tiruvārūr particularly concerning the Tarumapuram ātīṉam properties. Court cases between Government and trustees are also a regular feature. These costly court actions are the legacies of the British rule.

The Recent Past

The British passed the control of temples and other institutions into the hands of the social elites - the Brāhmaṇas and upper caste non-Brāhmaṇas, thereby entrenching the elite in society. With the rise of the Justice Party a new upper strata of non-Brāhmaṇas got involved in temple politics. P.T. Rajan supported one of the trustees in the Tiruvārūr temple.

The D.K. and D.M.K. movements started on a very atheistic note. Under E.V. Ramasamy Naicker's statue in the centre of

Thañjāvūr is written "There is no God. He who worships God is an idiot. He who prays to God is a fool".

Yet it was under the DMK chief ministership of M.Karuānidhi that the Tiruvārūr *tēṛ* (chariot) began to be drawn in a procession after a lapse of twelve years due to disputes between the trustees. The occasion was marked by great pomp and splendour. The Government Photographic Unit was out to get it on film and a poem was composed on the deity and the minister. Coming close to the present time, a big *Kumbhābhiṣēkam* ceremony took place in 1986. It was under the D.M.K. Government that temples like Paḻaṉi which had never had a *Kumbhābhiṣēkam* before had one and over seven hundred temples have been renovated.

The temples, since 1959, are under the management of the H.R. & C.E. Board (Hindu Religious and Charitable Endowments Board) consisting of a full-fledged minister, a commissioner and three deputy commissioners. The Commissioner has a right to appoint trustees in all large temples, i.e. those with over Rs. 20,000 as annual income. Six C.P.I. (Communist Party of India) members are temple trustees. Traditionalists like the Śaṅkarācārya are also being gradually drawn into the orbit; Śaṅkarācārya of Kāñcī the younger pontiff, i.e. the second in command (there are three - the eldest pontiff has retired from adminstrative functions and the youngest is still receiving instruction) has opened Āgama classes for Harijans. Government organised *Samapanti pōcaṉai* (dinners to all served at the the same time to break taboos against commensality) in temples are the means by which the idea of egalitarianism and non-casteism are legitimised.

In 1983 the birthday of Rājēndra Cōḻa was celebrated by the Government agencies including the Tamiḻnāḍu Archaeological Department at Gaṅgaikoṇḍacōḻapuram. The previous year witnessed the birthday celebrations of Rājarāja at Thañjāvūr.

In 1986 the temples were asked to contribute to the Tamiḻ Conference, which was basically a platform for the assertion of Tamiḻ cultural consciousness. Temples, as organs of legitimation, are now used to legitimise Tamiḻ cultural nationalism as an ideology. The statues of Marx, Lenin and Tiruvaḷḷuvar are often juxtaposed in public gatherings. A new ideology is now presented through the old media, legitimised through means used and evolved over the centuries. The Hindu temple remains today the legitimiser of not only power but a new ideology - that of Tamil̲ cultural nationalism. Tamil̲ *arcan̲ais*, non-Brahmin priesthood, open access to temples for all, a common temple fund used for secular purposes such as eye-clinics, educational institutions and the like - such are the modern aspirations for the new role of the temple. In all this Tiruvārūr has had very little part to play. Not receiving any sizeable cash donation and its lands tied in legal disputes and the fact that tenants do not pay their rents to the temple regularly have made this a poor temple, earning less than Rs. 60 thousand per year.

At the time of writing, great changes are appearing in the religio-political scene of India with "Hindutva", the new wave of Hinduism acquiring a strong religio-political identity. Ancient temples like Tiruvārūr have not yet been drawn into the new wave.

Before concluding this discussion it would be interesting to see wherein lies the tenacity of this institution and also to see how not only the temple but the social history of the last three centuries is perceived and interpreted by a contemporary historian of the Tirāviṭa Kal̲akam mould.

Regarding the tenacity of the temple as an institution, Appadorai[154] suggests three possible reasons for the persistence of temples as an arena of politics. These are according to him:

1) "Cultural continuity";
2) "Structural virtuosity", which he basically defines as adaptability as an institution to accommodate different requirements;
3) "Political utility" in the sense of providing the right suprafamilial and cross-caste mechanism to express political ambitions.

As far as Tamil̲ culturalist interpretation of history is concerned it is interesting to quote from a typical comment on Vijayanagara period of Tamil̲ history by a DK historian: "The invaders mostly from the northern areas moved into the land and reduced the Tamil̲s to servitude", and then proceeds as to how 'the Āryans', the 'Kannaḍas', the 'Telegus' and 'Marāṭhās' conquered the Tamil̲s, who being deprived of lands and possessions and temple associations "found themselves reduced to the status of untouchables". While talking of the Brāhmaṇas he says, "The association that they claimed with the world of the celestials and the collusion that they established with the rulers of the land ensured for them a tryrannical sway over the rest of the population". He talks of the Satī of 47 women, wives of the Cētupati of Ramnad, supervised by Brāhmaṇas as a case of the decadence of Brāhmaṇa ethics. He describes the Brāhmaṇas of the 19th and 20th centuries as "promoting the monotonous *bhārata nāṭya*" at the cost of Tamil̲ local dances. He then refers to the inscription which states that Veḷḷāḷas decided to kill twenty-three Nāṭārs for some unspecified offence as an example of atrocities on the Tamil̲ population. He further speaks of caste Hindus snatching land from "native Tamil̲s".[155]

While all the atrocities he states took place and are no doubt indicators of a stagnant closed civilization when looked at from the sociological point of view, what is significant is the focus on the 'Āryan', 'alien' and 'Brāhman' models of tyrants. The Cētupatis of Ramnad, whose wives were forced to commit suicide were Tamil̲ Maṟavas. The Veḷḷāḷas who drove out the Veḷḷaināṭṭārs were in all probability Tamil̲ cultivators and the Veḷḷaināṭṭārs were possibly foreigners, for they were the ones who were forbidden to marry Tamil̲ girls, settle in Tamil̲ lands, etc. They were basically being driven out of Tamil̲nāḍu. Bharatanāṭyam was *revived* by Rukmini Devi Arundel and her contemporaries from disrepute. It was the prerogative of the Devadāsīs, who claim to be Icai Veḷḷāḷas only very recently. They were otherwise mostly low caste Tamil̲s. Lastly, to classify the Vijayanagara rulers as 'Āryan' is based on rather tenuous grounds.

Thus the model of the 'oppressed' is drawn both from Marxist and Tamil̲ nationalist viewpoints with the anti-Brāhmaṇa 'anti-Āryan' slant. In this cultural conflict, temple priests as repositories of a tradition, which itself is in question, find themselves without the necessary intellectual, economic or social confidence to conduct their lives with meaning and dignity.

Temples are now bringing in more money. Tyāgarāja has more *Mucukundashasranāma* performed now for him than before. The fees for this *Arccaṉai* are high by Indian standards, for it costs Rs. 2,000 to have this ritual performed. Priests are essential for its performance. Yet their legal and, even more so, their religious validity as custodians of Āgamic lore is itself only vaguely accepted. Fuller, in his book on the Mīṉākṣī Temple has studied their present plight. Thus, caught between a growing religious consciousness amongst the educated, who demand well informed priests on one hand, an official state policy of secularism, which does not favour government funded classes for the priests on the other, and an Anti-Brāhmaṇa, Anti-Āgama Tamiḻ consciousness on the third front, the social status of Tamiḻ temple priests is precarious. The young of these traditional priestly families are abandoning their familial call in quest of a more upwardly mobile socio-economic status.

NOTES

1. Kulke, Herman, 'Jagannātha as the State deity under the Gajapatis of Orissa', in A. Eschmann, Kulke and Tripathi (ed.), *The Cult of Jagannātha and the Regional Tradition of Orissa*, p. 199. (From hereon referred to as 'Kulke'.)
2. *Ibid.*
3. Geertz, Clifford, 'The Javanese Kijaji: the Changing Role of a Cultural Broker' in *Comparative Studies in Sociology and History*, Vol. 2, 1959-60, pp. 228-49 where he describes a similar phenomenon in a more modern Javanese context.
4. Kulke, *op. cit.*, p. 125.
5. Kulke, *op. cit.*, p. 143. The Tillai—three thousand were known from before the time of Kulōttuṅga I. It is only the inclusion of priests from Veṅgi into this group that was an accretion.
6. Srinivas, M.N., *Religion and Society among the Coorgs of South India*, 1952, p.30. See also Staal, J.F., 'Sanskrit and Sanskritization' in *J.A.S.*, XIX, 2 (1960), 163-76.
7. Redfield, R., *Peasant Society and Culture: Anthropological Approach to Civilization*, set the anthropologists thinking on these lines and it has since been developed by others such as Singer, M., who discusses the means by which such an interaction takes place. Singer, M., *When a Great Tradition Modernizes*. See also *Traditional India: Structure and Change*, by the same author.
8. Marriot, M., *Village India*. See also his 'Changing channels of cultural transmission in Indian civilization' in Ray, V.F. (ed.), *Intermediate Societies*.
9. Eschmann, A., 'Hinduization of Tribal Deities in Orissa: The Śākta Śaiva Typology', in Kulke , *op. cit.*, Ch. IV, especially p. 79.
10. Harvey, C.E., *History of Burma*, Introduction. See also Maung Htin Aung, *Folk Elements in Burmese Buddhism*, O.U.P., 1962, pp. 4 and 107.
11. See note 9 above.
12. Pl.VIII. There is no icon, just a passage. For the Purāṇic myths see *Skanda Purāṇa, Nagara Khaṇḍa*.
13. Krishnamurthy, C., 'The Tiruvoṟṟiyūr Temple', unpublished Ph.D. thesis, University of Madras, 1956.
14. Induchudan, V.T., *The Secret Chamber, A historical, anthropological and philosophical study of the Koduṅgallūr Temple*, Trichur, Cochin Devasvom Board, 1969. Vaṭṭappāṟiayammaṉ's Kaṇṇaki origins are still remembered in the ritu-

als. It is an *uvacan̲* priest who offers worship to her and human sacrifices were offered until fairly recent times. The oral traditions preserve stories of Kaṇṇaki's entrance into Tiruvoṟṟiyūr and in a rage interrupting a game of dice between Śiva and Pārvatī. Śiva is believed to have created the nude figure of a Bhairava and in her modesty she stayed in her own shrine. Her name Vaṭṭappāṟai may relate to the Pattiṉi cult. See Obeyesekere, Gananath, *The Cult of the Goddess Pattiṉi*, Chicago and London, University of Chicago Press, 1984, p. 557 where he refers to a class of priests called Vaṭṭanti or Vaṭṭati etc. who are priests from the *Komput Viḷaiyāṭṭu* ritual associated with Kaṇṇaki. He also refers to a betel stand called Vaṭṭa, *op. cit.*, p. 562, again connected with the ritual. The word means round and the *Viṭaṅka* at Tiruvāymūr is said to perform the dance pattern called *Vaṭṭaṉaiyāṭal*. All this could well have been connected with Kaṇṇaki worship. *Kōvalan̲ katai*, a folk ballad tells the story of Vaṭṭappāṟai being thrown into the well by Śaṅkara. (*Kōvalan̲katai, Madras 1975*, p.63)

15. In normal less important processional rites the Candraśēkhara image is regarded as the representative of the Somāskanda, who in turn has become identified with the Viṭaṅka.
16. Shulaman, D., *Tamiḻ Temple Myths*, p. 124.
17. *Ibid.*
18. Eschmann, see note 9 above.
19. Sastri, K.A.N., *The Culture and History of the Tamiḻs*, p. 19, and Mīnakshī, C., *Administration and Social Life under the Pallavas*, pp. 213-38. This is by no means certain.
20. Raman, K.V., *The Early History of the Madras Region*, pp. 191-92. For a list of Jaina villages in Cōḻa country see Mahālingam, T.V., *Mackenzie Manuscripts*, p. 268, Mss. No. 69.
    Also *Camaṇa ūrkaḷiṉ jāpitā* (A list of Jaina sites), a handwritten mss. dated 1819 in U.Ve Cāmināta Iyer Library, Tiruvānmiyūr , gives a list of places where Jainism was practised.
21. Spencer, George W., 'The Sacred Geography of the Tamiḻ Śaivite Hymns', in *Numen*, Vol. 17, pp. 237 and 238, especially the map tracing the district-wise distribution of Śaivite sacred places mentioned in the *Tēvāram* hymns.
22. *S.I.I.*, Vol. I., Nos. 33 and 34 v. 3 in both. No. 33 v. 3 runs:
    'This mountain resembles the diadem of the Cōḻa province; this temple of Hara its chief jewel". Ins. 34 v. 3 Siva is said to have asked the Pallava king, "How could I standing in a temple on earth view the great power of the Cōḻas or the river Kāvērī?" The term Cōḻa is presumably used here in a territorial and not a political sense, indicating the Cōḻa territorial origins of the Somāskanda.
23. In the list of shrines visited by the Nāyaṉmār 160 shrines are recorded in Thañjāvūr, 31 in South Arcot, 8 in North Arcot, 18 in Tiruccirapalli, 20 in Chingleput, 4 in Madurai, 7 in Ramanāthapuram, 3 in Coimbatore, 1 in Salem. This phenomenon of including local pre-Āgamic deities into the Āgamic fold is visible in the case of antill deities, subterranean caverns, worship of pillar (Ēkāmranātha), Kaṇṇaki, Vaḷḷi etc.
24. Dirks, Nicholas B., 'Political Authority and Structural Change in Early South Indian History', in *I.E.S.H.R.*, Vol. 13, No. 21 (1976).
25. Stein, Burton, 'All the Kings' Mana: Prespectives on Kingship in medieval South India', in Richards, J.F. (ed.), *Kingship and Authority in South India*, pp. 115-67.

26. Berger, P., *The Sacred Canopy*, p. 29.
27. Larsen, G.J., 'Modernisation and Religious Legitimation in India', in Bardwell Smith (ed.), *Religion and Legitimation of Power in South Asia*, p. 29.
28. *Ibid.*
29. *Vide Infra*, Chapter II.
30. Hart III, George L., 'Ancient Tamil̲ Literature: Its Scholarly Past and Future'. in Stein, Burton (ed.), *Essays on South India*, pp. 52-53.
31. Subramanian, N., *History of Tamil̲nāḍu*. p. 32
32. *Vide Infra* Chapter VI.
33. *Epigraphia Indica, Vol. 12, No. 28.*
34. This persistent symbol keeps cropping up even in profound philosophical literature like the *Tirumantiram*. e.g. 4th Tantra, v. 907: '*Por̲pātam kāṇalām puttirar uṇṭākum*" - 'by beholding his golden feet sons would be conceived'. The two concepts *Tyāga* and *bhōga* are the two antipodes of the cult and occur repeatedly in such a manner in the *Mucukundasahasranāmam* and in the *padas* of Shāhāji.
35. Ghose, Rajeshwari, *Śaivism in Indonesia in the Hindu Javanese Period*, unpublished M.A.Thesis, University of Hong Kong, 1966, sp. chapter on Iconographical Parallels and Opposites.
36. Dirks, *op. cit.*, p. 149. The role of these *ājñāpatis* and *madhyasthas* has probably been overemphasised by Dirks and by Stein, 'All the Kings' Mana ...' and in his *Peasant, State and Society in Medieval South India*. While they seem to have been important local people as signatories of grants, their power seems often to stem from the king who chooses them to act in such a capacity. The power seems to vary considerably. Sometimes the wording in Pallava and Cōl̲a inscriptions suggest that the *vijñāpatis* were the people on the spot - the local power, in others simply semi-officials. From Tiruvārūr we get several records in which a local man 'recommends' the grant to the king. In such cases it seems that the initiative and a high degree of power seem to rest on the *ajñāpati* or *madhyastha*. The tone in some of these epigraphs seems to be one of simply a 'royal blessing' on a deed already worked out. See *S.I.I.* XVII, 595, where the deity Vītiviṭaṅkapperumāḷ approves the transfers of land at the instance of a *Tiruvāykkēḷvi*. 591 and 593 also portray similar situations and come from the Tiruvārūr temple.
37. *Ibid.*
38. Dirks, *op. cit.*, p. 145. He emphasizes this close structural link between *dāna* and 'kingship' by observing "the endowed institution or individual(s) became actualized expressions of sovereignty, and in that sense made equivalent in ritual terms to the King". See also Hocart, *Kings and Councillors*.
39. Appadorai, Arjun, *Worship and Conflict under Colonial Rule*, p. 34.
40. *Ibid.*
41. Stein, Burton, 'All the Kings' Mana ...", p. 115.
42. *Ibid.*, p. 135.
43. *Vide Infra* Chapter VI.
44. Appar's earlier espousal of Jainism, his later denunciation of the faith and the Pallava king's persecution of the newly converted Appar and finally the king's conviction of the superiority of the Śaiva faith of Appar and his adopting it are all told with great relish in the *Periya Purāṇam, Tirunāvukkaracu Purāṇam*, vv. 1266/1 - 1694/429. A series of miraculous escapes from the 'tortures' arranged by the king on the machinations of the Jains is also

recounted with great panache. In his own hymns Appar often repents his espousal of the Jaina faith (eg. IV.39, IV.102 etc.) In VI. 241 he refers to the tortures that the king subjected him to and seeing that no torture affected him the king himself got converted. In the *Periya purāṇam, Tirunāvukkaracu Purāṇam* (1561.296,and 1562.297) the Palaiyāṟai episode is recounted.

45. *Peiya Purāṇam. Taṇṭiyaṭikaḷ Purāṇam*, vv. 3592/1 - 3617/26.
46. *Periya Purāṇam* vv. 2576-2753 recounts the incident. For the actual enactment see Ramaswami Ayyangar, M.S., *Studies in South Indian Jainism*, Pt. I, p. 79 (2nd Ed. Delhi, 1982). He refers to the paintings of this incident at the Golden Lily Taṉk Maṇṭapa and the "five of the twelve annual festivals" in which this is enacted. For royal presence in episodes relating to *bhakti* poets see Spencer, George W., 'Religious Networks and Royal Influence in 11th Century South India', *J.E.S.H. of Orient.*, Vol. 11-12 (1968-69). For a reproduction in black and white of the painted panels see Dessigane, R. and Filliozat, J *La Legende Des Jeux De Civa A Madurai*, Pondicherry 1960, pl.XXXIII 18-19.
47. Dirks, *op. cit.*, p. 144.
48. The Pāṇḍyas were one of the oldest ruling families in Tamiḻnāḍu from Caṅkam times but their power was eclipsed by the Kalabhras and later the Cōḻas. Cuntara Pāṇṭiyaṉ revived it by defeating the Cōḻas and performed a Vīrābhiṣēka in Paḻaiyāṟu and assumed epithets like *'Cōnāṭukoṇṭaruḷiyē'* (the conqueror of Cōḻanāṭu).
49. Śiva as Ugra Pāṇḍya comes to Madurai from Kailāsa. Mīṉākṣī is the local bride, the territorial goddess. See Shulman, D., *Tamiḻ Temple Myths*, p. 51. See also Fuller, C.J., *Servants of the Goddess*, p. 20. For the variants in the myths and the legitimation of Nāyaka power see Jeyachundran, A.V. *Madurai Temple Complex*, Ph.D thesis, Madurai Kamaraj University, 1982.
50. Stein, Burton, 'All the Kings' Mana ...', p. 117. See also Kailasapathy, R., *Tamiḻ Heroic Poetry*, p. 86.
51. Stein, Burton, 'All the Kings' Mana ...', p. 117.
52. We know from Tiruvārūr *Līlai, kōvai, nānmaṇimālai* and a whole host of literature on Tyāgarāja that Vītiviṭaṅkaṉ was Tyāgarāja. We also know that Tyāgarāja was a Somāskanda and hence our identification of Vītiviṭaṅkaṉ with Somāskanda. Several iconic concepts are known at a fairly early period and actual iconic representations of the 'idea' seem to have occcurred at a later date or at any rate we only know of later art works.
53. Cēramāṉ Perumāḷ was a Cēra King. Kōcceṅkaṇaṉ was a Cōḻa king and so was Pukaḻccōḻar. Neṭumāṟaṉ was a Pāṇḍya King. Maṅkaiyaṟkaraciyār was his queen. Aiyaṭikaḷ and Kaḻaṟciṅka were Pallavas and Kūṟṟuvas belonged to Koṭumpālūr chief's family. There were several petty chiefs.
54. *Vide Infra* Chapter II under Religious Topography.
55. See Bernard Cohn and McKim Mariott, 'Networks and Centres in the Integration of Indian Civilization', *J.S.R.*, Vol. I, No. I, September 1958, 1-9. Also McKim Marriott, 'Changing Channels of Cultural Transmission in Indian Civilization', *J.S.R.*, Vol. IV, Nos. 1-2 (Mar-Sept) 1961, 13-25.
56. *Vide Infra* Chapter II.
57. Ponnusamy, S., *Sri Thyagaraja Temple, Thiruvarur*, p. 30.
58. *ARE 1912*, Nos. 158 of Kō-Vijaya Aparājitavarman; 161 and 163 and 180 of the same king; 162 of Nṛpatuṅgavarman; 174 of Kampavarman, 188 of Kampavikramavarman; 189 of Kampavarman and 190 of Aparājita Vikrama, etc.

59. 180 of *ARE 1912* gives the name of Cōḻamālīśvara. *ARE 1912-13*, Reports, para 18 refers to Aṟiñjīśvara shrine. See Suresh B. Pillai, 'The Rājarājēśvaram' (2nd Int. Tamiḻ Conference, Kuala Lumpur) where he points out that of a sampling of 174 Cōḻa temples, 49 were named after Cōḻa rulers.
60. Stein, Burton, *Peasant State and Society in Medieval South India*, Stein's conception of the 'Segmentary State' is basically against the idea that pre-Vijayanagara South Indian society was feudal. Stein believes that several nuclear institutions were organised pyramidally but only in an ideological or ritual union under the sovereign. In the segments political control was exercised by local elite. While it seems that he has clearly pointed out that it was not a centralised bureaucratic 'Byzantine' empire as held by K.A.N. Sastri and others, he seems to go to the other extreme of presenting the Cōḻa rulers as universally weak and that *nāṭu, periyanāṭu, capai (Sabha,) Ur, Nakarattār* etc., were in control. He bases his argument on the absence of a centrally devised taxation system with booty from war being one of the main sources of wealth, which too was often channelled through *brahmadēyas, dēvadānas* and other 'nuclear'institutions.The king *vis a vis* the temple, the institution of primary concern for this work, seems to have exercised 'administrative' rather than 'Legislative' power as suggested by Appadorai, *op. cit.* and seems to have interfered directly in temple accounts, disputes, etc. Stein contends that Cōḻamaṇṭalam was very much centrally controlled and next in order of the exercise of central power was Toṇṭaimaṇṭalam. The peripheral areas were left to nuclear institutions. Since the Tyāgarāja Cult was predominant only in these two zones, direct royal manoeuvring of the cult is noticeable. See also Stein, 'Agrarian Integration in South India' in Frykenberyg, R. (ed.), *Land Control and Social Structure in Indian History*, pp. 175-216.
61. *S.I.I.*, Vol. II, p. 20.
62. Visvanathan, N. (ed.) Shāhāji *Tyāgēśapada*, p. 224. *"Tyāgaika lōlurē dēva Tañjēśvarārūre"* - 'The Tyaga who is the Lord of Tañjai and Ārūr' and p. 101, *"Tyāga Bṛhadīsaśivaka"* equating them.
63. The king who found the *Tēvāram* in Chidambaram as recorded in the *Periya Purāṇam* has been equated by historians with Rājarāja I. This identity is on internal evidence and chronology and is by no means proved beyond doubt. For a summary of the different arguments see Balasubramanian, S.R., *Middle Cōḻa Temples*, p. 79 footnote. Vellaivaranar and T.V.S. Pantarattar equate the king with Āditya II. See Pandarattar, T.V.S., *Piṟkāla Ccoḻarvaralāṟu* (*History of the later Cōḻas* (in Tamiḻ) and *Paṉṉiruttirumuṟaikaḷ* of Vellaivaranar. However, as shown in the main body of the text, a 14th century work directly equates the king who found the Tēvāram with Rājarāja.
64. See Somasundaram, J.M., *Cōḻar Kālakkōyiṟ Paṇikaḷ*, Thañjāvūr temple tradition believes this.
65. Visvanathan N., (ed.), *Tyāgēśapadas*, p. 49.
66. *Ibid.*, p. 101.
67. See also *Mucukundasahasranāmam* inv. 254
68. *Kalveṭṭukaḷ*, Madras Tamiḻnāḍu Archaeological Department Publication, p. 44.
69. Sivaramamurti, C., *South Indian Paintings*, 1968, pp. 82 and 87. The Cōḻa paintings in the dark passage around the main cell was uncovered by S.K. Govindaswamy in 1930. For a line drawing of Cēramāṉ on his caparisoned and prancing horse see Sivaramamurti, *op. cit.*, fig. 41. See also

Balasubrahmanyam, S.R., *Middle Cōḻa Temples*, p. 31.

70. For the traditional links between Tiruvārūr and Thañjāvūr see U. Ve Cāminata Iyer's introduction to the *Tañjai Peruvuṭaiyār Ulā* of Civakoḻuntu Tēcikar, where the editor discusses the links between the two temples under Rājarāja I and revival of these special links under the Marāṭhās.
71. See note 70 above and Bibliography.
72. *S.I.I.* Vol. II, No. 38. *S.I.I.*, II *Reports*, paras 48 and 68. *ARE 1907*, No. 360. *ARE 1912-211*. *S.I.I.*, Vol. II, No. 65. See also Sastri, K.A.N., 'The Economy of South Indian Temple in the Cōḻa Period', in *Mālavīya Commemoration Volume*.
73. *S.I.I.*, Vol. II, p. 20 ff.
74. Personal communication by Kurukkaḷ and Śivatāṅkis of Tiruvoṟṟiyūr temple, 27th July 1983. Though the term 'left' and 'right' were not assigned to the Tiruvārūr Devadāsīs they were classified as belonging to 'Tyāgarāja' and 'Kamalāmpāl' and officiated as separate categories of dancers. The terms 'Iṭaṅkai' and 'Valaṅkai' have puzzled scholars for so long. It could well have originally been a division of Śiva and Śakti worshippers.
75. See Bibliography for a list of his works. The theme of the 'Segmentary State' has been expressed in several of his works.
76. Burton Stein has been criticised by Kenneth R. Hall for not giving due importaṉce to the 'nagaram' as a unit and his failure to deal adequately with the market forces, See Hall, Kenneth R., 'Peasant State and Society in Cōḻa Times' in *I.E.S.H.R.*, 1981,Vol.XVIII, Nos. 3 and 4, p. 394. See also by the same auṭhor, *Trade and Statecraft in the Age of the Cōḻas*, Delhi, 1980.
77. Spencer, George W., 'Religious Networks and Royal Influence in 11th Century South India', *Journal of the Economic and Social History of the Orient*, Vol. 11-12 (1968-69.)
78. Spencer, George W., 'Royal Initiative under Rājarāja I', *I.E.S.H.R.*, 7. No. 4 (December 1970) pp. 431-42. See also George Spencer's 'Temple Money Lending and Livestock Redistribution in Early Taṉjore', *I.E.S.H.R.*, V. (1968) pp. 270-293. See also Stein, Burton, 'The Economic Function of a Medieval South Indian Temple', in *J.A.S.* XIX, 2 (1960), 163-176. For actual figures of livestock etc., see *S.I.I.* Vol. II, 63 and 94 and also 64 and 95. The first two list the shepherds. The latter gives the names of other than royal donors. In all 2,832 cows, 1,644 ewes and 30 she-buffaloes were donated.
79. For the transactional nature of Hindu temples see Stein, Burton, c.f. note 78 above. *S.I.I.*, Vol. II, 91 mentions three major sources of wealth. 1) King's own treasury; 2) booty in war siezed during wars with Cēras and Pāṇḍyas 3) taxes.
80. Personal Communication July 1983.
81. Nāgasāmy, R., *Gaṅgaikoṇḍa cōḻapuram*, State Department of Archaeology, Tamiḻnāḍu, 1970, pp. 13-14.
82. From Jayavartman II who established his capital at Kulen plateau to Jayavarman VII at Bayon, there has been a continuous change of capitals accompanied by the building of royal temples in Khmer history. Jayavarman II (802-50), after freeing himself from Javanese dominance erected a *linga* of Śiva, the 'symbol of his royal power' on the Kulen plateau. Indravarman (877-889) built his royal temple at Bakong; Yaśōvarman (889-909) at Bakheng and was the patron of the complex network of hydraulic works at Angkor. Jayavarman IV (921-24) moved his capital to Kokher, as he was an usurper and wanted to be away from the erstwhile capital. This tradition was contin-

ued until Sūryavarman II (1113-50) built Angkor Vat and Jayavarman VII (1181-1219), the Bayon.

83. See Goswami, B.B. and Horab. S.G., *Cāmuṇḍēśvarī Temple in Mysore*, Calcutta, Anthropological Survey of India, Memoir No. 35, 1975.
84. Strangely enough no inscriptions of the time of Rājēndra I have come from Gaṅgaikoṇṭacolpuram. It is only in the time of Vīrarājēndra (*ARE 1892* No. 82) that the above epithet of Rājēndra and other details of his endowments of the temple are recorded. The style of this inscription which is also reproduced in *S.I.I.* Vol. IV, No. 529, is very similar to the inscriptions of Rājarāja I from Thañjāvūr. In all 340 kalañju of gold and 1,100,000 kalams of paddy are recorded in this inscription as endowments to the temple.
85. *ARE 1892*. Cited by Nagaswamy, R., *op. cit*.
86. Subramanian, T.N., (ed.), *South Indian Temple Inscriptions* Vol. II, p. 643, No. 676.
87. Ponnusamy, S., *Śrī Tyāgarāja Temple at Tirvārūr*, State Department of Archaelogy, Tamilnāḍu, 1972, p. 51.
88. *Ibid.*
89. The Paravai image at Tiruvārūr has been recently stolen and now Cuntarar stands alone waiting for a new image to arrive. (Information as in February 1984). The Cuntarar and Paravai images at Thañjāvūr were set up by an officer of the king, *S.I.I.*, Vol. II, No. 38. Several of these Viṭaṅka images seem to have strong territorial affiliations. Tillai Viṭaṅkar, Tañjai Viṭaṅkar, 'Āraṉiya Viṭaṅka' (*Vide Infra* Ch. II) and so on. Though it is tempting to conclude from this that they were territorial gods - there are some exceptions to this rule, such as Puvaiviṭaṅkar (Bhuvanaviṭaṅkar.)
90. See 165 of *ARE 1912* which refers to a Viḷupparaiyar of Kāraṇai.
91. The Vijayadaśamī festival has always strong royal connotations. Carol Breckenridge has discussed this ritual with relation to the Cētupatis of Ramnaḍ. See Breckenridge, Carol Appadorai, 'From Protector to Litigant - Changing Relations Between Hindu Temples and the Rājā of Ramnaḍ', in *I.E.S.H.R.*, Vol. IV, 1977, pp. 75-106.
92. *SII Vol. II, No.38*
93. *S.I.I.* Vol. II, No. 6, records Kuntavi's installation of the image of her parents. *SII Vol.II, 95, para 82* records that Īśāna Śiva, the royal guru set up an image of himself.
94. *SII Vol.V*, no.521. Also *ARE 1894*, 219 and 222. Temples were connected to other temples through royal donors, myths, etc. Rājēndra I built Tyāgarāja temples in stone at both Tiruvārūr and Tiruvorriyūr which were connected through Cuntaramūrtināyaṉār. There are several such examples. *Vide Infra*, Chapter II.
95. *ARE 1956-57* contain several epigraphs from this temple.
96. S.R. Balasubrahmanyan, *op. cit.*, p. 114. For Cōḻīśvaram temple, *Ibid.*, pp. 374-5.
97. *Ibid.*, p. 267. *ARE 1965-66*, Nos. 440 and 448.
98. *ARE 1950-51*, nos. 246-269, for inscriptions. See L'Hernault, *Iconographie ...*, p 30 for a photograph of the Tiruvāymūr Somāskanda.
99. Balasubramanian, S.R., *Early Cōḻa Art*, p. 184.
100. Jagannāthan, K.V. Ed. *Caṅkara Rājēndra Cōḻan Ulā* Tiruvanmiyur, U.Vē Cāminàta Iyer Library, 1977. Zvelebil, K.V., *A History of Tamil Literature*, p. 188.

101. *Divyasūricaritra* XVIII, v. 84 cited by K.A.N. Sastri *Cōḻas* p. 297, footnote 42)
102. Sastri, op.cit p. 294
103. Kulke, Herman, *Cidambaramāhātmya* (in German), but he mentions it in brief in the English summary. Also his article, 'Funktionale Erklaerung eines Soedindischen Māhātmyas. Die Legende Hiranyavarmans und das Leden des Cōḻa Koenigs Kulōttuṅga I; in *Saeculum*, XX (1969), 412-422.
104. Epigraphs of Vikramacōḻa refer to famine and several instances of people selling themselves as slaves to the temple. See Sastri, K.A.N., *Cōḻas*. p.344 See *ARE Reports, 1900,* para 24, *ARE 1910 Reports*, para 10 and *ARE Reports 1935,* para 14. In all these references are made to floods and famine. 276 of *1901* states clearly "The times became bad, the village was ruined and the ryots had fled". 151 of *1934-35* speaks of restrictions on sale of land at time of distress. The interesting thing to note is that in the *Kanta Purāṇam* Mucukuntaṉ is said to have gone to heaven since the land was ravaged by a subterranean fire. (*Vide Infra*, Chapter IV). Mucukuntaṉ married a daughter of Vīrabāhu and establised a *new* kingdom with the heavenly damsels brought down to the earth. This rings very close to truth. Kulōttuṅga I had started a new era and floods swept in the reign of Vikramacōḻa. They were both combined in the myth.
105. Vikramacōḻa's munificence to Chidambaram is recorded in several inscriptions. See *ARE Reports 1913*, para. 34.
106. *Ibid.*
107. He has been identified with Kirimikaṇṭaṉ of the Vaiṣṇava traditions and persecutor of Rāmānuja.
108. *Kulōttuṅgacōḻaṉulā*. Vide Infra Chapter III, f.n. 51.
109. *ARE of 1901*, No. 269. (*S.I.I.*, Vol. VII, No. 485) See *Periya Purāṇam, Tirunāṭṭucciṟappu*, v. 35, *Tirunakaracciṟappu*, v. 13.
110. *Ibid.*
111. Subramanian, N., *History of Tamiḻnāḍu*, p. 254.
112. *Ibid.*, p. 256.
113. *E.I.*, Vol. XXXI, 1955-56, p. 224 ff. *ARE 1924*, no. 433. Also *Kulōttuṅgaṉcōḻaṉulā*
114. *Ibid.*
115. *E.I.*, Vol. XXXI, p. 226.
116. Sethuraman, N., *Aruḷuṭaiya Cōḻa Maṇṭalam*, has strange theories by which he equates Rājādhirāja with Etirilāperumāḷ and takes him to be the regent. The strangeness lies in his methodology for the author attributes his theory to para-sensory perception in deciphering the mystery of succession. He believed that figures from history presented the story to him in a dream.
117. Zvelebil, op. cit p. 188. See Note 100 above.
118. *Ibid.* See Mu. Arunachalam, *History of Tamiḻ Literature* (in Tamiḻ), 13th century, p. 406. (*Tamiḻ Iḻakkiya Varalāṟu Patiṉmūṉṟām Nūṟṟāṇṭu*). See note 100 above.
119. Mu Arunachalam, *op. cit.*, pp. 407 and 408.
    He states that this *Ulā* is published in *Maturai-CenTamiḻ*, Vol. 16, cited *op. cit.*, p. 406. The reference appears to be wrong since I could not find it in Vol. 16.
120. *Ibid.*
121. See U.Vē Cāmināta Iyer, Introduction to *Tiyākarājalīlaikaḷ*. The story occurs in *Līlai* No. 1, vv. 3-31 of Piḷḷai, Mīṉātcicuntaram, *Tiyākarājalīlaikaḷ*.
122. The Maṉunīti Cōḻan myth seems to have captured the imagination of rulers in Sri Lanka and Thailand. In Śrī Laṅka Maṉunīti is substituted by Ellara, (*Mahāvaṁśa*) see *Epigraphia Zeylonnica*, iii, 1-47. A popular Thai legend how

Rāma Kamhaeng placed a bell of justice and whenever it was rung he would appear personally and sit on the royal seat called the Maṅgkaśilā, which he had placed between two palm trees. This stone throne was discovered by Moṅgkūṭ when he was a monk and he brought it to Bangkok. It is now placed in the Great Hall of the Dusit Palace.

123. Ātma Tēcikar, *Cōḻamaṇṭalaśatakam*, v. 86.
124. Kulke, *op. vit.*, p. 149, Ch, VII, p. 150.
125. *Ibid.*
126. *Ibid.*
127. Sastri, K.A.N., *Cōḻas*, p. 328. See *E.I.* XV, pp. 101 and 103.
128. Mahāliṅgam, T.V. (ed.), *Mackenzie Maṉuscripts*, records several myths about Kulōttuṅga.
129. Kā. Kōvintaṉ, (ed.), *Kūttaṉ Tamiḻ*, Madras, 1957.p.1
130. Piccāṇṭārkōyil Irācakōpāla Piḷḷai (ed.). *Tiyākarājalīlaikaḷ*.
131. Stein,Burton, 'Agrarian Integration ..." in Frykenberg, (ed.), *op. cit.*
132. Spencer, George W., 'Sacred Geography of the Śaivite Hymns', *Numen* 17. See Map, showing the distribution of temples referred to in *Tēvāram*.
133. The marked change between the Pallava-Cōḻa and Vijayanagara period seems to have been focussed on the more contractual nature of relationships between the central government and feudatories Vijayanagara rule. Nevertheless, temples and sectarian matters played an important role.
134. Stein, Burton, 'Agrarian Integration ...' in Frykenberg (ed.), *op.cit.* p. 207.
135. Appadorai, Arjun, *Worship and Conflict in the Colonial Period*. Also note 136 below.
136. Baliga, B.S. *Handbook*, Madras, 1957, p. 62.
137. The early Vijyanagara kings were othodox Śaivas and their tutelary deity was Virūpākṣa. The *Prapannāmṛtam*, a celebrated Vaiṣṇava work explains this change in strange terms. It is said that the ghosts of the relatives killed by the King Virūpākṣa bothered the monarch and they were pacified by Vaiṣṇavas reading out the Rāmāyaṇa to them. Cited by T.V. Mahalingam, *Administration and social life under Vijayanagara*. p. 321, f.n. 68. During Acyuta Rāya's rule (1529-42) the devotion extended to Gōvindarāja once more became a major controversial issue in the Chidambaram temple. In 1597 Kṛṣṇappa Nāyaka renovated the Viṣṇu shrine despite violent opposition by the Śaiva priests who went to the extent of committing suicide in protest. See Mahalingam, T.V., *op. cit.*, pp. 325 and 330. Debates between sectarian leaders were often held in the presence of the king. This sectarian rivalry continued throughout the 19th century.
138. There are numerous examples of such debates. Appaya Dīkṣita, an Advaitin debated against Tātācārya a Vaṭakalai Vaiṣṇava. A Mādhva leader debated against a Vīraśaiva.
139. The Gōḷaki Maṭha was popular till the 15th century. 213 of *1924* of Narasiṅgarāya Dharmāraṇya from Pirāṉmalai in Tirupputtur taluq, Ramnad district, refers to a gift of the village of Kīḻaikkūṭalur by Eppuli Nāyakar as a *maṭhapuram* to Pāṇḍimaṇḍalādhipati (Tamiḻ *Pāṇṭimaṇṭalātipati*). Pāṇṭināṭṭumutaliyār of the Bhikṣāmahāsantāṉa alias "Lakṣādhyāyi Santāṉa and the Gōḷaki maṭha was the presiding pontiff of an Aṟupattimūvartirumaṭam alias Dakṣiṇa Kailāsam". This made the identification of the maṭha foolproof. References to this maṭha occur from 1555 and with great regularity. 525 of *1962/63* of Sadāśivāraya's reign mentions this maṭha Santāṉa from

Perumparrappuliyūr. The pontiff is called Tiruppunavāśal Mutaliyār and a grant of 1785 Śaka = 1863 A.D. records an endowment for a *maṭhapuram*. A group of records of this period come from Kōvilūr in Tiruppatur taluq from the Korravālīśvara temple.

140. Mahalingam, T.V., *Administration and Social Life under Vijayanagar*, pp. 116, 117 and 20. He refers to two instances of government interference in enforcing *svadharma*. Kṛṣṇadēvarāya had appointed a sectarian leader to enquire and punish the delinquents among the worshippers of the Rāmānuja order.

141. *Ibid.*, p. 116.

142. *ARE 1916*, No. 325. For Iṭaṅkai Valaṅkai conflicts see *ARE 1913* p. 109. Also M. Śrinivasa Aiyangar, *Tamil Studies*, Madras, 1914, p. 95. See also Beck, Brenda, 'The Right Left Division of South Indian Society', in *J.A.S.*, Vol. XXIX, No. 4, August 1970, pp. 779-98. Also her *Peasant Society in Koṅku*, especially p. 74, and Appadorai, Arjun, 'Right and Left hand Castes in South India', *I.E.S.H.R.*, Vol. XI, Nos. 2-3 June-Sept., 1974, pp. 216-59. The fact that 'Right-handed' and 'Left-handed' castes could be related to the Tāntric mode of worship does not seem to have received enough attention. For conflicts between Maravars and Nāḍārs (Nāṭṭārs) see Hardgrave, R., *The Nāḍārs of Tamilnāḍu: the Political Culture of a Community in Change*, University of California Press, Berkeley, 1969. The Maravas moved upward in the caste structure with the establishment of the first Maravar Cētupati in 1604 A.D. The Tiruvārūr temple had a special Toṇṭaimān *mariyātai* for the Cētupatis, which has recently been discontinued. (Personal communication, Kurukkaḷ Candraśēkhara Nāyiṇār, July 1982). Thus they were allowed into the temples, but the Nāṭṭārs were not received in Maravar-managed temple. The Nāṭṭārs were however allowed in Thañjāvūr temples. This led to the famous 'Kaumuthi Temple case' of the 1920s which was both a caste and a temple-entry dispute.

143. Examples are provided by the one referred to above in footnote 140 which refers to a conflict between Veḷḷāḷars and Veḷḷaināṭṭārs. See *ARE 1917* Reports, Para. 55. Inscription No. 325 of *ARE 1916* on the "Kulaśēkharamuṭaiyār temple" at Kalliḍaśkuricci records the above dispute. See also 309 and 378 of *ARE 1916* from the temple at Ambāsamudram which refers to conflicts in Kammāḷa community. The 12th century Tiruvārūr epigraph regarding Rathakāras and Kammāḷas has been discussed in detail in Chapter VI.

144. *ARE 1912*, Reports. *ARE 1913*, paras, 6, 24 and 5.

145. *Bōsalavaṁśāvali*, a Sanskrit Mss. of Sarfoji's time in the Thañjāvūr Sarasvati Mahal Library.p.36.

146. Subramanian. K.R. The *Marātha Rājās of Tanjore*, p. 33.

147. For a mention of some paintings in the British Collection *Vide Infra* Chapter II. For the vast corpus of literature on Tyāgarāja written during the Marāṭhā period see Subramanian, K.R., op.cit.

148. *Viṣṇu Śāhendra Vilāsam*, Tanjore Saraswatī Mahāl Series.

149. Visvanathan, N., (ed.), *Tyāgēśa Padas* of Shāhāji. Introduction.

150. *A Triennial Catalogue of Manuscripts*, Vol. 2, part 1, c (Sanskrit) of the Madras Oriental Manuscripts Library, (Mss. D. 530- D. 534.) is a work by Shāhāji called *Tyāgarājavinōdacaritra Prabandha*. It is composed in a hybrid language mixing Telugu, Marāṭhī, Tamil and Sanskrit. It is a work on dance and is dedicated to Tyāgarāja and his Dance. It uses 7 *ragas* and 7 *talas*. To the best of my knowledge this has not been published.

151. *Tyāgarājakavacam* Mss. Sarasvatī Mahal, Thañjāvūr, B. 8393 D 22264, '*Tripta-*

sundarasaṅgītā rasanām pātu mē'niśam'.

152. Mahālingam, T.V., 'The Nawābs of the Carnatic and Hindu Temples' in his *Readings in South Indian History*, Delhi, 1977, pp. 192-95.
153. Kennedy, R., 'Status and Control of Temples in Tamilnāḍu', in *I.E.S.H.R.*, 1974 (June-September), Vol. XI, pp. 260-88. The local trustees became all important because as pointed out by the above author the British were the new rulers and they had right of supervision and regulation but were really outsiders with no legitimation through temples. He cites Ramanatha Iyer, *Endowments Acts*, p. 4. to show the effects it has on Brāhmaṇas who acquired trusteeships which had not belonged to them earlier. Thus for example until 1,830 *pūcāris* at Paḻaṉi were non-brāhmaṇas. It was during the 1860s that the landlords of the Vaṭapātimaṅgalam estate became the trustees of the Tiruvārūr and Vedāraṇyam temples. Several law suits in the 1920s and 30s were between them and the *pantāracaṉṉiti* of the Tiruppukaḷūr Maṭha.
154. Appadurai, *Worship and Conflict* ...
155. Rajayya, K., *History of Tamilnāḍu*. p.301.

Chapter Ten

POSTSCRIPT

Several questions were posed in the introduction with the hope of being able to follow the working and logic of a regional cult of Tamilnāḍu, through a process of historical evolution. The first task was to define the essential characteristics of a cult within the rather amorphous framework of Hinduism. A constellation of elements such as a sacred locus, an icon or a chthonic symbol, a shrine, a compendium of myths, a plethora of rites, an edifying metaphysics, a cultic personnel and a pilgrimage tradition, all these carefully nourished by powerful patrons, were seen to provide the parameters of the cult studied. The Tyāgarāja cult of Tiruvārūr was taken as a case study and some of the general conclusions were drawn by treating it as an archetypal Tamil̲ Śaiva cult.

The next issue was to trace the manner in which a locotheistic cult could become a regional cult by a process of networking and creating the idea of sacred geography. Antiquity and the revelation of the sacred were the important notions that determined the nodal points within such a network. A network could be further expanded to include other nodal points. This was done by attributing to them a sacred character by virtue of their association with the primary nodal points. Thus sacrality was assumed by association with another sacred spot and this association was provided by myths. The circulation of myths was accomplished in the early days of an emerging cult by itinerant minstrel poets. Gradually these poets were themselves regarded as a holy collective and their visit to a spot with possibly a special sanctity to the autochthonous beliefs of the people sanctified the spot for the "higher Āgamic" religion and incorporated it into the fast expanding cultic geography. These poets were subsequently canonised by the Tamil̲ Śaiva or Vaiṣṇava traditions. In the case of the Tyāgarāja cult of Tiruvārūr this expansion of cultic topography was the achievement of the Śaiva collective called the *nāyan̲mār*, particularly the three singer poets whose anthology of hymns was called the *Tēvāram*. In fact it will be more true to say that the lines of the cultic topography were given a clarity by the subsequent hagiologists of this trio.

Furthermore, links were established between one cluster of sacred cultic points with another cluster belonging, albeit to an allied cult. Hence, fairly complex inter cultic and intra-cultic boundaries were drawn of the sacred realm. Thus the Tiruvārūr Tyāgarāja cult was extended to include at first seven cultic centres and later several more, some of which were based on episodes in the 'lives' of the saint poets as recorded in their hagiographies. Sometimes a common philosophical theme such as the divine dance, which as a dance of knowledge revealed the metaphysical Truth to the devotee linked several sites with dance as its focal soteriological motif. The Tyāgarāja of Tiruvārūr, the performer of the metaphysical "*ajapā*" dance was linked through the theme of the divine dance with the Naṭarāja of Chidambaram, and the sacred shrine at Chidambaram was a central point of an even larger networking system.

This was possible because at a philosophical level there was the constant reminder that though the local manifestation is rooted to the soil, it is also the vision of the universal God, and hence the locotheistic deity could assume henotheistic proportions. The *Tēvāram* hymns themselves exhibit henotheistic tendencies as well as an emphasis on the *locus sanctus*. Hence, deities retained a territorial identity but often lost their iconographic particularity in the general spirit of henotheism, so predominant in these hymns. The iconographic particularity belongs to the realm of the Āgamas, not of *bhakti*.

Nevertheless, the notion of the sacred had to peneterate the subconscious of the culture and any new imported idioms of the sacred had to be superimposed on these sub-strata of beliefs. The result was that the cultic symbol became multi-vocal. It was in the case of the Tyāgarāja cult the worship of an anthill, a subterranean cavern, a Somāskanda icon, a symbol of universal Breath and so on and so forth.

One of the main focuses of this research was on deconstructing the world view of the cultic believers. This world view was shaped by many streams of thought propagated by several schools. This cultic association was developed by piling ever expanding layers of symbolism on to the icon. Thus Tyāgarāja was a fertility symbol, a paradigmatic sovereign, a palladium of Cōḻa royalty, a Tamiḻ icon, an agent of Sanskrit-Tamiḻ synthesis, and a divine dancer whose *'ajapā'* and *'haṁsa'* dance encompasses a maze of doctrinal synthesis drawn from Vedic, Āgamic, and Śrī-Vidyā sources. The Tyāgarāja is also the great grammarian, the expounder of the Āgamic metaphysics of speech; he is all this and more. He is the friend of the lowly and the downtrodden and grants secret visions to those who are prohibited by the rules of the organised faith to enter his temples. He is often portrayed as the mediator in certain important socio-religious issues. For within the cult are seen several powerful dichotomies. In the world of myths the Tyāgarāja is multi layered and in this sense is typical of a cultic personality within the Hindu fold. Believers chose a particular set of messages, to suit their own ethos which, in turn, helped in the social construction of their 'reality'. Thus grew a kind of pluralism of beliefs and approaches towards the divine under a cultic umbrella. This was justified by a specific kind of universalism which believed that though Reality is One it manifests itself as many. The many manifestations were then graded in a hierarchic manner as various levels of truth. This was a distinctly Hindu brand of universalism, pluralism and relativism arranged in an unique manner into a highly hierarchic structure. In more recent times it has led into classifying anyone who is not anything else such as a Christian, Muslim or Parsee etc. as a Hindu.

The methodology therefore oscillated between a mainly historical enquiry as to what happened when, and an ahistorical methodology of peeling layers of myths and imageries in trying to understand the culture that gave shape to the cult and its world view. The historical enquiry has looked at the growth of the two institutions of the temple and the *maṭha* or monastic organisations, the latter mainly in their capacity as trustees of temples, in and around Tiruvārūr. In attempting this, only those institutions with direct or indirect connections to the Tyāgarāja cult have been dealt with. Thus, selection of institutions studied has been restricted to those with cultic associations and playing a prominent part in Tiruvārūr and its environs.

Chronologically speaking, the periods of the Pallavas, and even more so of the Cōḻas, have received much greater attention, as it is during these periods that a major shift occurred in Tamiḻ religion when temples and cults enshrined therein attained a new importance and evolved new forms of organisations. The Post-

Cōḻa period saw the weakening of this cult. It was resucitated for a short period under the Marāṭhās and then dwindled once more into relative obscurity.

This work has looked at the cultic temple as a dynamic and versatile institution, which could be a centre of social protest. However, more often than not, it acted as an agent through which all charismatic protests were tamed and institutionalised. Hence, the temple as an acculturating agent had and still has tremendous potential for politicisation. Traditionally the king was a noble royal icon, whose nobility lay, amidst other qualities, in his munificence to the sacred temples of his realm. His court poets sang of his greatness by highlighting his devotion to the chosen deity. This gave the cult and the temple a capacity to play an important role in the legitimising of power. In the case of the Tamiḻ kings it played the additional role of providing them with an acceptance by the north Indian monarchs as fellow members of a cultural elite. It also brought several sub cultural regions of the realm under a larger cultural orbit dominated by the sacral presence of the monarch.

The Tyāgarāja Cult was not the spontaneous product of an outburst of primitve genius. It was a well tailored court cult, fostered by the sovereigns of the realm. This conclusion has been arrived at primarily by studying the origin myth (Chapter 4) and by tracing the development of the Somāskanda iconography (Chapter 2).

From the beginning, the Tyāgarāja cult was associated with Cōḻamaṇṭalam. The land of the Cōḻas was the realm of Tyāgarāja; the icon in turn was brought to this earth from the heavens by a noble Cōḻa monarch. When the Cōḻa monarch was hurt in a duel the deity bled, striking terror in the heart of the enemy. At a moment of crisis the deity or a mysterious person associated with the deity came to save the Cōḻa monarchy. The world of myths is rich with such legitimatory tales. It is this utter devotion of the monarch to a deity, his humble role *vis-a-vis* the deity, his act of kenosis that underpinned the ruler's high status.

On the social front when regulations forbade the untouchable to enter the temple, divine vision was provided for the unfortunate man, as long as he did not gatecrash into the temple. Thus the role models were created and conformity brought rewards in the form of temple 'honours'. Cultural integration brought shared social ideas and through myths shared social legitimations. Legitimation, as pointed out by Berger, is different from the body of ideas existing in a society at any given period for they are mostly pre-theoretical and pre-reflexive in character, while ideas are consciously worked out.

One conclusion that became apparent from this study was that Tamiḻ medieval society was neither as static and consistently 'orthodox' nor as systematically Sanskritic-Brāhmaṇa dominated as present day Tamiḻ nationalists would have us believe.

What did however emerge from this study was that both Orthodoxy and Protest Movements were couched in ambivalent terms and the system survived by shifts and countershifts. Nākaikkārōṇam, one of the Tyāgarāja centres, was a renowned centre of the Pāśupatas, who at one level were dissenters (Chapter 6) and at another were the upholders of orthodoxy; '*gṛhastha*' or householder Pāśupatas were hereditary trustees of "higher" Āgamic temples.

Every protest movement soon got bifurcated into an orthodox and a heterodox school and the heterodox end of the spectrum gradually got absorbed into mainstream orthodoxy by being provided with respectability. Co-option of protest leaders into the orthodox fold, at one end acknowledged their new way of looking at things, and on the other abstracted and intellectualised their ideology to such abstruse heights that at a mundane social structural level they had become completely innocuous. Myths, rituals, rites and "honour" system were the means by which such an acculturation took place.

The temple was the place where fierce or unorthodox ideas could be tamed and institutionalised. It was also the ideal agent for the "routinisation of charisma" - all charismatic movements once accepted and propagated by the temple lost their anti-establishment character. The temple priest as one of the chief personnel of this acculturating process was regarded as much less pure than the Tamiḻ Brāhmaṇa scholar who could afford not to compromise and live in his own ivory tower of purity. Hence the temple priest could not even enter into matrimony with the Vedic Brāhmaṇa. By being symbolically equated with the temple, a structure which has survived through skilful compromises, the *kurukkaḷ* or temple priest had to finally compromise his own purity.

Thus temples and temple cults succeeded in articulating an overall monism under which were subsumed a variety of particularisms all neatly ordered into a hierarchic framework. Most rival beliefs were absorbed as a caste and given a place in the hierarchical scale and accommodated philosophically by accepting the two notions of pluralism and relativism, thereby creating as stated earlier, a very Hindu brand of universalism. This universalism accepted all other religions but assumed a superiority because it saw itself as superior to those faiths which expressed what in its opinion was narrow particularisms.

As an unarticulated, yet strong undercurrent running through the whole research was the question of continuity and change. How much of a study of the past can throw light on understanding the present? Secularism in India as enshrined in the Constitution is vastly different from the manner in which secularism is understood in western democracies or for that matter in socialist countries like China. In India it is interpreted as equality of all religions. India is a highly religious civilisation; an attempt to keep religion out of the political process is proving increasingly difficult. What then is the nature of the religious experience?

Tamiḻ nationalism of the 20th century, which began as anti northern, anti-Āryan, anti-Brāhmaṇa and finally anti-Hindu movement soon settled down to a kind of recognisable orthodoxy. No form of cultural nationalism, however avowedly atheistic, could completely avoid the religious idiom - it was the most immediate language of the masses. Thus, Ramasami Naicker, the D.K. leader, and an avowed atheist, wanted Tamiḻ *arccaṉai* to replace Sanskrit. He thundered in a public meeting: "What business has a God in Tamiḻnāḍu if he does not want Tamiḻ?" So at one level he was an atheist at another a pragmatist Tamiḻ nationalist, who was instinctively aware of the power of the Tamiḻ *arccaṉai* issue in mobilising the masses. He was a religious Tamiḻ *bhakta* who burnt the Tamiḻ Vēda, the *Periya Purāṇam* and acted as a temple trustee, all at the same time.

Even political sycophancy is expressed in the sacred idioms of the 'mother' figure, when the Chief Minister happens to be a commanding female figure, as is the case in Tamiḻnāḍu at the time of writing. Despite a rationalist secularist garb, traditional imageries keep resurfacing and without batting an eyelid erstwhile atheistic DMK leaders can claim Murukaṉ to be the great

Tamiḻan. Further north in the region of Maharashtra, protest movements of the 1950s, which converted their followers to Buddhism as a protest against Hinduism's inequities have, sooner or later been engulfed by the affective emotive stance of the militant Shivsena, with its symbols drawn from the Hindu cultic god Gaṇapati and fused with historical Marāṭhā heroes such as Shivaji.

Closer to our times, archaelogy and history have become highly politicised. The birthplace of Rāma- the precise spot where the locotheistic presence revealed itself, is a matter of vital importance to large sections of the community. Whether a cultic shrine existed at that very spot is no longer only a matter of religious concern but has become a current political and legal issue. The sacred presence is revealed by a "miraculous and sudden" appearance of icons. New myths, newly fashioned rituals, reworking of an ancient pilgrimage tradition, a pan-Indian sacred network meticulously constructed through a processional icon being ritually taken all across the pan-Indian sacred topography of the Rāma cult provide the essential system of communication for the newly emerging religio-political forces that have been labelled under the blanket term 'Hindutva'. Maṭhas or monastic establishments with their ritual personnel have been co-opted and the most effective crowd gatherers are those who assume the mantle of the religeuse - the two most prominent women in the neo-Hindu movement are known by their epithets as Sannyāsinī and Sādhvī.

Socially shared legitimacies are as important as socially shared ideas. Symbolic resonances, evocations and associations literally reek with surfeit of meanings and when used effectively by a speaker of the new Hindu forum the message burrows deep in the minds of the audience going well beyond the articulated words.

Bibliography

Tamil Texts, by Title

Aiṅkuṟunūṟu, E. S. Rajam, Ed., Madras 1957.

Caṅkara Rājēndra Cōḻaṉulā Ed. Ki.Va. Jakannātan, U.Ve Cāmināta Iyer Press, Tiruvāṉmiyūr, 1977.

Cātinūl of Kamalai Nānappirakācar, Madras: Kaḷānidhi Press, 1875. A paper mss. of this work with notes by U. Ve Cāminātaiyar is available in the U. Ve Cāminātaiyar Library at Tiruvāṉmiyūr. Also Ed. Cantiracēkara Nāṭṭār, Madras, 1875

Cēkkiḻārnāyaṉār Purāṇam of Umāpaticivācāriyār. in the same volume as the *Tiruttoṇṭar Mākkatai* (TSISSP, Madurai, 1970).

Cilappatikāram of Iḷaṅkōvaṭikaḷ, with Arumpatavurai and the commentary of Aṭiyārkkunallār, Ed. by U. Ve Cāminātaiyar, Madras, 9th Ed. 1978.

Cilappatikāram, Trans. V.R. Ramachandra Diksitar, *The Śilappatikāram*, Madras 1939.

Citampara Purāṇam with commentary by Pe. Irāmaliṅkapiḷḷai, Madras, 1906.

Civañāṉacittiyār of Aruṇanti, *Cupakkam*, Tarumapuram, 1962.

Civañāṉacittiyār, with Civañāna yōgin's commentary, TSISSP,1940.

Civañāṉacittiyār, Trans, with text, K. Śivarāmaṉ, Kāśimutt, Tiruppaṉantāḷ, 1950.

Civapūcai akaval of Ñāṉapirakācapaṭṭārakar with notes by G.K. Cuppiramaṇiamutaliyār, Madras, 1958.

Cōḻamaṇṭalacatakam of Ātmanāta Tēcikar (of) Vēlur, Ed., Cōmacuntara Tēcikar, Mayunar, 1916

Cūṭāmaṇi Nikaṇṭu, Maturai, Tamiḻ Caṅkam Press, 1922.

Īrācarācacōḻaṉulā, Ed. Caṅku Pulavar, TSISSP, 1974.

Īṭṭiyeḻupatu of Oṭṭakkūttar, *Kūttaṉ Tamiḻ*, with notes by Kā. Kōvintaṉ, Madras 1957.

Kāciyāraṇyamāhātmyam (Prose rendering), Madras 1915, This is a Śiva temple at Ālaṅkuṭi.

Kaliṅkattupparaṇi, of Cayaṅkoṇṭār, with commentary, A.V. Kaṉṉaiya Nāyuṭu, Madras 1944.

Kaliṅkattupparaṇi, Ed. S. Rājam, Madras 1960.

Kaliṅkattupparaṇi, Trans. by V. Kanakasabhai Piḷḷai, Tamil Historical Texts, No. 2., The *Indian Antiquary*, vol. 19, 1890,pp. 329-40.

Kamalālayaccirappu eṉṉum Tiruvārūr Purāṇam of Citamparam Maraiñāṉacampanta Nāyaṉār. Ed. Ca. Caccitānanta Piḷḷai, U.Ve Cāminātaiyar Library Publication, Adyar 1961.

Kamalāmpikāmāhātmyam Ed. Na.Cuppiramaṇi Iyer., Śri Raṅgam, Vāṇi Vilās Press, 1956.

Kamalālayapurāṇam incomplete mss. See Tanjore Saraswati Mahal Library Tamil mss. catalogue, No. 319.

Kāñcipurāṇam of Kacciyappamuṉivar, Ed. Kāñci Nākaliṅka Mutaliyār, Madras 1910.

Kāntāpurāṇam of Kacciyappacivācāriār, with commentary by ma. Ti. Pāṉukavi, 2 vols., Madras 1907.

Kāntāpurāṇam 2 volumes Ed. A. Ramanathan, Madras 1974

Kāntāpurāṇam, Trans. R. Dessigane and P.Z. Pattabiraman, *La Légende de Skanda selon le Kandapurāṇam tamoul et l'Iconographie*, Pondicherry 1967.

Kṣētra Veṇpā of Aiyaṭikaḷ kāṭavarkōṉ, See *Patiṉōrām Tirumurai*.

Kōvalaṅkatai, Madras, 1975.

Kōvilpurāṇam of Umāpati Civācāriar, Ed. Kāñcīpuram Capāpati Mutaliyār, Madras 1967.

Kulōttuṅkacōlaṉulā of Oṭṭakkūttar, see *Mūvar Uḷā*.

Kulōttuṅkaṉ Piḷḷaittamiḻ of Oṭṭakkūttar, Ed. T.S. Kaṅkātaraṉ, Tanjore Saraswati Mahāl Publications, Thañjāvur, 1974.

Maṇimēkalai of Cīttalai Cāttaṉār, Ed. Na. Mu. Veṅkatacāmi Nāṭṭār and Auvai Cu. Turaicāmi Piḷḷai, 2nd Edition, Madras, TSISSP, Madras 1951.

Maturaimāṉmiyam of Citamparacuvāmi, Ed. A. Cuntaranāta Piḷḷai, Maturai, 1908.

Mūvar Uḷā, Ed. A. Gopala Aiyar, Madras, 1926.

Pallakki Sevā Prabandham (Telugu opera of Shāhāji Mahārāja) 1684-1710, Ed. P. Sambamoorthy, Madras, 1955.

Paṅkuṉi Uttira Pācuram of A.S. Turaicāmi Piḷḷai, 1924 (on Tiruvārūr Tiyākarāja).I.O.L mss.

Paṇṭāra Cāttiram, with introduction by K. Subramanya Piḷḷai, Tiruvāvaṭuturai Ātīṉam, 1931.

Paṇṭāra Cāttiraṅkaḷ, Śivabhogasāram and other works with modern commentary and trans. Tarumapuram Ātīṉam 1947.

Patiṉōrām Tirumurai, Śrī Vaikuṇṭam, 1963.

Pattuppāṭṭu with Nacciṉārkkiṉiyār Urai, Ed. with commentary,

Cāminātaiyar, Madras,1889.

Periya Purāṇam Eṉṉum Tiruttoṇṭar Purāṇam, Ed., C.K. Cuppiramaṇi Mutaliyār, Kōvai Tamiḻccaṅkam, Coimbatore 1937 in 7 vols.

——, Ed. Irākava Aiyaṅkār, Maturai, 1935.

Tiruttoṇṭar Mākkatai, TSISSP, Madras, 1977

Piṅkalanikaṇṭu, Ed. Civaṉ Piḷḷai, Madras 1890.

Takkayākapparaṇi of Oṭṭakkūttar, with old commentary, Ed. U. Ve. Cāminātaiyar, Madras, 1945.

Tamiḻnāvalarcaritai, Ed. Cāmi Tillai Naṭeca Ceṭṭiyār, Madras 1916.

Tañjai Peruvuṭaiyār Uḷā of Koṭṭaiyyūr Civakkoḻuntu Tēcikar, in *Koṭṭayūr Civakkoḻuntu Tēcikar Pirapanta Tiraṭṭu*, Tiruvāṉmiyūr, U.Ve. Cāmināta Iyer Library, 1932.

Tēvāram, 7 vols., Tarumapuram Ātīṉam,1953-64.

Tēvāram. volume I Tirumuṟai I-III. Tiruñāṉacampantar Tēvarappatikaṅkaḷ, volume II. Tirumuṟai IV-VII. Tirunāvukkaracar, Cuntaramūrti patikaṅkaḷ. Ed. Kayapākkam Catāciva Ceṭṭiyār. Madras, SISSP, 1973.

Tēvasthāṉa Carukkam of Tiyākarāyamutali, 1913 (I.O.L.unpublished cat. P Tam C 2116).

Tirimūrtimalaipurāṇavacaṉam of Aruṇācala Kavuṇṭar, Madras 1936.

Tirukkaccūr Tiyākarācar, Government Oriental mss. Library, Madras, mss. nos. 1492, 1493.

Tirukkāṟayiltalavaralāṟu by Ca. Taṇṭapāṇi Tēcikar, Madras, 1943.

Tirukkāṟayiṟpurāṇam, Ed. Citamparaceṭṭiyār and Vēlucāmi Kavirāyar, Madras 1924.

Tirukkuvaḷaittalavaralāṟum Tōttiraṅkaḷum, Tarumapuram Ātīṉam 1972.

Tirumantiram of Tirumūlar, with commentary by Pa. Irāmanāta Piḷḷai, 2nd Ed., Madras, SSP,1957.

Tirumantiram, with notes by Veḷḷaivāraṇar, TSISSP, 1957.

Tirumullaivāyilpurāṇam of Vaṭuaknāta Tēcikar, Cīrkāḻi, 1927.

Tirumurukāṟṟuppaṭai—See *Pattuppāṭṭu*.

Tirunākaikkārōṇappurāṇam of Tiricirapuram Mīnātcicuntaram Piḷḷai, Madras, 1869, New Ed. Devasthānam, 1980.

Tirunaḷḷāṟuppurāṇam, Kumpakōṇam, 1935.

Tiruppērūrppurāṇam, of Kacciyappamuṉivar, Madras, 1930.

Tiruppōrūrttalapurāṇa carittira carukkam, Tiruppōrur, 1934.

Tiruvācakam of Māṇikkavācakar, with a commentary by Cuvāmi Citpavānanta, Śrī Rāmakṛṣṇa Tapōvaṉam, Tirupparāyittuṟai

Post, 1970.
Tiruvālavāyuṭaiyār Tiruviḷaiyātaṟpurāṇam of Perumpaṟṟappuliyūr Nampi, Ed., U. Ve Cāminātaiyar, Madras 1906.
Tiruvamparmākālappurāṇam of Tiricirapuram Mīnātcicuntaram Piḷḷai, Tiruvāṉmiyūr, 1965. Also—
Tiruvāṉmiyūr U.Ve.Cāmināta Iyer Library, unpublished mss. No. 391/Serial 405. It is a short work of 59 pages.
Tiruvāṉmiyūrañjali Ed. N.S.Citamparam, Śrī Maṟuntīcuvaracuvāmi Tēvasthānam, 1962.
Tiruvāṉmiyūr Kalitturai Antāti, Ed. E.S. Varatarāja Iyer, U.Ve Cāmināta Iyer Press, Adyar,1964.
Tiruvāṉmiyūrttala Purāṇa Vacaṉam, Vicuvanātaṉ, Madras Makātēva Adyar Library Press 1966.
Tiruvārūrkkōvai of Ellappa Nāyiṉār, Ed. U. V. Cāminātaiyar, Madras, 1937.
Tiruvārūr Tiruppatikaṅkaḷ, Tarumapuram Ātīṉam, 1981.
Tiruvārūr Mummaṇikkōvai of Cēramāṉ Perumāḷ, See *Patiṉōrām Tirumuṟai*.
Tiruvārūr Nāṉmaṇimālai of Kumarakuruparacuvāmikaḷ, with a prose commentary by Ka.Caṇmukacuntaram Ceṭṭiyār, Tarumapuram Ātīṉam, 1943.
Tiruvārūr Nāṉmaṇimālai, with commentary by Paṭṭucāmi Ōtuvār Tiruppanantāḷ, 1962.
Tiruvārūr oru tuṟai kkōvai of Kīḻvēlur Kurucāmi, Madras Govt. Oriental Mss. Library.
Tiruvārūr Paḷḷu of Kamalaiñāṉappirakācar, Ed. Cōmacuntara Tēcikar, Madras, B. N. Press, no date.
Tiruvārūr Paṅkuṉi Uttira vaḻinaṭaippāṭam of T.B. Iraṅkacāmi Piḷḷai, 1911 (Tam b/59) I.O.L catalogue in progress.
Tiruvārūr Paṉmaṇimālai of Vaidyanātha Tēcikar. I.O.L Mss.
Tiruvārūrppāti Tiruvoṟṟiyūrppāti Veṇpāvantāti of Tiyākarāca Ceṭṭiyār, Madras, no date.
Tiruvārūr Purāṇam of Campantamuṉivar, Ed., Tiruvārūr Cāmināta Tēcikar, Madras 1894.
Tiruvārūr Purāṇa Vacaṉam by Pāṉu Kavi, Madras 1918.
Tiruvārūr Tiyākarācalīlai of Tiricirapuram Mīnātcicuntaram Piḷḷai, with an introduction by U. Ve. Cāminātaiyar, Madras,1928.
Tiruvārūr Uḷā of Anantakavi Vīra Rākavaṉ, Ed., U. Ve. Cāminātaiyar, Madras, 1902.
Tiruvaruṭpayaṉ of Umāpati Civācāriār, Madras, 1958.

Tiruviḷaiyātaṟ Purāṇam of Parañcōti Muṉivar, with commentary by Na.Mu.Vēṅkaṭacāmi Nāṭṭār, 2 vols., Madras, SISSP, 1965.

Tiruviḷaiyātaṟ Purāṇam Maturai Kāṇṭam 1973.

Tiruviḷaiyātaṟ Purāṇam trans. william Taylor, Oriental *Historical Manuscripts* vol.1, Madras,1835.

Tiruviḷaiyātaṟ Purāṇam, Trans.R. Dessigane, P.Z. Pattabiraman and J. Filliozat, *La Légendé des jeux de Civa à Madurai d'après le textes et les peintures,* 2 vols., Pondicherry 1960.

Tiruvoṟṟiyūrkkōvai, anon., Tiruvāṉmiyūr U. Ve. Cāmināta Iyer Library mss. 426, consists of 460 verses sung in praise of the deities of Tiruvoṟṟiyūr.

Tiruvoṟṟiyūr Kṣēttirattiṉ makimaiyum makāṉkaḷiṉ stutiyum, Madras 1924.

Tiruvoṟṟiyūr Tiyāka Taṅkacinṭu of Āṟumukanāyaka, (I.O.L Cat Tam A 932).

Tiruvoṟṟiyūr Tiyākēca patikam of Muṉicāmi Mutaliyār, 1892, British Library Tamil Mss. 13170 e 47(3).

Tiruvoṟṟiyūrppatikam of Taṇṭapāṇi Cuvāmaikaḷ. (I.O.L Cat Tam A 931)

Tiruvoṟṟiyūrppurāṇam of Tiruvoṟṟiyūr Ñāna Pirakācar, with commentary by Capāpti Mutaliyār, Madras, 1869.

Tiruvoṟṟiyūrppurāṇa vacaṉam, by Pāṉukavi, Madras 1918.

Tiruvoṟṟiyūr Māṇikka Tiyākar Pukaḻ Mālai Ed. Irāmāliṅkaṭikaḷ, TSISSP,1973.

Tiruvoṟṟiyūr Tiyākarāca temmāṅku, I.O.L.Cat Tam A 849).

Tiruvoṟṟiyūrvaḻinaṭaipāṭam, mainly ślokas and stuti - a call to worship Gods and Goddesses (I.O.L. Cat number Ptam A 484)

Tiruvoṟṟiyūr Vaṭivuṭaiyammai Pukaḻ Mālai, Ed. Irāmaliṅkaṭikaḷ, TSISSP,1973.

Tiyākarācacāmi Ulā, Anon., (on Tirukkoḻili Tiyākarāca), Tarumapuram Ātīṉam 1972.

Tiyākarāca Kaḻineṭil, Tanjore Saraswathi Mahāl Library, mss. no. 349.

Tiyākarācalīlaikaḷ in 4 Vols., Ed. G. Irācakōpāla Piḷḷai, Vāṇi Vilās Press, Śrīraṅgam, 1952-64.

Tiyākarācastuti, Government Oriental Manuscript Library, Madras, mss. no. 1491

Tiyākēśastuti of Śrīnivāsa Mutaliyār (I.O.L. P Tam. c 631)

Tiyāka Paḷḷu, attributed to Kamalai Ñāṉappirakācar, mss. in TSML. mss. no. 609.47 folio.

Tiyākēcar Kuṟavañci, Ed., Ve. Prēmalatā, TSML Publication, No. 130, Thañjāvūr, 1970; TSML library, No. 606.

Śrī Tiyākēcar Pirapantaṅkaḷ, Ed., S. Kalyānacuntaraiyar, Madras, 1946. (This is a collection of three works, *Tiyākēcar Kuṟavañci*, Anon; *Tiruvārūr maruntu Veṇpāmālai* by Tiyākarāca Ceṭṭiyār; and *Tiyākēcar Tālāṭṭu*, Anon; collected by Irācakōpāla Piḷḷai.

Tiyākēca Tiruviḷaiyāṭṭakaval, Anon., Madras Government Oriental Mss. Library R 6656. (This strangely enough passes off the Tiruviḷaiyāṭals of Cuntarēśvarar of Maturai as the Tiyāka Viḷaiyātals. Only a few are mentioned incomplete)

Uṇmai Viḷakkam of Maṉavācakam Kaṭantār, with modern commentary by K. Vajjiravēl Mutaliyār, Tarumapuram Ātīṉam, 1954.

Uṇmai Viḷakkam, Trans. J. M. Nallaswāmi Piḷḷai, Madras 1929.

Vētāraṇṇiya Purāṇam of Akōratēvar, Madras 1898.

Vetāraṇṇiya Purāṇam of Parañcotimuṉivar, Ed., Ma.Somāskanda Paṭṭar, Madras. 1898.

Secondary Sources in Tamil by Authors

Aruṇācalam, Mu. *Tamiḻ Iḷakkiya Varalāṟu* Pattām, Patinoṉṟām, Paṉṉiraṇṭām, Patiṉāṉkām, Patināṟām (parts I and II), Nūṟṟāṇṭu Gandhi Vidyalaya, Tiruciṟṟampalam, 1972, 1971, 1973, 1969, 1977 and 1975 respectively. The sequence of these volumes does not follow a chronological order.

Avinācilinkam Ceṭṭiyār, Ti. Cu. et al., Ed., *Kalaikkaḷañciyam*, 10 vols., Madras, 1954-68.

Bhāskara Toṇṭaimāṉ *Vēṅkaṭam Mutal Kumari Varai*, 4 vols. Madras 1960-67.

Catāciva Paṇṭārattār, T.V., *Tamiḻ Iḷakkiya Varalāṟu 250-600 A.D.*, 2nd Ed. Aṇṇāmalainakar, 1957.

——, *Piṟkālaccōḻarvaralāṟu*, Aṇṇāmalai, 1958.

——, 'Tēvāram eṉṉum peyar viḷakku', in *Ceṉ Tamiḻccelvi*, Vol. 23, pp.305-10.

Ceṅkalvarāya Piḷḷai, Vā.Cu. *Tēvāra Oḷineṟi:* Cuntarar, 1963, Campantar, (from 1-100), (from 101-265), Śaīva Siddhānta Press, 1963.

Cuntaram Piḷḷai *Tirunaḷḷātṟṟuttalavaralāṟu*, Tirunaḷḷāṟu Tēvasthāṉam, 1964.

Irācamāṇikkanār, Mā *Periya Purāṇa Ārāycci*, Madras, 1978.

Irāmanāta Piḷḷai, Pā, *Tēvārat Tiruppatikattiraṭṭu* (Campantar), (Appar) TSSP, Madras, 1964.

Cōmacuntara Tēcikar, S., *Tamiḻppulavarkaḷ Varalāṟu*, Patināṟām Nūṟṟāṇṭu, Madras, P.N. Press 1939.

Kiruṣṇacāmi,Ve. *Tamiḻil taḷapurāṇa Iḷakkiyam*, Nākarkōyil, 1974

Rāmaśeṣan, R. Ed., *Aruṇakirinātar aṭiccuvaṭṭil*, Cuvāmimalai,1981.

Raṅkarāmānuja Ayyaṅkār, Ār., *Śrī Kiruti Maṇi Mālai*, Vol. V, Madras 1953/

Subramaṇiam, P. *Meykīrtikaḷ*, Madras, International Institute of Tamil Studies, 1983.

Taṇṭapāṇi Tēcikar, S., *Tiruvārūr*, Tarumapuram Ātīṉam, no date

——, *Tiruvārūrttalavaralāṟu*, Tiruvārūr, Śrī Tyāgarājasvāmi Tēvasthāṉam, 1955.

——, *Vētāraṇṇiyattala Varalāṟu*, Vētāraṇṇiyam Tēvasthāṉam, 1975.

Veḷḷaivāraṇaṉ, Kā., *Paṉṉirutirumuṟai Varalāṟu* Aṇṇāmalai, 1969, 1972.

Vēṅkatacāmi Avarkaḷ, Mayilai Cīni, *Camaṇamum Tamiḻum*, TSISSP, 1980

——, *Pauttamum Tamiḻum*,TSISSP,1980.

Vēṅkaṭarāmayya, Kā. Mā., *Kalāveṭṭil Tēvāramūvar* Madras 1977.

Sanskrit Texts by Title

Āditya Purāṇam. TSML Sanskrit mss. no. 7165 and 7166.

Ahīśakuṭi in praise of Valmīkanātha. Also mss. Extracts from Brahma Kaivalya Purāṇam TSML B1919.13,1920, TD 10070.

Ajapābhāgaḥ Government Oriental Mss. Library Madras.

Ajapādattātreyakavacādayaḥ, TSML SKT. mss. supp. no. 978 B12215

Ajapā Gāyatrī TSML Sanskrit mss. I. 15539. B.6903. With minor variations D 15540-6905. With further variation in D15543-6904. With minor differences D. 15544-6908. See also B.12091 D. 1892 and D-12265-(7if c.v.) MOL SKt. mss. numbers 5852-59, D7733, D5860, D 14174.

Ajapā Gāyatrī Kalpa (in Telegu script) MOL D7732 and R 823(b) in Devanāgarī Script and D 24

Ajapāgāyatrī mantra TSML Skt. mss. D15542. B.6907.

Ajapā Gāyatrī Nivedana BISM 44/25

Ajapā Gāyatrī Paddhati RASB VIII B.6521, 6522.

Ajapāgāyatrīpuraścaraṇa RASB Cat. of skt. mss. VIIB 6520. This is in Bengali script and claims to be part of the *Nārāyaṇopaniṣad*.

Ajapā Gāyatrī Stotra Sanskrit mss. in the Library of the Calcutta Sanskrit College.

Ajapāgāyatrī Vidhānam, MOL 15302 and TSML SKt. mss. supp. no. 331. B. 6986.

Ajapaikadeśamātram 448b B.7098 (TSML Skt. Mss.)

Ajapājapakramaḥ, RASB Skt. mss VIII B. 65290 and 6521. Also 6521 and 6522 with minor variations. VIII B. 6520 claims to by a Śaṅkarācārya and from the text Kulamūlāvatāra.

Ajapāmahimādāyaḥ TSML Skt. Mss. 257 B6909.

Ajapā Rahasyam, by Govinda Gopāla Mukhopadhyāy (in *Suṣamā, Sanskrit University Journal*) 1957.

Ajapā Vidhānam, Adyar Mss. Lib. 25 No.24 and MOL R.323 (g). TSML Skt. mss. 260 B. 6909.

Brahma Upadeśa An incomplete mss. in TSML Skt. mss. B.7098, supp. 4486.

Brahmavaivarta Purāṇam, Vedāraṇya Māhātmyam: Tanjore Saraswati Mahal No. 10112-14, pp. 6949-50.

Caṇḍakauśika of Kṣemesvara, Ed. and trans. Śibāni Dāsgupta, Calcutta, Asiatic Society, 1962.

Canna Basava Purāṇa Trans, G. Wurth, *JBBRAS* VII (1864-6), pp. 98-221.

Caturdaṇḍi Prakāśikā of Veṅkaṭamakhin, Madras, Music Academy 1934.

Coḷa Campu of Virupākṣa Kavi, Ed., V. Raghavan, TSML Series, No.55.

Daksiṇāmūrtisaṁhitā Banaras, 1937 (No. 61 of Princess of Wales Sanskrit Series).

Devī Kalottarāgama, Gr. with Notes. Ed. Kailāśa Piḷḷai, Jaffna, 1923.

Gheraṇḍa Saṁhitā Sanskrit Samsthān, Bareilly, 1974

Gorakṣa śataka, Ed. Kuvalyānandaswāmī, (Ed. and Trans.), Varāṇasī.

Gorakṣa Siddhānta Saṅgraha, Ed. Gopināth Kavirāj, Princess of Wales Saraswati Bhavana Tests, No.18, Banaras 1925.

Haṁsopaniṣad, TSML Skt. mss. B.6909. D15538 and B6906. Also D.15541.

Hāṭakeśvara Māhātmyam from Nagara Khaṇḍa No.10282-95, (47 pages). Also 7044.

Iśādi Aṣṭottara Upaniṣad, Ed. Babu Śivprasād Raghorām, Varāṇasī 1937. This compendium includes all the so-called Yogic

Upaniṣads mentioned in this work.
Kāḷikā Purāṇa Bombay 1891
Kāmakalāvilāsa of Puṇyānanda. Ed., N. Subramaṇiaṉ with Tamil Trans., Madras 1942.
Kāmākṣī Vilāsa, Bangalore, 1968.
Kamalālaya Māhātmyam TSML SKT. mss. No. B.1845-D10332.
Kāmikāgamam Pūrvabhāga (kriyāpāda) Grantha script. Ed. with Tamil Trans Aḻakappa Mutalyiār, Madras.
Kāñcī Māhātmya, Ed. P.B. Anantachariar, Kāñchipuram, 1906.
Kāraṇāgamam (Nityārcanavidhi), Ed., Coimbatore Irācaliṅkakurukkaḷ, Coimbatore, 1969.
Mahānirvāṇṇ Tantra, Ed. and trans. John Woodroffe as *The Great Liberation*, Ed., Norman Brown, Poona, American Institute of Indian Studies, 1965.
Maitrāyaṇīya Upaniṣad, Ed. and Trans. J.A.B. Van Buitenen. The Hague, Mouton & Co., 1962.
Mālatī Mādhava, Ed. R.G. Bhandarkar, Bombay, 1905.
Mantra mahodadhi, Varāṇasī, 1919.
Matta Vilāsa of Mahendravarman, Ed., T. Gaṇapati Śāstri,Trivandrum, 1917.
Matta Vilāsa, Trans, L.D. Barnett in *BSOAS V* (1830), pp.697-710.
Mucukundasahasranāmam, Ed., V. Raghavan, Madras, 1959.
Mucukunda Sahasranāmam, Handwritten litany from Candraśēkhara Nāyiṉār, Kurukkaḷ of Tyāgarājasvāmi temple at Tiruvārūram.(Minor differences)
New Catalogues Catalogorum, Ed., C., Kunhan Raja, Madras,1949.
Niṣadhacarita of Śrī Harṣa, Ed., Gopināth Kavirāj, Sampurnānanda and Sanskrit University, Varāṇasī, 1969.
Prabodhacandrodaya, Ed. K.K. Handiqui, Poona, 1956.
Puṇḍarīkapura Māhātmyam, TSML mss. No. 9715 (6803-5).
Puraścaryārṇava in 3 vols., Ed., Śrī Paṇḍita Muralī Dhar Jha, Banaras, Tara printing works, 1902.
Ratnatrayam of Śrīkaṇṭhācārya with Aghora Śiva's commentary Devakottah, 1926.
Rudrayāmala, Varāṇasī, Sampurṇānand Sanskrit University Press.
Śabdakalpadruma Vol. 1, Ed., Rādhākāntadeva, Chowkambha, Sanskrit Series, 93
Sakalādhikāra, attributed to Agastya, Ed. with English Introduction and Tamil Trans. by K. Vāsudeva Śāstrī TSML 92, Grantha Tanjore, 1961.

Śaradātilaka, Bareilly, Sanskrit Saṁsthān, 1980.

Sārasvatīyacitrakarmaśāstra, Ed., with Tamil Trans. by K.S. Subrahmaṇiya Śāstri, TSML Series NO. 87, 1960.

Sarvadarśana Saṅgraha, by Mādhavācārya, (Son of Śāyaṇa) with commentary by Vāsudev Śāstri Abhyaṅkara. Ānandāśrama Samskrita Granṭhāvali No.51, Poona 1906.

Sarvadevavilāsa, Ed. V. Raghavan, Adyar Library Pamphlet, Series, No. 33, Madras 1958.

Ṣaṭcakranirūpaṇam, Ed. Arthur Avalon, Calcutta, 1913.

Saundaryalaharī of Śaṅkara, Madras the Theosophical Society, Adyar, 1965.

Siddhāntasārāvalī, Gr. Ed., with Tamil notes, Madras, the South Indian Arcaka Association, 1975.

Śilparatna by Śrīkumāra, TSML Series No.90, 1961.

Śivabhaktavilāsa (as told by Agastya) of Haradatta, Grantha script., Ed. S. Rājaśāstri, Madras, Vāṇī Bhūṣan Press, 1970.

Śivabhaktavilāsa, mss. In Devanāgarī characters in Tanjore Saraswati Mahal Library. (no number) This is the version followed in the body of the work.

Śivabhaktavilāsa of Upamanyu, Ed. Mahāmahopādhyāya Karuṅkulam Śrī Krishna Śastrikaḷ, Madras Law Journal Press 1931.

Skanda Purāṇa, Bombay, Veṅkaṭeśvara Press (This is the North Indian rendering).

Śrī Navanāthanavaratnamālāmañjūṣā of Bhāskararāya, unpublished mss. in the possesssion of Paṇḍit Vaṭuknāth Śāstri Khiṣṭe of Varāṇasī of the Bhāskararāya *guruparamparā*.

Śrī Skanda Mahāpurāṇam, Ed., Ceṅkālipuram Anantarāma Dīkṣitar, 2 Vols, Cēlam, 1964 (This is purported to be taken from the *Śivarahasyakhaṇḍa* of the *Śaṅkarasaṁhitā*.

Śrī Purāṇam, Ed., Veṅkaṭarājulu Reḍḍiyār, Madras, 1946.

Sundaramūrti Aṣṭōttaram See under *Mucukundasahasranāmam*

Tañjaimāhātmiyam of Brahmāṇda Purāṇa, TSML 10480 and 10481, (7118-tt, 21 pages).

Tyāgarāja Aṣṭakam Madras Oriental Manuscript Library. mss. no. R.84D

Tyāgarāja Kavacam TSML mss. D.2265-B-12466.

Tyāgarāja Māhātmyam, TSML. mss. B.1848-9621. (This is a compendium of works collected from ten Purāṇas) by Parama Śivānanda Sarasvatī of the Śaṅkarācārya Maṭha of Kāñci.

Tyāgarājanāmāvali, see under *Mucukundasahasranāmam*.

Tyāgarājasahasranāmāvaḷi, TSML mss. B. 7441-D-22272.
Tyāgeśa Stuti Madras Govt. Oriental Manuscript Library, R. 5874.
Laghu Upaniṣadaḥ, Minor Upanisads (2nd series) containing ten Upaniṣads in English trans. by K. Nārāyaṇaswāmi Aiyar, Madras Śriṅgeri Maṭha Samiti, 1967.
Yogatantragranthamālā, Ed. V.V. Dviveda, Varāṇasī, 1968.

Marathi

Agastya Bhakta Vilāsa of Virūpākṣa Kavi, Ed. V. Śrinivāsachāri, TSML Series, No.57, Tanjore, 1952.
Tyāgarāja Māhātmya of Rāma Paṇḍita, TSML, Thañjāvūr.
Tyāgeśa Padas of Shāhāji Mahārāj, Ed., Na. Viśvanāthan, TSML Thañjāvūr, 1980.

Telegu

Pallakī Sevā Prabandham of Shāhāji Mahārāj, Ed., P. Sambamoorthy, Madras, 1955.
Tyāgeśapadamulu of Shāhāji Mahārāj. Several mss. in the TSML in Devanāgarī script. In praise of Tyāgeśa. The collection includes 103 *Śṛṅgārapadas*, 50 bhaktipadas, 5 bhāvapadas, 9 vairāgya padas, 14 *hāsyapadas*, 24 *nītipadas*, 3 *maṅgalapāṭṭu*.

Hindi

Nirbhaya Vilās (also called Gītagovinda) by Khemrāj Śrī Kṛṣṇadās. Bombay, Śrī Veṅkaṭīeśvara Press, 1981.

Epigraphy

Annual Report on (South Indian) Epigraphy, Madras Government Press, 1887 referred to as ARE and A.R.E. in the work.
Corpus Inscriptionum Indicarum Government of India, Department of Archaeology, referred to as CII.
Damilica ('Journal of the Tamil Nadu State Department of Archaeology'), Madras, 1970.
Epigraphia Indica, Delhi/Calcutta: Archaeological Survey of India, 1892 - Bombay 1872-1923 referred to as EI
Epigraphia Tamilica: A Journal of Tamil Epigraphy (Jaffna, Sri

Lanka Archaeological Society,1971.
Indian Antiquary, Bombay 1872-1923.
Indian Epigraphy, Delhi, Motital Banarsidas, 1965.
"A Bibliography of South Indian Epigraphy", Noboru Karashima in *Journal of Asian and African Studies*, Institute for the study of Languages and Cultures of Asia and Africa, Tokyo, No.6, 1973, pp.151-63.
Krishnamacharlu, C.R., *List of Inscriptions copied by the Office of the Superintendent for Epigraphy*, Delhi, Manager of Publications, 1941.
Krishnamacharlu, C.R. *Subject Index to the Annual Reports on South Indian Epigraphy from 1887-1936*, Delhi, Manager of publications, 1940.
Nagasamy, R., *Seminar on Inscriptions*, Madras, Books (India) Private Ltd., 1966.
Rangacharya, V. (Ed.), *A Topographical List of the Inscriptions of the Madras Presidency collected till 1915 with notes and reference*, Madras Government Press, 1919.
Sircar, D. C., *Indian Epigraphical Glossary*, Delhi, Motilal Banarsidass, 1965.
South Indian Inscriptions ('Publication of the Archaelogical Survey of India), Madras Government Press, 1890, Vols. I-XXIII available, referred to as SII.
Studies in Indian Epigraphy, Journal of Epigraphical Society of India, Mysore, 1974.
Transactions of the Archeological Survey of South India, Publication of the Archaeological Society of South India, Madras, 1955.
Subramanian, T. N. (Ed.), *South Indian Temple Inscriptions*, Madras Government, Oriental Series 157, 3 vols. Madras Government Oriental Manuscript Library, 1953-7.

Tamil

Kalāveṭṭil Tēvāramūvar d. Kā Mā. Veṅkaṭarāmayyā, Madras, 1977.
Meykīrtikaḷ by Subramaṇian, P., Madras International Institute on Tamil Studies 1983.
Tañjai Peruvuṭaiyār Kōyil Kalveṭṭukaḷ, Ed. Nākasāmi, Irā. Tamilnāḍu Government Archaeological Survey, Madras 1966.
Tamil̲nāṭṭu Ceppu Tirumēṉikaḷ, Ed. Irāmacāmi, Me. Cu. (Tamil̲nāḍu

Government Archaeological Survey), Madras 1976.

Miscellaneous

Abbot, J., *The key of Power: A Study of Indian Ritual and Belief* London 1932.

Agarwala, V. S., 'One Hundred and One names of prāṇa in Vedic Literature', *Indian Culture* 5 (1983) p. 285ff.

Aiyangar, S.K., *Hindu Administrative Institution in South India*, Madras, University of Madras, 1929.

Aiyar, Kalyanasundaram R., 'South Indian Serpent Lore' QJMS,Vol. 21-22 p. 424 ff.

Aiyar, Subramania K.V., 'Origin and Decline of Buddhism and Jainism in South India', in *IA* Vol. 40 1911, p. 218ff.

Appadurai, Arjun and Breckenridge, C., 'The South Indian Temple: Authority, Honour and Redistribution' *Contributions to Indian Sociology* (NS) 10, pp. 187;21.

——, 'From Protector to Litigant: Changing Relations between Hindu Temples and the Raja of Ramnad', *IESHR* Vol. XIV 1977, Jan-march pp. 75-107.

Aryan, K. C. *the Little Goddess* New Delhi, Rekha Prakashan 1980.

Awasthi, A. B. K., *Studies in Skanda Purāṇa* Part I, Lucknow, Kailash Prakashan 1965.

Ayyar, Jagadisa, P.V., *South Indian Shrines* Madras, Times Publishing Co., 1920.

Ayyar, Jagadisa, P.V. *Festivities*, Madras, Higginbothams Ltd., 1920.

Ayyar, Narayana, C.V., *Origin and Early History of Śaivism in South India*, Madras, University of Madras 1936.

Ayyar, Subramania, A.V., *The Poetry and Philosophy of the Tamil Siddhars*, Tirunelveli 1957.

Baj, S.R., 'The Juristic Personality of an Idol in Hindu Philosophy', *Jaipur Journal* 3 1963 pp. 220-236.

Baker, C., (see also under Washbrook, D.A.) and Washbrook *Political Institutions and Political Change 1880-1940*, Delhi, Macmillan 1975.

Balasubramanyam, S.R., *Early Chola Temples* Part I, Faridabad, Thomson Press 1975.

——, *Middle Chola Temples*, Bombay Asia Publishing House

1966
——, *Later Chola Temples*
——, *Four Chola Temples* Bombay 1963.
Banerjea, Jitendranath, *Development of Hindu Iconography*, Calcutta, University of Calcutta 1954.
Barnet, M.R., *The Politics of Cultural Nationalism in India*, Princeton, Princeton University Press 1976.
Barnett, S. A., 'The Process of withdrawal in South Indian Caste' in Singer, Milton, Ed., *Enterpreneurship and the Modernisation of Occupations in South Asia*, Durham, N.C.Duke University Press 1974 pp. 179-204.
Barrett, Douglas, *Early Chola Architecture and Sculpture,806-1014*, London, Faber and Faber Ltd. 1974.
Beal, Alan, 'Conflict and Interlocal Festivals in South India' in *Journal of Asian Studies* Vol.23 (1964, June).
Beck, Brenda, 'The Right-Left division of South Indian society', *Journal of Asian Studies* Vol. XXIX no. 4 August 1970, p. 779-9f.
——, *Peasant Society in Koṅku*, Vancouver, University of British Columbia 1972.
Berger., P., *The Sacred Canopy: Elements of a Sociological Theory of Religion*, Garden city, New York, Double Day & Co. 1967.
Beteille, Andre, *Caste, Class and Power, Changing Patterns of Stratification in a Tanjore Village*, Berkeley 1965.
——, 'Organization of Temples in a Tanjore Village' in *History of Religions* Vol. V 1965; 66. pp. 74-92.
Bhandarkar, R.G., *Vaiṣṇavism, Śaivism and other Minor Religious Systems*, Strassburg 1913.
Bhandarkar, D.R., 'Lakulīśa' ARE 1906-7 pp. 179-92.
Bharadwaj, S.M., *Hindu Places of Pilgrimage in India* (A study in Cultural Geography), Berkeley, University of California Press 1973.
Bharati, Agehananda, *The Tantric Tradition*, London, Rider & Co., 1965.
Bhatt, N. R. (Ed.), *Rauravāgama* 2 vols., Pondicherry, 1961.
Bhootalingam, M., *Movement in Stone*, New Delhi Somani 1969.
Bloomfield, M., *A Vedic Concordance* Cambridge, Massachusetts 1906.
Bodewitz, H. W., *Jaiminīya Brāhmaṇa I, 1-65* Trans and Commentary with a study of Agnihotra and Pranagnihotra, Leiden,

E.J. Brill 1973.

Bolle, Kees W., 'Speaking of a Place' in Kitagawa, J.H. and Long, C. Ed., *Myths and Symbols, Studies in Honour of Mircea Eliade,* Chicago 1969.

Boner, Alice and others (Ed.) *Vāstuśāstra Upaniṣad - the Essence of Form in Sacred Art,* Varāṇasī 1981.

Breckenridge, Carol Appadurai, *The Śrī Mīnākṣi Sundareśvarar Temple: Worship and Endowments in South India 1833;1925* unpublished Ph.D. thesis, University of Wisconsin, Madison 1976.

Breckenridge, C., See under Appadurai.

Briggs, G.W., *Gorakhnāth and Kānphāṭa Yōgīs* 2nd Ed. Motilal Banarsidas 1982.

Brown, Norman W. (Ed.), *Saundaryalaharī,* Harvard Oriental Series, Cambridge, Vol.43, Harvard University Press, 1958.

Buitenen, Van. J.A.B., *The Maitrāyaṇīya Upaniṣad* (See under Sanskrit Titles above)

Cenkner, William, 'The Śaṅkarāchārya and Hindu Orthodoxy in Contemporary Perspective' Proc of 1st International Symposium on Asian Studies 4, SOAS, pp. 785-96.

Census of India 1961, Vol. IX Part XI D.

Chakraborti, H.P., *Pāśupata Sūtra,* Calcutta 1970.

Chakravarti, Chintaharan, 'The Soma or Sauma Sect of Śaivas'in *Indian Historical Quartely* VIII 1932 pp. 221-3.

——, *Tantras: Studies on their Religion and Literature,* Calcutta 1963.

Chandra, Pramod, 'The Kaula Kāpālika Cults at Khajurāho' in *Lalit Kalā* No. 1-2 (1955-56) pp.98-107.

Chattopadhyaya, D., *Lokāyata,* Delhi 1959.

Chettiyar, C.M.R., "Social Legislation in Ancient South India' in *QJMS* 31, 1930 PP. 341-343; *QJMS* 1937 PP.65-77.

Clark, John, *Differences between a Cult and Religions,* Pamphlet issued by Council of Mind Abuse, Toronto 1981.

Clothey, F.W., *The Many Faces of Murukaṉ: the History and Meaning of a South Indian God,* The Hague, Mouton Publishers 1978.

——, *Rhythms and Intent. Ritual Studies from South India,* Madras 1983.

——, *Religion and Historical Process in South Asia,* Madras 1981.

Cohn, B.S. and Marriott, M., 'Networks and Centres in the Integration of Indian Civilization', *Journal of Social Research* No.1

September 1958 pp.1-9.

Coomaraswany, A.K. *The Dance of Śiva*, New York 1978.

Custead, H., *The Iconography of Śiva Naṭarāja as an Indian Synthesis of Non Aryan and Aryan Conception of Divinity* unpublished Ph.D. thesis, Florida State University 1974.

Das, Bhagavan, *Concordance to the Yogasūtra of Patañjali and Bhāṣya of Vyāsa*, Benares, The Kāśī Vidyāpīṭha, 1938.

Das Veena, *Structure and Cognition: Aspects of Hindu Caste and Ritual*, Delhi, O.U.P.1977.

Dasgupta, S.B., *Obscure Religious Cults*, Calcutta, University of Calcutta, Firma K.L. Mukhopadhaya 1962.

Dasgupta, S.N., *History of Indian Philosophy*, Vol V, Cambridge University Press 1955.

Dave, J. H., *Immortal India* 4 Vols., Bombay 1959-61.

Derrett, J. D. M., 'Two epigraphs on Rathakāras and Kammāḷas' in *K.A. Nilakantasastri 80th Birthday Felicitation Volume* Madras 1971 pp. 32-5.

Derrett, J. D. M. Reprint of above in *Essays in Classical and Modern HIndu Law* Vol. I, London, E. J. Brill 1976.

Derrett, J. D. M. 'Modes of Sannyāsīs and the Reform of a South Indian Maṭha carried out in 1854', in *JAOS* 54, 1974 p.67ff.

Desroche, Henri, *Sociologie Religeusses* Paris 1968.

Dessigane, R., *Les Lēgendes Çivaites de Kāñcīpuram*, Pondicherry, Institut Francaise d' Indologie, 1964.

Dessigane, R., Pattabiraman, P. Z. et Filliozat, J., *La Légende des jeux de Çiva à Madurai d'après les Textes les Peintures*, Pondicherry, Instituut Francais d'Indologie, 1960.

Deussen, Paul, *The Philosphy of the Upaniṣads*, trans.Rev. A. S. Geden, Delhi, Oriental Publishers 1972.

Deussen, Paul, *Sixty Upaniṣads of the Vedas*, Trans. V.M. Bedekar and G. B. Palsule, Benaras, Motilal Banarsidas, 1980.

Devakunjari, D., *Madurai through the Ages: from Earliest Times to 1801 A.D.*, Madras, Society for Archaeological and Epigraphical Research 1979.

Devasenapathi, V.A., *Śaiva Siddhānta*, Madras, University of Madras 1958.

Devasenapathi, V.A., *Of Human Bondage and Divine Grace*,Annamalai 1, 1963.

——, *Kāmakkōṭṭam, Nāyaṉmārs and Ādiśankara*, Madras, Madras University Press, 1975.

Dhavamony, Maria Susai, *Love of God according to Śaiva Siddhānta: A Study in the Mysticism and Theology of Śaivism*, Oxford University Press 1971.

Diehl, G., *Instrument and Purpose: Studies in Rites and Rituals in South India*, London, Gleerup 1956.

Dietrich, Gabriele, *Religion and Peoples' Organization in East Thañjāvūr*, Madras, Christan Literary Society, 1977.

Dirks, N. B., 'Political Authority and Structural Change in Early South Indian History' in *IESHR* Vol. 13, 1976 pp. 125-157.

Divanji, P.C., 'The Māheśvara cult and its Offshoots', in *Journals of the Asiatic Society of Bombay* XXX 1955, Part II pp.16-22.

——, 'Lakulīśa of Kāravān and his Pāśupata Culture' *Journal of Gujrat Research Society* XVII, 1955 p. 267;74.

Draguhn, Werner, *Entwicklungsbewussts ein und Wirtschaftliche Entwickling in Indien* (with a short English summary), Weisbaden, 1970.

Dubreuil, Jouveau, *Iconography of Southern India*, Trans. A. C. Martin, Paris 1937.

Dumont, Louis, *Religion, Politics and History in India*, Paris, Mouton 1970.

Eisenstadt, B. N., Kahane, R. and Shulman, D., *Orthodoxy, Heterodoxy and Dissent in India*, Mouton, Berlin, New York and Amsterdam 1984.

Eliade, Mircea, *Yoga: Immortality and Freedom* Routledge, Kegan and Paul 1958.

——, *The Sacred and the Profane*, Trans. William R.Transk, and Kitagawa, Joseph, New York 1959.

——,(Ed.), 'Methodological Remarks on the Study of Religious Symbolism' in *History of Religions: Essays on Methodology*, Chicago, Chicago University Press, 1959

Elmore, W.T., *Dravidian Gods in Modern Hinduism*, Omaha, Nebraska 1915, reprinted Madras 1924.

Eschmann, A., Kulke, H. and Tripathi, G. C. (eds.), *The Cult of Jagannāth and the Regional Tradition of Orissa*, New Delhi, Manohar 1978.

Farquahar, J.N., *An Outline of the Religious Literature of India*, Delhi 1969.

——, 'Temple and Image worship in Hinduism', in *JRAS*, 1928, pp. 15-23.

Filliozat, J., see Dessigane, R.

Francis, T. Dayanand, *Rāmaliṅgaswāmy*, Bangalore n.d.
Freeman, James H., *Power and Leadership in a Changing Temple of India*, unpublished Ph.D. thesis, Harvard, 1982.
Fuchs, Stephen, *Rebellious Prophets. A study of Messianic Movements in Indian Religion*, New York, Asia Publishing House 1965.
Fuller, C. J. 'The Madurai Mīnākṣī Priests 1937-80', Paper presented to 7th European Conference on Modern South Asia Studies, SOAS, London 7th-11th July 1981.
Fuller, C. J. *Servants of the Goddess* Cambridge Studies in Social Anthropology, Cambridge University Press 1984.
Galanter, Marc, 'The Religious Aspect of Caste: a Legal View', in Smith, D.E., *South Asian Politics and Religion* Princeton, University of Princeton Press 1966.
Geertz, Clifford, 'The Javanese Kijaji: the Changing Role of a Cultural Broker' in *Comparative Studies in Sociology and History 1959-60*, p.225-249.
Geertz, Clifford, 'Religion as a Cultural System' in Banton, Michael, Ed., *Anthropological Approaches to the Study of Religion*, London 1966.
Ghurye, G. S. *Indian Sādhus*, Bombay, Popular Book Depot, 1953.
Gnanambal, K., *Religious Institution and Caste Panchayats in South India*, Calcutta, Anthropological Survey 1973.
Gombrich, E. H., *Art and Illusion: a Study of the Psychology of Pictoral Representation*, London, Phaidon Press 1968, specially, chapter on *Symbolic Images*.
Gonda, J., *Ancient Indian Kingship from a Religious point of view*, Leiden, Brill 1966.
——, *Change and Continuity in Indian Religion* The Hague, Mouton 1965.
——, *Viṣṇuism and Śivaism*, London 1970.
——, 'Medieval Religious Literature in Sanskrit' in *History of Indian Literature*, Vol. II, Weisbaden, Otto Harrowitz 1977.
Gopalakrishnan, M.S., 'Goddess Kāli' in *JMU* 1975, Vol.47, p.74ff.
Gopalakrishnan, M.S., 'Mother Goddess and Snake worship' in *JMU*, 1973-74, Vol. 45-46, pp.53-56.
Goswami, B. B. and Morab, S. G., *Chāmuṇḍēśvarī Temple in Mysore*, Calcutta, Anthropological Survery of India Memoirs No.35.
Goudriaan, Teun and Gupta, Samyukta, 'Hindu Tāntric and Śākta

Literature' in Gonda, J. (Ed.), *A History of Indian Literature* Vol. II, Weisbaden 1981.

Govindacharya, A., *The Holy Life of the Alvars or the Draviḍa Saints*, Mysore 1902.

Hara, Mimoru, Nakulīśa Pāśupata Darśanam' in *Indo-Iranian Journal* Vol.2, 1957-58, p.8-32.

Hardgrave, Robert., *Nāḍārs of Tamiḻnāḍu*, Berkeley and Los Angeles, 1969.

Hart, George L., *The Poems of Ancient Tamil* Berkeley 1975.

——, *Related Cultural and Literary Elements in Ancient Tamiḻ and Indo Āryan*, Ph.D. thesis, Harvard, 1969.

——, 'The Relation betweem Tamil and Classical Sanskrit Literature', in Gonda, J. (Ed.) *A History of Indian Literature* Vol. X, Weisbaden, 1976.

——, 'Ancient Tamil Literature: Its Scholarly Past and Future' in Stein, Burton (Ed.) *Essays on South India*, (see Stein).

Hemingway, F. R., *Tanjore District Gazetteer* 1915.

Heine-Geldern, R., *Conceptions of State and Kingship in South East Asia*, Ithaca, Cornell University 1960.

Hoisington, Henry R., trans. 'Śiva Prakāśam' 'Light of Śiva' in *JAOS* IV (1854) PP. 125-244.

Induchudan, V. T., *The Secret Chamber*, Trichur, Cochin Devasrom Board 1969.

Ingalls, Daniel H. H., 'Cynics and Pāśupatas; the Seeking of Dishonour' in *Harvard Teleological Review* IV, 4, October 1962.

Irschick, Eugene, *Politics and Social Conflict in South India, Non-Brahmin Movement and Tamil Separatism* 1916-29, Berkeley, University of California, 1969.

Ishwaran, K., 'Bhakti Tradition and Modernisation' in Lele, Jayant Ed. *Tradition and Modernity in Bhakti Tradition*, Leiden, E.J. Brill 1981.

Jacob, G. A., *A Concordance to the Principal Upaniṣads and Bhagavad Gītā* 1891, Reprinted Benaras 1963, 1971.

Jouveau, Dubreuil G., see under Dubreuil.

Jesudasan, C. and Jesudasan H., *A History of Tamil Literature*, Calcutta, 1961.

Jagadisa Ayyar, P. V., see under Ayyar.

Kailasapathy, K., *Tamil Herioc Poetry*, Oxford 1968.

Kalyanasundaramaiyar, R., 'South Indian Serpent Lore' in *QJMS*, Vol. 21-22, p.426ff.

Kandiah, A., *A criticial study of early Tamil̲ Śaiva Bhakti Literature with special reference to Tēvāram*, Ph.D. Thesis, London, SOAS 1973.

Karashima, Noboru, Subbarayulu, Y., Matsui, Toru (Eds.),*A Concordance of the Names in Cola Inscriptions* 3 Vols.,Madurai, Sarvodaya Ilakkiya Paṇṇai 1978.

Karmarkar, A. P., 'The Vrātya or Dravidian Systems ' in *The Religions of India* Vol. 1, Lonvala 1950.

Karve, Iravati, 'On the Road' in *Journal of Asian Studies* XXII, 1 1962, pp.13-27.

Kearns, J. F., 'The Right and Left Hand Castes' in *IA* Vol.5, December 1976.

Kennedy, R., 'Control of Temples in Tamil̲nāḍu' in *IESHR* II 2-3, pp.260-90.

Kingsbury, F. and Phillips, G. E., *Hymns of the Tamil Śaivite Saints* Calcutta 1921.

Kinsley, R., *The Sword and the Flute,* Berkeley and Los Angeles, 1975.

Krishnamurthy, C. *The Tiruvor̲r̲iyūr Temple* unpublished Ph.D. Thesis, University of Madras, July 1951.

Krishnamurthy, S. R. *A Study of the Cultural Development in Cola Period*, Annamalai, Annamalai University 1966.

Krishna Sastri, *South Indian Images of Gods and Goddesses,* Madras 1916.

Kulke, Hermann, *Cidambaramāhātmya* Weisbaden 1970.

——, see under Eschmann.

——, 'King Anaṅgabhīma III', in *JRASB* 1983.

Kuppuswamy, Gouri and Hariharan, M., *Glimpses of Indian Music*, Madras, Sandeep Prakashan, 1982.

Lal, Rai Bahadur Hira 'The Goḷakī Maṭha' *Journal of the Bihar and Orissa Research Society* XIII 1927, pp. 137-44.

Law, B.C. *Holy Places of India*, Calcutta 1940.

Lele, Jayant (Ed.), *Tradition and Modernity in Bhakti Movements*,Leiden, E. J. Brill 1981.

L' Hernault, Francoise, *L'Iconographie de Subrahmanya au Tamil-nad* Pondicherry, Instituut francaise d'Indologie, 1978.

Lockwood, M., Siromoney, G. and Dayanand P., *Mahābalipuram Studies*, Madras, The Christian Literary Society 1974.

Lorenzen, David N., *The Kāpālikas and Kālāmukhas; Two Lost Śaivite Sects*, New Delhi, Thomson Press Ltd. 1972.

Macdonell, A. A., *A History of Sanskrit Literature*, Heinemann, London 1900, Reprints 1905, 1925, 1928.

Mahalingam, T. V., *Administration and Social Life under Vijayanagara*, Madras, University of Madras 1940.

——, 'The Pāśupatas in South India' in *Journal of Indian History* XXVII (1949) pp. 43-53.

——, 'A family of Pāśupata Gṛhasthas at Jambukēśvaram' in *Journal of Oriental Research*, Madras, XV 1957 pp. 79-85.

——, *'Kāñcīpuram in early South Indian History*, Madras, Asia Publishing House 1969.

——, *'South Indian Polity*, Madras, University of Madras, 1955.

——, (Ed.), *Mackenzie Manuscripts* vol. I (Tamil̲ and Malayālam) Vol. II (Telegu and Kannaḍa), Madras, University of Madras 1972.

——, 'Social Legislation in Medieval South India' in *Readings in South Indian History* . Ed. S. Gupta, Gen.Ed. K. S. Ramachandran, Delhi. 1977.

——, *Studies in the South Indian Temple Complex*, Dharwar 1970.

Majumdar, B. P., 'Lakulīśa Pāśupatas and their Temples in Medieval India', in *Journal of Bihar Research Society*, XXXIX, 1953, pp.1-9.

Marr, J. R., Review of Kulke, *BSOAS* 35, pp.639-40.

Marr, J. R., Review of William Y. Willets, *An Illustrated Annotated Annual Bibliography of Mahābalipuram on the Coromandel Coast of India 1582-1962*, in *BSOAS*, 30, 1976, p.421.

Marr, J.R., 'The Periya Purāṇam frieze at Tārācuram: Episodes in the Lives of the Tamil Śaiva Saints' in *BSOAS*, Vol. XLII Part 2, 1979, pp.268-289.

Miller, David and Dorothy Wertz, *Hindu Monastic Life. Monks and Monasteries of Bhubaneswar*, Montreal, 1976.

Minaksi, C., *Administration and Social Life Under the Pallavas*, Madras, Madras University Historical Series No. 137 1938.

Mirashi, V. V. (Ed.) *Corpus Inscriptionum Indicarum* vol. IV, Part 1, Introduction, Calcutta, 1955.

Mirashi, V. V., 'The Śaiva Ācāryas of Mattamayūra clan', in *IHQ*, 1950, March, vol. XXVI, pp. 1-16.

Mishra, K., *The Cult of Jagannāth*, Calcutta, Firma K. L. Mukhopadhya 1971.

Moffatt, M. *An Untouchable Community in South India: Struc-*

ture and Consensus, Princeton 1979.
Mukhopadhyaya, Govinda Gopala, 'Ajapārahasyam' in *Suṣamā*, Varāṇasī, Sanskrit University Journal Śrāvaṇa 2022.
Nagasamy, R., 'Śiva Worship as gleaned from Appar's Devāram' in *Śaiva Siddhānta* 1, 1966, pp.49-61.
Nagasamy, R., '*Gangaikoṇḍa Chōḷapuram*, State Department of Archaelogy, Tamilnad 1970.
Nagasamy, R. and Gros F., *Uttaramērūr*, Pondicherry 1970 (in French).
Nagasamy, R., *Art and Culture of Tamiḻnāḍu*, Madras, Tamiḻnāḍu Government 1972.
Nallaswami Piḷḷai, J.N. *The Periya Purāṇam: The Lives of Śaiva Saints*, Madras 1924.
Nambi, Arooran, *Glimpses of Tamiḻ Culture Based on Periyapurāṇam*, Madurai, Kooḍal Publishers 1977.
Nambi, Arooran, *Tamil Renaissance and Dravidian Nationalism 1905-44*, Madurai 1980.
Natarajan, B., *The City of the Cosmic Dance, Chidambaram*, New Delhi 1974.
Nilakanta Sastri, See under Sastri.
Oddie, G. A., 'The Character, Role and Significance of Non-Brāhmaṇa Śaivite Mutts in Tanjore District in 19th Century', Paper presented to the 7th European Conference on South Asian Studies, London SOAS.
Obeyesekere, Gananath, *The Cult of the Goddess Pattiṉi*, Chicago and London, University of Chicago Press 1984.
O'Flaherty, Wendy D., *Hindu Myths*, Harmondsworth, 1975.
——, *Asceticism and Eroticism in the Mythology of Śiva*, London, O.U.P. 1973.
——, *The origin of Heresy in Hindu Mythology*, Oxford 1973.
——, *Women, Androgynes and Beasts*, Chicago, University of Chicago Press 1980.
——, *The Origin of Evil in Hindu Mythology*, Berkeley, University of California 1976.
——, *Dreams, Illusions and Other Realities*, Chicago, London, University of Chicago Press 1984.
——, (Ed.), *Karma and Rebirth in Classical Indian Traditions* Berkeley, University of California Press 1980.
——, and Derrett, J.D.M., *The Concept of Duty in South Asia*, Vikas and SOAS 1978.

Otto, Rudolf, *The Idea of the Holy*, trans. John W. Harvey, London, O.U.P. 1925.

Pai, D. A., *Monograph on the Religious Sects in India among the Hindus*, Bombay, The Times Press 1928.

Pal, P., Hindu *Religion and Iconology According to the Tantrasāra of Āgamavāgīśa*, Los Angeles, Vicitra Press, 1983.

Pandey, K. C., *Abhinavagupta: A Historical and Philosphical Study*, Banaras 1935.

Pandey, K. C. 'Śaiva Siddhānta and the Philosophy of Grammar', in *Bhāskarī* Vol. III p.xcvi, xcviii.

Paranjoti, Violet, *Śaiva Siddhānta*, London, Luzac & Co. 1938.

Pathak, V. S., *Śaiva Cults in Northern India (700-1220 A.D.)*, Banaras 1960.

Patthar, Virasami, *The Temple and its Significance*, Tiruccirapalli, might be *Vani* Vilas Press, 1974.

Piḷḷai, Lokanatha, *A Descriptive Catalogue of the Tamil Mss.* in the Tanjore Maharaja Serfoji's Library, Tanjore, 1964.

Piḷḷai, K.K. *The Sucīndram Temple* Madras, Kalakshetra Publications, 1953.

Piḷḷai, Chidambaram P., *Right of Temple Entry*, Nagercoil 1933.

Piḷḷai, Suresh B., 'Rājarājeesvaram at Tañcāvūr, *Proc. of 1st International Seminar of Tamiḻ Studies*, Kuala Lumpur, International Association of Tamiḻ Research 1968, pp. 439-43.

——, *Introduction to the Study of Temple Art*, Tanjore, Equator 1978.

Piḷḷai, Subramanian G., 'Tree Worship and Ophiolatry in Tamilnad', in *Journal of Andhra University* 12 (1943), pp.70-2.

Ponnusamy, S., *Śrī Thyāgarāja Temple, Tiruvārūr* Madras, State Department of Archeology 1972.

Pott, P. H., *Yoga and Yantra*, The Hague, M. Nijhoff 1966.

Presler, Henry H., *Primitive Religion in India* Serampore, and Christian Society 1971.

Presler, Franklin, 'The Legitimation of Religious Policy in Tamilnad' in Smith, Bardwell (Ed.), *Religion and Legitimation of Power in South Asia* Leiden, E. J. Brill 1978.

Raghavan, V. (Ed.), *Cola Campū* of Virūpākṣa, TSML Series No.55.

——, Introduction to *Sri Tyāgarāja Mucukunda Sahasranāmāvaḷi*, Madras 1959.

——, 'The Sūtasaṁhitā' in *Annals of Bhandarkar Oriental Research Institute* Vol. 22, 1941, pp.236-53.

——, 'Methods of Popular Religious Instruction in South India' in Singer, Milton (Ed.), *Traditional India* (see Singer).
——, *Abhinavagupta and his works*, Varāṇasī, Chaukhambha Orientalia 1980.
——, 'Variety and Integration in the Pattern of Indian Culture', in *Journal of Asian Studies*, vol. 15, August 1956, pp.497-506.
——, *The Great Integrators, The Saint Singers of India*, New Delhi, Ministry of Information 1979.
——, *New Catalogues Catalogorum*, Madras, Madras University Sanskrit Series, 18, 26, 28, vols. 1-8 (1984), Madras 1949.
——, (Ed.), *Sāhendra Vilāsa, A Sanskrit Poem of the Life of King Shāhāji of Tanjore 1684-1710 of Śrīdhara Venkateśa Ayyāvāḷ*, TSML Series No.54, Tanjore 1958.
——, (Ed.) *The Sarvadeva Vilāsa, an Anonymous Sanskrit Champū Kāvya*, Adyar Library, Madras, 1958.
——, *Yantras or Mechanical Contrivances in Ancient India*, The Indian Institute of Culture, Trans. 10, Bangalore, 1952.
——, Introduction to *Tiyākarājalīlaikaḷ* (See Tamil books above).
Rajamanikkam, M., *The Development of Śaivism in South India, (*A.D. *300-1300)*, Tarumapuram Ātīṉam Publication No.554, 1964.
Rajamanikkam, M., 'The Tamil Śaiva Mutts under Colas (900-1300 A.D.)', in *Essays in Philosphy Presented to T. M. P. Mahadevan on his 50th birthday* Madras 1962.
Rajan, S. unpublished work (in cards), *Encyclopaedia of Important Names and Epithets in Tamil Literature till 10th century* A.D. (in progress), Madras.
Rajayyan, K., *Rise and Fall of the Pōligārs of Tamiḻnāḍu*, Madras, University of Madras, 1974.
——, *History of Tamiḻnāḍu 1563-1982*, Madurai 1982.
Ramachandra, Diksitar V. R., *The Lalitā Cult*, Madras 1942.
——, 'Migration of Legends' in *Annals of the Bhandarkar Oriental Institute*, 15, 1933-34, pp.212-19.
Ramachandra Mudaliyar Avargal D.B., 'Mudaliyār' in *QJMS* Vol. 10 1919-20, pp. 289-99.
Ramakrishana Ayyer, V.G., *The Economy of a South Indian Temple*, Annamalai Nagar, Annamalai University, 1946.
Raman, K. V., *Sri Varadarāja Temple, Kañcī*, New Delhi 1975.
——, 'Iconographic Concepts and Forms from Early Tamil Sources', in *Reports of Seminars Bulletin of Institute of Traditional Cultures*, Madras 1957.

Ramanujan, A., *Speaking of Śiva*, Harmondsworth 1973.
——, *Hymns for the Drowning*, Princeton 1981.
——, *Interior Landscape*, Indiana University Press,1967.
Ramesan, N., *Temples and Legends of Andhra Pradesh*, Bombay, 1962.
Ranade, R.D., *A Constructive Survey of Upaniṣadic Philosophy*, Bombay Baratiya Vidya Bhavan 1968.
Rangasamy, Dorai M. A., 'The Tiruttoṇṭattokai of Ārūrar', in *Journal of Madras University* 1957, pp. 75-84.
Rangasamy, Dorai M.A., (Turai Iraṅkacāmi), 'Rise of Temple Cult in Śaivism with Special Reference to Tēvāram', in *Annuals of Oriental Reserach*, Vol. XII, 1954-55, p.7ff
——, *The Religion and Philosophy of Tēvaram*, 2 vols., Madras, University of Madras 1959.
Rao, T.A. Gopinath, *Elements of Hindu Iconography* 2 vols., Madras 1914 in four parts, Varāṇasī, Delhi Indological Book House 1971.
Redfield, Robert, *The Little Community and Peasant Society and Culture*, Chicago, University of Chicago Press 1956, reprinted 1969.
Richards, John F., *Kingship and Authority in South Asia*, Wisconsin University Press 1977.
Sastri, H. Krishnan, *South Indian Images of Gods and Goddesses*, Madras 1916.
Sastri, K. A. Nilkantha, *The Colas*, Madras University Historical Series No. 9, 2 Vols. (in three), Madras 1935-37
Sastri, K. A. Nilakantha, *Development of Religion in South India*, Madras 1963.
Sastri, K. A. Nilkantha, *The Culture and History of the Tamils*, Calcutta, K.L. Mukhopadhyaya, 1964.
Sethu Piḷḷai, R. P., 'Sacred Place Names in Tamilnad', in *Proc. of All India Oriental Conference*, 13th Session, Nagpur 1946, Nagpur 1951 III. pp. 143-54.
Sharma, R. K. *The Temple of Caunsat Yoginī*, Bhopal 1978.
Sharma, R. S., *Śudras in Ancient India*, Delhi 1955.
Shulman, D. D., see Eisenstadt, *Orthodoxy, Heterodoxy and Dissent*.
——, *The Mythology of the Tamil Śaiva Tala Purāṇam*, Ph.D. thesis, SOAS, London 1976.
——, *Tamil Temple Myths*, Princeton 1981.

——, 'On the Pre History of Tyāgarāja Cult at Tiruvārūr', in *Art and Archaeology Research Papers* 13, 1978, pp. 55-58.

Silverberg, J. (Ed), *Social Mobility in the Caste Systems in India*, The Hague, Mouton, 1968.

Singer, Milton, *Traditional India Structure and Change*, Jaipur 1978.

Sivaramamurti, C., *South Indian Paintings*, New Delhi National Museum 1968.

——, *Naṭarāja in Art, Thought and Literature*, New Delhi, 1974.

——, *Śatarudrīya*, New Delhi 1976.

——, *Royal Conquest and Cultural Migrations in South India and Deccan*, Calcutta, Indian Museum 1955.

——, *Four Chola Temples*, New Delhi 1978.

Śivaraman, K., *Śaivism in Philosophical Perspective*, Delhi, Motilal Banarsidas, 1973.

Soundararajan, K. V., 'Cult in Pallava Times', in *Transactions of Archaeological Society of South India 1962-65*.

Soundararajan, K. V., 'Rājasiṁha's Temples in Pallava Times', in *Transactions of Archaeological Society of South India, 1962-65*.

Spencer, George, 'The Sacred Geography of the Śaivite Hymns', in *Numen*, 17, 1970, pp 232-44.

——, 'Temple Money Lending and Livestock Redistribution', in *IESHR* 5, 3, 1968, pp. 277-93.

——, 'Networks and Royal Influence in 11th Century South India', in *IESHR*, Vol. 7, No. 4, December 1970, pp.431-42.

——, 'The Politics of Plunder - The Coḷas in 11th Century Ceylon', in *Journal of Asian Studies*, Vol. 35 May 1976, pp. 405-19.

——, *'Royal Leadership and Imperial Conquest in Medieval South India, The Naval Expedition of Rājendra Cōḻa I (1025 A.D)*, unpublished Ph.D., thesis, Department of History, University of California, Berkeley 1967.

Srinivasan, K. R., *Cave Temples of the Pallavs*, Kanpur, Job Press Pub. Ltd., 1968.

——, *Some Aspects of Religion as Revealed by Early Monuments and Literature of the South*, Madras, Madras University 1960.

——, 'Tirukāmakoṭṭam', in *Proc. of All India Oriental Conference 1946*, Nagpur, 1981 III, pp. 50-6.

——, *South Indian Tèmples*, New Delhi National Book Trust, 1972.

Srinivasan, P. R., 'A Tiruvoṟṟiyūr Sanskrit Inscription', in *Journal of Oriental Research,* Madras, Vol. 32, pp.12-15.

Srinivasan, T. N., *A Handbook of South Indian Images. An Introduction to the Study of Hindu Iconography,* Tirupathi Devasthanam.

Stein, Burton, 'Brāhmaṇa and Peasant in Early South Indian History', in *Adyar Library Bulletin,* Vol. 31-32, 1967-68, (V. Raghavan Felicitations Volume)

——, 'All the King's Mana: Perspective on Kingship in Medieval South India', in Richards, J. F. Ed. *Kingship and Authority in South India,* Wisconsin University Press 1977.

——, *Peasant, State and Society in Medieval South India,* Delhi, Oxford University Press 1980.

——,Ed. *Essays on South India,* Honolulu Asian Studies Program, University of Hawaii, (Asian Studies at Hawaii, No. 15).

——,Ed. *South Indian Temples: An Analytical Reconsideration,* New Delhi, Vikas Publishing House, 1978.

Subramanian, N., *Pre-Pallavan Tamil Index,* Madras 1966.

——, *History of Tamilnad (to A.D. 1336),* Madurai, Koodal Publishers, 1st Ed. 1972, 2nd Ed. 1976.

Subramanian, T.N., *South Indian Temple Inscriptions (See under Epigraphy)*

Swamy, B.G.L., *Chidambaram,* Mysore, Geeta Book House, 1979.

Thurston, E. and Rangachari K., *Castes and Tribes of Southern India,* 6 Vols., Madras 1909.

Turner, V. and Edith, *Image and Pilgrimage in Christian Culture,* Oxford 1978.

Turner, V., *The Ritual Process: Structure and Anti Structure,* Chicago, University of Chicago Press, 1969.

Turner, V., *Dramas, Fields and Metaphors: Symbolic Action in Human Society,* Ithaca, Cornell University 1974.

Upadhyaya, G. P., *Brāhmaṇas in Ancient India,* New Delhi, Munshiram Manoharlal, 1979.

——, 'The Origins and Functions of Tīrthas', *Proc, of Indian History Congress,* 1976, pp.126-30.

Vanamamalai, N., 'Skanda Murugan Synthesis', in Nagasamy, R. Ed., *South Indian Studies,* Vol. II, pp. 8-30.

Venkataswamy, M.S., *The Seven Dances of Śiva,* Madras 1948.

Vogel, J.P., *Indian Serpent Lore,* London 1926.

Wadley, Susan S., *The powers of the Tamil Women,* Syracuse 1980.

Washbrook, D. A., *The Emergence of Provincial Politics*, Cambridge, Cambridge University Press, 1976.

Washbrook, D. A., and Baker, C. J. B., *South India, Political Institutions and Political Changes 1880-1940*, Delhi, Macmillan Co. of India, 1975.

Watts, Alan, W., *The Supreme Identity*, New York Press, 1967.

Weber, Max, *The Religion of India*, New York Free Press, 1967.

Werbner, R. A., *Regional Cults*, London, Academic Press, 1977.

Whitehead, Henry, *The Village Gods of South India*, Oxford, Oxford University Press, 1916.

Wirz, Vol Paul, Katiragama, *The Holiest Place In Ceylon*, Colombo, 1966.

Zvelebil, K. V., *The Smile of Murukan*, Leiden, E.J. Brill, 1973.

——, *History of Tamil Literature*, Leiden, 1975.

——, *Tamil Literature*, Weisbaden, 1974.

——, *Tirumurukaṉ*, Madras International Institute of Tamil Culture, Adyar, 1969.

——, *Poets of Power*, London 1970

——, 'Valli and Murukan, a Dravidian Myth', Indo-Iranian Journal 19, 1977, pp.227-46.

INDEX

Abhinavagupta, Tantraloka, 114
Abhiseka kattalai, 256-7
Acaleśvara shrine, at Tiruvārūr, 299
Acalpuram, 64
Adhirajendra (1067/68-1071), 319
Adi Śaiva Brāhmaṇas, 136
Adi Śaivas, 240
Adiśeṣa, 100
Aditya I (c.a. 871-907 A.D.), 299
Adityavarman of Sumatra, 175
Āgamas, 97, 109, categories in the descent of the soul, 119-20, a collective term, 140-1
Āgamic tradition, 136, 138-43
Agastya Bhakta Vilāsa, 180
Agastya, the Tamiḻ culture hero, Vijayanagara king's claims, 342
Agents of acculturation, (the nāyaṉmār and ālvārs as), 289
Agrahāraṃ, 136
Aiyatikaḷ Katavarkon, 297
Ajapā, 11, iconology, 97-134, its equation with 21, 600 breaths, 163
Ajapā mantaraṃ, 46, 158, Pl.
Ajapā yantraṃ, 68, a 51 syllabled diagram, 114, Pl.
Ajapā-Haṁsa, dance of Tiruvārūr as the conceptual archetype, 100
Ajapā mantra, 271
Ajapāgāyatri, 109
Ajapānatanam, 106
Ājñāpatis, local chieftains, 293
Aksarapīṭha, 69
Aḻitter, 266
Aḻuṭaiyanampi, 147
Ambedkar, 276
Ammaṉ shrines, 221
Ammāṅkatevi, the daughter of Rajendra I, mother of Kuloṭṭunga I, 318
Ampar, 171
Anādi Śiva, an epithet of Siva, 240
Ānanda Tāṇḍava, 100, of Dārukāvana repeated in Chidambaram, 299
Ānandagiri's Śaṅkaravijayam, 161
Ānandarāya Makhin's Vidyapariṇayana, 161
Anaṅgabhīma III, royal patron of Jagannātha cult, 333
Anapāya, an epithet of Śiva assumed by Kulottuṅga II, 331
Āṇava, 112, 168
Ancient boundary of Tiruvārūr, and Vijayadasami rites, 313-4
Annadāna kaṭṭalai, 254-5, 260
Annual rites, in Tiruvārūr temple, 140
Antecedents of the Manunīti myth, 326
Anthill, 18
Antinomian ethics of nāyaṉmār, 144
antiquity, as sacred, 308-9
Anuloma, 265
Anuśaivas, as ksatriyas and temple entry, 240
Apāna, 103
Appadorai, 204, 294, 343, 352
Appar, 1, 40, and Vedas 137, and Āgamas,139, 295, installing worship of Naminanti at Tiruvārūr, 298
Appaya Dikṣita, (honourific form Dikṣitar) 142, commentary on, 259
Arcaka Association, and hereditary priesthood, 265
Architectural positioning, of Tyāgarāja shrines, 304, fig.
Ardhayāma kaṭṭalai, 256
Aruḷnandi Śivācārya, 271-2
Aruḷnandi's disciple Māṟaiñānacampantar, 271-2
Arunācalam, Mu., 78, 169, 270
Aruṇācalatampirāṉ, 257
Arupattimūvarcaritam, 172
Ārūran, 39
'Āryan', 2
Āṭavaḷḷān, (and honourific Āṭavaḷḷār) 25, identity of, 301-2
Atheistic radicalism, early Tirāviṭa ideology, 276
Atipattanāyaṉār, 62
Ātiviṭaṅka, of Tirukkaṟāyiḻ, dance form of Kukkuṭa, 99
Ātiviṭaṅkaṉ, 61
Atiyārkkunaḷḷār, 78
Attavirattānam, 55

Auditory meditations, 106
Autochthonous beliefs, 365
Avanivitaṅka, (honorofic form Avanivitaṅkar), 63, of Tirukoḻili, and dance form of Piruṅka, 99
Avantara Śaivas and temple entry, 240-1

Backward communities, 269
Bādus, in Jagannatha temple, 229
Baker and Washbrook, role of temples in local politics, 204
Barnett, 273
Barnett, 220
Bauddhas, 156
Berger, and process of legitimation, 290
Bhairavāgamās, 161
Bhakti, 1, 97, 288, 347, as a bond of synthesis, 143, as charisma, 199
Bhandarkar, 151
Bhāskararāya, 91, 162, 347
Bhavabhuti's Mālatīmādhava, 161
Bhikṣā maṭha, 150, 165, See also Lakṣādhyāyī, Goḻaki and Kiḻaimatha.
Bhogamūrti, Tyāgarāja as, 293
Bhonsle rulers of Thañjāvūr, 255
Bilingual charters, 299
Bindu, 106, 108
Brahmadeya,(s) 136, 292
Brāhmaṇa mathas, and their conflict with Veḷḷāḷa maṭhas, 257
'Brāhmaṇa', 2
Brāhmaṇas and Sabhās, 293, as teachers, 137
Brahmarandhra, 115
Brahmarāyar, 239
Brahmasūtra Bhāṣya, 159
Brahmotsavam, 225
Breckeṉridge,Carol, 204
Bṛhadaraṉyaka Upaniṣad, 107
Brick Tyāgarāja shrine , converted into stone, by Paṟavai, 312
British Government and temples, 349
Brother saints, worship of, 297
Buddhism, 215
Buddhists, 289
Burton Stein, 203, 221, 263, 274, 292
Cakkiḻiyār, 214
Cakrās, 107
Camāpantipocanam, Govt. directed eating together sessions, 275
Campantamunivar, author of Tiruvārūrppurāṇam, (1592 A.D.), 59, 83
Campantar, 24, 291 his equating Śiva with Veda,137, with Āgama, 138-9
Caṇḍāla, 173-4, 213
Candrakalāgama, 161
Candraśekhara kurukkaḷ, of Tiruvārūr, 313
Caṅkam Coḻas, 292
Caṅka Mahārāja, 324
Cankaracevakan, son of Caṅka Mahāraja, helps the Coḻas, 324
Caṅkaracoḻanulā, 317-24
Caṅkili, 64, 146
Cārvāka, and materialist school, 161
Caste-affiliations, of Nāyaṉmār, 206
Caste composition of temple trustees, 255
Cātinūl of Kamalaiñānappirakācar, 268-73
Caturānana , 152-3, 157, 301, 313
Caturānana maṭha, 153
Caturvedimaṅgalam, 136
Caunṣat yogini, 164
Cayankoṇṭāṉ's Kalinkattupparaṇi, 320
Cekkiḻār, 32
Celva Tiruvārūr, 166, 261
Cempiyāṉ Mahādevi builds the Aṟaneri shrine, 301, 312
Ceṅkuntar, 241, (s), the nine warriors of Muṟukaṉ, 79
Cenna Bāsava Purāṇa, 172
Ceṟṟūr, 65
Ceṟuttunai, 144
Ceṭṭitteṟu Ñānappirakācar, 201
Ceṭṭiyār and Mutaliyār community, 280
Cetupatis of Ramnād, patrons of Rameśvaram, 205
Cevappa Nāyaka, 169
Cevappa Nāyaka and Raghunātha Nāyaka, 343
Chidambaram Piḷḷai, 259
Citampara rahasyam, 68
Chidambaram, 68, 299

Cilappatikāram, 77, and Manunīti myth, 327
Civañanapotam, 258
Co-option of protest leaders, 369
Coḻa connection in the other Saptaviṭaṅka sites, 315
Coḻa Monarchy and Tiyākarājalīlaikaḷ, 338
Coḻa paintings in the temple of Thañjāvūr, 305
Coḻa Siva, 22
Coḻa bronze of Somāskanda, 21-2
Coḻa-Cāḻukya line, 319
Coḻa Mucukuntan, 296
Coḻa Mahārāja image taken in procession, 313
Coḻa, Cera and Pāṇḍya, the ancient tripartite division, 296
Coḻamaṇṭalacatakam of Ātma Tecikar, 332
Coḻamaṇṭalam, 7, 43, 290, Tyāgarāja as territorial emblem of, 263
Coḻas, 222, 287
Coḻentiraciṅka Veḻaikkāran, 325
Coḻentiraciṅka, epithet assumed by Rājarāja I, 325
Comacimāṟanār, 176, 218
Comacuntara Mutaliyār, Tiruvārūr temple trustee, 255, Late V.I. Comacuntara Mutaliyār of Vaṭapātimaṅgalam, 201
Commentary of Kauṇḍinya on the Pāśupatasūtra, 159
Communal tensions, 269
"communitas", 4, 6, 144
Concept of 'acapai' in the Tirumantiram, 110
Conflict between the sannyāsis of Sūryanārāyaṇarkoil and Veḷḷāla, 270
Conflicts between Veḷḷaḷas and Veḷḷannāṭṭārs, 345
Corporate mobility of the Veḷḷāla community, 260
Corporate mobility, of a caste, 219
Court-temple symbiosis, 295
Court cult, 368
Cult, 3-7, 311
Cultic geography, 55, 365
Cultural integration, 368
Cuntarar, 1, 43, 146, 169, 257
Cuntara pāṇṭiyan, as the royal and divine consort, 296
Cuntarapāṇṭiyan canṭi, 310
Cuntaraviṭaṅkar, of Tirunākaikāroṇam, dance form, 60
Cuntareśvara-Mīnākṣi, 287
Curse pronounced by God Siva of Tiruvārūr, 320
Cuvāminatakurukkaḻ, President of South Indian Arcaka Association, 187

Dakṣiṇa Goḷakī maṭha, 164, 340, See Kiḻai maṭha, Goḷaki and bhikṣāmaṭha
Daksinameru Vitankar, 32, 302, 304, and Ātāvallān, 302
Dakṣināmūrti Saṁhita, 104, 121
Dakṣināmūrti, and Tiruvārūr temple, 236
Dalhousie, 60, 349
Dalit, 276
Dana, as a paradigm of monarchy, 294-5
Dāsa mārga, 143
Dasa Mahāvidyas, 175
Dasāris, officers of religious department under Vijayanagara, 345
Deity, polluted by contact, 210
Deity speaking, 318, 330
Deity Vītiviṭankan making grants, 317
Deity as the ruler, 317
Deity's inscriptions, 326
Derrett, and the caste arbitration epigraph at Tiruvārūr, 267
Devadānas, 292
Dhaky, 67, 316
Dharma, 209
Dhvani, 117
Differences between the Vedas and the Āgamas, 140
Diṇḍima, 167
Dirks, dāna as paradigm, 294-5
Divyasūricaritra, and prophesy of the downfall of Coḻas, 319
DMK and the Tiruvārūr ter, 351
Doctrine of Lapse, 60, 349
Donor (upāyakara), and his socio-religious status, 204

Dravida Brāhmaṇas, 164
Dravidavyakaraṇaguru, 109
Durvāsa, 148, 164

Egalitarianism vs. non-egalitarianism, 6
Ekāmranatān Uḷā, reference to Mutaliyār, 261
Ellappanāyanār, author of Tiruvārūrkkovai, 60
Epigraphical evidence, worship of nāyanmār icons, 147
Equality of all religions, 370
Eschmann, 229, 289
Eternal Verbum, 118
Etirilāpperumāḷ, the son of Neriyutaiyapperumal, 323
Etymological meaning of Somaskanda, 29
"exclusiveness vs. inclusiveness", 6
Eyarkon Kalikkāmanāyanār, 170

Festivals, 239
Fifty-one letters of the alphabet, 113-4
Fisherman, Saint Atipattanāyanār, 60
Folk-Court syntheses, 56
Fuller, Chris, 136

Gaṅgadevī, wife of Kampanna, 342
Gangaikoṇḍacoḷāpuram temple, (spelt in the Tamil form Kaṅkaikoṇṭacoḷāpuram) loss of its royal status, 310
Garbhagṛha, 201
Garlandmaker, and temple entry issue, 212
Gaulīśa, of Tiruvoṟṟiyūr, 153
Gavamāyana sattra, Vedic rite, 152
Gāyatrī, 109
"generic vs. particularistic relationships", 6
Geocentricity, 5
Ghurye, 162
Gñanaṃbāl, K. 218
Goḷaki sampradāya, 150, (maṭha), 164-5, 340-1, See also Bhiksa, Laksādhyāyī, Kīḻai, Cantāna , 233
Gorakṣa samhita, 121
Govinda Dikṣita, (1550-60), 259
Great and Little Traditions, 288
Gṛhastha Pasupatas as custodians of temples, 157
Gross speech (varṇa), as an Agamic category, 109

H.R. & C.E. Board, 60, 260, 351
Hālasya Māhātmyam, 202
Haṁsa, 11
Haṁsa nāda, 108
Haṁsanāṭanaṁ, 97
Haṁsapaṭanātanam, 99
Hamsopanisad, 105, 107-8
Harihara I and his vow to restore dharma, 342
Harsa's Naiṣaddhacarita, 160
Hart, 292
Hāṭakeśvara, 59, 76, 289
Henolocotheism, 115
High caste and low caste Veḷḷāḷas, 258
Hindu Law, 254
Hindu jurists, 265
Hindu brand of universalism, pluralism and relativism, 370
Hinduisation, 288
Hindutva, 205
Hiraṇyavarman myth of Chidambaram, 320
Hoisington, 151
Homa, 136
Homakuṇḍa, myth of Tirunīlakaṇṭa yāḻpānar and Campantar, 207
Honour, bestowed by temples, 295
Horizontal Legitimation, 290
Hultsch, 167

Icai Veḷḷāla, 230
Icon of Cuntaramūrtināyanār, 147, and Paravai, 312
Iconology of the Tyāgarāja image, 88
Image of Coḻarāja, 313
Images of Rajendra and Paravai, 312
Ināms, 256
Iñcikollā, 177
Incorporative kingship, 295-7
Indispensable helper, 318
Indra, 77, 227, and six Tyāgarāja replicas, 80, 82, 84
Inscription from Taxila in Kharosti script, referring to hassa, 106
Internal economy, the kattaḷai system

of Tiruvārūr temple, 254
Irācakopāla Pillai, Editor of Tiyākarājalīlaikaḷ, 181
Irācarācacoḷanulā, 80
Iṟai, 292
Islam, seen as a cultural threat, 264
Iṭakkal, 64
Itaṅkaī, 235
Itinerant ministrel poets, 365
Īṭṭiyelz-upattu of Oṭṭakkūttar, 39, 76, 321, Controversy over its genuineness, 336-7

Jagannātha of Puri, 5, 229, 287
Jaimini, (Hindu jurist), 267
Jaina and Baudha faith, 56
Jaina faith, 210
Jaina centres, 290
Jainas, 160, 290
Jarāsandha, 159
Jātavarāman, Cuntarapantiya (1251-68 A.D.), 340
Justice Party, 310, 350

Kacciyappamunivar, 81
Kaikkolaperumpaṭai, Itaṅkkai and valaṅkai(martial) groups of , 270
Kaikkoḷar, 238, 241
Kālabharas, 210, 289
Kaḻal, 98
Kaḻalnilai, 98
Kālāmukha temples, 154
Kālāmukha, 154
Kālāmukha mathas, 155
Kaḻarciṅkar, 144, a Pallava king, 297
Kaliṅga war, 320
Kāmadahana, 83
Kāmakalā = śabdabrahmaṉ, 121
Kāmakoṭṭams, 38, 67, 221
Kāmaksi of Kañci, 60
Kamalaī Ñānappirakācar, 201, 273
Kamalālaya, 6
Kamalālayaciṟappu (1547 A.D.), 17, 59, 82
Kamalāmpāl, the dancer,grandmother of Tilakkammā, 233
Kamalāmpikai and Raudra Durga or Eriñcakkoṟṟavai, 64
Kamalāmpikai, 58, 60
Kamalanaṭanam, 63, 99
Kammālas, 265-7
Kampanna Oḍeyar, the Vijayanagara ruler and "Mohammedans", 342
Kanakadāsa, 208
Kaṇimuṟṟattu, 263
Kaṅkaikoṇṭa, 310
Kannaki merged into Kāli, 289
Kannaki becomes Vaṭṭapāṟaiyammaṉ, 289
Kannappan, 186
Kantapurānam, 81, 98
Kantatai Maṟaiñānacampantar, 271
Kāpālika, 61, (s) 155, See Tantrics
Kāppu, bond between folk and Āgamic temples, 223
Karaikkāḷ Ammaiyār, 19, 62
Kāraṇai Viṭaṅkar, 65, 150, 313
Karkata Veḷḷāḷa, 220, 239
Karma, 112
Karmarkar, 151
Karuṇākara Toṇṭaimān, 320, and Tyāgarāja, 332
Karūr, 79
Karve, Iravati, 208
Kauḻa mārga and Comācimāṟanār Episode, 169-81
Kaṭapāyādi system, 163
Kaṭikamāṟayans, 278
Kaṭimaram, and Coḷa kingship rituals, 314
Kaṭṭaḷais, 60, 203, 253, at Tiruvārūr, 257
Kausitaki Upaniṣad, 103
Kāverī, 7, 290
Kāyārohana, 37, 150
Kāyārohanasvāmi, 60
Khajuraho, Caunṣaṭ Yogini temple, 164
Kiḻai maṭha, See also Dakṣiṇa Goḷaki, Goḷaki, Bhikṣā and Kiḻai maṭha, 261, 341
King as the Vedic sacrificer, 293
King as a noble royal icon, 368
Kīrtivarman, the Chandeḷḷa king of Jejākabhukti, 160
Kiṭāraṅkoṇṭān, boundary of Tiruvārūr, 314
Kodiya maṭha, a Kālāmukha maṭha, 154
Koḷḷa maṭha at Vārāṇasi, 262
Koṇṭi, 231, 232, and mariyātai, 233,

Konṭi vamcam, 313
Konṭimakaḷir, 232
Konṭiyammā, a dancer at the temple, 234
Koṟṟavai, 20
Kotumpālūr chiefs, 300
Kotuṅkolur, 289
Koyil Tirumalam, 177
Krishna Sastri, 302
Kriyā Dīpika and Sannyāsa Paddhati, 169
Kriyā Dīkṣā, 169
Krodhabhaṭṭāraka, (epithet of Durvāsa) and Tiruvārūr, 149
Kukais or non-Brāhmaṇa maṭhas destroyed by order of the king, 260
Kukkuṭanaṭanam, 998
Kulke, 287, 320, 332
Kulottuṅga I, 318
Kulottuṅga II (1133-50) 318, 320-1, expansion of temple rites at Tiruvārūr, 331, "as a fanatic Śaiva, 332, and the image of Govindarāja of Chidambaram, 68
Kulottuṅga III (1178-1218), 322, 325, 331
Kulottuṅkacoḻacarittram, 335
Kulottuṅkacoḻanulā, 323
Kulottuṅkakkōvai, 324
Kulotuṅga, 260
Kumāṟakuruparar,author of Tiruvārūrṇānmanimālai, 39, 60, 90
Kumbhābhiṣekam, 275
Kumudi temple case, 210
Kuṇḍalini, 37, 107
Kuṇḍaliṇi yoga, 148, 161
Kuñjitapādam, spokesman for Madhyāhna Brāhmaṇas, 177
Kuntavi, 302
Kurukkaḷ, heirarchy vis a vis Vedic priest, 136
Kuṭantaikkāroṇam, 150
Kūṭas, 148

L'Hernault, 36, 37
Lakṣādhyāyī matha, 166, 168, See also Goḻaki, Bhiksā
Lakṣādhyāyī Caṅtāna, 262
Lakulīśa, founder of Pāśupatas, 150
Lalita, 163
Lalitāsahasranāmam, 174
Larsen, 291
Latchappa, the musician, 231
Later Coḻas and the Revival of Tyāgarāja Myths, 316

Legal suits, 254
Legitimation, 287, 290-1
Levels of truth, 367
Lockwood, 15, 37
Lokāyatikas, 156
Lord of Tiruvārūr, 7
Lord of Udipi, 208
Lord of Pūṅkoyil, 329
Lorenzen, 151, 161

Mackenzie Mss., 211
Madhughūrnitalolākṣī, 174
Madhughūrnitaraktākṣī, 174
Madhuravijayam, 342
Madhyama, 117
Madhyāhna Brāhmaṇas, alt. pariahs, 176
Mahābalipuram, 14, 21
Mahābhārata, 20, 159
Mahāliṅgam, 162
Mahāmeruviṭaṅkar and Tañjaiviṭaṅkar, 302
Mahāśaivas, 240
Mahāvrati Bādarāyana, 154
Mahāvṛtikaḷmaṭam, 154
Mahāvṛtins, 150-5
Mahendravarman (580-630 A.D.), 12, 289, conversion to Śaivism, 295, 299
Maheśvara 159, 169, and Siva Yogis, 255
Maitrāyaṇīya Upaniṣad, 103
Makiḻam tree, 65, 147
Mālatī Mādhava, 161
Malkāpuram inscription, 164
Mānakañcaranāyaṉār Purāṇam, 150
Manarkaḷ, 65
Māṇikkaṉācciyār, a courtesan devotee, 233
Māṇikkavācakar, 145
Manimekaḻai, 327
Maṅunīti Myth, 317, and Vikramacola, 326, developed by Cekkiḻir, 329
Māṟa Somayaji Kaivalya Prāpti, a mss., 172

Māṟai, Tamil for Veda, 136, 137
Māṟaiñānacampantar, 59
Mārāṭha patronage of Sanskrit and Telegu, 347
Māṟathas, 59, and Tyāgarāja, 346
Mārāṭhi version of the Agastya Bhakta Vilāsa, 180
Maṟavar, and temple issue, 205
Mariyātai, (honour system in temples) 204, 223
Mātaṅga, 174
Mātaṅgas, an untouchable caste, 214
Mātaṅginītantra, 175
Maṭhādhipatis, 60, 254, 261
Maṭhas, 224, as trustees of temples, 60, 253, 255
Mattalam, a drum, 224
Mattamāyūra and the Goḻakī Maṭha, 164
Mattamāyūramārga, 163
Mattavilāsaprahasana, 161
Māyā, 118, 168
Meister and Dhaky, 221
Metaphysics of the Tyāgarāja cult, 97
Meykaṇṭa parampara, 261
Meykantār, 112, 258, 271, 273
Meykīrtti, 298
Mimic tableau, and Coḷa royalty rites, 314
Mīnākṣi - Cuntareśvara of Madurai, 5, 60, 296
Mīnākṣi as Taṭātakai, 296
Mīnātcicuntaram Piḷḷai, 112, 182
Mirashi, 164
Mitākṣara, 267
Moccakkulam maṭha, 257
Moffatt, Michael, 214
Mucukundasahasranāmam, 9, 30, 38, 106, 138, 146, 162, 202, 331, 333
Mucukuntaṉ, 20, 63, 79, 83
Mucukuntarājña caritram, 85
Mudras, 141
Mukhamaṇṭapa, 136
Mukundasahasranāmam, 63, 140
Mulādhāra, 115
Murukaṉ, 19
Muslims, 216
Mutaliyār maṭhas, 261
Mutaliyārs of Lakṣādhyāyī santāna, 167
Mutaliyārs at Celva Tiruvārūr, 262
Muṭṭukārar, the uvacaṉ as the drummer, 224
Mūvar Uḷā., 80, 328
Myths in 12th century literature and Coḷa epigraphs, 316

Nādabindopaniṣad and reference to Haṁsayoga, 105
Nāgabilā, 59, 76
Nāgapaṭṭanam, (modern for Nakaikkaroṇam, Tam. Nākappaṭṭanam) 60, 150, 290, 315
Nagasamy, 162, 309
Nākaviṭaṅka (Nakaraviṭaṅkar) at Tirunaḷḷāṟu, dance form of 99, 62
Nakulīśa Pāśupata Darṣaṇa of Mādhvācārya, 158
Nallaswami Pillai, J.M. 2, 173
Nallūr, 65, 66
Nallūrppurāṇam, 66
Namiṉanti, 144, (yaṭikaḷ), 207
Nampiyāṇṭār Nampi,171, 206, 303
Ñānacampantar, 43, comments on Jainas and Buddhists, 137
Ñānacampantar, a kārkaṭa Veḷḷāḷa, 258
Ñānanacampantar, the founder of Tarumapuram ātīnam, 201
Ñānapirakāca paṇṭāram, 257
Nandivarman II, 294
Naṅkai Paravai (Paṟavai Anukkiyār) donated, 312
Nantanār, 145
Nantan,the untouchable puḷaiyar, 208
Nārpatt ennāyiravar, 263
Nāṭarāja, 24, 68, 257
Nātha sampradāya, 162
Nateśan, V., 231
Native elite, 350
Nats, of Burma, 289
Navavīras, 336
Nāyanmār, 1, 19, 97, and bigotted despising of Jainas and Bauddhas, 143, of Pallava royal families, 265297, and the Pallava Process of Incorporative kingship, 295
Nayiṇār, the priests at Tiruvārūr temple, 239
Neriyuṭaiperumān, a man or woman, 324

Netumāṟan, 295
Networking tradition, 55, 365
New emerging structures of patronage, 254
New state temples, 287
Nigamic, 135
Nīlakaṇṭa Śastri, 323
Nīlaviṭaṅka, of Tiruvāymūr, dance form Kamala, 62, 99
Nilāyatākṣī, 61
Nilotpalāmpāḷ, 36
Nirañjana guru, 153, and Caturānana Paṇḍita, 300
Nirguṇa Brāhmaṇa, 136
Nirguṇa, 289
Nityārcanāvidhi' of the Kāraṇāgama, 240
Nityas, 163
Nityaṣodasīkārṇavam, 163
Niyamaneṟi, 139
Noboru Karashima, 68, 238
Nodal points, 365
Nūl vaḻi, 139
Nyāsa, 109

O'Flaherty, Wendy, 8, 156, 159, 215
Om, 109
Orissan and Tamil tradition, 287
Ostracisation, by caste organisations, 220
Oṭṭakūttan, (and honourofic Oṭṭakūttar), 9, 39, 320
Otuvar, 188, 203, 239-41
Oymānāṭu, the ancient name of Toṇṭaimaṇṭalam, 292

Paintings of Tyāgarāja, Nāyakka and Marāṭha, 347
Paḻaiyanūrutaiyān Vetavanamuṭaiyāṉ Ammai Āppaṉ with the epithet Viluppaṟaiyan, 237
Paḻaiyāṟu, 65-6
Paḻani, 276
Pālas, 166
Palladium of sovereignty, 77
Pallava Somāskanda model, 14
Pallava model of Kingship, 292
Pallava Siṁhavarman, 297
Pallavaṟāyan, a donor, 277
Pallavarāyan Perunampi, 313, the loyal general, 323
Pallavas, 287
Pan, 304
Pan-Indian world of royal dharma, 290
Pañcadāsi, 148
Pañcakrośa, 314
Pañcākṣara, 111
Pañchapāṇḍavas, 313
Pāṇḍya king Netumāṟan and Jainas, 289, 295
Pāṇḍyas and Vijayanagara kings, offerings of food to temples, 253
Pāṇḍyas of Madurai, and Mīnākṣi cult, 287
Paṅkuni Uttiram festival, 120, 225, 235, 257
Paṇtāra Canniti, 158, 258
Paṇtārams, 225, 256
Parā vāk 98, or nada, 117, 120
Paramāṟayars, 236 (see also Brahmāṟayars)
Parañjoti, 296
Parāntaka I (907-955 A.D.), 301, 311
Parārthapūja, performed by initiated priests, 240
Pāraśaivas, priests and congregation of non-Āgamic temples, 224
Paṟavai, 64, 147, (nacciyar), 212, 233
Parāvaratarankam, 99
Parigraha śakti, 118
Parivaṭṭam, as symbol of temple honour, 204
Pāśupata, 150, 156
Pāśupata centres, 150
Pāśupata maṭha, 150
Pāśupata order of monks as celibates (brahmacāris), 157
Pāśupata Sūtra, 158
Pāśupatas divided into *śrauta* and *aśrauta*, 162
Paśyanti, 117
Pāṭal peṟṟa talaṅkaḷ, 55
Pāṭalpeṟṟataḷām, 28
Patañjali's Yogasūtra, 101
Pathak, 151
Pati, paśu and pāśa, categories in Śaiva Siddhānta, 142, 168
Patron of the poet Cekkiḻiār, 321
Paṭṭīcuram, 65
Paṭṭināppaḷai, 232

Paṭṭinātha, 66
Peri Cetti, 167, 258
Periya Purāṇam, 1, 2, 8, 32, 137, 170, 172, 200, 211, 218, 257, 297, 317
Periya maṭha, 256, painted on the Tevācirīya maṇṭapam, 271
Persecution of Jainas, 295
Persecution of the Vaiṣṇava philosopher, 319
Peruvelur, 65
"peripherality vs. centrality", 6
"processual symbols", 99
Pippalāḍa, 142
Piruṅka(skt. Bhṛṅga) natanam, 99
Pitārikoyil ammaṉ pucāri,(priest) 223, see also uvācaṉ,
Piṭāriyammaṉ, 67, 203
Piṭāriyamman koyil, 222
Pīṭha, 6
Pluralism of beliefs, 361
Political statement of Rājarāja, 302
Political history of the later Coḷas, 318
Politics and Śaivism, 322
Ponnusamy, 312
Prabodhacandrodaya, 160
Prāṇa, 101-3, 119, 142, Prāṇa and apāna, 105-6, as breath, 21, 600 times in a day, 122
Prāṇa upakāri, 318
Prasádam, food distribution, 204
Praṣṇopaniṣad, 103, 142
Prathamasākhins, 177-8
Pratiloma, 265
Pratyabhijña, 28, 112
Pre-Rājasiṁha style, 16
Presler, 275
Primordial Sound, 100
Problem of succession to the throne, 321
Protest movements,bifurcated into orthodox and heterodox, 369
Pseudo-scripture, Āgamas as, 142
Ptolemy, 61
Puliyūr became Chidambaram, 299
Pūṅkoyil Nampi, playwright honoured by deity, 334
Puri, 287
Puṟṟitaṅkoṇṭāṉ, 58, 76, Sanskritised, 290
Puruṣa Śūktam, 135
Putra mārga, of Campantar,143
Puvaniviṭaṅka, of Tirumaṟaikkāṭu, dance form of Haṁsapādanaṭanam, (honourofic) Puvaniviṭaṅkar, 61, 99

Raghavan, V. 154
Rājādhirāja II (1163/66- 1179/82), 237, succession problems, 318, 323
Rajamanickam, 167, 261
Rajan, P.T., 310
Rājan kaṭṭalai, 255
Rājarāja and Rajendra, 35
Rājarāja III, the last of the Imperial Coḷas, taken prisoner(1250), 339
Rājarāja I, 287, and state temple at Thañjāvūr, 306, importing antiquity, 308 and Dakṣiṇameriviṭaṅkar, 305, 302, association with Cuntarar, 271,inscriptions, 268, hearing Tevāram, 303, and the Cola State Cult, 306
Rājarājaviṭaṅkar, 257
Rājarājeśvaranāṭakam, 335
'Rājasiṁha style', 12
Rājasiṁha (680-700 A.D.) and Somāskandas, 12, 297
Rājendra I, 287, bringing the waters of the Ganges, 311, builds Tyāgarāja shrine, 313, and the State Cult, 310
Rājendracola, 153
Rajoguṇa, 303
Rājrarājeśvaram, 302
Rāmānuja, 155
Ramasvami Naicker, 2, 218, 276
Rao, Gopinath 175
Rashtriya Svayam Sevak Sangh, 205
Rathakāras, 268
Rāyī, 142
Reciting of the Vedas in temples, 135
Redistribution (viniyokam), 204
Regional Cults and Hindu Tradition., 4
Regional chiefs called 'mantāḷikas, 321
Regional loyalty, 287
Relationship between Āgama and Śiva, 138
Religio-political shrine dedicated to Manunīti, 329
Religious topography, 5

Religious synthesis, 3
Ritual parallels between Tiruvārūr and Thañjāvūr, 304
Root metaphors, 11, 99
Route taken by the deity of Ārūr, 65, 298
Routinization of Charisma, (Weber's view) 200
Royal cult, 3
Rudra Paśupati nāyaṉār, 150
Rudracamakam, 135

Sabarimalai, 310
Śabda Brahmaṇ, 98, 106, 118
Śabdakalpadrumaḥ of Rādhākānta Deva, definition of Ajapā, 105
Śabdavāda, the school of Grammarians, 99, - vadins , 109
Sacred clusters, 55, 297-8
Ṣaddarśana Samuccaya, 158
Śaīva Siddhānta, 2, 98, 108, 168
Śaiva collective, 1
Śaiva-smārta framework, 135
Śaiva Dīkṣā, of Āgamic tradition, 136
Śaiva kurukkaḷ, 136
Śaiva Siddhānta maṭhas, 258
Śaiva Sannyāsa Paddhaṭi, 270
Samāna, 103
Samayācāryas, 345
Sambhoh Āḻā Sundara, alter ego of Śiva, issues invitation to festivals, 240
Samprokṣanam, Ritual cleansing of temple, 225
Sanātana dharma, 215
Śaṅkara, 158
Śaṅkarācārya (honourofic *cariar*), 159, 218
Śaṅkarādhyāya, 172
"Sanskritic", 2
Sanskritic tradition and the Tamil fold, 299
Sanskritisation, 288
Sapta viṭaṅkatalaṅkal., 37, 55, 57
Sapta viṭanka kṣetras, 57
Sapta-viṭaṅka, 57
Saptamātṛka, 67, 221
Saptasṭaḷam, 55
Sarabhendra Bhūpāla Kuravañci by Koṭṭayin Civakoḻuntu, 348
Sarvadarśanasaṁgraha, 158
Sarfoji II (1798-1833), 346
Sarvadevavilāsa, 154
Sectarian leaders, 264, 341
Secularism, 370
Segmentary state, 301
Sen, Chitrabhānu 152
Sethuraman, N., 323
Shāhāji (1684-1710), 90, 346
Shahājirājapuram, 347
Shahendra Vilāsa, 347
Shared social legitimations, 369
Shift of political capitals, 287
Shulman, David Dean, 76, 86
Siddha, (Tamil Cittar) 97, 112
Siddhantic, 135
Śiva Bhakta Vilāsa, 172
Śiva as Spirit of the Vedas, 137
Śiva as "god of Tamils', 7
Śiva as the 'southerner, 43, as the Dancer, 41
Śivācārya, 188
Śivadrohin, 322
Śivāgamas, twenty eight according to Śaiva Siddhānta, 141
Śivāpādaśekhara, 302
Śivarahasyaskhaṇḍa, 18, 87
Sivaraman, K., 117
Six daily rites in the Tiruvārūr temple, 139
Skanda Mahā purāṇam, 172
Social arbitration, 268
Soḍasīmantra, 161
Śoham, 107
Soma Siddhānta, 153, 166
Somakaṇṭha, Ālayapraveśavidhi, (temple entry), 210
Somasiddhāntin, 150
Somāskanda as ritual imperative, 18
Somāskanda as a Pallava innovation, 29
Somāskanda as one of the lilāmūrti, 17
Somāskanda image on the rear wall, 12-3
Somāskanda panels, 12-3
Somāskanda, 2, 11-5, 37, 77
Somāskanda as the leitmotif, 12, 293
Somāskanda later called Tyāgarāja, 287
Somāskanda associated with Coḻa

territory, 291
Somāskanda, its debut, 12, 291, 297
Somāskanda as palladium of Pallava sovereignty, 297
Somāskandas as high reliefs, 14
Soundarararajan, K.V., 12, 36
Sound zones of consciousness, 110
South Indian pilgrimage tradition, 298
South India Archaka Association, 210
Special endowments called *kaṭṭalais*, 254
Specific kind of universalism, 367
Spencer, George, 203, 308
Spandana, 100
Sphoṭavāda, 109
Śri Vidyā, 18, 38, 09, 148
Śrī Purāṇam, 147
Śrī Śūktam, 135
Śrikaṇṭhabhāṣya, 161
Śrinātha Navaratnamālā Manjuṣā by Bhāskararāya, 162
Srirańgam, 264
Sṛṅgāramañjarī Shahājīyam, 348
State-sponsored religion, 222
Stein,Burton, 261-2
Subramanian, T.N. 323
Succession issue, 322
Śuddha māyā as jñāna śakti, a Śaiva Siddhānta postulate, 108
Śūdrā, 212
Śukla Yajur Veda, 107, 178
Sūkṣmanāda, 109
Sumatra, 175
Sundaramūrtyaṣṭottaram, 213
Sūra Saṁhāra, 81
Ṣūryanārāyaṇa koyil maṭha, 169
Svadharma, 209, 215
Svayambhū liṅga, 37
Swāmimalai, 276
Sword of the Pāṇṭiyan, 342
Symbiotic relationship, between Āgamic and non Āgamic temples, 222
Syncretistic concept, 89
Systems maintaining, 217, 220

Taittirīyas, 178
Talaiyālaṅkāṭu, 65
Talicaṭṭaṅkuti, 65
Tamiḷ identity, 43
Tamiḷ cultural nationalism, 2, 351, 370
Tamiḷ-Sanskritic synthesis, 56
Tamiḷ linguistic consciousness, 138
Tamiḷ religiosity, 276
Tamiḷ consciousness, 276, 351
Tamiḷ tradition a pan-Indian acceptability, 299
Tamiḷ Conference, 351
Tamiḷ nationalism, 169, 370
Tampirān, 225
Tānattār, 254-257
Tanjore Gazetteer of 1915., 176
Taṇṭiyaṭikaḻ, 58, 144, 295
Tantrasāra of Kṛṣṇānanda of Bengal, 175
Tantrasāra of Abinavagupta, 175
Tantric, 135, 148-76
Tārācuram frieze, 173, temple at of 1150 A.D., 322
Tarumāpuram Ātīnam, 63, 168, 203, 255, 257-8
Taṭātakai, 146
Tāyumānavar, 141
Tecikar, 225
Temple building and Sanskritisation, of the Nāyaṇmār, 138
Temple Donors and their Caste Affiliations, 277
Temple politics, 350
Temple priest, 369
Teṇṇavan, the 'southerner, 43
Territorial tripartite division, 296
Tevāciriya mantapam, 1, 35, 263
Tevāram, 1, 7-8, 12, 23, 136, 291, 365
Tevaraṭiyār, myths, rites and honour schemes, 203, 230-5, some sold to the temple, 235
Thañjāvūr Saraswati Mahal Library, 172
Thañjāvūr style, 347
Thañjāvūr, 304, 342-3, the British take over, in 1787, 349
Tillai—three thousand, 68
Thurston, 224, 259
Tilakammā, from Koṇṭi family, temple dancer, 203, 232
Tillai Uḷā, 261
Tirāviṭa munneṭra kaḻakam, 20
Tirāviṭa Kaḻakam, 2, ideology,and Tamil historiography, 351-2

Tirāviṭa movement, 276
Tiricirāpuram Minatchicuntaram Piḷḷai, 176
Tīrtha, 6
Tirucirrāmpaḷa Mutaliyār, 261
Tirukaccūr, 64
Tirukkāṟavācal, 258, 315, ancient Tirukkāṟāyil, 57, 61, 99, 315
Tirukkoḻili, 56, 90, also Tirukkuvalai, 62-3, 99, 258, 316
Tirumala Nāyakka, 296
Tirumaṅkai Āḻvār, 60
Tirumantiram, 8, 112
Tirumaṟaikkāṭu (or Vedāraṇyam), 61, 99, 316
Tirumukham, (temple invitation) 239
Tirumūlar, 98, 138, and the dance of Siva, 110-2
Tirumuṟaikaṇṭapurāṇam of Umāpati Civācārya, 14th C, 303
Tirunākaikkāroṇam, (see also Nāgapaṭṭaṇam), 60, 99
Tirunaḷḷāṟu, 62, 99, 258, 316
Tirunīḷākaṇṭa, the paṇar, player of yāl (lute) 207
Tirunīlakaṇṭa, the 'potter, 206
Tirupati, 264, temple, 345
Tiruppukaḻūr, 257, 260
Tiruppuvanam, (Tribhuvanam), 322
Tiruttoṇṭarttiruvantāti, 171, 206
Tiruttoṇṭātakai, 1, 146, 171
Tiruvaiyāṟu Māhātmyam, 259
Tiruvaiyāṟu, 315
Tiruvampalacakṟam, 112
Tiruvampar Puraṇam, 176
Tiruvamparmākālam, 214
Tiruvānmiyūr, 64, 65
Tiruvārūr, 1, 14, 56, 60, 65, 312-4
Tiruvārūr literati, 59
Tiruvārūr Ulā, 57
Tiruvārūr Ajapānaṭanam or Haṁsanaṭanam, 99
Tiruvārūr Temple and its 55 major shrines, 255
Tiruvārūr and Tyāgarāja , as nodal points of sacred cluster, 298
Tiruvārūr , sanskritised names, 299
Tiruvārūrkkoi, 39, 143
Tiruvārūrppurāṇaṃ, 22
Tiruvāykeḻvi, 154
Tiruvāymūr, 57, 62, 99, 316
Tiruvicaippā , mention of Meru Viṭaṅkar, 302
Tiruviḷaiyāṭṭal Purāṇam of Perumpaṟṟapuliyūrnampi, 296
Tiruviḷaiyātalppuranam, of Parañjoti, 340, 396
Tiruviḷaiyātarpurāṇam, 201
Tiruvoṟṟiyūr, 34, 64, 76, 146, 281
Tiruvoṟṟiyūr Purāṇam, 153, 165
Tiruvoṟṟiyūr and Ganga- Pallava records, 299
Tiruvoṟṟiyūr, Padmanāṭanaṃ, 99
Tiruvoṟṟiyūrppurāṇam,by Ñānapirakācar, (16th century A.D.), 64
Tirvavātaturai ātīnam, 259
Tiyākarāja Mutaliyār, 255
Tiyākarājakalineṭil, 201
Tiyākarājalīlaīkalḷ 181-9, 200, 223, 212-1
Tiyākarājalīlaikaḷ by Tiricirapuram Minatchicuntaram Pillai, 202, 324
Tiyākarājalīlaikaḷ, of Irācakopāla Piḷḷai, 181
Tolkappiyam, 137
Toṇṭaimān, 89
Toṇṭaimanṇṭalam, 29, 263, 292
Toṇṭaimaṇṭalam Veḷḷāla Community, 263
Trikā, 98, 120, 148
Turairaṅkacāmi (also spelt Dorai Rangasami), 263
Turner, 6
Tyāgarāja, 5
Tyāgarāja as a Smārta-Śri Vidyā symbol, 90
Tyāgarāja Cult and general Śaiva context, 135-189ff.
Tyāgarāja intervenes on behalf of Paravai, 170
Tyāgarāja as the model Vedin, 138
Tyāgarāja brought to earth by a Cola king., 77
Tyāgarāja in the bosom of Tirumaḷ, 79
Tyāgarāja origin myth, 76, 79
Tyāgarāja icon, 11
Tyāgarāja Mutaliyār of Vaṭapātimaṅkalam,(trustee) 234
Tyāgarāja paṇṭāram, 256
Tyāgarāja, Ritual equality with the

mulabera, 304
Tyāgarāja shrine, 309, and the State Cult, 311
Tyāgarāja as symbol of, Fertility of man, 303
Tyāgarāja cult and Imperial Cola, 301-4
Tyāgarāja Mahātmyam, 348, 86
Tyāgarāja Typology, 25
Tyāgarāja Vilāsam, 348
Tyāgarājanāmāvaḷi, 213
Tyāgeśa Padas, 348
Tyāgeśa kuravañci, 347
Typologies of absorption, into Hindu sects, 289
Udāna, 103
Ugradevatas, 67
Uḷtuṟai kaṭṭaḷai, 255
Umāpati Śīvācāra, excommunicated, 272
Uncrowned son, also called Caṅkaracoḻan, 318
Uṇmai Viḷakkam by Mānavācakam Kaṭantār, 112
Uṇmaṇi, 110, 120
Uṇmatta naṭanam, 99
Upanisadic thought, 215
Upaniṣads, 97
Uṟavi poḻi naṭam., 112
Utcamayam, 151
Utpaladeva, 113
Utsavabera of Cuntareśvarar of Madurai, Somāskanda, 296
Uttaramerur temple inscription, 226
Uvācaṉ, (hereditary priest of pitari temple) and temple mariyātai, 203, 224-6

Vācaspatyam, 105
Vāgiśa Bhaṭṭa, 153, 160
Vaikharī, 116
Vaipputalaṅkal, 55
Vaiṣeśikas, 159
Vaiṣṇavite substratum, 68
Vaittiyaliṅka Paṇṭāracanniti, 260
Vājasaneyī, 107, 178
Vākyapadīya, 106
Valaṅkai, 235, 269
Valaṅkai Velaikkāra paṭaikaḷilār, 270
Valmīkanātha, 18, 59, 76
Vālpeṟṟakaikkoḷar, 270
Vama Pasupata, 161
Varṇadharma, 215 (āśrama), 345
Vastuśāstra Upaniṣad, 142
Vaṭakiḻmaṭam of Celva Tiruvārūr, 262
Vaṭivuṭaiyammaṉ and Vaṭṭapāṟai, 64
Vattanaiyāṭal, 63
Vaṭṭapāṟaiyamman, 221
Vaṭuknāth Śastri Khiṣṭe, 162
Vedic-Āgamic, 56
Vedic, 135-142, Vedic priest chants from ardhamaṇṭapa, hierarchy, 136
Vedic Pāśupata, 161
Vegetarianism, in Tiyākarājalīlaikaḷ, 216
Vegetarians, 258-9
Veḷākkuṟicci maṭham, 158, 203, 256-7, and married clerics, 256
Veḷḷaivāranar, 78
Veḷḷāla Śaiva maṭhas, 222
Veḷḷāla sanyāsiṅs, 345
Veḷḷāḷās, 169, 258
Veḷḷāḷas, custodians of temple lands, 257
Veṅkatamākhin, 40, 259
Venkatasubba Ayyar, editor, Pallavarayānpeṭṭai ins., 323
Vertical Legitimation, 288-90
Vetavanamuttaiyān Ammaiyappan, alias Rājarāja Viḻupparaiyan, 322
Vijayadaśami, 313
Vijayanagara dynasty, 264
Vikramacoḻa and break in succession, 317, 323
Vikramāṅkadevacarita of Bilhaṇa, description of chaos in Coḷa state, 320
Viḻuppaṟaiyaṉ, 235, (s) 238
Viḻupperumār, 235-8
Vīrabāhu, the chief of the nine warriors, 79
Vīṟacoḻanukkar, 242, 335
Vīracoḻanukkuvijayam, 311, (Vīrānukkuvijayam), 334
Viramitrodaya of Mitramiśra, 160
Viraṇmiṇṭa, 56, (honorofic miṇṭār) 147, 170, (nāyaṉār), excommunicating Cuntarar, 263
Vīraśaivas, 169
Virupākṣa Kavi, 172

Viśālākṣi of Kāsī, 60
Viśhva Hindu Pariṣad, 205
Viṣṇu, 82, 320
Viṭaldev of Pāndharapūr, 5, 208
Viṭaṅka, 12, 29-39, undescribed, 302
(Viṭankar=honourific form of viṭankan
and viṭaṅka) 31, 99
Vitelvitukiśvara, Coḻamāḷīśvara, 300
Vītiviṭaṅka Tyāgarāja or Vītiviṭaṅṅkar,
(an) 34, 37, 99, 291
Vyākaraṇa mantapa, 106, 155
Vyākaraṇadānapperumāḻ, 106, 155

Wearing white robes, Veḷḷaāḷa,
married clerics 256
Weber, 199
White (Śukla) Yajurveda, 178
Williams, Monier, 105
Word (śabda) and its meaning (artha),
109
World as the Word, 109
World view of the cultic believers, 366

Yājñavalkya, 265
Yānaiyerumperumpaṟaiyan, (myths
and temple honours) 203, 226-8,
Yantras, 101, 141
Yoga Sūtras, 101
Yogasūtra of Patañjali, 151
Yogic, 135
Yoṇi pūjā, 149
Yuvarāja,the Kakaṭiya king, 164

Zvelebil, 78, 115, 324

ILLUSTRATIONS

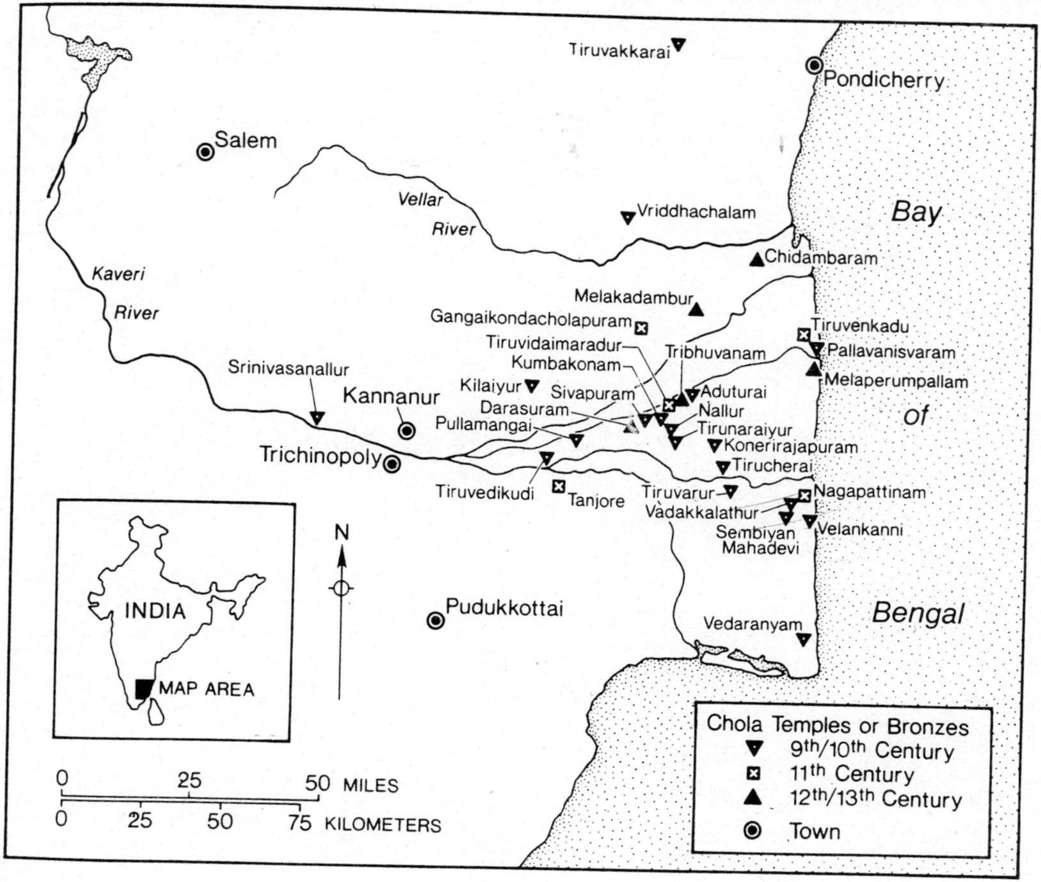
Tiruvakkarai
Pondicherry
Salem
Vellar
River
Vriddhachalam
Bay
Chidambaram
Kaveri
River
Melakadambur
Gangaikondacholapuram
Tiruvenkadu
Tiruvidaimaradur
Tribhuvanam
Pallavanisvaram
Kumbakonam
Melaperumpallam
Srinivasanallur
Kilaiyur
Sivapuram
Aduturai
Kannanur
Darasuram
Nallur
of
Pullamangai
Tirunaraiyur
Konerirajapuram
Trichinopoly
Tirucherai
Tiruvedikudi
Tanjore
Tiruvarur
Nagapattinam
Vadakkalathur
Sembiyan
Mahadevi
Velankanni
N
INDIA
Pudukkottai
Bengal
Vedaranyam
MAP AREA
Chola Temples or Bronzes
9th/10th Century
11th Century
12th/13th Century
Town
0
25
50 MILES
0
25
50
75 KILOMETERS

Plan 1: Tyāgarāja Temple Complex at Tiruvārūr

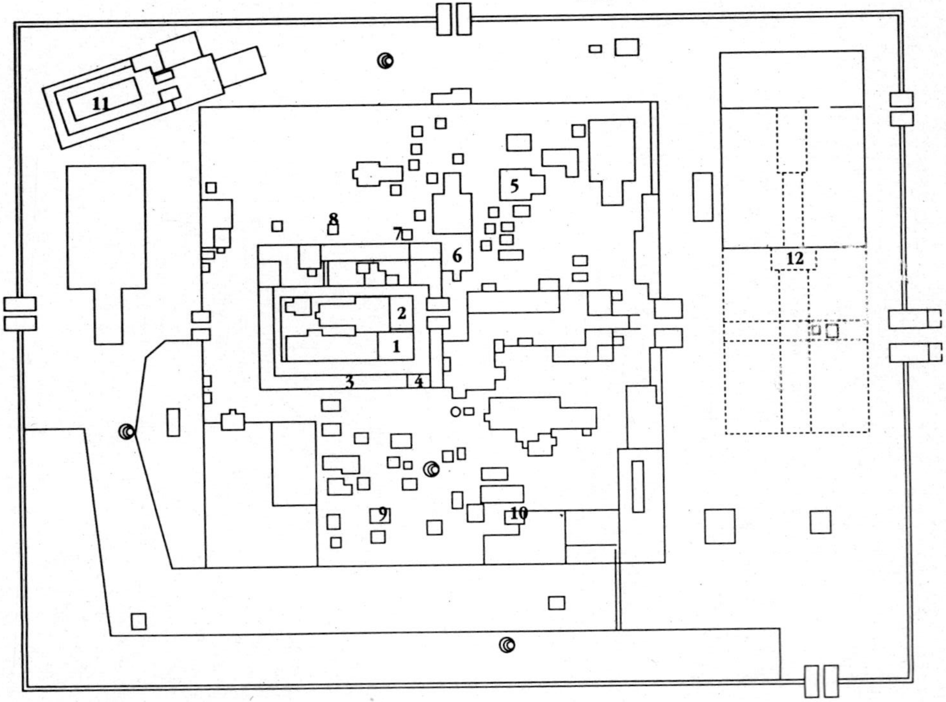

1. TYĀGARĀJA
2. VALMĪKANĀTHA [PRESIDING DEITY] Tamil:PUṞṞITĀṄKOṆṬAN
3. Sixtythree nāyaṉmār shrine
4. Shrine for the Tevāram Trio
5. YĀGASĀLAI [It is on a lintel at the entrance door where the Somayāji episode is painted]
6. Nilotpalāmpāḷ
7. ROUDRA DURGĀ [Koṟṟavai]
8. HĀṬAKEŚVARA, a nāgabila
9. CERAMĀṈ PERUMĀL
10. MUCUKŪṄDEŚVARA, a LINGA
11. KAMALĀMPĀḶ Shrine
12. TEVĀCIRṞIYA MAṆṬAPAM [Where Cuntarar is believed to have composed his TIRUṬṬOṆṬATOKAI]

Plan 2: Tyāgarāja Temple at Tirukkuvaḷai

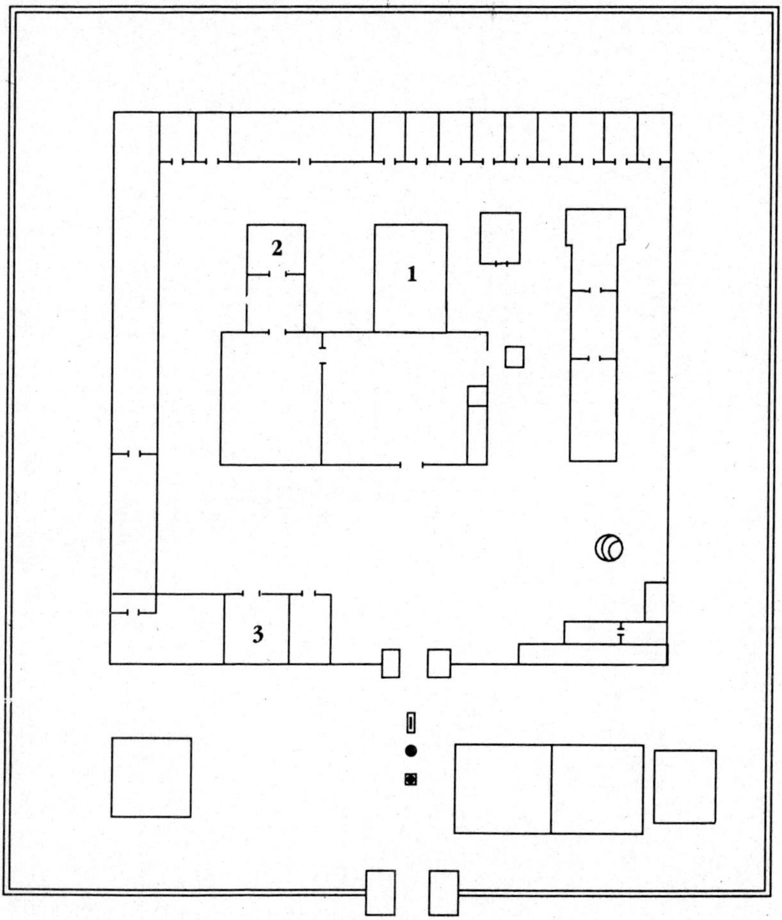

1. BRAHMAPURĪŚVARA [presiding deity]
2. TYĀGARĀJA
3. CUNTARAR

Plan 3: Tyāgarāja Temple at Tiruvoṟṟiyūr

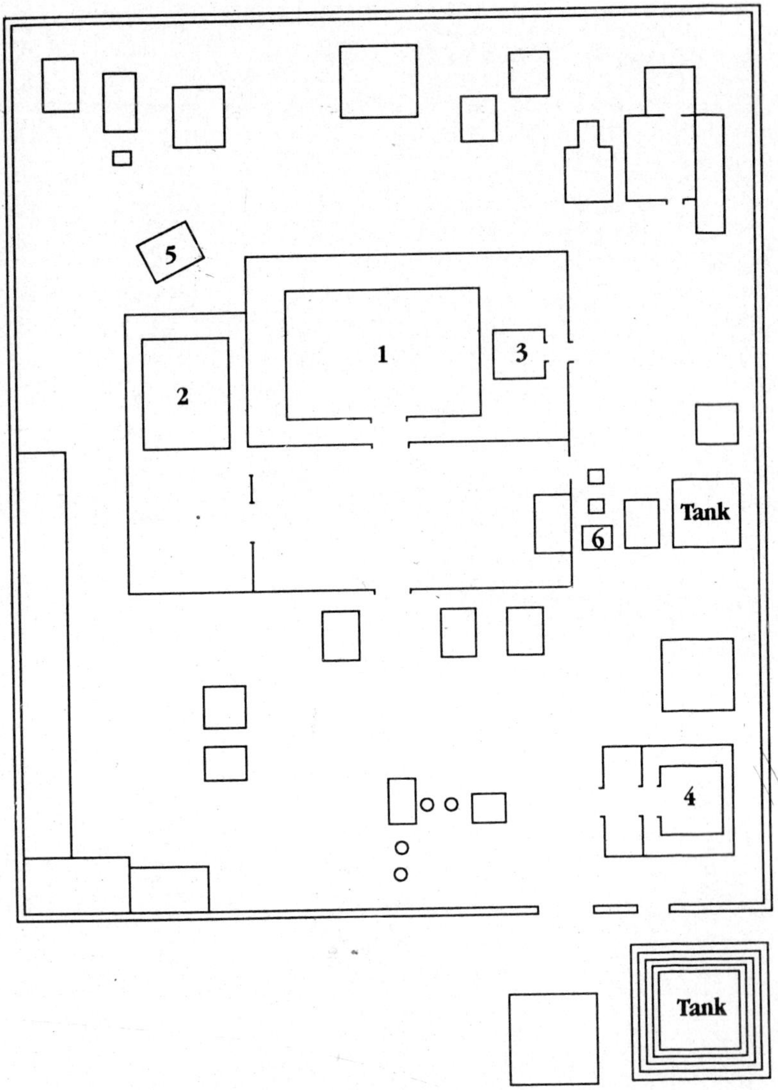

1. Ādipurīśvara (Presiding deity)
2. Tyāgarāja
3. Vaṭṭapāṟaiyammaṅ (Kāli))
4. Tripurasundari
5. Gaulīśvara (Lakulisvara)
6. Makilan Tree

Pl. I. Pallava Somāskanda from Mahābalipuram.

Pl. II. Pallava painting of Somāskanda, from Kailāsanātha Temple at Kañcī, kindly lent by Dr. J.R. Marr.

Pl. III. Marāṭhā painting of Somāskanda.

Pl. IV. Somāskanda in the dado of the Rājanārāyaṇa maṇṭapa.

Pl. V. Reclining Viṣṇu with Somāskanda in his bosom on silver doorway, entrance to Tyāgarāja shrine.

Pl. VI. Reclining Viṣṇu on a niche in the wall.

Pl. VII. Entrance to Tyāgarāja shrine.

Pl. VIII. Hāṭakēśvara, a cavern or nāgabila.

Pl. IX. Paintings of seven replicas of Tyāgarāja in the Tēvāciriyamaṇṭapam.

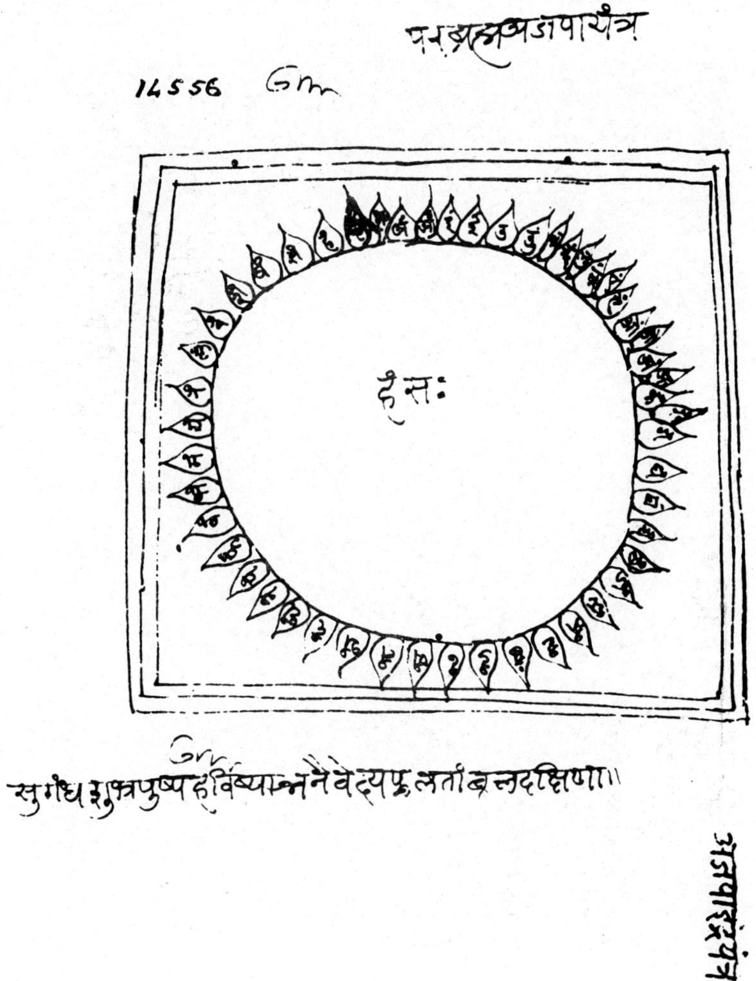

Pl. X. Ajapā Yantra.

Pl. XI. Pañcamukhavādyam and uvācan̲ playing it.

Pl. XII. *Periya maṭam*, the paṇṭāracaṉṉiti in white, receiving temple honours during Tyāgarāja processional rite: painting on the wall of Tēvāciriyamaṇṭapam.

Pl. XIII. Yoni pūjā, on pillar.

Pl. XIV. *Yāṉaiyērum perum paṟaiyaṉ*, with regalia, the present holder of the honour—Mr. Kaṅkāṭaraṉ and family.

Pl. XV. Icon of Cuntaramūrtināyaṉār.

Pl. XVI. Cuntaramūrtināyaṉār in Marāṭhā attire, Nīlōpalāmpāḷ shrine.

Pl. XVII. Cōmacimāṟaṉār episode painted on the lintel of the yāgaśālā.

Pl. XVIII. Cōmācimāṟaṉār episode on the wall of the Nīlōpalāmpāḷ shrine.

Pl. XIX. Cōḻarāja.

Pl. XX. Maṉunīti's shrine.

Pl. XXI. A festival painted on Tēvāciriya maṇṭapam.

Pl. XXII. The kurukkaḷ Cantiracēkaranāyiṉār Candraśekhara) at the Tiruvārūr temple.

Pl. XXIII. Tārācuram frieze.

Pl. XXIV. Tārācuram frieze.